The Theory of Contracts in Islamic Law

A Comparative Analysis With Particular Reference To The Modern Legislation in Kuwait, Bahrain and The United Arab Emirates

Series General Editor

Dr. Mark S. W. Hoyle

Titles in the Series

Islamic Law of Personal Status, (2 Ed.), Jamal J. Nasir

The Status of Women Under Islamic Law, Jamal J. Nasir

Islamic Family Law, Chibli Mallat and Jane Connors (eds)

Mixed Courts of Egypt, Mark S.W. Hoyle

Arab and Islamic Laws Series

The Theory of Contracts in Islamic Law:

A Comparative Analysis With Particuar Reference To The Modern Legislation In Kuwait, Bahrain and The United Arab Emirates

First Edition

Dr. S. E. Rayner

Graham & Trotman
A member of Wolters Kluwer Academic Publishers
LONDON/DORDRECHT/BOSTON

Graham & Trotman Ltd.
Sterling House
66 Wilton Road
London SW1V 1DE

Kluwer Academic Publishers Group
101 Philip Drive
Assinippi Park
Norwell, MA 02061 USA

First published 1991

British Library Cataloguing in Publication Data

Rayner, S. E.
The theory of contracts in Islamic law.–
(Arab and Islamic laws series)
I. Title II. Series
340.59

ISBN 1-85333-617-3 Series ISBN 1-85333-414-6

Library of Congress Cataloguing-in-Publication Data

Rayner, S. E. (Susan E.)
The theory of Contracts in Islamic Law : a comparative analysis with particular reference to the modern legislation in Kuwait, Bahrain and the United Arab Emirates / S.E. Rayner. — 1st ed.
p. cm. — (Arab and Islamic Laws Series)
Includes bibliographical references and index.
ISBN 1-85333-617-3
1. Contracts (Islamic Law) 2. Contracts–Persian Gulf States.
I. Title. II. Series.
LAW
346.536′02—dc 20
[345.36062] 91-24356
CIP

Printed and bound in Great Britain by
Hartnolls Ltd., Bodmin, Cornwall

FOREWORD

by

Dr. Doreen Hinchcliffe
Barrister-at-law, Grays Inn

A great deal has been written about traditional principles as laid down by the jurists of the four main Schools of Islamic Law and much academic ink has been spilt in examining the continuous process of adapting Classical principles to changing conditions by various means of extension and interpretation.

However, the explosion of commerce in recent years in the Gulf States has made all too clear the inadequacy of that approach and the pressing need to develop new codes of law which remain "Islamic" but are also more suited to current commercial realities.

The Law of Contract lies at the heart of all legal systems including that of Islam. Dr. Rayner takes the Contract of Sale as the basis of all contracts in Islamic Law and traces its principles from the earliest period of Islamic Jurisprudence to the most recent codifications adopted in the Gulf States of Kuwait, Bahrain and the United Arab Emirates, enhancing the comparative aspect of her work with examples drawn from Roman, Civil and Common Law as appropriate.

This book is the first comprehensive examination of the new codes of the major states of the Gulf region. In addition to being of great academic interest to all students of Islamic and Middle Eastern Law, it also sheds useful light on many of the problems which confront the ever-increasing number of practitioners in the area who are involved daily, for example, in the problems of Interest and Options. Interest, as *Ribā*, has always been of particular concern to Muslim lawyers. Options also feature regularly in modern commercial law, but sit uneasily in Islamic Jurisprudence because of its attitude towards any form of uncertainty in Contracts.

The book also examines in depth the provisions of the new codes regarding void and voidable contracts, a further example of the attempt of these codes to meet wider needs and yet remain true to the spirit of the *Sharī'a*.

DEDICATION

I dedicate this work to the memory of
Honora Rayner
whom I love and honour.

TABLE OF CONTENTS

TRANSLITERATION

ARABIC	Transcription	ARABIC	Transcription
ء	ʾ	ض	ḍ
أ إ أ	A I U	ط	ṭ
ا	ā	ظ	ẓ
ب	b	ع	ʿ
ت	t	غ	gh
ث	th	ف	f
ج	j	ق	q
ح	ḥ	ك	k
خ	kh	ل	l
د	d	م	m
ذ	dh	ن	n
ر	r	ه	h
ز	z	و	w (ū, aw, au)
س	s	ى	y (ī, ay, ai)
ش	sh		
ص	ṣ		

PREFACE

The last century has witnessed a buffeting of the world of Islam by internal and external crises of major proportions. The progressive decline of the Ottoman Empire in the face of European imperial, industrial and economic might prompted a quest in the early twentieth century for the very roots of an Islamic identity.

The last three decades, in particular, have witnessed a heightening and deepening of Islamic consciousness in Muslim communities throughout the world. The recent resurgence of the Islamic ethos - at once spiritual, cultural, social, economic and political in all its manifestations - is essentially a nativist response : Islam and its fundamental precepts are being re-examined in the light of the modern age. It is a response which has been diverse both in its activity and in its intensity.

The search for an Islamic identity in the Gulf, in contrast to the more revolutionary nature of the Iranian and Saudi Islamicist manifestations, has produced a relatively non-militant and essentially populist fundamentalism. It is the nature of this kind of fundamentalism not so much to challenge Islam itself directly, but, rather, to re-examine certain precepts of establishment Islam in the light of modern circumstances.

The legal response has been as pervasive as that manifested in other societal institutions. Where it has occurred at its most extreme, the traces of establishment Islam have almost, if not completely, been erased. In other areas, the ground remains relatively undisturbed. In the realm of contract and general commercial law, the discernible trend now seems to be towards a forging together of establishment and modernist Islam. The Gulf States in particular, where the rulers have responded with modern legal reforms coupled with a strengthening of the Islamic identity, provide most interesting subjects for legal and historical investigation.

To a significant degree, the search for an Islamic identity within the law, has been without a single reformative or organizational epicentre : the movement has been flavoured by the local character of each Nation responding to a legislative crisis within its own environment. Yet to the extent that legislative exigences within each National State are similar, the Islamic reform of legislation could eventually assume a transnational character.

The primary concern of this study is to examine the historical roots and systematization of the theory of contracts according to the classical law of Islam. It is also concerned, in so far as a theoretical study of this sort is able, to chart the dichotomy between legal theory and practice as it developed from the early centuries of Islam. In this respect the consonance of the Divine Sources of the law are weighed against the eclectic sources and legal methodologies, and the influence of both is marked throughout the exposition of the system of contracts. In a similar respect, an objective view is given to the way in which the more rigid or established laws have either resisted or been accommodated to adjust to social change.

Against this backcloth are placed the modern codifications of the three Gulf States of Bahrain, Kuwait and the United Arab Emirates. The choice of these three is deliberate, for they are illustrative of an evolving pattern which has enfolded during the course of the last three decades within the socio-legal-political environment of the Arab Islamic World. Several Characteristics define this milieu :

(1) All three have suffered substantial western economic and cultural penetration of the region in the context of rapid modernization;

(2) All three are under the dynastic rule of Sunni families, where the population consists of a significant proportion of Shi'ite concentration;

(3) All three manifest a political and economic dominance of the native Arab minority over increasing non-indigenous populations;

(4) All three labour under influential power rivalries and pressures from powerful neighbouring States, such as Saudi Arabia, Iran, Iraq, Pakistan, Israel, Syria and Jordan.[1]

The Nation States chosen for this study represent three stages of a modern era of legislation in the realm of Contracts. The Bahrain Contracts Code, enacted in 1969, represents the emergence from colonial protectoral status to independence, and characteristically retains significant echoes of the Common Law influence. A decade later, the Civil Code enacted in Kuwait in 1980 represents the height of pan-Arabism. It is reflective both of the declining codification process which consisted of adaptations of the French and sundry other European Civil laws, and of the individual and liberal identity that Kuwait assumed throughout the course of its rapid and affluent modernisation. The Federal Civil Code of the State of the United Arab

---

1 I am indebted to R. Hrair Dekmejian, *Islam In Revolution : Fundamentalism In The Arab World,* (New York, 1985) p.149 and *passim*, for the sociological outline of the modern Islamic transition.

Emirates, reflects the most modern era of Arab Islamic legislation. A demographic mosaic of seven Shaikhdoms, whose dynastic, tribal and economic conflicts had hitherto appeared intractable, it is undergoing a federal experiment with mixed success : the requirements of rulers to sacrifice their individual prerogatives for the common good, the dynastic rivalries and persistent antagonism between the largest units of the Federation, Abu Dhabi and Dubai, the exacerbating disparities in power, wealth, tribal and boundary disputes, and the external pressure of umbrella powers such as Saudi Arabia are all creating diverse tensions within the Federal entity. The status of the contract laws within this Federation belies, and yet reflects, these tensions. In 1971, the Emirates of Dubai and Sharjah enacted a Contracts Code which backdated to the end of the British jurisdiction, and which is remarkably similar to the Bahrain Contract Code of 1969. The present status of this code over the contract laws of these Emirates is uncertain: its predominance became engrained during the 1970's by the reluctance of the Federal Union to join the rush into codification during the pan-Arabism era. It was not until sixteen years later that this code was superceded, in part, by the Federal Civil Code of 1987. The Federal Civil Code does not, however, expressly repeal the Dubai Contract Code, and so to the extent that the 1971 code is not contradictory to the Federal Civil Code, it is presumably still valid within the Emirates of Dubai and Sharjah. It is to be noted too that the Courts Laws operating within these Emirates are both National and Federal.

The enactment of the Federal Civil Code in 1987 emphasised the wisdom of the UAE hesitation to codify prior to the settling out of the most vibrant of post-Independence tensions. The conceptual myopia, induced by the spate of mid-century codifications and echoed in certain degrees by the results of pan-Arabism legislation, tended to dismiss or underestimate the regenerative capacity of Islamic legal ethics. Moreover, it tended to ignore, or at best, merely pay lip-service to, the causative position of Islam as the focus of cultural identity for the modern Arab society. In their search for a careful, studied and balanced synthesis of Muslim ethics and modern exigencies, the Federal States produced a civil code based closely on the Jordanian Civil Code. The importance of both the Jordanian and the UAE codifications is their acknowledgement of the true role of Islam at the core of Arab ideology. For this reason, the newer UAE code may well become a model itself for future legislation within the Arab Islamic Civilisation.

The ideal approach to this subject requires a culturally indigenous perspective based on the diachronic development of the theology, jurisprudence, history and the opinions of the Islamic theorists. The present study therefore seeks to focus its attention primarily on the nativist perspective of the law, and more particularly, the law of Contract in Islam.

The emphasis is on the Sunni conception of this law. The decision to restrict the study to this sect is not least due to the exhausting plethora of references and divergences of opinion between its constituent rites. A similar study in the English language has, in any event, already been undertaken with its emphasis on the Shi'a conception of contract, and is still eminently worthy of reference.[2] Nevertheless, the decisive factor to concentrate on the Sunni exposition of contract lay in the reasoning that despite the predominant, but politically insubstantial Shi'a population within the jurisdiction of Bahrain, the significant Shi'a population of the UAE (30 percent), and the large minority Twelver Shi'a population of Kuwait (24 percent), the legal regimes of all three are *de facto* Sunni by virtue of the ruling dynastic families.

It has been attempted, during the course of this work, to construct a diachronic framework of the evolution of Islamic contractual theory. The intention to outline the Pre-Islamic and early Islamic origins of the commercial arena in order to demonstrate the existing system onto which the Islamic theoretical rules were imposed, is severely hampered by the fact that little information of this nature is actually extant today.

The almost complete absence of literary evidence, whether in the form of documents or records, from the first few centuries of the Islamic era is one of the most unfortunate handicaps under which any researcher in Islamic history (and in this case, the historical origins of the contractual theory), must labour.[3] Moreover, while from the ninth century, the Arabic sources contain lengthy accounts of the early political and religious life of Islam, and the theoretical opinions of the jurists according to the schools of Islamic Law, there are no legal archives or documents which reveal the working law and its practical applications.

It was not until the period of the Cairo Genīza documents, from the eleventh to the thirteenth centuries, that we have been provided with examples of actual contracts.[4] Even then, the limitations of geographical location, local customs and school doctrines must be kept in mind when treating such documents as general examples; In truth, they can only serve as specific examples of that area and doctrine within a specified era. The same reservations must needs apply to the earlier Arabic papyri, whose

---

2 Parviz Owsia, *A Comparative Study of the Conclusion of Contracts in Persian, Islamic French and English Law*, (Unpublished Ph D Thesis; London SOAS, 1965)

3 For discussion and attempted explanation of this problem, see J. Sauvaget, *Introduction à l'Histoire de l'Orient Musulman*, (Paris, 1961) pp.18-23

4 See Goitein, 'The Cairo Genîza as a source for the History of Muslim Civilization', *Studia Islamica*, III (1955); and *idem.*, 'The Documents of the Cairo Genîza, as a Source for Mediterranean Social History', *Journal of the American Oriental Society*, LXXX (1960); and Norman Golb, 'Legal Documents from the Cairo Genizah', *Jewish Social Studies*, XX (1958)

relevance is generally restricted to Egypt.[5]

Our information concerning the law of early Islam is therefore gleaned entirely from the legal treatises and collections of *Aḥādīth* produced by the various exponents of the differing Schools of Islamic Law. With regard to modern sources, the same preoccupation with theory, as opposed to practice, has been kept to. This is not only in the interests of a balanced comparison, but also because of the impossibility of attaining consistent evidence of the law in practice. The modern courts of the three constitutional areas under study do not resort, as a rule, to precedent. It is usually only the Supreme Court of each jurisdiction which issues principles of precedence for the lower courts. Moreover, reporting of cases outside the Supreme Courts is either non-existent, or unofficial and therefore unattainable to the ordinary lay-man or non-practising lawyer. For this reason, illustration by resource to cases has been kept to a minimum.

The major sources which have been consistently referred to for the preparation of this study have included at least one main primary source pertaining to each School of Classical Law, and the comparative works : Sanhūrī's *Maṣādir al-Ḥaqq Fī al-Fiqh al-Islāmī*; Jazīrī's *Kitāb al-Fiqh 'Alā al-Madhāhib al-Arba'a*; and Y. Linant de Bellefond's first volume of *Traité de Droit Musulman Comparé*. For the modern Civil Codes, the Civil Codes of the three areas have been referred to either in their official Arabic versions (which were the only satisfactory versions available to me at the outset), or in the translations noted from time to time in the text. In particular, as regards the UAE, the later studies have been prepared in conjunction with Mr. James Whelan's admirable translation of the Civil Code; Mr. Whelan was also kind enough to provide me with the Arabic copy of the circulated provisional Commercial Code of the UAE. The official Arabic texts of the Kuwaiti Civil and Commercial Codes, and the Explanatory Memorandum thereto have been used throughout, and therefore the translations of these references are my own.

The official English version of the Bahraini Contract Code has been used in close conjunction with the Arabic translation of the same, while all other Bahraini and Egyptian prototype Codes have been used in their official Arabic versions except as noted otherwise in the text.

Several invaluable English handbooks have been of constant reference, once published, namely, The late Professor Coulson's *Commercial Law in the Gulf States*, (1984); Nabil Saleh's *Unlawful Gain and Legitimate Profit in Islamic Law*, (1986); and W.M. Ballantyne's *Commercial Law in the Arab Middle East : The Gulf States*, (1986).

---

[5] A Grohmann, *From the World of Arabic Papyri*, (Cairo, 1952); and *idem.*, *Einführung Und Chrestomathie Zur Arabischen Papyruskunde*, (Prague, 1955)

Where references to Arabic or European works are multiple, this is because preparation has been undertaken at various different locations. Editions available in one library in one country may have differed, therefore, from those in the principal libraries used in the United Kingdom, namely, Cambridge University Library, Cambridge University Oriental Faculty Library, the Library of the School of African and Oriental Studies in London, the British Library, and the Institute of Advanced Legal Studies.

It must be remarked that the whole subject of slaves and incidences arising in contracts pertaining to slaves has been assiduously avoided where other examples have been provided by the jurists, as the conditions relating to slave trading are no longer relevant. Where only slave examples exist, or where they have provided useful light in relation to other contractual institutions, however, mention has been made of them.

It must be stated also that all references to codifications of modern constitutions are current to 1990. The references to Kuwaiti law are, naturally, pertinent to the status prior to August 1990.

This dissertation, then, proposes a comparative exposition of the role of contract in traditional Islamic law. It attempts a comparison between the traditional principles as exposed by the early jurisconsults of the four main schools, and those precepts contained within the modern codifications of the independent Nation-States of Kuwait, Bahrain, and the Federal State of the UAE. Occasional comparative references are also made to Roman, Civil, and Common law concepts, and to articles derived from the codes of other Arab constitutions.

In the first section, an investigation is made of the muslim legal dichotomy between theory and practice; the classical exposition of legal sources is set against the development and possibly eclectic origins of jurisprudential methodologies. A cursory evaluation is made of the Qur'anic reform of contract on pre-existing tenets. Thereafter follows a detailed exegesis of the principles of the Islamic contract of Sale, which forms the analogous premise for all contracts in Islamic law. The constituent elements of contract are itemised and discussed, along with their effects.

A similar exposition is given of void and voidable contracts, with particular reference to the nullities of contract, the various invalidities of consent, the Islamic concepts of *Ribā* and *Gharar*, and the Rights of Option.

The overall aim of this book is to emphasise the continuing importance of Islamic contractual precepts within the modern codifications of the Arab Gulf states. It is hoped that through its publication, it may urge a wider comprehension of these principles within the realms of comparative law and international commercial relations.

S.E.R.
Cambridge, April 1991

We are all bowmen in this place.
The pattern of the birds against the sky
Our arrows overprint, and then they die.
But it is also common to our race
That when the birds fall down we weep.
Reason's a thing we dimly see in sleep.

Conway Power : Guide to a Disturbed Planet

إتقوا دعوة المظلوم

فإنه

ليس بينها و بين السماء حجابا

«قول مأثور»

ACKNOWLEDGEMENTS

The task of preparing this work has been greatly facilitated by the help and encouragement of others whose contribution I would like to acknowledge. I am particularly indebted to Dr. Andreas Zürcher and Ciba Geigy AG of Basle, Switzerland, without whose generous financial support and encouragement this study would never have been possible.

I am particularly grateful to Professor David S. Pearl, who supervised the preparation of this work for submission as a Ph D thesis at the University of Cambridge. He gave kindly and generously of his hard-pressed time to offer his experienced advice and constructive critical remarks. I am indebted to him for his efforts and encouragement.

From my previous studies I wish to extend my gratitude to Professor M.A. Shaban, formerly Professor of Arabic Studies at Exeter University, who not only encouraged me to progress to further academia, but also helped to secure the sponsorship from Ciba Geigy.

I am also indebted to Dr. Doreen Hinchcliffe, Barrister-at-Law, Grays Inn and Lecturer at the School of Oriental and African Studies, for initially awakening my interest in the study of Islamic law and for directing my attention to contracts in particular. I am deeply appreciative of all the help and encouragement she has afforded me over the years.

My thanks are also due to the former Master of Fitzwilliam College, Cambridge, Sir James C. Holt, who made available to me a valuable contribution from the Fitzwilliam College Research Fund towards the financing of my field trip. I would also like to thank the Fitzwilliam College Society for their equally valuable contribution towards the field trip. Furthermore, I wish to record my gratitude to the law firm of Clifford Chance, and in particular Mr. Jeremy Carver, Mr. James Whelan, Mr. Essam al-Tamīmī and the staff of the law offices in Dubai, Sharjah and Bahrain, who offered me the most generous of financial and practical help for my field trip undertaken in the Arab Gulf States in the latter part of 1987.

In Kuwait, I am most indebted to Dr. Muḥammad Mubārak Belāl, and Dr. Ghānem al-Najjār, who made my research in their country easier by their offers of help beyond the expectations of friendship; to Mr. Ḥassan al-Matrūkh who gave unbegrudgingly of his time to guide my way around the Kuwaiti courts; to Dr. 'Abd al-Rasūl 'Abd al-Riḍā, Head of the Kuwaiti

State Department for Legal Advice and Legislation, for his time and help in providing me with all the relevant Kuwaiti Codes, and for allowing me to interview him at length; and to the Dean, Dr. ʻĀdel Ṭabṭabāʻī, and learned Professors of Kuwait University Faculty of Law, notably Dr. Aḥmad al-Samdān, Dr. ʻImād Aḥmad al-Amīr, and Dr. Rashīd al-Anezī, who all allowed me to discuss the Kuwaiti Codes and legal system with them, and gave valuable opinions in return. In Bahrain, my research was made not only easier, but immensely more profitable by the kindness and hospitality proffered by Moḥsin al-Marhūn, Yūsuf A. Yateem, and Dr. Hāshim al-Bāsh.

Many thanks should also go to the staff of the Squire Law Library in Cambridge, especially to its Librarian Mr. Keith McVeigh and Mr. Peter Zawada; to the staff at Cambridge University library; the staff at the Oriental Faculty Library in Cambridge; the Head librarian and staff of Kuwait University Law Library; the staff of the Institute of Advanced Legal Studies; and the British Library; all of whose extremely competent services and tolerance were always offered so willingly. My gratitude is extended to Maggie Carr of the University of Cambridge Computing Service, who helped in designing the flags for the Arabic transliteration used in the text, and who shared with me a small part of her vast knowledge of the GCAL Text Processing System. My thanks also to the plethora of other helpers, notably, Dr. Desmond Schmidt, Rupert W.G. Moss-Eccardt and Dr. Irsān El-Husein for their contributions in the preparation of the final manuscript.

I am very grateful for the offer to publish made by Mr Fergal Martin of Graham & Trotman. His enthusiasm and patience during the metamorphosis of my Ph D thesis into a book provided encouragement during the frustrations. My thanks also to Dr. Mark Hoyle for his support and suggestions.

In addition, I am indebted to numerous friends and colleagues for their encouragement, advice and practical help. In particular, I should like to mention Dr. Rashīd al-Anezī, my colleague both here and in Kuwait, who has been a constant source of debate and encouragement; ʻAbd al-Raḥmān Benḥamādī; Sulaymān and ʻĀlia H. Sālem; Alain Joffé (LLM); Dr. Sawwād Shawwāf; Anne Habiby and the Department of Land Economy, University of Cambridge; Dr. Peter Gaunt and especial thanks to Jonathan Bradbury.

Finally, to my parents, Sarah Elizabeth and Terence Rayner, my family; and to Jonathan Lowe, for their unfailing support and faith throughout the years and their encouragement and patience during my research, I offer my most loving and appreciative thanks.

S.E.R.
Cambridge, April 1991

Chapter 1

THE MUSLIM LEGAL DICHOTOMY

Throughout Muslim legal history, the unresolved relationship between traditional legal theory and changing social practice has been a pervasive cause of conflict.[1]

The traditional Islamic theory is that the primary source of law is of Divine origin,[2] revealed in stages[3] to the Prophet Muḥammad as the Will of God, and embodied in the Holy *Qur'ān*.[4]

The Prophet's own *ad hoc* legal decisions, his deeds, utterances and unspoken approval (*Fi'l, Qaul, Taqrīr*) are regarded as divinely inspired; they form the second of the primary sources of Islamic law, and are known as *Sunna*.[5] They are recorded in a corpus of *Ḥadīth* literature, which, together with the *Qur'ān*, form the primary sources of the *Sharī'a* (literally : "Pathway").

The *Sharī'a*, being of a religious nature and therefore sacred, not only embodies those aspects of law recognizable as such by western secular standards, but also includes religious ethics to govern every aspect of a Muslim's life. For this reason the *Sharī'a* is more aptly called a "Doctrine

---

1 This relationship has been acknowledged as one of the fundamental problems of legal philosophies: W. Friedmann, *Law in a Changing Society*, (London, 1964), p.19.; See also Vida, G. Levi Della, 'Dominant Ideas In The Formation of Islamic Culture', *The Crozier Quarterly*, 21 (July, 1944) p.215 f.

2 *Qur'ān*, (II,23), (X,38), (XI,13) and n. 2289 to *Ṣūra* (XVII,89) of A. Yusuf Ali, *The Holy Qur'ān : Text, Translation and Commentary*, (Islamic Foundation; Leicester, 1975)

3 *Qur'ān*, (XVII,106), (XXV, 32),(LXXVI,23), (LXXXVII,6-7)

4 *Qur'ān*, (X,15-16), (XI,12-14), (XLVI,9)

5 *Encyclopaedia of Islam*, vol. IV, p.555. For an etymological and semantic analysis of the usages of the term *Sunna*, See Z.I. Ansari, 'Juristic Terminology Before Shāfi'ī: A Semantic Analysis with Special Reference to Kufa,' *Arabica*, XIX, (Oct.1972) iii, pp.259-282.

of Duties",[6] or "a guide to mankind".[7] It is in this respect that Islamic law differs so fundamentally from any secular system.[8]

Upon the Prophet's death in al-Madīna in year 11 of the Hijra (632 AD), access to the Divine Revelation became sealed, and the *Sharī'a*, in theory, became immutably valid for eternity. Two years after the death of the Prophet the revelations which had been communicated piecemeal to him during his lifetime were collected together by the first Caliph, Abū Bakr, resulting in the compilation of the Holy *Qur'ān*. At the inception of Islam there were various different readings of the *Qur'ān*, which were gradually reduced to seven in number.[9] A decade later these were revised and a new public edition was issued by the third *Khalīfa*, 'Uthmān. The *Qur'ān* represents the earthly record of the Mother Book (*Umm al-Kitāb*),[10] which, according to Muslim legal theory, embodied the divine law in co-existence with God Himself, and which may be called the embodiment of a Universal Law or the Law of Nature.[11]

The classical theory of the sources of Islamic law was formulated by Muḥammad Ibn Idrīs al-Shāfi'ī (d.822).[12] Al-Shāfi'ī was the first to establish the precedence of the Prophet as the second source of law; this he derived

---

6 The Arabic term "*Ḥuqūq*" meaning "rights" lays more emphasis on what a Muslim should do as a duty rather than what he is entitled to claim as a right. Moreover, *Ḥuqūq* are divided into divine and human rights, the latter necessarily subordinate to the former. J. Schacht, *Introduction to Islamic Law*, (Oxford, 1966), pp.200-201.

7 *Qur'ān*, (III,3)

8 Ernst Klingmuller, 'Le Concept de Légalité dans le Droit Islamique', in *Rapports Généraux au VIe Congrès International de Droit Comparé*, at Hambourg, 30 July-4 August, 1962 (Brussels, 1964), pp.205-221; I. Goldziher, *Introduction to Islamic Theology and Law*, (1910; transl. 1981) 3, N.B. See also Schacht's article 'Sharī'a', in *Encyclopoedia of Islam*, Vol. IV, p.321

9 Presently, a single reading is accepted by the majority Muslim body: See H.A.R. Gibb, *Mohammedanism: An Historical Survey*, 34 (Second Edn. with Revisions, 1970, 1973); and J. Makdisi, 'Islamic Law Bibliography', *Law Library Journal*, 78 (1986) p.103

10 *Qur'ān*, (XLIII:4) : "And verily, it is in the Mother of the Book in Our Presence, high (in dignity), full of Wisdom." See also, A. Yusuf Ali, *ibid.*, (III,7), n.347, p.123

11 For a comparative approach of the character of Islamic Law as combined with the doctrines of western philosophers, see Muhammad Muslehuddin, *Philosophy of Islamic Law and the Orientalists*, (Lahore, n.d.) pp.21 ff. and *passim*.

12 In his treatise *al-Risāla*, (Cairo, 1321 AH), translated in Khadduri, *Islamic Jurisprudence*, (Baltimore, 1961) pp. 227-229. For al-Shāfi'ī himself, see Bishop, 'Al-Shāfi'ī (Muḥammad Ibn Idrīs) Founder of a Law School', *The Moslem World*, 19 (1929) pp.156-175; and A. Hassan, 'Al-Shāfi'ī's Role in The Development of Islamic Jurisprudence', *Islamic Studies*, 5 (1966) pp.239-273

from the Qur'ānic injunction to "Obey God and His Prophet".[13] The *Sunna* of the Prophet are recorded in *Aḥādīth, (sing. Ḥadīth)*, whose narrators are listed in a 'chain' of transmission (*Isnād*) preceding the text. The authenticity of the *Ḥadīth* was not only the subject of greatest controversy in early Islamic legal history, it was also the earliest example of legislative eclecticism.[14] The subject-matter of Traditions could not be questioned objectively because the Prophet's decisions were regarded as divinely inspired. Only the *Isnād* could be challenged,[15] and for this reason the acceptance of al-Shāfi'ī's legal theory, which delineated rules governing the authenticity of the *Ḥadīth*,[16] "drastically changed the relationship between legal doctrine and Ḥadīth".[17] Regional *Aḥādīth* which had assisted in the formulation of local school doctrines and substantive laws prior to al-Shāfi'ī's classical theory continued to hold their sway thereafter. There is, for example, little deviation between the early Ḥanafī authors such as Abū Yūsuf and al-Shaybānī, and later medieval views such as those expounded by Sarakhsī and Marghīnānī.[18] Prophetic traditions which did not comply with a school's doctrine would be rejected by the early lawyers,[19] or accommodated into the early treatises with little or no attempt at tailoring the doctrine to its principles. It would often simply lie extraneously and unexplained, an obvious incongruity within the doctrinal exposition of any

13 See Schacht, *The Origins of Muhammadan Jurisprudence*, (Oxford, 1950); H.A.R. Gibb, *Mohammedanism*, (New York, 1962), p.90ff; A. Guillaume, *The Traditions of Islam: An Introduction to the Study of the Ḥadīth Literature*, (Oxford, 1924), *passim*. Sheikh Alī el-Khafīf, 'Sunna's Role in Expounding Islamic Rulings and Refutation of Suspicions cast on its authenticity', *Islamic Culture*, (Oct. 1968), p.242; and *idem.*, (Jan. 1969), Vol. XLIII, No. 1, pp. 55-60; and N.J. Coulson, *A History of Islamic Law*, (Edinburgh, 1964), pp. 53-61. The authoritative exposition of the al-Ash'arī classical Islamic doctrine can be found in 'Abd al-Qāhir al-Baghḍāḍī's *Uṣūl al-Dīn*, (Istanbul, 1928), Vol. I; also H.A.R. Gibb, 'Constitution Organization', in Ed. Khadduri and Liebesny, *Law In The Middle East*, (Washington, D.C., 1955), p.7

14 Schacht, *Origins of Muhammedan Jurisprudence*, *op.cit.*, p.4; and R. Brunschvig, 'Polémique Médiévales autour du Rite de Malik,' *al-Andalus*, XV, (1950), pp. 377-435.

15 See Aghnides, *Mohammedan Theories of Finance*, (New York, 1916) pp.1-117; and N.J. Coulson, *A History of Islamic Law*, (Edinburgh, 1964) pp.62-70. For discussion on *Isnād* and distribution of transmission theories, See G. Juynboll, *Muslim Tradition: Studies in Chronology, Provenance and Authorship of Early Ḥadīth*, (Cambridge, 1983), pp. 206f; M. Cook, *Early Muslim Dogma*, (Cambridge, 1981), pp. 107f.; P. Crone, *Roman, Provincial and Islamic Law*, (Cambridge, 1987), pp. 25-31; J. Schacht, *Origins*, *op.cit.*, pp. 117f.

16 al-Shāfi'ī, *Ikhtilāf al-Ḥadīth*, printed in the margin of *Kitāb al-Umm*, (Cairo, 1325 AH)

17 P.Crone, *Roman, Provincial and Islamic Law*, *op.cit.*, p.25

18 The same may be said of the Mālikī school. See Schacht, *Introduction*, p.59; Crone, *ibid.*, p.26. Even the Shāfi'ī school introduced little of innovation and certainly nothing beyond the Medinese tradition in the post-Shāfi'ī era.

19 Coulson, 'Doctrine and Practice in Islam', *Bulletin of the School of Oriental and African Studies*, XVIII, 2, (1956) p.225; J. Schacht, *Origins*, *op.cit.*, pp. 62ff

one school.[20] It has also been known for a *Qāḍī* to have given judgment contrary to a *Ḥadīth* for pragmatic reasons.[21] It is a facet of the Imāmī school that only Prophetic traditions transmitted by Imāms carried any significance. Consequently, their *Aḥādīth* continue to reflect school doctrine.[22] This virtually unchanged reflection of the substantive law indicates that a lesser significance was accorded to al-Shāfi'ī's classical formulation than theorists would have us believe.

It has been suggested that the shift from archaic to classical law is the result of a parachronism and that in fact it preceded the advent of al-Shāfi'ī's theory of classical law.[23] The sparsity of documentation during the first two hundred years of the Hijra has meant that the early extant *Ḥadīth* assume vital importance in the reconstruction of the development of the law in that period.[24] The significance of this alleged parachronism cannot be underestimated. The proposition that: "in terms of substantial law the crucial battles had been fought before [al-Shāfi'ī]" of necessity compromises any claims made by theorists that the law evolved from embryonic beginnings to classical formulation between 620 and about 820 AD.[25]

Al-Shāfi'ī's theory was that only Prophetic *Ḥadīth*, authenticated by acknowledged *Isnād* could be admitted as sound. The *Ḥadīth* which were considered as sound have been collected together by religious scholars of the third/ninth century. Two collections known as the *Ṣaḥiḥān* are amongst those recognised as of prime authority, those made by Muḥammad al-

---

20 Juynboll, *Muslim Tradition: Studies in Chronology, Provenance and Authorship of Early Ḥadīth, op.cit.*; *idem.*, *The Authenticity of the Tradition Literature; Discussions in Modern Egypt*, (Leiden, 1969); Abdallah Knoun, 'Ḥadīth its Scientific and Religious Value', *Islamic Culture*, Vol. XLIII, No.3, (July 1969, Hyderabad), pp.215-231; Crone, *ibid.*, p.25. For general references, See Th. W. Juynboll, 'Ḥadīth' *Shorter Encyclopoedia of Islam*, (Leiden, 1961), pp.116-121; and M.A. Anees and A.N. Athar, *Guide to Sīra and Ḥadīth Literature In Western Languages*, (London and New York, 1986) Ignaz Goldziher was the first western scholar to expose the authenticity of a large proportion of the *Ḥadīth* to serious criticism. He considered the greater part of it to be "the result of the religious historical and social development of Islam during the first two centuries." Goldziher, *Muslim studies*, transl. by C.R. Barber and S.M. Stern, vol II, (London, 1971), p.19.

21 Coulson mentions two: Muḥammad b. Abī Bakr, and 'Umar b. 'Abd al-'Azīz. 'Doctrine and Practice in Islam', *Bulletin of the School of Oriental and African Studies*, XVIII, 2, (1956), p.225

22 See Ibn Babūyah, *Man Lā Yaḥḍuruhu al-Faqīh*, Ed. H.M. Al-Khurshān, (Tehran, 1390); P.Crone, *ibid.*, pp. 25-26, nn. 41-42 (p.122)

23 Crone, *ibid.*, p.26

24 Early *Aḥādīth* collections include: *al-Muṣannaf* of 'Abd al-Razzāq b. Hammām al-San'ānī, (d. 826) ed. H.R. al-A'zamī (Beirut, 1970-1972); *al-Muṣannaf*, of Ibn Abī Shayba (d. 849), compiled in *Kitāb al-Muṣannaf Fī al-Aḥādīth wa al-Athār*, ed. M.A. al-Nadwī, (Bombay, 1979-1983); Bayhaqī, *Kitāb al-Sunan al-Kubrā*, (Hyderabad, 1344-1355)

25 Crone, *ibid.*, pp. 26-27

Bukhārī (d.256/870),[26] and Muslim b. al-Hajjāj (d.261/875). Soon after, four other collections, those of Abū Dāwūd al-Sijistānī (d.275/889), al-Tirmidhī (d.279/892), al-Nasā'ī (d.309/915), and Ibn Māja al-Qazwīnī (d.273/897)[27] achieved only slightly less respect. Together they form the six canonical Sunan, although various other collections followed later and achieved varying degrees of acceptability.[28]

Modern historians, however, have shown increasing scepticism towards the chronology of al-Shāfi'ī's theory. An acknowledged expert in the field of Ḥadīth has recently shown that numerous Prophetic Traditions are proven to have originated as statements made by early lawyers.[29] The emerging rule of thumb evinced by modern historians therefore, is that Prophetic Traditions postdate those ascribed to the Companions of the Prophet, which in turn postdate those ascribed to the early *Fuqahā'*. The deduction that a perfect *Isnād* should postdate an imperfect one naturally follows, for as Crone states : "After all, the better a tradition conforms to the criteria evolved in the time of Shāfi'ī, the more likely it is to date from the time in which these criteria were evolved."[30] Coulson's theory that "an alleged ruling of the Prophet should be tentatively accepted as such unless some reason can be adduced as to why it should be regarded as fictitious",[31] seems to be losing support among contemporary scholars.[32] His dispute that a false *Isnād*, is insufficient to discredit the content of the *Ḥadīth*, was refuted in no uncertain terms by Schacht.[33] Schacht's own dating of legal *Ḥadīth* (from about 700-800 AD) is

---

26 According to estimates, only approximately 7000 out of 600,000 Traditions were preserved as authentic by al-Bukhārī. Al-Bukhārī himself expressed doubts about some 2,500 of even these. See A. Guillaume, *The Traditions of Islam, An Introduction to the Study of the Ḥadīth Literature*, (Oxford, 1924) pp.23ff.

27 Dates of death in parentheses are listed firstly according to the Islamic calendar, and secondly according to the Gregorian calendar.

28 For the orthodox view of *Ḥadīth*, See M.Z. Siddiqi, *Ḥadīth Literature; Its Origins, Development, Special Features and Criticism*, (Calcutta University, 1961); See also B. Ducati, 'Rationalismus und Tradition im Mohammedanischen Recht-Die am Meisten Juridische der Muslimischen Rechtschulen', *Islamica*, (Leipzig, 1927), 3, pp. 214-218

29 G. Juynboll, *Muslim Tradition, op.cit.*, p. 15f; See also Crone, *ibid.*, p.31

30 P. Crone, *ibid.*, p.31

31 *History of Islamic Law, op.cit.*, pp. 64ff

32 *Cf.* discussion in Ahmad, Anis, 'Scientific Approach to Fiqh and Social Sciences in Islam', in: *International Conference on 'Science in Islamic Polity-Its Past, Present and Future', 19-24 Nov. 1983: Abstracts of Papers*, (Islamabad: Ministry of Science); Ayub, Muhammad (Allama Hafiz), 'Mischief against Hadith Exposed - (Maulana Ayub's) Crushing Reply to Rejectionists,' *Islamic Order*, (Karachi, 1984) 6 (3) pp.47-65; and the literature quoted in Anees and Athar, *Guide to Sīra and Ḥadīth Literature in Western Languages*, (London/New York, 1986) pp. 295-296

33 See Schacht's review, 'Modernism and Traditionalism in a History of Islamic Law', in *Middle East Studies*, (1965), pp. 392ff.; Also Crone, *Roman, Provincial and Islamic Law op.cit.*, pp. 30 n. 59, and 33 n. 78

the theory which presently holds sway among modern historians.[34] Further demonstrations pursued by Crone have proffered evidence that it was the lawyers who moulded the Prophetic *Ḥadīth* to their rules.[35] Whether the lawyers did this through unintentional subjective interpretation (due to their removal from the Prophet himself), or similarly discriminate memories, or by intended design is not known, and is probably now impossible for us to discover. What the conclusions of these historians do purport is that a major chasm lies between al-Shāfi'ī's theory of the evolution of Islamic Law, and the theory of evolution in practice as evinced by modern scholars. The controversial chronology and attributions of *Aḥādīth* having remained undiscovered or unaccepted for centuries, have naturally played a considerable part in formulating the methodologies of the evolving law. Their role, however, is engrained within Muslim legal history. Now entrenched as a primary source in the *Sharī'a*, and confirmed by time and consensus, it is unlikely that any new interpretation of their authenticity would result in a reassessment of *Aḥādīth* as a primary source.[36] It is not likely, therefore, that new misgivings as to the authenticity of this source will open significant "doors of neo-*Ijtihād*" in the future. To overthrow the validity of *Ḥadīth* contribution to the law would effectively be to undermine the whole foundation of the classical law. This is a task which even the secular legislative councils of today would be reluctant to undertake. The questions surrounding the *Ḥadīth* are unresolved; and until certain proof of the development of the law in its early stages can be furnished, the subject of the *Ḥadīth* will undoubtedly remain the most important example of the dichotomy between theory and practice in Islamic law.

1. RA'Y

In the first three centuries of the Hijra, the comprehensibility of the sources of Divine Ordinance (the *Qur'ān* and the *Sunna*) had already been qualified. At the height of the Umayyad Dynasty,[37] the Islamic conquests had expanded into countries beyond the Arabian Peninsular, such as Yemen (by 628 AD), Southern Mesopotamia (by 633 AD), Damascus (635 AD), Egypt (639 AD), Persia (640 AD), Tripolitania (647 AD), and even as far as

---

34 See for example, Crone, *Roman, Provincial and Islamic Law*, *op.cit.*, p.31; *idem.*, *Slaves On Horses, The Evolution of Islamic Polity*, (Cambridge, 1980), Ch. 1; *idem.*, *Meccan Trade and The Rise of Islam*, (Oxford, 1987), Ch. 9

35 Crone, *ibid.*, pp. 31-33

36 A staunch defence of the Sunna's authenticity is propounded by Sheikh Alī al-Khafīf, 'Sunna's Role in Expounding Islamic Rulings and Refutation of Suspicions cast on its Authenticity', *Islamic Culture*, (Oct. 1968) pp.242 ff. and Vol. XLIII, No.1 (Jan. 1969) pp.55-65

37 The Umayyad Dynasty followed the rules of the first four Caliphs; It lasted from 661-750 AD. See Lewis, B. *The Arabs In History*, (London, 1966)

Central Asia, North Africa, Spain and France (661-715).[38] New legal problems were therefore encountered which lay beyond the scope of previous Arab experience. Khadduri writes : "The development of Islamic law would have been less complex and the differences among the jurists probably less controversial and confusing if the Muslim community had remained confined to Arabia."[39] The Caliphs, Governors and *Qāḍīs*, whose offices were introduced by the Umayyads to help govern the expanding Muslim Empire, were obliged to resort to their own personal opinions (*ra'y*) to supplement divine legislation and customary law.[40] Thus the practice of individual *Ijtihād* (originally, discretion or estimate) resulted in a multitude of individual opinions arising in points of law.[41] In the public domain, the general uniformity of law prevailed, but in the private law diversity was rife.

In theory, the use of *Ra'y* was the discretionary exercise of a thoughtful, weighed and rational opinion which did not contradict either of the primary sources. Traditions, some of which were certainly forged, were cited to sanction the use of *Ra'y*[42] which provided a certain measure of flexibility in dealing with legal problems throughout the expanding empire, but which also allowed for a diversification of solutions which countered the Islamic ideal of unification.[43] In practice therefore, a wide latitude in the development of the law existed from the period following the Prophet's death (632 AD). Ra'y, local customs and administrative regulations of the early Caliphs all contributed towards the corpus of law to which the early Muslim 'Empire' had access.

---

38 For the course and effects of the conquests, see Macdonald, *Development of Muslim Theology, Jurisprudence and Constitutional Theory*, (Beirut, 1965), pp.82-83.

39 Majid Khadduri, 'Nature and Sources of Islamic Law: Customary Law and Islamic Law', in 'Symposium on Muslim Law', Part I, *The George Washington Law Review*, XXII, (Oct., 1953) I, p.11

40 See "Omar's Instructions to the Qāḍī", in *The Journal Of The Royal Asiatic Society*, (London, April 1910) by Du Margoliouth, pp.312 : The second *Khalīfa* instructs "Use your brains about those matters that perplex you, to which neither law nor practice seems to apply."

41 For the doctrine of *Ijtihād*, See Coulson, *A History of Islamic Law*, (Edinburgh, 1964) pp.59-60, 76-77, 102, 129.

42 Macdonald cites such a Tradition, probably forged, in which the Prophet who has commissioned a judge to supervise legal affairs in al-Yaman, asks him on what he would base his legal decisions. "On the *Qur'ān*," the judge replies. "But if that contains nothing to the purpose?" "Then upon your usage." "But if that also fails you?" "Then I will follow my own opinion." Muhammad is reported to have approved the Judge's answer. D.B. Macdonald, *Development of Muslim Theology, Jurisprudence and Constitutional Theory*, (Beirut, 1965), p.86

43 Khadduri, 'Nature and Sources of Islam: Customary Law and Islamic Law,' Symposium on Muslim Law, I, *The George Washington Law Review*, 22, (Oct. 1953), p.11

During this early period, the first of the schools of Islamic law were formed. The Mālikī school was set up in Medina by Mālik (179/795), a practising judge;[44] while in Kūfa, what was later to become the Ḥanafī school was set up by Ḥammad Ibn Sulaymān (120/738) and named after Abū Ḥanīfa (150/767).[45] Scholars grouped themselves together on a regional basis, and further schools were to be found in Basra, Syria and Egypt.

In the last decade of Umayyad rule, the more pious scholars of these regional schools united in their growing dissatisfaction with the interference into the law by governmental authorities. With the overthrow of the Umayyad Caliphate in 750 AD, and the accompanying rejection of impious Umayyad practices, legal scholars were charged by the "Islamic" 'Abbāsids to redefine the constitutional basis of the new Islamic State. It was at this point of political initiative that the doctrinal split between the Sunni and Shi'ite schools of Islam occurred. The Sunni scholars fulfilled their undertaking of defining the legal basis for the new 'Abbāsid society of Muslims; while on the other hand, an alternative ideological view of the Caliphate was propounded by the Imām Ja'far al-Ṣādiq, the sixth Shi'a Imām. Al-Ṣādiq rejected the 'Abbāsid claim to political governance and asserted that the leadership of the Muslim community was vested in him by virtue of his direct descent from the Prophet.[46]

By the early 'Abbāsid era, the lawyers and *Fuqahā'* of these early rites had grouped themselves into two camps : members of the Medinese school were known as *Ahl al-Ḥadīth* (Traditionalists); while the Ḥanafīs of Iraq were known as the *Ahl al-Ra'y* (Rationalists).[47] The Traditionalists appeared as an opposition movement within the ancient schools of law, advocating greater strictness and rigorism in the adherence to the classical sources.[48] Their counterparts opposed this idealistic attitude, and developed new doctrines whose main concern was with the practical efficacy of the

44 Mālik recorded the prevailing civil and criminal laws of the Medinese region in his *Muwaṭṭa'* : See Goldziher, 'Fikh', *Shorter Encyclopoedia of Islam*, (1953) pp.102,104; N. Aghnides, *Mohammedan Theories of Finance (With An Introduction to Mohammedan Law and a Bibliography)*, (New York, 1916; 1969) pp.169f.

45 It included Abū Ḥanīfa's two prominent disciples Abū Yūsuf (182/795) and Shaybānī (189/804)

46 See Gibb, H.A.R., 'Some considerations on the Sunni Theory of the Caliphate', 3 *Archives d'Histoire du Droit Oriental*, (1948) pp.401-410

47 The terms have also been applied to other schools and some confusion exists in the secondary sources regarding their application. For clarification of this, see G. Makdisi, *The Rise of Colleges: Institutions of Learning in Islam and The West*, (Edinburgh, 1981) pp.3-4. Amin calls the *Ahl al-Ra'y* 'Methodologists', and groups them as Ḥanafī and Shāfi'ī schools. The *Ahl al-Ḥadīth* "later represented the Mālikī and Ḥanbalī schools". Amin, S.H., *Middle East Legal Systems*, (Glasgow, 1985)

48 See Coulson, *A History of Islamic Law, op.cit.*, pp.52, 56, 61

Sharī'a.[49] The extent to which these doctrines were applied no doubt depended upon the complexity of the societal need for flexibility within the law. The schools of Madīna and Kūfa were alike in their primary legal methodology, but their systems of law differed considerably. This is not surprising, for the circumstances and populations of these centres were radically different in nature : Madīna, home to the first real Muslim community,[50] although benefitting from the influx of converts both during and after Muḥammad's lifetime, had long been a settled establishment and urban cosmopolis; Kūfa, on the other hand, had originated as a military encampment, situated in proximity to the newly conquered territories of the East, and had become a city populated by expatriate soldiers, *Dhimmī*s and neophyte Muslims. The political and social differences in these centres was thus reflected in the systems of law which had developed in their respective communities. We could expect, therefore, that the cosmopolitan nature of Iraqi Kūfan society would have greater need for rationalisation within the legal sources than that of Madīna.[51] There is also opinion to the effect that the Mālikī *Fuqahā'* withdrew from public life in order to escape the influence of political authorities asking for *Fatwā*s and legalizing expedients (*Muḥallilāt*).[52] The Ḥanafīs were apparently willing to serve the political authorities in this respect through the use of *Ḥiyal* (Legal Devices). The division of the early Mālikī and Ḥanafī rites into their respective schools[53] is not, however, as clear-cut as its convenience would suggest, as the Mālikī 'Traditionalists' also resorted to flexible legislation when the need arose.[54]

2. THE INFLUENCE OF FOREIGN LAW

At this time too, the Muslim legal caste came under the influence of other legal cultures, a fact which is borne out, according to Hugues[55] and

49 On *Ahl al-Ra'y*, see Coulson, *ibid.*, pp.52, 61

50 Although Mecca was the birthplace of Islam, Madīna was the first community, a significant proportion of whose inhabitants lived according to Muslim tenets.

51 Bello Daura, 'A Brief Account of the Development of the Four Sunni Schools of Law, and Some Recent Developments', 2 *Journal of Islamic and Comparative Law*, (1968) pp.1,4

52 On the arbitrary interference of rulers and government officials, see H.A.R. Gibb, 'An Interpretation of Islamic History', *Muslim World*, XIV, (1955), pp. 4-15, 121-133

53 Coulson interprets the distinction as between 'the lawyer and the moralist'. 'Doctrine and Practice in Islam', *Bulletin of the School of Oriental and African Studies*, XVIII, 2, (1956), p.225

54 See section 'Amal *infra*.

55 H. Hugues, 'Les Origines du Droit Musulman', *La France Judiciaire*, (1879-1880). p. 171

Goldziher, by the term *Ra'y* itself.[56] *Ra'y*, Goldziher states, is a literal translation of the Roman *Responsa* or *opinio prudentium*. This argument is refuted by Crone and Cook,[57] who point out that there is no such expression as *opinio prudentium* in Roman Law, and that the *Responsa prudentium* related more readily to *Fatāwā*. Applying the rationale that by the time of the Arab conquests Roman law had long ceased to be a jurists' law, Crone and Cook conclude that the Arabs did not translate directly from the Latin. Muslim *Ra'y*, they assert, is more closely related to Judaic *da'at* and *sevara* than it is to the Roman legal opinions.[58]

The term *Ra'y* is merely a case in point. Whether the origins of the concept are ultimately determined to be Roman, Jewish or from any other legal culture, the accepted fact is that the Middle East, at the inception of the Islamic legal system, did not constitute a legal vacuum which the conquerors were bound to fill with an Arabian law of their own.[59] The Development of the law required more than mere recourse to the primary sources, and since no constitutionalised authority existed to regulate the development, nor any system of judicial precedent, the corpus of the law at this stage became a hybrid collection of customs, borrowed practices, flexible measures and unofficial doctrines which were all eventually incorporated into the body proper of Islamic law by means of consensus (*Ijmā'*).

The extent to which other legal systems influenced Muslim law has long been disputed. This is not least because of the Muslim belief that the *Sharī'a* is an unprecedented, immutable and comprehensive world order, derived exclusively from the Word of God and conduct of the Prophet.[60] The influence of the legal scholars on the development of the law is generally

---

56 I. Goldziher, 'The Principles of Law in Islam', in H.S. Williams (ed.), *The Historians' History of the World*, (London, 1907), vol. VIII, p. 297; *ibid.*, *Muhammedanische Studien*, (Halle, 1889-1890), vol. II, p.76; *ibid.*, 'A Muhammadán jogtudomány eredetéröl', *A Magyar Tudományos Akadémia*, Értehezéseh a nyelv-és széptudományok köréböl kötet XI, (Budapest, 1884), p.11; *ibid.*, 'Die Religion des Islams' in P. Hinneberg (ed.), *Die Kultur des Gegenwart*, vol. I, part iii, (Berlin and Leipzig, 1906), p.102; *ibid.*, 'Fikh' in *Encyclopaedia of Islam*, *op.cit.*, p.101

57 P. Crone and M. Cook, *Hagarism the Making of the Islamic World*, (Cambridge, 1977), p.151

58 Crone and Cook, *Hagarism*, *op.cit.*, pp.37ff; Crone, *Roman, Provincial and Islamic Law*, *op.cit.*, pp.103-103

59 Contrary to the impression given by C.A. Nallino, 'Considerazioni sui Rapporti fra diritto romano et diritto musulmano' in his *Raccolta di Scritti editi e inediti*, vol. IV, (Rome, 1942); and S.V. Fitzgerald, 'The Alleged Debt of Islamic to Roman Law', *The Law Quarterly Review*, (1951). Crone, *Roman, Provincial and Islamic Law*, *op.cit.*, p.92

60 See, for example, Savvas Pacha, who having originally ascribed to the Roman Law influence theory, later adheres to this 'pure muslim' theory : *Études Sur la Théorie du Droit Musulman*, vol. I, (Paris, 1982) pp. xvi ff, xxi

admitted,[61] but the extent to which they themselves were influenced by other legal cultures causes some variance of opinion among modern authors. Santillana defiantly protests that Islamic law cannot have been conceived by parthenogenesis.[62] In concordance, Maḥmaṣānī states : "There is no need to point out that Islamic Law constitutes an original system, unborrowed and underived from any alien patterns, and hence totally independent from the Roman system."[63] He goes on to assert that Islamic Law is recognised as having "its own special origins and its own glorious history".[64] Badr also rejects the proposition that Islamic law was influenced by either the Roman or Jewish legal systems.[65] He argues that the Roman legal system was totally alien to the new world order created by Islam; he also doubts the probability of the Roman law ever having been translated into Arabic. Emphasizing that Muslim contact with the Byzantine Empire was minimal, he suggests that if any foreign influence had been exerted on the *Sharī'a* it should have been Sassanid, for the Muslim Empire came into closer contact with the Sassanian Empire. Further, Badr goes on to argue that Jewish influence was precluded by the fact that inter-trading between the Jews and the Arabs was kept to a minimum and did not therefore constitute a likely contact for the reception of cultural elements. In support, he points out that all Jews were exiled from Madīna by the year 627 AD after trading hostilities with the Arabs.[66]

A more substantial argument against the direct influence of Roman law upon the Islamic legal system could have been concluded in that in character and intention, the two systems differ radically. Where Roman law always remains in its abstract and academic, a lawyer's law : *nominem causa omne jus constitutum*, Islamic law is primarily a system of casuistics concerned with the relation of the individual human soul to God.

On the other side of the fence, however, we find authors arguing that Islam was formulated on an eclectic basis. Ever since the writings of H.

---

61 See Andreas B. Schwartz, 'Der Einfluss der Professoren auf die Rechtsentwicklung im Laufe der Jahrhunderte', in Elemer Balogh, Ed. 3 *Mémoires de l'Académie Internationale de Droit Comparé*, (1953) p.43

62 D. Santillana, Review of M. Fathy in *Revista degli Studi Orientali* (1916-1918), p.766

63 S. Maḥmaṣānī, 'The Principles of International Law in the Light of Islamic Doctrine', *Recueil Des Cours*, (1966) I, pp.221-222

64 Maḥmaṣānī and al-Azhar University Delegates to the International Conference on Comparative Law, The Hague, 1937

65 G.M. Badr, 'Islamic Law : Its Relation to Other Legal Systems', *American Journal of Comparative Law*, vol.26 (1978) pp.192-4

66 Badr, *ibid.*. For criticism of these arguments, see below. cf. Bousquet, 'Le Mystère de la Formation et des Origines du Fiqh', *Revue Algérien, Tunisienne et Marocaine de Législation et de Jurisprudence*, 66 (1947), who argues that Islamic law was not significantly influenced by Roman, Canon or Parsi law, but only in part, in the spirit of the Talmud.

Reland in 1708[67] and his successors D. Gatteschi,[68] and Sheldon Amos[69] in the nineteenth century, arguments have been advanced for the case of Roman influence upon Islamic doctrines.[70] Of these arguments, the principal are : the lack of Qur'ānic legislation together with the spread of Islam to provinces which sustained Roman law and its studies; the rapid growth and development of Islamic law in its infancy; and the generally stubborn resistance of legal institutions to change. Their assertions that Islamic law is "Roman law in Arab dress" led Crone to conclude that these early proponents of Roman influence rather "overstated their case".[71] Indeed, it is known that no study of Roman legal institutions was undertaken by the Islamic jurisprudents,[72] but the parallel terminology and institutions between the two have indeed proven hard to resist. Enger, writing in 1853, remarked on the parallel terminology in the subjects of taxation and ownership.[73] Van den Berg, soon after, highlighted similar parallels relating to sale and hire.[74] This itself was taken up and expanded by Von Kremer, in his *Culturgeschichte* where he expounded his theory that the doctrines of Roman law were introduced indirectly into Islamic law through other notions and borrowings, especially from the Jews.[75] An *a priori* case for Roman influence was also suggested by Schram-Nielson,[76] who notes parallels between Roman and Islamic law in the field of liability and compensation. His example is followed by several other authors, although it should be stated that their cases are less convincing due to the lack of

---

67 H. Reland, *Dissertationes Miscellaneae*, trajecti ad Rhenum, (1706-1708), vol. III, pp. 3ff.

68 Domenico Gatteschi, *Manuale Di Diritto Pubblico e Privato Ottomano*, (Alexandria, 1865)

69 Sheldon Amos, *The History and Principles of The Civil Law Of Rome*, (London, 1883)

70 P. Crone, *Roman, Provincial and Islamic Law*, (Cambridge, 1987), pp. 1-4, and *passim*; cf. also Saba Habachy, on the reception of concepts which he alleges to have originated with the Roman jurisconsults, in his 'The System of Nullities In Muslim Law', *American Journal of Comparative Law*, 13 (1964) pp. 62,72

71 Crone, *ibid.*, p.2

72 A. Von Kremer, *Culturgeschichte Des Orients Unter Den chalifen*, (Vienna, 1875-1877), Vol.I, Ch. 9

73 M. Enger, (Ed.) *Maverdii Constitutiones Politicae*, (Bonn, 1853), pp.xiv, 14 ff., 22 ff.

74 L.W.C. Van den Berg, *De Contractu 'do ut des' Iure Mohammedano*, (Leiden and Batavia, 1868), pp.17 ff. and *passim*.

75 Von Kremer, *Culturgeschichte*, Vol. I, pp.532 ff.

76 E. Schram-Nielson, *Studier Over Erstatningsloeren i Islamisk Ret*, (Copenhagen, 1945), p.29

demonstration.[77]

The theory that Islamic law owes more to Jewish influences than was previously admitted has been steadily gaining ground since Abraham Geiger's study in 1823.[78] Badr's arguments are swiftly swept aside when it is remembered that the assimilation of legal principles took place over some two hundred years,[79] in which time there was plenty of opportunity for contact between the cultures, besides which, the formation of the law was not localised to Mecca and Madīna but was spread over the conquered territories. Jewish, or other, influences which had been assimilated into provincial laws could have preceded the Islamic inception, and therefore could have been the result of indirect borrowing, as suggested by Van Kremer.

Crone argues, more convincingly, that Roman law disappeared from the Near Eastern Provinces simultaneously with the Roman state. The only real system which she will admit that the Arabs encountered in the Near Eastern provinces therefore, was that of the Jews. In fact, her own thesis for the influence of provincial laws rules out neither, as will be seen.[80]

Among the later Islamicists, Goldziher, for example, maintains that the similarities between Roman and Islamic law indicate a large scale influence

---

77 See A. Fattal, *Le Statut Légal des Non-Musulmans en Pays d'Islam*, (Beirut, 1958), p.75; M. Daoualibi, *La Jurisprudence dans le Droit Islamique*, (Paris, 1941), pp. 135ff; M. Hamidullah, *Muslim Conduct of State*, (Hyderabad, 1945). p.36; and *ibid.*, 'Influence of Roman Law on Muslim Law', *Journal of the Hyderabad Academy*, (1943)

78 Abraham Geiger, *Was Hat Mohammed Aus Dem Judentum Aufgenommen*, (Bonn, 1823). Translated by F.M. Young, under the title *Judaism and Islam*, (New York, 1970); Thereafter a vast literature has since developed on the subject. See, for example, Y. Meron 'Points de Contact des Droits Juif et Musulman', *Studia Islamica*, vol.LX (1984); Maḥmaṣānī, *Philosophy of Jurisprudence In Islam*, (Engl. Transl. by F. Ziadeh) (Leiden, 1961) pp.136-146 [3rd Ed. Arabic (Beirut 1961) pp.246-260]; and Judith Wegner, 'Islamic and Talmudic Jurisprudence: The Four Roots of Islamic Law and Their Talmudic Counterparts,' 26 *American Journal of Legal History*, (1982) pp.25 ff.

79 Contrary to the suggestion made by Fitzgerald that the main principles of the law had been worked out in Madīna before it had been carried West by disciples of Mālik in the latter half of the Eighth century A.D. See Fitzgerald, 'The Alleged Debt of Islamic to Roman Law', *The Law Quarterly Review*, (1951) p.85

80 P. Crone, *Roman, Provincial and Islamic Law*, *op.cit.*, p.92; and see below.

of Roman law upon Islamic law.[81] He regarded Roman Law as 'one of the chief sources of Islamite jurisprudence', and follows up this assertion with demonstrations. Goldziher has been accused, in later times, of consistently exploiting a "structural similarity between the concepts of early Roman and Islamic law to postulate a genetic relationship between the two without regard for the fact that it was with late Roman law that the Arabs came into conflict".[82] Regarding *Fiqh*, for example, he construes *Fiqh* and *Faqīh* as loan translations of the latin *(juris)prudentia* and *(juris)prudens*;[83] *Fatwā*, he equates with *Responsa prudentium*,[84] whereas both translations appear less plausible in the face of the information brought to light by Nicholas and Fitzgerald that the *prudentes* of Rome disappeared some four centuries before the conquests.[85] Similarly, Goldziher's correspondence of *Maṣlaḥa* with the Roman standard of *Utilitas Publica*,[86] and *Istishāb* with the Roman *Praesumptiones* have been shown to have missed the mark. Later authorities have emphasised the closer parallel between both concepts and their Jewish equivalents.[87]

Meron compares Muslim and Jewish theories of contract and finds various similarities (such as obligation falling upon the debtor; the notion of

---

81 I. Goldziher, 2 *Muhammedanische Studien*, (reprint 1961) p.75, n.18. For other authors maintaining this view see the literature cited here. He pursues his arguments in his other works, *inter alia*, : 'The Principles of Law in Islam' in H.S. Williams (ed.), *The Historians' History of the World*, (London, 1907), vol. VIII, p.296; See also his *Muhammedanische Studien*, (Halle 1889-1890), vol. I, p 188n; *idem*., 'Die Religion des Islams', in P. Hinneberg (ed.), *Die Kultur der Gegenwart*, vol. I, part iii, (Berlin and Leipzig, 1906) p. 102; and *idem*., 'Fikh' in *Encyclopaedia of Islam* *1*, *op.cit*., (written c. 1913) p. 102. See also Crone, *Roman, Provincial and Islamic Law, op.cit*., pp.102-106. Santillana accentuates the features common to Islamic and to Roman law in his original draft of the *Code Civil et Commercial Tunisien. Avant-Projet Discuté et Adopté au Rapport de M. D. Santillana*, (Imprimérie Générale; Tunis, 1899), known as the *Code Santillana*, part of which was enacted in 1906 as the Tunisian Code of Obligations and Contracts.

82 Crone, *Roman, Provincial and Islamic Law*, *op.cit*., p.103

83 Goldziher, *Principles*, p.296; *Jogtudomany*, p.19

84 *idem*., Jogtudomány, p.19

85 B. Nicholas, *An Introduction to Roman Law*, (Oxford, 1962) p.30; Fitzgerald, *Alleged Debt*, pp. 96ff; Crone, *Roman, Provincial and Islamic Law*, p.103

86 *Principles*, p.297; *idem*., 'Das Prinzip des Istishab in der Muhammedanischen Gesetzwissenschaft', *Wiener Zeitschrift für die Kunde des Morgenlandes*, (1887), p.183n; *idem*., 'Fikh', *Encyclopaedia of Islam*, p.103

87 For instance, the concept of *Maṣlaḥa* has more in common with the latin *utilitas causa receptum*, but even more so with the Rabbinic *Mippene tiqqun ha-'olam*, or *mippene tiqqanah*. *Istishāb* is more closely paralleled with the Jewish *Hazaqa*; Goldziher appears to have been aware of this fact (*Das Prinzip*, p.185) but suppressed it for reasons of his own. Crone, *Roman, Provincial and Islamic Law*, pp.102-196, who also provides an acceptable explanation of Goldziher's stance.

Person taking second place) between the two systems.[88]

Due to lack of documentation in the early Islamic era we can only hypothesize as to how extensive these external influences really were. Crone writes, in this context :

> "Umayyad law thus cannot be studied directly. Classical law, on the other hand, is usually too finished a product for the identification of origins. The evidence must thus come from pre-classical law, the earliest law of the scholars, which can be reconstructed partly from early *Ḥadīth* and partly from a systematic comparison of Sunni and heretical law, archaic elements being fairly common in the latter. This certainly is not first-class evidence, and arguments for Roman influence can probably never be as decisive as those for Jewish origins; but it is the best we have."[89]

In one study, Schacht attempts to show that the formation of Muslim law was an act of borrowing from the ancient legal systems.[90] In a later study, Schacht argues that foreign legal influence was introduced into Islamic law primarily by converts to Islam, and more particularly by advocate orators. He maintains that it was probably these people who introduced alien concepts into the Muslim legal system, rather than any serious studying of the Byzantine and Roman legal institutes by the Islamic jurists, whom he suggests, did not read Latin at that time.[91] The argument is plausible considering the large-scale conversion of *Dhimmīs* to Islam in the early years of the conquests. Conversion, or at least lip-service, was probably

---

88 Y. Meron, 'Points de Contact des Droits Juif et Musulman', *Studia Islamica* vol. LX (1984) p.85. Chehata is at variance with this point, and states that the Muslim theory of contract bears no similarity with any other legal system. Cf. Chehata, *Théorie Générale de l'Obligation en Droit Musulman*, (Cairo, 1936; reprinted Paris 1969) p.180

89 Crone, *ibid.*, p.16

90 J. Schacht, 'Foreign Elements in Ancient Islamic Law', *Journal of Comparative Legislation and International Law*, (1950), 32 [Series III] 3-4: 9ff. In his *Origins*, (p.100), he had supported Goldziher's acceptance of Roman law influence, but he had had a change of mind by the time he had written his *Introduction* (p.21).

91 Joseph Schacht, *Introduction to Islamic Law*, (Oxford, 1966) pp.6-8

encouraged by the financial constraints of the *Jizya* poll tax.[92] This would therefore constitute a new, but not insignificant, body of Muslims who could be expected to have retained their own customs and practices, so long as such practices did not conflict with the dictates of their new religion. This point is particularly pertinent in the field of commercial practices which, primarily, were unlikely to have been regulated by theological authorities in the previous religious persuasions of the converts ; and secondly, in the light of the fact that the primary sources of Islam do not provide comprehensive guidance to commercial practice even within the Islamic system.

It would not seem unreasonable, therefore, to postulate that commercial jurisprudence in particular, based primarily on the precepts dictated by the *Qur'ān* and the *Sharī'a*, was probably reinforced by the processes of its early *Fiqh* through the absorption of foreign customs and practices into each locality.[93] With the passage of time, the foreign elements would have merged with the local so as to make them indeterminable; the net result would be a body of provincial laws made up of an assimilation of all the influences of the locality.

If this theory is accepted, whether as an active result of the *Dhimmīs*, or as a passive result of Arab contact with engrained provincial laws, then the question of foreign law influence must be reformulated. No longer do we need to consider the possibilities and effects of each legal system in separation. Rather, the examination need only concentrate on the contribution of provincial law, including such elements of individual foreign

---

92 This tax on non-Muslim subjects was not, in theory, supposed to be either heavy or unjust; however, the very exhortations against this would seem to indicate that this was not always the case in practice. Cf.Abū Yūsuf, *Kitāb al-Kharāj*, (Cairo, 1302 AH) pp.69-85; al-Ṭabarī, *Ta'rīkh al-Rusul wa al-Mulūk*, (Leiden, 1879-1901) Vol.I, pp.2497, 2665; Ibn Qudāma, *Kitāb al-Mughnī*, (Cairo, 1341-48 AH) Vol. VIII, p.445; al-Kāsānī, *Kitāb al-Badā'i' al-Ṣanā'i' Fī Tartīb al-Sharā'i'*, (Cairo, 1909-1910; 1327-1328 AH) Vol. VII, p.111; al-Shāfi'ī, *Kitāb al-Umm*, (Cairo, 1321-1326) Vol. IV, p.120; al-Shaybānī, *Kitāb al-Aṣl*, (Cairo, 1954) Vol. XI, pp.141-2; al-Sarakhsī, *Kitāb al-Mabsūṭ*, (Cairo, 1913) Vol. IX, p.119; *Qur'ān*, (IX: 29); Yusuf Ali, *The Holy Qur'ān, op.cit*, p. 447, n. 1281. We do know that as there is no fixed amount for *Jizya*, unlike the *Zakāt*, the levy was decided by ruling authorities from time to time. See al-Ṭūsī, *Masā'il al-Khilāf*, (Iran, n.d.) vol. II, p.200; al-Shāfi'ī, *Kitāb al-Umm, op.cit.*, IV, p.122; A.R.I. Doi, *Non-Muslims Under Sharī'ah*, (London, 1983) pp. 55-61; A. Abel, 'La djizya : tribut ou rancom?', *Studia Islamica*, XXXII, (1970), pp. 5ff; Dennett, *Conversion and the Poll Tax in Early Islam*, (Cambridge, 1950); Emary, *La Conception de L'Impôt Chez les Musulmans*, (Paris, 1930)

93 This argument finds support with Crone, who, in relation to her example of *Kitāba* states: "Its continuance demonstrates that Arab manumitters did indeed pay attention to the legal practices of their non Arab subjects." Crone, *Roman, Provincial and Islamic Law*, *op.cit.*, p.64

laws as it may have contained.[94] The theory is a convincing one and comfortable. Not only is it mutually inclusive of all the above-mentioned foreign law influences, but it will easily accommodate any of the rarer suggestions so long as they may be shown to have been extant at some time within those geographical domains into which the Islamic 'constitutions' extended. The theory thus incorporates in the term "Provincial laws" the whole concept of custom, while at the same time, it admits of the varying celerity and extent of the assimilation process. For it must be deemed most unlikely that the far-flung provinces of the Islamic conquered territories all progressed in the same identical pattern. As Maine points out, "Societies do not advance concurrently, but at different rates of progress".[95] Hence we find that certain areas of the law bear more evidence of external influence than others.[96] In this context, therefore, we must take account not only of the customs and practices brought into the Islamic societies and absorbed by the indigenous populations, but also of the customs and practices which, inevitably, must have been accumulated by the muslim merchants and travellers during the course of their business abroad. O'Leary, in support of his thesis that the elements of culture (including social structure and law) have the distinguishing factor that they are all learned by intercourse, and never inherited,[97] propounds the chief ways in which 'Culture' percolated into pre-Islamic Arabia. The first, he states, was by the formation of colonies or outposts to cultivate the soil or exploit mines; The second was by the opening up of regular trade routes across the desert and the formation of alliances with the Arabs through whose territory they passed, and who, in return for subsidies, abstained from interfering with the caravans, while keeping off other Arab raiders; The third and not insignificant method he suggests is by the formation of marts and settlements along the frontiers, which allowed cultural influences to filter into the tribal hinterlands.[98]

Indeed, O'Leary's proposal is in harmony with Crone's emphasis on Jewish influence.[99] He asserts that in the centuries immediately prior to Islam, Arabia witnessed an outspread of Judaism, as an anti-Hellenistic movement, which was manifested in the scattering of Jewish colonies particularly in the settled plains along the Ḥijāzī mountain ridge which

---

94 Crone states: "The more we belittle the contribution of Roman law, the more we make a case for that of *provincial* law, not for that of Arabia." *Roman, Provincial and Islamic Law*, p.92

95 *Ancient Law*, (London, 1977) p.71

96 See section 1.9 on Legal Methodology

97 O'Leary, *Arabia Before Muhammad*, (London, 1927) p.24

98 *ibid.*, p.25

99 Crone does not make reference to O'Leary's work of 1927, which is surprising, for his interpretation of the Tradition at large is as constructive as hers is destructive.

delineated the North-south trade route.[100] The chief of these was at Yathrib, a colony of Jewish artisans and agriculturists.[101] Later known as Madīna, it was the city where

> "the community of Islam took coherent shape and where the basis of its jurisprudence was laid. But there to begin with, the Prophet assumed the customary law of the city, he varied it and added to it, but the common law of Yathrib was the starting point and that common law was the law of the Jewish colony. So far therefore as Muslim jurisprudence is concerned we must admit this Jewish basis."[102]

Thus, according to O'Leary, the common law in the market of Yathrib, as opposed to the customary tribal law, was not exclusively of Arab origin, but already established by the Jewish colonists. In spite of asserting Judaism as the expression of anti-Hellenism, O'Leary explains that the Jewish tradition contained a certain measure of Graeco-Roman law which had filtered down through the rabbinical academies of Galilee and Babylon, and was an inheritance from the days when the more progressive and flourishing section of Judaism was drawing inspiration from Hellenism.[103]

Nor were these colonies exclusively Jewish, according to Islamic Tradition. Reports tell of Syrian and Abyssinian colonies scattered around. The Tradition also relates of a clearly marked sphere of Byzantine influence along the Ḥijāz, and a similar sphere of Persian influence to the East and South.[104] Thus Arabia, if we are to believe the Tradition, was far from remote. Through the constant contact with surrounding empires and cultures, whether encountered directly, indirectly, within the Ḥijāz, or without, the influences of these peripheral cultures must have percolated through to the Ḥijāzī hinterlands. As commerce was perhaps the most obvious way by

---

100 O'Leary, *ibid.*, pp. 22-23, 171

101 O'Leary, *ibid.*, p. 105; The Jewish colonists of Yathrib were grouped in three tribes with Arabic names: the Banū Qaynūqa', the Banū an-Nādir, and the Banū Quraiza. O'Leary suggests on the authority of Yāqūt that the Banū Qaynūqa were possibly North-Arab, Idumaean or Nabataen, in other words, Arabs who had turned Jews. The other two tribes are held to have been Judaean who moved into Arabia sometime around the first century AD. (O'Leary, *ibid.*, pp. 173-174). He also attests active Jewish propaganda and conversion in the South (*ibid.*, pp.175-176).

102 O'Leary, *ibid.*, p. 171

103 O'Leary, *ibid.*, pp. 171, 175; Mittwoch, *Zur Entstehungsgeschichte des Islamischen Gebets und Kultus*, (Berlin, 1913); See also Pringsheim, Fritz, *The Greek Law of Sale*, (Weimar, 1950); and Taubenschlag, Raphael, *The Law of Graeco-Roman Egypt In the Light of the Papyri: 332 BC-640 AD*, (New York, 1944)

104 Which O'Leary states had been preceded by Egyptian and Babylonian influences 'which go back to a remote antiquity'. (*ibid.*, p.22)

which this process was implemented, it is not unlikely that the customs regulating whatever trade was engaged in at this time in the Arabian peninsula were the most vulnerable to these external influences.

It would indeed seem reasonable to suggest that the whole effect of these contacts would have been a unifying or assimilating influence on the institutions of any given order. In this context, Saleh states, in opposition to the argument proffered by Badr, that the situation of mercantile cities on trade routes, and Arab involvement in trading caravans makes it "difficult to support the alleged theory that such an international merchant society escaped foreign influences. Arabia, especially Hijaz, by the mid-seventh century AD was a cauldron of ideas, religions and trade."[105]

The basis of this argument finds an extremely interesting parallel in another theory proffered by Crone. This theory is established on scattered evidence[106] that the Near East formed a legal unit in Hellenistic times, and still formed such a unit on the eve of the conquests. The legal unit is attested to have varied from location to location,[107] but to have all added up to '*ein grosses ganzen*', much like the Greek legal *Koinē*.[108] Thus the legal unit would be "known to and understood throughout the provinces which were to form the heartlands of Islam" :

> "To some extent law in Arabia would thus appear to have been Near Eastern law, or an archaic version thereof, not simply tribal law unique to the peninsula. Now given the familiarity of the Arabs with the legal *Koinē* on the one hand, and the prevalence of this *Koinē* in the future heartlands of Islam, it is tempting to speculate that it was this *Koinē* which came to form the substratum of the Sharī'a : if the Sharī'a is provincial law recast with Jewish concepts at its backbone and numerous Jewish (and other foreign) elements in its substantive provisions, it would not be surprising that it fails to resemble any known legal system."[109]

Thus the theory also answers, in part, the claim of the Traditionalists that Islamic law is unprecedented and unique.

---

105 Nabil Saleh, *The General Principles of Saudi Arabian and Omani Company Laws*, (London, 1981) p.2

106 L. Mitteis, *Reichsrecht und Volksrecht in den Östlichen Provinzen des Römischen Kaiserreichs*, (Leipzig, 1891), p.62; *idem.*, 'Zwei Griechische Rechtsurkunden aus Kurdistan', *Zeitschrift der Savigny-Stiftung für Rechtsgeschichte*, (1915) p.426

107 E. Sachau, (ed. and transl.) *Syrische Rechtsbücher*, (Berlin, 1907-1914) vol.III, pp.8-9

108 Mitteis, *Reichsrecht und Volksrecht*, p.61

109 Crone, *Roman, Provincial and Islamic Law*, p.93

Specific inferences of similarities between the Muslim and foreign legal systems will be itemized throughout the text in support of the argument that Muslim law has always, in practice at least, remained susceptible to the influence of foreign legal institutes. At the same time, however, it must be remarked that mere similarity is not necessarily sufficient evidence of borrowing. Examples of similarity may give an exaggerated impression when mention of the many differences between Muslim, Roman and other legal systems is omitted. It remains to be said that similarities and infiltration of foreign elements are almost inevitable between legal systems. Those similarities which exist between Muslim and other legal institutes must not, therefore, be taken out of true perspective.[110]

3. SECONDARY SOURCES OF LAW

Where lacunae existed in the primary sources, secondary sources were developed by means of the human intellect, gaining their authority from Qur'ānic verses and Prophetic maxims.[111] These secondary sources of *Qiyās* (analogical deduction)[112] and *Ijmā'* (Consensus of Opinion) completed the four official sources of the *Sharī'a.*[113]

The Mālikī jurist Shihāb al-Dīn al-Qarāfī (d.1285) defined *Qiyās* as "establishing the applicability of a ruling in one case to another case on the

[110] For a full examination of the arguments involved here, see Maḥmaṣānī, *Falsafat al-Tashrī' Fī al-Islām*, (Translated by F. Ziadeh :Leiden, 1961) pp.136-145; also Goldziher, *Introduction to Islamic Theology and Law, op.cit.*, n.1 at 50; Schacht, *The Origins of Muhammedan Jurisprudence*, (First Edn. 1950, with corrections 1953) pp.85-86

[111] For example, the source of *Ijmā'* , or 'Consensus of Opinion' derives from the Prophet's maxim "My community will never agree upon an error." See the *Sunan* of al-Tirmidhī, (Cairo, n.d.) and Abū Dāwūd al-Sijistānī (Cairo, n.d.) 4 Vols.

[112] See Ahmad Hasan, 'The Critique of *Qiyās*', *Islamic Studies*, XXII, pp.31-35; Ibn Ḥazm did not recognise *Qiyās* as a source of law (he did recognise it in the deduction of Physical Sciences). He did not consider it a Muslim's duty to seek for the causes of the Divine Commands. See Afghānī's Introduction to Ibn Ḥazm's *Mulakhkhaṣ Ibṭāl al-Qiyās wa al-Ra'y*, (Damascus, 1960) pp.11-13; and Ibn Ḥazm, *al-Iḥkām Fī Uṣūl al-Aḥkām*, (Cairo, 1347 AH) VII, pp.55-56; The Shi'ites also reject *Qiyās* unless the cause of the rule of law is clearly mentioned in the text and the same cause is found in the parallel case : See, for example, Ibn Shahīd al-Thānī, *Ma'ālim al-Uṣūl*, (Tehran 1379 AH) p.402

[113] The four sources as recognised by al-Shāfi'ī were never recognised by the Khārijīs, the Wahhābīs or the Shi'a. See Wensinck's article, 'Sunna', in *Encyclopoedia of Islam*, 1, Vol. IV, p.557. Al-Shāfi'ī called '*Qiyās*' '*Ijtihād*', and did not permit of any other method of arriving at a legal opinion (*Fatwā*) or making a judgment (*Ḥukm*) outside these four sources of law. He was opposed to the use of arbitrary opinion (*Ra'y*) or other unofficial legal reasoning: Shāfi'ī, *Kitāb al-Risāla*, (Cairo 1321/1903) 66 [4-5,18-20], 69 [17-18], 70 [31-33]; M. Khadduri, (transl.) in *Islamic Jurisprudence: Shafi'i's Risāla*, (1961); also Shāfi'ī, *Kitāb al-Umm*, (Cairo/Bulaq, 1325/1907) Vol. VII, 270; [33] 272

grounds of their similarity, with respect to the attribute upon which the ruling is based."[114] *Qiyās* has its limitations as a source of law, as Subkī has pointed out.[115] It cannot apply to natural functions or ancient, long-established practice, nor can it be based on any of the abrogated verses of the *Qur'ān*. The practice of *Qiyās* also courted casuistry and diversity of opinion, even within the schools, as is shown by divergences within the Ḥanafī school.[116]

Theoretically, *Ijmā'* meant the consensus of the Islamic community, but eventually it devolved from the legal scholars, or *Mujtahidīn*.[117] The consensus of opinion (*Ijmā'*) sanctioned any law obtained by *Qiyās* as valid and enforceable. It was only pure idealism that prevented the recognition that such unfettered opinion would eventually lead to abuse.[118]

In the practice of the law, the early jurists supplemented the four official sources with a corpus of 'tertiary sources': these were highly technical ideas and institutions far beyond the scope and implications of Qur'ānic legislation. Consensus, for instance, precluded differences of opinion (*Khilāf*), which sought solution through publicly conducted disputation (*Munāẓara*).[119] Juristic speculations (*Ra'y*), conjectures (*Ẓann*) and preferences (*Istiḥsān*) were employed by the jurisconsults to form a diversity of arbitrary legal decisions.[120]

By the third century AH, the elaboration of jurisprudence had reached the point of mere abstract casuistry. Moreover, opinions on points of law had become so diverse among the different schools that, in the interests of uniformity, further processes of independent and analogical reasoning were

114 al-Qarāfī, *Sharḥ Tanqīḥ al-Fuṣūl Fī 'Ilm al-Uṣūl*, published as Chapter II in *al-Dhakhīra*, (A Collection of Qarāfī's writings) (Cairo, 1961) I, 119; For *Qiyās generally, see also Kerr, M.H., Islamic reform : The Political and Legal Theories of Muhammad Abduh and Rashid Rida*, (Berkeley, 1966) pp.66-79

115 Subkī, *Jam' al-Jawāmi'*, (Cairo, 1354 AH) II, 176-178

116 see Abū Yūsuf's *Kitāb al-Kharāj*, (Cairo, 1302 AH) pp.36,39

117 al-'Āmilī, *Ma'ālim al-Dīn*, (Lucknow, 1301 AH) p.99. The Ẓāhirīs upheld only the *Ijmā'* of the Prophet's Companions. See also J. Makdisi, 'Islamic Law Bibliography' *op.cit.*, p.106; Hassan, *The Doctrine of Ijmā' in Islam*, (Islamabad, 1978); G.F. Hourani, 'The Basis of Authority of Consensus in Sunnite Islam', *Studia Islamica*, 21 (1964) pp.13-60; and M.Z. Madina, *The Classical Doctrine of Consensus in Islam*, (Chicago: Dept. of Photoduplication, University of Chicago Library, 1957).

118 R. Levy, *The Social Structure of Islam*, (Cambridge, 1969) p.167

119 For which, see G. Makdisi, 'The Scholastic Method in Medieval Education : An Inquiry Into Its Origins in Law and Theology', 49 *Speculum*, (1974) pp.640 f.

120 See, for example, Coulson, *A History of Islamic Law*, (Edinburgh, 1964) p.60

restricted : the "*doors of Ijtihād* " were firmly closed.[121] In principle therefore, the classical ideal of the immutable *Sharī'a* held sway for some nine centuries.[122] In practice, however, the changing demands of society required variable implementations in the law. The *Sharī'a*, set in a rigid mould by the doctrine of *Taqlīd* (Imitation),[123] was unable to accommodate these demands and the changes that were made came of necessity from the sub-strata of legal administration.[124]

The need to co-ordinate even the strictest theoretical ideals with actual practice gave rise to various methodologies of incorporating provisions to fit social change.

> "Usages had grown up and taken fast hold which were in the teeth of all traditions. These usages were in the individual life, in the constitution of the state, and in the rules and decisions of the law courts. The pious theologian and lawyer might rage against them as he chose ; they were there, firmly rooted, immovable. They were not arbitrary changes, but had come about in the process of time through the revolutions of circumstances and varying conditions."[125]

The law therefore continued to develop through the following centuries by means of an independent arrangement of doctrine, an originality of argument

---

121 Shāṭibī, *al-Muwāfaqāt Fī al-Uṣūl al-Shar'iyya*, (Cairo, 1341 AH) IV, 132-135. See Hallaq, *The Gate of Ijtihād: A Study in Islamic Legal History*, (Ann Arbor, Michigan: University Microfilms International, 1983); Maḥmaṣānī explains the cause of the 'fossilization of legal rules' as the fall of Baghdad and the steady decline and stagnation of the Arab civilization. See his article 'The Principles of International Law in the Light of Islamic Doctrine', *Recueil Des Cours*, I, p.221

122 J.N.D. Anderson, *Law Reform in the Muslim World*, (London, 1976), p.7; and J. Schacht, *Introduction to Islamic Law*, *op. cit.* , p.202.

123 Technically *Taqlīd* means 'acting on the word of another without *Ḥujja* (proof)': Ibn al-Ḥājj, *al-Taqrīr wa al-Taḥbīr*, commentary on *al-Taḥrīr*, by Ibn al-Hammām (Bulaq, 1316 AH) III, p.340. See also, Nyazee, 'The Scope of Taqlīd', *Islamic Studies*, XXII (4) (1983) pp.1-29. Ibn Taymiyya (682/1283) rejected the doctrine of *Taqlīd* on the basis that he considered it bad practice to follow the authenticity of anyone other than the Prophet in religion and law. He did not, however, advocate a reopening of the Doors of *Ijtihād*, but rather to reinterpret the primary sources afresh thereby to reach novel conclusions regarding many muslim law institutions.

124 Schacht, *An Introduction to Islamic Law*, (Oxford, 1964) 70-73; Milliot, *Introduction á L'Étude du Droit Musulman*, (1958) 150-151; 3 Ibn Khaldūn: The Muqaddimah An Introduction to History, 8-9 (transl. F. Rosenthal, 1958); Anderson, 'Law as a Social Force In Islamic Culture and History', 20 *Bulletin of the School of Oriental and African Studies*, 13, 16 (1957); Y. Linant de Bellefonds, *Traité de Droit Musulman Comparé*, I, 20-22 (1965)

125 Macdonald, *Development of Muslim Theology, Jurisprudence and Constitutional Theory*, (*op.cit.*), p.105

and an evolving use of legal terminology.[126]

4. ḤIYAL

The open practice of accommodating the law to fit social change and usage had now become tempered by the doctrine of *Taqlīd.* The official surface of the law remained calm, but rippling underneath the surface, "underground doctrines" became discernible in the prevailing positive law.[127] A vast body of literature of "*Ḥiyal*", or Legal Stratagems was established by the jurists[128] to circumvent legal concepts proving too ideal to be practicable.[129] The earliest *Ḥiyal*, were simple evasions by merchants, but at the hands of zealous jurists these devices were developed into a series of complex and pedantically elaborate "masterpieces of legal construction."[130]

The *Ḥiyal* would conform to the letter of the law, and would therefore be acceptable on purely legal grounds; but in their betrayal of the spirit of the law, they would prove objectionable to the moralist.[131] An example is *Bay' al-Wafā'*, a contract which allegedly evolved in the fifth or sixth century AH

---

126 J. Makdisi, 'Islamic Law Bibliography' *op.cit*, pp.108-109; See also Meron, 'The Development of Legal Thought in Hanafi Texts', 30 *Studia Islamica*, 73, 90-91 (1969); cf. Chehata, *Études de Droit Musulman*, (1971) who acknowledges the attempt at innovation within the law, but who rejects the thesis that the structure of the law was altered (*id.* at p.40). On *Fatāwā* of legal scholars, see G. Makdisi, 'Interaction between Islam and the West', *Revue des Études Islamiques*, 44, (1976) pp.287, 300-302, and G. Makdisi, *The Rise of Colleges: Institutions of Learning in Islam and the West*, (Edinburgh, 1981) pp. 290-291 who state that the activity of *Ijtihād* was not weakened seriously until the seventh/thirteenth century, and then it was the doing of the governing power rather than the strictures of Islamic doctrine.

127 Roman law resolved this conflict by distinguishing between *jus civile* and *jus honorarium*, whereas English Common Law retained its flexibility through the doctrine of Equity.

128 For example, Abū al-Su'ūd; See Schacht's article 'Abū al-Su'ūd', in *The Encyclopoedia of Islam*, (New Edn. Leiden, 1960) p.152

129 See J. Schacht's article '*Ḥiyal*', in the *Encyclopaedia of Islam*, (New Edition: Leiden, 1971), Vol. III, pp.511-512; also I. Goldziher, *Die Zâhiriten, Ihre Lehr-System und Ihre Geschichte*, (Leipzig, 1884), pp.68f; and Schacht's article, 'Die Arabische Hiyal-Literature,' in *Islam*, XV, (1926), pp.211-232. R. Brunschvig, 'De la Fiction Légale dans L'Islam Mediéval', *Studia Islamica*, XXXII, (1970), pp. 41ff..

130 J. Schacht, *Introduction to Islamic Law*, *op.cit*, p.80. Schacht notes here that similar devices existed in the Jewish Canonical and Roman legal systems. The Roman devices differed from the Islamic *Ḥiyal*, in that they provided a legal framework for new requirements in legal practice with the minimum of innovation, whilst the Islamic *Ḥiyal* provide for the circumvention of existing provisions.

131 See the list of examples given by the Shāfi'ī jurist Sulāmī , *Qawā'id al-Aḥkām Fī Maṣāliḥ al-Anām*, 2 Vols in 1, (1388/1968); and the Mālikī jurist, Shihāb al-Dīn Aḥmad b. Idrīs al-Qarāfī, *Kitāb al-Ummiyya Fī Idrāk al-Niyya*, (Furūq Edn, Cairo, 1344 AH); and *id.*, *Sharḥ Tanqīḥ al-Fuṣūl Fī Ikhtiṣār al-Maḥṣūl Fī Uṣūl*, (Cairo, 1393/1973)

in order to circumvent the prohibition against *Ribā*. The seller effectively defers payment of the price in a contract of sale. In essence, the 'sale' is a loan for usufruct where the debtor 'sells' his property to the creditor on condition that it is returned upon his repayment of the price. In the interim the debtor has use of the price, while the creditor has use of the property which constitutes the object of the 'sale' in consideration for the price paid to the debtor. The objections of the moralists to this transaction are plain to see. Firstly, if the transaction is that of sale, it constitutes sale with a condition, which was forbidden by the prophet;[132] and secondly, it can be argued to constitute a contract of pledge: in which case, the creditor may not have use of the pledged object as a right. This contract would therefore not be permitted.[133]

Schacht describes the *Ḥiyal* as a "*modus vivendi*" between theory and practice, but the extent to which the four Sunni schools regard *Ḥiyal* as theoretically acceptable varies. The Ḥanafīs, being the most liberally disposed towards the concept, nevertheless invalidate those *Ḥiyal* causing prejudice to a third party or which incorporate individually reprehensible operations. On the whole though, the Ḥanafīs are more inclined to accept *Ḥiyal* as legally valid rather than concern themselves with moral evaluation of the practice.[134] The Mālikīs, on the other hand, were more concerned with the moral considerations of *Ḥiyal*, and condemned the majority of devices. In fact, any necessity to resort to *Ḥiyal* was probably quite satisfactorily covered by the Mālikī doctrine of *'Amal.*

The majority opinion of the Ḥanbalī school is to distinguish the lawful *Ḥiyal* from the forbidden and invalid.[135] Here the Ḥanbalī school adopts a tolerant approach, which contrasts favourably with the extremist neo-Ḥanbalī approach of Ibn Taymiyya. In his view that both *Ḥiyal* and *Taḥlīl* (Resolution) are invalid, Ibn Taymiyya can be more easily identified with the Traditionalists, such as al-Bukhārī, who characteristically rejected *Ḥiyal* and produced sustained polemics against the concept.[136]

Finally, the Shāfi'īs regard *Ḥiyal* as generally reprehensible; they are nevertheless disposed to recognise the concept as legally valid for the sake

---

132 Ibn 'Ābidīn, *Radd al-Muḥtār 'alā al-Durr al-Mukhtār*, 8 Vols., (Cairo, 1386-89/1966-69), IV, p.341

133 El-Hassan, 'Freedom of Contract, The doctrine of Frustration, and Sanctity of Contracts in Sudan Law and Islamic Law', *Arab Law Quarterly*, Vol. I (1) (Nov. 1985) pp.51-59, at 55.

134 The major Ḥanafī treatises on *Ḥiyal*, were written by Abū Yūsuf and Shaybānī, *Kitāb al-Makhārij Fī al-Ḥiyal*, Ed. Joseph Schacht (Leipzig, 1930), an appreciation of whose works may be found in Khaṣṣāf, *Kitāb al-Ḥiyal wa al-Makhārij*, (Hanover, 1923).

135 The proponent of this Ḥanbalī opinion was Ibn Qayyim al-Jawziyya (d. 751 AH/ 1350 AD), a disciple of Ibn Taymiyya.

136 See, for example, al-Bukhārī's *al-Jāmi' al-Ṣaḥīḥ*, (Cairo, n.d.) 9 vols.

of practicability.[137]

It may be deduced therefore that in the realm of *Ḥiyal* it is the Ḥanafī school which is more liberal in its recognition of the importance of the application of the law in practice over the strict dogmas of the *Sharī'a*. The recognised need throughout the schools of law to circumvent the theory eventually established an uneasy conciliation between the traditional theorists (the *'Ulamā'*) and the practical administrators (the political authorities). The *'Ulamā'* therefore formulated doctrines which were able to relinquish Muslims from their obligation to observe the more strict provisions of the *Sharī'a*.

5. MAṢ LAḤA

The legal consideration of *Maṣlaḥa* (literally, "Human Good")[138] was treated by Shāṭibī and other jurists, such as Qarāfī,[139] as an independent principle of legal theory although it has never been officially recognised as such by the body of *'Ulamā'*.

Istiṣlāḥ was resorted to in cases where the strict application of *Qiyās* would have led to irrational or unnecessarily harsh results. The contract of *Istiṣnā'* (manufacture) finds its legality through this principle: if, for example, a person buys leather on the stipulation that it should be made into a specific article, the contract would normally be voidable on the grounds that it included a stipulation which is extraneous to the object of contract. As it is a generally adopted procedure in normal commercial life however, the contract is considered as valid through the effects of Maṣlaḥa.[140] Similar contracts made lawful by the application of Maṣlaḥa are the customary hire of a wet nurse for consideration of her food and clothing;[141] and the contract of sale in which non-fungibles are pledged as security for the price.[142]

---

137 The Shāfi'ī view is contained in Qazwīnī's treatise, *Kitāb al-Ḥiyal fī al-Fiqh*, edited by J. Schacht, (Hanover, 1924).

138 Ghazālī defines *Maṣlaḥa* as "Consideration for what is aimed at for mankind in the law" (*al-Muḥāfaẓa 'alā Maqsūd al-Sharī'a...min al-Khalq*) and the averting of corruption (*daf' al-Mafsada*). See Paret, *Encyclopoedia of Islam*, p.25; and Tyan, E., 'Méthodologies et Sources du Droit en Islam (Istiḥsān, Istiṣlāh and Siyāsa Shariyya)', *Studia Islamica*, X (1959) pp.79-110. The doctrine of *Ḍarūra* is almost synonymous with Maṣlaḥa, although it was more sparingly used.

139 Shāṭibi, *al-Muwāfaqāt Fī al-Uṣūl al-Shar'iyya*, (Cairo, 1341) IV, pp.116-118. The principle champions of Istiṣlāḥ were the Mālikīs: Mālik, *al-Mudawwana al-Kubrā*, [Narrated by Saḥnūn] (Cairo, 1323) XVI, 217. For further references see Paret's article in *Encyclopoedia of Islam*, pp.258 ff.

140 Schacht, *Introduction*, p.152

141 Schacht, *Introduction*, p.155

142 *idem*, p.146. This contract would otherwise have been *Fāsid* because pledging and security constitute separate contracts from that of sale.

The radical medieval proponent of *Maṣlaḥa*, Najm al-Dīn Tawfī (d. 716 AH)[143] asserted that *Maṣlaḥa* is a necessity and takes precedence over every other *Sharīʿa* principle.[144] Tawfī based his conviction upon the Prophet's formula *Lā Ḍarāra wa lā ḍirāra fī al-Islām* (In Islam there is no injury or malicious damage).[145] Tawfī claims that the concept of *Maṣlaḥa* was the only acceptable means of retrieving order out of the chaos instigated by the dichotomy between theory and practice in Muslim legal tradition. For him the principal provision of the *Sharīʿa* is for utilitarianism :

> "And let it not be said that the law knows better what are one man's interests and that his interests can therefore be surmised by the law's indications. We have established that regard for these interests is indeed one of the indications of the law, if not the most important and specific of them. Let us therefore give it precedence that it may achieve these interests."[146]

Tawfī's is an extremist's view of the concept of *Maṣlaḥa* as an accommodating principle within the structure of the law. At the other end of the scale, Ibn Taymiyya promotes his misgivings on the principle by lamenting the use of *Maṣlaḥa* by rulers. He asserts that the *Sharīʿa* has not neglected "Human Good" and that if man thinks he can assume a *Maṣlaḥa* which is not represented in the law, then he is either imagining his own version of *Maṣlaḥa*, or the law has already indicated it without his having recognised it. The concept was also violently criticised by the Shāfiʿīs, who accused it of opening the door to legislative creation,[147] arbitrarism and rendering the law vulnerable to serious abuse. Ghazālī ranked both *Istiḥsān* and *Istiṣlāh* among the *Uṣūl Mawhūma*, the 'imaginary sources' of the law.[148] The neo-Ḥanbalī school in general took a more lenient view,

---

143 Tawfī was considered a Ḥanbalī, but in reality he was an independent *Mujtahid*. For his biography, see Shaṭṭī, *Mukhtaṣar Ṭabaqāt al-Ḥanābila*, (Damascus, 1339 AH) pp.52ff

144 Tawfī, *Risāla Fī al-Maṣāliḥ al-Mursala (Majmūʿ Rasāʾil Fī Uṣūl al-Fiqh*, (Beirut, 1324) pp.37-70 [Published in R. Riḍā's periodical *Al-Manār*, IX (1324) 745-770. See M. Muslehuddin, *Islamic Jurisprudence and the Rule of Necessity and Need*, (Islamabad, 1975)

145 Ḥadīth No. 32 of the Shāfiʿīte jurist al-Nawāwī (d. 670 AH). Tawfī's commentary 'Sharḥ al-Ḥadīth al-Thānī wa al-Thalāthīn Min al-Arbaʿīn al-Nawāwiyya,' is published in *Majmūʿ al-Rasāʾil Fī Uṣūl al-Fiqh*, (Beirut, 1324 AH).

146 Muṣṭafā Zayd, *al-Maṣlaḥa Fī al-Tashrīʿ al-Islāmī wa Najm al-Dīn al-Tawfī*, (Cairo, 1954), Appendix p. 48. Also cited in Kerr, *Islamic Reform, op.cit.*, p.100.

147 See the Mālikī report of al-Shāṭibī, *Kitāb al-Iʿtiṣām*, 2 vols. (Cairo, 1295 AH) II, 113

148 Ghazālī, *Kitāb al-Mustasfā Min ʿIlm al-Uṣūl*, 2 Vols. (Bulaq, 1322 and 1324; Cairo, 1937/1356) I, 283 ff.

differentiating between the concerns of the *'Ibādāt* and those of the *'Adāt* : in matters of worship everything has been definitively determined by God and the Prophet; for the rest, that is, the organization of material life, the *'Ulamā'* are free to exercise their right of *Ijtihād.* In general therefore, *Maṣlaḥa* was seen as a dynamic characteristic of Islamic legal theory, and as a concept of goodwill and reconciliation which accorded the law the scope for permutation.[149] It is this stance which has provided the interpretation for modern *Istiṣlāḥ,* and which is adhered to in effecting modern legislative changes necessitated by commercial activites of the present era.[150]

6. ISTIḤSĀN

The parallel concept of *Istiḥsān* provided the jurists[151] with an opportunity for flexibility within the immutable theory by the intervention of principles based on the justification of "Choosing for the better".[152] *Istiḥsān* forms a rational method for determining decisions when particular cases are not regulated by the incontrovertible authority of the *Qur'ān, Sunna* or *Ijmā',* or when conflicting principles, drawn from the primary sources, compete for consideration. It is an equitable concept which is based, like the concept of *Qiyās,* on the determination of the cause (*'Illa*) underlying an

---

149 R. Paret's article '*Istiḥsān* and *Istiṣlāḥ*' in the *Shorter Encyclopaedia of Islam,* (New Edition, Leiden, 1978), Vol.IV, pp.255-259. Also M. Khadduri, 'The Maṣlaḥa (Public Interest) and 'Illa (Cause) in Islamic Law', *New York Journal of International Law and Politics,* 12 (1979) pp.213-217; Tyan, E., 'Méthodologies et Sources du Droit en Islam (Istiḥsān, Istiṣlāh and Siyāsa Shariyya)', *Studia Islamica,* X (1959) pp.79-110; Chehata, 'L'Equité en Tant que Sources du Droit Hanafite', II *Studia Islamica,* XXV (1966) pp.123-128; and F. Rahman, 'Towards Reformulating the Methodology of Islamic Law : Sheikh Yamani on "Public Interest" in Islamic Law', *New York University Journal of International Law and Politics,* 12 (1979) pp.219-224

150 Ahmad 'Aziz, '*Iṣlāḥ*', *Encyclopoedia of Islam,* vol. IV, (Leiden, 1978) p.154; David Suratgar, 'The Development of Legal Systems', in *An Introduction to Business Law of the Middle East,* (ed. Russell) p.5; Bagby, Ihsan A., 'The Issue of Maṣlaḥa in Classical Islamic Legal Theory', *International Journal of Islamic and Arabic Studies,* Vol. II (1985) No.2 (Bloomington, Indiana, USA) pp.1-11

151 The advocates of *Istiḥsān* belong for the most part to the Ḥanafīs. The main body of Shāfi'ī and Ḥanbalī schools refute its validity although it is unclear whether this applies only to *Istiḥsān* based on expediency. See Jawda Hilāl, 'Istiḥsān wa Maṣāliḥ Mursalat,' in *Usbū' al-Fiqh al-Islāmī Mahrajān Ibn Taymiyya,* (Damascus, 1966), p.244. Ibn Qudāma and Ya'qūb acknowledge the validity of Istiḥsān: Ibn Qudāma, *Rawḍat al-Naẓīr,* p. 26 of a MSS in the al-Azhar Library 284 cited in Saleh, *The general Principles of Saudi Arabian and Omani Company Law,* (London, 1981) p.22, FN. 21

152 Paret, *idem.*; Al-Shāfi'ī fundamentally rejected *Istiḥsān* as a "loophole for arbitrary decision". He stated: "God has not permitted any man since His messenger to present views (*Qaul*) unless from knowledge that was complete before him." Shāfi'ī, *Kitāb al-Risāla Fī 'Ilm al-Uṣūl,* (Cairo, 1321) p.70

existing legal rule.[153] The difference between the two principles of *Qiyās* and *Istiḥsān* is that *Istiḥsān* arises from the exercise of conscience for the promotion of a more equitable result.[154] It is precluded from a subjective interpretation by the fact that it must be justified by a provision in the *Qur'ān, Sunna, Ijmā'* or by a cause. *Istiḥsān* provides a systematic and rational process of reasoning which, because it is based on equitable considerations, may override the occasionally inequitable results of legalistic analogy, however manifest.[155] It could also modify an existing or injurious custom where the application of strict *Qiyās* would lead to an unnecessarily harsh result. For this reason it has been compared with both the Common Law principle of Equity, and the American concept of reasoned distinction of precedent.[156]

7. 'AMAL

From the end of the ninth century (the fifteenth century AD) in Morocco,[157] the jurisdiction of the *Qāḍīs* combined with the action of

153 Ibn Taymiyya treats *Istiḥsān* in conjunction with the Doctrine of Utility or Public Interests, *Maṣālih Mursala*, in *Majmū'at al-Rasā'il wa al-Masā'il*, 5 Vols. (Cairo, 1341-1349/1923-1931) V, pp.22 ff. See also Makdisi's report 'Ibn Taiymīya's Autograph Manuscript on Istiḥsān: Materials for the Study of Islamic Legal Thought', in *Arabic and Islamic Legal studies in Honour of H.A.R. Gibb*, (Leiden, 1965) pp.446-479, who states that Ibn Taymiyya's only known full-length work *Istiḥsān* is preserved in a Manuscript in the Ẓāhiriyya Library, Damascus, *Majmū'*, 91 Folios 325a-333b (n.d.;n.p.). But it is also discussed in his *Uṣūl al-Fiqh*, (written in conjunction with his father and grandfather) preserved in a Manuscript in the Egyptian National Library [Dār al-Kutub MS *Uṣūl al-Fiqh*, 150, Folios 178b-180a.

154 It finds an equivalent doctrine, *Istidlāl*, meaning 'reasoning, inference' in the Shāfi'ī, Ḥanbalī and Ja'farī schools. Maḥmaṣānī, 'Principles of International Law In the Light of Islamic Doctrine', *Recueil Des Cours*, I (1966), likens these tertiary sources to similar 'Reason and Equity sources' to be found in the Roman Praetorian Edicts, and the law as administered by the early English chancellors (pp.230-231).

155 Maḥmaṣānī, *Falsafat al-Tashrī' Fī al-Islām*, (1975 edn. in Arabic), pp. 190 ff.

156 See John Makdisi's Article: 'Legal Logic and Equity in Islamic Law,' in *The American Journal of Comparative Law*, vol.33 (1985) pp.63-92. Makdisi suggests that were *Istiḥsān* to be given a translation within the context of American legal terminology, it might be called the "reasoned distinction of *Qiyās* (reasoning by analogy)." *idem.*, p.92; See also Suratgar, 'The Development of Legal Systems', *op.cit*, who states that it constituted a form of equity, though not the Anglo-Saxon idea of equity (p.4). Chehata favours the Roman *Benignitas Juris* comparison over the Aristotelian sense of 'Equity'. see his 'Equité en Tant que Sources', *op.cit*, p.137

157 A similar tendency prevailed in Andalucia, where judges following the "practice of Cordova" entered into compendia of formularies (*Wathā'iq*) *Responsa* (*Fatāwā*) and regulations (*Qawānīn*), as partly incorporated in Ibn 'Aṣim's commentary *Tuḥfat al-Ḥukkām Fī Niqāṭ al-'Uqūd wa al-Aḥkām*, (Cairo, 1355 AH) transl. by Bercher, *Al 'Acimiyya ou Tuh'fat al-H'ukkam fi Nukat al-'Uqoud wa al-Ah'kam: "Le Present Fait aux Juges Touchant Les Points Délicats des Contrats et des Jugements"*, (Algiers, 1958)

municipal authorities to give consideration to prevailing institutions of custom over the stricter doctrines of the Mālikī school. Isolated or anomalous opinions (*Shādhdh*) could be determined by the *Qāḍī* as preferable to the predominant opinion (*Mashhūr*), thus leading to temporary pragmatic solutions to legal problems.[158]

Mālik is reported to have said : 'There were many scholars among the *Tāb'iūn* who used to relate and transmit *Ḥadīth* and say "We are not ignorant of this Ḥadīth, but the practice is established to the contrary"'.[159] The doctrine of *'Amal* (Judicial Practice), once recognised and recorded by notable jurists,[160] found a prominent place in the legal system. The concept of *'Amal* did not try to change strict legal theory in any way, but rather gave recognition to the fact that actual conditions did not permit strict theory to be translated into practice. The philosophy behind the concept of *'Amal* was that it was preferable to attempt to control practice as much as possible rather than to outlaw it, while simultaneously casting a protective screen around the *Sharī'a*.[161] Under the auspices of *'Amal* those institutions otherwise rejected by strict Mālikī doctrine were licitly incorporated into the orbit of the *Sharī'a* on the principle that "judicial practice prevails over the best attested opinion."[162] *'Amal* thus amounted to the upholding of local custom and *Aḥādīth* as preferable sources of law as against the free and arbitrary use of *Ra'y* and *Qiyās*.[163]

8. TRIBUNALS

From the dawn of Islam up until the 'Abbāsid Revolution, one of the most important organs for the practical application of the *Sharī'a* was the

---

158 cf. J. Berque's article '*'Amal*', in the *Encyclopaedia of Islam*, (New Edition), Vol.I, (Leiden, 1960), pp.427-429; also *Ibid*., *Essai sur la Méthode Juridique Maghrébine*, (Rabat, 1944). *'Amal* was first attested as of regulative force by L. Milliot in his *Démembrements du Habous*, (Paris, 1918) pp.23-30. See also his 'Coûtumes et Jurisprudence Musulmans ('Orf et 'Amal) in *Rapports Généraux au Ve Congrès International de Droit Comparé*, (Brussells, 1960) pp.179-183

159 cf. Coulson, 'Doctrine and Practice In Islam', *BSOAS*, XVIII, 2, (1956), p.225

160 See, for example, the *Lāmiyya* of 'Alī al-Zaqqāq (d. 912 AH) on pp.129-152 following text in Ibn 'Aṣim, *Matn al-'Aṣimiyya*, (Cairo, n.d.). Also transl. by Merad Ben 'Ali Ould Abdelkader, 'La "Lāmiyya" ou "Zaqqāqia" du Jurisconsulte Marocain : Zaqqāq', (Casablanca, 1927) *Revue Algérienne, Tunisienne et Marocaine de Législation et de Jurisprudence*, 41 (1925) pp.35-54; 42 (1926) pp.1-8, 17-42.

161 Schacht, *Introduction to Islamic Law*, *op.cit*., pp. 61-62.

162 *idem*., p. 62; The Moroccan Mālikī *'Amal* is held to mirror a predecessor in Madīna. For the history of *'Amal* in Morocco, see Ḥajjwī, *al-Fikr al-Sāmī*, (Fez, n.d.) Vol. IV, 226 ff., transl. J. Berque, *Essai Sur La Méthode Juridique Magrébine*, (1944) pp.120ff.

163 See Mālik Ibn Anas, *al-Muwaṭṭa'*, (Cairo, 1280 AH) II, 378; Levy, *The Social Structure of Islam, op.cit*., p.172

Judge (*Qāḍī*).[164] The *Qāḍī* was delegate of the Provincial Governor or Caliph, and was expected to follow the law as expounded by the established *Fuqahā'* in their legal treatises. In this task, he could seek the consultation of a *Muftī*.[165] The administration of justice was not, however, left to the office of *Qāḍī* alone. Other tribunals, such as the police (*Shurṭa*), the officials of the Investigation of complaints (*Naẓār Fī al-Maẓālim*)[166] and the Market Inspector (*Muḥtasib*) shared the administration.[167]

---

164 Schacht, *Introduction*, pp. 37-52, 74-75; Concerning the activities of an integral Judge, see the typical example of a letter probably written by 'Umar Ibn al-Shaṭṭāb to Abū Mūsā al-'Ash'arī, translated by Tyan, E., in *Histoire de l'Organisation Judiciaire en Pays d'Islam*, (Leiden, 1960) p.23, where other bibliographical notes may also be found; and Schimmel, A., 'Chalif und Qādī im Spätmittelalterlichen Ägyptien', *Welt Islams*, vol. 24, p.1 ff.; See also Spies on Muḥammad Ibn al-Ḥasan al-Shaybānī (b.132 AH/749 AD), who was the first *Qāḍī al-Quḍāt* of Islam and a statesman at the 'Abbāsid Court: 'Un Grand Juriste Musulman: Mohammed Ibn al-Ḥasan al-Shaibānī', *Rapports Généraux au Ve Congrès International de Droit Comparé*, I (Brussels, 1960) pp.125-129; See also Coulson, 'Doctrine and Practice in Islam', *Bulletin of the School of Oriental and African Studies*, XVIII (2) (1956) pp.211-226

165 The duties of Judges are listed in works called *Ādāb al-Qāḍī*; See, for example, al-Jassās al-Rāzī, *Sharḥ Kitāb Adāb al-Qāḍī*, (latter work by al-Khaṣṣāf) ed. F. Ziadeh, (Cairo, 1978); and A.A.A. Fyzee, 'The *Adāb al-Qāḍī* in Islamic Law' *Malaya Law Review*, 6 (1964) pp.406-416; Their decisions are recorded in registers called *Sijills*. See Chehata, *Droit Musulman: Applications au Proche-Orient*, (Paris, 1970) p.27; H.I. Hassan, 'Judiciary System from the Rise of Islam to 567 AH (AD 1171)', *The Islamic Quarterly*, 7 (1963) pp.23-30; and Bellefonds, 'Ḳanun', *Encyclopoedia of Islam*, Vol.IV (New Edition: Leiden, 1978) pp.556-557

166 H.F. Amedroz, 'The Maẓālim Jurisdiction in the Aḥkām Sulṭaniyya of Mawardi', *The Journal of the Royal Asiatic Society*, (1911) pp.635-674; and *id.*, 'The Office of Kadi in the Ahkam Sultaniyya of Mawardi', 2 *The Journal of the Royal Asiatic Society*, (1910) pp.761-796; M.I. Khalīl, 'Wālī al-Maẓālim or the Muslim Ombudsman', *Journal of Islamic and Comparative Law*, 6 (1969-76) pp.1-9

167 I.M. al-Husaini, 'Hisba in Islam', *The Islamic Quarterly*, 10 (1966) pp.69-83; Wickens, 'Al-Jarsīfī on the *Ḥisba*', *The Islamic Quarterly*, 3 (1956) pp.176-187; 'Abd al-Raḥmān Ibn Naṣr al-Shayzarī, *Nihāyat al-Rutba Fī Ṭalab al-Ḥisba*, Ed. al-Bāz al-'Arīnī, (Cairo, 1365/1946) transl. by W. Behrnauer in *Journal Asiatique*, 5me Séries, XVI, pp.347-352, and XVII, pp.1-76; E. Tyan, *Histoire de l'Organisation Judiciaire en Pays d'Islam*, (First edn, 1943; Second Edn, Leiden, 1960); Tyan, 'Judicial Organisation' in *Law In The Middle East*, vol.I: *Origin and Development of Islamic Law*, ed. M. Khadduri and H. Liebesny (Washington, D.C., 1955) pp.236-278; H.F. Amedroz, 'The Hisba Jurisdiction in the Aḥkām Sulṭaniyya of Mawardi', *The Journal of the Royal Asiatic Society*, (1916) pp.77-101, 287-314

The *Muḥtasib* was the "keeper of public morals".[168] His tasks included the prevention of frauds and commercial knavery in markets and elsewhere. He exercised his supervision over all traders and artisans by daily patrols through the markets, either by himself, or by his assistants;[169] for which the scholars have drawn up guidelines.[170]

These tribunals, which dealt directly with the practical application of the law, did not always apply the strict doctrines of the *Sharī'a*. The Caliph's discretionary powers of *Siyāsa Shar'iyya* (Canonical Statecraft)[171] and *Takhṣīṣ al-Quḍā'* were often the resource in practice for more practical considerations and extended the jurisdiction of non-Sharī'a courts in matters

---

168 Levy, *The Social Structure of Islam, op.cit.*, p.336. Gaudefroy-Demombynes suggests that the *Muḥtasib* perpetuates the Greco-Roman *aedile*, ['Sur Les Origines de la Justice Musulmane', *Mélanges Syriens Offerts á René Dussaud*, (Paris, 1939) vol. II, p.828] and *Agoranomos*, or *Ṣāḥib al-Sūq*: see *ibid.*, 'Un Magistrat Musulman = Le Mohtasib', *Le Journal des Savants*, (Paris, 1947) pp.36ff. This is supported by Foster, B.R., in his article 'Agoranomos and Muhtasib', *Journal of the Economic and Social History of the Orient*, (1970); Schacht also asserts the view that the 'Abbāsid *Muḥtasib* is an Islamised version of the Byzantine *Agoranomos*: see his *Introduction, op.cit.*, p.25, and *id.*, 'Droit Byzantin', *op.cit.*, p.207; and Mantran, R., 'Ḥisba', *Encyclopoedia of Islam*, (New Edition, Leiden, 1971) Ed. B. Lewis, V.L. Ménage, Ch. Pellat and J. Schacht. Vol III, pp.485-490; See also D. Sperber, 'On the term Heshbar', *Tarbiz*, (1969-1970) pp.96ff. (In Hebrew with English Summary); and *id.*, 'On the Office of the Agoronomos in Roman Palestine', *Zeitschrift der Deutschen Morgenländischen Gesellschaft*, (1977) who suggests that *Muḥtasib* and *Ṣāḥib al-Sūq* are likely derivatives of the Greek terms. Crone (*Roman, Provincial and Islamic Law, op.cit.*, Appendix III: 'The Muhtasib', pp. 107-108) notes the interchangeability of the terms *Logistēs* and *Agoronomos* practiced by the Jews, and their frequent transliteration as *Ḥashban* or *Ba'l-ha-suq*. She concludes that the Arabic institution of *Muḥtasib* therefore derived from the antique official under a Jewish terminology (*ibid.*, p.108)

169 Maqrīzī, *Khiṭāṭ*, 2 vols., (Bulāq, 1270 AH) I, p.463

170 See, for example, Abū al-Faḍl Ja'far b. 'Alī al-Dimashqī, *Kitāb al-Ishāra Ilā Maḥāsin al-Tijāra*, (Cairo, 1318); and 'Abd al-Raḥmān Ibn Naṣr al-Shayzarī, *Nihāyat al-Rutba Fī Ṭalab al-Ḥisba*, (Cairo, 1365/1946) transl. by W. Behrnauer in *Journal Asiatique*, 5meSér. XVI, pp.347-392; and *ibid.*, XVII, pp.1-76

171 E. Tyan, 'Méthodolgie et Sources du Droit en Islam (*Istiḥsān, Istiṣlāḥ, Siyāsa Šar'iyya*)' *Studia Islamica*, 10 (1959) pp.79-109; H. Laoust, *Le Traité de Droit Public d'Ibn Taimiyya, Traduction Annotée de la Siyassa Shar'iya*, (Beirut, 1948)

of a civil or criminal nature.[172]

1. CUSTOM

It has now been acknowledged that custom (*'Urf*)[173] too has had an extensive influence on the formulation of Islamic Law.[174] Custom infiltrated the *Fiqh* in a number of different ways. Firstly, pre- and early Islamic customs were incorporated among the body of *Sharī'a* principles often by tacit acceptance of prevailing practice.[175] *Muḍāraba* itself was allegedly a pre-Islamic institution, and is thus justified on the basis of custom, for it is not strictly based on the *Qur'ān* or *Sunna*.[176]

---

172 The famed work describing these administrative tribunals is al-Māwardī, *Kitāb al-Aḥkām al-Sulṭāniyya wa al-Wilāyāt al-Dīniyya*, (Cairo, 1393/1973); also transl. by Count Léon Ostrorog, *El-Aḥkām Es-Soulthania : Traité de Droit Public Musulman d'Abou'l Ḥassan 'Alī Ibn Moḥammad Ibn Ḥabīb El-Mawerdi*, 2 Vols., (Paris, 1900, 1901, 1906): [New Edn.: *Le Droit du Califat*, (Paris 1925)]; also transl. by E. Fagnan, *Les Statuts Gouvernementaux ou Règles de Droit Public et Administratif*, (Algiers, 1915). Sources thereon are rare in early Islam, although many more describing Ottoman administration exist. See, for example, R. Jennings, 'Kadi, Court and Legal Procedure in Seventeenth Century Ottoman Kayseri', *Studia Islamica*, 48 (1978) pp.133-172; Jennings, 'Limitations of the Judicial Powers of the Kadi in Seventeenth Century Ottoman Kayseri', *Studia Islamica*, 50 (1979) pp.151-184; Savvas-Pacha, *Le Tribunal Musulman*, (Paris, 1902)

173 *'Urf*, literally: 'accepted', denotes the unwritten laws of local custom and is synonymous here with *'ādāt* which refers to products of long-standing convention, or deliberate adoptions of expediency according to circumstances. See Levy, *Social Structure of Islam*, (Cambridge, 1969) p.248. Khallāf defines custom as that which the people practise (in their legal relations) in speech or deed, including the common custom and private custom : *al-Siyāsa al-Shar'īyya*, (Cairo, 1977) p.145. Al-Zarqā' defines custom as any legal rule practised by any human community in their legal life even when promulgated by temporal legislative authority : *al-Madhkhal al-Fiqh : al-'Amm*, (Damascus, 1965) Prt.II, p.838; See also Aḥmad al-Samdān, 'Muslim Private International Law', *Majallat al-Ḥuqūq*, (Kuwait Univ. Faculty of Law and Shar'īa: Jumād I, 1402/March 1982) pp.243-244

174 Schacht wrote :"Islamic jurisprudence ignores custom as an official source of Islamic law." ('Problems of Modern Islamic Legislation', in Nolte, *The Modern Middle East*, (New York, 1963) p.182). See also : Anderson, *Law Reform In The Muslim World*, *op.cit.*, p.10; Goldziher, *Zâhiriten*, p.204; Levy, *Social Structure of Islam*, (Cambridge, 1969) pp.243,248; Chelhod, J., 'La Place de la Coûtume dans le Fiqh Primitif et sa Permanence dans Les Sociétés Arabes à Tradition Orale', *Studia Islamica*, LXIV (1986) pp.19-37; M. Muslehuddin, *Philosophy of Islamic Law and the Orientalists*, (Lahore, n.d.) pp.18,19,21 : The recognition by Savigny of the role of custom is comparable here with Islamic practice.

175 See Maḥmaṣānī, 'Principles of International Law in the Light of Islamic Doctrine', *Recueil Des Cours*, p.231; and section 1 *supra*.

176 Islamic Research Institution, *Landlord and Peasant in Early Islam*, (Islamabad, 1977) pp.12-28; Ziaul Haque, 'Some Forms of Ribā al-Faḍl', *Islamic Studies*, 22: IV (1983) p.76

Mālik is attested to have cited practices from the *Jāhiliyya* (Pre-Islam): for instance, a revenue case concerning the Caliph 'Umār, where a tithe was levied on the first waters of a newly-opened well, is said to reflect pre-Islamic custom.[177] The consensus of school opinion concerning *Jāhilī* custom was divided:

(1) The Ḥanafīs and Mālikīs officially validated those customary practices not abrogated by the *Qur'ān*,[178] whilst others asserted that the all-encompassing reformist essence of the *Qur'ān* superceded all systems preceding it, including customary practices.

(2) A number of *Ḥadīth* were based upon customs, called *sunna*,[179]

(3) Customary practices in Madīna were regarded by Imām Mālik as sufficient consensus of opinion to provide a source of law in the absence of specific texts.[180]

(4) Customs emanating from exigences of *Ḍarūra*, *Istiḥsān*, *Istiṣlāḥ* and other tertiary rational sources were eventually accepted into the *Fiqh* by consensus.[181]

(5) Some customs and provincial practice of the conquered territories prevailed against the confrontation of the new religion, either because of lacunae in the formulated laws of Islam, or because these customs were so well engrained as to withstand the doctrinal exigences of a

---

177 See Mālik, *al-Muwaṭṭa'*, (With Commentary by al-Zurqānī: Cairo, 1280 AH) II, 76.

178 see Margoliouth, 'Omar's Instructions to the Kadi', *Journal of the Royal Asiatic Society*, (April, 1910) p.314; al-Sarakhsī, *Kitāb al-Mabsūṭ : Sharḥ al-Kāfī*, (Cairo, 1913) XV, pp.171-172

179 To be distinguished from Sunna, or practices of the Prophet. See, for example, on testamentary dispositions and a rule which the Imāmīs claim was the customary law of Madīna prior to the Prophet's arrival there: Ibn Babūyah, *'Ilal al-Sharā'i'*, (Najaf, 1963) pp. 566ff; Ṭūsī, *Tahdhīb al-Aḥkām*, ed. H.M. al-Khurshān (Tehran, 1390); *idem.*, Kitāb al-Istibṣār, Ed. H.M. al-Khurshān (Tehran, 1390); Coulson, *History*, *op.cit.*, pp. 65ff.; D.S. Powers 'The Will of Sa'd b. Abî Waqqâs : A Reassessment', *Studia Islamica*, (1983); R.M. Speight, 'The Will of Sa'd b. a. Waqqās: The Growth of a Tradition', *Der Islam*, (1973); Crone, *Roman, Provincial and Islamic Law op.cit.*, p.93

180 See section 'Amal, *supra*; and Mālik, *Al-Muwaṭṭa'*, *op.cit.*, III, PP. 134-136, who admits sales of bales by specification from a list, because it was accepted and established practice and devoid of *Gharar*. See also Schacht, *Origins, op.cit*, p.64

181 See Maḥmaṣānī, *Falsafat al-Tashrī' fī al-Islām*, (Trans. F. Ziadeh) *op.cit.*, p.132; and Maḥmaṣānī, 'Principles', *Recueil Des Cours, op.cit*, p.231

new and 'foreign' authority.[182]

Udovitch writes: "The extent to which Islamic Law made an accommodation with customary commercial practice is evidenced by the very existence of an entire genre of legal writings known as *Shurūṭ* (legal formulae) literature."[183]

An additional reason may be attributed to a regulation apparently passed by 'Umar, to the effect that no new lands should be held by Muslims. Macdonald surmises that the reason behind the regulation was to preserve Arab stock as a warrior caste of *Mujtahidīn*, but it also meant that the indigenous populations of the conquered territories were left more or less to their own devices, apart from the obligatory payment of the *Jizya* poll tax. The practices and customs which preceded the Islamic conquests were therefore not subsequently restrained.[184]

Through the processes of time and assimilation these practices came to lose their non-Islamic identity and became accepted as part of the law. Coulson writes : "Over the whole of the Umayyad period standards and norms of foreign law (Sassanian Persian as well as Roman law) gradually infiltrated into legal practice, so that Muslim jurisprudence in the mid-eighth century could take them for granted when conscious knowledge of their origin had been lost."[185] Despite the dominant role played by custom, it was not incorporated among the official sources of the *Sharī'a*.[186] This may be due, in part, to the initial lack of formal recognition given to custom by al-Shāfi'ī; in part it may also be due to the cautionary prophesy of the Prophet : "Verily you shall imitate the *sunan* of those who were before you, inch for inch, ell for ell, span for span, if they were to crawl into a lizard's hole, you

---

182 Crone, *Roman, Provincial and Islamic Law*, *op.cit.*, p.92 :"Substantially, it was thus provincial practice which went into the Sharī'a in this particular case; Roman law contributed only in so far as it was part of the practice." See also Dwyer, Daisy Hilse, 'Is Middle Eastern Behaviour Distinctive? Toward a Political Analysis of Knowledge of the Law.' (Paper published by Columbia University) pp.46ff.; Thompson, J.H., and Reischauer, R.D., (Eds.) *Modernization of the Arab World*, (Princeton, 1966) pp. 37-51

183 Udovitch, Partnership and Profit in Medieval Islam, (Princeton, 1970) p.9

184 D.B. Macdonald, *Development of Muslim Theology, Jurisprudence and Constitutional Theory*, (Beirut, 1965) p.15

185 *A History of Islamic Law*, (Edinburgh, 1964), p.28; See also *id.*, 'Muslim Custom and Case-Law', *Die Welt Des Islams*, N.S. 6 (1959) pp.13-24

186 Schacht, *Introduction to Islamic Law*, *op. cit.*, pp.62,77-78 ; and *idem.*, 'Problems of Modern Islamic Legislation' in R.H. Nolte (Ed.) *The Modern Middle East*, (New York, 1963), p. 182.

should follow after them."[187] Abū Ḥanīfa was one of the few early jurists who "looked into the practices followed by the people in their transactions, because such practices constitute the customary usage on which he based his opinion".[188] Later jurists, however, have been prepared to acknowledge the significant role of custom throughout the formulation of the law.[189] The diversity of laws and the positive sciences based upon them among different communities is a constant theme of Islamic political philosophy.[190] Indeed,

---

[187] Aḥmad b. Ḥanbal, *al-Musnād*, (Cairo, 1313 AH) ii, 327; *Encyclopoedia of Islam*, I, vol IV, p.555. Dr. al-Samdān affirms that it is valid to state that "to any community they belong, temporal rules (ie., rules initiated by men) are equal, in the view of the divine law, as sources regulating the acquisition of rights and the fulfilment of obligations" whenever the case calls for their application and to the extent that they do not contradict the Shar'īa: 'Muslim Private International Law', *Majallat al-Ḥuqūq*, (Jumād I, 1402) p.243. Zuja Gökalp (d.1924), the Turkish poet/sociologist defined *'Urf* as "the value judgments of a people or of a given community", which cannot be based on the same level as the divinely revealed law. A similar argument was submitted by Jalāl Nūrī Bey in *Ijtihād al-Islam*, (Constantinople, 1913; Arabic transl. Cairo, 1920) pp.42 ff. See Gibb, *Modern Trends in Islam*, (Chicago, 1947) p.92, and n.5. The al-Azhar view is published in *Nūr al-Islām*, (Cairo, n.d.) I, 534-540 : Jurists are prepared to admit local custom when not contradictory to the divine Text or Traditions.

[188] Abū Zahra, *Abu Hanifa: His Life, His Age, His Opinions and His Methodology*, (1947) p.350

[189] For instance, the neo-Ḥanbalī jurist, Ibn Qayyim al-Jawziyya, in his *'Ilām al-Muwaqqi'īn 'An Rabb al-'Alamīn*, (Cairo, n.d.) vol. III, at 66-67; al-Zarqā' *al-Madhkhal, op.cit.*, I, 147, 852-859-9; Khallāf, *Maṣādir al-Tashrī' al-Islāmī Fīmā Lā Naṣṣa Fīh*, (Kuwait, 1970) p.49, 145-149; Gerber, H., 'Sharia, Kanun and Custom in the Ottoman Law: the Court Records of Seventeenth Century Bursa', *International Journal of Turkish Studies*, 2(1) (1981) pp.131-147; 'Allāl al-Fāsī, *Risālat al-Maghrib*, (Rabat, 7 Nov. 1949) Fr. transl. in *Échanges*, (Rabat) French Series No. 8 of 25 Dec. 1949; Engl. Transl. in Schacht, 'Problems of Modern Islamic Legislation', *Studia Islamica*, XII (1960) p.127; and Maḥmaṣānī's forward to Nabil Saleh, *General Principles of Saudi Arabian and Omani Company Laws*, (London, 1981) p.x

[190] See, for example, Ikhwān al-Ṣafā, *Rasā'il Ikhwān al-Ṣafā wa-Khillān al-Wafā*, ed. Khayr al-Dīn al-Ziriklī, (Cairo, 1347/1928), IV, 22,25; al-Fārābī, *Kitāb Taḥsīl al-Sa'āda*, (Hyderabad, 1345 AH), 35; *idem*, *Ihsā' al-'Ulūm*, (La Statistique des Sciences), ed. Osman Amine, (Second Edn; Cairo, 1949), 45:3, 107:9 ff; Ibn Sīnā (Avicenna), *Fī Aqsām al-'Ulūm al-'Aqliyya*, in *Tis' Rasā'il Fī al-Ḥikma wa al-Ṭabi'iyyāt*, (Cairo, 1326/1908), 108:9; Ibn Rushd (Averroes), *Tahāfut al-Tahāfut (Incohérence de l'Incohérence)*, ed. M. Boryges [Bibliotheca Arabica Scholasticorum, Séries Arabe, Vol. III], (Beirut, 1930), pp. 581-582; Ibn Khaldūn, *Muqaddima Ibn Khaldūn (Prolégomènes d'Ebn Khaldoun)*, ed. É.M. Quatremère ('Notice et extraits des Manuscrits de la Bibliothèque du Roi et autres Bibliothèques, publiés par l'Institut Impérial de France', Vols. 16-18), (Paris 1858), corresponding to *Kitāb al-'Ibar wa Dīwān_al-Mubtada' wa al-Khabar Fī Ayyām al-'Arab wa al-'Ajam wa al-Barbar wa man 'Aṣarahum min Dhawī al-Sulṭān al-Akbar*, ed. Naṣr al-Ḥurīnī, (7 vols.; Bulaq, 1284/1867) II, 387; III, 243: 19-13; I, 364 :9; III, 90:17-18. It was generally acknowledged that general principles could be applied in particular communitites and situations, leaving room for the faculty of prudence to resolve actual decisions in particular acts. See Muhsin Mahdi, *Ibn Khaldun's Philosophy of History*, (London, 1957: Second Impression 1971), p.75

Schacht goes so far as to suggest that custom has always coexisted with the *Sharī'a*, while remaining outside the recognition of its strict theory.[191]

Within the sphere of civil and commercial transactions particularly, this incongruity concerning the role of custom within the *Sharī'a* has achieved gradual clarification by means of legislation. For example, Article 45 of the *Majella* states: "What is directed by custom is as though directed by law".[192] In the modern codes, the confusion concerning the role of custom has been greatly reconciled by the legal priority afforded to it in the applied law of the courts. The Qaṭari Civil and Commercial Code states : "In the absence of an applicable provision, the judge shall ajudicate according to custom. Special custom and local custom shall prevail over general custom".[193] An identical provision is to be found in the Kuwaiti Civil Code, Article 1. Here custom is given priority over the principles of the *Sharī'a.* In the new Bahraini Commercial Code too, custom is allotted a higher priority than that of the *Sharī'a.* In the absence of specific agreement between the parties concerned,[194] or any relevant provision in the commercial code or any other code relating to commercial matters,[195] the Judge is directed to apply the principles of commercial custom. Special custom shall be preferred over general custom[196] and principles of custom take precedence over the laws relating to civil matters, the principles of the Islamic *Sharī'a* and the principles of natural law and justice.[197]

This constitutes a modification from the former order of priority in sources of law, as set out in the Bahraini constitution. The Judicature Law of 1971 states : "In the event the judge finds no provision of law capable of application he shall deduce the basis of his judgment from the principles of the *Sharī'a* and the provisions thereof, and in the absence of any such provision, Custom shall be applied. A particular Custom shall be preferred

---

191 Schacht, *Introduction to Islamic Law*, *op. cit.*, p. 76ff.

192 See also Arts. 36, 37, 39, 40 (which states that a custom may change the meaning of a law and a law may change with the passing of time), 43 (which states that a matter in accordance with custom is accepted as a contractual obligation even if it is not made part of the text of the agreement), and 45 (A Rule established by custom has the same force as a rule established by law). Also see the translation of the *Majella*, Hooper, *The Civil Law of Palestine and TransJordan*, (1933) pp.20-21

193 Art. 4 of the Qaṭari Civil and Commercial Code, Law No. 16 of 1971; Art. 179 (c) of the Omani Commercial companies' Law cites established commercial practices among the criteria for settling commercial disputes. See N. Saleh, *General Principles of Saudi Arabian and Omani Company Laws, op.cit.*, pp.6-7; and the Explanatory Memorandum introducing the draft bill of Saudi Companies' Regulation, which recognises usages of trade as a source of law.

194 Commercial Code of Bahrain, Law no. 7 of 1987, Art. 2(1)

195 *ibid.*, Art. 2(2)

196 *ibid.*, Art. 2 (2)

197 *ibid.*, Art. 2(3);

to a general Custom, and in the absence of Custom the tenets of natural law or the principles of equity and good conscience shall be applied."[198] It may be taken for granted that Article 2 of the new Commercial Code supercedes these provisions in the Judicature Law of 1971, despite the absence of express directions thereto. It may be argued, however, that this order of priority may only apply to commercial matters, and that the order as dictated by the Judicature Law of 1971 still stands for other areas of the law, notwithstanding express indications to the contrary in those laws concerned.

In the UAE Civil Code, custom is also a subordinate source to the Shar'īa (Article 1), and may be resorted to only after all four schools of Sunni Fiqh have been consulted, and then must not contravene public order or morals. The custom applying to a particular Emirate applies only to that Emirate. The role of custom is outlined further in a later section :[199] Recognised custom, that is, custom which is 'of long duration and continuing, or prevalent', whether it is general or particular, is binding.[200] Actual facts may be established by reference to custom;[201] customary usage amounts to evidence of rights and obligations and shall be abided by;[202] and whatever custom regards as impossible (*al-Mumtana'*), shall be deemed impossible in fact.[203] Commonplace custom shall be given preference over exceptional;[204] and that which is either established by custom, or constitutes an obligation under custom, has the same force as an expressly stipulated condition.[205]

Custom is now seen, therefore, as an important complementary source of law, which may be used by judges and jurists to furnish principles determining the rights and obligations of litigating parties.[206] It is difficult to assess the exact extent to which custom has infiltrated the law over the centuries of its formation. Equally, it is difficult to discover even the approximate number of contemporary cases which require that reference be

---

198 Translation taken from W.M. Ballantyne's article in *The Arab Law Quarterly*, 2 (4), Nov. 1987, pp.352-356.

199 Articles 46-51 in the Section on 'Certain Jurisprudential Maxims and Rules of Interpretation' in Part II of the UAE Civil Code

200 UAE Civil Code, Art. 46 (1) and 46 (2)

201 UAE Civil Code, Art. 46 (3)

202 UAE Civil Code, Art. 47

203 UAE Civil Code, Art. 48

204 UAE Civil Code, Art. 49

205 UAE Civil Code, Arts. 50, 51 and 264

206 Muṣṭafā al-Zarqā', *al-Madkhāl al-Fiqh : al-'Āmm*, (Damascus, 1965), Part I, pp. 147. See also, 'Abd al-Wahhāb Khallāf, *Maṣādir al-Tashrī' al-Islāmī Fīmā Lā Nassa Fīh*, (Kuwait, 1970), pp. 146, 149; and *Majella*, Arts. 36-45.

made to custom in the absence of codified provisions.[207]

This leads us to the question : 'What establishes a custom ?' The *Majella* answers this question by stating that the custom must be continuous or preponderant.[208] By 'preponderant', it means 'commonly known'. This is the interpretation that has been adopted by the Civil Code of the UAE.[209] Fyzee states that the burden of proof lies heavily upon the party relying on the validity of a custom as against the application of the general law. This party must, firstly, plead the custom; and secondly, he must clearly prove that he is governed by that custom and not by the general law. Moreover, there is no presumption in favour, and the requirement that the custom be of long duration and not opposed to public policy, pertains to all accounts.[210]

Certain questions and problems regarding custom do remain. In the Kuwaiti Courts in the 1960's, a certain confusion reigned because of the non-indigenous character of the judiciary and lawyers, who had little knowledge of the Traditional law, while the court officials were ignorant of the national system which superceded it.[211] The same problem may be said to exist to a certain extent as yet, for contemporary courts of the three Gulf States still retain non-indigenous judiciary, a large proportion of which are Egyptian, Syrian or Palestinian, and who cannot be expected to know of the local customs. They are therefore dependent on the advice of counsel and/or legal advisers and experts.[212]

With the emergence of modern legal systems, it would appear to be inevitable that in comparison with its influence in the formative period of Muslim law, custom should now play a relatively minor role as a source of law. Indeed, Maḥmaṣānī states that custom as a source of law has suffered a continual decline with the emergence of law courts and the codification of laws.[213]

It cannot be said that the role of custom has been altogether clarified even within the constitutions and codifications of the modern Gulf States.

---

207 Due to the lack of published, systematised official reporting of cases in the constitutions concerned.

208 Art. 41

209 Compare *Majella*, Art.41 and 40 with UAE Civil Code, Art. 46(2)

210 Fyzee, A.A.A., *Outlines of Muhammedan Law*, (1974) p.67

211 Liebesny, *The Law of the Near and Middle East, op.cit*, p.110

212 In India/Pakistan, a different problem arose, in that customary Muslim laws of the Khojas, Sunni Bohoras, Molesalām Girāsias and Mophahs in Madras and Malabar have been retained by non-Muslims of the locality. The question which arose regarding the application of custom in such circumstances, was tackled in *Abdul Hussein v Sona Dero*, (1917) 45 *IA*. 10; Cases 94 : Held: it must firstly be ascertained whether the custom is proved, and this being so becomes a question of fact; secondly, it must be ascertained whether the custom is binding, and this is a question of law. See Fyzee, *Outlines of Muhammedan Law*, (Delhi, Fourth Edn. 1974) pp.64-76

213 Maḥmaṣānī, *Falsafat al-Tashrī' Fī al-Islām, op.cit.*, p.131

Certain questions remain, as yet, unanswered : To what extent, for example, are customs of other Muslim States recognised in commercial litigation in the three Gulf States, especially those customs dominant in other Gulf States, Egypt and Jordan ? Similarly, given the precedence of Custom over the *Sharī'a* in the new Bahraini Commercial code, may such tenets of custom be applied, even if they are in contradiction to the *Sharī'a* ? Furthermore, does the Bahraini Commercial Code of 1987 supercede the Judicature Law of 1971 in the matter of the hierarchy of sources of law, despite the lack of any mention of the latter's repeal in that new code ?

10. LEGAL METHODOLOGY

While the traditional jurists were reluctant to recognise the concept of the historical evolution of their law, the actual historicity of the *Sharī'a* has been explicitly proven by the development of Islamic legal methodology.[214] Together with those elements of tertiary doctrines, custom, prevailing practice and external influences such as foreign laws, it provided the means of circumventing strict legal theory in the interests of an equitable and practical system of justice.

Schacht argues that both the assimilation of non-Islamic elements into the corpus of Islamic law in the formative period, and the assimilation of practice by the theory are merely stages in the same process.[215] In his opinion, the process of influence is not precluded by the passage of time between legal systems.[216] From an external viewpoint, the process would appear as one of modification upon the positive core of the law; from within, however, it is seen as a more acceptable "expansion" by Islamic jurisprudence into new areas. Schacht affirms that the consequence of this process is an equilibrium between theory and practice strong enough for any closed society but which lacked the force to withstand the impact of modern

---

214 Coulson, *Conflicts and Tension in Islamic Jurisprudence*, (Chicago U.P., 1969), pp.58-76

215 Schacht, 'Problems of Modern Islamic Legislation,' *Studia Islamica*, XII, (1960), p. 140

216 'Vom Babylonischen Zum Islamischen Recht', *Orientalische Literaturzeitung*, (1927), p.664; Liebesny, 'Comparative Legal History: Its Role In The Analysis Of Islamic and Modern Near Eastern Legal Institutions', in *American Journal of Comparative Law*, 20 (1972), pp. 38-39

Western culture.[217]

It becomes clear therefore, that any analysis of Islamic commercial law which does not take into account the influence of historicity and methodology on the evolution of its principles, would be far from complete.

In this context, modern scholars divided the subject-matter of the *Sharī'a* into three broad categories according to variability and the effect that positive law had upon it.[218]

In the first category are the religious tenets, and the laws of personal status, that is, Family law,[219] the laws of Succession, Inheritance, Gift and *Waqf*.[220] These laws are regarded as the least permeated by external influences and therefore the most consistently "Islamic".

The second category consists of the commercial laws, or, in Schacht's terminology, the laws of Contract and Obligation.[221] These have experienced a variable degree of infiltration by non-Islamic elements and lie somewhere

---

217 See also, on this subject, Schacht's 'Foreign Elements In Ancient Islamic Law', *Mémoires de l'Académie Internationale de Droit Comparé*, (1955); *idem.*, 'Modernism and Traditionalism In A History Of Islamic Law', *Middle East Studies*, (1965), (Review of N.J. Coulson); *idem.*, 'Pre-Islamic Background and Early Development of Jurisprudence', in M. Khadduri and H.J. Liebesny (eds.), *Law In The Middle East*, vol. I (Washington, 1955); *idem.*, 'Droit Byzantin et Droit Musulman', (Accademia Nazionale dei Lincei, Fondazione Allesandro Volta, Atti dei Convegni), no. 12, (Rome, 1957); and *idem*, 'Remarques Sur La Transmission De La Pensée Greques Aux Arabes', *Histoire De La Médicine*, (1952).

218 It is believed that Bergstrasser was the first scholar to distinguish the various subject-matters of the *Sharī'a*. Udovitch, *Partnership and Profit in Medieval Islam*, (Princeton, 1970), p.7.

219 In Tunisia in 1947 by the Minister of Justice, the Grand Muftī Muḥammad b. Jā'iṭ, appointed a commission charged with codifying the Family Law in an integration of Mālikī and Ḥanafī doctrines. This attempt was later abandoned due to political upheavals in Tunisia, and the drafts were destroyed in 1950. A similar project had been abandoned in 1927 in Saudi Arabia due to resistance from Legal Scholars. See VIII *Oriente Moderno*, (1928) pp.36-38; Nallino, C.A., *Raccolta di Scritti*, I (Rome, 1939) p.79; and Schacht, 'Problems of Modern Islamic Legislation', *Studia Islamica*, XII (1960) p.123

220 The Institution of Private family Waqf was abolished in Egypt by the 1946 Law of Waqf, and by similar models in Syria and Lebanon in 1947. Public Waqfs were abolished in Tunisia in 1956, and assets of existing waqfs were made the property of the state.

221 Although Schacht in an early statement in an article entitled 'Islamic Law' in the *Encyclopedia of Social Sciences*, (Old Edition), (New York, 1932), Vol. VIII, p.348, agrees with Hurgronje that Islamic Commercial Law remained, for the most part, obsolete. c.f. G.H. Bousquet and J. Schacht (Eds.), *Selected Works of C. Snouck Hurgronje*, (Leiden, 1957), p.260.

between the other two categories.[222]

The third category encompasses the areas of fiscal, constitutional and criminal law. These areas have always remained flexible in the path of social change.[223] Indeed, Bergstrasser considered the laws in this category as diverging the furthest, if not completely, from the Islamic formulation.[224]

We can see therefore that the reception of institutions from one legal system into another, and the evolution of assimilated doctrines of that latter system may be instigated in two ways, namely :

(1) The nonsystematic and unstated : that is, unofficially, as in early Islamic law

(2) The systematic : that is, as part of a clearly defined public policy.[225]

It is the second option which the Islamic governments of the nineteenth century chose in order to instigate the reception of foreign legal institutions, and which eventually led to the wholesale codification movements of the last century. It was also the election of this policy which has led to the resurgence of old conflicts between theory and practice into a vibrant modern dichotomy.[226]

---

222 But cf. Levy, *The Social Structure of Islam*, (Cambridge, 1969) who states (at p.255) : 'It is in the sphere of trade and commerce that the greatest gap is visible between theory and practice.' To argue the point would necessitate a comparative analysis of Islamic and modern commercial laws as against those in the fiscal, constitutional and criminal domains, which is clearly outside the scope of this study.

223 Claude Cahen, 'Body Politic,' in Grunebaum, *Unity and Variety in Muslim Civilization*, (Chicago, 1955), p.139.

224 Udovitch, *Partnership and Profit, op.cit.*, p.7.

225 H.J. Liebesny, 'Comparative Legal History: Its Role In The Analysis Of Islamic and Modern Near Eastern Legal Institutions', in *American Journal of Comparative Law*, 20 (1972), p.38 n.1

226 See further, Varga, Csaba, 'Modernization of Law and its Codification Trends in the Afro-Asiatic Legal Development', *Studies In Developing Countries*, No.88 (Institute for World Economics of the Hungarian Academy of Sciences: Budapest, 1976); Tedeschi, G., 'The Movement for Codification In The Moslem Countries - Its Relationship with Western Legal Systems', (Report to the Vth International Congress of Comparative Law: Jerusalem, n.d.); Wassel, Mohamed, 'The Islamic Law, Its Application as it was Revealed in the Qur'ān and its Adaptability to Cultural Change', *Hamdard Islamicus*, 6(1) (1983) pp.53-61

Chapter 2

THE MODERN DICHOTOMY

The modern cleft between theory and practice in Islamic Law finds its roots in the arguments of two opposing schools of thought[1] which were brought to the forefront of Muslim legal philosophy by the reformist movements of the late nineteenth century.[2]

The upholders of theory are the Islamicists or Muslim Traditionalists who maintain that Islamic Law is immutable and hence not adaptable to social change. Orientalists such as Goldziher, Bergsträsser[3] and Hurgronje[4] played down the importance of theoretical Fiqh, almost dismissing it entirely for the best part of the Classical Period, since, they claimed, it was never enforced. Udovitch writes :

> "The Fiqh had very little to do with actual practice. It was only of theoretical significance and was developed by the religious scholars according to the paradigm of what they considered to be a golden age, namely, the period of the first caliphs. The religious legal scholars saw their task as that of

---

1 Termed by Schacht as the 'lawyers and the Islamicists'. See Schacht, 'The Present State of the Studies in Islamic Law', in *Atti del Terzo Congresso di Studi Arabi e Islamici*, (Naples, 1967) pp. 621-622

2 The challenge to the traditional muslim theory was initiated by the two reformist intellectuals, Muḥammad 'Abdūh and Muḥammad Rashīd Riḍā. For the substance of their ideas, see Rashīd Riḍā's biography of 'Abdūh : *Ta'rīkh al-Ustādh al-Imām al-Shaikh Muḥammad 'Abduh*, (Cairo, 1931), 3 Vols; and M.H. Kerr, *Islamic Reform : The Political and Legal Theories of Muḥammad 'Abduh and Rashīd Riḍā*, (Berkeley, 1966); and *idem.*, 'Rashīd Riḍā and Legal Reform', *Muslim World*, L (1960) pp.99-108; 170-181.

3 Bergsträsser, *Grundzüge des Islamischen Rechts*, publ. by J. Schacht, (Berlin, 1935); cf. J.H. Kramers, 'Droit de l'Islam et Droit Islamique', in *Analecta Orientalia; Posthumous Writings and Selected Minor Works of J.H. Kramers*, vol. II (Leiden, 1956) p.67

4 Hurgronje, *Revue de l'Histoire des Religions*, XXXVII (1898) in Bousquet and Schacht (Eds.) *Selected Works of C. Snouk Hurgronje*, (Leiden, 1957), p.256

> creating an ideal doctrine of how things ought to be and the fact that things were not as they ought to be can be amply documented by the numerous references to transgressions of the law. The law was destined for the ideal society and did not take into account the needs of the corrupt world. As Hurgronje summed it up: '...all classes of the muslim community have exhibited in practice an indifference to the sacred law in all its fulness quite equal to the reverence with which they regard it in theory.'"[5]

Such Islamicists as Bergsträsser, Hurgronje and Schacht contend that the immutability of the law derives from three main points of departure. The first is that the absolute and divine nature of Islam prohibits change in its concepts and institutions. The second is that the nature of development in its formative period isolated Islamic law from the institutions of social and legal evolution, that is, the state and the courts. The third is that as the *Sharī'a* had failed to develop an adequate methodology of legal change, it was, of necessity, immutable.[6]

Opposed to these persuasions, the muslim reformers or "liberal Islamicists" of the latter century argued for the adaptability of the *Sharī'a*, that is, its openness to change according to social conditions.

These modernists, who include such contemporary lawyers as Ṣubḥī Maḥmaṣānī, Professor 'Abd al-Razzāq al-Sanhūrī, Y. Linant de Bellefonds, Van den Berg[7] and Morand[8] contend that Islam and the *Sharī'a* are meant to provide viable socio-political institutions which must be adaptable to, and serve the interests of, man in all ages. They assert that in its present state the *Sharī'a* is inadequate to support the trappings and institutions of a

---

5 Udovitch, *Partnership and Profit In Medieval Islam*, (Princeton, 1970), pp. 5-6. This seems to have been refuted later by Udovitch and Gerber in relation to the law of Commenda Partnerships : See H. Gerber, 'The Muslim Law of Partnerships in Ottoman Court Records', in *Studia Islamica*, LIII, pp. 114-119; and Koundes, P. Nicholas, 'The Influence of Islamic Law on Contemporary Middle Eastern Legal Systems : The Formation and Binding Force of Contracts', *Columbia Journal of Transnational Law*, vol.9 (2) (Fall, 1970) pp.384-435

6 For discussion, see Masud, *Islamic Legal Philosophy - A Study of Abū Isḥāq al-Shāṭibī's Life and Thought*, (Islamabad, 1977)

7 L.W.C. Van den Berg, *Minhâdj aṭ-Ṭālibīn, Texte Arabe Publié avec Traduction et Notations*, (Batavia, 1862-1884), which received staunch criticism from Hurgronje in his Review, *Revue de l'Histoire des Religions, op.cit.*, pp.1-22, 174-203 in Bousquet and Schacht (Eds.), *Selected Works of C. Snouk Hurgronje, op.cit.*, pp.214-255

8 Morand, *Introduction à l'Étude du Droit Musulman Algérien*, (Algiers, 1921; 1961) pp. 108-112; and *id.*, *Avant-Projet de Code Présenté à la Commission de Codification du Droit Musulman*, (Algiers, 1916)

modern social, political and economic community. They point out that since at least three-fifths of the *Sharī'a* depends on human reasoning, the *Sharī'a* must always be a recognised instrument for man's development.[9] While the *Qur'ān* and *Sunna* are immutable, however, interpretations by human reason are subject to change in proportion to the extent of knowledge and experience which man acquires in certain ages. Thus the *Sharī'a* must be adaptable or be broken.

In questioning the immutability of Islamic law, the arguments of the modernists, and those of their opponents, seem to hinge upon the very same points, namely : the fundamental concept of Islamic law, the history of its sources and development, and the resource of methodology in the light of social change. In view of the fact that both contentions pertain not to the actual historicity of legal change but rather, to the legal theory behind it, it is worth considering whether it is not the interpretation of the concept of "Islamic Law" which is at the root of the problem.

The ambiguity *apropos* "Islamic Law" seems to originate in a confusion between "*Sharī'a*" and "*Fiqh*", where the *Sharī'a* is the law consisting of the four sources recognised by al-Shāfi'ī;[10] while *Fiqh* is the science of knowing the law, as developed by subsequent jurisprudents.[11]

The inherent ambiguity of these terms is resolved somewhat by Kerr, who perceived four levels of meaning implicit in the general idea of juristic theory :

(1) The Divine Will, "the sole metaphysical reality upon which all creation and material or moral relationships depend for their existence."

---

9 Blaustein, A.P., and Flanz, G.H., (Eds.) *Modern Constitutions of The World*, vol. XIV, pp.1-2. But see the distinctions made between the use of *Sharī'a* and *Fiqh* in this context, *infra*.

10 Ṭabarī gave an early definition of *Sharī'a* as comprising the laws of inheritance, Ḥadd punishments, commandments and prohibitions. Later it became understood as "Allāh's commandments relating to the activities of man of which those that relate to ethics are taken out and classed as *Adāb*." Schacht, *'Sharī'a'*, *Encyclopoedia of Islam*, vol. IV, pp.320-324, at 320

11 Schacht, *'Fikh'*, *Encyclopoedia of Islam*, vol. II, (Leiden, 1965) pp.886-891. For the distinction between Natural (*Ṭabi'iyya*) sciences, transmitted (*Naqliyya*) sciences, and the primary legal sciences (*'Ulūm al-Shar'iyya*), see Ibn Khaldūn, *Muqaddimāt Ibn Khaldūn*, corresponding to *Kitāb al-'Ibar*, *op.cit.*, II, 385:3-12; and M. Mahdi, *Ibn Khaldun's Philosophy of History*, (London 1957, 1971) pp. 73-75. Ibn Khaldūn states that the essential difference between the philosophic and positive sciences is their ultimate source, which is human reason and the Prophet-Legislator respectively.

(2) The spiritual relationship between man and God.

(3) The normative relationship between man and man, that is, the perfect terms of law conceived by God and imperfectly applied by man.

(4) Non-normative relationships : the world of matter; appearances; and circumstances.[12]

In applying the areas of law to these levels, we could say that the *Sharī'a* covers the first, while *Fiqh* encompasses both the second and third levels, although not comprehensively. The third level would include, for example, social change, which could also be found indirectly in the second and fourth stages. The immutability view seems to confuse both *Sharī'a* and *Fiqh* as inseparable elements of the law; while the adaptability view is really referring to the third level meaning of *Fiqh*, yet confusing it with the first level meaning of "*Sharī'a*".[13]

Borrowing the metaphor of the muslim scholars, if the *Sharī'a* is considered as the trunk of the legal tree (*Uṣūl*), the *Fiqh* is discernible as the science of its branches (*Farū'*); whereupon it becomes easier to distinguish between the various subject-matters of *Fiqh*.[14] This argument would lead us to infer that "Islamic legal theory" must consequently mean the science of "*Uṣūl al-Fiqh*", that is, the principles and methods of interpretation (which includes those of *Maṣlaḥa*, custom and other 'unofficial' tertiary doctrines) according to which *Fiqh* is arrived at rather than the methods and principles of *Fiqh* itself.[15]

The view of the conservative traditionists, contending that the law is divine and immutable, therefore refers to the *Sharī'a* rather than the Fiqh. The arguments relating to the nature, adaptability and practice of the law are made in reference to *Fiqh*.[16] Once the areas of *Sharī'a* and *Fiqh* are thus demarcated, the apparent ambiguity and inconsistency between the opposing schools of legal philosophy becomes somewhat reconciled.

---

12 M.H. Kerr, *Islamic Reform, op. cit.*, pp.21-22.

13 Muhammad Khalid Masud, *Islamic Legal Philosophy : A Study of Abū Isḥāq al-Shāṭibī's Life and Thought*, (Islamabad: Pakistan, 1977) pp.22-23.

14 Abou'l Hassan Ali Ibn Mohammad Ibn Habib El-Mawerdi, *El-Ahkam Es-Soulthania : Traité de Droit Public Musulman*, transl. by Count Léon Ostrorog, (Paris, 1900), p.2.

15 Masud, *op.cit.* , p.24.

16 Said Ramadan, 'Islamic Law: Its Scope and Equity, (First Edn., London?, 1961; Second Edn., 1970)

The equilibrium which evolved between theory and practice up until the nineteenth century had been spread over the mild vacillations of thirteen hundred years. During this time, Islam had been confronted with sectarianism and two waves of Hellenism, but had met nothing comparable with what Watt calls "the new Dawn" or the technological aftermath of the Industrial Revolution in the West.[17] The emergence of the modern secular state was one of the most important corollaries of the integration of the Middle East into the modern political, economic and technological order dominated by the Western States.[18] The growth and development of the Muslim secular state must therefore be seen as both a reflection of the new world order, and as a reaction to the changes taking place within its broad structure. There are, however, two essential points to note in the process of assimilation and integration as it ocurred in the Middle East. Firstly, whereas the West had experienced a period of acculturation to the new age of technology and modernity over a span of three or four centuries, and had changed its institutions accordingly, modernity came to the Middle East with unexpected force and cataclysmic impact in the nineteenth century.[19] In the light of Western military and economic supremacy, the Middle Eastern states sought to redress the balance of world power by carrying out major reforms in the central institutions and reorganization of government. Both internal and external expectations were that the East could carry out this "defensive modernization"[20] almost overnight to accommodate the new means to wealth, power and worldly status that had been lost with the

---

17 W.M. Watt, *Islamic Philosophy and Theology*, (Edinburgh,1962), p.173.

18 Philip S. Khoury, 'Islamic Revivalism and the Crisis of the Secular State in the Arab World: An Historical Appraisal,' in *Arab Resources: The Transformation of a Society*, I. Ibrahim, (Ed.), (London; Center for Contemporary Arab Studies, Washington, D.C., 1983) pp.215-216; Hourani, A., *The Ottoman Background of the Modern Middle East*, (University of Carreras Arabic Lecture, 1969)

19 Holt, Lambton and Lewis (Eds.), *The Cambridge History of Islam*, (Cambridge, 1977) Vol 2B, pp. 703 ff.; Velidedeoglu, Hifzi Verdet, 'Le Mouvement de Codification dans les Pays Musulmans - Ses Rapports avec les Mouvements Juridiques Occidentaux', (Rapport Général Présenté au Ve Congrès de l'Académie Internationale de Droit Comparé à Bruxelles : 4-9 Aug. 1958) [Annales de la Faculté de Droit d'Istanbul], VIII (1959) pp.130-178 (Brussels, 1960)

20 The term is coined by Khoury, 'Islamic Revivalism and the Crisis of the Secular State', *op.cit.*, p.216 to mean the creation of new expectations (*idem.*, p.221)

decline of the Ottoman Empire.[21] Moreover, many of the Gulf countries were not exposed to the onslaught of technological advancement until well into this century, when the discovery of oil and its incipient technological and economic corollaries meant that the West brought its manpower, machinery and attendant legal institutions into the oil states. In these countries therefore, the impact, when it eventually came, was not only rapid, but also more extreme.

The Middle Eastern institutions accordingly changed, aided distinctly by the new educational and communications systems,[22] but the pace of cultural assimilation rarely proceeds at the same rate as actual mobilization (that is, institutional change), and integration therefore becomes spasmodic and uneven. Those slower processes of culture, engrained customs and traditional philosophies fall behind, resulting in an increasingly differentiating society, and the creation of tension between its component parts. In particular, in the field of law, the modern states underwent a certain loss of muslim identity. In several constitutions, of which the most extreme example is Turkey,[23] the *Fiqh* and *Sharīʿa* had been replaced almost entirely in some areas by the indiscriminate reception of western codifications into their systems of law.[24]

The new "Secular Islamic Legislation"[25] sought its legitimacy in a controversial flinging open of the 'doors of *Ijtihād*'. In the interests of a

---

21 This impact was initiated by Napoleon Bonaparte's invasion of Egypt in 1798. For this and the accruing social and philosophical consequences, see A. Hourani, *Arabic Thought in the Liberal Age, 1798-1939*, (London, 1970) and *idem.*, *The Emergence of the Modern Middle East*, (London, 1981); and Hrair, Dekmejian R., 'The Anatomy of Islamic Revival: Legitimacy Crisis, Ethnic Conflict and the Search for Islamic Alternatives', *Middle East Journal*, 34 (Winter, 1980) pp.1-12; Udovitch, *The Islamic Middle East, 700-1900 : Studies in Economic and Social History*, (Princeton, N.Jersey, 1981)

22 See Holt *et al*, *The Cambridge History of Islam*, *op.cit.*, Vol. 2B, pp.704-709

23 Sauser-Hall, *La Réception des Droits Européans en Turquie, Extrait du Recueil de Travaux Publié par la Faculté de l'Université de Genève*, (1938); Ansay, Tugrul *et al*, *Introduction to Turkish Law*, (Ankara, Society of Comparative Law, 2nd Ed., 1978); Anderson, 'The Movement Towards Codification in Turkey, Cyprus and The Arab World', *Indian Yearbook of International Affairs*, (1958) pp.125-142. Turkey derived sources for its new codes from Switzerland, Italy and Germany. See also Heyd, Uriel, *Revival of Islam in Modern Turkey*, [Lecture delivered 28 March, 1968 : Jerusalem Hebrew University, 1968) which indicates the present reversal of this trend, in societal terms at least.

24 For instance, the Egyptian Penal, Commercial and Maritime Codes basically modelled on French Law; the Egyptian Criminal Code of 1927 and the Turkish Criminal Code of 1926 are of Italian inspiration; the Libyan Criminal Code now operative is French based. Coulson, *A History of Islamic Law*, pp.152-153

25 Coined by Schacht in 'Problems of Modern Islamic Legislation', *Studia Islamica*, *op.cit*, pp.116, 120

logical necessity to incorporate the novel principles of the twentieth century and its concomitant institutions, the rejection of *Taqlīd* was accepted by all but the most stubborn of traditionalists as the lesser of two evils: to recognise the body of the law as a living, progressive organism relevant to the modern day; or to reject it as a dead and rigid antique.[26]

The methodology employed by the modern jurists in their *Ijtihād* is no less eclectic than that used by the their eighth century predecessors, as a reading of any of the Memoranda accompanying the neoteric codes of the mid-twentieth century would illustrate. As a consequence, the codes enacted at this time are at best a reflection of the prevalent noumenon of the age : that 'West is implicitly best'. The integration of Islamic principles into the otherwise universally imitated codes seems to resemble arbitrary and somewhat forced interpretations of the Classical *Fiqh* twisted into correspondence with the secular contexts, rather than *vice versa.* The legal modernists wanted revisionism at the cost of Islam; yet they were not prepared to abandon altogether the cultural and spiritual ascendancy of their Islamic heritage. Therefore token representations of the Classical tradition were interspersed among the code provisions, partially thwarting the abhorrence of the Traditional jurists, and proving, perhaps, the firm hold that the religious tradition has on the minds of even the most modern of jurists.

Among the laws of Obligations and Contracts, Turkey, in 1926, abandoned the *Majella* for an adaptation of the Swiss Civil Code; The Lebanese Law of Obligations and Contracts of 1932 was based squarely on

26 Siddiqi, H., 'Iqbal's Legal Philosophy and the Reconstruction of Islamic Law', 2 *Progressive Islam*, No.s 3-4 (Amsterdam, 1955) pp.14 ff.; and Badr, Gamal Moursi, 'Law in the Middle East: Origin and development of Islamic Law : A Review', *Tulane Law Review*, 30 (1955-1956) pp.451-460. The development of modernist legal thought remained under the shadow of the *Ijtihād* problem in Pakistan. This may be contrasted to the official adoption of legal modernism in, for example, the North African countries such as Tunisia. See Schacht, 'Problems of Modern Islamic Legislation', *Studia Islamica*, XII (1960) pp.116-117.

27 Cardahi, Choucri, 'Le Projet de Code des Obligations du Liban', 60 *Bulletin de la Société de Legislation Comparée*, (1931) at p.611

28 Egyptian Civil Code, Promulgated 16 July 1948; Came into Force 15 Oct. 1949. Issued as Law No. 131 of 1948; See Michael Davies, *Business Law in Egypt*, (Deventer: Netherlands, 1984) pp.191-221; Anderson, 'Law Reform in Egypt 1850-1950', in *Political and Social Change in Modern Egypt*, ed. P.M. Holt, (Oxford, 1968) pp.20-30; Badr, Gamal Moursi, 'The New Egyptian Civil Code and the Unification of the Laws of the Arab Countries', *Tulane Law Review*, 30 (1955-1956) pp.299-304

French law;[27] while the Egyptian 1949 law,[28] and therefore the Iraqi[29] and Syrian laws which devolved from it, were derived from the French model.[30] The revision of existing legislation was accompanied by the introduction of secular courts to apply the new laws.[31] Simultaneously, large rationalized bureaucracies supported by the new secular institutions and managed by civilian and military elites educated in secular liberal philosophies were to weaken the influence of religious institutions and scholars. The tensions created by these changes in the *status quo* eventually led to state intervention and control of these institutions in the twentieth century.

The second point to note is the apparent lack of intention by the instigators of this process to amend or reverse the disparities created by the new order.[32] The Muslim World has witnessed a number of efforts on the part of fundamentalists or religious influentials to remedy the loss of religious monopoly over the law, but in countries such as Egypt, the constitutions remain stubbornly secular.

A new look is now being given among the Gulf States to the "embryonic beginnings of a process of the Islamicisation of foreign elements such as

29 Iraqi Civil Code of 1953 : "A merger of foreign and Islamic elements is the outstanding feature of the Iraqi Civil code promulgated in 1953. Many of its rules were derived from the Ḥanafī Codification of the *Majella* and from traditional *Sharī'a* texts, while other provisions, on such matters as Insurance and aleatory contracts, rest squarely on European sources." Coulson, *A History of Islamic Law, op.cit.*, p.218; For the Iraqi background to the promulgation of this code, see Amin, S.H., *Middle East Legal Systems*, (Glasgow, 1985) Chpt. 4, pp.150-242

30 Coulson, *A History of Islamic Law*, p.152. For the constitution of Egypt, see G. Flanz and F. Shafik, in A.P. Blaustein and G.H. Flanz, (Eds.), *Modern Constitutions of the World*, (New York, Dec. 1985) Vol. V (11/84); For Syria, see P.B. Heller, in *ibid.*, Vol. XV (6/74); and Khany, Riad, 'The Legal System of Syria', *Comparative Law Yearbook*, Vol. I, 1977 (Center For International Legal Studies, The Netherlands, 1978) pp. 137-152.

31 Anderson, 'Codification in the Muslim World: Some Reflections', *Rabels Zeitschrift für Ausländisches und Internationales Privatrecht*, XXX (Tubingen, 1966) pp.241-153; Coulson, *A History of Islamic Law*, pp.152-3, 156; Adams, C.C., *Islam and Modernism in Egypt*, (Oxford, 1933); Liebesny, 'Impact of Western Law In the Countries of the Near East', *George Washingtom Law Review*, 22 (1953-1954) pp.127 ff.; A.B. Schwartz, 'La Reception et l'Assimilation des Droits Étrangers', 2 *Introduction à l'Étude du droit Comparé; Recueil d'Études en l'Honneur d'Edouard Lambert*, (1938) pp.581-590; Brinton, J.Y., *The Mixed Courts of Egypt*, (Second Edn: New Haven/London, 1968); Kerr, 'The Emergence of a Socialist Ideology in Egypt', 16 *Middle East Journal*, (1962) pp.127-144; Bellefonds, Y. Linant de, 'Immutabilité du Droit Musulman et Réformes Législatives en Égypte', *Revue International de Droit Comparé*, Vol. VII (Paris, Jan-Mar 1955) pp.5-34

32 Khoury, P., 'Islamic Revivalism and the Crisis of the Secular State,' *op.cit.*, p.221

had taken place in the first two centuries of Islam".[33] Codifications are being revised in relation to their compatibility with the original tenets and nature of the *Sharīʻa*; and more attention is being paid to the Islamic identity of the law and its origins. In short, the process of westernization in the legal systems of the Arab Gulf is being checked in the light of Islamic Revivalism.

This process was, in fact, begun by Egypt. Its promulgation in 1949 of the Civil Code claimed to have attempted a "compromise between the traditional Islamic and modern western systems".[34] The result was an amalgam of extant Egyptian law,[35] comtemporary civil codes, and some principles of the *Sharīʻa*. Rather less of the latter were in fact incorporated than the Memorandum would have us believe; but the Code did provide that, in matters not specifically regulated by the code, the courts should follow "customary law, the principles of Islamic law, or the principles of

---

33 Coulson, *A History of Islamic Law*, p.153; For the background of the Gulf States, see Liebesny, 'Administration and Legal Development in Arabia: The Persian Gulf Principalities', *Middle East Journal*, X (1) (1956) pp.33-42; Dougherty, James E., 'Religion and Law', *The Persian Gulf States: A General Survey*, [Ed. A.J. Cottrell *et al*] (Baltimore/London, 1980) pp. 281 ff., at pp.302-313; Bonderman, D., 'Modernization and Changing Perceptions of Islamic Law', *Harvard Law Review*, 81 (1968) pp.1169-1193; and Brown, L. Carl, 'The Middle East: Patterns of Change, 1947-1987', *The Middle East Journal*, 41 (1) (Middle East Institute, Washington, D.C., Winter, 1987) pp.26-39. For English translations of the various codes of these States, see Hall, Marjorie J., (Ed.) *The Business Laws of the United Arab Emirates*, (London, 1979)

34 As Coulson points out, "the debt owed to traditional *Sharīʻa* law was slight, for more than three-quarters of the code was derived directly from the previous Egyptian codes of 1875 and 1883". (Coulson, *A History of Islamic Law, op.cit.*, p.153); Likewise, Schacht states: "Whatever the explanatory note of the Egyptian Civil Code of 1949 may say, Islamic Law has not become one of its constituent elements to any degree greater than it had been in its predecessor." ('Problems of Modern Islamic Jurisprudence' *op.cit.*, p.122). See also, Liebesny, 'Religious Law and westernisation in the Moslem Near East', *American Journal of Comparative Law*, Vol. 2 (1953) pp.492-504. Only the Islamic institutions of *Shufʻa, Ḥawāla, Khiyār al-Sharṭ, Salam* and the rule disregarding enforcement of debts arising out of the sale of intoxicating liquor were highlighted. It was the **attitude** towards integration which was novel.

35 Notably, the Egyptian codes of 1875 and 1883. See Anderson, 'The Sharīʻa and Civil Law (the debt owed by the new Civil Codes of Egypt and Syria to the Sharīʻa'), in *Islamic Quarterly*, (1954) pp.29-46; and Chehata, Chafik, 'Le Code Civil Français et son Influence dans le Bassin Méditerranéan', *Egypt: La Semaine Internationale de Droit*, (Paris, 1954); and *idem.*, 'Les Survivances Musulmanes dans La Codification du Droit Civil Egyptien', *Revue International de Droit Comparé*, (1965) pp. 839-853

36 Egyptian Civil Code, 1949, Art.1. See also Coulson, *A History of Islamic Law*, p.153; and *cf.* Sanhūrī, 'Le Droit Comme Élément de Reforme du Code Civil Égyptien', 2 *Recueil d'Études en l'Honneur d'Edouard Lambert*, (Paris, 1938) pp.621-642.

Natural Justice".[36] The Civil Codes of Iraq[37] and Syria[38] followed close on Egypt's heels.[39] The Iraqi Code was supposedly modelled on the *Majella*, and the 1949 Egyptian Code.[40] It was held to represent "a remarkable synthesis of an ancient legal system, age-old local usages and the most modern legal theories", but articles of the former were distinctly repealed or overruled by the new codification.[41]

Before the discovery of oil deposits in the Gulf, the Principalities of Kuwait, Bahrain, Qatar, and the Trucial States had been little more than tribal-based city states.[42] They were small, sparsely populated settlements with marine-based livelihoods, which held little interest for the outside world. Hence, they had all eluded the direct authority of the Ottoman Empire.[43] Until India's Independence in 1947, the British Persian Gulf was

---

37 Civil Code of Iraq, Law No.3 of 1951; (enacted Sept 8), effective as of Sept 8, 1953.

38 Civil Code of Syria, 1949

39 Sanhūrī speaks of "the Arab civil Code" in that the three codes are so similar: *al-'Ālim al-'Arabī*, II (Cairo, 1953) pp.5-29. See also Muḥammad 'Alī 'Arafa, *al-Taqnīn al-Madanī al-Jadīd*, (Cairo, 1949). Sanhūrī's statement was qualified by A. d'Emilia in 'Intorno Alla Moderna Attiuità Legislativa di Alcuna Paesi Musulmani nel Campo del Diritto Privato', 33 *Oriente Moderno*, (1953) pp.301-321; and *ibid.*, *Annuario di Diritto Comparato e di Studi Legislativi*, XXXII (1957) pp.82-117, at 117

40 The first draft was submitted by Sanhūrī on June 15, 1936: al-Sanhūrī, *Document No.1, Sale and Barter, Selected Sample from Western Legislation III and IV Majallat al-Qaḍā'*, (1936) pp.229-394. The committee was disbanded for political reasons and when it reconvened a new source was used : the Egyptian Civil Code of 1949. The second Draft was prepared by a group of distinguished jurists led by Professor Sanhūrī, who was assisted by Professor Munīr al-Qāḍī (Professor of *Majella* at Iraq Law College). (See Jwaideh, 'The New Civil Code of Iraq', *The George Washington Law Review*, vol. 22 (1953-4) pp.176-186, at p.176).

41 For example, Art. 64 of the Code of Civil and Commercial Procedure, Law No. 13 of 1968, published in the *Egyptian Official Gazette : al-Jarīda al-Ra'smiyya*, No. 19 of 9/5/1968. The 1968 law supercedes the 1949 Code, which, in turn, superceded the 1883 Code. All these were basically French procedures with modifications drawn from various western codes. The 1968 Code obviated the 'defects' of the *Majella*, and liberated the courts from its rigidity. In contracts of sale, see also Art. 64 of the Civil Code, which contradicts fundamental Islamic rules of object of contract. See Jwaideh, 'The New Civil Code of Iraq', *The George Washington Law Review*, vol. 22 (1953-4) p.179; and *International Encyclopoedia of Comparative Law*, Vol. I, 'National Reports', (Completed Dec. 1972)

42 Miles, *The Countries and Tribes of the Persian Gulf*, (London, 1966);

43 For details and dates of treaty relations with Great Britain, see Liebesny, H.J., 'International Relations of Arabia: The Dependent Areas', *The Middle East Journal*, Vol. I (Washington, D.C., 1947) pp. 148-165; al-Baharna, Husain M., *The Legal Status of the Arabian Gulf States*, (Manchester, 1981); and Abi-Saab, G.M., 'The Newly Independent States and the Rules of International Law: An Outline', *Howard Law Journal*, Vol. VIII (1962) pp.95-121, at p.106.

subordinated administratively to the Government of India, through the acolyte offices of the India office in Bombay. Thus laws applied through the judicial office of the British Political Resident in the Gulf were English as applied in India. In 1949 these principalities were listed as Protected States in Sch. 2 to the *British Protectorates, Protected States and Protected Persons Order In Council 1949/140.*[44]

Bahrain became a British Protected State in 1892, in which the Crown exercised extra-territorial jurisdiction over British subjects. It continued to be a Protected State until 15 August 1971,[45] when the Crown's protection over and jurisdiction in Bahrain were terminated.[46]

In Kuwait, in 1899 an agreement had been made with the Sheikh whereby the British Crown would protect Kuwait from Turkey. Kuwait thereupon became a Protected State in which the Crown exercised extra-territorial jurisdiction over British subjects (although it may be that such jurisdiction was already being exercised prior to 1890.[47] Kuwait continued to be a Protected State until 1 July 1961, accordingly listed as such in the 1949/140 Order in Council. In mid-1961, the United Kingdom and Kuwait agreed that the 1899 treaty relations should be terminated, and on 1 July 1961, Kuwait therefore became a fully independent State. It was not until 6 December 1961, however, that Kuwait was removed from Sch. 2 of the 1949 Order in Council.[48]

The Trucial States first came under British influence in the 1820's as a result of efforts to curb piracy and slavery. Some time after this the Crown gradually assumed extra-territorial jurisdiction over British subjects. By 1892 British Protection had formally been extended to each of the seven

---

[44] *The British Protectorates, Protected States and Protected Persons Order In Council 1949/140*, Sch. 2 referred to the Persian Gulf States as comprising "Koweit, Bahrein, and Qatar, and the Trucial Sheikhdoms of Oman, *viz*: Abu Dhabi, Ajman, Dibai, Kalba, Ras al Khaimah, Shajak and Umm al Quaiwain." See the Order, S.5 (2) and Second Schedule, pp. 358, 362-363. See also British Nationality Act, 1948; Parry, Clive, *Nationality and Citizenship Laws of the Commonwealth and of the Republic of Ireland*, Vol. II (London, 1960) Section 339, Note 19 at pp. 1044-1045; and L. Fransman's *British Nationality Law*, (London, 1989) at pp. 318, 496, 808, 1924-1027.

[45] *British Protectorates, Protected States and Protected Persons Order In Council 1949/140 (Sch.2); the British Protectorates, Protected States and Protected Persons Order In Council 1965/1864 Sch.3) and the British Protectorates, Protected States and Protected Persons Order In Council 1969/1832 (Sch.2)*. No reference to Bahrain has been made in the subsequent Orders.

[46] *The Termination of Special Treaty Relations between the United Kingdom and Bahrain, 1971, Cmnd 4827*. See Fransman, *ibid*., p.319.

[47] Fransman, *ibid*., p.496.

[48] British Protectorates, Protected States and Protected Persons (Amendment) Order In Council 1961/2325.

Sheikhdoms (Dubai, Sharjah, Ra‘s al-Khaimah, Ajmān, Umm al-Qawain, Abu Dhabi and Kalba). The Trucial States continued to be Protected States at the commencement of the British Nationality Act in 1948 and were identified as such in the 1949/140 Order in Council. There was no clear Nationality Law in force in the Sheikhdoms at the time, and for the purposes of S.12 (1) of the 1949/140 Order in Council, they were treated as *Protectorates*, so far as ascertaining the persons who, by virtue of their connection with the Sheikhdoms, were statutory British Protected Persons.[49] Kalba was removed from Sch.2 to 1949/140 Order in Council and Fujairah was added on 30 July 1952[50] when Kalba's territory became part of Sharjah and other territories belonging to Sharjah formed the new State of Fujairah. The Trucial States remained Protected States until, by agreement with the United Kingdom, the Crowns's protection and jurisdiction terminated as of 2 December 1971.[51]

From 1949, therefore, maintaining quasi-authority under British protection, the judicial systems were somewhat reorganised on a more local basis by Orders-In-Council.[52] This same era saw a general development of the individual nationalist states in the Gulf. The evolution of each towards independence and beyond, and the legislative ‘mobilisation’ undertaken by each Government has varied significantly between the three States under study, as will become clear.[53] In Bahrain, the express laws to be applied were (1) Specified enactments of the Indian Legislature and British Acts of Parliament; (2) Orders-In-Council and other regulations;[54] (3) A residual jurisdiction based on ‘Justice, Equity and good conscience’. What remained of the British enactments by 1970, when Bahrain achieved its independence, have gradually been replaced by National Codes. The first of these was the

---

49 British Protectorates, Protected States and Protected Persons Order In Council 1949/140 S.12 (2). Fransman, *ibid.*, p.808.

50 By the British Protected States [Fujaira and Kalba] Order In Council 1952/141.

51 Termination of Special Treaty Relations Between the United Kingdom and the Trucial States, dated 1 December 1971, Cmnd 4941. Fransman, *ibid.*, p.808.

52 These are itemised in Ballantyne, *Commercial Law In The Arab Middle East : The Gulf States*, (London, 1986)

53 Carter, L.N., ‘Gulf Cooperation Council’, *Persian Gulf States : Country Studies*, Ed. R.F. Nyrop (Second Edn. Washington, 1985) Kuwait: pp.72-141; Qatar: pp.191-237; UAE: pp.239-305

54 As according to S.12 of the Bahrain order of 1959

Constitution, promulgated in December, 1973.[55] Of the rest, the most important for our purposes, the Contract Code of 1969, has not been subject to re-codification in the light of civil law provisions but remains wholly based on English law principles, as influenced by Indian statute. As Bahrain encouraged International Offshore Banking Units, Bahrain had more urgent need, perhaps, than the other constitutions under study to legislate rapidly and efficiently upon Independence. It received the first influx of large numbers of foreign workers,[56] and this is reflected in the promulgation of essential laws regulating labour, contractual and commercial relations. It was not until 1988, however, that a comprehensive Commercial Code was promulgated in Bahrain.[57]

In Kuwait, the impact of the oil revenues was sudden. From a relatively poor community with few resources outside pearl fishing and the dhow trade, Kuwait became a financial giant, an immensely rich state, possessing only a finite number of self-investment resources.[58] The administrative system could hardly have been expected to have kept up with the rapidity of development. In 1938, public pressure mounted for the creation of a legislative assembly. A fourteen-member council under the presidency of ʻAbdallāh al-Ṣabāḥ (then Crown Prince), convened to draw up a document of five articles, approved by the Amīr on 2 July 1938, and regarded by some as the first Kuwaiti Constitution.

The demise of this legislative assembly came about largely because of the British reluctance to deal with a council rather than one man, but a subsequent similar council, and eventually, a number of consultative committees and government departments were set up, each headed by members of the ruling family, Āl-Ṣabāh. All legislation emanated from the ruler, there being no legislative council. The Supreme Council, which aided the Amīr in legislative and administrative matters, was replaced in 1962 by the Council of Ministers.

---

55 Larkin, Patricia E., in A.P. Blaustein and G.H. Flanz, (Eds.), *Modern Constitutions of the World*, (New York, Dec. 1985) Vol. II (6/85); See also, *International Encyclopoedia of Comparative Law*, Vol. IB (Completed July 1972); Miles, *The Countries and Tribes of the Persian Gulf, op.cit.*; and Ballantyne, *Legal Development in Arabia*, (London, 1980) pp. 59,66 and *passim*.

56 See Birks, J.S., and Sinclair, C.A., *The Nature and Progress of Labour Importing : The Arabian Gulf States*, (International Labour Office Working Paper, Geneva, 1977)

57 Bahrain Commercial Code, No. 7 of 1987: Official Gazette 26 March, 1987.

58 See Hakima, Ahmad Mustafa Abu, *The Modern History of Kuwait : 1750-1965*, (London, 1983) particularly at pp.93-106; Hijazi, A., 'Kuwait : Development From a Semitribal, Semicolonial Society to Democracy and Sovereignty', 13 *American Journal of Comparative Law*, (1964) pp. 428-437; J. Daniels, *Kuwait Journey*, (London, 1971); Dickson, *Kuwait and Her Neighbours*, (1956)

On June 19, 1961 with the termination of the 1899 agreement with the British, "an act that was tantamount to Kuwait's achieving full independence",[59] British jurisdiction in Kuwait came to an end. The newly elected fourteen-member Council of Ministers drafted the Constitution, which was signed by the Amīr on 11 November 1962.[60] This Constitution[61] remained unchanged until August 1976 when four articles concerning the dissolution of the legislature and the freedom of the press were suspended. These articles were reinstated four years later and the constitution remained intact until 1981. In 1982 the Government submitted sixteen constitutional amendments which were formally dropped in May 1983. Discussions have nonetheless infrequently arisen since on the need to amend the constitution in the light of the past two and a half decades of independence, and the co-existence of monarchical and "tribocratic"[62] forms of government.[63] Up until this time, in matters other than personal status (which are still governed by the *Sharī'a* courts), the Ottoman *Majella* was retained in Kuwait. As the *Majella* was based mainly on the Ḥanafī school, while the ruling family of Kuwait belonged to the Mālikī school, it obviously had its drawbacks. It was abrogated in 1981 by the new Civil Code, Law No 67 of 1980. In 1939, customs and conventions governing pearl-fishing crews and their employers were codified, and commercial disputes were sent to special commercial tribunals to be settled. The judicial system of Kuwait laid particular emphasis on the idea of arbitration and conciliation, and it is here that the old Arab system is still clearly visible, even though the

---

59 *Persian Gulf States: Country Studies*, Ed. Nyrop *op.cit.*, p.119

60 Reproduced in *International Encyclopoedia of Comparative Law*, 'Kuwait', (19 June 1961); and *al-Kuwait al-Yaum*, Spec. Issue of 12 Nov. 1962. Abu Zayyad, Fuad S., 'Kuwait', in *Yearbook of Commercial Arbitration*, (The Netherlands, 1979) pp.139-147; Yunus, As'ad, *Commercial Arbitration and Legal System in Kuwait*, (Kuwait, 1978); Europa Publications Limited, 'Kuwait', in *The Europa Yearbook : A World Survey*, (London, 1984) See also, Baaklini, Abdo I., 'Legislatures in the Gulf Area : The Experience of Kuwait, 1961-1976', *International Journal of Middle Eastern Studies*, 14 (1982) p. 362; Kiran, B., and Jain, 'Constitution and the Law in the State of Kuwait : Highlights and Sidelights', *Islamic and Comparative Law Quarterly*, Vol. VI (4) (Dec. 1986) Ed. T. Mahmood, pp.231 ff.

61 The Constitution of 1963 comprised 5 basic chapters : Systems of government; Guiding principles of society; General rights and duties; Divisions of power and State's authorities; Final Provisions. See Blaustein, Eric B., 'Kuwait', in *Modern Constitutions of The World*, Blaustein, A.P., and Flanz, G.H., (Eds.) Vol. VIII (12/71) (New York, Dec. 1985); Schacht, Lewis and pellat, (Eds.), *Dustūr: A Survey of the Constitutions of the Arab and Muslim States*, (Leiden, 1966) 'Kuwait': pp.101-103.

62 A term employed increasingly frequently in reference to the merger of modern "democracy" and the traditional tribal/feudal political system of Kuwait.

63 *Persian Gulf Studies, op.cit*, p.119.

systematisation and codification has largely obscured it in other respects.[64]

Shortly after British jurisdiction came to an end, the ruler invited Sanhūrī to draw up what was to become the Commercial Code, Law No. 2 of 1961. The Second Book of this code is comprised of provisions on contracts modelled on those found in the Egyptian Civil Code. It was the *Majella* which remained the Civil Law of Kuwait in name, but in application it was to the provisions of the 1961 Commercial Code that the courts made resource.[65]

During 1975/6, Assembly debates regarding oil and social policies and general Middle Eastern politics had been growing increasingly strident. Concern with the increasing disparities in personal wealth within Kuwait had led on occasion to explicit verbal attacks on the Āl Ṣabāḥ. In mid-August 1976, the Assembly, in sympathy with the Arab Nationalist opposition, championed the Palestinian cause.[66] This was in direct opposition with the Government's officially neutral position : these activities had been viewed by the Āl Ṣabāḥ as dangerous to Kuwait's internal security and contrary to its foreign policy interest, and therefore, on August 19 1976, after thirteen years of legislation, the *'Amīr* dissolved the National Assembly, suspended the four suffrage provisions in its Constitution, and embarked on an "evaluation" of its legislative and democratic processes.[67]

Despite this enormous upheaval, the institutions and enactments established by Kuwait continued, in the interim, to serve as a model for the other Gulf States. Meanwhile, there was no attempt by the Kuwaiti

---

64 See, generally, Ballantyne, *Legal Development In Arabia, op.cit.*; and Pillar and Kumar, 'The Political and Legal Status of Kuwait', II *International and comparative Law Quarterly*, (1962) at p.108; Statutory Laws and Regulations of the Kuwaiti State for this period are recorded in *The Persian Gulf Gazette*, No.s 1-32 (1953-1961); and *Al-Kuwait al-Yaum*, (Kuwaiti Official Gazette) Supp. No.s 253-373 (Dec. 1959 - April 1962)

65 Ebraheem, Hasan Ali al-, 'Jurisdictional Changes in Kuwait', *World Today*, (1960) pp.39-40; See also Kabeel, Soraya M., *Select Bibliography on Kuwait and the Arabian Gulf*, (Kuwait, 1969); and Winstone, H.V.F., *Kuwait : Prospect and Reality*, (London, 1972)

66 By adopting a pro-Palestinian resolution condemning Syrian involvement in the Lebanese Civil War. *Persian Gulf Studies, op.cit.*, p.128

67 Baaklini, Abdo I., 'Legislatures in the Gulf Area : The Experience of Kuwait, 1961-1976', *International Journal of Middle Eastern Studies*, 14 (1982) states that the reasons for the suspension of the legislature in Kuwait are twofold: political and structural. The political reasons were those substantive issues over which the legislature and executive collided, and which threatened National Security; while the structural reasons were inherent weaknesses in the system concerning the legitimacy of authority to rule (See pp.373-374). Baaklini suggests that the very strength of the legislature, together with the extension of its authority into foreign policy, inter-Arab politics and National Security, made it intolerable to the executive. (p.374)

Government to undertake any "evaluation" of the democratic process until the success of the Iranian revolution in 1979, which shattered the tranquility of the Gulf. Immediately after, the Government announced the formation of a special commission to carry this out, thus hastily providing a representative institution to legitimize its authority in the face of the rising fundamentalism which had begun its sweep of the area. In March 1981 another, reshuffled, legislative assembly was convened and entrusted with the responsibility of drafting a new constitution and ratifying the basic structures of the State. The character of this assembly, no doubt fashioned by the new emphasis which had developed in Arab politics during the previous five years, showed early signs of the predominance of tribal leaders (traditionally the element most loyal to the Āl Ṣabāḥ),[68] loyal moderates and technocrats,[69] the Shi'a contingent[70] and Sunni fundamentalist representation;[71] with this came a rejection of the altruistic pro-Western and nationalistic elements of the previous Council of Ministers.[72] During 1982-1983 the fundamentalists, who constituted the only effective remaining opposition, introduced numerous initiatives designed to enforce greater compliance with Islamic practice, such as the prohibition of importation of alcohol, segregation of schoolrooms by sex, and restriction of citizenship to Muslim nationals. Repeated attempts by the fundamentalists to amend the Constitution so that the *Sharīʿa* would be the sole source of Kuwaiti law have remained unsuccessful.

The Commercial Code of 1961[73] and the *Majella* were abrogated in 1980 by new Civil and Commercial codes which were drafted by a commission headed by three distinguished Egyptian lawyers. A new Civil Code, Law no. 67, was enacted in 1980 and became law on 25 February 1981.[74] In his Introduction to the Code, Sheikh Salman claimed that "Its provisions are in harmony with the schools of Islamic Jurisprudence, to the extent that there is no provision in it, which cannot be supported by any one such school or

---

68 Bedouin tribal leaders won 23 out of 50 seats being contested.

69 Won 13 seats.

70 Who had won 10 seats in 1975, won only 4 in 1981.

71 Won 5 seats, and constituted a new element in the Assembly elections.

72 Baaklini, Abdo I., 'Legislatures in the Gulf Area : The Experience of Kuwait, 1961-1976', *International Journal of Middle Eastern Studies*, 14 (1982) pp. 359-379, at pp.359, 362,

73 For a discussion of this law, see Kassim, 'The New Civil Code of Kuwait', *Middle East Executive Report*, (Feb. 1962) at pp.2,3.

74 Kuwait Civil Code, Law No. 67 of 1980.

[is] in conflict with the Sharia."[75] The new Civil Code abrogated the *Majella*, and Law No. 6 of 1961, recognising liabilities arising out of unlawful acts ('The Tort Law'). It was accompanied by the new Code of Civil Procedure; the new Commercial Code, Law No. 68 of 1980; and the Code of Maritime Commerce, Law No. 28 of 1980. A Commercial Companies Code, Law No. 15 of 1960, had been promulgated towards the end of British Jurisdiction in 1960 and was based on the French Civil/Egyptian model. The new Civil Code of Kuwait is "Derived from Islamic Principles in accordance with the Constitution, consistent with its principles and in conformity with the realities of Kuwait and its Traditions."[76]

In early 1987, the parliament of Kuwait was dissolved and all legislative duties passed to the Government. There has been no further legislation by parliament since this time.

Prior to 1971, the Trucial states were under effective British protection, brought about by a series of treaties and agreements which had climaxed in May 1853 in the Treaty of Maritime Peace in Perpetuity. This treaty was strengthened later in the century by identical, separate treaties between Britain and each of the Trucial coast rulers. In 1951, Britain set up the Trucial States Council of the 7 rulers.[77] In 1968, due to changes in policy, the British Government announced its intention to withdraw its force, terminate its position and obligations in the Gulf, and effectively abrogate its treaties with the Trucial States by the end of 1971. In February 1968, the representatives of the seven Trucial States, Bahrain and Qatar met, and on 30 March announced the provisional formation of the Federation of Arab Emirates. Due to boundary disputes, the resurgence of old dynastic quarrels and an inability to agree on details of precedence and organisation, Bahrain and Qatar shortly withdrew from this arrangement, choosing to remain separate and independent, while the seventh Emirate, Ra's al-Khaima, acceded to the union in February 1972.[78]

A draft provisional Federal Constitution was promulgated in December,

[75] Isa A. Huneidi, 'Twenty-Five Years of Civil Law System in Kuwait', *Arab Law Quarterly*, 1 (2) (Feb.1986) pp.216-219, at p.218

[76] Introduction by Sheikh Salman, p.12 of the Official Arabic Civil Code of Kuwait, published by the Kuwaiti *Majlis al-Wuzarā'*.

[77] To meet semi-annually, and presided over by the British Polical Officer. This council afforded the 'Amīrs the opportunity to define areas of common interest.

[78] *Persian Gulf Studies, op.cit.*, pp.283, 245-246.

1971, but remains temporary to this day.[79] In its draft form it follows the precedent set by the 1963 Kuwaiti Constitution, with five additional chapters which define the inter-Emirate relationships with each other and the Union, and which delimit the Federal powers and functions. Initially, the Federal State was seemingly reluctant to rush into modernising legislation projects with the same fervency as Bahrain and Kuwait. This reluctance was no doubt due initially to the conservatism of the rulers, jealous of their traditional perogatives, and the lack of articulate political constituencies among Emirati citizens,[80] but the new Federation also demonstrated a similar reluctance to borrow either wholesale or arbitrarily from the continental model adopted by Egypt and Kuwait. The price it paid for such reluctance was that up until 1987, the State suffered serious lacunae in its legislation, and in practice, much borrowing and reference to the codes of Kuwait and Egypt took place. Ultimately, however, the reluctance of the Federal State to rush this important process has seemingly paid off. In its search for the harmonious combination of Islamic tradition and modern tenets, the Federation took the Jordanian Civil Code of 1976 as its model. It was the Jordanian Code of 1976 which had started the new Islamised trend : the "true" reassessment of Islamic principles within a modern code. Significantly, Article 7 of the Provisional Constitution of the UAE determines that the Islamic *Sharīʿa* shall be **a** main source of legislation within the Federation. In the law setting up the Supreme Court, however, the *Sharīʿa* is determined as **the** main source of reference and so, in effect, the *Sharīʿa* is afforded its role as primary source of law within the Federation.[81] In the Civil Code, Article 1 states that where a question is not covered by a specific provision in the text of the code, the Judge is to have regard to the 'most appropriate solution from the schools of Imām Mālik and Imām Aḥmad bin Ḥanbal, and if none is found there, then from the schools of Imām al-Shāfiʿī and Imām Abū Ḥanafa as most befits.' Article 2

[79] The Provisional Constitution was enacted on July 18, 1971, (the product of more than three year's bargaining among the rulers) and has been reaffirmed every five years thence. See 'Document: The Provisional Constitution of the United Arab Emirates', *Middle East Journal*, 26 (3) (1972) pp.307-325; also Bassiouni, Cherif, and Dyba, M.E., in A.P. Blaustein and G.H. Flanz (Eds.), *Modern Constitutions of the World*, VII, (New York, Dec. 1985) 'United Arab Emirates', Vol. XVI (8/82); and H.M. al-Baharna, 'United Arab Emirates', in *International Encyclopoedia of Comparative Law: National Reports*, pp. U:53-U:57. The Constitution is likely to remain provisional for the forseeable future, whilst the Emirate politics of leadership between Abu Dhabi and Dubai remain at issue.

[80] *Persian Gulf Studies, op.cit.*, p.283.

[81] The only Gulf State which states the *Sharīʿa* as **the** main source of law in its constitution is Qaṭar.

determines that in the understanding, construction and interpretation of the provisions contained therein, it is the rules and principles of the Islamic *Fiqh* which are to be relied upon, while Article 27 of the same code states that it shall not be possible to apply the provisions of a law specified in the section governing Private International Law : choice of Law, if such provisions are contrary to the Islamic *Sharī'a*, public order or morals in the State of the United Arab Emirates.

The enactment of the Federal Civil Code was long awaited,[82] for until the promulgation of this code, the only legislation in the UAE specifically covering Obligations and Contracts was the Contract Code of Dubai and Sharjah.[83] This code, was largely based on Indian Law, and contains little of Islamic origins. All other states of the UAE were meanwhile obliged to operate without a civil code.

The new Federal code, however, is the most realistic and careful attempt in the modern Arab Gulf to correlate principles derived from the *Fiqh* together with the most modern precepts of practical legislation.[84] Because it is based on the Jordanian Civil Code,[85] this code constitutes a marked departure from the Egyptian-Iraqi-Syrian-Kuwaiti model with its combination of French civil law and symbolistic attentions to Islamic principles. The attempts to synthesise Islamic tenets into a modern exposition in the UAE Code has been met with appraisal, and it is this trend which is now likely to set the prototype for future promulgations within the Arab Gulf States. Already, Bahrain has produced a new Commercial Code, which, in its intent (if not in its content) manifests the desire to follow suit.[86]

As yet, a Federal Code of Civil Procedure has not been enacted. The Emirate States presently refer to the Code of Civil Procedure of Abu

---

82 Union Law No. 5 of 1985 Issuing the Code of Civil Transactions for the United Arab Emirates, [Effective as from March 1986], *UAE Official Gazette*, No 158,(Dec. 1985)

83 *Dubai Contract Law*, of 15 July 1971

84 Ballantyne, 'The New Civil Code of the United Arab Emirates: A Further Reassertion of the Shari'a', *Arab Law Quarterly*, vol. I (3) (May 1986) pp.245-264; and *id.*, 'The Sharia: A Speech to the IBA Conference in Cairo, on Arab Comparative and Commercial Law, 15-18 Feb. 1987', *Arab Law Quarterly*, 2 (1) (Feb. 1987) p.28: ("and unlike Kuwait, there is no Commercial Code to dissolve it"). See also Edge, Ian, 'Comparative Commercial Law of Egypt and The Arabian Gulf', *Cleveland State Law Review*, Vol. 34, No.1 (1985-1986); and Sloane, 'The Status of Islamic Law In The Commercial World', *International Lawyer*, (Fall 1988) 22(3) p.758.

85 Law No. 43 of 1976

86 See Ballantyne, 'Note on the New Commercial Code of Bahrain (Decree Law 7/1987)', *Arab Law Quarterly*, vol.2 (4) (Nov. 1987) pp.352 ff.

Dhabi.[87]

The present era of modern Islamic reform, and the search for a "New *Ijtihād*", can be compared to some extent to the first formative period in the doctrinal development of the *Sharī'a*.[88] The acceptance of a modern *Ijtihād* is becoming widespread.[89] Muhammad Iqbal stated: "The claim of the present generation of muslim liberals to re-interpret the foundational legal principles, in the light of their own experience and the altered conditions of modern life is, in my opinion, perfectly justified...each generation, guided but unhampered by the work of its predecessors, should be permitted to solve its own problems."[90] Even in Saudi Arabia, the legitimacy of *Ijtihād* has been recognised. Until 1961, a Saudi court was required to apply the *responsa* in Ḥanbalī texts. Recourse was occasionally had to a certain *Ijtihād* made in reference to Ḥanbalī scholars, other than the official judicial references. Such decisions could result in arguments involving the Judicial Board of Scrutiny (Appellate Court). In 1961, a Decree[91] was issued which states: "The Judicial Board of Scrutiny can only object to a decision taken by a court if this decision does not comply with the *Qur'ān*, the *Sunna* and the *Ijmā'*, ie. Consensus. If this were the case, the judge in question would be asked to withdraw his judgment."[92] With the enactment of this regulation, the Saudi judge is thereby accorded the freedom to apply Islamic law generally, and is not limited to the precepts of the Ḥanbalī texts.

The right to exercise *Ijtihād* is similarly recognised in the United Arab Emirates, although, on an individual level, it is more likened to *Ra'y*, and is

---

87 Abu Dhabi Code of Civil Procedure, 1970.

88 Schacht wrote in 1960 : "The fact is that only now, after an interval of more than 1200 years, a situation has arisen comparable to that in which an Islamic jurisprudence arose for the first time." Schacht, 'Problems of Modern Islamic Legislation,' *Studia Islamica*, XII, (1960) pp.99-129.

89 I am assured of this by several practising and academic lawyers of the Arab Gulf States, notably, Dr. 'Adel Ṭabṭabā'ī, Dean of the Faculty of Law, University of Kuwait; Dr. Aḥmad al-Samdān, Professor in Private International Law, University of Kuwait; and Dr. 'Abd al-Rasūl Riḍā, Head of the State Department for Legal Advice and Legislation, Kuwait; in personal interviews conducted 6 and 10 October, 1987.

90 Muhammad Iqbal, *The Reconstruction of Religious Thought in Islam*, (Lahore, 1930, Reprinted 1968); Also cited in Pearl, 'Codification in Islamic Law', *JLA*, Vol. II (1979) p.167 n. This view was repeatedly confirmed during interviews conducted with academic lawyers, practising lawyers and legislative ministers in the three Gulf states under study during late 1987. The proviso for Neo-*Ijtihād* seems to be that the *Mujtahid* is a recognised expert in the field under revision.

91 Saudi Arabia: Cabinet Decree No. 16-3-1336, issued on 20-10-81 AH; See Muhammad I. Ali and Abdul W.A. Sulaiman, 'Recent Judicial Developments in Saudi Arabia', *Journal of Islamic and Comparative Law*, vol. 3 (1968) p.12

92 Saudi Arabia: Cabinet Decree No. 16-3-1336, Article 6

restricted to the expression of that opinion in published legal articles and journals. For the judicial exercise of *Ijtihād*, certain axiomatic guidelines are stated in the civil code, rather in the nature of the maxims set out in the *Majella. Ijtihād* may not be exercised in the case of provisions with definite import, where resort may be had to the principles of the four Schools of Sunni law, or where there is some local or general custom to govern the question.[93] Article 30, for example, states that "Exceptions may not be used by analogy, nor may their interpretations be extended." Likewise, Article 41 states: "No analogies may be drawn from what is shown to be contrary to analogy" (ie. outside the normal course of events).

The conclusions of this search for a "New *Ijtihād*" will inevitably affect the course of the legislation of Contract Laws, and all their attendant branches, in the Islamic constitutions in the future. In accordance with the recommendation given by the Conference of Arab Ministers of Justice in Morocco in 1980, of the need to codify Islamic law in all Arab countries, and the reaffirmation of this recommendation in Jedda in 1981, the process of codification is now well established within the Arab world, with the exception of Saudi Arabia and Oman. These latter countries do nevertheless issue Regulations (*'Anẓima*; sing. *Niẓām*) from time to time.[94] Additionally, the Islamic Research council of al-Azhar is continuing a process of codifying Islamic Law according to the four schools. Whether this will be done on a comparative basis along the lines of Sanhūrī's work,[95] or whether (and to be preferred) it is being compiled in four separate studies is not clear. The project is nevertheless a welcome and awesome undertaking. It will no doubt provide the definitive reference for all future Islamic legislation, once it is completed, as present resource to a multitude of badly or non-indexed tomes makes reference to the early *Fuqahā'* a cumbersome and time-consuming pursuit.

---

93 UAE Civil Code, Art. 1; See also Kuwaiti Civil Code, Art 1.

94 For the respective Laws and Constitutions, see Ballantyne, *Register of the Laws of the Arabian Gulf*, (London, 1985); *id.*, 'The Constitutions of the Gulf States: A Comparative Study', *Arab Law Quarterly*, 1(2) (Feb. 1986) pp.158-176; Nabil Saleh, 'Les Lois Régissant Le Commerce Dans Le Sultanat d'Oman', *Revue Trimestrielle De Droit Commercial*, (Paris, 1974); Hill, 'The Commercial Legal System of the Sultanate of Oman', 17 *International Lawyer*, (3) (Summer, 1983) pp.507-534; Davis, Helen M., *Constitutions, Electoral Laws, Treaties of States in the Near and Middle East*, (Durham, N.Carolina, 1947) is still relevant in parts. The High Committee for the Codification of Islamic Law was presided over by the Egyptian Jurisprudential Counsellor, 'Alī 'Alī Manṣūr. There are still a number of draft laws not yet promulgated, including the Draft Commercial Law.

95 *Maṣādir al-Ḥaqq fī al-Fiqh al-Islāmī*, (6 Vols.; Cairo 1954-9)

A further improvement has been made as regards public access to the new promulgations of these jurisdictions. The gazetting of laws is now obligatory in Bahrain, Kuwait,[96] the UAE,[97] Qatar[98] and Oman.[99]

Thence, what of the possibility of the States of the Gulf Co-operation Council joining together in the future to enact a unified set of codes ? Despite the similarities in general, principles of their individual Civil and Commercial Codes as do differ in detail, such as the particular significance afforded to the *Sharī'a*, together with the political factors that such unification would entail, render the concept most unlikely, notwithstanding its obvious benefits.[100]

If, in the interests of the uniformity of world legal systems, the contract laws continue to assume an increasing volume of internationally accepted principles at the expense of Islamic tenets such as the prohibition of *Ribā*, or Unjust Enrichment, the laws of contracts and obligations will indubitably lose their muslim character and identity.

If, on the other hand, the Middle East decides to take a renewed look at the position of Islamic injunctions and their compatibility with modern commerce in the light of the developed legal methodology - and this appears to be the aim of the new islamised trend characterised by Jordan and the UAE - then the laws of obligation and contracts will reassume their muslim character by returning Islam to its crucial and central role within the law.

Through its own evolution, the corpus of Islamic law as it stands today is richer and more comprehensive than in the first formative period of its evolution. It is also, perhaps, more rigid. It therefore remains to be seen whether the law can repeat the process of Islamicization upon the new doctrines it has encountered in the twentieth century, that they may be assimilated into the accepted body of the *Fiqh* in a similar manner to the "underground doctrines" of previous centuries.

---

96 The first Kuwaiti Gazette was issued in 1954. Saudi Arabia also has a gazette, *Umm al-Qūra*, (Held in the British Library), but there is no law making it obligatory.

97 Gazettes for the UAE (Federal state) have been issued since 1971 (Inchoate holding in the UAE Embassy, London); Abu Dhabi has issued its Gazette since 1968 (with a new series beginning in 1972); Dubai since 1971; Ra's al-Khaima since 1969; Sharjah does not have an offical Gazette and legislation ensues courtesy of the Chamber of Commerce.

98 Issued since 1961, (9/72 missing)

99 Issued since 1971.

100 This view has been endorsed by the personal opinions of Drs. Ṭabṭabā'ī, Samdān and Riḍā in interviews conducted personally with them on 6, 6, and 10 October 1987, respectively.

Chapter 3

THE HISTORICAL EVOLUTION OF COMMERCIAL LAW

1. EARLY ISLAMIC COMMERCE

> "The Islamic modification of the positive contents of this material (Ḥanafī commercial laws) is sporadic, uneven, and in many cases, minimal. Islam's formal contribution was very much conditioned by the underlying raw material."[1]

In the field of commerce the historical evolution of the structure of the law is of prime significance. It has already been noted that the laws of contract and obligation have been exposed to a variable degree of infiltration by external elements to Islam.[2] The most significant example of this is the role played by pre-Islamic commercial customs in the Islamic principles of commerce. These customs consisted of an amalgam of indigenous and external practices which, by the rise of Islam, had become correlated with, and integrated into, an historico-cultural unity. Joseph Schacht writes:

> "The substratum, the subject-matter of Islamic law is to a great extent not originally Islamic, let alone Koranic; it became Islamic law only through having the categories of Islamic jurisprudence imposed upon it."[3]

Likewise, Coulson writes:

---

1 A.L. Udovitch, *Partnership and Profit In Medieval Islam*, (Princeton, New Jersey : 1970), p.254

2 See Chapter One, Section 1.2 on Foreign Law Influence, *supra*.

3 Joseph Schacht, 'Problems of Modern Islamic Legislation', *Studia Islamica*, XII (1960) p.100

> "The starting point was the review of local practice, legal and popular, in the light of the principles of conduct enshrined in the *Qur'ān.* Institutions and activities were individually considered, then approved or rejected according to whether they measured up or fell short of these criteria."[4]

On the basis that the transfusion of these pre-Islamic customs was a transfusion between the micro-cultural communal practices extant in the regions of *Jāhilī* Ḥijāz, and the macro-cultural commercial practices employed by international traffickers, with whom the Arab merchants came into contact, we may sumise that the status of commercial and contractual principles at the rise of Islam was the product of teleological and paradigmatic development : regulations were formulated to govern both new and pre-existing practices only when the community posed questions regarding such practices, or when these practices ran contrary to the spirit of the new order. It is therefore likely that the mark made upon the commercial order of the Arab hinterlands by Islam was mainly reformative. It was not until successive centuries, that the principles of contracts and obligations took on the forms in which they are set out in the *Fiqh* expositions as a result of the attention paid to the contextualised development of the law by the early Muslim casuists.

2. THE TRADITIONAL CONCEPTION OF PRE-ISLAMIC COMMERCE

In order to comprehend fully the formulation of commercial law within Islam, it is essential to seek the basis upon which Islam founded its commercial principles : the existing practices and commercial customs indigenous to Pre-Islamic trading. As Saleh states, the prevalent belief concerning early Muslims is of "hoardes of warring Bedouins" living in otherwise tribally secluded nomadism.[5] Any reading of the *Dīwān* poetry will confirm this belief, but while it is true that the vast proportion of the Arab hinterland consisted of mountain and desert unsuitable for permanent habitation, it must also be remembered that the inception of Islam took place in Mecca and Madīna (then known as Yathrib), which were among several settled communities nestled among the hills and plains between the two mountain ridges of the Hijāz which ran North-South from the Gulf of

---

4 N.J. Coulson, *A History of Islamic Law*, (Edinburgh University Press, 1964), p.38

5 See Strabo, *The Geography of Strabo*, (Transl. H.L. Jones; London, 1930; repr. 1966) 8 Vols, Vol VII, Bk. 16:IV 1-2 (p.309) Nabil A. Saleh, *The General Principles of Saudi Arabian and Omani Company Laws: Statutes and Sharia*, (London 1981), p.1

Aqaba to Sana'a.[6] Up until very recently, it was consistently argued by western orientalists that these settled sites were prosperous mercantile communities, in the pre-Islamic period, due to their location at the nodal points of numerous trade routes scouring Arabia from East to West, and North to South.[7] Most of the information for these submissions has been based on the first studies of the subject by Lammens[8] and Kister.[9] It has been faithfully reproduced since by successive historians, such as Watt,[10] Shaban,[11] Rodinson,[12] and Hitti.[13]

Kister has attempted to show how the relationships between the settled communities of Mecca and Madīna were conspicuously linked through the expanding international trade network involving the two great powers of the time, the Byzantine and Sassanian Empires.[14] In early times, most South Arabian trade is reported to have come up through the Hijāz to Syria and Egypt through the medium of the Yemeni and Sabean commercial agents.[15] These Arabs were believed to have taken over the produce of the Hadramawt, Dhofar and imports from India at Sana'a, and conveyed it all

---

6 O'Leary, *Arabia Before Muhammad*, (London, 1927) pp.3,8,. O'Leary states that the Arab tribes settled in Madīna were Yemenites, while the Meccans belonged to a Northern group. The Meccans were pro-Byzantine 'as might be expected from their close commercial relations with Syria' (p.17).

7 Hussein states that most trade was conveyed overland due to the dangers to Red Sea navigation from pirates and coral reefs. See Raef T.A. Hussein, 'The Early Arabian Trade and Marketing', *Islamic Culture*, vol. LIX, no.4, Oct. 1985, p.366. On the "Incense Road", see Hermann Schreiber, *Merchants, Pilgrims and Highwaymen*, (New York, 1962) p.79

8 H. Lammens, *L'Arabie Occidentale Avant L'Hégire*, (Beirut, 1928); *id.*, *La Meque à la Veille de l'Hégire*, (Reprinted from Mélanges de l'Université St. Joseph, Vol. IX) (Beirut, 1924: Original pagination) p.118; *id.*, 'La République Marchande de la Meque vers l'an 600 de Notre Ère', *Bulletin de l'Institut Égyptien*, (5th Series) IV (1910) pp.23-54; *id.*, *La Cité Arabe de Ṭāif à la Veille de l'Hégire*, (Reprinted from Mélanges de l'Université St. Joseph, Vol. VIII) (Beirut, 1922: Original pagination)

9 M.J. Kister, 'Mecca and Tamīm: Aspects of their Relations', *Journal of Economic and Social History of the Orient*, (1965), pp.116-117; *id.*, 'Some Reports Concerning Mecca from Jāhiliyya to Islam', *Journal of the Economic and Social History of the Orient*, 15 (1972).

10 Watt, *Muhammad at Mecca*, (Oxford, 1953) p.3; *id.*, *Muhammad at Medina*, (Oxford, 1956); *id.*, *Muhammad, Prophet and Statesman*, (Oxford, 1964)

11 Shaban, *Islamic History : New Interpretation*, I (Cambridge, 1971) pp. 2ff.

12 Rodinson, M., *Mohammad*, (London, 1971) p.39

13 Hitti, P.K., *Capital Cities of Arab Islam*, (Minneapolis, 1973) p.5

14 M.J. Kister, 'Mecca and Tamīm', *Journal of Economic and Social History of the Orient*, (1965), pp.116-117; See also: Maḥmaṣānī, *al-Naẓariyyat al-'Amma li al-Mūjibāt wa al-'Uqūd*, 2 Vols, (Beirut, 1948),Vol I. p.27.

15 N.A. Faris (Ed.), *The Arab Heritage*, (New Jersey, 1946) p.42

up to Teima. O'Leary states that Mecca and Madīna rose to importance with the revival of the Hijāzi trade route when Red Sea shipping declined.[16] He asserts that Mecca "was important as connecting with a crossroad which went around the north side of the Ruba' al-Khali by way of ar-Riad to Gerrha on the Persian Gulf". He dates the revival of the Hijāzi route and the Mecca-Riyāḍ route as contemporaneous, although he attributes Mecca with previous importance as a 'station' on the Hijāzi north-south route, on the basis of the sources. The supposition is that the role of the Sabean commercial agents was therefore later transferred to the Nabatean Arabs, who were in time succeeded by the Ḥijāzī Arabs.[17] Reports are given of transactions conducted between competitive commodity traders in the bazaars of the nodal centres.[18]

In early Islam, therefore, Orientalist tradition has it that "Commerce was indeed at its peak, and Arabia, before and after the rise of Islam, was frantically involved in trade."[19] Histories relate lists of the commodities traded : spices, silks, perfumes, precious stones and pearls, drugs, iron, hides and furs, timber, and later, slaves.[20]

The Pre-Islamic Arabs were not only regarded as intermediaries exposed to the influence of passing merchants, but were themselves believed to have organized trading caravans in pursuit of profit through commerce.[21] Shaban writes:

> "It is impossible to think of Makka in terms other than trade; its only *raison d'être* was trade. It was first established as a

---

16 O'Leary *Arabia Before Muhammad, op.cit.*, pp. 78, 105

17 O'Leary, *op.cit.*, p. 181

18 Ernst Samhaber, *Merchants Make History*, (New York, 1964) p.95. Annual fairs (called *'Ukāẓ*, were held during the sacred months between Nakhlah and Taīf in the Ḥijāz for the purpose of displaying local works and for the exchange of trade. cf. Philip K. Hitti, *The History of The Arabs*, (New York, 1967) pp.93-94

19 Saleh, *op. cit.*, p.1.

20 For Western sources on pre-Islamic trading, see also : G. Hourani, *Arab Seafaring*, (Princeton, 1951); S. Huzayyin, *Arabia and the Far East*, (Cairo, 1942); H. Lammens, *L'Arabie Occidentale Avant L'Hégire*, (Beirut, 1928); H. Philby, *The Background of Islam*, (Alexandria, 1937); E. Warmington, *The Commerce Between The Roman Empire and India*, (Cambridge, 1928); and Claude Cohen's article 'Economy, Society, Institutions', in *The Cambridge History of Islam*, Vol. 2B, p. 524

21 M.H. Haykal, *Ḥayāt Muḥammad*, (13th Ed.:In Arabic), p. 115

local trading centre around a religious shrine."[22]

Thus from the earliest information we have on Mecca, historians have consistently regarded its religious and trading practices as inseparably linked. The prestige of its local trade, they assert, was enhanced by its prestige as a religious sanctuary, which was itself an aspect of its trading system.[23]

Kister states that through conflict, the Byzantine and Sassanian decline created the expedient political vacuum which led, at the end of the sixth century, to the rise of Mecca as an eminent trading nucleus.[24] This in turn resulted in a series of commercial treatying between Mecca and the Byzantine Emperor. Such treaties, he says, took the form of business associations which enabled the safe passage of merchants from other parts of the Arab hinterland and beyond, through Mecca. These pacts were termed *Īlāf*.[25]

The acceptance of this "*Pax Meccana*" by surrounding tribes was interpreted by later historians as an expression of their acknowledgement of

---

22 M.A. Shaban, *Islamic History : New Interpretation*, I (Cambridge, 1971), p3. De Lacy O'Leary states : "Its importance was purely commercial." *op.cit*, p.182; F.M. Donner describes Mecca as "a typical...combination of pilgrim center and marketplace." cf. *The Early Islamic conquests*, (Princeton, 1981), p.51.

23 Shaban, *op.cit*., p.3. It has been held that the exports in greatest demand, frankincense, myrrh and spices, were themselves utilised for religious purposes: see Hussein, 'Early Arabian Trade', *op.cit*. pp. 368-369. (The fact that they were largely Arab exports is disputed by Crone, *Meccan Trade*, pp.48-107.) See also A. Abel, 'L'Incidence de l'Activité Commerciale de la Mekke Sur Son Développement Urbain', in *Dalla Tribu Allo Stato*, (Académie Naz. dei Lincei; Rome, 1962), pp. 124-136; H. Lammens, 'La Republique marchande de la Meque vers l'an 600 de notre Ère', *Bulletin de L'Institute Égyptien*, 5th Series, 4 (1910) pp. 33ff.; Margoliouth, *Mohammad and The Rise of Islam*, (London, 1971) p.39; P.K. Hitti, *Capital Cities of Arab Islam*, (Minneapolis, 1973) p.5; M.J. Kister, 'Some Reports Concerning Mecca from Jāhiliyya to Islam', *Journal of the Economic and Social History of the Orient*, 15 (1972) p.76

24 O'Leary, *op.cit*, p.205 f.

25 The *Īlāf* pacts (covenants of security and safeguard) and the Quraysh in Mecca are referred to in the *Qur'ān, Sūra* (CVI:1-4). See also A. Yusuf Ali's commentary, *The Holy Qur'ān: Text, Translation and Commentary*, (Leicester, 1975), p.1794. The general interpretation comes from Ibn Kalbī's *Īlāf* Tradition : Ibn Ḥabīb, *Kitāb al-Munammaq*, Ed. K.H. Fāriq (Hyderabad, 1964) p.32; Ya'qūbī, *Ta'rīkh*, Ed. M.T. Houtsma, 2 Vols. (Leiden, 1883) I: 280ff. Ismā'īl b. al-Qāsim al-Qālī, *Kitāb Dhayl al-Amālī wa al-Nawādir*, (Cairo, 1926) p.199; Kister, 'Mecca and Tamīm', p.250; Sulayman b. Sālim al-Kalā'ī, *Kitāb al-Iktifā'*, part I, Ed. H. Massé (Algiers/Paris, 1931) pp.207ff; Tha'ālibī, 'Abd al-Mālik b. Muḥammad al-, *Thimār al-Qulūb*, Ed. M.A.-F. Ibrāhīm (Cairo, 1965) p.115; Maṣ'ūdī, *Murūj al-Dhahab*, Ed./Transl. C. Barbier de Meynard and P. de Courteille, as *Maçoudi, Les Prairies d'Or*, (Paris, 1861-77); O'Leary, *Arabia Before Muhammad*, p.181 : The interpretation of the *Īlāf* pacts has not yet been unanimously concluded upon. Kister treats them as inter-tribal, but they are also understood to have been more of an 'international' nature.

Mecca's status as a trading centre. The merchants were thus able to travel to Syria under the protection of the tribes along their route, sell their goods, and on their return share their profits with their tribal partners.[26] In this way these early *Īlāf* pacts benefitted both the merchants and their surrounding communities.[27]

O'Leary attributes the effectiveness of such charters to the "honourable and punctilious" manner in which the tribes promising protection carried out their agreements. It was common for those parties whose protection proved ineffective, even through no fault of their own, to return the payment due to them.[28]

Wāqidī describes pre-Islamic Mecca as a *Jamā'a* or republic.[29] O'Leary interprets this as meaning that Mecca consisted of a collection of tribal camps which all combined together into a confederacy for the purpose of trade. He suggests that this confederacy formed a *Mala'*, or general assembly, at which commercial enterprises were planned on the lines of a *Majlis* or council.[30]

3. CRONE'S REFUTATION OF THE TRADITION

In her work *Meccan Trade and the Rise of Islam*,[31] Patricia Crone has significantly undermined this Orientalist conception of pre-Islamic Mecca as a sophisticated and commercially "frantic" society. By attempting to show

---

26 Tradition relates that Muḥammad's Great-Grandfather, Hāshim, was one of the first to form such systems of treaties for merchants of Mecca visiting Syria with the Byzantine Emperor, from whom he obtained permission to sell leather and clothing there; See Muḥammad Ibn Ḥabīb, *Kitāb al-Munammaq*, ed. K.A. Fāriq (Hyderabad, 1964), p.32; Ismā'īl b. al-Qāsim al-Qālī, *Kitāb Dhayl al-Amālī wa al-Nawādir*, (Cairo, 1926). p.199; Ya'qūbī, *Ta'rīkh*, ed. M.T. Houtsma, 2 vols. (Leiden, 1883) I, 280f. Either he or his three brothers were also alleged to have procured treaties from the Persian and Abyssinian rulers. cf. Kister, 'Mecca and Tamīm', *op.cit.*, p.117-121, -163; and Crone, *Meccan Trade*, pp.98ff

27 Udovitch states that the commenda agreement, parallel to these *Īlāf* pacts, found its origins not amongst the Arabs, but can be traced back to at least the Babylonians, for mention is made of such pacts in the Babylonian *Talmud*, (Baba Mesi'a, chpt. 5) and the *Corpus Iuris Civilis*, of Justinian. Udovitch, *op.cit.*, p.8. He also notes that "the treatment of partnership and commenda in Islamic legal treatises remained essentially the same from the time of Shaybānī to that of the Ottoman Majellah". *ibid.*, p.14; Udovitch, 'At the Origin of the Western Commenda: Islam, Israel, Byzantium?' *Speculum*, 37 (1962) pp.198-207

28 O'Leary, *op.cit.*, p.179

29 Wāqidī, *Kitāb al-Maghāzī*, 59,3; O'Leary, *op.cit.*, p.183

30 O'Leary, *op.cit.*. p.183

31 Patricia crone, *Meccan Trade and the Rise of Islam*, (Oxford/Princeton, 1987)

the evidence upon which Kister, Lammens, Watt *et al* relied to have been either fabricated by early exegetes, or misinterpreted by later orientalist historians, Crone has clearly sown serious doubt as regards the truth of the Tradition. The commonly-held conceptions of the scale of pre-Islamic Meccan trade, the wealth of its commodities, and its status as a nodal point between important trade routes have been shaken by her work.

By detailed re-investigation of the original Arabic texts, Crone concludes that their mutual imcompatibility and contradictory nature are telling clues to their complete fabrication on the part of the exegetes. These exegetes, she suggests, were 'storytellers',[32] more interested in projecting a continual Tradition for the societal needs for Islam, venerating its origins and sanctity, rather than representing the true historical facts. She claims that the basis of the political tension which occurred uniquely at the end of the Sixth century, and resulted in the transferral of political authority to Mecca, and the inception there of the new Muslim religion, was not brought about by its previously alleged importance and wealth generated by commerce.[33] Nor, she holds, did Mecca's wealth develop through trade generated from its importance as a religious sanctuary.[34]

While acknowledging the existence of limited trading within the Meccan environs, Crone states that there is neither logical base nor testimonial evidence for large-scale pre-Islamic Meccan trading. This is the key issue, the sticking point in the history of Muḥammad's origins and the foundation of the Meccan society and commercial laws. The first point of Crone's contention concerns Mecca's situation at the intersection of major trading routes : On the basis of Bulliet,[35] She states that these claims are quite wrong : Mecca lies, she asserts, at the bottom of a steep barren valley, and "only by the most tortured map reading can it be described as a natural crossroads".[36]

Secondly, Crone rejects a major proportion of the 'exotic' commodities previously believed to have reached the markets of Mecca.[37] She asserts that

---

32 Crone, *ibid.*, p.243

33 Crone, *ibid.*, p.243

34 Crone, *ibid*, pp. 168-199, particularly at 173

35 Bulliet, R.W., *The Camel and The wheel*, (Cambridge, Mass., 1975) p.105 and n.40

36 Bulliet, *ibid.*, p.105; Crone, *Meccan Trade*, pp.6-7. The fact that Mecca had religious sanctuary and a brackish well, "*Zamzam*", were not sufficient advantages in themselves, for so did other rather more realistic natural halts, like Ṭā'if, which actually lay on the 'incense route'. According to Bulliet (and *Pace* Crone) "The only reason for Mecca to grow into a great trading centre was that it was able somehow to force trade under its control".

37 see Chapters II and III in her *Meccan Trade*.

the international trade of the Meccans consisted of the humble articles of perfume (exported from the Yemen), leather, clothing, animals and miscellaneous foodstuffs.[38] Further, similar and superior specimens of the same commodities traded were being traded elsewhere around the Arab peninsular, and in Syria, which is the only international destination of any importance which she accepts.

Although the Yemen and Ethiopia are discussed as probable, but less frequent destinations for Meccan commodities, Crone concludes that on the whole, Meccan trade was local,[39] and was generated by Arab needs rather than the commercial exigencies of surrounding empires.[40] The proposition that the Quraysh made the Īlāf agreements she also rejects. The term, she postulates, if it really was the technical term for such an institution, would not have perplexed the later scholars in its etymology; however, it was unknown, even as to its number and pronunciation.[41]

Nevertheless, Crone, although generally sceptical of the scale of Meccan trading *per se*, acknowledges the importance of the general trade enjoyed by Arabia, and, in addition, Mecca's religious sanctuary. She attributes the popularity of any Meccan produce that may have been traded to this rather than to any supreme quality of its commodities.[42]

One point which seems to be beyond dispute in this now controversial issue, is that **Arab** trade was healthy. The pilgrim fairs of 'Ukāz, Dhū al-Majāz, Majanna and Minā which took place annually in the environs of Ṭā'if, are generally accepted by historians. Crone suggests that trading was by pilgrims, and only occurred in the first three of these. Mecca, Minā and 'Arafa (another religious sanctuary), she asserts, were not included.[43]

> "All our stereotyped notions about the relationship between the Meccan sanctuary and Meccan trade, in fact, apply to the pilgrim fairs...it was these *ḥarams* that were objects of a pre-Islamic pilgrimage, generating trade, and it was here that disputes were settled and debts repaid. Whatever the precise

---

[38] Crone, *Meccan Trade*, pp.12-108, particularly at 107

[39] Crone, *Meccan Trade*, pp.149

[40] Crone, *Meccan Trade*, pp.149, 151

[41] Crone, *Meccan Trade*, p.212

[42] Crone, *Meccan Trade and The Rise of Islam, op.cit.*, pp.100, 142, 160 and chpt.8: pp.168f

[43] Crone, *Meccan Trade*, pp.171-173: Mecca, being a city with a permanent population, a shrine endowed with guardians, and owned by a specific tribe (rather than a desert sanctuary, unowned) does not belong in the complex of pilgrim fairs, she states (p.174).

> relationship between these sanctuaries, it was they which mattered for Qurashī trade: in commercial terms the *ḥaram* of Mecca was redundant".[44]

This point is pertinent to us whatever conclusion we are to reach regarding the Tradition at large.[45] Because Arab trade generally, as opposed to Meccan trade specifically, is accepted as having been pre-eminent throughout the Peninsula and internationally, we may still assume that the integration of international commercial institutions and customs did, in fact, occur. If we are to accept Crone's refutation of the Tradition, of course, we have no finite sources to work on and this remains a conjecture. Non-Arab sources also testify to this Arab trading some time previous to the rise of Islam, however,[46] and it seems quite safe to assume that the longer the time given for integration, the more engrained and less distiguishable they may have become. We must, at any rate, treat information regarding late pre-Islamic and early Islamic commerce with caution, bearing in mind that these histories may have been as subject to the dictates of later Muslim lawyers and exegetes, as the religious tenets referred to above.[47]

4. EARLY ISLAMIC COMMERCIAL OPERATIONS

According to Tradition, the most prevalent means of merchant practice in Pre-Islamic Arabia were firstly, by partnership agreement (*Mushāraka*), and secondly, by receiving goods on the basis of a commenda partnership

---

44 Crone, *Meccan Trade*, p.185

45 Crone effectively rejects all Tradition regarding this issue as spurious story-telling, ("The entire tradition is tendentious, its aim being the elaboration of an Arabian *Heilsgeschichte*") (p.230) on the basis that it will not comply with modern historical methodology. Having the normal methodological arbitrary system applied, it results in contradiction and confusion and must therefore be rejected *in toto*, although this leaves us with precious little indigenous sources. Crone is, however, blissfully aware of her own "methodological arbitrariness", and the indefensible weakness of "minimal source criticism" (p.92)

46 See, for instance, Strabo, *Geography, op.cit.*, Vol VII, Bk. 16:IV 1-2 (p.309); Scarce, J.M., 'Preserving the Arab Gulf Culture', 1 *The Arab Gulf Journal*, Vol. 6, No. 1 (April 1986) p.60; Leeman, W.F., *Foreign Trade in the Old Babylonian Period*, (Leiden, 1960); That the tradition was continued is testified in various sources, See, for example, Lopez, R.S., and Raymond, I.W., *Medieval Trade in the Mediterranean World*, (London, 1955)

47 Chapter One, *supra*.

(*Qirāḍ/Muḍāraba*).[48] These methods provided unlimited scope for progress : potential investors would entrust capital or merchandise to the agent merchants on the understanding that the merchant would trade with it in foreign parts and then return the principal sum to the investor along with a previously agreed share of the profits (or alternatively, the losses). The merchant retains the surplus profit in payment for his labour but does not participate in the material losses (other than having wasted his time and effort), which are borne exclusively by the investors. Alternatively, a merchant was able to combine his capital with that of the investors in a bilateral commenda. In such an enterprise, the merchant would enjoy the total profit from his own injected capital.[49]

The benefits of these kinds of trading enterprises were therefore shared by any capitalist willing to invest in the merchants' activities. Strabo, describing every Arab as a natural merchant, relates the degree of vigorous community involvement in Meccan trade, and the esteem accorded to the merchant class.[50] Wāqidī tells of all members of the Meccan community who owned anything, including women, investing in trading caravans and commercial enterprises to Syria : "Few caravans set forth in which the whole population, men and women, had not a financial interest. On their return, every one received a part of the profits proportionate to his stake and the number of shares subscribed."[51] This pervasive 'mercantile mentality' has also been attested to in later Islamic communities, such as Bursa,[52] Fāṭimid and 'Ayyūbid Fustāṭ (Medieval Cairo)[53] and Ottoman Kayseri.[54]

A further method of trading commenda, according to the Tradition, was practiced by using state monies as capital for the merchants' business

---

48 Ibn Ḥazm, *al-Muḥallā*, (Cairo, 1347-52 AH), 11 Vols; Vol. 8, p.247 on *Muḍāraba*; and Kāsānī, *Badā'i' al-Ṣanā'i' Fī Tartīb al-Sharā'i'*, (Cairo, 1328 AH), 7 Vols; Vol. 6, p.57. *Cambridge History Of Islam*, Eds. P.M. Holt, A.K.S. Lambton, B. Lewis; (Cambridge, 1977), p.525. *Qirāḍ* is the Mālikī and Shāfi'ī name for *Muḍāraba*.

49 Udovitch, *op.cit.*, p.170

50 Strabo, *Geography, op.cit.*, Vol VII, Bk. 16:IV, 23

51 Wāqidī, *Kitāb al-Maghāzī*, (Ed. M. Jones; Oxford, 1966) 3 Vols.; I, 19,21 ff.; Lammens, *Islam: Beliefs and Institutions*, (London, 1968), pp.15-16. O'Leary, *Arabia Before Muhammad*, p. 183. Also quoted in Saleh, *op.cit.*, p.2

52 Halil Inalcik, 'Bursa', in Encyclopoedia of Islam^2 (Ed. Lewis, Pellat and Schacht) Vol. I, Fasc. 12 (London/Leiden, 1958) pp.1333-1336; also, Inalcik, 'Bursa and the Commerce of the Levant', *Journal of the Economic and Social History of the Orient*, 3, (1960), 133ff.

53 S.D. Goitein, *Mediterranean Society*, 2 vols (Berkeley and Los Angeles, 1967-1972)

54 R. Jennings, 'Loans and Credit in Early Seventeenth Century Ottoman Judicial Records', *Journal of the Economic and Social History of the Orient*, 16 (1973) pp.168-216, particularly 191ff.

ventures. These monies were collected from taxes and employed as in *Qirāḍ* investments.[55]

Udovitch states : "Pooling resources, whether in the form of cash, goods skills or a combination of these, is one of the indispensable components of any extended commercial activity."[56]

The Tradition reports that the commercial pooling of resources by partnership and commenda ventures was extant and widely practiced in Mecca in the period preceding the Prophet's lifetime.[57] There is little evidence to suggest that any of the pacts or business associations of the time were either legislated or evidenced in writing; the ventures depended on veracity and good faith. Contracts were secured by the word of honour of the respective parties, and remedies for non-performance and breach of promise were referred to the tribal chiefs or other notables for settlement.

Apart from the commenda and partnership contracts, there are reports that contracts of Agency,[58] *Salam*, (future delivery)[59] normal sale,[60] mortgage,[61] *Ju'āla*,[62] *'Umra*,[63] and hire[64] were also extant and practised prior to Islam. If such contracts were established, it is likely that these pre-Islamic contract forms provided the original models for the parallel contracts sanctioned by Islam. Where the form of the pre-Islamic models does not correspond in detail with the the later Islamic version, it may be that this is the result of the process of Islamisation: the stamping of the law and pactice with a peculiarly Islamic identity, in this case by the application of the processes of *Ijmā'*, *Qiyās* and *Istiṣlāḥ*.

---

55 *Cambridge History of Islam*, vol. 2B, p.525

56 *Partnership and Pofit, op.cit.*, p.3

57 Qālī, *Kitāb dhayl al-Amālī wa al-Nawādir*, p.199: the tribesmen in this version receive the capital of the profit. In Tha'ālibī's version, the Quraysh get a cut of the *Ribḥ* as well : *Thimā al-Qulūb, op.cit.*, p.116; but see Crone's refutation of this *Supra*.

58 It is believed that Byzantine agents operated in Mecca prior to Islam for mainly commercial reasons, although the tentative suggestion that they were also spies has also been advanced. cf. O'Leary, *op.cit.*, p.184; Lammens, *La Meque, op.cit.*, p.257; Wāqidī, *op.cit.*, pp.58-9

59 *al-Lu'lu' wa al-Marjān*, (Cairo, 1949) Vol 2, p.180

60 Ibn Rushd, *al-Muqqadamāt al-Muḥamidāt Libayan mā 'qtadathu al-Rusūm al-Mudawwana min al-Aḥkām al-Sharī'a wa al-Taḥsilāt al-Muḥkamāt (al-Shār'iyāt) li Ummahāt Masā'ilhā al-Mushkilāt*, 2 vols. in 1; (Cairo, 1332 AH), vol 2, p.222

61 *Subul al-Salam*, (Al-Bābī al-Ḥalabī Press, 1372 AH), vol. 3, p.52

62 Ibn Rushd, *al-Muqadamāt al-Muḥamidāt*, vol 2, p.305

63 al-Shawkānī, *Nayl al-Awṭār: Sharḥ Muntaqā al-Akhbar*, (Cairo, 1347 AH), 8 Vols.; vol. 6, p.15

64 Ibn Rushd, *Bidāyat al-Mujtahid Wa Nihāyat al-Muqtaṣid*, (Cairo, 1966), 2 Vols., vol. 2, p.224

Secondary sources allege that by the end of the seventh century, banking, proto-banking and money-changing practices had developed also, advanced by the powerful groups of Persian, Basran and Jewish financiers, and often the merchants themselves. O'Leary suggests that in pre-Islamic Hijāz, the resting places of the caravan routes would often develop into the clearing houses of the wealthy financiers.[65] On the basis of Crone's refutation, it would seem unlikely that Mecca could have constituted such a centre. It is more probable that such a development could only have arisen in Mecca after its escalation to importance at the end of the seventh century.

By the mid-eighth century, fairly complex credit transactions are known to have been widespread in the Islamic world, notably some three to four centuries earlier than such practices appeared in the West.[66] Our information regarding these transactions in the period from the dawn of Islam until the eleventh century is gleaned almost entirely from non-documentary sources. Such as there is, is derived from theoretical legal sources supported by the occasional reference in chronicles, geographical works or *belles-lettres*. The early Ḥanafī jurist al-Shaybānī, for example, writes of provisions for buying and selling on credit in a manner which suggests that it was well-known practice.[67]

It therefore seems to be apparent that credit instruments such as cheques, and *Ḥawala* (payment of a debt through the transfer of a claim) were widely used amongst the merchant classes, as were letters of credit and bills of exchange.[68] These early negotiable instruments in the form of written obligations were known as *Suftaja* (letter of credit or bill of exchange), and were credited as being "the first and most important forms of commercial credit papers in the medieval Near East."[69] "In private commerce *Suftaja*s for as large a sum as 42,000 Dinars are attested to in the trans-Saharan trade,

---

65 Hussein, 'Early Arabian Trade', *op.cit.*, p.374; O'Leary, *Arabia Before Muhammad*, p.182; Watt, *Muhammad at Mecca*, pp. 19, 72

66 See W.J. Fischel, *Jews In the Economic and Political Life of Medieval Islam*, (London, 1937), pp. 1-44; A.L. Udovitch, 'Reflections on the Institutions of Credits and Banking In The Medieval Islamic Near East,' *Studia Islamica*, XLI, pp. 5-7

67 al-Shaybānī, *Kitāb al-Aṣl*, [Kitāb al-Sharika], MS. Dār al-Kutub al-Miṣriyya, Fiqh Ḥanafī, 34 folios, 57b and 61b : "wa yabi'u bi al-naqd wa al-naṣīa" (he [the partner] may sell for cash and credit); Udovitch, *ibid.*, p.8

68 See Karl Polanyi, Conrad M. Avensberg and Harry W. Pearson, *Trade and Market in the Early Empires*, (Illinois, 1957) p.175; A. Lewis, *Naval Power and Trade In The Mediterranean AD 500 to 1100*, (Princeton, New Jersey, 1951), p. 171. These instruments are also documented in the Arabic Papyri from Egypt and in the chronicles of the ninth and tenth centuries. See also Schacht, *Introduction to Islamic Law*, *op.cit.*, pp. 148-9.

69 Udovitch, *ibid.*, p.10

and for much larger sums in Iraq involving the remittance to the central government of provincial revenues by tax farmers."[70] Other instructional credit papers such as the *Ruqa'a* and the *Shakk* supplemented the *Hawala* and *Suftaja* as regards payment, transfer or deposit of funds with bankers or money-changers.[71]

The late eighth century also testifies to the existence of credit partnerships, where the capital of the partnership is entirely of credit, usually resting on the good reputation of the partners.[72]

According to Watt *et al*, the transition from the fourth to the fifth century had witnessed the apogee of the bourgeoisie which was reflected in a new economy in which feudalistic trends became dominant.[73] By the mid-sixth century, the supposition is that a conflict had arisen between the tribal-nomadic, the old Persian Aristocratic outlook, and the mercantile capitalistic environment of Mecca whose bazaars and markets reflected a deterioration of public ethics.[74] Exploitation, most particularly from moneylenders, was rife. The merchants now belonged to an elitist class and were thereby exposed to ideal opportunities to swell their already vast wealth through their trading.[75]

The theory of moral malaise in Mecca is rejected absolutely by Crone as wrong, inadequate and familiar.[76] She acknowledges from the rapid rise of Islam in the Peninsula that there must have been a fundamental change with accompanying spiritual crisis that was unique to the mid-seventh century.[77]

---

70 A. Mez, *The Renaissance of Islam*, (transl. S. Khuda Bakhsh and D.S. Margoliouth, (Patna, 1937), p. 470, quoting Ibn Hawqal; Fischel, *Jews in the Economic and Political Life of Medieval Islam*, *op.cit.*, p.19; Udovitch, 'Reflections on the Institutions of Credits and Banking in the Medieval Near East', *op.cit.*, p.10

71 Udovitch, *ibid.*, pp. 11,17; cf. also, W.J. Fischel, 'The Origin of Banking in Medieval Islam', *Journal of the Royal Asiatic Society*, (1933), pp. 339-352.

72 Sarakhsī called these partnerships "partnerships of the penniless": *Sharikāt al-Mafālis*. *al-Mabsūṭ*, vol. II, p.152; They were also known as *Sharikāt al-Wujūh*: Partnerships of the Faces. Udovitch, *ibid.*, p.11

73 Watt, *Muhammad at Mecca, op.cit.; id., Muhammad at Medina, op.cit.; id., Muhammad, Prophet and Statesman, op.cit.; id., Islam and The Integration of Society*, (London, 1961); *The Cambridge History of Islam*, op.cit.; S.D. Goitein, *Studies in Islamic History and Institutions*, (Leiden, 1966) p.218

74 The contempt of the bedouin for the merchant profession may be witnessed in the *Ḥamāsa*, of Buḥturī, a collection of classical Arabic poetry containing three chapters devoted to bedouin poems condemning both Arab and Persian mercantile practices : Buḥturī, *Ḥamāsa*, (Cairo, 1929) pp.413-32, chpts. 171-3. *cf.* C.A. Nallino, *La Littérature Arabe*, (trad. into the French by Ch. Pellat (Paris 1950) pp.144-6

75 Watt, *Muhammad, Prophet and Statesman, op.cit.*, pp.48-51

76 *Meccan Trade*, pp.231-233.

77 *Meccan Trade*, p.237

But, she states, "The novelty of the solution lay in the idea of divinely validated state structures; and it was Muḥammad's state, not his supposed blueprint for social reform, which had such powerful effect on the rest of Arabia".[78]

Replacing our reliance upon the Tradition, we are told that those Meccans with a ready source of capital, including the Caliph and tribal chiefs, were able to invest in the merchants' trading in order to accumulate their wealth.[79] According to the interpretation given by Watt to these traditions therefore, in the Prophet's time there was a tendency in Mecca for wealth to be concentrated in the hands of the rich to the exclusion of the poor.[80]

It would not seem illogical to infer from this controversy surrounding the status of trade at the inception of Islam, that the traders, whether of Mecca, or of Arabia as a whole, formed a distinctive 'professional' cadre. From the nature of the assimilation of commercial customs, it naturally seems to follow that the early implicit regulations concerning commerce within the new Islamic community would have been largely developed by this professional cadre themselves. Prior to his realization of Prophethood, we are told, Muḥammad had himself been a merchant[81] and a member of the attested trading clan of Quraysh.[82] The Prophet's first wife, Khadīja, is reported to have employed Muḥammad as a mercantile agent (*Amīn*) in

---

78 *Meccan Trade*, pp.236. "Muhammad was neither a social reformer nor a resolver of spiritual doubts: he was the creator of a people." (p.237) "What he had to offer was a programme of Arab state formation and conquest: the creation of an *umma*, the initiation of *jihād*." (p.241) The presumption tentatively suggested by Crone is that "Islam originated as a nativist movement", in other words, its immense success lay in a primitive reaction to alien domination. This theory, if accepted, would be explanatory of the *Qur'ān*'s emphasis on its unprecedented, immutable essence, and the 'nationality' of the religion.

79 Saleh, *op.cit.*, p.3

80 Watt, *Muhammad at Mecca*, pp.19, 72 ff.; and based on Watt, *cf.* Shaban, *Islamic History*, p.8

81 One account in the *Sīra* relates that he was taken up to Baṣra when he was only 12 years old: Ibn Hishām (d.834), *Kitāb Sīrat Rasūl Allāh*, (Eg. Ed. Bulaq, 1295 AH) ; Ed. F. Wüstenfeld, *Das Leben Muhammads Nach Muhammad Ibn Ishâk*, (Göttingen, 1858-60) p.115. Another reports a trip made when he was 25 years old: Ibn Hishām, *op.cit.*, p.119. See also Muḥammad Ibn Sa'd. *al-Ṭabaqāt al-Kubrā*, 8 vols (Beirut, 1957-60) I: 120,129,153,156. That Muḥammad was a merchant is also attested by non-Arab sources: See, for instance, Sebeos (attrib.) *Histoire d'Héraclius*, transl. F. Macler (Paris, 1904) p.95; I. Guidi *et al*, (Eds. & Transl.) *Chronica Minora*, CSCO, Scriptores Syri:Third Series, Vol. IV (Louvain, 1903-1907) p.326=250

82 Watt, *Muhammad at Mecca*, p.33. The name "Quraysh" derives from "Taqrish" which means 'from trading and getting profit.' al-Jihāẓ, (d. 255 AH) MSS. in British Museum OR. 3188, fo. 267

Syria prior to their marriage[83] thus the Prophet had first-hand knowledge of the mercantile practices of his day. If the Meccans had deteriorated into an unsavoury 'supereminence of wealth' as Watt suggests,[84] at least the Prophet would have been aware of its harmful social effects upon his new community of believers, and as a concerned statesman would have sought to remedy these effects. The earliest schools too (formed about a century after the Hijra) consisted of congeries of scholars who often made their livelihoods as merchants and shopkeepers, discussing law in their spare time.[85] As merchants, neither Muhammad nor the early scholars would have "advocated the destruction of [Makkan] trade, [t]he[y] can only have suggested means to maintain and strengthen it."[86]

Whether or not the Prophet was aware of an unjust imbalance in society, it cannot be denied that the teaching he pursued took 'moderation' as its keyword. This is principally the reason why Watt has suggested that Muḥammad was a reformer[87] and that Islam created a kind of welfare state.[88]

The theory that the Islamic era did indeed bring reform to the field of pre-Islamic commerce, rather than a completely new system which

---

83 'Abd al-Ḥamid Jauda al-Saḥḥār, *Khadīja Bint Khuwaylid*, (Cairo, 1967). Others state that he went on her behalf to Ḥubāsha : al-Ṣan'ānī, *al-Muṣannaf*, Ed. H.-R. al-A'ẓamī, 11 Vols. (Beirut, 1970-1972); Ḥassān al-Thābit, *Dīwān*, Ed. W.N. 'Arafat (London, 1971) II, 310; Yāqūt b. 'Abdallāh, *Kitāb Mu'jam al-Buldān*, Ed. F. Wüstenfeld, 6 Vols. (Leipzig, 1866-1873) II:192 ff.; Haykal (*op.cit.*, pp. 137-138) is more inclined to think that the business relationship between the Prophet and Khadīja was that of a commenda agreement rather than agency; This may be borne out by the meaning of *Amīn*, which translates as 'trustworthy' or 'faithful' instead of the more usual term for agent, *Wakīl*, or the term *Niyāba* corresponding to the french *Répresentation*, which in this author's view is the most probable interpretation for the business relationship between Muḥammad and Khadīja. The disparity is not, however, important for our immediate purposes. The account is rejected by Crone as 'ficticious'. She points out that the Tradition that Muḥammad traded in partnership with Sā'ib b. Abī al-Sā'ib in the Jāhiliyya does not allude to another partnership with, or agency for, Khadīja (*Meccan Trade*, p.220 n. 81). The latter Tradition comes from Shaybānī, *al-Kasb*, ed. S. Zakkār, (Damascus, 1980) p.36; and Azraqī, *Kitāb Akhbār Makka*, ed. F. Wüstenfeld (Leipzig, 1858) p.471

84 Watt, *Muhammad at Mecca*, pp. 72-78

85 Crone, *Roman, Provincial and Islamic Law*, p.20; Schacht, *Origins*, pp.6ff.; *idem.*, *Introduction* pp.28ff.; H.J. Cohen, 'The Economic Background and Secular Occupation of Muslim Jurisprudents and Traditionalists in the Classical Period of Islam', *The Journal of the Economic and Social History of the Orient*, (1970)

86 Shaban, *op.cit.*, p.8

87 Watt, *Muhammad at Mecca*, pp. 19,72; The Islamic social reform is also acknowledged by Maḥmaṣānī, 'The Principles of International Law in the Light of Islamic Doctrine', *Recueil Des Cours*, I (1966) p.221

88 The view of Islam as creating a "welfare state" in an economic context is also held by Qureshi; see his *The Economic and Social System of Islam*, (Lahore, 1979) pp.65 ff

superceded all other practices, is extremely attractive. The maxims contained in the Qur'ān regarding commerce are sufficiently general to pre-suppose a welcome continuation of all that was just and fair in the Jāhilī commercial systems. Trade was to be encouraged and considered as a highly honourable occupation,[89] but the excessive pursuit of wealth at the expense of deprivation of one's neighbours was discouraged.[90] The maxim of Islam was "Justice for all based on co-operation by all,"[91] but if Crone's theory is correct, and trade was not practised on a large scale before the rise of Islam, then might we not have expected to find rather more guidelines to commercial transactions, than we do ?[92] The absence of any explanation of the *Ribā* prohibition, for instance, would seem to indicate that the concept was perfectly understood at that time, and was not in need of explanatory addenda. The implication from this is that interest demands were a severe problem at the inception of Islam, and that the Prophet reformed society of their exploitative nature. In other words, the theories of "a programme of Arab state formation and conquest: the creation of an *umma*," and that of a reformist, welfare state, are not, in fact, mutually exclusive.

5. THE QUR'ANIC REFORM OF COMMERCE

Crone's refutation of the status of Mecca as a major trading centre prior to Islam, together with the theory that Islam merely reformed the principles of pre-Islamic trading practices in paradigmatic fashion, may yet go some way in explaining the general sparsity of commercial provisions to be found in the Qur'ān.

The *Qur'ān* in Muslim theory both supercedes and encompasses all matters.[93] In commercial practice however, it may equally be argued that the lacunae in the Qur'ān concerning commercial regulation are due to the inherent nature of commerce itself. A merchant was taught his profession by

---

89 cf. the literature by the mystic Sulāmī (d.941-1021), particularly his *Kitāb Ādāb al-Ṣuḥba*, ed. M.J. Kister (Jerusalem, 1954) p. 54 ff.

90 Sulāmī says: "When you leave your house for the bazaar, do so with the intention of satisfying the wants of a Muslim; if, in addition, you make a profit, regard this as a favour granted to you by God and a blessing bestowed on your customer for your sake." *Kitāb Adāb al-Ṣuḥba*, *op.cit.* , p.54; also quoted in S.D. Goitein, *Studies in Islamic History and Institutions*, *op.cit*, p.227

91 Shaban, *op.cit*., pp. 9.and 15

92 This argument may, of course, work the other way : Family Law ethics, which affect every individual in the Muslim Community, receive exhaustive explanation in the primary sources. This is, however, an important area of the *'Ibādāt*, in which Islam could not afford lacunae, or allow custom to intervene.

93 Based on *Qur'ān*, (V:155), (XIV:89), (XIII:2), (VI:38)

his kin or peers and all merchants followed an almost internationalised system of commercial methods with variation according to local customs.[94] Markets were regulated by custom (*sunna*) subject to the new Islamic restrictions imposed upon merchants for the general benefit of the community. It might have been expected that the *Qur'ān*, given the alleged importance of trade during the Prophet's lifetime and in the growing Muslim community during the Madīnan period and the later Meccan era, should, at least, have formulated a skeletal code of obligations concerning commercial transactions. This was not the case, for those regulations governing commerce that are to be found in the *Qur'ān* are more like paradigmatic "occasional hints" than clear instructions, and must be sifted out from among the usually lengthy passages of general exhortations.[95] Duties in the *Qur'ān* consist of two types. The first, *Farḍ al-'Ayn*, is the duty imposed on the individual, and commercial duties fall under this heading. The second, *Farḍ al-Kifāya*, is the essential duty encumbent upon the community such as the election of a caliph.[96]

Most of the Qur'ānic dictates concerning commercial transactions were revealed during the Madīnan period. However, the Meccan period also produced some secular prescriptions and almost certainly nurtured the beginnings of the later Madīnan injunctions. An example of this is the prohibition of *Ribā* which was first formulated in Mecca as a moral exhortation, but which was later condemned outright in the Madīnan era.[97] Duties regarding commerce are expressed in the *Qur'ān* as either positive or negative injunctions. The positive exhortations can be categorized as those directing meticulous honesty, consideration and delicacy in business relations and, above all, fair dealing :

> "Give just weight and full measure"[98]

---

[94] *Cambridge History of Islam*, Vol.2B, p.525

[95] Levy, *Social Structure of Islam*, (Cambridge, 1969), p.153

[96] Although, much later, al-Ghazālī alludes to the pursuit of business also as a religious duty (*Fard al-Kifāya*). cf. H. Ritter, 'Ein Arabisches Handbuch der Handelwissenschaft,' *Der Islam*, VII, (Berlin, 1917) p.41

[97] Shaikh Draz, 'L'Usure en Droit Musulman', in *Travaux de la semaine Internationale de Droit Musulman* (Sirey, France, 1953), pp. 147-8; See also N.A. Saleh, *Unlawful Gain and Legitimate Profit in Islamic Law : Ribā, Gharar and Islamic Banking*, (Cambridge, 1986) p.2

[98] *Qur'ān*, (VI:153). This and subsequent translations will be taken from A. Yusef Ali, *The Holy Qur'ān: Text, Translation and Commentary*, (The Islamic Foundation: Leicester, 1975), unless otherwise stated.

> "Give full measure when you measure, and weigh with even scales. That is fair and better in the end"[99]

> "Deal justly; Justice is nearer to true piety"[100]

> "Woe to those that deal in fraud (*Tatfīf*); those who, when they have to receive by measure from men, exact full measure; but when they have to give by measure or weight to men, give less than due."[101]

A Muslim is required to fulfil his obligations, but if his business partner through hardship is forced to request cancellation of the contract, he should not insist upon execution.

> "oh you who believe, fulfil all obligations."[102]

> "Keep your promises. You are accountable for all that you promise."[103]

The negative exhortations are the reforming elements imposed by Islam on commerce. These exhortations all derive from the Islamic abhorrence of unjustified enrichment, and comprise six distinguishable instructions:

(1) The prohibition of usurping another's property
("Oh you who believe, eat not each other's property by wrong means")[104]

(2) The prohibition of *Ribā*, (Usury, Interest)
("That which you seek to increase by usury will not be blessed by Allah")[105]
("God has permitted sale and prohibited usury")[106]

---

99 *Qur'ān*, (XVII:35)

100 *Qur'ān*, (V:8)

101 *Qur'ān*, (LXXXIII:1-3). Fraud here is taken in the general sense of the spirit of injustice. See also *Qur'ān*, (LV:8), (XXVI:1), (XI:86)

102 *Qur'ān*, (V:1)

103 *Qur'ān*, (XVII:34). See also (VI:153)

104 *Qur'ān*, (IV:29). See also (II:88)

105 *Qur'ān*, (XXX:39)

106 *Qur'ān*, (II:75)

(3) The prohibition of *Gharar* (Risk) which includes any element of uncertainty.

(4) The prohibition of hoarding or monopoly[107]

(5) The prohibition of *Maysir* (Gambling or aleatory transactions)[108]

(6) The prohibition of bribery[109]

It may be seen, therefore, that these Qur'ānic injunctions are peripheral adjudications covering isolated situations which are interspersed without sequence or system throughout the text of the *Qur'ān*.[110] Thus it is not unreasonable to surmise that the prevailing law providing for the regulation of commercial affairs in the early Islamic community was that of the pre-Islamic customary tribal law.[111] In addition, we may assume that those trading practices which prevailed among the merchants of the Mediterranean, Red Sea, Indian Ocean and trade routes along the Arab hinterlands, in short, any merchants with whom the Arab traders came into contact, whether directly or indirectly, may have been assimilated to a lesser or greater degree into the prevailing customary practices if not disconsonant with the Qur'ān.

Mercantile practice continued its tradition of oral transmission even in the era after the Divine Revelation. Now, however, theoretically at least, customary mercantile activities were tempered by the few provisions which Islam had introduced for a more beneficial and equitable society.

---

107 *Qur'ān*, (CIV:1-4) : This is one of the rarer, earlier Meccan suras. see also *ibid.*, (XII:8) and S.A. Ali, *Economic Foundations of Islam*, (Calcutta, 1964), pp. 162, 168. Ghazālī relates a Tradition : "It is difficult for a rich man to enter the gates of heaven" and in explanation, states: "Hoarding of wealth is condemned because it develops sensual appetites, greed, *etc.*, and the love of the world which are all fatal to the spiritual aspirant." *Iḥyā' 'Ulūm al-Dīn*, transl. Behari (1972), p.166. See also *Qur'ān*, (CII:1)

108 *Qur'ān*, (V:3), (V:91)

109 *Qur'ān*, (II:188)

110 In this respect it has been suggested that these Qur'ānic injunctions may be likened to the Homeric "*Themistes*" commands. See Sir H. Maine, *Ancient Law*, (London 1917), pp.3-5

111 C.A. Nallino, 'Considerazione sui rapporti fra diritto romano et diritto musulmano', *Raccolta di Scritti Editi e Inediti*, vol. IV (Rome, 1942) p.88, argues that since there must have been a highly developed law in the commercial Ḥijāz we may assume that it was the customary law of the Ḥijāz which was assimilated into the *Sharī'a*.

There are numerous theories regarding the reason for the piecemeal nature of Qur'ānic legislation in the sphere of commerce : the circumstances in which the *Qur'ān* was revealed; the time lapse of two decades before it was officially recorded; the nature of its recording and subsequent abrogations; the alleged exclusively moral content of the *Qur'ān*, and so on. One of the most plausible reasons would seem to be the fact that commerce throughout the area we now know as the Middle East was already a well-established concern at the time of Islam, regulated by custom, and practiced among a reasonably elite minority to which Muḥammad himself was party.[112] On closer examination of the ancient law codes of the Near and Middle East,[113] we find that the casuistic development of Islamic law parallels that of the model of paradigmatic laws which preceded it. Thus the *ad hoc* injunctions conveyed by Muḥammad during his prophecy may have been the products of similar paradigmatic development.[114] The Prophet's general policy seems to have been to introduce as few innovations as possible into the ordinary mode of life, other than the direct religious ethics (*'Ibādāt*),[115] and to accept the continuation of the common moral patterns of his tribe and community, except where social reform was evidently called for.[116] It may be noted that the prohibitions are classified as *Ḥarām* (forbidden) and

---

112 This argument is not harmed by Crone's refutation of the status of pre-Islamic Meccan trade, for she acknowledges that by the seventh century, Mecca had become a thriving urban centre. See her *Meccan Trade, op.cit.*, pp.

113 Finkelstein, J.J., 'The Ox That Gored', (Prepared for Publication by M. de J. Ellis) *American Philosophical Society*, Vol.71, Part 2 (Philadelphia, 1981) pp.14 ff.; Goetze, A., 'The Laws of Eshnunna Discovered at Tell Harmal', *Sumer*, 4 (1948) pp.63 ff.; *id.*, *The Laws of Eshnunna*, (Annual of the American Schools of Oriental Research) 31 (New Haven, 1956); G.R. Driver and J.C. Miles, *The Babylonian Laws*, (2 Vols.:Oxford, 1953-1955); Finet, A., *Le Code de Hammourabi*, (Paris, 1973)

114 Compare: Hammurapi; Leviticus 25,26; Lipit-Ishtar; Eshnuna , for which, see authors cited in previous note. The *Sharī'a* may be distinguished from these ancient law codes by the fact that it may also be characterised as apodictic (which was previously unique to the Biblical law among the laws of the ancient Near East) in that in certain areas, clear delimitations are given, such as the regulation of family and inheritance issues; and that it is imbued with the recompensatory spirit of restitution, such as in liabilities arising from torts. In the field of contracts and obligations, it is the paradigmatic character of the law which holds sway.

115 It is also reported that the prophet was commanded to resort to mutual consultation (*Mushāwara*) in matters concerning rights of war and people. In this context, he is reported to have said: "If I command you about religious affairs, follow it; and if I command you about worldly affairs, you are more aware of your worldly affairs." Cited in Hasan, 'The Critique of Qiyās' *Studia Islamica, op.cit.*, p.38

116 Levy, *Social Structure of Islam, op.cit.*, p.193. There is a *Ḥadīth* reporting that the Prophet said to Sa'īb : "Look to those moral practices you had in the *Jāhiliyya* and apply them in Islam...", Aḥmad b. Ḥanbal, *Musnād*, (Cairo, 1313AH) (6 Vols), III,425.

therefore they assume a status parallel to the most abhorrent criminal practices in Islam. Paradoxically, however, the *Ḥarām* commercial practices are not accompanied by guidance for penalties to be imposed upon their violation. The sanction given in each case is rather of a moral and divine nature[117] and stands in contrast to the more extreme and unaccommodating sanctions (*Ḥudūd*) imposed upon criminal malefactions such as adultery and fornication, theft, highway robbery, false accusation of *Zinā*, drinking alcohol and apostasy.[118]

Nor are the prohibited commercial practices listed above readily classified into the same category of crimes as *Qiṣās* (retribution) and homicide, for which the *Sharī'a* provided *Ta'zīr* (discretionary) punishments, and the institution of *Diyya* (bloodmoney payments).[119] These are offences of criminal law which are of a primarily private recompensatory nature and are therefore remedied by the individual victim (or the courts at his instigation) rather than by the state. Despite their classification as *Ḥarām*, it would appear that the violation of commercial law provisions, such as *Ribā*, is regarded more as a personal sin deserving of Divine retribution than as a crime deserving of public worldly sanction.[120]

To a pious Muslim, personal divine sanction is indeed a far greater deterrent against illegal practices than any comparable legal or social sanction. However, when it is considered that the deliberate commission of such *Ḥarām* practices is not likely in the first instance to originate from the pious Muslim, such dependence on moral sanctions reflects a somewhat optimistic idealism.[121] As such, Qur'ānic remedies pertaining to commercial transgressions appear wholly inadequate in comparison with the strength of

---

117 For example the *Ḥadīth* quoted by Ibn Mājah and al-Ḥakīm: "A trustworthy and an honest and truthful businessman will rise up with martyrs on the day of resurrection." Also the *Ḥadīth* quoted by al-Tirmīdhī : "A truthful and trustworthy trader will rise up with the Prophets, the Righteous and the Martyrs." Quoted in Abdur Rahman I. Doi, *Sharī'a: The Islamic Law* (London, 1984), p.350

118 Sheikh Ibrāḥīm Ibn Muḥammad Ibn Sālim Ibn Duyān, *Manār al-Sabīl*, in explanation of the Ḥanbalī text *Al-Dalīl*, transl. by George M. Baroody as *Crime and Punishment Under Islamic Law*, (London, 1979; Second Edn.) : *Hudud*: pp.47 ff.

119 Ibn Duyān's *Manār al-Sabīl*, in G.M. Baroody (transl.), *Crime and Punishment*, *op.cit.*: *Ta'zīr*: pp. 84ff; *Diyah*: pp.35-46

120 David and Brierley explain: "The real sanction for these obligations is the state of sin into which the believer neglecting them will fall. For this reason Muslim Law often shows very little interest in the civil sanction attached to the violation of its prescribed rules." René David and John E.C. Brierley, *Major Legal Systems In The World Today: An Introduction to the Comparative Study of Law*, (London, 1968), p.386

121 Aristotle states: "For most people obey necessity rather than argument, and punishments rather than the sense of what is noble." *Nicomathean Ethics*, (Oxford, 1980),X,9, p.271

their prohibition.

The important concept of pooling resources, whose existence prior to Islam has been ascertained above, is one of the few customary commercial practices which is alluded to in the *Qur'ān*. The allusions to partnership in the *Qur'ān* imply the general acceptance of this method of mercantile management rather than state its express permissibility. For example, *Qur'ān*, (II:220): "If ye mix their affairs with yours"; and *Qur'ān*, (XXXVIII:24): "Truly many are the partners who wrong each other".[122] However there are *Sunna* which expressly allude to partnership[123] and it is thought that Muḥammad himself may have entered into partnership with the wealthy widow, Khadīja, whom he later married.[124]

---

122 See also: *Qur'ān*, (XVIII:19) and (XXXIX:29)

123 For example, "Allah says I am third with two partners unless he betrays the other."

124 See Section 4, *Supra*.

Chapter 4

THE ISLAMIC PRINCIPLES OF CONTRACT

1. GENERAL PRINCIPLES

The fundamental principles which lie at the root of all commercial operations in any legal system, not excluding Islamic law, are to be found in the principles governing the law of contract and the regulations of obligations arising therefrom. The principles of contract in modern Islamic legal systems are regarded as civil law principles and therefore are contained in the respective Civil Laws of the Islamic nation states. They are used as a fundamental basis for commercial law transactions and are frequently referred to in this respect.[1] In recent promulgations however, the distinction between civil and commercial activities has been emphasized[2] and this must be borne in mind when dealing with modern commercial transactions, the various prohibitions, remedies and effects, and merchant obligations as regards commercial book-keeping, registration in commercial registers, and the composition and provision of insolvency.

It is generally argued that Islamic Law knows no general theory of contract.[3] This argument is based on the method of development of the system of Islamic contracts by the *Fuqahā'* (Jurists), who categorized each contract into classes of nominate contracts (*'Uqūd al-Mu'ayyana*) with their own distinctive rules. However, as has been shown above, the primary

---

1 See, for example, Article 2 of the Kuwaiti Commercial Code, (Law No. 68 of 1980) which states: "If no commercial custom is existing then the Civil Code provisions shall be applied."

2 For example, Art.9 of the Kuwaiti Commercial Code of 1980. See also, 'Azīz al-'Akīlī, *Al-Mūjiz Fī Sharḥ Qānūn al-Tijāra al-Kuwaitī*, (Kuwait, 1978), pp.8-9

3 Schacht, *Introduction to Muslim Law, op.cit.*; Y. Linant de Bellefonds, *Traité de Droit Musulman Comparé*, (Paris, 1965) 2 Vols; Vol. I, pp.53-54; Chafik Chehata, 'Le Droit du Contrat et des Obligations Musulmans', *Droit Musulman: Applications au Proche-Orient*, (Dalloz: Paris, 1970), p.124 (Art.164) Maḥmaṣānī, *al-Naẓariyyat al-'Amma li al-Mūjibāt wa al-'Uqūd, op.cit.*, vol V.

sources of the law formulated only the very broadest principles which are applicable to all classes. The Qur'ānic injunction "*'Aufū bi al-'Uqūd*": "Fulfil your Obligations" is the fundamental principle which governs the sanctity of all contracts, whether private, public civil or commercial.[4] Indeed, it has been shown that according to the strict sanctity of valid contracts in Muslim law, a national Islamic state has no vested right to cancel or alter a contract by unilateral action, whether such action takes the form of an administrative, judicial or even legislative act.[5] Similarly, Muslim law does not discriminate against foreigners or non-Muslims in matters of contract, and apart from certain exceptions dictated by the state of war, the Muslim community has a duty to respect its contractual obligations towards aliens and non-Muslims.[6]

Likewise the prohibitions and the limitations upon validity provided by the Islamic sources were applicable to all contracts prior to the later allowances in certain cases made by the *Fuqahā'*. Further, one of the most important concepts in the Islamic law of obligations, that of the role of mutual consent, is given its authority by the *Qur'ān* and *Aḥādīth*.[7]

The Arabic word for contract is "*'Aqd*" (Plural: *'Uqūd*). It is derived from the root verb "*'Aqada*" which means to tie or bind.[8] The Arabic term is loosely employed to describe all manifestations of the will which tie their

---

4 A similar importance was given to oral obligations in Roman Law: "Oxen are bound by their horns and men by their words; a simple promise or covenant is worth as much as the stipulations of Roman law". *Institutes Coutumières*, III, tit.I, 2 (transl. from the French)

5 See Hamidulla, *Muslim Conduct of State*, (Revised Ed. 1945) p. 145, n.4, which states: "Party and Judge cannot be in one and the same person, not even the caliph." Sarakhsī, *al-Mabsūt*, (Cairo, 1324-1331 AH) vol.16, p.73 recites a Tradition reporting that even the Prophet and the first four Caliphs submitted their disputes to arbitration.

6 Based on *Qur'ān*, (IX:4): "Fulfil their covenant up to (the end of) its period; Allah loves those who show piety." The state of war does not in itself justify violation of contracts entered into with foreigners. See Hamidullah, *Muslim Conduct of State*, *op.cit.* , p.130.

7 *Qur'ān*, (IV:29): "Oh you who believe! Squander not your wealth among yourselves in vanity, except it be a trade by mutual consent." The Prophet is reported to have said: "It is not lawful to take the property of a Muslim except by his consent." Also: "Sale is by consent." Hamid, 'Mutual Assent in the Formation of Contracts in Islamic Law', *Journal of Islamic and Comparative Law*, Vol.7, (1977), p.41

8 The term *'Aqd* has been etymologically defined by 'Alī al-Rāzī (d.370 AH) whose definition appears in Muḥammad Yūsuf Mūsā, *al-Amwāl wa Naẓariyyat al-'Aqd*, (Cairo, 1953), p.258

author to the obligations arising therefrom.[9] The most common use of the word however is to denote synallagmatic transactions (*Mu'āwadāt*) which are concluded by an offer (*Ijāb*) and an acceptance (*Qabūl*). The term *'Aqd* is also used by the jurists to denote dispositions of property by will (*mortis causa*) which are concluded by the offer of one party only, such as gift (*Hiba*), guarantee (*Ḍamān*), *Waqf* bequests, the remission of debts and the archaic liberation of slaves. Mere juristic acts such as marriage (*Nikāḥ*) and divorce (*Ṭalāq*) which do not necessarily involve the concept of consideration also fall under the heading of *'Uqūd*.[10] For this reason, Chehata divides the term *'Aqd* into two notions of contract:

(1) The umbrella term to cover a large spectrum of general legal acts and obligations.

(2) The bilateral act concreting the relation of privity between two interested parties.[11]

Chehata attributes the reason for such wide application to the fact that the term *'Aqd* is only used once in the *Qur'ān* and that is in reference to a marriage contract. A derivative form *'Uqda* is more commonly encountered, which is more consistent with the latin term *Contractus*, but it is the form *'Aqd* which was preferred by the Islamic jurists and which therefore appears in the legal treatises.[12]

Recently, however, the application of the term *'Aqd* has become subject to disagreement. Modernists are more inclined to apply *'Aqd* only to bilateral contracts as it appears in western laws, and this is how it is defined in most modern civil codes of the Islamic nation states. This may constitute in itself indications of an increasing tendency towards uniformity with the

---

9 *al-Taṣarrufāt al-Qawliyya* are thereby distinguished from *al-Taṣarrufāt al-Fi'liyya* (material acts), which form the basis of the theory of civil responsibility for torts (*Ḍamān*). Literally meaning 'Transactions by word of mouth', *al-Taṣarrufāt al-Qawliyya* can be construed *lato sensu* to cover any comprehensible manifestation of the will of the parties. cf. Saba Habachy, 'The System of Nullities in Muslim Law', *American Journal of Comparative Law*, vol. 13, (1964), p.62.

10 *'Uqūd* also corresponds to the French 'Extrapatrimonial' contracts (such as marriage, repudiation, oath, manumission) which are obligations the object of which is not the satisfaction of financial or economic interest of the 'creditor'. See Weill and Terré, *Précis Dalloz: Droit Civil: Les Obligations*, (3rd Ed.; Paris, 1980) p.6. The sphere of the term is therefore much wider than that understood by 'contract' in the common law.

11 Chafik Chehata, *op.cit.*, p.124, Art.165

12 Chehata, *op.cit.*, p.124

West in the field of obligations, for it is clearly moving away from the wider Islamic interpretation of the term, and towards the more precise definitions employed in western systems. Other unilateral engagements are defined by other terms such as *Taṣarruf* (Disposition) or *Iltizām* (Obligation), but neither of these terms are totally satisfactory in meaning. The modernists, who are more concerned with identifying the different reciprocal and *ex uno latere* obligations arising from bilateral and unilateral contracts, accuse the early jurists of allowing a certain confusion to exist by not distinguishing between these two types of obligations. They claim that every *'Aqd* transaction is also a *Taṣarruf* but that not every *Taṣarruf* is an *'Aqd.*[13] The more conservative contingent prefer not to depart from the approach of the early jurists and continue to use the term *'Aqd* in its original, broader application.[14]

The fundamental notion of a "general theory of contract" is probably too occidental and systematic an approach to impose on the underlying principles of contract in the early Islamic era. Milliot writes : "The Muslim jurist resists abstraction, systematization and codification. He will avoid generalization and even definition."[15] Indeed, until the codification of the Ottoman *Majella,*[16] civil principles were interspersed among all other areas of the law.[17] Even the *Majella* could not provide an explicit general theory governing obligations and contracts : Pertinent rules are scattered

---

13 'Alī al-Khaffīf, *Aḥkām al-Mu'āmalāt*, (Cairo, 1941) p.138; Sanhūrī, *Maṣādir al-Ḥaqq Fī al-Fiqh al-Islāmī*, (6 Vols.; Cairo 1954-9) I, p.74; Bellefonds, *Traité, op.cit.*, pp.63-64

14 Aḥmad Ibrāhīm, *al-Qānūn wa al-Iqtiṣād*, (1934), IV, p.644f. ; and Bellefonds, *op.cit.*, p.61-62

15 L. Milliot, 'La Pensée Juridique de l'Islam', *Revue Internationale de Droit Comparé*, (1954), p.448 David and Brierley construe the lack of systematization (*inter alia*) in Muslim Law as a resulting characteristic of the fact that "as a science it was formed and stabilized during the Middle Ages". *Major Legal Systems in the World Today*, (London, 1968), p.393

16 The *Majella*, introduced 1869-1876, was a product of a reform movement in the Ottoman Empire which started in 1939 with the Gülhane Charter. It represents the earliest example of an official promulgation of the Civil law principles of the Ḥanafī School of Islam by the authority of the Ottoman Empire. It has been translated into English as *The Civil Law of Palestine and Trans-Jordan*, by C.A. Hooper, (Jerusalem, 1933); and also by Tyser, C.R., Demetriades, D.G., and Haqqi, Ismail, *The Mejelle*, (Lahore, 1967; Cyprus, 1901). See also S.S. Onar, 'The Majella', in *Law In the Middle East*, (Eds. Khadduri and Liebesny) *op.cit.*, pp.292-308

17 Schacht held that Ibn al-Muqaffa''s plea for a codification of Islamic Law was influenced by a Sassanian precedent. His view has been subsequently refuted. cf Schacht, *Origins*, p.95 and *idem.*, *Introduction*, pp. 21f.; Goitein, 'A Turning Point in the History of the Muslim State', *Islamic Culture*, (1949) p.128; Crone, *Roman, Provincial and Islamic Law*, p.118 n.113

unsystematically throughout the *Majella*'s sixteen books.[18] The early jurists were more inclined to exercise subtle analyses of specific contracts rather than to formulate broad principles of theory. This fact may be tentatively attributed to the jejune of broad Qur'ānic provisions on commerce, in conjunction with the prominent role played by mercantile custom in the market. Rare attempts at a general theory are to be found among the early jurists, but they do not so much formulate water-tight theories as to deduce several general principles from the libraries of commentaries and exegeses produced by their predecessors or contemporaries.[19] Such an attempt was made by the neo-Ḥanbalī jurist, Ibn Taymiyya, who devoted a chapter of his *Fatāwā*[20] to the principles governing contracts in general. However, these principles appear so vague and broad that they really cannot be termed more than mere affirmations or truisms. It seems that Ibn Nujaym attempted a similar systematisation, but his efforts also lack any true or watertight classifications. His second principle, for example, states : "In order to judge an act it is necessary to discover the intention behind it". The philosophy is sound enough, but as a broad principle rather than as a specific rule. Indeed certain treatises contradict the principle in that they would give effect to the declared intention of the parties rather than the 'real' intention.[21] Most of Ibn Nujaym's statements tend to be consequences which do not always coincide with the principle, such as "An end must be put to all which may cause damage"; "Necessity renders legal that which is prohibited"; and "That which is justified by excuse ceases with its disappearance".

Recently however, within the last four decades or so, works have been produced[22] which impose a continually increasing importance on general theories, derived in abstract hindsight from the series of specific contracts

---

18 The sixteen books of the *Majella* are: Sale; Hire; Guarantee; Transfer of Debt; Pledges; Trusts and Trusteeship; Gift; Wrongful Appropriation and Destruction; Interdiction, Constraint and Preemption; Joint Ownership; Agency; Settlement and Release; Admissions; Actions; Evidence and Administration of Oath; Administration of Justice by the Court

19 See for example, Ibn Nujaym's *al-Ashbāh wa al-Naẓā'ir*, (Cairo, 1298 AH); Imām al-Suyūṭī's *al-Ashbāh wa al-Naẓā'ir*, (Cairo, 1359 AH); and Ibn Rajab's *al-Qawā'id al-Fiqhiyya*, (Cairo, 1933).

20 Ibn Taymiyya, *Majmū'a Fatāwā*, 5 Vols, (Cairo, 1326-1329 AH), p.387 ff.

21 Soliman Morcos and W. Faraq in *al-Qānūn wa al-Iqtiṣād*, (Sept. 1952)

22 Mainly by University Professors teaching modern law in Middle Eastern Universities. Most prominent are Ṣubḥī Maḥmaṣānī's *al-Naẓariyyat al-'Amma li al-Mūjibāt wa al-'Uqūd*, *op.cit*, p.30; 'Abd al-Razzāq as-Sanhūrī, *Maṣādir al-Ḥaqq Fī al-Fiqh al-Islāmī*, *op.cit*., p.46; and Yūsuf Mūsā, *al-Amwāl wa Naẓariyyat al-'Aqd*, (Cairo, 1953) p.44

and their regulations formulated by the early jurists.[23] The general theories of today cover such elements as impediments to consent, classification of legal acts and their effects, and a *resumé* of the various options (*Khiyārāt*) open to the parties for remedy.

It is true that the contract of sale provided a premise for analogy. The majority of legal treatises all contain a chapter on *Bay'* in which important ground rules are provided for contracts in general.[24]

2. FREEDOM OF CONTRACT

The concept of Freedom of Contract in Islamic law operates around rather diverse principles, in that the question as discussed by the jurists makes as the primary presumption the fact that no contract which derogates from any principle of the *Sharī'a* may be validly concluded. This presumption thus automatically sets the doctrine against Freedom of Contract as it is understood in the West, for the parties to a private transaction are only free to determine the terms and object of their agreement subject to the strictures placed upon them by the *Sharī'a*. Thus a contract providing for *Ribā* is no more valid, according to classical doctrines, than a contract whose object (*Maḥall*) is illegal, or whose object of contract (*al-Ma'qūd 'alayh*) is prohibited.

The classical discussions concerning Freedom of Contract do not therefore turn on the possibility of enforcing questionable contractual terms consented to within the private agreement. Rather, the discussions cover the possibility of enforcing variant contractual types, that is, outside the scope of the nominate contracts established by the early *Fuqahā'*.[25]

It is necessary to note that the exceptions between the Islamic nominate contracts far outweigh the generalities. It is this fact which prompts modern authors to state that Islamic law is a law of contracts rather than a law of

---

[23] Both Schacht ('Problems of Modern Islamic Legislation' *op.cit.*, p.108) and Hurgronje (*Verspreide Geschriften*, (Leipzig, 1923-1927) IV, ii, pp.260 ff.) considered the traditional law incompatible with being codified: "Every codification must subtly distort it" (Schacht, *ibid.*, p.108).

[24] cf., for example, in the Ḥanafī school: al-Kāsānī, *Kitāb al-Badā'i' al-Ṣanā'i'*, (Cairo, 1909-1910); Ibn 'Abidīn, *al-Radd al-Muḥtār*, (Cairo, 1324); Ibn al-Hammām, *Fatḥ al-Qadīr*, (Cairo, 1315-1318); In the Mālikī school: Dardīr, *al-Sharḥ al-Ṣaghīr*, (Cairo, 1972); In the Ḥanbalī school: Ibn Qudāma, *al-Mughnī*, (Cairo, 1341); In the Shāfi'ī school: al-Shīrāzī, *al-Muhadhdhab*, (Cairo, 1343)

[25] But *Cf.* Saba Habachy, 'Property, Right and Contract in Muslim Law', *Columbia Law Review*, Vol. 62 (1962) pp.450 ff. who emphasises *Pacta Sunt Servanda* (p.463), and that the contract is the 'Sharī'a of the parties' (p.467).

contract.[26] This same basis was employed to substantiate the argument that Islam does not recognize freedom of contract.

The protagonists of the view against freedom of contract in Islamic law[27] hold that the list of nominate contracts is closed to new forms. They argue that the interpretation of the Qur'ānic verse :

> "For whosoever transgresses Allāh's limits are wrongdoers";[28]

and the verse :

> "And whosoever disobeys Allāh and His Messenger and transgresses His limits will enter into the fire and will dwell there forever";[29]

in conjunction with an *Ḥadīth* of the Prophet reporting that Muḥammad said:

> "How can men stipulate conditions which are not in the Book of God? All conditions that are not in the Book of God are invalid, be it a hundred conditions. God's judgment is more true and His conditions are more binding" ;[30]

and a Tradition reputed to have been given on the authority of 'Ā'isha, that the Prophet said : "If anyone does a deed which we have not commanded, it shall be repudiated" ;[31] effectively asserts the conclusion that all contracts and conditions, not proven by text or consensus of opinion, or made outside

---

[26] See N.J. Coulson, *Commercial Law in the Gulf States*, (London, 1984), pp.17, 27-31; and Maḥmaṣānī, 'Transactions In The Sharī'a', in *Law In The Middle East*, (Ed. Khadduri and Liebesny) (Washington, 1955), p.185; and Joesph Schacht, *Introduction to Muslim Law, op.cit.*, pp.144 ff. This may therefore form a substantive point in the argument for Roman influence in Islamic Law.

[27] The most extreme protagonists are the Ẓāhirīs (the followers of, firstly Abū Dāwūd b. 'Alī, and secondly, Ibn Ḥazm of Spain) who recognize only seven valid conditions in a contract of sale. Ibn Ḥazm, *al-Muḥallā*, (Egypt, 1347 AH) vol.VIII, p.412 Some Ibāḍī authors also argue that "unless there is permission prohibition is the rule." See 'Abdallāh Ibn Ḥamīd al-Salīmī, *Kitāb Sharḥ Ṭal'at al-Shams 'Alā al-Alāfiyāt*, (2 Vols.: Egypt, n.d.) Vol.II pp.183-191.

[28] *Qur'ān*, (II:229)

[29] *Qur'ān*, (IV:14)

[30] Imām al-Zabaydī, *al-Tajrīd al-Ṣarīḥ li-Aḥādīth al-Jāmi' al-Ṣaḥīḥ*, (Būlāq, 1287 AH) I, 147

[31] Ibn Ḥazm, *al-Iḥkām Fī Uṣūl al-Aḥkām*, (Cairo, 1347 AH) Vol. XXXII

any express rule of law permitting them, are *prima facie* invalid. If the legality of such contracts or conditions was not proven, they declared both contract and condition void.[32] It is also argued that the same presumption should apply to all obligations, and that the Qur'ānic verse enjoining Muslims to so honour their obligations is only relevant to those obligations expressly permitted by rule of law.[33]

The advocates of freedom of contract in Islamic Law (*Ahl al-Ibāḥa*) form the majority opinion of the Ḥanbalī school. Non-restriction of nominate contract types is therefore the general rule in this school.[34] Like their counterparts, they also base their argument on the *Qur'ān* and *Ḥadīth* texts. They quote the sanctity of contract verses in the *Qur'ān*,[35] together with *Aḥādīth* of a similar vein[36] to conclude that the injunction to fulfil all contracts and undertakings is unqualified and absolute.[37] Further, on the basis of the Qur'ānic verse : "He has explained to you that which is forbidden to you", and a *Ḥadīth Ṣaḥīḥ* related by al-Tirmīdhī to the effect that "Every agreement is lawful among Muslims except one which declares forbidden that which is allowed, or declares allowed that which is forbidden",[38] the advocates of freedom of contract argue that there is a natural presumption of legality subject to the Qur'ānic prohibitions. The counter argument these proponents present to the Ẓāhirīs' posture that every condition which is not in the *Qur'ān* is void, is simply to construe the *Ḥadīth* as meaning 'every condition which is not contrary to the Qur'ān and *Sunna*', rather than every condition which is not dealt with by the primary sources.[39]

Apart from the general religious delimitations placed on the freedom of contract, the law does provide for considerable intervention by a judge to reconstruct or readjust an existing contractual obligation. Thus extra-

---

32 Ibn Taymiyya, *Fatāwā*, op.cit., III, 323

33 M.E. Hamid, 'Islamic Law of Contract or Contracts?' in *Journal of Islamic and Comparative Law*, vol.3 (1969), p.9. This is contrary to the understanding expressed by Professor Mūsā in his article, 'The Liberty of the Individual in Contracts and Conditions According to Islamic Law', *Islamic Quarterly*, 2, (1955), p.82

34 El-Hassan, 'Freedom of Contract, The Doctrine of Frustration, and Sanctity of Contracts in Sudan Law and Islamic Law', *Arab Law Quarterly*, Vol. I(1) (Nov. 1985) pp.51-59, at p. 54

35 *Qur'ān*, (V:1), (VI:153), (XVII:34)

36 For instance, the Prophet is reported to have said : "The conditions most deserving of fulfilment are those whereby you make a woman lawful unto you", which was interpreted as meaning that all conditions relating to contracts deserve to be fulfilled.

37 See Ibn Ḥazm, *al-Iḥkām Fī Uṣūl al-Aḥkām, op.cit.*, Vol. V, pp.2-49

38 *Fatāwā Ibn Taymiyya, op.cit.*, III, 333; al-Shāṭibī, *al-Muwāfaqāt*, V, pp.305-307

39 Musa, 'The Liberty of the Individual in Contracts and Conditions According to Islamic Law', *Islamic Quarterly*, vol. II (Dec.1955), p. 84

contractual obligations may be imposed upon the parties by this judicial intervention.[40] A debtor who fails to meet his contractual term would not be ordered to settle interest payments agreed upon in the contract, but may be allowed by the court to make payment at a later date or by installments.

A court could also intervene, for example, in a case of *Istighlāl* (Unfair advantage), where a disproportion of obligation exists between the contracting parties, to readjust those obligations in a more 'equitable' manner.[41]

The system of Judicial Intervention[42] may therefore set aside the private arrangements of the contracting parties by seeking justification in an Islamic system of 'equity'. The intervention nevertheless operates in conjunction with the high esteem accorded to sanctity of contracts in Islam.

An argument which is gaining more force in the modern era, is that the only condition required according to Qur'ānic stipulation for the validity of any contract is the mutual consent of the contracting parties.[43] This philosophy is derived from the doctrines of freedom of contract of liberal nineteenth-century Europe, "when the economic laws of the market were considered to be the best safeguards of justice between the parties".[44] These advocates thereby conclude that subject to such consent, and such prohibitions and limitations[45] as yet set down by the law, every contract is valid whether or not they coincide with any of the recognized nominate

---

40 Amin, S.H., *Islamic Law In The Contemporary World*, (Glasgow, 1985) pp.46-47

41 See Chapters 6.5 and 6.6 on *Istighlāl* and *Force Majeure, infra.*

42 The Ministry of Justice in Iraq, in a working paper entitled *Legal System Reform*, approved by the revolutionary Command Council in 1977, recommended further law reform in order to extend the possibility of judicial intervention in the sphere of contractual relations. Iraq, *al-Waqai al-Irāqiyya*, (Official Gazette) (1977) No.37; See also Amin, *Islamic Law in the Contemporary world, op.cit.*, p.59

43 *Qur'ān*, (IV:29): "Oh you who believe, squander not your wealth among yourselves in vanity, except it be a trade by mutual consent". The Prophet is also reported to have said: "It is not lawful to take the property of a Muslim except by his consent", and "Sale is by consent". Hamid, *op.cit.*, p.41

44 Amin, S.H., *Islamic Law in the Contemporary World, op.cit.*, p.47

45 Basically, Islamic law does not recognise a statute of limitations. There is an *Ḥadīth* attributed to the Prophet which states "The right of a Muslim is not extinguished by the passage of time". See 'Abd al-Jalīl al-Rāwī, 'Principles on the Islamic Law of Contracts', *The George Washington Law Review*, XXII, (1953-4) p.38. In practice, certain limitations have been established. The *Majella* stipulates that actions referring to debt, inheritance, real estate held in absolute ownership and others could not be brought after fifteen years had elapsed. Modern legislation does recognise a statute of limitations: periods differ depending on subject-matter, and regulations are provided in the relevant sections of the Civil Law Codes of the respective countries.

contracts.[46]

Ibn Taymiyya writes :

> "If proper fulfilment of obligations and due respect for covenants are prescribed by the Lawgiver, it follows that the general rule is that contracts are valid. It would have been meaningless to give effect to contracts and recognize the legality of their objectives, unless these conditions were themselves valid."[47]

In the manner of their exegesis, it is admitted, the jurists' treatises would tend to affirm the opposite conclusion, but it is submitted that the purpose behind such expositions was not to limit the scope of contracts as suggested by the Ẓāhirīs, but is merely an unintended result of the process of Islamicisation upon contracts which were extant in the era prior to Islam. In addition, the majority of jurists themselves make no indication that the scope of contracts exposed by them in the systems of nominate contracts should be closed. There is, therefore, a reasonable presumption that all contracts are valid subject to their being expressly forbidden by rule of law, or that they contain voidable stipulations, or contravene Islamic prohibitions (especially those of *Ribā, Maysir* and *Gharar*), or public policy or morals.[48]

In 1961, in Damascus, the Congress of the Week of Islamic Law fervently accepted this thesis against a system of numerous nominate contracts. It was stated that as the parties are free to make contracts of their own choice, all kinds of contract would be acceptable providing that they do not contradict the basic principles of the *Sharī'a* law of contract and the

---

46 Ibn Ḥazm, *Al-Iḥkām Fī Uṣūl al-Aḥkām*, op.cit., pp.2-49; But see *Fatāwā Ibn Taymiyya, op.cit.*, pp.323-324, which notes the vacillation of the other schools on the validity of contracts whose effects and purpose are analogous to other innominate contracts, or whose effects and purpose are inconsistent with those of other nominate contracts. cf. also Musa, 'The Liberty of the Individual In Contracts and Conditions According to Islamic Law', *Islamic Quarterly*, 2, (1955), p.82

47 *Fatāwā* of Sheikh al-Islām Takī al-Dīn Aḥmad Ibn Taymiyya, *'Mabhath al- 'Uqūd'*, (Chapter on Contracts), Vol.III, (cairo, 1326-1329 AH), p.387 ff.

48 *Cf.* Ibn Qayyim al-Jawziyya : "Nothing is unlawful unless it is declared to be so by God and His Apostle....in human transactions and contracts, the general rule is that they are valid, unless there is legal evidence that they are unlawful or forbidden......where the law is silent about them, the transaction or the contract is valid." *I'lām al-Muwaqqi'īn 'An Rab al-'Alamīn*, 4 Vols; (Cairo, n.d.) vol.I, p.299ff.; Milliot, *Introduction à l'Étude du Droit Musulman, op.cit.*, p.205

generally acknowledged principles of Islam.[49]

Arab States follow suit, the majority of which do not restrict the ability of the parties to enter into a contract freely. Contracts containing elements of *Gharar*, for example, are explicitly allowed by the civil Codes of Egypt,[50] Iraq,[51] Kuwait,[52] and Dubai and Sharjah.[53]

Recent assimilation of civil law contracts into modern Islamic codes is evidence enough that this is the common point of view throughout the Muslim world today. Article 126 of the newly enacted United Arab Emirates Federal Civil Code, for example, provides that a contract may contain various incidents and in general, "any other thing which is not prohibited by a provision of the law and is not contrary to public order or morals."[54]

Similarly, the principle is upheld by the new Commercial Code of Bahrain. Article 2 of this law states : "There shall apply to commercial matters that which the two contracting parties have agreed upon provided that such agreement does not conflict with mandatory legislative provisions."[55]

---

49 Ernst Klingmuller, 'The Concept and Development of Insurance In Islamic Countries', *Islamic Culture*, Vol. XLIII, No.1, (Hyderabad, Jan. 1969), p.36. Schacht took the stance against Freedom of Contract simply on the basis that the list of *Sharī'a* prohibitions is too restrictive. See his *Introduction, op.cit.*, (1964) at p.144 : "[L]iberty of contract would be incompatible with the ethical control of legal transactions".

50 Egyptian Civil Code, No. 131 of 1948, Arts. 131, 265

51 Anderson, *Law Reform in the Muslim World, op.cit.*, p.97

52 Kuwaiti Commercial Code, Decree Law No. 68 of 1980, allows the sale of property not yet in existence (Art. 130), and the sale of goods where the risk exists that those goods may perish prior to delivery (Art. 121); and a contract lacking a price term if the intention is to use the market price or a price fixed by a third party (Arts. 124, 125). The Kuwaiti Civil Code, Law No. 67 of 1980, allows contracts for the sale of something not yet in existence (Art. 168)

53 Dubai Law of Contract, 1971 allows contracts which are conditional upon future events (Arts. 36, 37). It is not altogether clear whether this law has been superceded by the Federal civil Code, even though that code is operative also in Dubai and Sharjah.

54 United Arab Emirates Federal Law of Civil Transactions, *UAE Official Gazette*, No. 158, (Dec. 1985), Art. 126(d). See also: *Dubai Contract Law*, of 15 July 1971, Art.2 : "Nothing contained herein shall affect any usage or custom of trade, or any term of a contract which is not inconsistent with the provisions of this law". See also the *Qatar Civil and Commercial Law*, Law No. 16 of 1971 : Art.2, which recognises the *Pacta sunt servanda* rule; and Art.4, which states that in the absence of express provisions the judge shall decide in accordance with custom. Reference may also be made here to the construction of contracts, for which see section thereon, section 4, Arts. 257-266 of the Federal Civil Code of the UAE.

55 Law No. 7 of 1987. For the text and comments upon this enactment, see W.M. Ballantyne, *Commercial Law In The Arab Middle East : The Gulf States*, (London, 1986), Appendices XVII and XVIII at pp. 279 ff, 313 ff; and *idem.*, *Arab Law Quarterly*, 2(4), Nov. 1987, pp.352-356

Thus, although the *Sharīʿa* does not recognise the concept of a holder in due course, nor an unconditional guarantee,[56] because they were unknown to the early *Fuqahā'*, these concepts, which do not offend against any *Sharīʿa* principles, may be integrated into the ambit of the law by means of modern legislation.[57] Such has been the case in Saudi Arabia, where a holder in due course on a negotiable instrument is now recognised.[58]

Two remarks must be made at this stage regarding the principle of Freedom of Contract in its modern exposition. The first is that although the general subscription seems to be towards *autonomie de la volonté*,[59] the position with regard to contractual agreements between parties which are basically contrary to the *Sharīʿa* prescriptions, is unclear. Where codes give provisos to the precedence of contractual agreements, these are generally where such agreements are contrary to 'mandatory legislative provisions',[60] or 'public morals'.[61] The question of such agreements being contrary to the *Sharīʿa* prohibitions, which was tackled and made abundantly clear by the memorandum of the 1961 Damascus congress, is now studiously avoided in the Civil Codes. We are only left to presume that the non-inclusion of the *Sharīʿa* prohibitions in the provisos, is due to the abundantly clear instructions in the respective constitutions to follow dictates of the *Sharīʿa* law where no specific provisions of the relevant codified law exist. For example, article 75 in the UAE Provisional Federal Constitution states that "the Supreme Federal Court is required to apply the principles of the *Sharʿīa* and all Federal legislation, together with the laws in force in each Emirate, established custom and usage, and internationally recognised

---

56 Coulson, *Commercial Law op.cit.*, pp.1-5

57 Sloane, 'Status of Islamic Law in the Modern Commercial World', *International Lawyer*, (Fall, 1988) 22 (3) pp. 749 and 758

58 Saudi Arabia : Negotiable Instruments Regulation, Royal Decree No. 37 (11.X. 1383 AH) Art. 17; See also Kuwaiti Commercial Code, Art. 429; and Iraqi Law of Commerce, Law No. 30 (1984) Arts. 57 and 59

59 Amin clarifies the distinction between 'Freedom of Contract' and *Autonomie de la Volonté* (*Islamic Law in the Contemporary World, op.cit.*, p.46) : Freedom of contract, he says, is "a matter of legal policy stating that individuals are free to change their rights as they please." Conversely, *Autonomie de le volonté* is "a juristic principle stating that the free will of the individuals produces changes in rights." Thus Freedom of contract serves to demarcate the scope within which *Autonomie* is permitted to operate. Freedom of Contract allows parties complete liberty to determine the form, content and term of their agreements, and delimits the powers of the State to interfere in those contractual agreements. Islamic law clearly does not recognise Freedom of Contract by this definition, yet it does permit *Autonomie de la Volonté*.

60 For example, Art. 2(1) of Bahrain Commercial Code, No. 7/1987; Art. 2 of Dubai Contract Law, 1971; Art. 126 of UAE Federal Civil Code, 1986.

61 eg. Art. 126 of UAE Civil Code, 1986

principles of law, equity and natural justice to the extent that none of the foregoing are inconsistent with or repugnant to the *Sharī'a* or UAE Federal law."

The situation is clarified somewhat with regard to the Commercial Codes, however, even if such clarification is patently against the spirit of the 1961 memorandum. In two of the three constitutions under study, express authority is stated for the judicial enforcement of contractual agreements for the payment of interest on commercial loans : thus the *Sharī'a* doctrine of *Ribā* is openly defied.[62] The position in the UAE, although somewhat obscure at the time of enactment of the Federal Civil Code in 1980, has now been brought into harmony with Bahrain and Kuwait by an amendment which excludes the Civil Code provisions from governing Commercial Loans. The Provisional Draft of the Federal Commercial Code of the UAE does, however, recognise and enforce interest payments on commercial loans.

Secondly, it bears remark that if the legislative councils had adopted a contrary position, and gone against the *Autonomie de la volonté*, then this would have had an extremely limiting effect on the present modern Civil and Commercial Codes of the Middle Eastern states. Recognition of the freedom to contract has meant that these codes have been able to assimilate a whole corpus of otherwise alien and invalid contracts into their legal systems.[63] Throughout the course of the past century alone, the scope of commercial contracts in particular has expanded to an extent impossibly beyond the imaginations of the early *Fuqahā'*. To have limited the constitutions of these states to the Islamic set of nominate and innominate contracts alone would have been to seriously jeopardise the progress and economy of these countries. Indeed, it would have been an act of throwing such a spanner into the vast machinery of international commercial relations as to have resulted in retrogressive paralysis.

---

62 Kuwait Commercial Code, Art. 102 (1) and (2); UAE Draft Commercial Code, Art. 100 states: "If two or more persons bind themselves in a commercial obligation, then they are liable for the performance of this obligation notwithstanding any provision of law or agreement to the contrary." See also Bahrain Commercial Code, No. 7 of 1987, Arts. 2 (1) and 76, subsections (2) and (3)

63 The assimilation of such contracts has been an essential feature of the positive and substantive law since the time of 'Umar I, due to the unanimous preference by jurists of the four major schools for the principle of *Ibāḥa*. The contracts of yesteryear, which initiated the principle, were concerned with such matters as the payment of fees to *Qur'ān* readers, Imāms and Muezzins. These were eventually approved due to the absence of texts in conflict with their effects. See further, M. Hamidulla, 'Sources of Islamic Law, A New Approach', 1 *Islamic Quarterly*, No. 4, (1954) pp. 207-208

This important principle has had its share of modern connotations. In its Geneva Award of August 23, 1958, the Arbitration Tribunal between Saudi Arabia and the Arabian American Oil Company (ARAMCO) held that a contract between the two parties (one being the Muslim state of Saudi Arabia) was legally valid and binding despite its innominate *Sui Generis* nature. The Tribunal stated :

> "In the Ḥanbalī School of Islamic law, respect for previously acquired private rights, and specially for contractual rights, is a principle just as fundamental as it is in the other legal systems of civilised states.
>
> This flows from the fact that valid contracts bind both parties and must be performed, for rights resulting from agreements concluded for due consideration are absolutely secure; when one party has granted certain rights to the other contracting party, it can no longer dispose of the same rights, totally or partially in favour of another party."[64]

In determining the legal nature of a concession contract, for which no provision had been made in Ḥanbalī law, HM Ibn Sa'ūd, the King of Saudi Arabia in his capacity as theocratic ruler filled the lacuna by adopting the solution of a mining concession.[65] The mining concession contract was therefore outside the scope of the Ḥanbalī nominate contracts. It was held that the concession contract did not conflict with the *Sharī'a* law, since it was in conformity with two fundamental principles of Islamic law, that is, the principle of liberty to contract within the limits of Divine Law, and the principle of respect for contracts.[66] The first principle of this decision was based on Ibn Taymiyya's statement :

---

[64] *The Geneva Award of 23 August 1958 between Saudi Arabia and ARAMCO*, is deposited in the archives of the Republic and Canton of Geneva. This quotation refers to the Onassis Agreement of 20 Jan 1954 (15 Jumad I, 1373) as quoted on pp.146-7 of the official typewritten English version of the Award, and pp.101-2 of the printed version.

[65] See generally, Seamen, B.W., 'Islamic Law and Modern Government : Saudi Arabia Supplements the Shari'a to Regulate Development', *Columbia Journal of Transnational Law*, Vol. XVIII (1980) No.3, pp.413-481

[66] *The Geneva Award of 23 August 1958 between Saudi Arabia and ARAMCO*, pp.55-56 of the printed version. See also Seaman, Bryant w., 'Islamic Law and Modern Government : Saudi Arabia Supplements the Shari'a to Regulate Development', *Columbia Journal of Transnational Law*, Vol. XVIII (1980) No.3, pp.413-481; and Shamma, 'Law and Lawyers in Saudi Arabia', 14 *International and comparative Law Quarterly*, (1965) pp.1034-1039

> "The following rule shall be obeyed : men shall be permitted to make all transactions they need, unless these transactions are forbidden by the Book or by the *Sunna*."[67]

The second principle of this decision was based on Ibn Taymiyya's opinion that Muslim law does not distinguish between treaties, public or administrative contracts or contracts of a civil or commercial nature, and that all contracts fall under the "*Pacta sunt Servanda*" rule because it is God Who is the witness of all contracts.[68]

3. THE ISLAMIC NOMINATE CONTRACTS

The development of Islamic contracts is therefore the result of the method undertaken by Muslim jurists to elaborate the very broad and piecemeal doctrines of the *Qur'ān* and *Sunna*, and to impose them on the pre-Islamic norms of practice. Every so often among the works of the early jurists it is possible to find a solution or a rule of a certain category which *a priori* seems restricted to that certain type, but which, if tested on other categories, allows a principle of a certain generality to emerge. The method followed by the jurists in the development of the system of nominate contracts (*al-'Uqūd al-Mu'ayyana*) was by applying the process of *Qiyās* to already existing contracts, and by authorising the resulting category with *Ḥadīth* or other legal sources. The Muslim psychology therefore tended to treat the law as paradigmatic : "made up of individual solutions, handed down from day to day in relation to the specific needs of the moment, rather than of general principles set forth *a priori* from which the appropriate inference will be drawn for each fresh situation. "[69]

The system used by the jurists to categorize the nominate contracts was to determine whether, in any given contract, right passed in ownership or possession, and whether consideration passed or otherwise.

---

67 H. Laoust, *Le Traité de Droit Public d'Ibn Taimiyya, Traduction Annotée de La Siyassa Shar'iya*, (Beirut, 1948), p.167

68 Habachy traces the religious nature of *Pacta Sunt Servanda* back to Pre-Islamic Semitic traditions. He states that "The *Ka'aba*, the Holy Shrine of Mecca, was the abode of their idols, who were witnesses and guarantors of their pacts." S. Habachy, 'Property, Right and Contract in Muslim Law', *Columbia Law Review*, 62 (1962) p.463. See also the unpublished opinion of Pofessor Abū Zahra cited in *idem.*, p.466; and Hans Wehberg, 'Pacta Sunt Servanda', *The American Journal of International Law*, vol.53, (1959) p.775; and Khalid M. Ishaq, 'Islam and Law In The Twenty-First Century', *Islamic and Comparative Law Quarterly*, (Sept.-Dec. 1985), V, p.181.

69 L. Milliot, 'La Pensée Juridique de l'Islam,' *Revue Internationale de Droit Comparé*, 1954, pp.441

The basic nominate contracts number four:

(1) *Bay'* (Sale) : Where right of ownership passes for consideration (*Tamlīk al-'Ayn bi-'Iwād*)

(2) *Hiba* (Gift) : Where right of ownership passes without consideration (*Tamlīk al-'Ayn bilā 'Iwād*)

(3) *Ijāra* (Hire) : Where transfer of possession occurs for consideration[70]

(4) *'Āriya* (Loan) : Where transfer of possession occurs without consideration[71]

Other nominate contracts include those of *Salam*, (a contract for delivery with prepayment),[72] *Muḍāraba* ([Sleeping] Partnership Agreement; Equity sharing between bank and client), *Sharika* (Partnership), Mortgage (*Rahn*), *Ju'āla*, *Wadī'a* (Deposit), *al-Muzāra'a* (an agricultural contract where the landlord provides the land, seed and plants, and the worker provides the labour) and *'Umra*.[73]

In a more recent exposition, Professor Sanhūrī lists the nominate contracts as six : Sale (*Bay'*), Gift (*Hiba*), Partnership (*Sharika*), Hire (*Ijāra*), Piecework (*Muqāwala*), and Agency (*Wakāla*).[74]

Whereas in modern civil codes we find that recognition is often given to the Islamic system of nominate contracts, most legislation today prescribes that the principles of civil codes should apply to nominate and non-nominative contracts.[75] Principles which are peculiar to certain contracts are normally established by special regulating provisions which may be

---

70 See Kamil Tyabji, *Limited Interests in Muhammedan Law*, (London, 1949) pp.55-85

71 The *'Āriya* contract is applicable only to non-fungibles. Schacht defines it as :"Putting another temporarily and gratuitously in possession of the use of a thing, the substance of which is not consumed by its use." *Introduction to Islamic Law, op.cit.*, p.157. He equates it to the *Commodatum* of Roman Law; But *cf.*, Udovitch, 'Reflections on the Institutions of Credits and Banking in the Medieval Islamic Near East', *Studia Islamica*, XLI (Paris, 1975) p.10

72 See Schacht's definition in *Introduction to Islamic law, op.cit.*, p.153; See p.104 and Section on *Salam*, Chapter V, Section 5.3.1 *infra.*,

73 The *'Umra* contract is an archaic form of an unconditional donation in perpetuity.

74 Sanhūrī, *al-Wasīṭ Fī Sharḥ al-Qānūn al-Madanī*, (Beirut, n.d.), vol. IV, part I, p.1

75 See, for example, UAE Federal Civil Code, Art. 128

contained either in the same civil code, or in accompanying legislation.[76]

The most important nominate contract is that of Sale (*Bay'*). Sale formed the prototype contract around which the other classes of contract were analogously developed. Indeed it is the chapters on sale (*Kitāb al-Buyū'*) in the various legal treatises which formed the basis for the jurists' procedure of analysis : several common principles of contract and laws of ownership may be gleaned from these chapters.[77]

76 See Art. 128 (2) of the Federal Civil Code of the UAE. Ballantyne suggests that in so regulating, the UAE legislators have allowed themselves an escape route for mitigation against the stringent *Sharī'a* rules : See his article, 'The New Civil Code of the United Arab Emirates: A Further Reassertion of the *Sharī'a*', *Arab Law Quarterly*, I (3) (May, 1986) p.262

77 Bellefonds, *Traité, op.cit.*, p.57. It is to be noted that in Ḥanafī works, chapters on Duress also contain a certain number of general dispositions of this character.

Chapter 5

THE CONTRACT OF SALE (BAY')

1. DEFINITION OF SALE

Ibn 'Arfa defines sale as : "A contract of obligation by which each party transfers to the other the property of something for other than simple usage or pleasure. An additional limitation is that the contract is commutative of which one of the considerations shall be of legal tender, and the other shall be a specific object other than gold or silver."[1]

Other jurists have been content with simpler definitions, for example, "the exchange of one commodity for another, one of which is called the object, and the other the price"; or "the transfer of ownership of property for another".[2]

The Ḥanafī authors classify definitions of sale according to two principal headings : Special Sales *(al-Bay' bi al-Ma'nā al-Khāṣṣ)*; and General Sales *(Bay' bi al-Ma'nā al-'Āmm)*. The special sales are then recategorised according to Meaning, Object and Price, as follows :-

---

1 Quoted in N. Seignette, *Code Musulman par Khalil: (Rite Malékite)*, (Algiers/Paris, 1878)

2 'Abd al-Raḥmān al-Jazīrī, *Kitāb al-Fiqh 'alā al-Madhāhib al-'Arba'*, (7th Edn. Dār 'Ahyā' al-Turāth al-'Arabī: Cairo) Vol. II, p.147 Corresponding to this is Art. 489 of the UAE Federal Civil Code : 'A Sale is the exchange of non-money property for money'. The definitions of modern commercial sales are narrower: Art. 93 of the Bahrain Commercial Code, Law No. 7 of 1987, (Official Gazette 26 March, 1987) states: "Sale is a contract in which the seller undertakes to deliver up the ownership of a thing in exchange for a consideration in money. If the exchange is for money and corpus (*'Ayn*), for the contract to be considered a sale, it is necessary that the monetary exchange exceed that of the corpus." A similar article is presently contained in Art. 115 (2) of the draft Federal Commercial Code of the UAE, but it expressly permits partial monetary payment in distinction to the provision contained in Art. 93 of the Bahraini Code. For this latter, See Ballantyne, W.M., 'Note on the New Commercial Code of Bahrain (Decree Law 7/1987)', *Arab Law Quarterly*, vol. 2 (4) (Nov. 1987) pp.352 ff.

(1) Categories of Sale According to Meaning

(a) *Nāfidh* : Confers benefit immediately

(b) *Mawqūf* : Confers benefit upon permission or ratification

(c) *Fāsid* : Confers benefit upon the taking of possession

(d) *Bāṭil* : Confers no benefit in its original state

(2) Categories of Sale According to Object

(a) *Muqāyaḍa*: Exchange of object for object ('Object Barter')[3]

(b) *Ṣarf* : Exchange of price for price ('Money Barter')[4]

(c) *Salam* : Sale with immediate payment and deferred delivery

(d) *Muṭlaq* : Absolute sale of object for money, whether immediately or deferred

(3) Categories According to Price

(a) *Tawliyya*: Resale at cost price

(b) *Murābaḥa*: Resale with profit increase

(c) *(Wa)dī'a*: Resale with loss

(d) *Musāwama*: Resale with agreement that no reference be made to the original cost price

In their treatment of the conditions of substantive areas of the law, the Muslim jurists analysed the constituent elements of contracts which formed the basic foundations by which a contract would become validly concluded. These elements are called *Arkān* (Pillars), of which the five most important for any nominate contract are to be found in the constituent elements of sale, as follows :

---

[3] In an exchange of a commodity for a commodity, neither of which is money payment, each of the two commodites constitute both the price and the object.

[4] Where both commoditites are money payments amounting to the 'sale of money' such as gold, silver, and suchlike. This category is sometimes referred to as *Bay' al-Dayn*, or 'sale of a debt'.

(1) An Agreement

(2) Consent and Intention to contract

(3) Contracting parties with capacity to contract

(4) An Object of sale and valid Cause

(5) Consideration

Sanhūrī, in this context, recognises seven component elements to any contract: These are : (1) The Congruence of offer and acceptance; (2) The unity (*Ittiḥād*) of the *Majlis* of contract; (3) Plurality of contractors (*Ta'addad*); (4) The intelligence (*'Aql*), or distinction (*Tamyīz*) of the contracting parties; (5) The Subject (*Maḥall*) is susceptible to delivery ; (6) The Object (*Maḥall*) defined or susceptible to delivery; and (7) The beneficial nature of the Object, in that it is permitted to be traded in (*Māl Mamlūk; Māl Mutaqawwim*).[5]

The definitions of contract make it immediately apparent that the pillars of contract as laid down in the chapters of sale are first and foremost for the application of the sale contract. Invariably they do constitute general principles, but in dealing with contracts such as hire and gift, it may not always be safe to assume sale as a prototype. Often a jurist will devote a separate chapter to such of these other contracts as he considers requires special explanation.

2. THE AGREEMENT : MAJLIS AL-'AQD

The jurists developed a system of formation of contract based upon the contractual séance called *Majlis al-'Aqd.*[6] The *Majlis* occurs in any natural place where the contractors meet to form their agreement. The agreement is

5 Sanhūrī, *Maṣādir al-Ḥaqq*, IV, pp.134-135

6 The Islamic *Majlis* may be contrasted with the Roman law principle of *Ex Intervallo* which arose out of the formalism of the system rather than from consensualism as in Islamic law.

7 The confluence of offer and acceptance is upheld in modern legislation. See Art.130 of the UAE Civil Code; Arts. 31-32 of the Kuwaiti Civil Code; and Art. 5 of the Bahrain Contract Law of 1969

formed by the linking[7] of an offer (*Ijāb*)[8] and an acceptance (*Qabūl*)[9] which may be either express (*Sarīḥan*), tacit (*Ḍamānan*), by conduct (*Mu'āṭāh*)[10] or by gesticulation (*Isharāt*) when the party is mute,[11] but for which there is no special form.[12]

In certain cases, acceptance may also be implied from a party's silence.[13]

2.1 Tense

The Islamic prohibition against *Gharar* covers any degree of uncertainty and therefore express stipulations must not be formed in the future tense but in the present or preterite (for example, *bay'tuka*, : I sold you).[14]

---

8 "Offer" is defined in the *Majella*, Art.101 as the statement made in the first place by one of the two contracting parties raising the subject between the parties. See also Art.39 of the Kuwait Civil Code and Art. 131 of the UAE Civil Code. Art.40 of the Kuwait Civil Code states that a publication, advertisement or a current price list or any other statement connected with offers or orders directed towards the public or individuals shall not be considered as implicit offers, notwithstanding any indication to the contrary given by the circumstances of the case; The UAE Civil Code contains an almost identical article (Art. 134 (2)) adding that such offers will only be treated as an 'invitation to contract', thus taking a leaf out of the Common Law books. See Treitel, *The Law of Contract*, (Sixth Edn) pp.8-9 and Case Law listed therein.

9 "Acceptance" is defined in the *Majella*, Art.102 as the statement made in the second place by the other party which completes the contract. It is required that acceptance be in accordance with the offer. See also Arts. 125 and 129 (c) of the UAE Federal Civil Code.

10 Dardīr, *al-Sharḥ al-Kabīr*, (Boulac, 1295 AH; 4 vols.), vol.III, p.3; and Kāsānī, *Badā'i' al-Ṣanā'i'*, *op.cit.*, V, p.134

11 Kāsānī, *op.cit.*, V, p.133-135; al-Hammām, *Fatḥ al-Qadīr*, (First Ed., Boulac, 1316) V, pp.456-462. See also Art. 132 UAE Federal Civil Code, which includes 'Such acts as are customary', or by an interchange of acts demonstrating the mutual consent, or by adopting any other course in respect of which the circumstances leave no doubt that they demonstrate mutual consent. Art. 34 of Kuwait's Civil Code expressly includes 'writing'.

12 Ḥaṭṭāb writes :"It is not necessary that the offer and acceptance are expressed in any special form; any word or sign which conveys the meaning of the offer and acceptance renders an obligatory character on the sale and most other contracts." *Mawāhib al-Jalīl*, (6 vols: Cairo, 1928), IV, P.229. See also Art. 65 of Kuwait's Civil Code; Arts. 131-132 inclusive of the UAE Civil Code; and Art. 4 of the Bahrain Contract Law of 1969

13 See Section : Consent and Intention to Contract, subsection 'Silence as an Expression of consent' *infra*, and Article 135 (1) and (2) of the UAE Civil Code; Art. 35 of the Kuwaiti Civil Code

14 *al-Hidāya*, by Marghīnānī, transl. by Charles Hamilton, (Delhi, 1982 ed.), Bk.XVI, p.241 Comtemporary writers accuse the early jurists of verbal formalism in relation to this rule. See Chehata (Shahāṭa), *al-Naẓariyya al-'Amma li al-Iltizāmāt Fī al-Shar'īa al-Islāmiyya*, (Cairo, 1939), pp.130-132. This detail of tenses is taken up in modern legislation solely by the UAE Civil Code. Art. 132 states that if the present time is intended, the expression of intent may be expressed in the imperitive.

2.2 *Unity of Time and Place*

Subject to certain Ḥanafī and Mālikī principles, the *Fiqh* has ruled that the double declaration of offer and acceptance from which the contract is concluded must take place almost simultaneously in the *Majlis*, whether it is a *Majlis* between the principals themselves or between their authorised representatives. At the moment that the parties separate, the offer falls and acceptance is rendered impossible. The offer must be renewed and a new *Majlis* created for the acceptance to have any legal effect after separation of the parties. Bellefonds questions the consistency of such a strict doctrine as the *Majlis al-'Aqd* in contrast to the broad concept of mutual consent (which will be examined below) and whether the two may be reconciled.[15] Bellefonds concludes that the *Majlis* theory arose from the very lack of formalism in the Muslim *Fiqh* in order to precisely ascertain the intention of the contracting parties. It may also derive from the importance placed on verbal declaration as opposed to written declaration of consent, which precludes a theory of unity of time and place. Bellefonds also refutes the suggestion made by Mūsā that the *Fiqh* established such a theory in the interests of the contracting parties.[16] Bellefonds regards this suggestion as insufficient explanation for the rigorous sanctions imposed by the *Fiqh* for non-observance of the rules of the *Majlis*, that is, absolute nullity (*Bāṭil*) of the contract.[17]

The *Majlis* therefore creates the essential unity of time and place necessary for the dual declarations of intention and consent.[18] All four schools are in agreement on this point, but variations in opinion arise out of certain situations concerning the *Majlis* and the extension of the offer.

2.2.1 *What Constitutes Termination of the Majlis ?*

The first point of divergence arises from the termination of the *Majlis* and whether the *Majlis* itself is unequivocably terminated by the separation of the parties, subject to the definition of "separation". Certain interruptions during the *Majlis* are held to terminate the *Majlis*, for example, stopping to pray, or discussing other subjects, changing positions or attitudes, or even

---

15 Bellefonds, *Traité, op.cit.*, pp.146-7

16 Muḥammad Yūsuf Mūsā, *al-Amwāl wa Naẓariyyat al-'Aqd*, (Cairo, 1953), p.258

17 Bellefonds, *Traité, op.cit.*, p.147

18 See Ibn Hammām, *Fatḥ al-Qadīr*, Vol. V, p.460: "The option of acceptance continues until the meeting breaks up because the meeting brings together what is apart. Its hours are deemed one hour to avoid hardship and to make things easy." See also Sanhūrī, *Maṣādir al-Ḥaqq, op.cit.*, Vol.2 p.23.

falling asleep![19]

Article 137 of the UAE Civil Code has pursued this moot-point and consequently determines that "If the parties concern themselves during the *Majlis* of the contract with extraneous matters, that shall be regarded as rejection of the matter in hand." Modern interpretation in the UAE is therefore likely to construe the *Majlis* as terminated when the parties embark on unrelated topics of conversation, or when they are interrupted, in a similar way to the constructions applied by the earlier Ḥanafī *Fuqahā'*.

2.2.2 Immediate Acceptance

The second divergence of opinion emanates from the question of whether acceptance should follow immediately from the offer, and the jurists' definition of "immediate" (*Ḥālan*). The majority of the schools allow the second party until the end of the *Majlis* to make his acceptance known, but the Shāfi'īs take the definition of "immediate" in its strictest sense. This interpretation would seem unnecessarily draconian if it were not for the fact that the Shāfi'īs also allow the acceptor to withdraw his acceptance once given, at any time before the *Majlis* comes to an end.[20]

2.2.3 Withdrawal of Offer prior to Acceptance

The third divergence of opinion relates to whether the offer may be withdrawn before acceptance is given. It is only the Mālikī school which seems to be at odds here, for all the other schools unequivocally accept the right of either party to withdraw their declarations during the period of the *Majlis*.[21] The Mālikīs however hold that the offeror must stand by his offer until it has received a response from the offeree.[22] The effects of this opinion are obviously mitigated by the rules governing termination of the *Majlis*: an offeror can simply terminate the *Majlis* by walking away from

---

19 The Ḥanafīs are particularly adamant on this view. cf. 'Alā' al-Dīn al-Kāsānī, *Badā'i' al-Ṣanā'i'*, *op.cit.*, Vol.V, pp.136 ff. The Mālikīs and Ḥanbalīs rely on custom and usage to determine the termination of the *Majlis* in such cases, by basing their opinion on Ibn Qudāma, *al-Mughnī*, (Cairo: Third Ed. 1367 AH; 9vols.), III, p.565. This seems to be the most logical solution, as it is not only consistent with the principle of intention, but also allows a judge to decide on the facts of each particular case in the incidence of dispute.

20 Sanhūrī, *Maṣādir al-Ḥaqq*, *op.cit.*, Vol.2, p.23; and Ramlī, *Nihāyat al-Muḥtāj*, (8 Vols; cairo 1938), Vol.3, p.370

21 See Ibn 'Ābidīn *Radd al-Muḥtār*, (1252 AH), vol.IV, p.29. This is also the case where offer and acceptance take place simultaneously: the withdrawn offer takes legal effect. See also Kāsānī, *Badā'i' al-Ṣanā'i'*, V, P.137

22 Mālik, *al-Muwaṭṭa*, (Cairo, 1310 :with commentary by al-Zurqānī) 4 Vols., III, 136

the offeree if he later regrets his offer.[23]

The Kuwaiti Civil Code determines in this context that the offer may be withdrawn at any time before it is linked with the acceptance.[24] If a term has been fixed for the offer to stand, however, whether by designation of the offeror, or from the circumstances of the case, or the nature of the offer, the offer must stand for the whole of that term. The offer therefore lapses only on the term's expiry.[25]

The UAE Civil Code takes up the predominant opinion of the *Fiqh* in this respect. Article 138 specifically allows repetition of the offer prior to acceptance. Repetition automatically revokes any previous offer, and it is the last offer before acceptance is given which is regarded as the valid one. The following article states, however, that if a time is fixed for the acceptance to be given, the offeror is bound to keep to his offer until such time as the term for acceptance has expired, thereby honouring the agreement made between the parties.[26] Article 139 (2) states that where this term is not determined by agreement between the parties, it may also be inferred from the circumstance of the case, or the nature of the transaction.

2.2.4 OPTION OF THE MAJLIS : (Khiyar al-Majlis)

The fourth difference of opinion between the schools arises from the question of revocation of offer and acceptance once given. Here the Mālikīs and Ḥanafīs hold that once a contract has been concluded by corresponding offer and acceptance, neither of the parties may retract their declarations, whether or not the *Majlis* has been terminated.[27] Contrastingly, the Ḥanbalīs and Shāfi‘īs regard such declarations as provisional for the duration of the *Majlis*.[28] In this respect they have formulated a principle of an "Option of

23 Bellefonds, *Traité, op.cit.*, p.151

24 Article 41 (1) Kuwaiti Civil Code

25 Art. 141 (2) Kuwaiti Civil Code

26 Art.139 (1) UAE Civil Code

27 Ibn ‘Abd al-Barr, quoted in al-Zurqānī's commentary on Imām Mālik's *al-Muwaṭṭa*, (Cairo 1910) III, p.137; and see Chapter 7.1 below.

28 See *Majella*, Arts. 183 and 184, where after offer and before acceptance, upon an indication of dissent by either party, the offer becomes void.

the *Majlis*" (*Khiyār al-Majlis*)[29] whereby, following declaration of consent in a bilateral contract, the parties may retract their declarations at any time prior to the termination of the *Majlis*.[30] This option is not recognised by the Mālikīs and Ḥanafīs, who view it as contrary to the Qur'ānic verse enjoining Muslims to fulfil their undertakings.[31]

The option is, however, taken up by the UAE Civil Code. Article 136 states that the contracting parties shall retain the option from the time the offer has been made to the time the *Majlis* is terminated. If the offer is withdrawn prior to its acceptance, or if either party says or does anything to demonstrate that he is resiling from it, the offer is avoided and no acceptance thereafter shall be of any effect.

Contracts Inter Praesentes

It follows that in a contract *inter praesentes* it is a necessary condition that the contracting parties actually hear each others' declarations.[32] This is a rigid condition strictly insisted upon by most schools[33] and rather belies the modern importance given to written documents of contract exchanged between parties who are not only neither deaf nor mute, but who are contracting *inter absentes*. Likewise, the majority opinion of the Ḥanafī

---

29 The option of *Majlis* is based on *Aḥādīth* attributed to the Prophet (*Isnād* = Mālik: Nāfi: Ibn 'Umar: Muḥammad) by Bukhārī, *al-Jāmi' al-Ṣaḥīḥ*, (Cairo, n.d.), and Muslim, *Ṣaḥīḥ*, (Cairo, 1334 AH) vol.V, 10, which state : "The two contracting parties have a right of option in a sale, as long as they have not separated." See Schacht, *Origins*, (Oxford, 1979) pp.159-160, who states that this option was not recognised by the very early schools of law, as is evidenced by a reading of Shaybānī. A Tradition from the Meccan Scholar 'Aṭā' in al-Shāfi'ī's *Kitāb al-Umm*, (Būlāq, 1321-1325) III, 3 contains a detailed statement in its favour, and because it shows no trace of the legal maxim embodied in the Tradition attributed to the Prophet, Schacht regards it as genuine. The ascription of a similar Tradition to Shurayḥ, however, he rejects as spurious, as put into circulation by Nāfī and projected back to the ancient Iraqi authority.

30 Ibn Qudāma, *al-Mughnī, op.cit.*, III, 562 ff. ; Abū Zahra, *Al-Milkiyya wa Naẓariyyat al-'Aqd*, (First Ed. 1939), p.176 ff. The option of *Majlis* is not relevant to those contracts designated *Ghayr Lāzim*, (not binding) which are always revocable by either party, such as deposit, etc.

31 *Qur'ān*, (V:1). Ibn al-Hammām, *Fatḥ al-Qadīr*, v, p.464

32 Sanhūrī, *Maṣādir al-Ḥaqq, op.cit.*, II, 55-56

33 But the Shāfi'īs require that the offer and acceptance be loud enough for the people in the *Majlis* to hear. This constitutes mere evidentiary value and it can therefore be deduced that communication is not a necessary requirement with the Shāfi'īs. See Hamid, 'Mutual Consent in the Formation of Contracts', *Journal of International and Comparative Law*, vol.VII, (1977), p.48; and more fully Hamid, 'The Role of Consent in the Formation of Contracts - A Comparative Study in English and Islamic Law', (Unpublished Ph D. Thesis, University of London, 1971)

school requires that revocation is only effective upon communication.[34]

Contracts Inter Absentes

In cases of contracts being formed *inter absentes* by means of representatives (or modern communications systems such as the telephone or telex), or by letter, the jurists have extended the theory of *Majlis* by construction.[35] The *Majlis* was held to open upon communication of the offer to the offeree and to take place where the offeree receives the offer.[36] The *Majlis inter absentes* terminates after a reasonable lapse of time during which the offeree has failed to respond, or upon the declaration of acceptance by the offeree.[37] On the construction of the usual theory of *Majlis* the jurists allow the offeree to suspend his declaration until he leaves the place of communication or turns his attention to another matter.[38] However, there is nothing to prevent the offer from being reiterated, and this therefore creates a new *Majlis*. For this purpose a written offer of marriage is considered by the Ḥanafī school as continual and perpetrates until it is withdrawn or responded to.[39] By analogy with contracts formed *inter praesentes* it would follow that the contract is concluded upon communication of acceptance reaching the offeror. However, this is not the opinion adopted by the *Fuqahā'*, and contracts between absent parties are in fact concluded at the time and place of acceptance, and therefore before communication of the acceptance has reached the offeror. This therefore forms an exception to the Ḥanafī rule of communication of acceptance between parties contracting in each other's presence. The conjunction of consent is presumed as existing from the point of time in which acceptance is pronounced.[40]

In the process of adoption from the European Civil law codes, this rule was reversed in modern Middle Eastern contracts codes enacted in the second half of the twentieth century. The contract *inter absentes* in the

---

34 See *al-Fatāwā al-'Ālmakīriyya*, 6 vols., (Cairo, 1323 AH), vol.III, p.11

35 Kāsānī, *op.cit.*, V, 138

36 Kāsānī, *Badā'i' al-Ṣanā'i'*, V, p.138; Ibn al-Hammām, *Fatḥ al-Qadīr*, V, p.461-462

37 Ibn al-Hammām, *Fatḥ al-Qadīr*, V, p.462

38 *The Hedaya*, (Transl. Hamilton) *op.cit.*, Bk.XVI, p.242. This rule is hyperthetical rather than practical as neither party will know when the other has left the *Majlis* if they are contracting *inter absentes*.

39 Ibn 'Ābidīn, *al-Radd al-Muḥtār*, *op.cit.*, IV, p.11. The reason for this is that the necessary witnesses may not be available at the time the offer is received.

40 Ibn 'Ābidīn, *op.cit.*, IV, p.11; Kāsānī, *Badā'i'*, *op.cit.*, V, p.138; Chafik Chehata, *Théorie Générale de l'Obligation en Droit Musulman*, (Cairo, 1936) p.61

Egyptian Civil Code[41] is now deemed conclusive when communication of the acceptance has reached the offeror, or when the communication has been put on a course of transmission to the offeror which was reasonably contemplated by the parties and which puts such communication beyond the power of its author.[42] In the classical formulation of contracts *inter absentes* the Option of *Majlis* is not applicable, and the offeror has the option to withdraw only until the offeree has communicated his declaration. This is the case whether or not the offeree had actually received communication of the revocation.[43] Following logically from the principles already given in the Egyptian prototype codes however, these statutes now permit the acceptance to be revoked prior to its communication to the offeror.[44] This stance bears out the important role given by Islamic law to the declaration of Will. To concord with the classical jurists would be to render that role ineffective in its true aim, that is, to communicate that will from its author to its intended recipient. By application therefore, in a situation whereby two contradictory declarations of will are emitted simultaneously, it is the first to reach the other party which will take effect. The second will be regarded as non-existent unless it is treated as a revocation where revocation is possible.[45]

With this new wave of codification therefore, a different result had emerged from that of the classical formulation of the theory of the *Majlis*. The difference occurs in the principle of intention of the contracting parties,[46] which is the second essential element to a contract of sale, and will be dealt with immediately below.

Contracting Inter Absentes : Modern Legislation

In the more recent codes the format of contracts made by telephone, telex and other such means of communication, has been modified. The justifications for the revised formats seem to be parallel to the original methodolgy formulated by the earlier *Fuqahā'*, and the theory of *Majlis* is adhered to where it may be logially possible : in the case of communications by telephone, it has therefore been possible to extend the *Majlis* theory with regard to the time sequence of the contractual session.

---

41 Art. 91 of the Egyptian Civil Code of 15 October 1949.

42 See also Dubai Contract Law of 15 July 1971, Art.6(2), which is derived from English Law influences.

43 Except in Mālikī law, where the same rule applies as for contracts formed *inter praesentes*.

44 See also, Dubai Contract Code, 1971, Art. 7 (2)

45 See Art. 127 of the Egyptian Civil Code of 1949.

46 Chafik Chehata, 'Volonté Réelle et Volonté Déclarée dans le Nouveau Code Civil Égyptien', in *Revue Internationale de Droit Comparé*, (April-June 1954) p.243

According to the 1980 Kuwaiti Civil Code, it is now presumed, that in contracts formed by correspondence, in the desire to prevent confusion arising, the offeror will specify a time limit within which he expects to receive a response from the offeree. The offer will therefore stand so long as that specified period has not elapsed. If the offeror has not specified such a time, the offer remains valid until acceptance is given, for as long as is deemed proper according to the circumstances of the case.[47] The period will take into account the due time taken for the communication to reach the offeree, for him to give it adequate consideration, and for his decision to reach the offeror.[48] If the acceptance does not reach the offeror within a reasonable period (which, again, is judged according to the specific circumstances of the case) then the offer is considered as having lapsed. This is so even if the offer has been sent on a course to the offeror, but has failed to reach him.[49] The contract by correspondence itself is deemed to have been made at the time and place in which the acceptance is brought to the knowledge of the offeror, unless there is contractual agreement, or a provision of law, or custom to the contrary.[50]

A contract made by telephone or such other means, is deemed to have been formed within a *Majlis*, and that *Majlis* exists in relation to the time of conclusion. As regards place of conclusion, however, the contract is deemed to have been concluded at the place where acceptance is received.[51] In other words, the contract is considered as formed between two absent parties who are conjoined in voice, and therefore the rule follows as for contract by correspondence in that it is concluded in the place where the offeror receives the acceptance. But it forms one *Majlis* in relation to its format and time.[52] Here, therefore, a different approach has been adopted, as from the previous Egyptian-prototype codes, even though Article 49 of the Kuwaiti code essentially retains the same result as those other models : the contract is deemed complete at the time and place that the acceptance comes to the knowledge of the offeror, notwithstanding agreement, provisions or laws to the contrary.[53]

---

47 Kuwaiti Civil Code, 1980, Art. 48 (1)

48 Kuwaiti Civil Code, 1980, Art. 48 (1)

49 Kuwaiti Civil Code, 1980, Art. 48 (2)

50 Kuwaiti Civil Code, 1980, Art. 49

51 Kuwaiti Civil Code, 1980, Art. 50

52 Memorandum to the Kuwaiti Civil Code, 1980, p. 66

53 Memorandum to the Kuwaiti Civil Code, 1980, pp. 64-65 : cf. Egyptian Civil Code, Art. 97; Libyan Civil Code, Art.97; Iraqi Civil Code, Art. 87; and Kuwaiti Civil Code Art. 112

In Bahrain, the position is the same, in that the communication of the proposal is complete when it comes to the knowledge of the person to whom it is made,[54] and communication of acceptance is complete when it has been brought to the knowledge of the proposer, or 'put in a course of transmission to him, the use of which was in the contemplation of the parties in all circumstances of the case, and which puts such communication out of the power of the acceptor'.[55] It can be noted that in this respect a parallel exists between the Bahraini code (derived from English Law principles) and the Egyptian prototype codes (derived from Civil Law origins). With regard to revocation of offer or acceptance, the Bahraini code also follows the example of the Egyptian prototype codes. Revocation is complete as against the person who makes it when it is put into a course of transmission to the person to whom it is made, so as to be out of the power of the person who makes it. As against the person to whom it is made, it is complete when it comes into his knowledge.[56] On this basis, we may presume that where acceptance and revocation of offer or acceptance conflict, here, as in the prototype codes, it is the first which reaches the person to whom it is made which stands. The situation is not explained within the code, however, and we may suppose that each case may be considered on its individual merits.

According to the UAE Civil Code, a contract made *inter absentes* is deemed to have been made at the time and place at which the offeror learns of the acceptance, unless there is agreement or a provision of law to the contrary.[57] As in the Kuwaiti Code[58] the offeror is deemed to have learned of the acceptance at the time and place at which such acceptance reaches him, unless there is evidence to the contrary.[59]

In contracts made by telephone or similar methods, the Kuwaiti model of the single *Majlis* regarding time and the *inter absentes* non-unity of *Majlis* regarding place is followed.[60]

---

[54] Bahrain Contract Law, 1969, Art. 6 (1)

[55] Bahrain Contract Law, 1969, Art. 6 (2)

[56] Bahrain Contract Law, 1969, Art. 6 (3)

[57] UAE Federal Civil Code, Art. 142 (1)

[58] Kuwaiti Civil Code, Art. 49

[59] UAE Federal Civil Code, Art. 142 (2)

[60] UAE Federal Civil Code, Art. 143

3. CONSENT AND INTENTION TO CONTRACT

Consent (*Riḍā*) to the contract, its form and principles is an example where the jurists have regulated detailed causes and ground rules on a broad Qur'ānic injunction. The *Qur'ān*[61] and *Aḥādīth*[62] determine that bilateral contracts can only take place by the free consent of the parties.[63]

Neither of these sources go so far as to explain how mutual consent may be ascertained and it was therefore by virtue of the reasoning of the jurists that a series of inductive regulations governing consent and intention has come about.[64]

Intention and consent have become the two fundamental precepts to any contract. However, this is not to say that the *Fiqh* in any way adopted a formalistic approach to the expression of the concordant wills of the contracting parties.[65]

3.1 Non-verbal Expressions of consent

It was determined that mere intention was not sufficient to conclude a bilateral contract[66] but that such intention could be most simply conveyed by verbal expression. Should verbal expression be impossible such as in cases where either of the parties are deaf, mute or absent, then Muslim law allows for that intention to be conveyed by other means. This may be by writing, by signs or gesticulations[67]

---

61 *Qur'ān*, (IV:29)

62 *al-A'māl bi al-Niyya*: 'Acts are valid according to the intention'; Goldziher, *Vorlesungen*, 45, *Encyclopaedia of Islam*, I, p.429

63 Bahrain Contract Law, Art. 15, defines consent: "Two or more persons are said to consent when they agree upon the same thing in the same sense." See also Art. 129 (a) of the Federal Civil Code of the UAE

64 For a comprehensive discussion of the subject, see Mohamed Al-Fatih Hamid, *The Roles of Consent in Formation of Contracts: A Comparative Study in English and Islamic Law*, (Unpublished PhD Thesis: University of London, 1971)

65 This principle has been carried into the codes which appeared in the Middle East in the post-World War II era. See for example, Art. 89 of the Egyptian Civil Code promulgated 15 October 1949 : "The contract is concluded when the two parties have exchanged two concordant expressions of will, without prejudice to the formalities imposed by the law for the conclusion of the contract." See section on Defect of Form, *infra*.

66 "What is in the breast is an intention and an intention without an act is not sufficient to conclude the contract". Shams al-Dīn al-Sarakhsī, *al-Mabsūṭ*, *op.cit*, Vol.13, p.46; See also Ibn 'Abidīn, *Radd al-Muḥtār*, Vol.4, p.17

67 All four schools allow deaf and dumb persons to contract by signs, there being no priority set by writing. This is certainly due to the high rate of illiteracy extant even to this day in the Middle East. cf. Ibn Nujaym, *al-Ashbāh wa al-Naẓā'ir*, (Cairo, 1298 AH), p.188; See also Arts. 90, 91 and 92 of the Egyptian Civil Code of 1949.

3.2 Silence as an Expression of consent

In certain cases where a person is required to indicate his position explicitly, silence may also be considered as an expression of positive intention.[68] Generally silence is not considered as having any significance except in cases where a response must be given and then it is considered as verbal acquiescence.[69] Cases where silence is deemed verbal acquiescence are :the virgin girl's consent to marriage; the acceptance of her dower by her guardian; the master's consent for his slave to enter into commercial transactions and the guardian's consent for his ward to enter into commercial transactions when both are done in the knowledge of the master or guardian; the silence of the beneficiary in non-contractual transactions such as *Waqf*, donation, and remission of debts, when an act is subordinate to the taking of possession. Also, a seller loses his right of retention if he sees that the buyer has taken possession of the goods without paying the price : if he remains silent, he loses his right of lien.

The position of the *Fiqh* regarding silence as an expression of consent to a contract has been adhered to in the UAE Federal Civil Code : Article 35 (1) denotes that a person who remains silent shall not be deemed to have made a statement of consent. However, silence in the face of a circumstance which requires a statement shall be regarded as an acceptance. This provision was originally formulated in the *Fiqh* with regard to the bashfulness of young girls whose hands were being requested in marriage contracts.

In particular, silence is deemed to be a manifestation of a positive response in modern legislation of the UAE, if there has already been prior dealing between the contracting parties and the new offer is related to such prior dealing, or if the offer will bring about a benefit to the person to whom it is made.[70]

Similarly in Kuwait, consideration may be given to implicit expressions of the will, so long as such expressions are not precluded by any law, or by the agreement itself, or when the nature of the transaction requires that the acceptance be explicit.[71]

---

68 On silence as consent see Maḥmaṣānī, *al-Naẓariyya al-'Āmma li al-Mūjibāt wa al-'Uqūd Fī al-Shar'ia al-Islāmiyya*, II, p.52 ff; and Ibn Nujaym, *al-Ashbāh wa al-Naẓā'ir*, (Cairo, 1298 AH), V, pp.78-79 whose opinion is reproduced in the *Majella*, Art. 67.

69 For a *resumé* of the different stance pertaining to the four schools, see Bellefonds, *Traité*, pp.141-145.

70 Art. 135 (2) of the Federal Civil Code of the UAE

71 Kuwait Civil Code, Art. 35

3.3 Ambiguous or Erroneous Expressions

Where words or expressions have given ambiguous (*Mubham*) or erroneous declarations of intention, regard was given by the early jurists to the real intention of the parties over the actual expressions used.[72]

Schacht states that the interpretation of *Niyya* was not strictly objective, but nor was it totally subjective. He submits that the declarations were scrutinised as to their particular meanings without regard to the intention claimed, to determine whether they might then be compatible with that *Niyya* latterly claimed. He also admits the tendency to restrict the effect of the declaration to mitigate the obligation resulting in evasion thereof.[73]

3.3.1 Talji'a Sales

Intention is also discussed in the treatises with regard to the fictional *Talji'a* sales. The *Talji'a* sale is an operation whereby a person wishes to dispose of his goods to prevent them from being confiscated, and secretly arranges with the supposed buyer that after the danger has passed he may recoup his property. An ostensible contract of sale is concluded, so that right of title is passed to the third person and confiscation is avoided but the intention has not been to conclude a contract of sale. The contract assumes the appearance of a sale for the benefit of observers, but the contract is in fact that of a pledge or deposit. The question asked by the jurists is whether the apparent seller has the authority to prove the secret agreement notwithstanding the ostensible act of sale. The Mālikīs and Ḥanbalīs argue that since a pre-condition of the contract of sale, that is, the intention of the parties, is missing, the sale is void. The Ḥanafīs[74] and Shāfi'īs however would declare the sale valid on the basis that the pre-conditions of the existence of the object of sale and the contract's being devoid of any defects, are present and sufficient to validate the contract.[75]

---

72 *Majella*, Art.3, which is based on Ibn Nujaym's statement in *al-Ashbāh, op.cit.*, p.12-27 : "It is necessary to consider the intention of the parties". The Ḥanafīs and Shāfi'īs seem in general to give meaning to the declared intention or its usual sense rather than the hidden intention. *Cf.* Bellefonds, 'Volonté Interne et Volonté Déclarée en Droit Musulman', in *Revue Internationale de Droit Comparé*, (1958), No.3 *Contra* Suyūṭī, *al-Ashbāh wa al-Naẓā'ir*, (Cairo, 1359 AH), p.111-113; 148; and Shāṭibī, *al-Muwāfaqāt*, II, pp.206-227; Shāfi'ī, *Kitāb al-Umm*, (7 vols. Cairo, 1321-1326 AH), p.65; and Sanhūrī, *Maṣādir al-Ḥaqq*, IV, pp.54-55

73 See Schacht, *Introduction, op,cit.*, (Oxford, 1979) pp.116-117;123

74 But see the remarks made by Abū Ḥanīfa's disciples, Muḥammad and Yūsuf, who are *contra* this view and declare the *Talji'a* sale null and void (*Bāṭil*) because it is a simulated (*Hazl*) sale. Discussed in Bellefonds, 'Volonté Interne et Volonté Déclarée en Droit Musulman', *Revue Internationale de Droit Comparé*, (1958) No.3, p.154

75 Ibn Qudāma, *al-Mughnī*, Vol.IV, p.214

The effects of the decisions of the *Fuqahā'* on the importance of declared intention have repurcussions on the systems of *Ḥiyal* which were devised for the very purpose of circumventing strict prohibitions on *Ribā*.

3.3.2 'Īna Sales

In the contract of *'Īna* for example, a contract comprising a credit sale and one sale or a double sale for immediate consideration is effectively a loan with interest :

> A wishes to borrow a sum of 100 Dinars from B who agrees to be repaid after three months the sum of 110 Dinars. A buys an object from C for 110 Dinars which they agree should be paid three months later. A then resells the same object to B for 100 Dinars which B pays immediately. A therefore finds himself in possession of 100 Dinars as seller and by title of the first sale three months later he reimburses 110 Dinars to C. B then sells the object to C for 110 Dinars. B will therefore have obtained the 10 Dinars interest which he would not have been able to demand openly.[76]

Although all transactions forming the *'Īna* contract are correct in themselves, when put together they merely mask a loan with interest which is prohibited in Islamic law according the rules of *Ribā*. Therefore, the Ḥanbalīs, in accordance with their principles and taking into account the illegal nature of the contract, condemn the *'Īna* contract and regard it as null and void.[77] The Shāfi'īs however, regard it as perfectly valid on the grounds that everyone has the right to sell an object at a diminished price to the one he himself paid. The *Ḥiyal* exert no influence on the validity of acts with the Shāfi'īs, accordingly, the *'Īna* sale is regarded as perfectly valid within the Shāfi'ī school. The Ḥanafīs are not unanimous in their decision regarding the *'Īna* sale.[78] Abū Ḥanīfa himself admits only the case where a third party buys from the buyer to resell to the seller. Muḥammad al-Shaybānī, however, admits the *'Īna* sale as valid, but he categorises it as *Makrūh* (blameworthy). It is Abū Yūsuf who provides the predominant opinion of the Ḥanafī school. He considers the sale as perfectly valid and not at all *Makrūh*.

---

76 Bellefonds, 'Volonté Interne et Volonté Déclarée en Droit Musulman', *Revue International de Droit Comparé*, *op.cit.*, (July-Sept 1958) p.520

77 Ibn Qudāma, *al-Mughnī, op.cit.*, IV, p.174 ff. See also Shāṭibī, *Al-Muwāfaqāt, op.cit*, II, pp.206-227

78 Ibn 'Ābidīn, *Radd al-Muḥtār, op.cit.*, IV, p.255

The status of the *'Īna* contract in the majority opinion of the Mālikī school is less tolerant; *'Īna* is not approved of, but it nevertheless forms a valid contract.[79]

It may be concluded therefore that the Mālikīs and Ḥanafīs give due effect to the real intention of the parties, but that as regards illicit motives both schools are reluctant to make such an uncertain element as motive a dependent factor of a legal act.[80] The Ḥanbalī school however, always gives precedence to real intention over declared intention.[81] In general, the tendency of Muslim law seems to be to give priority to the declared intention. Indeed, in the Shāfi'ī school this is not just a tendency but a doctrinal stance.[82]

The dichotomy between these doctrines has been taken up to a certain extent in the first codifications to be enacted in the Middle East. In the Egyptian Civil Code,[83] for example, Article 148 states : "The contract must be executed in accordance with its contents, in a manner which complies with the requirement of good faith."[84] This article therefore gives *a priori* importance to the declarations exchanged, but the notion of good faith provides a leeway for the contents of the declarations to be judicially interpreted through objective criteria.

The consequent result is that legislation has brought the treatment of the concept of intention around in a full circle to where the jurists had originally started : necessary legal effect appends to the declaration of intention, but where that declaration is unclear, interpretation must go beyond the declarations to discover the real intentions of the parties. Hence Article 150 of the Egyptian Civil Code of 1949 redeveloped original Islamic

---

79 Santillana, *Instituzioni di Diritto Musulmano Malechita*, Vol.II, p.396; Dardīr and Dasūqī, *Sharḥ al-Kabīr*, (4 vols.; Boulac, 1295 AH), vol. III, p.88 ff; Yūsuf Mūsā states in his *al-Amwāl wa Naẓariyyat al-'Aqd*, (Cairo, 1953), p.302 that Mālik himself regarded the *'Ina* contract as void, but that he was not followed in this respect by his disciples.

80 Sanhūrī, *Maṣādir al-Ḥaqq*, IV (1957) pp.54-55

81 Ibn Qayyim al-Jawziyya, *I'lām al-Muwaqqi'īn*, (Cairo, n.d.) vol. III, pp.106-107

82 Bellefonds, 'Volonté Interne et Volonté Déclarée en Droit Musulman', *Revue International de Droit Comparé, op.cit.*, (1958) No.3, p.521; cf. also Chafik Chehata, 'Volonté Réelle et Volonté Déclarée dans le Nouveau Code Civil Égyptien', [Lecture given at the Institute de Droit Comparé at the University of Paris on 5 March 1953] In *Revue Internationale de Droit Comparé*, (April-June 1954) pp.242-249.

83 Promulgated by Law No. 131 of 1948; Effective as from 15 October 1949.

84 The Draft to this code adds the phrase : "and to the customs of loyal dealing." It is somewhat surprising that this phrase was not retained in the eventual code as it would seem to add another positive objective criterion for the interpretation of intention in contracts.

principles by stating : "When the wording of a contract is clear it cannot be deviated from in order to ascertain by means of interpretation the intention of the parties. When a contract has to be construed, it is necessary to ascertain the common intention of the parties and to go beyond the literal meaning of the words, taking into account the nature of the transaction as well as that of loyalty and confidence which should exist between the parties in accordance with commercial usage."[85] Despite the fact that post-war legislation effected changes in the overall concept of intention, it must be noted that intention still retains its role as the substrata of the contract in the most recent Gulf legislation.[86]

In situations where expression of that intention is omitted, or is inadequately or ambiguously expressed judicial intervention is permitted in order to seek out the true intentions of the parties, thereby reinstating the views of the Ḥanbalī school in conjunction with the varying views of the other three schools.

Article 258 of the UAE Federal Civil Code states that in construing a contract, effect must be given to intentions and meanings, not artificial or mechanical expressions and deductions. (This is redolent of the maxims in the *Majella*). Where the content of a contract is clear, there is no room for abtuse construction in order to determine the intentions of the parties.[87] If no such clarity exists, then the joint intention of the parties must be sought without the restriction of the literal meaning of expressions used, but taking guidance from the nature of the transaction and also taking account of the good faith and trust between the parties in accordance with current custom in such transactions.

In the classical formulation of the concept of intention, a general principle took effect that if a declaration was made by a party who died shortly thereafter, the declaration was regarded as nonexistent *ab initio*, since by virtue of the idea of unity of intention, this intention was not complete. The same principle applied to parties who became incapacitated. However, the modern stance, in contradiction to both the previous Muslim principle and to the French Civil Code, treats the declared intention of the deceased as a perfect entity once it has reached its intended destination.

---

85 This is also the result of an eclectic compromise between the provisions of the French Civil Code and those of the German Civil Code. See Chehata, 'Volonté Réelle et Volonté Déclarée dans le Nouveau Code Civil Égyptien', *Revue Internationale de Droit Comparé, op.cit.*, (1954), p.248

86 See Art. 129 (a) of the UAE Federal Civil Code; and Arts. 131-135 inclusive which deal with ways in which intention and consent may be expressed. Kuwait Civil Code, Art. 38 (2). There is no mention of construction in the Bahraini Code.

87 UAE Federal Civil Code, Article 256

Moreover, even if that declared intention has not reached its destination at the time of its author's demise, it is still regarded as effective if it has been despatched and exists in a transitory state.[88]

In summary therefore, it is evident that the concept of intention in modern legislation in the Middle East retains the primary importance given to it by the early jurists as a pillar of any contract. In the implementation of the effects of intention however, it has been seen that modern legislators have attempted to draw out the general opinion of the schools in order to integrate these opinions in conjunction with the newer concepts pertaining in the modern European codes from which much of the new civil and commercial statutes were taken. The compromise is a fortunate one, and it may be said that the more divergent views of the slightly more orthodox Ḥanbalī school have not been compromised excessively by the modern statutes.

4. CONTRACTUAL CAPACITY (AHLIYYA)

The capacity of the parties to contract is a prime consideration of the validity of that contract. There is a natural presumption of capacity to contract subject to three categories of restrictions where a party belonging to one or more of those categories is interdicted[89] from contracting and therefore any contract entered into by him is null and void *ab initio*.

Capacity is generally governed by Family Law in Arab Islamic countries, but outlines of persons competent to contract are provided in the Civil codes. For the purposes of contract, the State, public departments or institutions, companies, corporate entities, private societies established by law, or any grouping of persons satisfying the legal properties of a judicial

---

[88] See Art.2 of the Egyptian Civil Code, promulgated by Law No.131 of 1948, effective as from 15 October 1949 : "If the author of the declaration dies, or becomes legally incapable before the declaration of intention takes effect, the declaration of intention shall be no less effective at the time it reaches the knowledge of the person for whom it was intended, unless the contrary is shown by the declaration of intention or by the nature of the transaction."

[89] The *Majella*, Art. 941 defines "interdiction" (*Ḥijr*) as "prohibiting any particular person from dealing with his own property". See Art. 85 (1) of the UAE Civil Code : "Every person who has reached the age of majority in possession of his mental powers and who has not been placed under a restriction, shall be of full capacity to exercise his rights laid down in this law and the laws deriving from it." The default in the Kuwaiti Civil Code is also of competency to contract subject to interdiction by the law on the grounds of incapacity or diminished capacity (Art. 84). Art. 13 of the Bahrain Contract Code reaffirms the presumption in favour of capacity: "Every person is competent who is of the age of majority and who is of sound mind, and is not disqualified from contracting."

person are given juristic personality and may therefore constitute a party to a contract.[90] Juridical persons enjoy all rights save those pertaining exclusively to the capacity of natural persons, within the limits laid down by the laws concerned.[91] Juridical persons must have a natural person to express their intentions,[92] and are subject to special laws pertaining to them, as detailed in the relevant sections of the codes.[93]

A provision which is expressed in the UAE Federal Civil Code, but which applies comprehensively elsewhere, is that no person may divest himself of his personal liberty or of his capacity, nor may he vary the concomitants thereof.[94]

4.1 Restrictions to Capacity

4.1.1 Majority

Every person entering into a contract must have reached the age of majority. Certain jurists[95] and modern legal systems[96] designate a specific age of majority, but most jurists specify that majority means having reached puberty. On the basis of a Qur'ānic verse[97] majority is linked to a manifestation of prudence (*Rushd*) but certain limited capacities may be granted to persons manifesting discernment or discretion (*Tamyīz*).[98] It was generally thought that prudence and puberty occurred at around the fifteenth year.[99] In any event, the minimum age of puberty was set at nine years for

---

90 Art. 92 UAE Federal Civil Code; See, also, the United Arab Emirates Federal Rule No.4 of 1980 'Regarding categorization of contractors', Arts. 1 and 2.

91 Art. 93 (1) and 93 (2) (b) of the UAE Civil Code

92 Art. 93 (3) of the UAE Civil Code

93 Art. 94 of the UAE Civil Code

94 Art. 89 of the UAE Civil Code

95 For example, Abū Ḥanīfa set the age of puberty to be seventeen. See Chafik Chehata, 'La Notion d'Incapacité en Droit Hanéfite' in *Études de Droit Musulman*, (Paris, 1971) pp.77-155; Brunschwig, R., 'Théorie Générale de la Capacité Chez Les Hanéfites Mediévaux', *Études d'Islamologie : Droit Musulman*, 2 (1976) pp.37-52; Tyan, E., 'La Condition Juridique de 'l'Absent' (*Mafkud*) en droit Musulman, Particulièrement dans le Madhab Hanéfite', *Studia Islamica*, 31 (1970) pp.249-256

96 Dubai Contract Law of 1971, Art.13 : "Every person is competent to contract who is of the age of majority according to the law to which he is subject..."

97 *Qur'ān*, (IV : 5) : "Make a trial of the orphans until they reach marriageable age. If you are then accustomed to their acting with prudence, hand over their property to them." See also the *Majella*, Arts. 968,981,982.

98 The Ottoman *Majella*, for instance, determines majority by whether a person is able to discern the difference between a sale and a purchase. (art.934).

99 Ibn Qudāma, *al-Mughnī*, *op.cit.*, IV, p.461

females and twelve for males.[100] All acts entered into by a minor are null and void, except where such acts are purely to the advantage of a minor of perfect understanding and which must be ratified by the guardian.[101] A minor of imperfect understanding may not make any valid disposition of his property even with his guardian's consent or ratification.[102]

Modern Legislation

The distinction between the age of majority and discretion is taken up by modern legislation in the Gulf states concerned.

Article 86 (1) of the Kuwaiti Civil Code states that a minor without discretion (*al-Ṣaghīr Ghayr al-Mumayyiz*) is without capacity; Article 86 (2) determines that any minor under seven years of age will be considered as being without discretion. Discerning minors may only enter into obligations which are beneficial to their maintenance (*Nafaqa*).[103] A discerning minor is so considered from the age of distinction (*Tamyīz*), which is determined subjectively in each case, until he reaches the age of prudence (*Rushd*) in males and females alike. At the age of fifteen years, a discerning minor has the capacity to conclude a contract of work (so long as it does not exceed one year), and to dispose of his salary awarded for that work, or any other benefit derived from it.[104] This salary may, however, be confiscated by the court on request of the parent, guardian or any other person with a vested interest in that minor's welfare.[105] At the age of eighteen years, a minor with discretion may establish a bequest.[106]

The age of prudence (*Rushd*) is reached when, at eighteen years, the minor's guardian discerns that he is capable of handling his own affairs and gives permission so to do.[107] This permission may be either absolute or restricted[108] and may be withdrawn once given, or further restricted after having been granted.[109] Permission, withdrawal or restriction is made in the

---

100 *The Hedaya*, (transl. Charles Hamilton), *op.cit*, Bk.XXXV, p.530

101 Maḥmaṣānī, *al-Naẓarīyya al-'āmma li al-Mūjibāt wa al-'Uqūd Fī al-Sharī'a al-Islāmīyya*, II, p.104

102 See the *Majella*, Art.966; and The Civil Code of Kuwait, Law No. 68 of 1980 (Law No. 1335, issued 29 Ṣafar 1401 AH; Law No. 2 of Jan 5, 1981)

103 Arts. 87 (1) and 93 (1) Kuwaiti Civil Code

104 Kuwaiti Civil Code, Art. 94 (1)

105 *ibid.*, Art. 94 (2)

106 *ibid.*, Art. 95

107 *ibid.*, Art. 88 (1)

108 *ibid.*, Art. 88 (2)

109 *ibid.*, Art.89

presence of an official witness.[110]

The court has the power to grant full or limited capacity to a minor upon request, if such capacity once given by a guardian has been withdrawn, if it determines that the grounds for the withdrawal by the guardian were baseless.[111] If the court so declines, the minor must wait for one year before he may resubmit his application.[112] A minor thus permitted (*Ṣaghīr Ma'dhūn*) is allowed to dispose of his affairs only within the bounds of that permission.[113] He is not, for instance, pemitted to lease out his property for periods exceeding one year.

Every person who has achieved *Rushd* has full capacity to enter into legal transactions so long as there is no judicial order that his guardianship or custody should continue.[114] The natural legal presumption of *Rushd* is at the age of twenty-one years in the kuwaiti jurisdiction.[115]

The position in the UAE Civil Code is similar. A minor lacking in discretion is competent to exercise his civil rights,[116] and every minor under the age of seven is considered not to have reached the age of discretion.[117] From the age of discretion until the age of majority, which Article 85 (2) sets at twenty-one lunar years, the minor is considered of defective capacity. Minors, be they male or female, are subject to the relevant laws concerning guardianship, tutelage and custody as set out fully in the respective provisions of the Civil Code.[118]

Neither the Bahrain Law of Contract and the Dubai Contract Law of 1971[119] define the age of majority, nor do they make the Islamic distinction between minors with discretion and minors without discretion.[120]

4.1.2 Sound Mind

The quality of a sound mind or prudence (*Rushd*) is a condition for contractual capacity. A lunatic (*Ma'tūh* or *Majnūn*), prodigal spendthrift (*Safīh*) or negligent person (*Dhū al-Ghafla*) is considered lacking in

110 *ibid.*, Art. 90

111 *ibid.*, Art.91 (1)

112 *ibid.*, Art. 91(2)

113 *ibid.*, Art. 92

114 *ibid.*, Art. 96 (1)

115 *ibid.*, Art. 96 (2)

116 UAE Civil Code, Law No. 67 of 1980, Art. 86 (1)

117 *ibid.*, Art. 86 (2)

118 *ibid.*, Art. 88

119 Article 13 in both Codes.

120 This is because they are both based on English Law, rather than the Islamic Fiqh.

discernment (*Tamyīz*) and therefore any act entered into by them is null and void (*Bāṭil*). Ibn Qudāma defines prudence in a person as the "protective safekeeping of his property and sound organization of his business."[121] The latter part of this definition assumed a more important sense for the purpose of determining whether a person was prudent, for a sound commercial sense took priority over moral probity or religious devoutness unless both were inextricably appropriate.[122] Whereas a *Majnūn*, who is characterised by abnormal and irrational behaviour is interdicted from entering into any valid contract, a *Ma'tūh* (partially or temporarily insane) is recognised as having lucid periods during which he is allowed to enter into certain valid transactions on a par with the discerning minor.

The concept of interdiction in these cases is based on voluntary will which is assumed to be non-existent in both minors and those of unsound mind. Similarly, the interdiction is imposed upon the spendthrift (Safīh), who is characterised by wasteful extravagance in commercial dealings. In this case, however, it is the duty of the court to assess the behaviour of a spendthrift, and to impose the interdiction upon him at its discretion. In the previous categories the incapacity is regarded as self-evident.

The *Fiqh* also provides that in similar situations to the *Ma'tūh*, where the will is temporarily absent, such as drunkenness, sleep and unconsciousness, no legal effect is to be given to any words or undertakings pronounced.[123] Drunkenness is a controversial issue with the *Fuqahā'*, due to the Qur'ānic prohibition of *Khamr*, and the *Fiqh*'s consequent analogous prohibition of alcohol.[124] The Ḥanafīs therefore distinguish between accidental and volontary drunkenness, giving legal effect to the acts entered into in the latter case in a moralistic attitude of just sanction.[125] The Mālikīs regard acts or declarations pronounced in a state of drunkenness as non-obligatory subject to later ratification; the Shāfi'īs and Ḥanbalīs consider them null or also void, subject to later ratification.[126]

---

[121] Ibn Qudāma, *al-Mughnī, op.cit.*, IV, p.456

[122] *idem.*, p.467

[123] Muḥammad Yūsuf Mūsā, *Naẓariyyat al-'Aqd, op.cit.*, p.332; See also Art.127 of the Draft Civil Code of Egypt, 1949

[124] *Qur'ān*, (II:219), (IV:43), (V:90-91).

[125] Ibn Nujaym, *al-Ashbāh, op.cit.*, p.124

[126] Maḥmaṣānī, *al-Naẓarīyya al-'Amma li al-Mūjibāt wa al-'Uqūd Fī al-Sharī'a al-Islāmīyya, op.cit.*, II, P.156. For discussion of the confusion regarding this tenet in the modern constitution of the UAE, see Ballantyne, *Commercial Law in the Arab Middle East: The Gulf States*, (London, 1986) pp.61-64

Modern Legislation

According to Article 97 (1) of the Kuwaiti Civil Code the *Majnūn* is devoid of all capacity, and all transactions entered into by him are void. If the madness is not absolute and the transaction takes place in a period of sanity then it is valid.[127] The *Ma'tūh* is governed according to the rules applicable to the discerning minor.[128] The madness or insanity of a person may be known or may be so determined by court judgment (Art. 100).

The transactions of the *Safīh* or *Dhū al-Ghafla* will, after determination of the judgment, be treated in the same way as the minor without discernment.[129] Any transactions arising from these persons before they are judged or proclaimed *Safīh* or *Dhū al-Ghafla* are neither *Bāṭil* nor voidable except where they have been concluded in collusion with the anticipation of the restriction, that is fraudulently, and with knowledge of the impending lack of capacity.

The *Safīh* or *Dhū al-Ghafla* may validly make *Waqf* or bequest dispositions if the court gives authority so to do.[130] The court has the power to give absolute or limited authorisation to a *Safīh* or *Dhū al-Ghafla* to handle his own affairs whether wholly, or in part. In special cases it may require the *Safīh* or *Dhū al-Ghafla* to give account of his affairs.[131] The court may also restrain or withdraw this authorisation if it sees just grounds for so doing.[132] Judgments so issued by the court are published according to a decision of the Minister of Justice.[133]

A *Safīh* who has been given permission to administer his affairs has capacity to enter into transactions within the bounds of that permission set by the court specifically for him.[134] He may also dispose of property in the interests of his own maintenance, in the same way as a discerning minor.[135] On request by the *Safīh*, his custodian, or anyone else with his interests at heart, the court may dispose of whatever is considered necessary for his

---

127 Kuwaiti Civil Code, Art. 98 (2)

128 Kuwaiti Civil Code, Art. 99. Rules for the discerning minor are contained in Art.87. See *Supra*.

129 *ibid.*, Art.101 (1); For Minor without discernment, see *ibid.*, Art. 87 *supra*.

130 *ibid.*, Art.102

131 *ibid.*, Art.103 (1)

132 *ibid.*, Art.103 (2)

133 *ibid.*, Art.103 (3)

134 *ibid.*, Art.104

135 *ibid.*, Art. 105 (1); For discerning minor, see Art.93

maintenance.[136] If the court has serious grounds for believing that the *Safīh* is squandering his assets, it may impound his access to those assets and entrust the administration of them to a party who will best determine the necessary expenditures from them on the *safīh* and his family.[137]

Like the Discerning minor, the *safīh* has the capacity to enter into a contract of employment, and to dispose of his salary, whether it be in cash or otherwise, within the same bounds as laid down in Article 94 in relation to the discerning minor.[138]

In the UAE Civil Code, Articles 85 and 86 (1) preclude an imbecile or insane person from exercising his civil rights on the grounds of defective consent. These persons are subject to similar law provisions as detailed in the Kuwaiti code. Persons who have reached the age of majority, but who have been proclaimed idiots or of unsound mind are also considered to have defective capacity under the law.[139] Similarly, they are subject to the relevant provisions laid down by the law.

In Bahrain, the natural presumption is of sound mind.[140] Sound mind is defined as being when, at the time of the contract a party is capable of understanding the contract and of forming a rational judgment as to its effect on his interests.[141] Therefore, a person who is usually of unsound mind but who is occasionally of sound mind, and who is lucid at the time of contracting, is considered to have transacted competently for the purpose of that specific disposition.[142] Similarly, in reverse, a person who is usually of sound mind but is occasionally of unsound mind, and who has contracted during a period of insanity, is considered to have acted without effective consent.[143] The ruling applies in a like manner to topics : A person of unsound mind may only make valid transactions in conjunction with those topics of which he has adequate comprehension, in that his mind is sound concerning them.[144]

In Western laws, the concept of unsound mind is not generally held to cover the issue of "death sickness". This concept does, however, often appear in the Arabic legal treaties under this heading, and for this reason,

---

136 *ibid.*, Art.105 (2)

137 *ibid.*, Art.105 (3)

138 *ibid.*, Art.106

139 UAE Civil Code, Art. 87

140 Bahrain Contract Law, Art. 13

141 *ibid.*, Art.14 (1)

142 *ibid.*, Art.14 (2)

143 *ibid.*, Art.14 (3)

144 *ibid.*, Art.14 (4)

the 'incapacity' caused by death sickness, and its effects will be treated under this heading, here.

In the Kuwaiti Civil Code, a sale made by a person with death sickness is governed by Articles 519 and 942 (relating to bequests made in Death Sickness). Nevertheless, Article 942 is not effective as against a third party of good intention when that third party has taken possession of the object for good compensation. In the UAE Code, *Marḍ al-Mawt* is defined as "an illness wherein a person cannot go about his normal business and in which the greater probability is that he will die in that condition prior to the expiration of one year".[145] *Marḍ al-Mawt* in according to this code also includes situations in which people fear death, and in which they normally die, notwithstanding that they may not, in fact, be sick.[146] This is an extension to the theories formulated by the earlier jurists, and is clearly susceptible to specific interpretation by the court in consideration of the facts of the case at issue. Certain difficulties may arise in relation to dispositions made by a person during what has been considered to be a death sickness and which have been challenged and annulled within a year. If that illness continues without deterioration beyond the year's course, may those dispositions be retroactively invalidated ?

According to UAE law, a sale of property by a person suffering from death Sickness to his heirs, or to a stranger for good compensation, or which comprises only a 'slight' element of cheating is deemed valid, and does not depend on the consent of the heirs, as would normally be the case.[147] If in such a sale, however, the price is less than the value of the object at the time of death, the sale is only effective as against the heirs if the excess amount of the value of the object does not exceed one third of the estate, including the object sold.[148] If the price difference is greater than the one third, the sale is not effective unless the heirs themselves affirm it, or the purchaser makes up two thirds of the value of the object. Otherwise, the heirs have the right to cancel the sale.[149] This rule applies to any sale made in death sickness, whether for good compensation or with slight disadvantage to the seller or obligees, when the debt exceeds the estate. The purchaser who wished such a sale to proceed may pay the true price, failing

---

[145] UAE Civil Code, Art. 597 (1): If his illness continues for more than a year, even and he remains in the same condition without getting worse, any dispositions made by that person are treated as those of a healthy person.

[146] UAE Civil Code, Art. 597 (2)

[147] UAE Civil Code, Art. 599: subject to Art. 600 below.

[148] *idem.*, Art. 599 (2)

[149] *idem.*, Art. 599 (3)

which the obligees shall have the right to cancel the sale.[150] If, however, the purchaser in such a case has disposed of the goods in such a way as to confer a right against consideration upon a third party acting in good faith, the sale may not be cancelled.[151] In such a case, it is permissible for the obligees of an estate which has been rendered insufficient to meet its debts to have recourse against the purchaser for the difference between the price and the value of the object, and the heirs shall have that right if the purchaser is one of them. If however, the purchaser is a stranger, then he must return such sum as will make up two thirds of the value of the object sold to the estate.

4.1.3 Legal Interdictions in the Interests of Third Parties

The *Fiqh* has set aside certain situations, where in the interests of relatives or third parties, a person is interdicted from disposing of his property.[152] Such dispositions made are suspended (*Mawqūf*) subject to ratification by the third parties concerned. The third party may confirm or annul the disposition. In the latter case the act becomes null and void.[153]

(1) **The Insolvent** (*al-Muflis*) : is interdicted from disposing of his property by the judge in the interests of his creditors.[154]

(2) **A person ill with Death Sickness** : Death Sickness is defined in the *Majella* as a "sickness where in the majority of cases death is imminent, and, in the case of a male, where such person is unable to deal with his affairs outside his home, and in the case of a female, where she is unable to deal with her domestic duties, death having occurred before the expiration of one year by reason of such illness, whether the sick person has been confined to bed or not."[155] Dispositions during Death Sickness are interdicted in the interests of the person's heirs or creditors.

---

150 *idem.*, Art. 600

151 UAE Civil Code, Art. 601 (1); Kuwaiti Civil Code, Art. 942

152 The jurists of the Ḥanafī and Mālikī schools

153 The Ḥanbalīs and Shāfi'īs do not recognise the right of the interested third person to ratify. They declare such acts by insolvents or persons in death sickness as null and void.

154 Sanhūrī, *Maṣādir al-Ḥaqq, op.cit.*, V, pp.180-192

155 *Majella*, Art.1595; For Death Sickness generally, see Hasan Kabalan, 'La Maladie de la Mort et la Peur de la Mort en Droit Musulman (Selon l'École Ḥanafīte)', 2 *Revue Judicaire Libanaise*, 33; and Fyzee, *Outlines of Muhammedan Law*, (3rd Ed.: London 1964) pp.363-365; Bellefonds, *Traité, op.cit.*, pp.262-277.

(3) **Virgin Mālikī Females** : Unmarried Mālikī women are considered as lacking full discernment. A Mālikī virgin girl is therefore interdicted from disposing of her property until she is married and has consummated that marriage.[156]

(4) **Miscellaneous Interdictions** : Mention must also be made here of the restriction imposed upon a pledgor disposing of a pledge before the pledgee has defaulted, for this would nullify the legal rights of the pledgee.

Similarly, city dwellers are not allowed to act as agents selling agricultural produce on behalf of country people, in the fear that the latter class would be prejudiced due to their ignorance of true market prices.[157] This is seen by some modern authors as an early attempt at consumer protection to prevent traders from cornering the market in basic foodstuffs in times of scarcity.[158]

Modern Legislation

The Kuwaiti Civil Code (Art. 107 (1)) determines that if a person suffers from a physical disability, such that it is difficult for him to be conversant with the circumstances of contracting; or if it is difficult for him to express his intention, especially if he is deaf and dumb, blind and deaf, or blind and dumb, the court may assign him a legal assistant who will co-operate in the transaction and see that his best interests are served. The assignment made by the court will be published to this effect.[159]

A court may also allow such legal assistants to operate single-handedly, by deputisation, when it determines that because of his difficulty in entering into transactions caused by some physical disability, the best interests of that party would be endangered by not transacting in a matter.[160]

Neither the UAE Civil Code nor the Bahrain Contract Law specifiy further defects to capacity as contained in the *Fiqh* or the respective articles referring to those persons 'not disqualified from contracting'.[161]

---

156 Ibn Qudāma, *al-Mughnī, op.cit.*, IV, p.463. This rule derives from Mālikī marriage principles, for which, see Pearl, *A Textbook on Muslim Law*, (London, 1979) p.44

157 See Khalīl's *Code Musulman*, (Transl. N. Seignette) *op.cit.*, p.90

158 See D.J. Hill and Abulbakar Sadiq Abbas, 'Comparative Survey of the Islamic Law and the Common Law Relating to the Sale of Goods,' in *Journal of Islamic and Comparaitve Law*, Vol.2 (1968), p.92

159 Kuwait Civil Code, Art.107 (2)

160 *ibid.*, Art.109

161 Such as UAE Civil Code, Art. 88; and Bahrain Contract Law, Art. 13

5. OBJECT OF CONTRACT (*AL-MA'QŪD ALAYH*)

The importance attached by the *Fuqahā'* to the concept of object by their detailed regulations, is explained partly by moral and religious considerations, and partly by their preoccupation with maintaining the balance between the diverse effects resulting from legal acts in conjunction with their efforts to prevent all aleatory or usurious transactions.[162]

The law of contract is based around the concept of Property (*al-Māl*).[163] Most schools require four conditions concerning the object which must be satisfied to effect a valid contract. These are : Legality; Existence; the property of being deliverable; and precise determination.[164]

5.1 Legality

The first is that the object must be legal (*Mubāḥ*), in that it is beneficial,[165] that it is a commodity capable of being traded in (*Māl Mutaqawwim*),[166] that its subject matter (*Maḥall*) and underlying cause (*Sabab*) are lawful,[167] and that it is not proscribed by Islamic law, public order or morals.[168]

Modern legislation governing legality of the object[169] states that property consists of "anything not forbidden by a provision of the law or contrary to public policy or morals."[170] The primary sources present a series of religious

---

162 Bellefonds, *Traité*, *op.cit.*, p.184

163 Schacht equivelates *Māl* to *Res in Commercio*, See his *Introduction*, (Oxford, 1979) p.134. The term *al-Māl* includes benefits derived from property and certain acts or services.

164 Sanhūrī, *Maṣādir al-Ḥaqq*, *op.cit.*, III, pp.13-111. The *Majella* also gives four conditions : Arts. 197-200; but See Kāsānī, *Badā'i' al-Ṣanā'i'*, *op.cit.*, V, p.138, who only gives three: Existence, legality and being capable of delivery.

165 See Article 208 of the Federal Civil Code of the UAE. The existence of such benefit is presumed unless there are indications to the contrary.

166 *Māl* has been defined as "[a]ll that has a commercial value"; or "[w]hose corporeal, usufructury and other rights of any kind the exchange of which is customary are to be regarded as property (*Māl*) of commercial value". Anderson, 'Islamic Law and Structural Variations in Property Law', *International Encyclopoedia of Comparative Law*, 2, (1975) at 103. For examples, see Chapter 6.1 'The Unlawful Object' below.

167 See, for example, Kuwait Civil Code, Art. 167: "The subject matter (*Maḥall*) of the obligation, out of which the contract arises, must be possible *in esse*. If it is not, the contract is void (*Bāṭil*)." And *idem.*, Art. 168.

168 See Khalīl's *Code Musulman*, (Transl. N.Seignette), *op.cit.*, p.13

169 Kuwait Civil Code, Arts. 167-175; UAE Civil Code, Art. 126; Bahrain Contract Law, Art. 12 (1).

170 UAE Federal Civil Code, Arts. 126 (d) and 205 (2); cf. Bahrain Contract Law, Art. 27 (1) and (2). See also Article 129 (b) which states that certain property may be prescribed as possible and lawfully dealt in.

prescriptions as to illegal substances, which must be included in contemplation of legal objects. These are listed in detail in the next chapter.[171] The object must be of use, in that the contract must contain lawful benefit to both contracting parties, whether it is a commodity or a service. The example of useless objects given by the *Fuqahā'* is that of small animals and vermin (*Ḥasharāt*),[172] and the exchange of a coin for a coin of the same value. Other examples overlap with the concept of inexistence and will be dealt with there. The presumption is that a contract will be held "to contain such lawful benefit unless there is evidence to the contrary."[173]

'Public policy or morals' would be likely to include, where specific mention is not made, any object, motivating purpose or underlying cause which the court may deem illegal. Such would be the case in, for instance, aleatory operations,[174] or contracts with immoral aims, where the court would look to the legal implications of the contract rather than the material object itself.[175] Bellefonds points up the variability of the notion of 'morally illicit' between the schools, depending on locality, customs and the particular era concerned. Originally, for instance, in Ḥanafī law it was prohibited to receive remuneration for teaching the Qur'ān or the *Fiqh*, or for directing prayers. With time, the Ḥanafī doctrine adopted the stance of the Shāfi'ī School in that a salary could be stipulated for these duties.[176]

The object of a contract may also constitute benefits derived from property, or a particular act or service.[177]

The contract must be lawful in its cause (*Sabab*). The term *Sabab* is rather a difficult concept to define satisfactorily : it is frequently mistranslated thereby confusing it with the distinguished concept of *Maḥall*. The UAE Civil Code defines *Sabab* as "the direct purpose aimed at by the

---

171 See Chapter 6.1 (p.155) on 'Nullities: Islamic Prohibited Commodities' *infra*.

172 Shīrāzī, *Kitāb al-Tanbīh Fī al-Fiqh*, (Ed. A.W.T. Juynboll; Leyden, 1879) p.95; Bellefonds, *Traité*, p.195.

173 UAE Civil Code, Art. 208 (2); see also Art. 208 (1)

174 Kuwait Civil Code, Art. 173; UAE Civil Code, Art. 204.

175 Bellefonds, *Traité*, *op.cit.*, p. 201 N.244. Although in some cases this may be circumvented by contractual clauses or special cases which apply to certain contracts (Art. 128 (2) UAE Civil Code). Under Article 2 of the Provisional Federal Constitution of the UAE, and Arts. 7 and 27 of the Civil Code, it would also presumably preclude contractual provisions which can be construed as contrary to the Sharī'a, although the extent of this argument is yet to be seen.

176 Bellefonds, *Traité*, pp.201-201, N. 245.

177 For example, UAE Civil Code No. 2 of 1987, Art. 126

contract", whereas *Maḥall* corresponds to the French *objet*,[178]

5.2 Right to Title

Inherent in the legality of the object is the condition that a person may not deliver into another's possession or transfer the right of ownership to a third party of, an object of which he is not himself the owner, without the authorisation of its legal owner or by virtue of delegated powers conferred upon him by that owner.[179]

5.3 Existence of the Object

The second principle governing the object of a contract is that the object must be in existence at the time of the contract. It is therefore illegal to sell the foetus of an animal before its birth, or the fruit which has not yet appeared on the tree.[180] Such sales are evidently contrary to the rule that the object of the contract should be in existence. Abū Dāwūd recites an *Ḥadīth* that Ibn Ḥazm asked the Prophet : "A man asked me to sell him something that I did not have; Should I go and buy it from the market?" The Prophet replied : "Do not sell what you do not have."[181]

The principle of Existence of the object becomes mitigated by the authorisation of *Salam* and *Istiṣnā'* contracts which provide respectfully for future provision of goods and future manufacture of goods. It follows that when the object of a contract is an actual thing it must be in existence at the time of the contract; but where the object is a provision, a promise to deliver or to manufacture, then the object of that promise does not have to be in existence at the time of the contract, but must be possible and defined, or capable of being defined and permissible.

The UAE Civil Code, which is generally the most 'Islamic' of the three Codes under study, recognises an agreement to contract in the future, so long as all of the essential matters of the intended contract, and the period within which it is to be made are specified.[182]

---

[178] UAE Civil Code, Art. 207 (1); See also Arts. 129 (c) and 207 (2). *Maḥall* is covered by the Kuwaiti Civil Code in Arts. 167-175, but other than stating that the motivating purpose must be possible *in esse*, this code provides no definition of the term. Mention is not made of the term in the Bahrain Contract Law, and 'lawful object' is translated into the Arabic as *li-Ghāyat mashrū'a* (for a legal purpose) - a complete divergence from the language of *Fiqh*-derived codes.

[179] Shāfi'ī, *Kitāb al-Umm*, (7 Vols.; Cairo, 1321-1326), vol. III, p.13; Henri Laoust, *Le Précis de Droit d'Ibn Qudāma*, (Beirut, 1950), Bk. VII, p.93;

[180] H. Laoust, *Le Précis de Droit d'Ibn Qudāma, op.cit.*, p.94. See Chapter on Nullities, *infra*.

[181] Abū Dāwūd al-Sijistānī, *al-Sunan*, (Cairo n.d.) 4 Vols; III, no. 3503.

[182] Art. 129 (b) of the UAE Civil Code.

5.3.1 Salam Contract

The term *Salam* forms the irregular verbal noun of the fourth declension of the Arabic root *Salima*, meaning 'to deliver up'. The term means 'advance payment'[183] or 'forward buying'.[184] Formally authorised by the Prophet,[185] the *Salam* contract is the sale of a thing which will be delivered to the purchaser on a future date. That future date must be set at the time of the contract.[186]

The requirement of the *Sharī'a* that a contract must be fulfilled within three days is impracticable in the case of the manufacture of a large quantity of goods. The *Salam* contract, by making payment in advance to secure an option on the goods to be made, therefore proved a likely expedient for evasion of onerous regulations.

Conditions of such future sales are that the goods must not be in existence or must be incapable of delivery at the time of contracting; full consideration must be paid, or the rate fixed at the time of concluding the contract.[187] Failure to do so results in a contract which is null and void. A *Salam* contract is also void if the buyer's consideration is in the form of a set-off, or negation of an existing debt.[188]

The jurists affixed the condition that the fungible object of a *salam* sale must be precisely determined as to quantity, quality and specific ascertainment. Non-fungibles such as precious stones, valuable paintings, animals and so on, which are unique, cannot by their nature comply with the condition of determination and are therefore not permitted to form the

---

183 Jazīrī, *Kitāb al-Fiqh, op.cit.*, p.303

184 Wehr, *A Dictionary of Modern Written Arabic*, (ed. J.M. Cowan : 3rd Edn.; New York, 1976), p. 425. For some extraordinary reason Furuqi does not include the term in his *Law Dictionary*, (3rd Edn.; Beirut, 1986)

185 See Ibn Qudāma, *al-Mughnī, op.cit.*, IV, p.275 ff; Kāsānī, *al-Badā'i', op.cit.*, V, pp.201-215; Marghīnānī, *al-Hidāya, op.cit.*, III, p.53 ff. See also T.W. Juynboll's article 'Salam', in *Encyclopaedia of Islam*, (London, 1934), p.89

186 The *Salam* contract does not compare with the Roman Law principle of *Res Speratae*, where the risk of future goods is immediately transferred to the buyer. Such a concept would be prohibited on the principle of uncertainty in Islamic Law.

187 Mālikī law permits consideration which is to be paid in kind (as opposed to cash), to be paid at a fixed term rather than immediately, but this is usually distinguished as a contract of *Mutuum* or the loan for use of goods. See Khalīl's *Code Musulman*, (Transl. N. Seignette), *op.cit.*, p.324 Cf. Santillana *Instituzioni di Diritto Musulmano Malechita, op.cit.*, II, p.171. Coulson states that a three-day grace period is allowed for full payment if the parties so agree: *Commercial Law, op.cit.*, p.21; See also Hill and Abbas, 'Comparative Survey of the Islamic Law and the Common Law Relating to the Sale of Goods', 2 *Journal of Islamic and comparative Law*, (1986) at p.97

188 Hill and Abbas, 'Comparative Survey of the Islamic Law and the Common Law Relating to the Sale of Goods', *op.cit.*, at p.97

objects of *salam* sales.[189] Property passes in a *Salam* sale at the time of delivery; risk therefore generally stays with the seller until the affixed term for delivery.[190]

The purchaser in a *Salam* contract, by his right of option of Inspection, may reject the goods on sight if they do not concord with their description at the time of contracting.[191]

The *Salam* contract is recognised in the Federal Civil Code of the UAE.[192] Article 129 (b) states that contracts for future consideration are valid providing that any uncertainty as to the essential details of the transaction is avoided. Therefore, the property must be such as can be specified by description and quantity; it must normally be available at the time of delivery;[193] and the contract must contain particulars of the nature, type, description and amount of the goods, and the time at which they are to be delivered.[194] Similarly, the price must be ascertained, both in amount and in the particular currency. The code expressly stipulates that a deferment of the price must not exceed three days,[195] and it must not consist of *ribawī* commodities, such as foodstuffs or money as against themselves.[196] A transaction involving the estate of a person not yet demised is not permitted to constitute the object of such a contract. This would contravene the rules governing object of contract.[197]

The Code specifically allows the buyer to dispose of the object of a contract by way of a Salam contract before taking possession of it.[198] This article therefore opens the door wide to such futures and stock market contracts as are in practice in contemporary commerce. It presumably also licences the buyer to buy spot commodities and sell them again, in other words, to engage in successive *Salam* sales, without ever having taken

---

189 Kāsānī, *al-Badā'i'*, *op.cit.*, V, p.201 f.

190 Except in the case of live animals, where risk passes to the purchaser at the time of the contract, subject to his right of recourse against the seller if the latter or a third party are at fault in case of loss or damage. See Khalīl's *Code Musulman*, (Transl. N. Seignette) *op.cit.*, p.319

191 Shīrāzī, *Kitāb al-Tanbīh*, *op.cit.*, pp.107-109; see Chapter on 'Options' *infra*, Section 5.

192 Article 568 defines *Salam* as 'for property the delivery of which is deferred, against a price payable immediately'.

193 UAE Civil Code, Art.569 (1)

194 *ibid.*, Art. 569 (2)

195 *ibid.*, Art. 570

196 *ibid.*, Art. 575

197 Ballantyne, 'The New Civil Code of the United Arab Emirates: A Further Reassertion of the Shari'a', *Arab Law Quarterly*, vol. I (3) (May 1986) pp.262-263

198 UAE Federal Civil Code, Art. 571

delivery of them.

The seller must deliver the goods to the purchaser, at the due term, at the place agreed in the contract, or if no place was specified, then at the place where the contract was made. Neither party is bound to deliver or take delivery of the goods at any other place, unless there is agreement to the contrary.[199]

Unlike the Classical stance on the subject, a condition of the UAE Code is that the impossibility of delivery of the object of a *Salam* contract at the due time, gives rise to an option to the buyer to wait until such time as the object becomes available, or to cancel the sale.[200] In the Classical law, the contract would be avoided for lack of a principle of the contract, namely, existence and delivery of the object. There has never been any obstacle, however, to the parties cancelling the first contract and making a second with a different term of delivery.

If the goods cease to exist after the buyer has received any part of them, he must wait for the remainder, unless the parties have come to a *pro rata* agreement,[201] or an agreement to supply goods of a like nature, or of a different nature subject to certain conditions.[202]

The incidence of *Istighlāl*, or fraud against a farmer in a *Salam* contract for produce may be adjusted by the court at the time of payment.[203] The other party is not bound, however, to accept the court's ruling and may instead recover the actual price paid to the seller, which releases the seller from that contract.[204] Any agreement or conditional clause purporting to nullify this right is null and void.[205]

If the seller dies before the term of delivery, the other party is afforded an Option to cancel the contract or to recover the price from the estate; he may also wait until the term, placing a restriction upon the estate to the amount due, or securing a guarantee of delivery from the heirs for the due date.[206]

---

199 *ibid.*, Art. 578

200 *ibid.*, Arts. 572, 576 (1). Moreover, in contracts of *Salam* dependent on the object appearing by a certain date, such as crops, the buyer must wait until the second appearance, if the delay in delivery is attributable to him.

201 *ibid.*, Art. 576 (2)

202 *ibid.*, Art. 577 : namely, (a) the substituted consideration must be exchanged immediately; (b) the substituted object must be as can properly form the subject of a *Salam* Sale; (c) the substitute must not be foodstuffs.

203 *ibid.*, Art. 574 (1)

204 *ibid.*, Art. 574 (2)

205 *ibid.*, Art. 574 (3)

206 *ibid.*, Art. 573

Where dispute arises as to the quantity of goods, or period of deferred payment, and neither party has independent evidence of the contract,[207] the benefit of the doubt is given to the party alleging the cutomary practice. Where such cannot be established, a compromise position is to be arrived at.[208] If it is the place of delivery which forms the subject of dispute, the party alleging delivery at the place of the *Majlis* is preferred. Where neither party so alleges, the place shall be the customary market place for those goods in the *Majlis* locality.[209]

5.3.2 Contract of Istiṣ nā ‘

The *Istiṣnā‘* contract is a contract in which the purchaser charges the seller to manufacture an object. In this contract no specification of time for delivery or passing of consideration is required.[210] The *Istiṣnā‘* contract defied the concept of *Qiyās* but came about by virtue of the concept of *Istiḥsān*. The reason for this was that analogy with the contract to deliver did not work because an object of the latter contract exists at the time of the contract, whereas the article to be manufactured does not. The equitable concept of *Istiḥsān* has, however, provided for the legality of a contract to manufacture, due to its practical necessity, by giving the object a fictional existence at the time of the contract.

An exception to the general rule of Existence of the Object is the sale of fruits which have appeared on the tree, but have not ripened and are not therefore in a state of immediate use at the time of the contract. This is unanimously considered a valid sale on the condition that the crops or fruit are harvested immediately so as to avoid the element of uncertainty.[211] In a similar case where harvesting is not immediate, the Shāfi‘īs, Mālikīs and Ḥanbalīs declare the sale null and void, basing their argument on the *Ḥadīth* by Bukhārī : "Do not sell the fruits before they have begun to ripen

---

207 Contrary to the Tradition of the Prophet which exhorts the recording of contracts to be made in the future. This will obviously not apply to certain commercial contracts requiring registration at a notary public. In Broking agencies, however, the only evidence of purchases are unnamed tickets, and these are therefore, theoretically at least, liable to dispute.

208 *ibid.*, Art. 579 (1)

209 *ibid.*, Art. 579 (2)

210 Kāsānī, *al-Badā'i'*, *op.cit*, V, p.2 ; and *The Mejelle*, (Transl. Tyser *et al*; Cyprus, 1901) p.53

211 Ibn Qudāma, *al-Mughnī*, *op.cit.*, vol.IV, p.81 f. sets out the arguments applied by the different schools.

[*Ṣalāḥ*]."[212] These schools declare any contract of this sort to be null when it either carries a clause stipulating that the fruit are to be left in their original state, or when it does not carry the clause that the fruit are to be harvested immediately. The Ḥanafī jurist Shaybānī regards the sale of unripe fruit before harvesting as perfectly valid by *Istiḥsān* and all the *Fatāwā* emanating from the Ḥanafī school conform to this opinion.[213] Abū Ḥanīfa himself and his disciple, Abū Yūsuf, however, declared *contra* this view that the sale would not be valid by analogical deduction.

The Ḥanbalī authors Ibn Taymiyya and his disciple Ibn Qayyim al-Jawziyya exclude the principle that the object must be in existence from their conditions of contract on the grounds that existence is encompassed by other conditions such as that of immediate delivery and precise determination of the object.[214] Ibn Taymiyya refutes any submission that the primary sources require this condition, and attributes the prohibitions of non-possessory sales to the Qur'ānic condemnation of aleatory contracts. He argues that if an object of a contract is capable of immediate delivery or is precisely determined in the minds of the contracting parties, it is of little significance whether the object actually exists at the time of the contract, and that exceptions will be encompassed by the rules governing *Salam*, *Istiṣnā'* and other contracts specifically permitted by *Qiyās*, *Istiṣlāḥ* or *Istiḥsān*.[215]

In modern legislation, *Istiṣnā'* contracts are generally explicitly recognised in provisions regulating commercial transactions. This is the case in Kuwait, where, for example, Article 120 of the Commercial Code states : "The sale of commercial goods which are not available at the time of contract but which may be prepared and made available at the time of delivery shall be valid."[216]

---

212 "Begun" is the operative word here, for it can be argued that a fruit begins to ripen as soon as it appears. The Prophet is reported to have defined *Ṣalāḥ* as "becoming red and yellow, that is, becoming edible." Cited in Bellefonds, *Traité*, *op.cit.*, p.190

213 see for example, *Majella*, Art.207

214 Ibn Taymiyya, *al-Qiyās Fī al-Shar' al-Islāmī*, (Cairo, n.d.) p.40; Laoust, *Contribution à Une Étude de la Méthodologie Canonique de Taki-d-Din Aḥmad B. Taimiya*, (Cairo, 1939) p.38

215 Bellefonds, *Traité*, *op.cit.*, p.191

216 The same provision is not included in the Bahraini Commercial Code (Law No. 7 of 1987). Nevertheless, it may be argued that the *Istiṣnā'* contract is implicitly permitted in the light of the role accorded to custom (and these contracts have become established according to commercial custom) and in accordance with Art. 2 (1) of the same code, which states that any commercial agreement will be valid so long as it does not contradict, firstly, what is agreed upon by the parties, and secondly, any relevant provision of law. See also Art 12 (1) of the Contract Law of Bahrain, 1969.

5.4 Certainty of Delivery

The third principle governing the object of a contract is that it must be capable of certain delivery. Where a contract consists of an obligation for performance, this performance must be capable of being executed immediately.[217] The classical jurists therefore prohibit the sale of a camel or slave which has fled, a bird in the air or a fish in water.[218] Likewise, a contract to perform a service which is not certainly possible such as an undertaking by a doctor to cure a person who is ill, is also void.[219] Bellefonds points out that the significance of this principle is directed at aleatory contracts rather than at implementing severe restrictions on the conditions and terms of a contract.[220] The overriding importance of all the conditions pertaining to the object is to prevent conflicts and unjustified profits arising out of uncertain or aleatory contracts. For this reason, the condition that the object must be capable of delivery or execution in Islamic law is also a judicial condition that the object must be in the ownership of the person intending to dispose of it, or that it must be capable of being performed.

5.5 Precise Determination of the Object

The final condition regarding the object of a contract is that it must be precisely determined as to its essence, its quantity and its value.[221] Similarly, where an object is an obligation of performance, it must be precisely determined as to its nature and its value.[222] In the case of benefits derived from property, acts, services or property not present at the time of contracting, the subject matter should be feasible and defined, or capable of definition and lawful.[223]

This is a principle which the *Fuqahā'* formulated in the interests of the parties, in order to prevent uncertainty and conflict between them in situations where a contract is rescinded or terminated for some cause, and either party is seeking a remedy. The principle has therefore received a great deal of attention from the jurists of all schools, and has been divided into

---

217 Kāsānī, *al-Badā'i'*, *op.cit.*, V, p.147; See also Articles 198, 209, 457, and 808 of the *Majella*.

218 Kāsānī, *al-Badā'i'*, *op.cit.*, V, p.147.

219 Ibn Ḥazm, *al-Muḥallā*, *op.cit.*, VIII, p.131

220 Bellefonds, *Traité*, *op.cit.*, p.192

221 Shīrāzī, *Kitāb al-Tanbīh*, *op.cit.*, p.95

222 Kāsānī, *al-Badā'i'*, *op.cit.*, V, p. 156 Shīrāzī, *al-Muhadhdhab*Fī Fiqh Madhhab al-Imām al-Shāfi'ī, 2 Vols. (Cairo, 1343 AH) I, p.262; Ibn Qudāma, *al-Mughnī*, *op.cit.*, IV, p. 29 f.

223 See UAE Civil Code, No. 2 of 1987, Art. 129 (b)

two categories. The first category is **Indetermination** which results in nullification (*Fāsid*) of the contract; the second is **non-serious Indetermination**, which does not affect the validity of the contract, but may be remedied by one of the parties under one or more of the various "Options of Recission" which were prescribed by the *Fiqh.*[224] Specifically relevant in this case, is the *Khiyār al-Ta'yīn* or 'Option of Determination', which is discussed in Chapter 7.3 *infra.*

With regard to the essence and quality of the object of contract, the determination given must be sufficient to render it distinguishable as the object. It is not therefore permissible to say "I will sell you one of the sheep from my flock", for this is insufficient description to distinguish the intended object (a sheep) from all other objects of that class (the rest of the sheep in the flock), and the contract would be considered *Fāsid.*

Article 203 (1) of the UAE Civil Code states : "In commutative contracts involving property, the subject matter must be specified in such a way as to avoid gross uncertainty by reference to it or to the place where it is located at the time of the contract, or a statement of its distinguishing characteristics and the amount thereof must be stated if it is measurable property or the like, so as to avoid gross uncertainty".

Goods sold in bulk are also subject to the condition of precise determination. Goods so sold must be viewed and their quantity must be at least capable of determination, even if that quantity is not known to the parties. There must be difficulties present in bulk sales which prevent the goods from being counted, weighed, or measured, and it must be customary for such goods not to be sold by the piece.[225] According to the Mālikī[226] and Ḥanafī schools[227] unseen goods cannot be sold in bulk. If inspected goods are sold in bulk, and only one of the parties to the contract has knowledge of the quantity involved, the party who is ignorant of the quantity will be able to rescind the contract by option upon discovery of his contractor's advantage.

According to the Ḥanafī and Mālikī schools, contracts concluded for goods which are not present or seen at the *Majlis*, are valid providing that a

---

224 See Sanhūrī, *Maṣādir al-Ḥaqq, op.cit.*, III, p.81, who compares the Islamic principles with those governing specific objects in the Western legal systems. See also 'The Islamic Rights of Option' Chapter 7 *infra.*

225 See Khalīl's *Code Musulman,* (Transl. N. Seignette), *op.cit.*, p.25

226 Khalīl's *Code Musulman,* (Transl. N. Seignette), *op.cit.*, pp.28-29

227 The Ḥanafī *Majella* states that if a price is specified for each part individually, the sale is valid. Thus a heap of grain unweighed can be sold for a stated price, unless a price has already been affixed for each unit of weight. See *The Mejelle,* (Transl. Tyser *et al*; Cyprus, 1901) p.26f.

precise description has been provided by the seller. Shīrāzī states that the Shāfi'ī school is divided in the matter of unseen commodities: One view is that such a sale is illegal; the other is that the sale is valid subject to the buyer's option of Inspection.[228] A description referring to an object of sale which is present and seen is of no consequence,[229] but the contrary applies when the object is not present at the *Majlis*. The *Majella* gives the example of a sale of a grey horse which is present at the *Majlis*, but which the seller refers to as brown. In such a case, the seller's offer is held to be good and the erroneous description is of no consequence. In the same circumstance where the horse is not present, and the seller refers to a grey horse as brown, the description is held to be satisfactory but the sale is not binding and the buyer is given the option of revoking the contract under the "Option of Inspection" (*Khiyār al-Ru'ya*).[230]

Similarly, where the seller describes goods to be sold as being of a certain quality, and the goods upon inspection prove to be of inferior quality or value, the Islamic abhorrence of unjustified enrichment allows for the purchaser to exercise an option, either to cancel the sale under the "Option of Misrepresentation", or to accept the goods for the whole of the fixed price.[231]

6. CONSIDERATION

Consideration in Islamic Law is not restricted to a monetary price, but may be in the form of another commodity. The Islamic prohibition against uncertainty requires that the price must be in existence and determined at the time of the contract and cannot be fixed at a later date with reference to the market price, nor can it be left subject to determination by a third party.[232] When the consideration consists of a monetary payment (as opposed to payment in kind), the jurists state that the currency must be in circulation and that its value and species must be determined exactly. In certain contracts such as money-changing (*Ṣarf*), a contract will be automatically declared null and void on the grounds of *Ribā* and *Gharar*, if there is any element of uncertainty regarding either the object or the consideration. If a merchant sells a commodity without agreement as to the time or manner of

228 Shīrāzī, *Kitāb al-Tanbīh Fī al-Fiqh*, (Ed. A.W.T. Juynboll; Leyden, 1879) p.95. See Chapter 7.5 below

229 UAE Civil Code, Art. 203 (2): "If the subject matter is known to both contracting parties, there is no requirement that it should be otherwise described or defined."

230 *Majella*, Art. 65

231 *Majella*, Art. 310

232 Khalīl's *Code Musulman*, (Transl. N. seignette), *op.cit.*, p.68

payment, and it is customary to obtain the price by weekly installments for such sales, then the contract of sale will be valid and interpreted according to this particular custom.[233]

If a type of currency unit is incompletely defined in the contract, custom will dictate that the currency will be construed as meaning the unit type most frequently in use in the country where the contract has been concluded.[234]

Due to the uncertainty in consideration which arises therefrom, there is no unanimous agreement among the jurists as to whether a rate fixed in respect of part of a consignment of goods may constitute a valid sale if applied to the whole consignment, where the exact quantity is not known.[235]

Detailed provision is made by the jurists for the time of payment.[236] A contract of sale must provide for the consideration, whether it is to be paid immediately at the *Majlis*, at some time in advance of delivery, or at an affixed term.[237]

In a *Salam* contract, if the consideration is fixed for a term, the general stipulation is that this term should not exceed three days, but some jurists allow an extension to this period according to customary practices.[238] Where a stipulation in a contract is made for consideration to be payed at term, that term must be certain and not dependent upon the occurrence of an uncertain event. A purchaser cannot therefore set the date of payment at "Harvest time", for this constitutes a variable description and would render the contract voidable for uncertainty, subject to proper fixing of a specific date for payment. Similarly, the *Khamīsa* contract, where the landlord leases land to a tenant on the condition that a portion of the rent paid amounts to one

---

233 For instance, in the Levant there is a custom for installments to be paid on Saturdays, which is called *al-Sabtiyya*; See Maḥmaṣānī, *Falsafat al-Tashrī' Fī al-Islām, op.cit.*, p.135.

234 Sanhūrī, *Maṣādir al-Ḥaqq*, III, pp.75-77; Ibn al-Hammām, *Fatḥ al-Qadīr*, V, pp.84-85; al-Nawāwī, *al-Majmū' : Sharḥ al-Muhadhdhab*, and its continuation by Taqī al-Dīn al-Subkī (Cairo, 1344-1353 AH) 12 Vols. IX, p.329; Ibn Qudāma, *al-Mughnī*, IV, p.217; Marghīnānī, *al-Hidāya, op.cit.*, III, p.18. See also J. Wakin, *The Function of Documents*, p.62, note 66 on irregularity of currency; and Nabil Saleh, *Unlawful Gain and Legitimate Profit in Islamic Law, op.cit.*, pp.62-63

235 Marghīnānī, *al-Hidāya*, (Transl. Hamilton), (2nd Ed.: Lahore, 1957) p.243-4

236 Hill and Abbas attribute this to the existence of widely scattered nomadic communities at the time the *Fiqh* was formed. See their 'Comparative Survey of the Islamic Law and the Common Law relating to the Sale of Goods,' in *Journal of Islamic and Comparative Law*, II (1968) p.97

237 Marghīnānī, *al-Hidāya*, (Transl. Hamilton), *op.cit.*, pp.242-248

238 Marghīnānī, *al-Hidāya*, (Transl. Hamilton), *op.cit.*, p. 303 According to the Ḥanafī school, payment in a *Salam* contract should take place prior to the end of the *Majlis al-'Aqd*. No accommodation is given therefore to consideration at term.

fifth of the produce of the land per annum, is a void contract according to the *Sharī'a*. This is because the transaction is based on pure speculation and risk (whether benefit is gained by the landlord or the tenant according to either a good or bad harvest), in that, firstly, the precise value of the one fifth portion is unascertainable at the conclusion of the contract; and secondly, the contract consists of foodstuffs subject to market price fluctuation. However, despite the evident element of *Ribā* in this contract, economic necessity has resulted in its widespread practice in times when there is little floating capital in a given society. The Mālikī jurists therefore recognise its validity through the concept of *Ḍarūra*, and it has become integrated into Mālikī *Fiqh* as a valid exception.[239]

6.1 Modern Legislation

Modern legislation shows itself relatively lenient in the rules pertaining to consideration as compared with the detailed regulations imposed by the earlier jurists.[240] Both the Kuwaiti Civil and Commercial Codes determine that if the contracting parties have not fixed the price for the transaction, the sale is not void if it appears from the agreement between the parties, or from the circumstances of the case that both parties intended to adopt the commercially recognised price or the prevailing market price.[241] Most modern codes now also permit the fixture of price for commercial transactions according to the market.[242] The construction of such agreements is usually detemined by the market price prevailing at the place and time fixed for delivery of the object. If there is no such market at the place and time of delivery, the prevailing market price will be that of the place recognised by custom.[243]

---

239 Coulson, *Conflicts and Tension in Islamic Jurisprudence*, (Chicago UP, 1969), pp.70-71

240 Art. 503 UAE Civil Code defines "price" as "that which the parties have agreed in consideration of the sale, whether it is greater or less than the value, and 'value' means the (true) value of goods, neither more nor less."

241 Kuwaiti Civil Code, Art. 460 (1); Kuwaiti Commercial Code, Art.124. See also the Draft Federal Commercial Code of the UAE, Art 116; and Bahrain Commercial Code, Law No.7 of 1987, Art. 100. The provisional UAE Commercial Code, Art 102 states that such price will be determined according to custom, or where no such custom exists, then the court has power to determine it.

242 Kuwaiti Civil Code, Art. 460 (1); Kuwait Commercial Code, Art.123; UAE Civil Code, Art. 504; UAE Federal Provisional Commercial Code, Art. 117; Bahrain Commercial Code, Art. 99

243 Kuwait Civil Code, Art. 460 (1); Kuwait Commercial Code, Art.123; UAE Civil Code, Art. 504; UAE Federal Provisional Commercial Code, Art. 117; Bahrain Commercial Code, Art. 99

The restriction is also lifted in modern legislation concerning prices fixed by third parties.[244] If the third person fails to specify the price for whatever reason, the buyer is liable to pay the market price as determined on the day of the conclusion of the contract. The judge is charged with affixing such prices as are indeterminable according to market prices on the day of contracting.[245]

In contracts of brokerage, as a comparison, modern legislation states that where remuneration of the broker is not specified by law or in the contract, it shall be determined according to custom or otherwise assessed by a judge according to the effort exerted by the broker and time spent by him in the performance of his brokerage work.[246] The Kuwaiti Civil Code dictates that where a price is determined according to weight, that weight shall be the net weight (*al-Wazn al-Ṣāfī*) unless the parties have specifically agreed, or custom decrees, otherwise.[247] Special conditions also apply to the Trust Sales of *Tawliyya, Ishrāka* (Association), *Murābaḥa* and *Waḍī'a,*[248] where the seller has an absolute duty to disclose the original cost price of the object, and the amount of profit or rebate.[249]

Whilst *Caveat Emptor* prevails as a leading principle in the Common Law of Sale,[250] the same concept finds no real seat amongst Muslim legal principles. The *Sharī'a* and *Fiqh* seek to assert above anything else the preclusion of unjustified enrichment, thereby manifesting greater legal protection for the buyer's interests. There is, therefore, an implied warranty for title and against defects in all cases, unless expressly and legally waived. Further, this principle is extended by the characteristically Islamic "series of Options" which the law permits to the transacting parties before certain contracts become binding. These options will be examined in relation to the muslim system of defective and voidable contracts which will comprise a

---

[244] Kuwait Commercial Code, Art.125; UAE Federal Provisional Commercial Code, Art. 118; Bahrain Commercial Code, Art. 101

[245] Commercial Code, Art.125; UAE Federal Provisional Commercial Code, Art. 118

[246] See Kuwait Commercial Code, Art.307; Bahrain Commercial Code, Art.205. A Judgement held in Kuwait Appeal Court that the Court has substantive powers to assess the salary of an agent : Appeal No. 119/87 from Commercial 27/1/82 *Majallat al-Qaḍā' wa al-Qānūn*, Rule No. 39, p.130

[247] Kuwaiti Civil Code, Art. 461

[248] See Chapter 6.3.10 on *Tadlīs bi al-'Ayb, infra.*

[249] Kuwaiti Civil Code, Art. 462; UAE Civil Code, Art.506

[250] See, for example, Holme's treatise on the theory of consideration, in *The Common Law*, (1881: ed. Howe, 1963) pp.227-230; and G. Gilmore, *The Death Of Contract*, *op.cit.*, p.18 : ("The balance wheel of the great machine")

further chapter.[251]

It may be seen therefore, that the conditions of contract imposed by the jurists are directed on the whole towards clarity of mutual consent. The jurists have striven to provide regulations governing transactions, which eliminate as far as possible any degree of uncertainty in transactions. These sometimes rather onerous conditions are imposed in the interests of fair and equitable transactions between all parties. At times, certain rules may seem pedantically superfluous, or ambiguously variant among the different schools. It may be surmised, however, that the overall objective of all the jurists of the four schools was to impose such reforming principles upon the prevailing practice simply in order to avoid any degree of uncertainty within the concept of consideration.

[251] See Chapter VII below

Chapter 6

VOID AND VOIDABLE CONTRACTS

Chapter 6.1

NULLITIES OF CONTRACT

The system of nullities in Islamic law is remarkably parallel to the equivalent institutions to be found in the Roman and some modern civil legal systems. However, in the same way that the jurists failed to elaborate a logical theory of obligations and contracts, they also failed to elaborate such a theory of nullities or impediments to the conclusion of contracts. Unable to resist the analogy, certain authors have been prompted by this observance to speculate upon the possible borrowing of Muslim law from the Roman theory of nullity.[1] The similarities are indeed striking; however, the fact that the system of nullities, like that of contracts and obligations, has been formed upon a religious foundation peculiar to Islam demarcates limits beyond which such comparisons must cease. The number of contracts which are absolutely null and void due to religious prohibitions stamp their own Islamic mark onto the personality of the law, for example; and the system of options to be found within the Muslim doctrine of nullity is indeed peculiar to that particular system.

In their treatment of nominate contracts Muslim jurists distinguished between the essential conditions upon which the valid conclusion of the contract depended, and conditions which may be regarded as less intrinsic to the transaction. The conditions in the former would affect all contracting parties; whereas those in the latter category might affect the binding force on only one of the parties concerned. Two scales were devised to express

---

1 S. Habachy, 'The System Of Nullities in Muslim Law', *American Journal of Comparative Law*, 13 (1964) p.62. For the Roman doctrine of Nullity see W.W. Buckland, *A Textbook of Roman Law: From Augustus to Justinian*, (Third Edn: Revised by P. Stein; Cambridge, 1975), p.180; R.W. Leage, *Roman Private Law*, (Third Edn: New York, 1967), *passim.*; R.W. Lee, *The Elements of Roman Law*, (Fourth Edn: London, 1956), *passim.*; B. Nicholas, *An Introduction to Roman Law*, (Oxford, 1962), *passim.*

the degrees of legal and religious validity.[2] The encompassing concept of the scale of legal validity is that of *Mashrū'*, literally meaning "legally recognised".[3] Within this concept the validity of legal contracts assumes the tripartite distinction between : *Ṣaḥīḥ* (valid) if both its nature (*Aṣl*) and circumstances (*Wasf*) are in accordance with the law; *Bāṭil* (Invalid, null and void); and *Fāsid* (Irregular or invalid or voidable) if its *Aṣl* is in accordance with the law but not its *Wasf*. Western orientalists like Schacht,[4] and Muslim authors such as Anṣārī[5] also include the category of *Makrūh* (reprehensible or disapproved) if the *Aṣl* and the *Wasf* correspond to legal requirements, but something forbidden is connected with it. The categorisations of contracts in the Fiqh treatises however, seldom resort to this term since the incidences of *Makrūh* are more commonly covered by the other three categories. It could be conveyed by the term *Ṣaḥīḥ* to mean "effective"; alternatively, it was also employed in earlier Fiqh to interchange with *Fāsid* and *Bāṭil*, even if the sense was not that in which they were necessarily used in later classical Fiqh literature.[6]

It seems to be the case with these terms of legal validity that their conceptual development somewhat preceded their terminological development.[7] Hence in the early Fiqh a range of alternative expressions or phrases would be used for what in later Fiqh could be expressed by recognised terminology. The fact that terms like *Makrūh* and *Ḥarām* were often employed interchangeably with *Ṣaḥīḥ* or *Bāṭil*[8] shows that the legal scale of an act was never altogether divorced from the religious value. This in itself was held to constitute an important aspect of the development of Islamic jurisprudence.[9] Thus, as with a contract that is *Makrūh*, the contract may be legally valid and therefore enforceable, and yet contain an element, which in religious terms is disapproved of.[10]

---

2 For the scale of religious validity, See Z.I. Anṣārī, 'Islamic Juristic Terminology Before Shāfi'ī - A Semantic Analysis With Special Reference To Kufa', *Arabica - Revue d'Études Arabes*, (1972) vol. 19(3), pp. 255-300; Schacht, *Introduction, op.cit.*, pp. 120-1.

3 Schacht, *Introduction, op.cit*, p.121

4 *ibid.*, p. 121

5 'Islamic Juristic Terminology', *Arabica*, p. 294

6 Abū Yūsuf, *Ikhtilāf Abī Ḥanīfa wa Ibn Abī Layla*, [ed. Abū al-Wafā' al-Afghānī], (Cairo, 1357 AH) *passim.*

7 See Anṣārī, *op.cit.*, pp. 295, 299

8 Hamilton, *The Hedaya, op.cit.*, p.266

9 Anṣārī, *op.cit.*, p.297

10 Hamilton, *The Hedaya, op.cit.*, p. 266

The supposition that the semantic development of legal terms lagged behind their conceptual development may also be discerned in the concept of *Ṣaḥīḥ*. The concept of "legally valid" was evidently in use long before the forms of expressing it as such were standardised. Hence a range of synonyms was used to convey the broader meanings of "legally effective" as it was later to be encompassed by *Ṣaḥīḥ*. *Lāzim* (binding), *Wājib* (obligatory), *Nāfidh* (operative); and *Jā'iz* (permissible) are among these.[11] The objective sense of *Jā'iz*, for example, is that the contract is unobjectionable in that it has been formed in conformity with the provisions of the law, and therefore, subjectively speaking, the contract is valid.[12]

The semantic evidence of the development of legal validity has been taken in conjunction with the development of other legal terms, such as the *Uṣūl al-Fiqh*, as a reflection of the general direction of the development of the Fiqh.[13] The appearance of elaborate terminology which may be discerned in legal treatises dating from the mid-second century of the Hijra, with their neat definitions and increasingly precise distinctions between terms, may be regarded as a reflection of the corresponding development of the Fiqh itself.

Anṣārī writes of "a more vivid *Uṣūl*-consciousness reflected in the growing recognition of distinctions between the various sources of positive doctrines, and its corollary, an increasing formalism and finesse in technical legal thought."[14] This is nowhere more apparent in the field of contracts than among the terms denoting legal validity, and the confusing interchanging of *Bāṭil* and *Fāsid* in particular. An extension of the effects of this development may be seen even more acutely by contrasting the works of modern authors such as Sanhūrī and Maḥmaṣānī against even the early Ḥanafī *fuqahā* such as Shaybānī, or the Shāfi'ī jurist, Shīrāzī. In the former, distinctions between the terms are, if not underlined, at least tacitly comprehended; In the latter, confusion reigns, for the terms are used as

---

11 Sanhūrī, *Maṣādir al-Ḥaqq*, IV, 133, divides the contract into Five categories : *Bāṭil, Fāsid, Mawqūf, Nāfidh* and *Lāzim*. The majority view is that the first two categories are not valid contracts, and that the latter three are valid contracts (*ibid.*, pp.134,138). He then discounts the category of *Nāfidh Lāzim* as an offshoot of validity and thus deals with it in conjunction with effects ensuing from contracts. The minority view of the Ḥanafīs treat the first three as invalid and the last two as valid: see Sanhūrī, *Maṣādir al-Ḥaqq*, IV, 138; Kāsānī, *Badā'i'; Ibn Nujaym treats the Mawqūf* contract as *Ṣaḥīḥ*.

12 Thus a contract in conformity with all provisions of the law is valid (*Ṣaḥīḥ*), binding (*Lāzim*), operative (*Nafīdh*), its conclusion is permissible (*Jā'iz*), and certain performances have become binding upon the parties (*Wājib*). Schacht, 'Problems of Modern Islamic Legislation', *Studia Islamica*, XII (1960) p.107; *idem.*, *Introduction*, *op.cit.*, p.122

13 Anṣārī, *op.cit.*, p.299

14 Anṣārī, *op.cit.*, p.299

synonyms for each other.

The distinction between *Fāsid* and *Bāṭil* was only recognised to a significant extent by the Ḥanafī school, which gave the terms two different and distinct meanings.[15] *Bāṭil*, it says, is when the pillars of the contract are breached, or when its cause is imperfect.[16] If one or more of the pillars are breached, such as when the contract issues from an insane person or a person lacking in competence, the contract is *Bāṭil* as though it has never been formed (*Ghayru Muta'aqqid*).[17] Similarly, if the underlying cause (*Sabab*) of the contract is dissolved, and it concerns the object of sale as, for example, when it constitutes one of the unlawful objects,[18] then the contract will also be considered as *Bāṭil*.

Fāsid, on the other hand, is defined as when something in the contract, other than a pillar or the cause, is defective. In other words, the contract is lawful in respect of its essence, but not with respect of its quality.[19] An example of this is when a defect or imbalance (*khalal*) occurs in the price. Thus a *Fāsid* sale of a commodity is binding (*Ṣaḥīḥ*) except for the irregular condition which constitutes the price; this renders the contract invalid upon the passing of possession. The buyer must pay its value in a lawful form.

Such irregularity can arise from lack of proper consent. Consent is impaired, for instance, if a contract has been formed by constraint or error. It can also arise from the insertion or stipulation of an irregular condition into the contract, or for a condition which is uncertain. For example A sells B a commodity on condition that he pays him a sum of money 'for as long as he lives'. This contract is clearly *Fāsid* for the uncertain condition of the length of A's life. To render the contract valid the term must be changed to a specific period, such as 'ten years'. Then, if the seller dies in the meantime, his title and duties will pass either to his heirs or to the treasury (*Bayt al-Māl*).[20] Thus a Ḥanafī contract may be *Fāsid* under five conditions: *Ikrāh* (Duress); *Gharar*; Harm or loss accompanying Delivery; A *Fāsid*

---

15 Sanhūrī, *Maṣādir al-Ḥaqq*, IV, (1957) pp.135-136; See also Arts. 209-212 of the United Arab Emirates Federal Law of Civil Transactions, issued Dec. 1985, Effective March 1986. *UAE Official Gazette*, No. 158, (Dec. 1985), [Hereinafter the UAE Federal Civil Code].

16 al-Jazīrī, *Kitāb al-Fiqh 'alā al-Madhāhib al-Arba'a*, (5 Vols.; Sixth Edn.; Beirut, n.d.), Vol. II, p.224

17 *ibid.*, p.224; Sanhūrī, *Maṣādir al-Ḥaqq*, IV, pp. 142-158

18 Charles Hamilton, *The Hedaya*, *op.cit.*, p.266; For Unlawful objects in contracts see below

19 Hamilton, *The Hedaya*, *op.cit.*, p. 266; Sanhūrī, *Maṣādir al-Ḥaqq*, IV, p.158

20 al-Jazīrī, *ibid.*, III, p.225

condition; *Ribā*.[21]

The remainder of the schools were content to use the terms *Bāṭil* and *Fāsid* without clear distinction and often employed them interchangeably at will. 'Abd al-Raḥmān al-Jazīrī, in his comparative volume on Fiqh, states that "*Fāsid* and *Bāṭil* have one meaning in relation to contracts of sale, for everything that is *Fāsid* is *Bāṭil* and *vice versa*; which is when one of the conditions or pillars ... is breached; *Fāsid* sales are all interdicted and it is incumbent upon people to avoid them."[22] This statement therefore applies to all schools other than the Ḥanafīs.

Further distinctions are made between *Muṭlaq* (Absolute) and *Nisbī* (Relative) nullity, contracts which are void *ab initio*, and contracts which are merely voidable. In addition, Islamic Law recognises contracts whose effects are suspended (*Mawqūf*) until ratification by the party who has been granted the option to annul the contract.[23] The *Mawqūf* contract also arises in cases of right to transfer ownership, such as where an unauthorised agent (*Fuḍūlī*) does not have full power to contract, such as in contracts of pledge or hire;[24] and where capacity is affected and awaits ratification by a guardian.[25] The categories of *Nisbī* and *Mawqūf* contracts are usually covered by the umbrella term of *Fāsid*, although they are to be distinguished. The Shāfi'īs reject the category of *Mawqūf*, treating it as a *Bāṭil* contract. They regard the elements of right to transfer ownership and capacity as essential elements of contract, rather than operative elements.[26] The Ḥanafīs treat the *Mawqūf* contract as invalid and the category is placed somewhere between the categories of *Bāṭil* and *Fāsid*.[27] These categories generally arise out of the operation of the series of options, which accord the right to ratify (*Imḍā'*), or to cancel (*Faskh*) a contract within a specified time limit. These rights in the first instance may issue from the law itself, or may be

---

21 Sanhūrī, *Maṣādir al-Ḥaqq*, IV, 137

22 'Abd al-Raḥmān al-Jazīrī, *Kitāb al-Fiqh 'Alā al-Madhāhib al-'Arba'a*(Seventh Printing: Beirut, n.d.), Vol. III, pp. 224-225

23 Sanhūrī, *Maṣādir al-Ḥaqq*, IV, 137; 195 ff. For *Mawqūf* contracts, see chapter on Duress, *infra*. The UAE Federal Civil Code also recognises contracts that are *Mawqūf*.

24 Sanhūrī, *Maṣādir al-Ḥaqq*, IV, 137

25 Sanhūrī, *Maṣādir al-Ḥaqq*, IV, 137-138

26 Sanhūrī, *Maṣādir al-Ḥaqq*, IV, 138

27 For the rest it depends on the various combinations of validity which are accepted with regard to *Mawqūf*. See, for instance, Sanhūrī, *Maṣādir al-Ḥaqq*, IV, 139-140; Ibn Nujaym, *Baḥr al-Rā'iq*, V, 277; and contracts under Duress *infra*. There is dispute as to whether contracts made in jest (*Hāzil*) are *Bāṭil* or *Fāsid*; Sanhūrī decides on the former, finding support in Sarakhsī, *al-Mabsūṭ*, XXIV, p.55. On *Mawqūf* see Zakī 'Abd al-Burr, *Majallat al-Qānūn wa al-Iqtiṣād*, XXV, pp.116-121

stipulated in the contract.[28] *Mawqūf* or suspended contracts are generally regarded as valid (*Ṣaḥīḥ*) contracts which depend upon the rights of the other party for their validity. They are formed without being conditional upon the passing of possession.[29]

The system of nullities in Islam takes its starting point from the *Qur'ān*, which provides the basic principles, morals and the fundamentals of Islamic public order for the guidance of the Muslim community. The Qur'ānic precepts take the effect of mandatory rules of good morals and public order. In principle therefore, any attempt by the contractors to exercise their freedom of contract to circumvent the Qur'ānic restrictions should prove ineffective : The contract is *Bāṭil* (null and void) as contrary to divine law. In practice, attempts to 'contract out of' these restrictions have sometimes been upheld by the courts. This may be due to a general imprecision of meaning and variable interpretation of the restriction in question, such as in the case of *Ribā*;[30] equally, it may be the result of an application of juristic method, such as *Istiḥsān*, which dictates that the interests of justice are better served by a logical development of the Qur'ānic precept through the *Fiqh*.[31]

The distinction that must derive from a comparison between nullities in Muslim law and that of Roman and other secular world legal systems is that violation of these basic rules in Islam is not merely against the common good, but also an offence against God.[32] Moreover, because such prohibitions are of a religious nature, they tend to be more numerous than similar civil restrictions. In character, they also have a tendency to be more idiosyncratic.

6.1.1 ABSOLUTE NULLITY

The only pre-eighteenth century jurist to have made any attempt at a general systematization of the theory of nullity is the neo-Ḥanbalī Ibn Taymiyya (661-728 AH/1262-1328 AD), who covered most of the salient points in his

---

28 Schacht, *Introduction, op.cit.*, pp. 121, 152

29 al-Jazīrī, *op.cit.*, p.224

30 See section on *Ribā*, below

31 See section on *Istiḥsān and Istiṣlāḥ*, and other juristic methods *supra*, Chapter One.

32 This comparison is to be found in Sanhūrī's exposition *Maṣādir al-Ḥaqq Fī'l Fiqh al-Islāmī: Naẓariyyat al-Sabab wa Naẓariyyat al-Buṭlān*, (Cairo, 1957) Vol. IV: Sanhūrī states that the Islamic system of nullities is wider than that covered by western systems (*ibid. IV, p.133)*

chapter on contracts in the *Fatāwā*.[33] It may be admissible however, to infer from the ocean of legal treatises and commentaries at least one generalisation concerning nullity according to the Sharī'a. This is that absolute nullity must be based on either a pillar or cause (*Sabab*) of the contract, and that this as often as not, concerns either the offer and acceptance, or the object of contract, or both.[34]

The Unlawful Object

When the four requirements of Legality,[35] existence,[36] the capability of being held in usufruct and delivered,[37] and the property of constituting lawful benefit, concerning the object are not realised at the time of contract, then the contract is void (*Bāṭil*).[38] Commodities which are not under individual control, not determinable, or are public property such as a mosque or a *waqf*, contravene the definition of *Māl Mutaqawwim*,[39] and may not constitute the object of a contract. Thus any contract purporting to sell, for example, air or water which cannot be secured; birds, fish, or animals not yet caught; or milk in the udder; minerals still in the earth;[40] is null and void.[41] Similarly, a contract to sell fruit yet unborne of the tree, a foetus in the womb or unborn (*bay' al-Malāqiḥ*) or impregnated livestock (*Habl al-Habla*) constitutes an illegal contract because the object is not in existence at the time of contracting.[42] Both the Kuwaiti Civil Code and the Federal

---

33 Sheikh al-Islām Takī Dīn Aḥmad Ibn Taymiyya, *Fatāwā*, (*Mabḥath al-'Uqūd*), [Cairo, 1326- 29], III, p.387ff.

34 'Abd al-Raḥmān al-Jazīrī, *Kitāb al-Fiqh*, *op.cit.*, III, pp. 224-225

35 See Section on the legality of object of contract, *supra*.

36 *Majella*, Art. 205 : "If the object does not exist the sale of it is invalid (*Bāṭil*)", eg. to sell fruit which has not yet appeared on the tree. Also see Art. 363; and Sanhūrī, *Maṣādir al-Ḥaqq*, IV, p.135. Exceptions are made in the case of *Salam* contracts, certain agricultural contracts and contracts for services or acts.

37 *Majella*, Art. 211 : "The sale of property (*Māl*) which is not *Mutaqavvim* is Bāṭil." *Mal Mutaqavvim (=Māl Mutaqawwim)* is explained in Art. 127 as "Thing the benefit of which is permissible by law to enjoy." See also Art.363; and Sanhūrī, *ibid.*, IV, p.135

38 Sanhūrī, *ibid.*, IV, p.135

39 See Footnote 37 above.

40 UAE Civil Code, Art. 612 (a) "that which is concealed in the earth until extracted and visible".

41 Shīrāzī, *Tanbīh*, p.94. But it is permitted to sell the leaves, blossom, or anything that might arise out of them. *Majella*, transl. C.R. Tyser, *et al.*, (Cyprus, 1901) p.26

42 Shīrāzī, *Tanbīh*, p.95; The *Hidāya*, regards these contracts as fraudulent, since there is a lack of certainty as to the true and quantitative existence of the object: Hamilton, *The Hedaya, op.cit.*, p.268, 270.

Civil Code of the UAE preclude the estate of a person still alive as an object of contract.[43] Some authors also include the sale of the seed of male animals for fecundation (*bay' al-mudāmin*) on the premise that such seed cannot constitute property (*Māl*).[44]

Secondly, the sale of any article which cannot be separated without harm (whether from its situation or from other commodities), and is not deliverable is invalid.[45] Thus a beam in the roof of a house would not be the lawful object of a contract as that beam could not be separated from the rest of the house without causing harm to the whole structure.[46]

Thirdly, goods which are deemed unlawful, or which offer no benefit (such as vermin, or wild animals not useful for hunting), or which have restricted disposal rights, such as articles of trifling value, holy, or, conversely, ritually impure things, or things without market value, are unlawful objects of contract.[47]

The Right to Title

This has been dealt with in Chapter 5.5.1 above.

Capacity

Due to the importance placed on the concept of will and consent, for any contract to be valid, not only does the consent of each contracting party

---

43 Art. 202 (2) of Law No.2 of 1987; See also Ballantyne, 'The New Civil Code of the United Arab Emirates: A Further Reassertion of the Shari'a', *Arab Law Quarterly*, vol. I (3) (May 1986) at p.263

44 al-Jazīrī, *ibid.* , p.225 Thus as seed cannot be sold, nor may animals be hired for stud on the premise that the contract amounts to *Gharar*, since the owner cannot be certain that the mare will foal. The semen of stud horses is also expressly forbidden in the UAE Civil Code, Art. 612 (b). The suggestion is that animals should rather be left to wander in season. Naturally, certain resistance to this prohibition was encountered and the practice of stud-hiring prevailed. This resulted in a degree of backtracking among the legal profession of Islam, and we now find authors who are tolerant of the limited and specific engaging of these sevices (*Ista'jara*). See al-Jazīrī, *ibid.*, p.225: The Mālikīs state that the hiring of a stallion for stud for a specific period or specified visits is a valid contract. If the period or number of visits is unspecified however, the contract is *Fāsid* for uncertainty.

45 Notwithstanding rules governing the sales of real properties. Hamilton, *The Hedaya, op.cit.*, p.268;

46 *Majella*, Art. 209 : "The sale of an object the delivery of which is impossible is invalid (*Bāṭil*)", eg. the sale of an escaped animal. See also Art. 363.

47 Shīrāzī, *Kitāb al-Tanbīh*, p.97; See also UAE Civil Code, No. 2 of 1987, Arts. 127 and 129(c).

have to be present, but it also has to be valid. Islamic law distinguishes between consent which is non-existent and that which is impeded or constrained.[48] Any contract, therefore, which is formed by a person lacking in capacity, such as a minor without distinction (*Ghayru Tamyīz*), a person whose competence is impaired through physical disablement (*Muta'awwah*), or who is suffering from death sickness,[49] a madman, a drunk or a jester, is formed in absence of consent and is null and void.[50]

Prohibited Commodities

The usufruct, sale and trading of certain "illegal" commodities, such as wine,[51] and pork,[52] are prohibited to Muslims. Any prospective Muslim buyer is therefore precluded from deriving any use or enjoyment from these commoditites and any likely contract would be void on the grounds of illegality.

Animals which have died without ritual slaughter (*Ḥalāl*), their flesh, bones and blood, cannot be sold (although they can be possessed and therefore eaten).[53]

Blood,[54] and idols are also forbidden commodities.

There is an *Ḥadīth* attributed to the Prophet[55] recording that he prohibited the sale of dogs with the exception of hunting or sheepdogs.[56] Therefore,

---

48 See the Section on Impediments to consent, *infra*, and Section IV on Capacity in Chapter V, *Supra*.

49 Sanhūrī, *Maṣādir al Ḥaqq*, IV, p.135

50 Sanhūrī, *Maṣādir al Ḥaqq*, (1960), II, p.104; *Majella*, Art. 362. There are exceptions to this rule however, for certain extrapatrimonial contracts are formed subject to these impediments. See Bellefonds, *Traité*, p.394; and section on Restrictions to Capacity, *supra*, Chapter 5.4.1.

51 *Qur'ān*, (II:219), (V:93,94)

52 *Qur'ān*, (II:173), (V:4), (VI:145), (XVI:115). See al-Shīrāzī, *al-Muhadhdhab*, (Cairo, 1343 AH); and Marghīnānī, *al-Hidāya*, *op.cit.*, III, p.32. The Ḥanafīs and Mālikīs recognise wine and pork as legal objects in contracts between non-Muslims.

53 *Qur'ān*, (II:173), (V:4), (VI:145), (XVI:115)

54 *Qur'ān*, (II:173), (V:4), (VI:145), (XVI:115)

55 Cited in Ibn Qudāma, *al-Mughnī*, (Cairo, 1341-48 AH) 12 Vols., IV, p.14; and *idem*., *Kitāb 'Umdat al-Aḥkām fī al-Fiqh 'Alā Madhhab al-Imām Aḥmad b. Ḥanbal*, (Damascus, 1352) fo. 66b, lines 12,3; (This Ḥadīth seems to be omitted from the Cairo edition of 1352 AH).

56 The sale and usufruct of hunting and service dogs which are considered to be of value, are permitted on the basis of a Prophetic Tradition : "Verily the Prophet forbade the costing of dogs and cats, except hunting dogs". Ibn Qudāma, *al-Mughnī*, (Third Edn: Cairo, 1367) vol. IV, pp. 252

most of the schools prohibit the sale of dogs except for hunting and service dogs.[57] The Mālikīs state that no dogs may constitute the object of a transaction for consideration, but that hunting and service dogs may be possessed and may form objects of transactions devoid of consideration.[58] However, the Ḥanafīs authorise the sale of all kinds of dogs, including domestic pets which perform no service. This ruling would seem to contravene the usefulness rule below, and is questioned by Kāsānī.[59]

All these commodities are impure (*Nājis, Mutanajjis*)[60] and therefore unlawful according to Islam. Necessity, however, can render these lawful in certain circumstances.[61]

Articles of public property also constitute forbidden commodities in private transactions. Thus a mosque cannot form the object of a private sale, for its use could not be passed exclusively to an individual.[62]

The person and attributes of a freedman are not regarded as *res in commercio* or *māl Mutaqawwim*, and cannot therefore be classified as commodities for the purpose of transactions.[63]

Certain other articles have also been itemised : the purchase of musical instruments, for instance, has been mentioned by Kāsānī as prohibited[64] on the basis that instruments can be used for immoral purposes; but as Abū Ḥanīfa points out, this is not sufficient reason to prohibit their purchase, which becomes an injustice for those wishing to put them to perfectly normal and other than immoral use. Service contracts of a dubious nature, are also outlawed on the basis of illegal *Maḥall* and *Sabab*.

The UAE Civil Code also lists contracts which are made prior to, and interrupted by, the Friday call to prayer as defective except in circumstances

---

57 See Schacht's Article 'Kalb' in *The Encyclopaedia of Islam, op.cit.*, Vol. V

58 Al-Zurqānī, *Sharḥ 'Alā Mukhtaṣar Khalīl*, (8 vols.; Cairo, 1307 AH), vol.V, p.17

59 Kāsānī, *al-Badā'i', op.cit.*, V, p.143

60 For specification of *Nājis*, see the following: *al-Fatāwā al-'Ālamgirīyya*, (Calcutta, 1828), I, pp.55-67; al-Marghīnānī, *Kifāya*, (Bombay, 1863), I, pp.15 ff., 41; Khalīl b. Isḥāq, *Mukhtaṣar*, (Paris, 1318/1900), S.3 ff.; al-Ghazālī, *al-Wajīz*, (Cairo, 1317), I, pp.6 ff.; al-Nawāwī, *Minhāj al-Ṭālibīn*, (Batavia, 1882), I, 36 ff.; al-Ramlī, *Nihāya al-Muḥtāj ilā Sharḥ al-Minhāj*, (Cairo, 1304), I, 166 ff.; Ibn Ḥajar al-Haythāmī, *Tuḥfa*, (Cairo, 1282), I, 71ff.; 'Abd al-Qādir b. 'Umar al-Shaybānī, *Dalīl al-Ṭālib*, with commentary by Mar'ī b. Yūsuf (Cairo, 1324-1326), I, 11 ff.; Goldziher, *Die Zâhiriten*, S.61 ff.

61 *Qur'ān*, (II,173); Ghazālī, *al-Iqtiṣād fī al-I'tiqād*, (Cairo, 1320 AH), p.107. Game is forbidden in sacred precincts or whilst dressed for the pilgrimage: *Qur'ān*,(V:2)

62 Muḥammad Abū Zahra, *al-Milkiyya wa Naẓariyyat al-'Aqd, op.cit.*, p.255 ff.

63 *Majella*, Art. 210

64 Kāsānī, *al-Badā'i'*, V, p.144

in extremis, or of compelling necessity.[65] Goods sold by way of forward sale which are rebought or sold (in a manner prejudicial to such forward sale) or, if having been bartered, are rebartered during the continuance of the period of the options of *Majlis*, or *Sharṭ*, are also defective according to the UAE Civil Code.[66]

A sale contract comprising an illegal object or *Maḥall* is *prima facie* void (*Bāṭil*).[67] Thus a contract made for property to be used to commit an offence, when one of the parties knows of this fact from the other, even if only by circumstantial evidence, is forbidden and defective.[68]

By the same reasoning, while the sale of forbidden goods for consideration is deemed void by the Ḥanafīs, if they are exchanged in the way of barter, the contract is merely considered *Fāsid*.[69]

Objects deemed illegal by the *Fiqh* generally retain this status within modern legislation.[70] Categories are no longer listed as in the *Fiqh* texts, but have been replaced by general phrases which cover the scope of 'immorality', and 'against public policy', and 'harmful to the person or property of a third party', or 'forbidden by law'. The latter refers to the legislation in effect in that locality.[71] It is not clear whether a court today would consider a contract between two persons for the sale of, for instance, alcohol or pork as void where dispute arises between those parties. It would

---

65 UAE Federal Civil Code, Law No. 2 of 1987, Art.613 (a)

66 *ibid.*, Art. 613 (c)

67 al-Jazīrī, *ibid.*, p.224; Hamilton, *The Hedaya*, *op.cit.*, p.266; But see M.M. Ali, *A Manual of Ḥadīth*, *op.cit.*, 17, p.300, notably his discussion of the legitimacy of trading in commodities which may not be eaten, and the contradictory *Aḥādīth*, (B34:112 and B24:61) which state, concerning dead animals, "only the eating thereof is forbidden". The point therefore remains somewhat controversial as to whether these commodities constitute legitimate objects of sale, especially in contracts between Non-Muslims, or Muslims and non-Muslims. In this context, see also Hamilton, *The Hedaya*, *op.cit.*, p.266

68 UAE Civil Code, Art. 613 (b)

69 Hamilton, *The Hedaya*, *op.cit.*, p.267. The direct sale of these items can be avoided, on occasion, by a formula which purports merely to transfer the owner's right of usufruct to a second party for consideration. The sale is invalid, but the owner has a right of possession (*Taṣarruf*) or a special interest (*Ikhtiṣāṣ*) which may be transferred to another for value received. See Sachau, *Muhammedanisches Recht*, (Berlin, 1897) p. 279 n.1, p.609 n.1

70 In Kuwaiti law this precept is contained in the Article governing *Maḥall*, Art. 167: "The motivating pupose must be legal, in that the nature of the contract to be formed must be possible *in esse*. UAE Civil Code, Art. 126 (d) in conjunction with Arts. 1 and 2. Bahrain Contract Law of 1969, Art.27 (2)

71 Bahrain Contract Law, Art.27 (1). Several specific circumstances are given in Arts. 612 and 613 of the UAE Civil Code: See above. See also Section on the exercise of rights in Kuwait's Civil Code, Art.30; and *ibid*, Art. 173

seem likely indeed, that a modern Bahraini Civil Court would be reluctant to interfere in the private arrangement between the parties in the case where a specific commodity is not outlawed by the legislation in effect under the categories listed above. In Kuwait, there is also no Civil Law provision against specific commodities, and guidelines must be derived from the sections on Intention and Cause (Arts. 167-178).

In the UAE, however, a case could be made for avoiding such a contract, on the basis that the object must be permissible to be dealt in[72] and must have a lawful purpose.[73] In addition, Article 52 of the UAE Civil Code states that where prohibition conflicts with an obligation, the prohibition shall take precedence. Article 1 of the Civil Code states that where the judge finds no provision in the Civil Code, he has to pass judgment according to the Islamic Sharī'a, in the first instance according to the Mālikī or Ḥanbalī Schools, and thereafter to the Shāfi'ī or Ḥanafī doctrines. Article 2 states that in the construction of the provisions contained in the UAE Civil Code, the principles of Islamic *Fiqh* shall be relied upon. Thus a construction of 'permissible to be dealt in' according to the reliance on the Sharī'a would mean that pork and alcohol (which are prohibited in all four schools of *Fiqh*) still constitute illegal objects of contract in the UAE. It would be expected therefore, that a UAE Court would not uphold such contracts for civil law purposes.[74]

With regard to commercial contracts in all three jurisdictions under study, again, it would seem unlikely that the court would interfere in the agreement between two parties, so long as the underlying intention (*Maḥall*) of the contract is not illegal. Although commercial transactions are based on the law of contracts, they are accorded a higher regard concerning sanctity and privity of contract, and are therefore less susceptible to judicial tampering. There is, as yet, however, no enacted commercial code within the UAE Federal legislation, and the situation is far from certain as it presently stands.

Consideration

Similarly, the consideration which must pass in commutative contracts must be lawful.[75] According to the Ḥanafī school however, a contract formed with irregular consideration is merely *Fāsid*. A contract formed for a legal object

---

72 UAE Federal Civil Code, Art. 129 (b)

73 UAE Federal Civil Code, Art. 129 (c)

74 See also Arts. 7 and 101 in the UAE Constitution.

75 See also section 'Consideration', Chapter V, *supra*.

to be paid for in an illegal commodity (such as wine), for example, is *Fāsid* according to the Ḥanafī School, but *Bāṭil* according to the remaining schools. The contract may be rendered *Ṣaḥīḥ* in the Ḥanafī rite by the removal of the irregular aspect : the illegal consideration must be exchanged for legal consideration.[76]

The same attention to minutiae is not given to these principles in the modern legislation as may be found in the Fiqh books. The Federal code of the UAE is, however, the closest echo. Article 204 of this code states: "If the object for consideration for the transaction consists of money the amount and kind thereof must be specified without any effect being accorded to increase or decrease in the value of such money at the time of payment." The same article is contained in Article 173 of the Kuwaiti Civil Code, and here it states that such variation will not be upheld even if it forms the subject of agreement between the parties. Ballantyne interprets this article as meaning that the code will recognise 'no exception which might otherwise be made due to modern inflationary circumstances.' In other words, it is a clear reflection of the *Sharī'a* interdiction against *Ribā*.[77]

Forbidden Jāhilī contracts

In addition to these categories there are a series of sales contracts dating from, and peculiar to, pre-Islamic market trading which have been expressly forbidden by the Prophet. These sales are uniformly based on conjecture and comprise elements of uncertainty which are unconscionable according to the strict rules of Islamic contract.

(i) The first species of forbidden contract was called *Muzābana*, or selling dates growing upon the tree in exchange for dates which have already been harvested. The quantity of dates on the tree amounts to mere conjecture, whilst the plucked dates may be computed : the equality of the exchange is therefore uncertain and the sale is prohibited.[78]

---

76 al-Jazīrī, *op.cit.* , III, p.224

77 Ballantyne, W.M., 'The New Civil Code of the United Arab Emirates: A Further Reassertion of the Shari'a', *Arab Law Quarterly*, vol. I (3) (May 1986) p.263; and *id.*, *Commercial Law*, pp.125 ff.

78 Ḥamilton, *The Hedaya, op.cit.*, pp. 268-269; Mālik Ibn Anas, *al-Muwaṭṭa'*, (Transl. 'A'isha Abdar-Raḥmān at-Tarjumana and Ya'qūb Johnson, Cambridge, 1982) Art. 31.13, pp.288-289; Suyūṭī, *Tanwīr al-Ḥawālik: Sharḥ Muwaṭṭa' al-Imām Mālik*, 3 Vols. (Cairo, 1348 AH) Vol. II, p.54 and by analogy the sale of grapes for raisins, and thus selling fresh fruit against dried fruit; or weighed commodities against unweighed or unmeasured; or the exchange of live animal for meat. *Muzābana* transactions are not permitted by the Mālikīs and Shāfi'īs.

(ii) The second species of forbidden contract is that of *Muḥāqala*, or the sale of grain while still growing in exchange for an "equal" quantity of harvested wheat.[79] The decisions on the sales of *Muḥāqala* and *Muzābana* thus amount to a prohibition of dealing in grain futures and other foodstuff commodities. This is significant in terms of the discussion on *Gharar (infra)*, for it is merely confirmation of the multiplicity of grounds which may be argued for the interpretation of the prohibition of Financial Futures and Stock commodities trading.

The law is extended by analogy to apply to all exchanges of foodstuffs, but variations in validity exist according to the Jurist's acknowledgement of mitigating circumstances of the contractors. Mālik determines that the analogous interpretation of *Muzābana* is 'Every purchase of which the amount is unknown by measure, weight or number, in exchange for something defined in weight, measure or number (*Juzāf*). He refers to the exchange not as a sale, but as a *Mukhāṭara* (risk).[80] Al-Shāfi'ī, for example, holds that these sales are lawful provided that they do not exceed a certain amount.[81] This is not contrary to the Prophet's prohibition of *Muzābana* in that he is reported to have specifically allowed the sale of Oraya (Wheat), where the exchange is for less than the five *Wasqs*. The more pedantic of the *'Ulamā'* chose to interpret this apparent anomaly not as a sale, but rather as a gift, making the practice more into a *Ḥīla* or *Mukhāṭara* than a legal exception in the requirements of necessity. Al-Shāfi'ī argues that the proper interpretation of this practice is that A promises B a gift of dates from his orchard. B thereupon enters A's orchard in order to collect the dates, but A is so abhorrent of this incursion into his home that he gives B the equivalent measure of cut dates instead. The right of property accompanying the seisin of a sale was never vested in the donee and so the cut dates given to him later are considered as a new gift.[82] The argument is outstanding only in its casuistry, for as a contract of sale for an unascertained object is null and void, so too is a contract of gift !

(iii) The third prohibited sale is that of *Mulāmasa*,[83] where the sale is determined by the purchaser touching the goods. Within this category also are *Munābadha* contracts, which are sales by throwing the goods to the

79 Hamilton, *ibid.*, p.269; Suyūṭī, *ibid.*, II, p.54

80 Suyūṭī, *Tanwīr al-Ḥawālik: Sharḥ Muwaṭṭa' al-Imām Mālik, op.cit.*, Vol. II, p.55

81 Reported to be five *Wasqs*: a *wasq* is literally a camel-load, and is equivalent to sixty *Ṣā's* . See Hamilton, *ibid.*, p.269

82 Hamilton, *The Hedaya, op.cit.*, p.269

83 Sale by touching without examination of the goods; Mālik, *al-Muwaṭṭa'*, (Translated by 'Aisha 'Abdarahmān at-Tarjumana and Ya'qūb Johnson : Cambridge, 1982), Art. 31.35, p.302

purchaser without allowing him to inspect them before the sale is concluded. The prohibited *Munābadha* sales include sales whose objects are determined by the chance casting of stones.[84] They are all speculative sales and forbidden on the grounds of *Maysir* (Gambling) and *Gharar*.[85]

6.1.2 DEFECT OF FORM

Due to the importance placed upon intention and mutual consent in Muslim nominate contracts,[86] the system is generally free from the fetters of external formalism which are to be found for instance, in the formalistic institutions of *Mancipatio* and *In Iure cessio*[87] in the early Roman classical law of contract,[88] and other archaic legal systems, as well as early European law.[89] Sanhūrī explains that the absence of formalities derives from the religious character of Muslim law.[90] Bellefonds attributes the lack of formalism not to the religious character (pointing out that Roman Law was more formalistic in its religious era) but to the exigences of early Islamic merchants who would reject any type of formalism, and also to the lack of any proper judicial system at the beginning of Islam.[91] The first of Bellefonds' arguments is not entirely convincing: the same argument could be used to reject the *Ribā* prohibition, and yet that prohibition remains with us. The second line of argument is also somewhat negated in the light of those

---

84 Hamilton, *The Hedaya*, *op.cit.*, p. 269

85 See the relevant sections in Chapter 6.7 below.

86 This principle of the *Fiqh* is taken up by Art. 257 of the Code of Civil Transactions for the United Arab Emirates, Law No.2 of 1987 which states : "The basis of the contract is the consent of the contracting parties and that which they undertake as a duty by entering into the contract." Also see Section on Consent, *supra*.

87 *Mancipatio* lasted until the Fourth century AD : Leage, *op.cit.*, pp. 192-194, particularly p.193. *In Iure Cessio* lasted out the Classical period but vanished soon after as a conveyance : See Leage, *ibid.* , p.195

88 See "Mancipatio": Jolowicz, *Historical Introduction to the Study of Roman Law*, (Second Ed., Cambridge 1952), p.145; "In iure Cessio", *idem*, p.150 and Appendix p.557; Formalism, *idem*, p.421 ff.; Buckland, *A Textbook of Roman Law*, *op.cit.*, p.265; But *cf.* Wakin, J.A., *The Function of Documents in Islamic Law : The Chapters on sales from Ṭaḥṭāwī's Kitāb al-Shurūṭ al-Kabīr; [Edited with an Introduction and Notes by J.A. Wakin]*, (Albany, Lebanon pr., 1972) p.38, who notes the later formalism, "the rigid structure and repetition of stereotyped phrases" on private legal documents and documents of state. She notes simultaneously that "the Arabic formulary does not seem to have become excessively overburdened in this respect."

89 W. Seagle distinguishes between the primitive, archaic and mature systems in his *The Quest for Law*, (New York, 1941) xv-xvi

90 *Maṣādir al-Ḥaqq*, I, 37

91 See Bellefonds, *Traité*, pp. 123-4

formalities which clearly did survive the 'uncertain' initial judicial period. This is notwithstanding the fact, of course, that the argument is hardly demonstrable due to the dearth of legal literature of the time.

Saleh proposes an alternative justification. He says : "The Islamic informality in the technique of contracting is the Qur'ān's concern to spare the Islamic community from any undue hardship (*Qur'ān* XXII,78); that concern being a distinctive feature of the teaching of Islam."[92] This was the explanation used by Ṭaḥāwī in the opening pages of his *Jāmi' al-Kabīr Fī al-Shurūṭ* : He said that God did not call for documents because this would have been oppressive; no-one would buy anything, not even food and water, without feeling obliged to draw up a written instrument.[93]

The actual reasons behind the Islamic position on formalism may well comprise a combination of all these, and other factors; the justification rests in the essence of Sanhūrī's proposition, echoed by Saleh, that the divine injuction 'O Ye who believe, fulfil your contracts' is a sufficient and finite guarantee for the respect of obligations.

Formalities which provide proof of contracts are not considered necessary in the light of the Qur'ānic verse (V:1).[94] Literacy during the first century of Islam and up to the present century was low in the Arab world. Agreements not committed to writing were the norm, and carried the same probatory force as those which were formally recorded. The testimony of those who witnessed the formation of the contract was considered sufficient to establish

---

[92] Nabil Saleh, 'Financial Transactions and the Islamic Theory of Obligations and Contracts', *Islamic Law and Finance*, (ed. C. Mallat; London, 1988) p.4

[93] Ṭaḥāwī, Aḥmad, *Kitāb al-Shuf'a Min al-Jāmi' al-Kabīr Fī al-Shurūṭ*, (Ed. J. Schacht) in 20 *Heidelberger Akademie der Wissenschaften*, 3 (1929-1930); Wakin, J.A., *The Function of Documents in Islamic Law*, (Albany, Lebanon pr., 1972) p.29

[94] 'O Ye who believe, fulfil (all) obligations', where obligations (*'Uqūd*) here implies the whole spectrum of human obligations: promises, social, state and commercial contracts, divine and nuptual contracts. The verse was considered of such importance by Ḥāfiz, 'Uthmān and the Fatḥ ur-Raḥmān, that it is numbered separately from the succeeding verses. See A. Yusuf Ali, *The Holy Qur'ān*, p.238, n.682

its existence.[95]

The *Sharī'a* does not, in principle, recognise a promise to contract.[96] The strictest rules require that offer and acceptance are expressed in the past or present tense, denoting the immediacy of time sequence between intention and contract. The extent to which the form of offer and acceptance are of importance in the formation of a contract varies from school to school. Sanhūrī, however, goes almost as far as to dismiss such vagaries as the rules determining verb tenses and language (Arabic), or predetermined phrases to be employed.[97] Nevertheless, Sanhūrī does acknowledge the classical view of the supercedence of intention and the will of the parties' over form and expression. He writes :

> "With regard to the form of the contract, the principle is that the expression of the intention will be taken into consideration if this expression is unequivocal .... but if the expression is not clear, then the intention, that is, the inner will of the parties, will be taken into account."[98]

We see the same prominent consideration afforded to the true will and consent in modern Islamic legal philosophy, as manifested by certain recent codes. Article 258 (1) of the UAE Federal Civil Code, for example, states : "That which is of consequence in contracts is intention and meaning, not expression or form." This is similar to Art. 3 of the *Majella* : "In contracts effect is given to the intention and meaning and not to the words and phrases."[99]

---

95 E. Tyan, 'Le Notariat et le Régime de la Preuve par Écrit dans la Pratique du Droit Musulman', *Annales de L'École Française de Droit de Beyrouth*, (Beirut, 1945) pp. 5-12, 72; Saleh, 'Financial Transactions and the Islamic Theory of Obligations and Contracts', *Islamic Law and Finance, op.cit.*; Wakin, J.A., *The Function of Documents in Islamic Law*, (Albany, Lebanon pr., 1972) pp.4-15, 30-71; Bajwa, M.A., 'Islam on the Law of Evidence', *The Review of Religions*, [Ed. A.Q. Niaz] Vol. XL, No.8 (Aug. 1941) pp.291-307; Grohmann, *From the World of Arabic Papyri*, (Cairo, 1952); Liebesny, *The Law of the Near and Middle East: Readings, Cases and Materials*, (Albany: New York, 1975) pp.261 ff.; Brunschvig, R., 'La Preuve en Droit Musulman', 2 *Études d'Islamologie*, (Paris, 1976) pp.201-216. Methods of proof and evidence are covered by Arts. 112-123 inclusive of the UAE Federal Civil Code, and follow *Sharī'a* principles.

96 This has been abandoned by modern legislation. Even the Federal Civil Code of the UAE recognises an agreement to agree in the future, so long as the period within which the contract is to be negotiated is specified (Art. 146)

97 Sanhūrī, *Maṣādir al-Ḥaqq*, II, p.90

98 *Maṣādir al-Ḥaqq*, II, p.90; Owsia, *op.cit.*, p.182

99 Hooper, *op.cit*, p.17

It may be remarked that the principal purpose for introducing formalities into a system of contracts is primarily to introduce clarity and to provide an unambiguous forum by which to express the parties' intentions. It may also serve to jolt the parties into a realisation of their responsibilities and duties regarding significant contracts. The disadvantages such formalities offer, however, are those of inflexibility and inconvenience. Nicholas states : "Primitive systems are given to the use of forms".[100] Most modern legal systems seek to escape these formalities wherever possible, and it may be suggested that in its lack of formalism, the Islamic Ṣunnī[101] contractual law manifested a sophistication that was ahead of its time.[102]

In contracts requiring a standard form, where that form is not observed, even if intention is without defect, no legal consequence may follow, nor are rights created. If, conversely, the form is observed but there is a defect of intention (by mistake or fraud), what then would be the consequence according to the Islamic philosophy of contract? If we were here dealing with Roman law, legal rights and recognition of the contract would indeed ensue, for form in Roman law is both essential and sufficient.[103]

Very few contracts in Islamic law require any special formality other than the expressions of offer and acceptance.[104] Ibn Taymiyya writes: "all contracts are automatically concluded by every word, or every act, which expresses their object beyond any possible doubt."[105]

Those contracts formed by acts (*Mu'āṭāh*) rather than the exchange of words, for instance when a buyer tenders money to a shopkeeper in exchange for goods in his hand, which the trader accepts undemurringly, do not require witnesses.[106]

However, a few contracts do remain subject to conditions, which, although not all are recognised as strict conditions of *form*, if omitted, would render the contract devoid of effect :

---

[100] B. Nicholas, *An Introduction to Roman Law*, (Oxford, 1962), p.61

[101] Owsia compares the less rigid approach of the Ṣunnī law here with the more formalistic Shi'ite schools, whose approach is "tinged with a ceremonious colouring." His speculations as to the reasons for this difference may be found in his thesis, *op.cit.*, at pp. 182 ff.

[102] Compare, for example, the formalistic laws of Byzantium and Sassania of the same era.

[103] See B. Nicholas, *An Introduction to Roman Law*, *op.cit.*, pp. 61-64; W.W. Buckland, *A Textbook of Roman Law*, *op.cit.*, passim; R.W. Leage, *Roman Private Law*, *op.cit.*, pp. 192-195; R.W. Lee, *The Elements of Roman Law*, *op.cit.*, p.116

[104] See, for example, UAE Civil Code No. 2 of 1987, Art. 130

[105] Henri Laoust, *Essai sur les Doctrines Sociales et Politiques de Taki-D-Din Ahmad B. Taimiya*, (Cairo, 1939), p.442; See also UAE Civil Code, Law No. 2 of 1987, Art. 132

[106] N. Saleh, 'Financial Transactions', in *Islamic Law and Finance*, *op.cit.*, p.3

(1) The contract of pledge depends on the transfer of possession to the pledgee.[107] In modern pledge and mortgage transactions, either physical or constructive possession of the pledge by title deed is required for the pledge to have valid effect. If possession of the pledge is not transferred the pledge is rendered incomplete and revocable.

(2) The contract of gift depends on the delivery of the object to the second party. Until delivery has been executed the contract remains revocable by the donor.[108]

(3) The contract of marriage: Muslim law deems the marriage contract as an ordinary contract subject to two conditions.[109] The first, which is applicable to all four schools, is that a certain number of witnesses are required.[110] The second condition is that the expressions employed must convey an unequivocal intention that the parties intend to become husband and wife.[111]

(4) The contract of *Salam*, being a contract involving future delivery requires immediate consideration to pass in order for it to be valid and not contrary to the rules of *Gharar*.[112]

(5) The contract of barter, by its very essence, requires immediate consideration to pass.

(6) The contract of *Mufāwaḍa* (unlimited mercantile partnership) is created either by mention of the term *Mufāwaḍa* itself, or by mention of every

---

107 *Majella*, Art. 706 which provides: "A contract of pledge is concluded by the offer and acceptance of the pledgor to the pledgee. If the pledge is not transferred to the effective possession of the pledgee, however, such contract is incomplete and revocable. The pledgor may, therefore, denounce such contract before the delivery of the pledge."

108 *Majella*, Art. 837: "A contract of gift is concluded by offer and acceptance. Upon taking delivery the contract becomes complete."

109 Ṣubḥī Maḥmaṣānī, *al-Naẓariyya al-'Āmma li al-Mūjibāt wa al-'Uqūd*, 2 vols., (Beirut, 1948) Vol. II, pp. 31-2.

110 See Bellefonds, *Traité*, I, p.126. The Mālikīs require witnesses *ad probationem*, for purposes of proof: Dardīr and Dasūqī, *al-Sharḥ al-Kabīr*, (Cairo, 1309 AH) II, p.199. The other schools require witnesses *ad solemnitatem*. See Muḥammad Abū Zahra, "*al-Zuwāj*" in *al-Milkiyya wa Naẓariyyāt al-'Aqd*, (First Edn., Cairo, 1939), p.46 ff.; Ibn Qudāma, *al-Mughnī*, *op.cit*., VI, p.450; al-Kāsānī, *al-Badā'i'*, *op.cit*., Vol.V, p.138.

111 The Shāfi'īs and Ḥanbalīs, for instance, insist on the use of the terms *Zawāj*, or *Nikāḥ*, based on the Qur'ānic employment of these terms for marriage; see, for example, *Qur'ān*, *Ṣūra* XXXIII.

112 See al-Jazīrī, *al-Fiqh 'alā al-Madhāhib al-Arba'a*, II, 397ff.; and Santillana, *Instituzione di Diritto Musulmano Malichita*, (Rome 1926-1938) vol. II, 168

single legal effect. Here effect is given only to formal declaration of the precise terms.[113]

(7) The contracts of *'Āriya*, (Hire) and *Qarḍ*, (Loan) are dependent for their legal effect on the taking possession of the object of the contract,[114] or delivery of the monies to the borrower.

The importance of this latter formality is emphasised by a decision of the Ra's al-Khaima Civil Court. In the case of *The Ra's al-Khaima Asphalt Company and The Bank of Oman v. Lloyds Bank (and others)*,[115] one of the Islamic formalities, namely that the monies of a *Qarḍ* loan should be delivered to the borrower for the contract of *Qarḍ* to be of effect, was not adhered to.

A contract for a loan of DM20,000,000 was made between a European businessman and the Ras al-Khaima Asphalt Company. The monies were to be delivered within the forthcoming week and were to be repaid by means of nine bills of exchange drawn on and accepted by the company and guaranteed by The Bank Of Oman. The loan monies never arrived, but the bills, having been discounted on the European Finance Market, were partly bought up by Lloyds Bank International Limited who naturally would seek restitution from the Asphalt Company. The latter, in conjunction with its guarantors, sought a judicial order to prevent the holders in due course of the bills from claiming restitution. The Senior Judge of Ra's al-Khaima, presiding in the Civil Court, held, in accordance with classical Islamic principles, that "The first defendant failed to perform his obligation of paying the sum of money agreed upon to Ras al-Khaima Asphalt Company. Accordingly the agreement concluded between Ras al-Khaima Asphalt Company and the first defendant is no contractual agreement at all and consequently the guarantee proffered by the Bank of Oman is totally devoid of legal effect."[116] There is no doubt that had the case taken place in any western jurisdiction, judgement would have been given for the defendants who were perfectly normal holders in due course. However, under the jurisdiction of Ra's al-Khaima, whose Courts Law of 1971 decrees that the law to be applied by the Civil Court is:

(i) The law expressly enacted in Ra's al-Khaima (in this case, the Contract Law of 1971);

---

113 Schacht, *Introduction, op.cit.*, p.116

114 Ibn 'Ābidīn, *Radd al-Muḥtār*, IV, p.531 ff.; Dardīr, *al-Sharḥ al-Ṣaghīr*, II, 121 ff.

115 Ra's al-Khaima Civil Court, Suit No. 397/78, September 1978; cited in Coulson, *Commercial Law, op.cit.*, p.1

116 Arabic court record of the Ra's al-Khaima Civil Court, Suit No. 397/78 : cited in Coulson, *Commercial Law, op.cit.*, pp.2-3

(ii) The provisions of the Islamic Sharī'a;

(iii) Custom and usage not contrary to the law, public policy or morals and the principles of natural justice, law and equity.[117]

The decision of the Ra's al-Khaima Civil Court, therefore, under the jurisdiction of the Shar'ia, is perfectly correct : The contract of loan was never accorded legal effect because of the failure to comply with a fundamental pillar of the contract. Therefore there was no loan to the Asphalt Company, and since a guarantee must relate to a binding debt, the guarantee was also without legal basis.[118]

Notwithstanding, a later decision by the UAE Federal Supreme Court, in a case concerning a contract between a construction company and Abū Dhabī Department of Social Services and Commercial Buildings to construct and maintain a building in Abū Dhabī, held that the obligations under a bank guarantee are independent of the underlying transaction, and that the performance bond of DH 600,000 represented an "absolute obligation" between the bank and the Department of Social Services, independent of the obligation between the Department of Social Services and the construction company.[119]

The Ra's al-Khaima case was significant for the proof it provided of the rigidity of Islamic principles in the face of Western banking dominance. In this respect alone, it stood rather as a lone pinacle. The later judgment, however, although inconsistent with preceding decisions (where such contracts have generally been avoided on the grounds of bad faith or fraud), does pull the UAE law more into line with international principles. The reversal of this principle is important : it may well serve as a useful parallel for future developments within the Islamic legal system, in particular with regard to the concept of *Ribā*.

The general trend with formalities however, has been to move away from the freedoms enjoyed by early contracting Muslims. To an increasing extent, written evidence is becoming the requisite. The complexities of modern commercial life have led not only to increased documentation in contracts; the current state of affairs renders it no longer advisable to enter into undocumented commercial contracts. Contracts which, a decade ago, would have covered one page of foolscap, would now be as likely to cover ten or twenty. Modern legislation too, has made its mark, and requires the formality of documentation for evidence at law. This is especially so within the fields of Company and Real Estate laws : Articles of Memoranda and

---

117 Ras al-Khaima Courts Law, 1971

118 Coulson, *Commercial Law*, *op.cit.*, p.3

119 *International Financial Law Review*, (Jan 1989).

Association; commercial Agency contracts; Company Registration; rent, mortgage and lease contracts must all be in writing and/or properly registered with Notaries Public.

6.1.3 EFFECTS OF SALES DEEMED VOID OR INVALID

Effects of sales deemed Bāṭil

Within the *Sharī'a* and modern legislation alike, void sales are of no effect and are legally non-existent.[120] No property rights are transferred and no liabilities are incurred by the purchaser in respect of the goods, whether or not he has taken possession of them with the consent of the seller.[121] Nor can void sales be validated, ratified, or amended by approval of the parties,[122] or by the passage of time.[123] Notwithstanding provisions of the law to the contrary, the effects of a void or voidable sale are to leave the contractors in the position in which they were prior to contracting.[124] According to the UAE Civil Code, however, if the void part is separately specified,[125] or if only a part is dependent upon grant of consent which has not been given, these parts may be severable.[126]

In cases of harm or destruction to the goods, therefore, it is the vendor who bears the cost or loss in void sales. It was generally held by the classical jurists that upon deeming nullity of contract once seisin has passed to the buyer, the object becomes as a trust in the hands of that buyer. The purchaser is not empowered to perform any act in respect of the object of sale and it is as if he merely retains seisin with the consent of the vendor.[127] Therefore, should the object perish whilst in his possession, he is not

[120] *Majella*, Art.370 : "A Sale which is void in its essential part (*Bāṭil*). Sanhūrī, *Maṣādir al-Ḥaqq*, IV, pp.145 ff. Kuwaiti Civil Code, Law no 67 of 1980, Art. 184, 187 (1) and (2); UAE Civil Code, Art. 210 (1).

[121] Hamilton, *Hedaya*, p.276

[122] Kuwaiti Civil Code, Law No. 67 of 1980, Art 185; Habachy, 'The System of Nullities in Muslim Law', *AJCL*, 13 (1964) p.72

[123] Kuwait Civil Code, Art.186 (1) and (2); UAE Civil Code, Art. 210 (1). The period of limitation is 15 years after the time of contracting : Kuwait Civil Code, Art 186 (2)

[124] Kuwaiti Civil Code, Law No. 67 of 1980, Art. 187 (1); Bahrain Contract Law, Arts. 66, 67.

[125] UAE Civil Code, Art. 211 (1)

[126] UAE Civil Code, Art. 211 (2)

[127] Hamilton, *The Hedaya*, p.267. This is generally held to be Abū Ḥanīfa's opinion.

liable.[128]

There is, however, dissenting opinion on this point. Some authors reject the deposit analogy, and hold instead that the purchaser should be answerable for harm or destruction to the object in the same way as if such harm should occur at his hands as an intending purchaser.[129]

Effects of sales deemed Fāsid

The schools of Islamic Law are divided as to the effects of invalid sales. The general rule is that voidable contracts can become valid through their ratification by the interested party, or because of prescription of the action which obstructs their validity.[130] The majority opinion is that, in an invalid sale, where the buyer has taken possession of the goods with the consent of the seller, and where both goods and consideration constitute property,[131] the right of ownership of the goods passes to the buyer. He is then responsible for loss or damage to the goods while they are in his possession.[132] Nevertheless, he is only liable for the value of the goods and not for the price, should the goods become harmed or perish in his possession.[133]

The main dissenter to this view is al-Shāfi'ī. Al-Shāfi'ī maintains that since it is forbidden and is in no respect sanctioned by the law, then no invalid sale can substantiate a right of property.[134] In al-Shāfi'ī's view therefore, an invalid sale assumes the same effect as sales which are void, on the grounds that their subject-matter does not constitute property, or that some essential pillar of the contract is lacking.

The counter claim given by the majority of scholars to this opinion is that so long as the object of sale and capacity of the parties is satisfactory, any other invalidating conditions are merely accessory circumstances. After seisin therefore, the right of property accrues to the purchaser by virtue of

---

128 For example, if B, in a void sale, receives an object by leave of S, it is not necessary for B to make compensation for the object if the object is destroyed other than by his fault whilst in his possession. This is because the object is in consequence of his receipt an *emanet* (ie. thing held in charge) in the possession of the purchaser : *Majella*, Art. 370

129 This is held to be the view of the two disciples. Hamilton, *ibid.*, p.267

130 Habachy, 'The System of Nullities in Muslim Law', *AJCL*, 13 (1964) p.72. Kuwait Civil Code, Arts. 181, 182; UAE Civil Code, Art. 212 (1)

131 ie., where goods and/or consideration do not constitute any of the commodities considered non-property, eg. carrion, wine, etc.

132 al-Shāfi'ī dissents. cf. Hamilton, *The Hedaya*, p.267; Sanhūrī, *Maṣādir al-Ḥaqq*, IV, pp.167 ff.

133 Hamilton, *The Hedaya*, pp. 275-276

134 Hamilton, *The Hedaya*, p. 276

the validity of the essential sale, but not by virtue of the invalidating accessory circumstances which are contrary to the law.[135]

The main proviso of this effect is, naturally, that seisin by the purchaser has already taken place. If this is not the case, then the right of property does not pass. The right of property which devolves from an invalid sale nevertheless remains weak and is dependent upon the passing of possession to have any effect. It stands to reason that right of ownership should not pass before possession, in order for the invalid circumstances to be removed.[136] To approve otherwise would mean that the law sanctions such invalidity. The established condition for invalid sales is that possession should pass with the consent of the seller. Such consent may be apparent, but according to a favourable construction of the law, may be implied. A purchaser taking seisin of a commodity at the place of sale or in full view of the seller, may be said to have the latter's consent by implication. This is because the contract of sale itself virtually guarantees the transfer of the right of ownership of the property to the purchaser. The burden therefore lies on the vendor to state his objection in such sales. If no objection on his part is forthcoming, the court will construe the transfer of seisin to have been made with his consent.[137]

In contracts for the sale of fungibles (*Mithlī*), the majority opinion is that such fungibles subject to loss or harm whilst in the possession of the buyer in an invalid sale should preferably be replaced by similar goods.[138] This was considered more equitable compensation than that of paying the seller the value of the lost goods.[139] In the case of non-fungibles (*Qīmī*), the buyer must give the seller the equivalent of their value on the day of delivery.[140] A further offshoot of the concept of *Gharar* is that Islamic law does not recognise the concept of consequential damages in rescinded contracts. Calculation of damages by the Sharī'a courts do not therefore take into account anticipated profits, due to the uncertainty of this matter.[141]

---

135 Hamilton, *The Hedaya.*, p.276; *Majella*, Art. 371 : "A *Bay' Fāsid*, after receipt, has a beneficial effect".

136 This is upheld by UAE Civil Code, Art. 212 (2)

137 Hamilton, *The Hedaya*, p.276. The same applies to the construction of consent in a contract of gift.

138 *Majella*, Art.371

139 Hamilton, *The Hedaya*, p.276

140 *Majella*, Art.371

141 Coulson, *Commercial Law in the Gulf States*, p.82; Sloane, 'The Status of Islamic Law In The Commercial World', *International Lawyer*, (Fall 1988) 22(3) p.747; Kuwait Civil Code, Art. 196 (2).

Invalid contracts may be annulled by either party prior to the passing of possession of the object.[142] Whilst the invalidating factor remains, the contract may also be annulled by either party after seisin. Where a sale is *Ghayru Lāzim* subject to the right of an option, only the person who has that right of option may annul an invalid contract.[143] Similarly, if the invalidity is incorporated in an invalid condition, only the party who has stipulated that condition may annul the contract.[144] Where the object has perished whilst in the buyer's possession, or if he has destroyed it, disposed of it, added to or subtracted from it, or changed it in such a way that it can no longer be regarded as the same object, there is no right for either party to annul the contract.[145]

A suspended contract (*Bay' Mawqūf*) has a beneficial effect only after leave has been given by the relevant party.[146]

It is a condition that if the seller wishes to resume the object of an annulled invalid sale he must first repay the purchase-money to the buyer. Until such restitution, the goods are held by the purchaser as a pledge.[147]

A purchaser may validly resell the object of an invalid sale by virtue of his proprietorship by seisin. This is so whether the invalidating quality exists in the object or in the consideration or exchange.[148] The second sale is contracted by virtual assent of the first seller by virtue of the effect bestowed upon him in the first sale. Secondly, the second sale, which is valid in both essence and qualities, cannot be obstructed in Islamic law by an invalid non-essential quality of a first sale.[149] This therefore forms the antithesis to, for instance, the sale of a house in which there is a right of *Shuf'a* (pre-emption). In the latter, the rights of the pre-empted party are not obstructed by the effects of a second sale, in that he has not forfeited his just title to the house. In both cases the rights of the individual supercede those rights devolved by law.[150] However, any conversion of the object of an invalid sale by the purchaser into whose possession the article has passed,

---

142 *Majella*, Art. 372 : "In a *Bay' Fāsid* either party has the right to annul the sale." Bahrain Contract Law, Art. 65; Kuwait Civil Code, Art. 182 (1); UAE Civil Code, Art. 212 (4)

143 *Majella*, Art. 376; Kuwait Civil Code, Art. 181; UAE Civil Code Art. 214.

144 Hamilton, *The Hedaya*, p.276

145 *Majella*, Art 372

146 *Majella*, Art. 377; UAE Civil Code, Art. 218.

147 Hamilton, *The Hedaya*, p.277; *Majella*, Art. 373

148 Hamilton, *The Hedaya*, p.277

149 *ibid.*, p.276

150 *ibid.*, p.276

whether by resale or by some manufacturing process entailing addition or diminution of the original object, automatically entails the lapse of the purchaser's right to annul the sale.[151]

In the case of real property which has been converted or altered, the view of Abū Ḥanīfa[152] is that based on the idea of perpetual possession. He thereby accords a higher right to the holder of pre-emption which precludes any rights of the seller to the property. The two disciples, dissenting, state that the property must be restored to its original state and returned to the seller.[153] In this case the rights of the pre-emptor, which are established by general law, are subordinate to the rights of the seller. Thus Muḥammad states, and is upheld by Abū Yūsuf, that where a purchaser, under an invalid sale, builds upon the ground he has purchased, the neighbour has no right of *Shuf'a* therein, anymore than he did previous to the purchase.[154]

The redemption of a pledge, on the other hand, restores the original right of the purchaser in an invalid sale to annul the original invalid contract.[155]

Upon the death of the seller, the purchaser has prior claim to the object of an invalid sale, and may sell that object in order to indemnify himself for the price he has paid. Should the sale realise a surplus over the original cost price paid by the purchaser, the surplus must be returned to any outstanding claimants, such as the seller's heirs or creditors.[156] Likewise, for surplus realised upon the resale of a non-fungible object of a previously invalid contract, the somewhat idealistic recommendation is that such surplus should be bestowed in charity. The surplus is regarded as unjustified and unearned, and therefore constitutes *Ribā*. In the case of fungibles, however, any such profits are legitimate and may be retained by the seller.[157] Thus if A sells B a thoroughbred horse for 5000 Dinars under an invalid contract, and subsequently both parties realise profits from resales, B must, according to this rule, bestow his profits from the resale of the specific object to some charity. A, meanwhile, may retain the profits from his subsequent exchange of the fungible purchase-monies.

The same reasoning is applied to profits acquired from objects in which no right of property exists, such as that made in the resale of usurped

---

151 Hamilton, *The Hedaya*, p.276

152 As related by Abū Yūsuf, who later admitted mistrust of his own memory; but the dispute is also related by Muḥammad.

153 *ibid.*, p.277

154 *al-Mabsūṭ*, cited in Hamilton, *The Hedaya*, p.277

155 Hamilton, *The Hedaya*, p.277

156 *ibid.*, p. 277 : In the same manner as the holder of a pawn.

157 *ibid.*, p.278

goods.[158] The absolute non-existence of the right occasioned by the usurpation is considered more important than the invalidity occasioned in the right of property. The consequence of this reasoning, however, defies logic and justice : while the resale profits of a specific object which has been usurped may be quite soundly denied to the usurper, the same profits of non-specific usurped articles (such as stolen monies) may be legitimately retained by the usurper!

Similarly, if A claims a debt owing to him by B of 1000 Dirhams, obtains payment, and later agrees with B that the debt was not due, the profits realised by him during the interim period, in which he legitimately possessed and perhaps processed these monies, are legally his. There is no obligation within the law for him to be denied such profits.[159]

---

158 *ibid.*, p.278

159 For the underlying regulations, see Hamilton, *The Hedaya*, p.278

Chapter 6.2

INVALIDITY OF CONSENT

Consent forms one of the major pillars (*'Arkān*) of the law of contract. The jurists recognised that the concept of ostensible consent is not necessarily conformative with intrinsic intention. Schacht writes,[1] and is echoed by Coulson,[2] : "A fundamental concept of the whole of Islamic religious law, be it concerned with worship or with law in the narrow sense, is the *Niyya* (intent)." They both go on to say that *Niyya* must be explicitly formulated, firstly in the mind of the contracting party concerned, and secondly, in its expression in a declaration of intention. It therefore develops from a state of mind into an act of will (similar to that of the Roman *Animus*), whose objective is to create legal effects. The Islamic stance however, gives an independent significance to the concept of *niyya* beyond that expressed as a manifestation of will. Imperfect, implicit, allusory (*Kināya*) or ambiguous (*Mubham*) declarations, for example, may be considered valid if the *Niyya* is present, and only the very faulty or illegal declarations are rejected as invalid if the *Niyya* is present.

The natural question to ask therefore, is how the court can tell whether the *Niyya* is present if its only formulation is in the mind of the contracting party ?

To this purpose, the jurists devolved a complex "network of legal casuistry"[3] in order to test the categories of declaration according to their validity in relation to *Niyya*. If a buyer, for instance, were to claim that his *Niyya* in concluding a contract of sale remained unfulfilled, the jurists would determine whether the given declaration at the conclusion of the contract is compatible with the *Niyya* he later claims. Such judgment is inherently

---

1 *Introduction, op.cit.*, p.116

2 *History Of Islamic Law, op.cit.*, p.116

3 Schacht, *Introduction, op.cit.*, p. 117

subjective, so the tendency developed to restrict the effect of such declarations so as to mitigate resulting obligations even to the point of evasion.[4] Islamic classical law does not restrict declaration to the narrow scope of verbal precision, but includes gestures (*Ishārāt*), silence, conclusive acts and inferred conditions or surrounding circumstances.

For this reason a series of impediments to consent in contracts was formulated. The formulation of impediments to consent did not form any general theory in the way French Civil Law formulated its "*Vices du Consentement*". Nevertheless, certain parallels may be drawn between the two systems in relation to the main categorisations of vitiating conditions. The same may be said for the Islamic system of options (*Khiyār, pl. Khiyārāt*) which create a power of unilateral rescission of the contract under conditions of vitiated consent. A party who had mistakenly entered into, or who had been unfairly or unwittingly forced or tricked into entering into a contract, was provided with a remedy against the effects of that contract. The jurists determined that consent which is impeded is consent which is conditional upon the cause of the contract, for the consent itself is present but is impaired and invalid : the apparent agreement between the parties is therefore not an actual agreement. The victim of the mistake, fraud or deceit, who is unaware of that fraud or deceit at the time of the contract, would, in all probability, have refrained from entering into that contract had he indeed known of the discrepant factor.[5] In these circumstances the contract becomes voidable (*Qābil li al-Ibṭāl*) with the right to avoid given to the contracting party whose consent was vitiated. It is with this same party that the burden of proof lies in establishing that the consent has been induced by factors which subsequently prove to have been misleading. Impediments may be pleaded on four grounds: Mistake; Fraud; Duress; and Effective constraint.[6]

6.2.1 MISTAKE (GHALAṬ)

The first impediment is that of Mistake (*Ghalaṭ*). There is, on the whole, relatively little discussion given to the concept of *Ghalaṭ* in the treatises. Sanhūrī concedes that Mistake is given the least consideration among the impediments to consent, despite the fact that it is the most conducive to dispute.[7] He classes it as the least obvious of defects due to its being, in all

---

4 Schacht, *ibid.*, p.117

5 Abdur Rahman I Doi, *Shari'ah: The Islamic Law*, (London, 1984), p.357

6 See Maḥmaṣānī, *al-Naẓariyya al-'Āmma li al-Mūjibāt wa al- 'Uqūd fī al-Sharī'a al-Islāmiyya*, II, pp.164-199.

7 Sanhūrī, *Maṣādir al-Ḥaqq*, II, p.112

probability, the most subjective defect to vitiate consent.[8] The principles of *Ghalaṭ* are certainly not to be found in any systematically theoretical exegesis among the Sharī'a authorities. This is a fact which merely compounds the difficulties experienced by modern authors in their attempts to compile any coherent theory of mistake. The latter, it has been remarked,[9] are reduced to equating mistake to the degree of ignorance (*Jahl*) on the part of the contracting parties which precludes a contract from being considered as binding.

The answer to this charge of 'neglect' on the part of the Muslim jurists -particularly Ḥanbalī and Shāfi'ī- lies in the particular structure of Islamic law. The jurists, it is contended, did not neglect the doctrine of Mistake so much as to incorporate it into the pillars of contract, the structure of options and other impediments to consent.[10]

The Muslim 'theories' of obligation are so detailed in their exigences as to the object of contract, for instance, that it would seem to preclude most areas for mistake prior to conclusion of the contract : the object must not only exist but must be in such a condition to be taken possession of; it must also be precisely determined in its substance, class, quality and value; the property must be identified;[11] and the intent to conclude the apparent contract must be genuine. Defects in any of the above will render the contract void *ab initio*. All these conditions placed by the Sharī'a upon the validity of the object may be argued to constitute preventative measures against Mistake.[12] Additionally, the order of priority accorded to Options in Islamic jurisprudence means that where circumstances so prevail, the contract may be more readily avoided through means of the Options of Defect (*Khiyār al-'Ayb*), Sight (*Khiyār al-Ru'ya*) and Description (*Khiyār al-Waṣf*).[13] Therefore in contracts where substantial or nominal Mistake has occurred as to the quality or attributes of the goods, these options will take

---

8 Sanhūrī, *Maṣādir al-Ḥaqq*, II, p.105; N. Saleh, *The General Principles of Saudi Arabian and Omani Company Laws (Statutes and Shar'ia)*, (London, 1981) p.38

9 Coulson, *Commercial Law, op.cit.*, p.67; Saleh, *General Principles, op.cit.*, p.37; S. Maḥmaṣānī, *General Theory, op.cit.*, II, p.420 (1972 Edn)

10 It may be noteworthy here that the two schools which give the least attention to Mistake, the Shāfi'īs and the Ḥanbalīs, are the schools which recognise the Option of *Majlis*. These same two schools also deny the validity of a contract of sale for an object which is not present.

11 Coulson, *Commercial Law, op.cit*, p.68

12 Bellefonds, *Traité*, p.384

13 Coulson, *Commercial Law, op.cit.*, p.67; Maḥmaṣānī, *General Theory, op.cit.*, II, p.423; Saleh, *General Principles, op.cit.*, p.38; Sanhūrī, *Maṣādir al-Ḥaqq, op.cit.*, II, p.121 ff; Sheikh 'Amr b. 'Alī al-Shammākhī, *Kitāb al-Iḍāḥ*, (Ibāḍi) IV Vols., (Lybia and Beirut, 1971) See also Chapter 7 below.

prior effect and it will only be in the final resort that a contract will be avoided for Mistake. Mistake as an Option (or *Khiyār al-Ghalaṭ*, as it would be called) does not strictly exist in the jurisprudence.[14]

In the light of the manifold solutions provided by these other doctrines it is hardly surprising that the Muslim doctors were reluctant to give the Doctrine of Mistake any substantial consideration.

Although discussion of Mistake is limited this does not necessarily mean that in the schools where its principles are found, there is only one accredited opinion. In this doctrine, as in many others, this is not the case, and so in order to avoid a chaos of contradictory dispositions only the prevalent opinions have been reproduced here.

Another difficulty concerning this doctrine is the lack of homology in vocabulary, not only between Islamic concepts and Western terms, but also between the terms employed within the schools. The usual term for error, *Ḥaṭā'*, for instance, is usually only applied in a legal sense in criminal law, to denote the absence of criminal intention.[15] It may yet be found within the *Fiqh* to refer to the Doctrine of Mistake.[16] The most usual term for Mistake is *Ghalaṭ*, which applies both to calculated and material error. In certain Mālikī texts, however, the term *Jahl* meaning 'Ignorance', is found to replace *Ghalaṭ*.[17] Serious misunderstandings are happily usually avoided in these exceptional cases for the context generally suffices to dissipate any ambiguities.

Mistake, which may be defined as a false or inexact representation of reality, may be made in regard to different elements of a contract. The *Fiqh*, like most of the Civil Law systems, is amenable to categorisation, and we may therefore divide this doctrine into several useful sections. Regarding perhaps the most important area of Mistake, the first two subsections concern the substance and quality of the object of contract, and comprise the discussions devoted to the manifestation of the will and consent of the contracting parties. The third section covers Mistake as to the contracting parties themselves; while the fourth section is concerned with Mistake made in consideration and the true value of the object of contract. The fifth category is Mistake made as to law.

---

14 Coulson, *Commercial Law, op.cit.*, p.67

15 Kāsānī, *al-Badā'i'*, VII, 271 f.; Ibn Qudāma; *al-Mughnī*, IX, 330f. (2nd Ed.)

16 For example, *Qatl al-Ḥaṭā'* is homicide : eg. al-Kāsānī, *al-Badā'i'*, VII, 335; also quoted on p.136 of Sanhūrī's *Maṣādir al-Ḥaqq*, Vol II.

17 For example, Ibn Nujaym, *Fatḥ al-Fanār bi-Sharḥ al-Manār*, III, 105

6.2.2 MISTAKE AS TO OBJECT OF CONTRACT

Islamic law conceives of Mistake as a substantive or intrinsic element capable of occurring only during the formation of a contractual agreement. This may occur through inadequacy of correspondence between the parties at the stages of offer and acceptance such as faulty transmission of the contractual declaration through a messenger, telex or suchlike. Similarly, it may be due to a misapprehension or misrepresentation as to the agreed terms, due to latent or patent ambiguities. Alternatively, the mistake could arise from an assumption as to the existence, quality or quantity of the contractual object, or to the nature or existence of the contract itself. It may originate in a computational error, an assumption as to a regulating principle of law, the capacity or identity of the other contracting party, or in a motive based on erroneous facts.[18]

In ascertaining the Cause of Mistake and thereby formulating provisions for its restitution, the desired aim of the legislator or jurisprudent must be to strike that delicate balance between the autonomous will of the individual (the subjective approach) and the respective interests of the parties to a contract (the objective approach).[19]

What provisions there are concerning Mistake are muddled and scattered among various locations in the books of *Fiqh*. More than occasionally they are to be found among the options of Description, Defect or Sight, and the first impression gained is that they form no coherent system at all. Certain texts, notably the Ḥanafī, deal with the concept not as a Doctrine of Mistake so much as a conditional element of the object of contract. An agreement on a *res extincta*, for example, which would be treated in the Common Law as a case of "common mistake", is regulated in Islamic law by rules concerning the existence of the subject matter.[20]

---

18 Mistake in the West is generally defined as "a belief that is not in accord with the facts." See, for example, the *I Restatement (Second) of Contracts*, S. 151 (1981) of the United States.

19 Wherein the law's primary concern is for the integrity of the transaction, but where the subjective-objective dichotomy exists. J. Makdisi, 'An Objective Approach to Contractual Mistake In Islamic Law', 3 *Boston University International Law Journal*, No. 2, (Summer, 1985), pp. 325; 333-334; Also Art. 1110 of the French Civil Code; and J. Ghestin, *La Notion D'Erreur Dans Le Droit Positif Actuel*, (Paris, 1971), pp. 4-5

20 See Sanhūrī *al-Wasīṭ, op.cit.*, Vol. I, pp. 289 ff. and *passim*. This compares with French law; See Parviz Owsia, *A Comparative Study of the conclusion of contracts in Persian, Islamic French and English Law*, (Unpublished Ph D Thesis; London SOAS, 1965), p.365 ; Alex Weill & François Terré, *Droit Civil : Les Obligations*, (Dalloz:Second Edn; Paris, 1975), pp.174-196

The Islamic concept of Mistake is inextricably bound to the notion of consent in Contract.[21] The law lacks a formulated theory because the provisions for Mistake are, in actuality, mostly preclusions or safeguards designed to prevent its very incidence. At the same time, however, cognisance is given to the limitations which must be, and have been throughout Western history, placed upon the scope of any Doctrine of Mistake.[22] If the incidence of Mistake were always to find remedy in non-performance or avoidance of the contract on the part of the mistaken party, the system of contract itself would become unpredictable and unreliable. It would thereby threaten to dispel the faith of the contractors upon which and in the interests of which, it may be argued, the system exists. Because Islamic law here is subjective, we find that a higher consideration is given to relief for Unilateral Mistake than in objective systems. In the latter, the expectations of the non-mistaken party and the security of contractual transactions take priority over the true will of the mistaken party because the mutual consent must be manifested in an external and formal manner.[23]

Mistake as to the object of contract is the most important category of Mistake since it incorporates Substantive Mistake, Mistake as to insubstantial qualities of the object, the controversy between continuing commercial relations and the maintenance of due respect for real consent. It also includes three different Options : the Options of Defect, Description and Inspection.[24]

---

21 This is also the case in modern legislation. See, for example, the *Explanatory Memoranda* to the Kuwaiti Civil Code, p.139

22 In Roman Law, for example, only a few types of Mistake concerning the nature of the transaction, or the identity of the subject matter of the contract were recognised as giving rise to relief by avoiding the contract *ab initio* . See McKeag, 'Mistake In Contract : A Study In Comparative Jurisprudence', 23/2 *Studies In History, Economics and Public Law*, (Columbia University, 1905), 3, pp. 23-24. Certain others, such as *error in materia*, of the object were said by some Roman authors to avoid the contract, but this point remained subject to dispute.

23 See Holmes, *The Common Law*, (1881: Ed. Howe, 1963), p.230; G. Gilmore, *The Death Of Contract*, (Ohio, 1974; 17th Reprint, 1986), p. 21, n. 41. See also *Bell v. Lever Bros Ltd*, [1932]. Lord Atkinson held at p.218: "A mistake will not affect assent unless it is the mistake of both parties, and is to the existence of some quality which makes the thing without the quality essentially different from the thing as it was believed to be." This was upheld in 1988 by Mr. Justice Steyn in *Associated Japanese Bank (International) Ltd. v. Crédit du Nord SA*, [1988] Q.B., who also established, *inter alia*, that "the law ought to uphold rather than destroy apparent contracts".

24 Sanhūrī includes only three options, for he does not recognise the Option of Mistake itself. *Maṣādir al-Ḥaqq*, II, 112, quoting Chafik Chehata, *al-Naẓariyya al-'Amma li al-Iltizāmāt fī al-Sharī'a al-Islāmiyya*, (Cairo, 1939), pp.145-7 who includes the 'Option of Mistake.'

Substantive Mistake

Substantive Mistake is categorised into two subsections which are distinguished from each other due to their different ensuing effects. The first is Mistake as to Meaning (*Ghalaṭ al-Maʿnā*); the second is Difference in the Desired (Insubstantial) Quality of the Object of Contract (*Fawāt al-waṣf al-marghūb fīh*).

The distinction between the categories of Substantial and Insubstantial qualities is somewhat indeterminate, if not arbitrary. The authors state that a piece of silk is substantially different from any other piece of cloth; as is a piece of cloth died red substantially different from one dyed yellow; or that a cloth from Nissapūr is to be distinguished in kind from one from Bokhāra.[25] The jurists therefore devised their system of distinguishing between these two categories not with regard to the material substance involved, but with regard to the usufruct of the object - the use to which it is intended to be put; and principally to the properties of that object that the contractor has in mind when he forms the contract.[26] The quality must therefore be material in the mind of the contracting party who is claiming Mistake; this is so whether it is clearly stated or merely implied. An exemplary case taken from the Ibāḍi Fiqh, for example, is the buying of an animal for its meat, after which the purchaser discovers the animal to be blind. The contract is not avoided here for the defect of blindness is hardly pertinent to the intended use of the transaction, that is, to obtain the meat.[27]

The Mālikī School on the other hand, does not consider Mistake a vitiating element of consent, whether the mistake purports to be to the substance or to an insubstantial quality of the object. In both cases, the contract is not binding because the object is not what has been stipulated and the contract is simply *Fāsid* (Void), in contradistinction to the status of non-existence (*Bāṭil*) given to the same Ḥanafī object.[28]

---

[25] *Fatāwā al-Hindiyya*, (Cairo, al-Muniyya ed.) III, 196.

[26] Marghīnānī, *al-Hidaya*, III. 35; Kāsānī, *al-Badā'i'*, V, 139; Ibn al-Hammām, *Fatḥ al-Qadīr*, V, 206 This compares with the French doctrine advanced by the *Villa Jacqueline*, Case (Cass. Civ. 23.11.1931) where a contract for an area of land was determined inadequate for the buyer's purpose, hence the term "Constructability". *Malinvaud Dalloz*, (1972) 'Chronique', pp.215 ff

[27] 'Abdallāh b. Ḥamīd b. Sallūm al-Sām al-Salīmī, *Jawhar al-Niẓām Fī 'Ilmay al-Adyān wa al-Aḥkām*, (Cairo, 1334 AH); Saleh, *General Principles*, *op.cit*., p. 38

[28] Bellefonds. *Traité*, p.391; For the distinction between *Fāsid and Bāṭil*, see 'Nullities of Contract', *supra*, and Sanhūrī, *Maṣādir al-Ḥaqq*, IV, pp.133,135-136

6.2.3 MISTAKE AS TO MEANING

According to the classical jurists, a mistake with regard to the substance (*Jins*) of the object of contract constitutes a just cause for voiding the contract *ab initio*.[29] The reasoning followed for rendering such contracts of Mistake as void (*Bāṭil*) is based on the concept of the object as a pillar of the contract, and the maxim that "what was intended has not happened, and what has happened was not intended". If the purpose of the obligation has been subject to Mistake, and is evidently not that which the parties originally intended, then the object of the contract is non-existent, and the contract itself becomes void for want of an essential condition. The example tendered by the jurists in their treatises in this respect, which would be treated in English Law under non-performance, but which is classed as 'Mistake' by the Muslim jurists, is commonly that of the stone sold as a sapphire which is subsequently realised to be mere glass.[30] Similarly, if the contract is for the sale of wheat and the object turns out to be flour or bread, the mistake is substantive and real, despite the fact that flour, wheat and bread are different stages of process of the same substance. The contract will be void for lack of agreement as to the meaning (the physical identity) of the expressed object.[31] Here the doctrine approaches that of the Roman *error in corpore*.[32]

Even if the species is the same, but an appreciable difference exists between the object which was contracted for and the usufruct of the intended object, then the contract is again void by virtue of mistake as to meaning. For instance if a cloth is sold in a different colour or pattern to the one intended, it is not in accordance with the purpose of the contractor; it may be arguable here that such a Mistake of Meaning may be actionable

---

29 See Sarakhsī, *al-Mabsūṭ*, XIII, 12; Kāsānī, *Badā'i'*, V, 139 ff.; Ibn Nujaym, *al-Ashbāh*, p.189; also Art. 121 (a) and (b) of the Egyptian Civil Code (law No. 131 of 1948); and *Majella*, Art. 208: "If the object is declared in kind (*Jins*) and the object proves to be of another kind the sale is invalid (*Bāṭil*)". For the rules for identifying the subject matter, see M.E. Hamid, 'Does the Islamic Law of Contract recognize a doctrine of Mistake?' in *Journal of Islamic and Comparative Law*, Vol.IV (1972), pp. 1-16

30 al-Kāsānī, *al-Badā'i'*, V, 139-40; Sarakhsī, *al-Mabsūṭ*, XIII, 12-13; Ibn al-Hammām, *Fatḥ al-Qadīr*, V, 206.

31 See Art. 121 (d) of the Egyptian Civil Code (Law No. 131 of 1948), but note Art. 147 (1) of the new Kuwaiti Civil Code (Law No. 67 of 1980) which states that it must be proven that both parties to a contract must have been deceived by the same error in order for the victim to nullify the contract on the grounds of Mistake.

32 Sanhūrī, *Maṣādir al-Ḥaqq*, II, 113, 114; For *error in corpore* see Nicholas, *An Introduction to Roman Law*, *op.cit.*, p.177; and Lee, *The Elements of Roman Law*, *op.cit.*, p.347

under the Option of Description.[33] In this respect the Islamic Doctrine of Mistake takes on a noticeably wider ambit than that, for instance, of the Common Law doctrines, which would render such contracts as merely voidable for Mistake.[34]

Mistake as to difference of a desired (insubstantial) quality of the object

When the mistake concerns an insubstantial quality (*Wasf*) of the contract, the object being of the same substance as that contracted for, the contract is regarded as valid but not binding and remedy is sought in Islamic law, not under *Ghalaṭ*, but either under the Options of Defect, or Description. If effected under the Option of Description the terms are even more precise in the Ḥanafī school and the holder of the option may seek remedy under the "Option for lack of a desired quality" (*Khiyār fawāt al-wasf al-marghūb*).[35]

The consequences of such sales are therefore of a more limited nature. For instance, if a seller represents the object as a ruby, and it is later deemed to be yellow,[36] the sale is valid because the mistake is not as to the substance of the object and is not deemed to have affected the usufruct intended by the purchaser and the true sale.[37] The object of such a contract is extant and thereby fulfils the essential contractual condition, but the representation made by the seller as to its quality is at fault and therefore renders the contract voidable.[38] Consent becomes vitiated and the purchaser is given an Option of Description (*Khiyār al-Wasf*), either to ratify the contract or to renounce it.[39]

A distinction exists here between the Ḥanbalī and the other schools of law. Where the contract is voidable at the option of the mistaken party, Ḥanbalī Fiqh allows the buyer who decides to ratify the contract and retain

---

33 See Sanhūrī, *Maṣādir al-Ḥaqq*, II, 114

34 The Common Law doctrines are "based on *external* manifestation of mutual assent". See 13 S. Williston, *A Treatise On The Law Of Contracts*, S.1536 (Third Edn.: 1970); and *Hotchkiss v. Nat'l City Bank of New York*, 200 F. 287, 293 (1911), dictum of Judge Learned Hand.

35 Bellefonds, *Traité*, p.385; al-Ḥaṭṭāb, *Mawāhib al-Jalīl*, vol.IV,p.466. Hamid, op.cit. p.6

36 Or as a cow which is discovered to be a bull, a ram which is a sheep, or a book by a certain author which is by another: Sanhūrī, *op.cit.*, II, 117.

37 *Fatāwā al-Hindiyya*, III, 140-1; al-Kāsānī, *al-Badā'i'*, V, 140; Ibn al-Hammām, *Fatḥ al-Qadīr*, V, 201; *Majella*, Arts. 72, 208, 310, 312

38 The example given by the jurists as to quality is where a sapphire is sold as a ruby or topaz. The object is in existence, for they are all precious stones, but the difference exists in the quality of the gem: In such cases the sale remains valid subject to the Option of Mistake granted to the purchaser.

39 Sanhūrī, *Maṣādir al-Ḥaqq*, vols. II, p.114 and IV, pp.248ff.

the object, to demand compensation for the diminution in value of that object so far as such diminution in value is attributable to that mistake.[40] This doctrine may also be found in the Ibāḍi school, but does not constitute a general rule of that school.[41] Some authors of the Ibāḍi school regard cancellation of contracts of Mistake as mandatory, while others recognise the right of option.[42]

The natural question which arises at this stage is with regard to the consequence of a contract where the object is referred to both nominally and demonstrably, and these two references do not concur. The Fiqh determines here that it is the nominal reference which applies. If the object does not comply with the nominal reference the contract becomes void for non-existence of the subject-matter. For example, if A shows B a stone to sell to him, which they both refer to as a sapphire, but which turns out to be a piece of glass, the subject-matter of the contract will be determined as a sapphire and the contract will become void for lack of subject-matter.[43] If, however, the stone sold turns out to be a ruby rather than a sapphire, the class of the subject-matter is the same and the contract remains valid subject to the buyer's Option of Description (*Khiyār al-Wasf*), since the subject-matter does not fit the description given by the seller.[44] It may be seen therefore that the primary concern of the jurists relates to the identification of the subject of the contract rather than the real intention of the parties.[45]

The *Hidāya*[46] states, in summary, that where the article referred to proves essentially different from what was mentioned, the sale is supposed to relate to the article named. If the article is of a different species, then the sale is null. If, on the other hand, the article referred to proves to be of the same species but of a different quality, then in this case the sale relates to the article referred to. If the article referred to is found to be of a different quality, the purchaser is accorded an option to rescind because the article is not of the quality contracted for.

An alternative reasoning is based not on the construction of error itself, but rather for common mistake between the two declared interests.[47] This

---

40 Maḥmaṣānī, *General Theory, op.cit.*, II, 423; Saleh, *General Principles, op.cit.*, p.38

41 al-Shammākhī, *Kitāb al-Īḍāḥ, op.cit.*, III, pp. 216, 250-1; Saleh, *General Principles, op.cit.*, p. 39

42 al-Shammākhī, *ibid.*; Saleh, *General Principles, op.cit.*, p.39

43 Kāsānī, *Badā'i' al-Ṣanā'i'*, V, p.140; Ramlī, *Nihāyat al-Muḥtāj*, Vol. III, p.454

44 Kāsānī, *Badā'i' al-Ṣanā'i'*, Vol. V, p.140

45 Bellefonds, *Traité*, pp.385-392; Hamid, op.cit. pp.7-8

46 Hamilton, *The Hedaya, op.cit.*, p.271

47 Chafik Chehata, *Droit Musulman*, (Paris, 1970) p.131

category of Mistake is important with regard to other contracts, and is discussed by the jurists under several other headings, such as Agency,[48] agricultural contracts,[49] acquittal,[50] bequest,[51] and hire.[52]

The will of the contracting party must generally be revealed to the other party at the time of the contract if the mistake is to be recognised at law. Alternatively, the intention must be evident to the other party at the time of contracting. In some rare instances however it has been held that revelation as to the true intention of the contracting party is not always necessary for Islamic *Fiqh* to determine that a mistake has occurred.[53] This particularly Islamic stance has been adhered to by the new codes only to a limited extent. Hamid notes that commercial usage has helped in bringing some degree of uniformity to the theory of Mistake as regards the subject matter of the contract.[54] He states that in the final analysis the "purpose" of the object of a contract must be determined with reference to commercial usage. If the object falls into a commercially different class for the purpose of the mercantile purchaser, the latter is at liberty to annul the contract under the Doctrine of Mistake. Article 193 of the new Federal Civil Code of the UAE, for example, states : "No regard shall be had for any mistake save in so far as it is contained in the form of the contract or demonstrated by the surrounding circumstances and conditions, or the nature of things, or custom."[55]

Here it may be said that the law will recognise technical errors of the contract and obvious mistakes in the declaration of the Parties' will or inferred intention. But beyond this, modern Islamic legislation does not go. In this respect therefore we see the marked approach of the UAE Code towards the more restrictive bounds of Western Civil systems.

This same tendency is clearly discernable in the Contract Law of Bahrain.[56] The Bahraini Code has been subjected to the influence of English Law, and this may be seen in the brevity of its articles on Mistake.

---

48 Ibn al-Hammām, *Fatḥ al-Qadīr*, VII, 27-8; al-Kāsānī, *al-Badā'i'*, VI, 23;

49 al-Kāsānī, *al-Badā'i'*, VI, 178

50 al-Kāsānī, *al-Badā'i'*, VII, 189;

51 al-Kāsānī, *al-Badā'i'*, VII, 335

52 al-Kāsānī, *al-Badā'i'*, IV, 181; Ibn al-Hammām, *Fatḥ al-Qadīr*, VIII, 60; Ibn 'Ābidīn, *Radd al-Muḥtār*, vol V, pp.4, 24.

53 Sanhūrī, *Maṣādir al-Ḥaqq*, II, 122

54 M. E. Hamid, 'Does the Islamic Law of Contract recognize the Doctrine of Mistake?', *Journal of Islamic and Comparative Law*, Vol.IV, (1972), p. 4

55 UAE Civil Code No. 2 of 1987

56 Bahrain, The Contract Law, 1969, Article 24

Moreover, the Bahraini Code only recognises mistakes made in respect to facts which are **essential** to the agreement;[57] Of equal importance is the specification that Mistake only invalidates an agreement where **both** parties to that agreement fall into the same mistake.[58]

The Code fails to give any interpretation of "essential" itself, and it may be presumed that it is the courts which are to determine its definition. In this context, however, reference to the Egyptian Civil Code may prove useful, for an "essential" mistake is here deemed to be "when its gravity is of such a degree that, if it had not been committed, the party who was mistaken would not have concluded the contract".[59] More particularly, a mistake is deemed to be essential, according to the Egyptian Code when :

> (1) "It has bearing on the quality of the goods, which the parties have considered essential or which must be deemed essential, taking into consideration the circumstances surrounding the contract and the good faith that should prevail in business relationships."
>
> (2) "It has a bearing on the identity, or on one of the qualities of the person with whom the contract is entered into, if this identity or this quality was the principal factor in the conclusion of the contract."[60]

A construction of the Bahrain articles on the foundation of this interpretation would clearly reinstate the wider ambit of the Islamic principles outlined in the Fiqh treatises. The Bahraini courts however, do not refer to the Egyptian codes or to the works of Professor Sanhūrī, unlike the courts of the UAE and Kuwait. Indeed, the Civil Code of the latter contains an article remarkably similar to that of Article 121 of the Egyptian Code quoted above.[61] Article 147 of the Kuwaiti Civil Code states:

> "If the party to a contract errs in such a way as to compel him to consent to the contract, ie., had he not erred he would

---

57 *ibid.*, Art. 24 (1)

58 *ibid.*, Art. 24 (1)

59 Egyptian Civil Code, (Law No. 131 of 1948), Article 121.

60 *ibid.*, Article 121 (a) and (b)

61 In the Explanatory Memorandum to the Kuwaiti Civil Code (p.139) the Egyptian Code is acknowledged as one of the sources of this article, along with 'other Arab codes', among which, the Kuwaiti Commercial Code.

> not have consented to the contract, then he shall retain the right to request that the contract become null and void. If the other party to the contract has made the same error without any influence from him, it will be possible to correct it or apprise him of it, or it will be feasible for him to notify him of it."[62]

The second clause of this article states that in the case of gifts, the same party retains the right to request that the contract become null and void without consideration of the participation of the other contracting party to the contract in the error or having to apprise him of it.[63]

A further 'new' principle is to be found in the Kuwaiti Code. Article 148 states that where a mistake in the contract does not render the contract illegal, but which is not brought to the attention of one of the contracting parties, the right of that party to nullify the contract is not lost.[64]

6.2.4 MISTAKE WITH STIPULATION OF INTENTION

The classic case of mistake as exposed by the early Muslim jurists is that of "error of expression", that is, where one word is used mistakenly for another : a case of *lapsus linguae*. In such cases the contract is regarded as having been concluded, for, as in the example of Duress, the declaration exists and has been issued by a party of full capacity, and is formed with all the requisite intention. It merely lacks consent (*Riḍā*), as in the example of Duress. Here, the *lapsus linguae* vitiates the declaration in a similar manner to the way the illicit act of Duress itself vitiates the resulting contract. In order to annul the contract on the basis of Mistake, the "victim" of the mistake assumes the burden of proof and must show that the mistake was a determining factor in his having entered into the contract.[65] Sanhūrī contrasts two situations: In the first, a seller sells a sapphire but calls it a stone without knowing that it is a sapphire. This will not be considered a mistake, as the seller does not reveal his intention to the buyer; indeed it is no different from his implied intention to sell the stone, due to his ignorance of its true essence. In the second case, the purchaser requests a piece of Mervian cloth valued at one Dinar; the seller produces a piece of cloth

---

[62] Kuwaiti Civil Code, (Law No. 67 of 1980) Art.147 (1); See also Explanatory Memorandum to the Kuwaiti Civil Code, pp. 139-140

[63] *ibid.*, Art. 147 (2)

[64] See Explanatory Memorandum to the Kuwaiti Civil Code, pp. 140-141

[65] Chafik Chehata, *Théorie Générale de l'Obligation en Droit Musulman*, p.124 ff.(French Edn.); Arts. 121 and 122 of the Egyptian Civil Code.

worth four Dinars. Here the mistake is discoverable and the seller is permitted to avoid the contract. The result would have been the same if the seller were to produce a piece of cloth for half a Dinar, for the Ḥanafī jurists do not distinguish between an object of superior or inferior value to that stipulated. In this matter the Shāfi'ī solution is diametrically opposed to that of the Ḥanafī's. Shīrāzī states that where an object is discovered to be superior to that stipulated, the buyer has no option to rescind the contract for Mistake.[66] This result is based on the more objective theory in that the mistake is expensive for the seller. It does not, however, take into consideration, (as the more subjective Ḥanafī theory does)[67] the fact that despite its superior value, the object may still be lacking in the substantial quality stipulated and desired by the purchaser, and may not, therefore, be in accordance with his consent.

The reasoning applies to questions of number : If a man sells 50 cloths for 1000 Dirhams and in actual fact the buyer finds 49 or 51, the buyer may claim the missing one or must return the extra, respectively. If the number is deficient, the contract is deemed *Fāsid* due to the ignorance of the price; for the price quoted is for 50 cloths and will not therefore correspond to the number actually delivered into the possession of the buyer.[68]

That the intention of the contracting parties is evident at the time of contracting may be argued in three ways: the intention may be expressly manifest so as to leave the other party with no doubt as to the former's intention; it may be tacitly deduced by indications, concomitants or the circumstances of the case; or the intention may be surmised from the necessary nature of things (*Ṭabā'i al-Ashyā'*).[69]

Manifest Expression of Intent

Muslim law divides manifest expression of intent into two formulae. The first is called Nomination (*al-Tasmiya*) and the second is designation or indication (*al-Ishāra*). Nomination represents the real will of the contracting party and indication represents the apparent will. If they coincide the contract is binding, but if they do not a series of combinations of solutions are provided by the *Fiqh*.

---

66 Shīrāzī, *al-Muhadhdhab*, I, 287

67 In general, Ḥanafī teaching is more objective than the other Sunni schools. The 'subjectivity' of the Ḥanafī doctrine mentioned here is thus only in relation to Mistake and is not a statement of general applicability.

68 Sarakhsī, *al-Mabsūṭ, op.cit.*, Vol. XII, p.2

69 Sanhūrī, *Maṣādir al-Ḥaqq*, II, 124; See also UAE Civil Code No.2 of 1987, Art. 193

In the first of Sanhūrī's contrasting situations given above, if the nomination of an article differs from an indication given, and thereby the true intention or will is different from the apparent intention, consideration is given to the real will rather than the apparent will, for the seller has been informed of the true intention of the buyer. If, however, the indication given refers to an object of a different substance to the one named, or to an object of the same substance but with an appreciable difference in usufruct, the mistake is that of meaning and the contract is void.

The Mālikīs here discuss sale by catalogue and arrive at the same solution: if the delivered article fails to fit its catalogue description, the buyer has an option to rescind the contract for Misdescription. But if he is satisfied upon delivery and later discovers the object to be inferior to its description then his former satisfaction is treated as a mistake.[70] If however, the object fits its description the contract is sound and, additionally, the buyer is denied the Option of Inspection.[71]

In the Ḥanafī school in the above case, where there is no difference in the use to which the object is put, the contract is formed on the basis of the indicated object, even if the buyer has given a description of a desired (insubstantial) quality which he later discovers is missing. His remedy will be in an Option of Description.[72]

Deduction of Intent from Circumstances of the Case

It is not necessary for manifestation of a contracting party's will to be express. The other party may be reasonably assumed to have tacitly understood or deduced his co-contractor's will from his accompanying circumstances or origin, and may therefore be expected to recognise a mistake. For instance, if someone sells a stone in a market for precious jewels, it may reasonably be assumed also to be of that category of value, even if it is not so expressed in the contract. Similarly, the sale of a male camel to a Bedouin who would obviously require a female for its milk, or of a female to a caravanner who would require a male for its strength, are mistakes recognisable from the circumstances of the contractor.[73]

Mistake having been established, the contractor is deemed to have the right of Option of Defect (*Khiyār al-'Ayb*), but the burden of proof does lie

---

[70] Dasūqī, *Ḥāshiyya 'Alā al-Sharḥ al-Kabīr*, vol III, 24-5; Mālik Ibn Anas, *al-Mudawwana al-Kubrā*, X, 44-45

[71] Sanhūrī, *Maṣādir al-Ḥaqq*, II, 127-8

[72] Sanhūrī, *Maṣādir al-Ḥaqq*, II, 125; Sarakhsī, *al-Mabsūṭ*, XIII, 12-13; Ibn Nujaym, *al-Ashbāh wa al-Naẓā'ir*, p.189

[73] Ibn 'Ābidīn, *Radd al-Muḥtār*, IV, 94

with the holder of that Option.[74] If proven satisfactorily, the intended characteristic is treated as a written condition of the contract.[75]

Custom is also regarded in this category as forming a part of the concomitant aspects of a case; custom is assumed to be within the bounds of knowledge of the contracting parties.[76]

Deduction of Intent from the "Nature of Things"

-The Option of Defect

The third method of deducing the intention of the contracting parties is alligned to the Option of Defect. This has been called an established option with an implied condition,[77] for there is an implied condition of guarantee concerning the soundness of the object, unless the contractor expressly inserts a condition of waiver against defects in the contract. That the soundness of an object is an implied condition in a contract is required by the very "Nature of Things" (*Ṭabā'i al-Ashyā'*).[78] Anything which appreciably diminishes the value of an object of ordinary commerce is regarded as a defect giving rise to an option. In this way, the Option of Defect is closely linked to the Doctrine of Mistake. It is, in fact, one of the many forms of remedy provided by the Islamic doctrine. In accordance with the rules governing the Option of Defect, however, a defect known by the buyer prior to taking possession of the object does not give rise to an option on his part. In such cases, his acceptance of the object is construed as tacit acceptance of the defect.[79]

Al-Kāsānī states in this context that the will of the buyer is that the object is sound, and that his will is a valid condition of the contract. Therefore, if the object is discovered to contain a defect, this condition of the buyer's will is lacking and the validity of the contract is affected, giving rise to the right of option. In support, he quotes the Qur'ānic verse : "Oh you who believe! Eat not up your property among yourselves in vanities; But let there be amongst you traffic and trade by mutual good will."[80]

---

[74] Sanhūrī, *Maṣādir al-Ḥaqq*, II, 128-9; Ibn Nujaym, *al-Baḥr al-Rā'iq*, VI, 26; See Chapter XII.4 below

[75] Ibn Nujaym, *al-Baḥr al-Rā'iq*, VI, 26; Ibn 'Ābidīn, *Radd al-Muḥtār*, IV, 94.

[76] Ibn Nujaym, *al-Baḥr al-Rā'iq*, VI, 25; See UAE Civil Code which also mentions custom in this context: Law No. 2 of 1987, Art. 193

[77] al-Kāsānī, *al-Badā'i'*, V, 273

[78] Sanhūrī, *Maṣādir al-Ḥaqq*, II, 130

[79] Sanhūrī, *Maṣādir al-Ḥaqq*, II, 130-131; al-Kāsānī, *al-Badā'i'*, V, pp. 274, 276, 282.

[80] *Qur'ān*,(IV:29) quoted in Kāsānī's *al-Badā'i'*, V, 274

6.2.5 NON-DISCLOSURE OF THE WILL (Khiyār al-Ru'ya)

It has been established in Islamic jurisprudence that if a contractor agrees to buy an object without having seen it, he is allowed an Option of Inspection, which gives him the right to ratify or rescind the contract when he does finally inspect the object. Such contracts are formed on the basis of the passing of possession rather than ownership and are avoided by the return of the object to the seller. Thus when the buyer contracts to buy an unseen article without disclosing his intention as to that article to the seller, and upon inspection he discovers that the article does not fit his original intention, he may seek remedy in Mistake under the title of the Option of Inspection.[81]

This doctrine, like that of the Option of Defect in Mistake, has its foundations in the role of the will of the contracting parties. A contract formed by the will of two parties cannot be valid when the will of one of those parties has been breached by mistake as to the intended object.[82]

Islamic law has taken a stance of 'tolerance' here in determining that a contract for an unseen object cannot become binding until it is inspected by the buyer and such a contract does not therefore depend on the buyer having to communicate his intention to his co-contractor at the time of the contract, nor on the possibility of such intention being deduced from custom or the circumstances of the contract. In this respect the Islamic ambit of the Doctrine of Mistake is somewhat wider than that of both Common and Civil Law systems. However, there are detailed rules determining the exercise of the Options of Defect and Inspection which prevent, as far as is possible, such a system from being constantly prone to exploitation. The majority of these rules are contained in the principles of the relevant options and will be discussed in the chapter on Options. Among the contemporary codes, recourse may be had to those articles which attempt to limit the scope of the doctrine of disclosed will within the ambit of Mistake. Article 124 of the Egyptian Civil Code, for example, states that : "A party who has committed a mistake cannot take advantage of the mistake in a manner contrary to the principles of good faith. Such a party, moreover, remains bound by the contract which he intended to conclude, if the other party shows that he is

---

81 al-Kāsānī, *al-Badā'i'*, V, 292; Sanhūrī, *Maṣādir al-Ḥaqq*, II, 132; IV, 248 : Sanhūrī quotes a Tradition of the Prophet in support of this doctrine : "Whoever buys something without seeing it has the option upon seeing it". See also Chapter on Options below.

82 al-Kāsānī, *al-Badā'i'*, V, 292

prepared to perform the contract."[83]

It merely remains to be said that the remedy in the Option of Inspection for Mistake is based both on an equitable notion for the continuance of healthy trade relations,[84] and for the protection of unwary consumers against the false, ambiguous, or unscrupulous commercial descriptions to which manufacturers and retailers occasionally resort.

6.2.6 MISTAKE AS TO PERSON

The doctrine of Mistake as to Person is not explicity formulated by the classical jurists, but certain resolutions may be adopted to form the general outline of a doctrine.

It almost goes without saying that Mistake as to Person does not affect the contract unless the persona of the contractor, or a substantive quality thereof, which gives rise to a mistake, is a legal cause of the contract. In most contracts Mistake as to the person with whom one is dealing is irrelevant because one is willing to contract with anyone. There are specific contracts in which a mistake as to the person of the co-contractor is however of significance, and it is in relation to these individual cases where the doctrine assumes any importance.[85] Should such a mistake occur in the formation of these specific contracts, the party who suffers by it is given the right to annul the contract.[86] This principle finds a parallel in the French Civil Law concept of *Intuitu Personae*[87] It may be contrasted to the English Common Law position where Mistake as to Person falls into the category of Mistakes which negate consent.[88]

This kind of mistake is most often mentioned in the *Fiqh* in relation to marriage contracts, where the person of the spouse is generally of prime consideration in the contract. The conclusion arrived at by modern authors like Sanhūrī however, distinguishes between qualities generally, and

---

83 Egyptian Civil Code, 1948 : Art. 124

84 Sanhūrī, *Maṣādir al-Ḥaqq*, II, 133

85 Sanhūrī, *Maṣādir al-Ḥaqq*, II 135-6

86 Reference is made here to "patrimonial" contracts, and details concerning the peculiar "Extrapatrimonial" contracts such as marriage, Repudiation, Oath, Manumission, etc., may be found in Bellefonds, *Traité*, p.394 ff. For the definition of 'extrapatrimonial' see section on restrictions to capacity, *supra*.

87 B. Nicholas, *French Law of Contract*, (London, 1982), p.92; See also Article 1110 of French Civil Code which states that Mistake as to the person with whom one intends to contract is not a cause of nullity "unless the consideration of this person is the principle cause of the agreement"; and Weill et Terré, "Erreur sur la Personne" in *Droit Civil Des Obligations*, (Précis Dalloz: Second Edition; Paris 1975)

88 Treitel, *Contract*, pp. 216 ff

essential qualities of the person, echoing the theory of annulment of marriage for certain impediments, which was indeed first postulated by the classical jurists. A Mistake as to essential qualities of the person in Sanhūrī's opinion therefore invalidates the marriage contract.[89]

Similarly, Mistake as to Person is mentioned in the unilateral contract of gift: the person of the donee generally constitutes a substantive aspect of the contract. A mistake as to his person therefore gives the donor the right to withdraw, or demand the return of, his gift.[90]

In the unilateral contract of bequest also, the person of the legatee is regarded as a cause of the contract. Al-Kāsānī states : "Among them (ie. the conditions of the pillar of contract) is the consent (*Riḍā*) of the testator because it is an offer of property or that which is connected with property, and there is no doubt that the will is an offer of property in all regards. Therefore, a bequest made in jest, or by compulsion or mistake (al-Khaṭi') is not valid, because these impediments are not in conjunction with the consent."[91] The same argument is applied to the contracts of pre-emption (*Shuf'a*)[92] and Agency (*Wakāla*), and the hire of a wet nurse.[93] In the contract of agency, however, Mistake pertains not so much to the identity of the person as to his substantive qualities. For example, a minor (*Ṣabiyy Mahjūr*) purporting to be an agent lacks capacity so to act. If a third party dealing with the agent believes the latter has proper capacity to contract and acquire his appropriate rights under the contract, this is a mistake in the substantial quality of the agent, that is, his capacity to acquire the rights of the contract. Thus the third party who deals unwittingly with such an agent

---

89 Sanhūrī, *Maṣādir al-Ḥaqq, op.cit.*, II, 135-6

90 This principle is not specific to the Doctrine of Mistake: the donor has the option to withdraw his gift even if he has not made a mistake as to the person of the donee. The right is absolute. See Sanhūrī, *Maṣādir al-Ḥaqq op.cit.*, II, 136. These unilateral contracts are included in the comprehension of the wider umbrella term of the Islamic *'Aqd*, and the Civil Law implication of *contrat*; even though they would not be considered in this context in Common Law analysis.

91 al-Kāsānī, *al-Badā'i', op.cit.*, VII, 335; Also cited in Sanhūrī, *Maṣādir al-Ḥaqq, op.cit.*, II, 136

92 Defined as "The right of a person to substitute himself for the purchaser in a complete sale of real property" (Ziadeh, at p.35). See al-Ṭaḥāwī, Aḥmad, *Kitāb al-Shuf'a Min al-Jāmi' al-Kabīr Fī al-Shurūṭ*, (Ed. J. Schacht) in 20 *Heidelberger Akademie der Wissenschaften*, 3 (1929-1930); and Ziadeh, F.J., 'Shufa'ah: Origins and Modern Doctrine', *Cleveland State Law Review*, 34 (1) (1985-1986) pp.35-46

93 Sanhūrī, *Maṣādir al-Ḥaqq, op.cit.*, II, 137-8; 142; Sarakhsī, *al-Mabsūṭ, op.cit.*, XIV, 105; Ibn Nujaym, *al-Baḥr al-Rā'iq, op.cit.*, VIII, 144; al-Khurshī, *Sharḥ Mukhtaṣar Sīdī Khalīl*, 8 Vols. in 4, (1318. Reprint, Beirut, n.d.) vol. VI, 173; Sheikh Zakarīyā al-Anṣārī, *Sharḥ al-Bahja al-Wardiyya.*, III, 279

may avoid the contract on the grounds of Mistake.[94]

The majority of texts relate that a buyer may never avoid the contract for Mistake when he contracts with an agent minor, whether he knows of the lack of capacity or not. However, Abū Yūsuf states that if the buyer is aware of the status of the agent minor, he is not allowed to avoid, whereas if he is mistaken unwittingly, he may be given the option to annul or perform.[95]

The Doctrine of Mistake as to Person is not, however, universally or definitively recognised, especially among modern authors. Sanhūrī is categoric enough in his stipulation that the person of the contractor is a determinant factor in the contract.[96] Chafik Chehata is less certain and states that the person may sometimes give rise to an action for Mistake.[97] Bellefonds, on the other hand, is not at all convinced by the arguments of the above authors and is rather more prepared to categorise these kinds of mistakes under 'misunderstandings as to the cause of the agreement, or imperative rules of law'.[98] Further, there are other modern commentators who never mention this category of mistake at all, let alone attempt to promote logical theories as to its determination.[99] Their reticence is reflected by the modern Codes of the Arab Gulf States: there is no article in the Kuwaiti, the Bahraini, nor even the Federal United Arab Emirates Civil Codes, which designates any space to "Person" in their articles on Mistake. It is especially surprising to find a lacuna of this sort in the Kuwaiti Code, since the Egyptian Code on which it is modelled contains an article in respect of Mistake as to Person.[100] It is nevertheless arguable that Mistake as

---

94 al-Kāsānī, *al-Badā'i'*, VI, 34

95 Sanhūrī, *Maṣādir al-Ḥaqq*, II 139

96 Sanhūrī, *Maṣādir al-Ḥaqq*, II 136

97 Chehata, *Théorie Générale de l'Obligation*, 126

98 Bellefonds, *Traité*, p.393

99 Cf. for instance, the works of Maḥmaṣānī, *al-Naẓariyya al-'Āmma li al-Mūjibāt wa al-'Uqūd, op.cit.*; Mūsā, *al-Amwāl wa Naẓariyyat al-'Aqd, op.cit.*; Aḥmad, *Baḥth Muqārin Mawḍū'uhū 'Uyūb al-Riḍā Fī 'Uqūd al-Mu'āwaḍāt al-Māliyya Fī al-Sharī'a al-Islāmiyya: al-Ghubna wa al-Tadlīs*, Vol. I, (Dār al-Maṭbū'āt al-Jāmi'iyya: College of Law, Alexandria University, Egypt, n.d.); 'Alī al-Khafīf, *al-Aḥkām al-Mu'āmalāt, op.cit.*; Abū Zahra, *al-Milkiyya wa Naẓariyyat al-'Aqd*, (First Ed. 1939)

100 Egyptian Civil Code, (Law No. 131 of 1948), Art. 121 (b) states that a contract may be set aside when it encompasses an essential mistake. An essential mistake may have, according to this article, "a bearing on the identity, or on one of the qualities of the person with whom the contract is entered into, if this quality was the principal factor in the conclusion of the contract."

to Person may be pleaded under Article 147 (1),[101] where the party can show that he would not have consented to the agreement had he not erred in the identity of the person of the other contracting party.

We see here then, in the more recent Codes of the three Arab Gulf states, a marked divergence away from both the classical exposition of Mistake as to Person in the Islamic Fiqh, and from that of the Civil Law system adopted by the first generation of Arab codifying countries.

6.2.7 MISTAKE AS TO VALUE : GHABN AL-FĀḤISH

Islamic law generally only recognises Mistake as to Value in conjunction with *Ghabn al-Fāḥish* (Flagrant Misrepresentation).[102] The *Majella*, defines *Ghabn al-Fāḥish* in its glossary as "Excessive deception in the value of goods"[103] but further definition is given in article 165 to the effect that "excessive deception" means not less than one-twentieth of the total price in respect of goods, one-tenth in respect of animals, and one-fifth in respect of real estate unless accompanied by verbal deception (*Taghrīr*) or fraud (*Tadlīs*).[104] In the latter cases, the misrepresentation appears in respect of the will as an expedient for the continuance of commercial relations. Article 356 of the *Majella* states : "If there is an excessive deception without fraud in a sale, the person who is deceived cannot annul the sale." Further, in Article 357 : "When one of the parties to a sale has defrauded the other and it has been ascertained that there has been excessive deception the person who is deceived can annul the sale." The doctrine is based on the lack of equivalence in the contract which would result in an injustice to one of the parties.

In the rare references to *Ghabn* concerning the value of a contract, as distinct from fraud and verbal deception, two main indications may be discerned: firstly, in the Ḥanafī, Shāfi'ī and Ḥanbalī schools, the *Fuqahā'* tend to concentrate on individuals or institutes most needful of public protection, such as the property of a minor, a *waqf* donor, or the treasury. If *Ghabn* occurs in transactions concerning these institutions, the contract may be rescinded for *Ghabn al-Fāḥish* and it is not a requirement that the *Ghabn*

---

[101] Article 147 (1) states, *inter alia*: "If the party to a contract errs in such a way as to compel him to consent to the contract, ie. had he not erred he would not have consented to the contract, then he shall retain the right to request that the contract become null and void".

[102] This is particularly prominent in the Ḥanbalī school : See Sanhūrī, *Maṣādir al-Ḥaqq*, *op.cit.*, II, 133 ff., 145

[103] Glossary, *Majella*, p.xiv

[104] See also comment to Kuwait Civil Code, Art. 163 (2) at the end of this section.

be accompanied by fraud or verbal deceit.[105] The provision of legislative welfare for vulnerable institutions has also been taken up by the recently promulgated Civil Code of the UAE.[106] Article 191 states that where a contract may not generally be cancelled on the basis of *Ghabn al-Fāḥish* without the accompaniment of Misrepresentation (*Taghrīr*), contracts in respect of property belonging to persons under restriction, *Waqf* or the State may be so cancelled.

Secondly, when Mistake as to the Value of the object is accompanied by a flagrant misrepresentation, it is not always necessary that it also be accompanied by verbal deceit for consideration to be given to *Ghabn*.[107] This is not the case in the Shāfi'ī school : Here it is held that a mistake accompanied by *Ghabn* alone does not give rise to rescission, but must also be accompanied by *Taghrīr*.[108]

The Ibāḍi school also mentions that a contract may be cancelled for any diminution in the value of the object, whether or not that diminution is a veritable defect. A somewhat irrational case is cited in this regard : A horse with a mark on its chest (*Makhū'*) was regarded of old with superstitious suspicion, such that its value immediately depreciated upon discovery of such a mark. In such cases the Ibāḍi school recognised avoidance of the contract by means of the Option of Defect, even though that defect did not affect the intended use of the horse, nor its strength.[109] Here the principle of the Ibāḍi school contrasts markedly with that of the other schools and must therefore be distinguished as contrary to the general doctrine.

Ghabn Accompanied by Taghrīr or Tadlīs

The general doctrine is that non-equivalence, accompanied by fraud may give rise to rescission of the contract, but this is not generally allowed as a basis for rescission or relief unless there is fraud.[110]

---

105 Sanhūrī, *Maṣādir al-Ḥaqq*, II 145; 148; *Majella*, Art.356; See also Art 124 of the Iraqi Civil Code; and Sarakhsī, *al-Mabsūṭ*, XV, 64-69

106 Federal Civil Code of the United Arab Emirates, Law No. 2 of 1987, Art. 191

107 Sanhūrī, *Maṣādir al-Ḥaqq*, II, 142-3. This contrasts with the general doctrine that flagrant misrepresentation must be accompanied by verbal deceit to give rise to rescission of the contract.

108 al-Anṣārī, *Sharḥ al-Bahja*, II, 455; al-Shirbīnī, *Mughnī al-Muḥtāj : Sharḥ Minhāj al-Ṭālibīn*, (Cairo, 1308 AH) II, 65

109 al-Shammākhī, *Kitāb al-Īḍāḥ*, *op.cit.*, III, 217-18; Saleh, *General Principles*, *op.cit.*, p. 39

110 Sanhūrī, *Maṣādir al-Ḥaqq*, II, 145

Ibn al-Hammām states that in a contract for the sale of property (*Qunya*) if the buyer is deceived in an exhorbitant way by the seller, he has the right to return the property to the buyer under the principle of *Ghabn*.[111]

There seems to be some dispute as to whether the seller, subject to the same mistake, may demand the return of the object. The majority opinion appears to think not. Further, Islamic sources are alleged to support the stance that a seller may deceive a buyer not only verbally, but also by indication (Dalāl), thereby resulting in the buyer's right to return the object.[112] Ibn 'Ābidīn seems to provide a more coherent picture of this rather vague doctrine. In his treatise on Avoidance for *Ghabn* unaccompanied by *Taghrīr*,[113] he suggests three different stances taken in Islamic Fiqh towards *Ghabn* and the rescission of sale. The first is that the sale is valid but may be rescinded absolutely; the second is that rescission is not absolute: the third is that if deceit has also occurred, rescission is absolute, but otherwise it is not. Ibn 'Ābidīn himself favoured the third solution[114] as, he states, do most of the *Fuqahā'*, for this is the solution which is ultimately most in harmony with public interest.

It is also the solution advanced by the *Majella*.[115] Additionally, the Shāfi'īs also hold that *Ghabn* does not give rise to rescission unless accompanied by *Taghrīr*,[116] and that *Ghabn* accompanied merely by mistake does not rescind the contract.[117] For instance, if a buyer buys a piece of glass in the belief that it is a jewel and he pays a considerable sum for it, or alternatively, if a seller sells a jewel believing that it is a piece of glass and receives a minor consideration for it, in the first case there is no option to the buyer, and in the second there is no option to the seller.[118] On the other hand, if the seller were to sell that jewel, calling it, or labelling it as a jewel, the Shāfi'īs hold that here *Ghabn* is accompanied by verbal deception (*Taghrīr*) and in this case the sale may be rescinded at the option of the buyer.[119]

---

111 Ibn al-Hammām, *al-Baḥr al-Rā'iq*, VI, 115-6

112 Sanhūrī, *Maṣādir al-Ḥaqq*, II, 143

113 Ibn 'Ābidīn, *Taḥbīr al-Taḥrīr fī Ibṭāl al-Qaḍā' bi al-Faskh bi al-Ghabn al-Fāḥish bilā Taghrīr.*

114 *idem*,. II, 7; and see further references quoted in Sanhūrī, *op.cit*, II, 144

115 See Articles 356 and 357 quoted above

116 al-Anṣārī, *Sharḥ al-Bahja*, II, 455

117 al-Shirbīnī, *Mughnī al-Muḥtāj Sharḥ al-Minhāj*, II, 65.

118 al-Shirbīnī, *Mughnī al-Muḥtāj*, II 65; al-Ramlī, *Nihāyat al-Muḥtāj 'ilā Sharḥ al-Minhāj*, IV, 74

119 Sanhūrī, *Maṣādir al-Ḥaqq*, II, 146

The Ḥanbalī school allows the option to rescind for *Ghabn* on three grounds, all of which require the accompaniment of *Taghrīr*: The first is sale to receive passengers and goods; the second is *al-Najsh*[120] and the third is for the contract of dispatch, when the carrier is unaware of the value of the commodity and does not deem it a condition of the contract. If he asks the contractor for indemnity and is deceived thereto, the carrier is given the option of *Ghabn* for it is accompanied by verbal deceit. This may also be classed as fraud and may be actionable under that title.[121] Additionally, it is to be noted that if rescission for *Ghabn* is incorporated into an agreement as a condition of the contract, then the rule of sanctity of contract admits that the contract may be rescinded on that basis.[122] Further, reference in cases of *Ghabn* must be made to the price of the commodities at the time of contract, bearing in mind the fluctuations of the market, and to the position of the buyer concerning whether or not he is assumed to have had knowledge of the proper price, or may have had means of discovering it.[123]

It may be surmised therefore that *Ghabn* leading to mistake in the value of an object does not generally give rise to an option to rescind, but that there are divergent opinions amongst the *Fuqahā'* even within the schools as to this doctrine. The majority view is that *Ghabn* accompanied by *Taghrīr*, whether verbal or by reasonable indication does permit rescission by the injured party. This is the view expressed in the Ḥanafī, Shāfi'ī and Ḥanbalī schools although the Baghdāḍī section of the Mālikī school proffers a divergent opinion. The Mālikīs hold that rescission is permissible here on three conditions: Firstly, where *Ghabn al-Fāḥish* occurs in a sale, other than at public auction and the *Ghabn al-Fāḥish* exceeds a third of the price, or is underpriced by a third or more in a purchase; Secondly, where it occurs in a sale whereby it may be determined that any reasonable person may have been so deceived, in which case consideration must be had to the price at the time of contracting. The prejudiced party must also be ascertained not to have had knowledge of the value prior to the contract, and that the co-contractor sought to deceive him on those grounds. The third condition is that the claim for *Ghabn* must proceed within one year of the action which gave rise to the deceit, so that longer lapses of time leading to breaches of agreement may not disrupt the ordinary continuance of trading relations.

---

120 For *al-Najsh* see its definition in the chapter on Active Fraud below.

121 Sanhūrī, *Maṣādir al-Ḥaqq*, II, 146

122 Tasūlī, *al-Bahja fī Sharḥ al-Tuḥfa*, (Latter by Ibn 'Āṣim) 2 vols. in 1 (Cairo, 1370/1951) II 106-7

123 Muḥammad b. 'Abd al-Zurqānī, *Sharḥ 'alā al-Mukhtaṣar Khalīl*, related in Tasūlī *op.cit*, II, 106-7

The Mālikīs therefore conclude that Mistake as to the value of the object of contract of a sale may occur, as long as the co-contractor (ie. the non-prejudiced party) knows or is assumed to know of that mistake; and as long as the prejudiced party processes his claim within the period of limitation.

The final two conditions of the Mālikī school are taken up in modern legislation. The Iraqi Civil Code[124] for instance, states that *Ghabn* may be pleaded where the needs of one of the parties have been exploited, or where he has been deliberately confused or intimidated into the agreement, or where he has been misinformed or is of subnormal intelligence. All of these would constitute manifestations of exploitation on the part of the other contracting party. Similarly, the UAE Civil Code[125] provides that where exploitation or conspiracy has been exerted in dispositions of property of subsequently restricted persons, the judge may avoid the contract despite the fact that the dispositions were made prior to the court's restriction. The limitation period is also set at one year in the Iraqi code, and similar provisions are provided by the Egyptian Civil Code,[126] the Syrian Civil Code,[127] and the Lebanese Code.[128]

The Kuwaiti Code (Article 166) follows suit, stating that the one-year period of limitation commences from the time of conclusion of the contract in relation to the state, other legal person or *Waqf* property; and from the date of resuming soundness of mind, or death in the case of restricted persons or those lacking capacity. In all cases, it lapses 15 years after conclusion of the contract. The Kuwaiti Code defines *Ghabn al-Fāḥish* as where, at the time of contracting, the value of the object exceeds one-fifth of its recognised value.[129] Claims may not be entertained in Kuwait for *Ghabn* relating to contracts of Auction (*al-Muzāyada*) or public tender (*al-Munāqaṣa*) where both have been conducted according to the law.[130]

In the UAE Civil Code the legislative committee evidently decided also not to stray too far from the accepted Islamic doctrine. Article 191 states that : "A contract may not be cancelled on the basis of a gross imbalance (*Ghabn al-Fāḥish*) in the absence of misrepresentation (*Taghrīr*), save in respect of property of a person under restriction, Waqf property and property

124 Art. 125 of the Iraqi Civil Code

125 UAE Civil Code, Law No. 2 of 1987, Article 170

126 Art.129

127 Art. 130 of the 1949 law

128 Art.129

129 Kuwait Civil Code, Art. 163 (2)

130 Article 165 of the Kuwaiti Civil Code.

of the state."[131] This is echoed by the Kuwaiti Civil Code, which substitutes "save in respect of special cases permitted by law".[132] The special cases, listed in the succeeding article, are 'against the state or other legal person; those legally defective in faculty; or regarding *Waqf* property.[133] It is to be noted that the right to cancel a contract for *Ghabn al-Fāḥish* and misrepresentation (*Taghrīr*) lapses on the death of the person having that right[134] This right may not therefore be inherited. The right also lapses upon any form of dealing regarding the subject matter of the contract, whether in part or whole, which may imply consent.[135] Thirdly, the right does not continue should the subject matter be consumed, damaged, or converted by the holder of that right, or should it be destroyed whilst in his possession.[136]

The Bahrain Contract Law mentions nothing of *Ghubn* in conjunction with mistake as to value. Article 24 (2) merely states that : "An erroneous opinion as to the value of the thing which forms the subject-matter of the agreement is not to be deemed a mistake as to a matter of fact".[137] This fact is not altogether surprising, given the indebtedness of the code to its British codifiers : the law with respect to mistake is clearly based on common law principles at the expense of the wider ambit afforded by the Islamic principles.

6.2.8 MISTAKE AS TO LAW

It is a general principle of civil law that a Mistake as to Law, like a mistake as to fact, may vitiate the consent of the contracting party.[138]

Bellefonds makes two pertinent points in the context of Mistake as to Law. The first is that despite the series of institutions established by the Sharī'a to prevent mistakes in the conclusion of legal acts, and the doctrines of Option and Mistake also established to regulate should mistakes occur nonetheless, none of these preventative or restitutative institutions provide for Mistake as to Law.[139] The second point Bellefonds makes is that the

---

131 UAE Civil Code No. 2 of 1987, Article 192

132 Kuwait Civil Code, Art.162

133 Kuwait Civil Code, Art. 163 (1)

134 *idem.*, Art. 192

135 *idem.* Art. 192

136 *idem.*, Art.192

137 Bahrain Contract Law, 1969; in force as from 25 D/Quida, 1389, corresponding to 1 Feb. 1970; Article 24 (2)

138 Sanhūrī, *al-Wasīt*, *op.cit.*, I, pp.301-2

139 Bellefonds, *Traité*, I, pp.410-416, at 410

Sharī'a, as formulated by the classical jurists, rarely distinguishes between the concept of Mistake as to Law and that of ignorance of the law.[140]

In the modern exposés of the principles of contract we find that the distinction is made between Mistake and ignorance of the law. Sanhūrī, citing Article 122 of the Egyptian Civil Code, states that whereas a Mistake as to Law (legislation to the contrary notwithstanding) renders the contract voidable (*Qābilan li al-Ibṭāl*), "ignorance of the law is no excuse".[141]

Article 122 of the Egyptian Civil Code itself states that a contract is voidable for Mistake in Law if the conditions of mistake in fact therein are fulfilled.[142]

The general maxim that "ignorance of the law is no excuse" with regard to Mistake is not always applicable in Islamic law. Among the compendiums on *Uṣūl al-Fiqh*, the principle to be found is that ignorance of the law is a valid excuse as long as it is not accompanied by negligence (*Taqṣīr*). So whoever is ignorant of the law and is negligent, is held answerable to this ignorance and it will not be considered a Mistake in Law; But whoever is ignorant of the law and is not negligent in that ignorance is excused his ignorance and it may be regarded as a Mistake as to Law.[143]

The primary assumption of Islamic Fiqh however, is that Mistake as to Law is not excusable. It cannot be excusable until it has been established that "special surrounding conditions rebut the charge of the assumed negligence regarding the ignorance as to the law."[144] Sanhūrī states in this context that if Islamic Fiqh can be accused here of a certain indulgence, it is only because the *Ḥudūd* penalties in particular admit of no judicial error.[145]

---

140 Bellefonds, *Traité*, pp.410-411; originally postulated by Milliot, *Introduction à l'Étude du Droit Musulman*, No. 221

141 *Lā yaftaraḍ fī aḥad innahu yajhal al-qānūn*. Sanhūrī, *al-Wasīṭ*, *op.cit.*, I, p. 302

142 See also Arts. 123 and 122 of the Syrian and Lebanese codes respectively.

143 Sanhūrī, *Maṣādir al-Ḥaqq*, II, 153; The case most frequently cited as an example of this principle is properly a criminal one : it concerns a non-Muslim who travels to an Islamic country, converts to Islam, and thereafter partakes of wine, unaware of its prohibition in Islam. This is contrasted with the situation of a *Dhimmī*, who commits *Zinā'* (adultery) after having converted to Islam. In the first case the mistake is permissible for it is a prohibition peculiar to Islam, of which a new convert newly arrived in a Muslim country is not expected to know. In the second case the mistake is without defence, whether for a Dhimmī or non-Dhimmī, for adultery is forbidden in all religions ; In any case, a Dhimmī who has been living in a Muslim country would be expected to know the laws of his country of domicile. See further, Sanhūrī, *Maṣādir al-Ḥaqq*, II, 154; Ibn Nujaym, *al-Ashbāh wa al-Naẓā'ir*, pp.167-8 and his *Fatḥ al-Fanār bi-Sharḥ al-Manār*, III, pp.105-6

144 Sanhūrī, *Maṣādir al-Ḥaqq*, II, 155

145 *idem*, II, 155

Thus, for instance, as the Ḥanafī author, al-Kāsānī, states, in a sale of movable property (*Manqūl; pl. Manqūlāt, Manqūla*), if a neighbour asks for a right of pre-emption to that property, and the buyer, thinking that his neighbour may legally have pre-emption over it,[146] submits that right of pre-emption to him, when later one of the two - either the holder of pre-emption or the original owner - wants to revoke the contract without the other's consent, he will not be able to because when the submission was made, it became a contract between them. Here, the buyer mistakenly thinks that pre-emption may be allowed on movable objects, which is a mistake in law in the Ḥanafī (and any other) school.[147] This ignorance may not be considered excusable because it encompasses negligence on the buyer's behalf. He is therefore not allowed to revoke the sale which he entered into due to ignorance, and the contract is binding upon him.[148]

The majority of codes recently promulgated in Muslim constitutions do tend to retain Mistake as to Law as constituting an impediment to consent.[149] It is to be noted however that this retention may be a reflection of Occidental Civil Law systems, rather than a true representation of the classical doctrines. One rather ironic example of the classical Fiqh exposed in the light of modern legislation is given by Professor Sanhūrī :

A lends B a sum of money in a *Qard* loan, with a stated profit or excess (*Fā'ida*) which exceeds the state imposed 7%. A is ignorant as to the limit imposed by the law. The lender in this case may not demand that the contract of loan be avoided by claiming Mistake as to Law, on the basis that he would not have lent his money if he had known that the limit of *Fā'ida* was only 7%. The loan remains valid, according to Sanhūrī, but the *Fā'ida* must be reduced to the legislated maximum.[150] In classical Fiqh, the same contract would be void for Ribā!

---

146 The Mālikī and Shāfi'ī doctrines restrict pre-emption to the co-owner; The Ḥanafī School also gives it to neighbours, sharers in a right of way, and sharers in a watercourse which irrigates their land. See al-Ṭaḥāwī, Aḥmad, *Kitāb al-Shufa'a Min al-Jāmi' al-Kabīr Fī al-Shurūṭ*, (Ed. J. Schacht) in 20 *Heidelberger Akademie der Wissenschaften*, 3 (1929-1930); and Ziadeh, F.J., 'Shufa'ah: Origins and Modern Doctrine', *Cleveland State Law Review*, 34 (1) (1985-1986) pp.35-46

147 Sanūrī, *Masādir al-Ḥaqq*, II, 156; *Shuf'a* is defined as "The right of a person to substitute himself for the purchaser in a complete sale of real property" : Ziadeh, 'Shufa'ah: Origins and Modern Doctrine', *Cleveland State Law Review*, 34 (1) (1985-1986) at p.35.

148 al-Kāsānī, *al-Badā'i'*, V, 151; Ibn Nujaym, *Fatḥ al-Fanār bi-Sharḥ al-Manār*, III, 106

149 See for example, Explanatory Memorandum to the Kuwaiti Civil Code, p.141, regarding Art. 148 of the latter

150 Sanhūrī, *al-Wasīṭ, op.cit.*, Vol. I, p. 307

It will perhaps illustrate the modern transition of these principles of the classical Fiqh to include the relevant passages of the modern Gulf codes here.

Article 196 of the UAE Civil Code states: "A contracting party shall have the right to cancel the contract if he makes a mistake of law and the conditions relating to a mistake of fact under Articles 193 and 195 are satisfied, unless the law provides otherwise."

The Bahraini Code of Contracts, (Article 25) states: "A contract is not voidable as to any law in force, but a mistake as to law not so in force has the same effect as a mistake of fact."

In the Kuwaiti Civil Code, there is no explicit mention of mistake as to law, even though there is mention in the Egyptian Civil Code from which the Kuwaiti Code is largely derived.[151] The Explanatory Memorandum to this Code, however, suggests that the tendency of legislation today is to give the same effect to Mistake as to Law as is given to Mistake as to fact. Both render the consent defective, and the contract voidable. It states that this occurs even in those countries which have not enacted this principle into any specific legislative text, as in France and Egypt under the old Civil Code, and in Kuwait under the new Commercial Code.[152]

6.2.9 CONCLUSION

We may conclude, therefore, that although error is perhaps the most pure and simple of all the impediments to a contract, the Muslim jurists rarely considered it as a sole criterion which might render a contract voidable. Instead, error is teamed with one or several other vitiating factors or options denoting the cause of that mistake. A purchaser who has been led to believe in the existence of certain characteristics or qualities in the commodity he has bought may rarely claim rectification under the title of Mistake alone, but, identifying the cause of his error, he claims misdescription or misrepresentation by the vendor who therefore bears the liability for the avoided contract. If the unhappy purchaser finds that the vendor has not made any contribution to the cause of the error, the purchaser himself assumes responsibility for the mistake and is without remedy at law.

Mistake is not therefore a question of ignorance or a wrong decision, but rather a doctrine which seeks to identify the underlying cause of the error. The error must generally have motivated the decision to contract to be actionable at all, and where such motivation or consent has been induced by

---

[151] Art. 122 of the 1948 law

[152] Explanatory Memorandum to the Kuwaiti Civil Code, p.141

deceit, misrepresentation or fraud, the Muslim jurists assign primary attention to the consent of the contracting parties.

The remedies regarding contracts subject to Mistake are almost always deduced in the light of the effect that the mistake and its concomitant cause has had on the consent of the contracting party.[153] Ultimately, the same effect has compromised or acted as a veritable impediment to his consent.

There are some commentators of Muslim Law who consider that the important role given to real consent - to the detriment of declared will and other accompanying risks to the stability of transactions - are exceptions to the general role of objectivism in the Fiqh.[154] It bears remark however, that this supposition by the commentators that Islamic Law is above all a system ruled by objectivism seems a little strange in the light of the traditional *exposé* of the Doctrine of Mistake.

Several of the modern codes seem also to be in similar doubts as to the objectivism of the Fiqh, and have imposed conditions, the attachment of which is indubitably to limit the scope of a doctrine which could otherwise prove potentially disruptive. Article 124 of the Egyptian Civil Code states that: "A party who has committed a mistake cannot take advantage of the mistake in a manner contrary to the principles of good faith. Such a party, moreover, remains bound by the contract which he intended to conclude, if the other party shows that he is prepared to perform the contract." The same principle is pursued in the Kuwaiti Code. Article 149 therein states: "One who has given consent by error shall not have the right to persist in that error by way of opposing the requirements of good faith. The other party, particularly, shall have the right, in his confrontation with the first party, to insist upon conclusion of the contract in a way that goes along with the truth as he knows it, without damaging himself."[155]

In the majority of the modern Codes too, statements concerning arithmetical errors, slips of the pen, or computational slips have been inserted, mention of which is infrequently found within the Fiqh treatises.[156] In all cases, such errors do not affect the validity of the contract, and therefore no option arises out of them. Needless to say, mistakes of this kind must nevertheless be rectified.[157]

---

153 See Explanatory Memorandum to Kuwaiti Civil Code, p.139

154 Chehata, *Essai d'une Théorie Générale de l'Obligation en Droit Musulman*, (French ed.) p.124 ff.

155 See Kuwait Explanatory Memorandum, p.141. This is derived from Art. 124 of the Egyptian Code with some modification.

156 Also Egyptian Civil Code, (Law No. 131 of 1948), Art. 123; Kuwaiti Civil Code (Law No. 67 of 1980), Art. 150

157 eg. Egyptian Civil Code, (Law No. 131 of 1948), Article 123

Chapter 6.3

FRAUD

6.3.1 Origins and General Discussion of Principles

The second impediment to consent in Islamic Law is that of Fraud (*Tadlīs, Taghrīr*). *Tadlīs* is itself generally considered not to have been of purely Islamic origin. As Bellefonds notes, in the Ḥanafī School, Fraud and *Ghabn* are not, in general, taken into consideration unless they occur together. Fraud is not, therefore, an impediment to consent on its own, in the sense given according to French Civil Law.[1] The requirement that Fraud is always accompanied by *Ghabn* to be an effective impediment to consent is not, however, altogether apparent according to the remaining Schools of Law.

The term *Tadlīs* is a second form noun from the root *DALLASA* meaning "to swindle or cheat".[2] It is held by Coulson to be an Arabized form of the Byzantine Greek *DOLOS*,[3] while Schacht states that "the Arabic term *dallas*, "to conceal a fault or defect in an article of merchandise from the purchaser", is derived from Latin *dolus*; the word entered Arabic through the channel of commercial practice at an early date, but it did not become a technical term for fraud in early Islamic law."[4]

---

1 Bellefonds, *Traité*, I, p.355

2 H. Wehr, *A Dictionary Of Modern Written Arabic*, (Ed. J.M. Cowan; Third Edn.; New York, 1976), p.290

3 N.J. Coulson, *A History of Islamic Law, op.cit.*, p.28; *idem.*, *Commercial Law In The Gulf States, op.cit.*, p.69, n.3. Coulson regards this as another example of the infiltration of foreign elements into the classical structure of Islamic doctrine.

4 Schacht, *An Introduction to Islamic Law*, (Oxford, 1964), p.9; P.Owsia, *op.cit.*, p.522 : FN.3; Commercial Fraud and immorality is condemned in the *Qur'ān* (XXIX: 36) by reference to the story of the Shu'ayb and Madyān peoples, who were commercial traffickers. The punishment for their 'Mischief on Earth' was a mighty tornado-like blast. See A. Yusuf Ali, *The Holy Qur'ān, op.cit.*, p.1038, n. 3458

In accordance with most doctrines of contract in Islamic law, there is no deviation in the exposition of the elements of fraud from the general Muslim disinclination to formulate theories. The principles of fraud, like those of many other concepts of contract, must be plucked from isolated cases of analysis from among the numerous tomes written by leading jurists.

Regardless of its probable eclectic origins, *Tadlīs* does not form a neat parallel concept of fraud with equivalent institutions elsewhere as may perhaps have been expected. Indeed, it remains somewhat removed conceptually from the Roman system of *Dolus*,[5] the French Civil Law concept of *Dol*,[6] or English Common Law Fraud.[7] Saleh goes so far as to suggest that the concept "if not unknown to the Shari'a, has not particularly recommended itself to Muslim legal scholars."[8] Primarily, *Tadlīs* and *Taghrīr* do not constitute regular "impediments" or "*vices du consentement*", although some authors have approached the Islamic concept as a defect in declaration.[9] The overriding concern which may be discerned in Islamic law through the vehicles of its teaching, - the *Qur'ān*, the *Sunna* and *Fiqh* works - is that trade is permitted so long as it is conducted honestly and in good faith. In every contract of sale, and *mutatis mutandis* of hire or service in Islamic law, there is an implied condition of merchantability of the goods (or suitability of the property or service for the proposed {declared} intention in a contract of hire or service). Arising therefrom is a warranty against defects in the goods sold. The consequence of such a principle is that every seller, hirer or contractor of services has a duty to disclose any defects, faults or unsuitability of the goods for their declared intended

5 For which, see W.W. Buckland, *A Textbook of Roman Law: From Augustus to Justinian*, (Third Edn. Revised by P. Stein; Cambridge, 1975) p.180; B. Nicholas, *An Introduction to Roman Law*, (Oxford, 1962), pp. 162 ff., 223; R.W. Leage, *Roman Private Law*, (London, 1932), p.379; R.W. Lee, *The Elements of Roman Law*, (Fourth Edn; London, 1956), p. 287 f. *Exceptio Doli* was introduced in the Edict of Aquilius Gallas in BC 66.

6 It is interesting to note that the distinction in terms between fraud in the formation of a contract (*dol*) and other fraud (*Fraude*) is only made in French law. See Georges Ripert et Jean Boulanger, *Traité de Droit Civil D'après le Traité de Planiol*, Vol. II, (Paris, 1957), p. 75, No. 178 : "Distinction du Dol et de la Fraude"; and José Vidal, *Essai D'une Théorie Générale de la Fraude en Droit Français*, (Paris, 1957), *passim.*; P. Owsia, *op. cit.*, p.523. For the principles of *dol* see : Alex Weill et François Terré, *Droit Civil : Les Obligations*, (Précis Dalloz : Second Edn; Paris, 1975), pp. 196-206; Ripert et Boulanger, *Traité de Droit Civil, op.cit* , pp. 75ff

7 Pollock on *Contracts*, (Thirteenth Edn; London, 1950) pp.264, 353, 451 ff; G.H. Treitel, *Contract*, (Sixth Edn; London, 1983) pp. 262-7, 429-32.

8 Saleh, *Unlawful Gain, op.cit.*, p. 116, where Saleh uses the term *Ghubn* translated as "lesion", in this context.

9 Schacht, *Introduction, op.cit.*, p. 117

purpose.[10]

The concept of fraud therefore lies comfortably against the broad Muslim equitable consideration against deception.[11]

This enables the concept to assume an even wider definition[12] than is given to the concept in Western laws. Islamic jurisprudence views fraud as a serious moral wrong.[13]

It consequently addressed means whereby a party subjected to, or exploited by, such a serious - and in the eyes of Islam - heinous deliberation, whether on the part of his co-contractor or of a third party, may be allowed a remedy in the rescission of the contract. A fraudulent contract is therefore a *Fāsid* (voidable) contract, for it has been formed with due formalities, legalities, consent and capacity of the parties. Its irregularity is generally only discoverable after formation. The fraudulent contract remains *Fāsid* until the disadvantaged party has exercised his right to revoke by option. If the contract is ratified at this point, the contractor affirms his consent to the known defect or fault in the object of that contract and has no further right to rescind. Secondly, it is considered by some[14] to be an unnecessary remedy in the same way as Mistake.[15] This is due to the considerable precautionary measures imposed upon the contracting parties in order to avoid the incidence of such nullifying factors.

An additional complication to the doctrine of Fraud in Islamic law is that it lacks a consistent approach. The field is divided between those authors who treat Fraud as a specific "option" which is regulated by its own individual principles in the contract of sale and which empowers the defrauded party to avoid the contract,[16] and those authors who "lump" the option of fraud (*Khiyār al-Tadlīs*) together with the other six options.[17] The latter viewpoint is based on the premise that the rules governing the option of fraud are not substantially different from those pertaining to the more important options[18] and therefore deserve no distinction or separate

---

10 Coulson, *Commercial Law, op.cit.*, p.65.

11 Such as "He who cheats is not one of us" (Saying of the Prophet); Coulson, *Commercial Law, op.cit.*, p.69; and: "One who deceives the other is liable for the consequence"; and "Deception should be redressed". See also P. Owsia, *op.cit.*, p. 522

12 For which, see below; Bellefonds, *Traité*, I, p.355 f.

13 Coulson, *Commercial Law, op.cit.*, p.70

14 Saleh, *Unlawful Gain, op.cit.*, p. 116

15 See supra, Chapter on Mistake

16 Bellefonds, *Traité, op.cit.*, II, pp.355 ff; Owsia, *op.cit.*, p.523

17 Coulson, *Commercial Law, op.cit.*, p.72; Saleh, *Unlawful Gain, op.cit.*, p. 61; Bellefonds, *Traité*, I, pp.355 ff.

18 Owsia, *op.cit.*, p. 523 and FN 5 for authors cited therein

categorisation.

The majority of authors, however, have been content to treat the instances of fraud on an *ad hoc* basis as they arise in their discussions of contracts. In these instances we therefore find that *Tadlīs* is often not even included among the system of options expounded.[19] The subject is encountered most frequently under "Sale" and is rarely consistently analysed in relation to any subject other than *Uberrimae fidei* contracts.

The result is, needless to say, not always perspicuous. The reasons for the inconsistent approach to fraud by generations of Muslim jurists may be accountable to several speculative causes. Firstly, as stated above, the concept is not originally Islamic[20] and is therefore likely to be of eclectic origins. Due to the reluctance of early classical theory to recognise non-Islamic elements of the law, the doctrine may therefore be assumed to have entered the sphere of Islamic jurisprudence in a piecemeal and unstructured fashion. Its failure to solicit any official formulation until quite late times would explain the lack of precise distinction of terminology or uniform interpretation which surrounds the whole concept.

6.3.2 TERMINOLOGY

The theory stated above is supported by the unrivalled number of different terms which are employed synonymously and without differentiation to denote the concepts of fraud, trickery and misrepresentation leading to imbalance. The most common among these are : *Tadlīs, Taghrīr, Ghushsh, Ghabn* (or *Ghubn*),[21] *Ghabn (Ghubn) al-Fāḥish*, and *Gharar*, which vary in precise meaning from fraud, trickery, deception, lesion or misrepresentation, gross misrepresentation, to imbalance respectively. Less common are : *Khallāb*,[22] *Khiyāna* (deception), *Iḥtiyāl, Iḥtiyāliyya*,[23] *Taḥāyul* or *Taḥayyul*

---

19 Saleh, *Unlawful Gain, op.cit.*, p.61

20 Coulson, *History of Islamic Law, op.cit.*, p.28; Schacht, *Introduction, op.cit.*, p.9 ; and *supra*

21 Hooper translates *Ghabn* as "Flagrant Misrepresentation without deceit": *Majella*, Art. 356; Hooper's Translation of the Majella, *op.cit.*, p.83. Ḥasan Aḥmad, *Baḥth Muqārin Mauḍū'uhū 'Uyūb al-Riḍā Fī 'Uqūd al-Mu'āwaḍāt al-Māliyya Fī al-Sharī'a al-Islāmiyya: Al-Ghubna wa al-Tadlīs*, Vol. I, (Dār al-Maṭbū'āt al-Jāmi'iyya: College of Law, Alexandria University, Egypt, n.d.) pp.72,73 explains the Jurists' definition of *Ghabn* as 'the disparity between the (two) exchanges in value'.

22 eg. *Sharḥ al-Kabīr*, in the margin of Ibn Qudāma's *al-Mughnī, op.cit.*, IV, pp.80-81

23 eg. Sanhūrī, *Maṣādir al-Ḥaqq*, II, 166; *idem.*, *al-Wasīṭ*, (Cairo, 1952), pp.320 ff.

24 eg. Sanhūrī, *al-Wasīṭ*, pp.321, 322

(trickery, deception, fraud), *Tadlīl* (deception),[24] *Īhām* (deception, fraud),[25] *Naṣb* (swindling),[26] and *Khadī'a* (deceit, trickery).[27] The theory is further strengthened by the lack of any attempt to distinguish or delineate the scope of even the major terms of *Tadlīs* or *Taghrīr* or *Ghabn.*[28]

It is submitted that a distinction exists between the terms *Tadlīs* and *Ghabn,* meaning "fraud", and "misrepresentation resulting in contractual imbalance", thus "non-equivalence of prestation" respectively. Closer analysis of the terms in their contexts seems to suggest that whereas *Tadlīs* usually encompasses deliberate deception, *Ghabn* may embrace both deliberate and/or unintentional misrepresentation. The terms *Tadlīs* and *Taghrīr* however, seem to be interchangeable. The submission is nevertheless difficult to prove, given the unwillingness of the employers of these terms to give even cursory definitions, and their frequent interchangings of the terms in the classical texts. It is generally believed that *Tadlīs* is the term adopted by the Mālikī school particularly for the concept of *Taghrīr.* If this is the case it rather belies the significance of the theories suggesting that the concept is of Byzantine or Greek origins, for the Mālikīs formed but a fraction of the Medinese.[29] It would denote therefore that the major term used to signify fraud in the Arabic would be *Taghrīr*, but the incidence of both this term and that of *Tadlīs* is by no means exclusive.[30]

The origins of *Taghrīr* have been less subject to investigation. Even the dating of the evolution of *Tadlīs* into Arabic, if such be the case, is unclear. It is to be remarked that neither of these terms occur at all frequently in the earliest texts, and not at all in any of the primary sources. Sanhūrī, in his comparative treatise[31] does nothing concrete to alleviate this problem, for at no stage does he attempt to trace the origins or define the scope of each term. Indeed, he himself cites from the classical authors without comment on their diverse use of synonyms.

In modern orientalist assaults on the subject moreover, we find that not only is there little conscious indication of the confusion at large, but that the

---

25 eg. *ibid.*, p.321

26 eg. *ibid.*, p. 319

27 eg. Sanhūrī, *Maṣādir al-Ḥaqq*, II, p.166; *ibid.*, *al-Wasīṭ*, p. 321; Bahrain Law of Contract, 1969, Article 20 (1)

28 But see the contemporary author Aḥmad, *Baḥth Muqārin, op.cit.*, p.73 : "Difference between *Ghabn* and *Taghrīr*".

29 Schacht, *Origins, op.cit.*, pp. 6-10

30 In the Bahrain Law of Contract, for example, while *Taghrīr* is found (Art. 21), so is the term *Ḥīla* (Article 20) meaning "trickery", where the parallel English version is "Fraud". *Tadlīs* in the same code corresponds to the English "Misrepresentation".

31 *Maṣādir al-Ḥaqq*, II, pp.157 ff

confusion and diversity of interpretation still continues. Polonymity in doctrines is discussed by Schiller.[32] He points out that the Arabic synonyms for 'deceit, fraud, artifice and ruse' in the same formulae had probably accumulated due to uncertainty whether the existing terms would indicate all that was intended by the formula.[33] A simple example may be seen in the use of the term *Ghabn*. In the classical treatises the script is, of course, unvowelled; it is therefore impossible, without given vocalisation, to determine how the term was pronounced. In more contemporary literature, where the term may sometimes be vocalised or transliterated, we come across a variance of vocalisation.[34]

The matter is not clarified by reference to standard dictionaries[35] which usually list both variations without preference; or to native Arabic-speaking lawyers, who seem to use either alternative in the same arbitrary fashion.

The rejoinder may well be that the transliteration or pronunciation of this term is of little matter. The confusion, however, which surrounds the precise vocalisation of the term *Ghabn*, merely manifests the tip of the iceberg in any investigation of the Islamic concept of Fraud and Misrepresentation in contracts. To the extent that there is no definitive decision upon the vocalisation of one of the main terms for fraud, nor even discussion as to

---

32 Schiller, 'Coptic Documents', *Zum Gegenwärtigen Stand der Juristischen Papyrusforschung, ZVRW*, LX (1957) p.203

33 Schiller, 'Coptic Law', *The Juridical Review*, XLIII (1931) p.222

34 Established orientalists such as Schacht, (*Introduction, op.cit.*, p.117), Coulson (*History of Islamic Law, op.cit..*, p.117), Bellefonds (*Traité, op.cit.*, p.356), Habachy, ('The System of Nullities in Islamic Law', *American Journal of Comparative Law*, 13, (1964), p.71), and Parviz Owsia (*op.cit.*, eg. p.534), refer to the term as *Ghabn*. Elsewhere it may be vocalised as *Ghubn* and this transliterated version is increasingly to be found in modern works on the subject, such as those by Saleh, (*Unlawful Gain, op.cit.*, pp. 52, 116), Anderson (*Law Reform In The Muslim World*, (London, 1976), pp. 94, 170), and the authoritative translation of the recent UAE civil code, (James Whelan, Translation of The Law of Civil Transactions of the State of the United Arab Emirates, No. 2 of 1987. Published in 3 *Business Laws of the United Arab Emirates*, [Suppl. 2, 1987]). Mr. Whelan translates the section entitled *al-Taghrīr wa al-Ghubn* as "Deception and Cheating". He adds a translator's note to the effect that *Ghubn* means "trickery or persuasion of a person to enter into an unconscionable bargain involving an imparity between the consideration moving from each party." (*ibid.* preceding Article 185). This is in accordance with the meaning given in the *Majella*, Art. 164. He goes on to use the term "Misrepresentation" for the Arabic *Taghrīr* in Arts. 185,186,190,191 and 192; and for the verb *Gharara* in Arts. 187 and 190; He translates *Ghubn* as "cheating" in Art. 189; and *Ghubn al-Fāḥish* as "Gross cheating" in Arts. 187,188,191 and 192.

35 H. Wehr, *A Dictionary of Modern Written Arabic, op.cit.*, p.665 lists both variations with no distinguishing remarks; H.S. Faruqi's *Law Dictionary*, (Librairie du Liban, Third Edn : Beirut, 1986), p.245 lists only *Ghubn* as a noun meaning "injustice, inequity, unfairness".

the variance of terms used, nor yet is there unanimity upon its status or significance as a doctrine relating to contracts.

6.3.3 MODERN THEORETICAL CONCEPT

In spite of the fact that agreement has been reached among the *Fuqahā'* concerning some elements of fraud, and that these points of convergence have been brought to light by Sanhūrī, it is the great Egyptian legist himself who emphasises the vulnerability of the Islamic concepts of *Tadlīs* and *Ghabn* to the trend outlined in the second tentative cause of inconsistency, namely, that of assimilation into the doctrinal format of Western systems.

In his comparative treatise *Maṣādir al-Ḥaqq*,[36] Sanhūrī argues for the construction of a doctrine of Islamic Fraud on the foundation pattern of the French doctrine of *Dol*, which is itself a model of the Roman system of *Dolus*. Sanhūrī's own exposé highlights the not altogether incongruous mixture of classical Islamic and Civil/Roman precepts. It is questionable whether, in the end, a subject approached from two completely different starting points may be left to perch unchallenged upon such an unstable bough. Nevertheless, the argument bears some force when, in conjunction with the assumed, but undocumented, eclectic origins of the Arabic *Dalasa*, it is remembered that the Latin adage *Fraus Omnia Corrumpit*[37] has equal and continuing validity in French Civil Law as an equitable consideration.[38] A hasty parallel may then be forged with the general dispensation of Islamic jurists against grave harm, lesion, imbalance, or unjustified enrichment between the parties to any contract, and their broad equitable consideration against deception.

This parallel has its limits though. As Schacht points out, "as regards fraud, there is little inclination to protect the victim; it manifests itself only in the case of 'grave deception' (*ghabn Fāḥish, laesio enormis*).[39] Mere verbal influence and general windowdressing are not regarded as sufficient cause for avoiding a contract unless accompanied by gross unjustified

---

36 *Maṣādir al-Ḥaqq*, II, pp.157 ff

37 "Fraud spoils everything"

38 René David, *French Law : Its Structure, Sources, and Methodology*, (Transl. by Michael Kindred), (Louisiana State University Press, 1972), pp.197-8. Even though no general code text articulates it: See Georges Ripert, *La Règle Morale dans les Obligations Civiles*, (Fourth Edn; Paris, 1949), pp. 287 ff, partic. 314 ff.

39 Schacht, *Introduction*, *op.cit.*, p.117

disproportion between the two parties' obligations.[40]

It may be surmised therefore that the doctrines of Fraud and Misrepresentation in Islamic classical law are so closely interrelated as to warrant simultaneous treatment. We have seen already that the element of Mistake as to Value is only recognised in conjunction with *Ghabn al-Fāḥish* or some other synonym denoting "grave deception", such as *Tadlīs* or *Taghrīr*.[41] In a similar manner *Tadlīs* and *Taghrīr* require in almost all cases to be accompanied by *Ghabn* or *Ghabn al-Fāḥish*, in order to constitute cause for avoiding the contract.

The question which remains to be asked at this point is : Upon what basis is the Islamic doctrine of Fraud construed ? The answers to this question, which follow, naturally lead us next to the question, posed by Coulson: "What kind of fraud gives the party deceived the remedy to rescind the contract ?"[42] Thereafter, having determined the principles of fraud in the classical law, a comparative look may be given to the situation regarding fraud as it exists firstly in the *Majella* and secondly in the modern codifications of the Nation States of Kuwait, The United Arab Emirates, and Bahrain.

6.3.4 DEFINITION AND INCIDENCE

The traditional definition of fraud is that it is the deliberate and deceitful causing to fall into mistake of the contracting party which persuades him to contract.[43]

Fraud as such must therefore constitute an impetus to contract. It is up to the judge in questions of dispute to determine this from the case concerned. He has the power to assess the total effect of the fraud on the defrauded contractor and to determine whether such fraud was sufficient to have induced him into contracting. In this matter he must seek guidance from the contract made between the parties, as well as certain elements in the personal situation of the defrauded party which may be relevant, such as his

---

40 For which see Chapter VI.2, Section on Mistake; Section 4, *supra*, and Chapter VI.5, Section 1 on *Istighlāl*: Disporportion of Obligation: This is particularly prominent among the Shāfi'ī jurists. See Sanhūrī, *Maṣādir al-Ḥaqq*, *op.cit.*, II. p.162

41 See Chapter VI.2 on Mistake, subsection 2:4

42 Coulson, *Commercial Law*, *op.cit.*, p.70

43 Sanhūrī, *Maṣādir al-Ḥaqq*, II, 157; the same principle is to be found in the Bahrain Law of Contract, 1969, based on the concept that consent which is not freely given, that is, which is induced, "when it would not have been given but for the influence of such coercion, Undue Influence, Fraud, Misrepresentation or Mistake". (Article 16 (5)); and in the Civil Codes of Kuwait (Art. 152) and the UAE (Arts. 187 and 191)

age, experience, intelligence, capacity and commercial knowledge.[44]

Mere verbal influence is not regarded as sufficient cause for avoiding a contract unless it is accompanied by gross[45] unjustified disproportion between the two parties' obligations (*Laesio Enormis*). The Ḥanbalī and Mālikī schools also require that it be accompanied by fraud.[46]

The general inclination in Islamic jurisprudence is to treat the Option of Fraud (*Khiyār al-Tadlīs*) which, in any case, can only be employed in regard to fraudulent acts, as a final resort. This option is usually only applied when the options of defect, sight, description,[47] and the rules of Mistake[48] cannot be properly invoked. Sanhūrī states that in the traditional doctrine fraud does not render the contract voidable (*Qābilan li al-Ibṭāl*) except by virtue of the mistake which was induced in the same contract.[49] He says, consequently, that the distinction between actionable fraud and non-actionable fraud rests upon whether or not the fraud is accompanied by mistake.[50] Mistake itself chiefly rests on the trilogy of options - Defect, Sight and Description - as shown above. However, Coulson is careful to distinguish the Option for Fraud from that for Defect. For while, he says, "concealment by the seller of a fault or defect in goods or services may amount to active fraud .... here the remedy lies in *Khiyār al-'Ayb*, so that it matters not whether the concealment is deliberate or accidental, by act or omission."[51] This point is important and must be borne in mind when attempting to answer the question "What kind of fraud gives the party deceived the remedy to rescind the contract ?" For while certain regulations impose limits on the scope of actionable fraud in Islamic law, just as in other systems of law, remedies in Islamic law may also be had by reference

---

44 Sanhūrī, *Maṣādir al-Ḥaqq*, II, 159

45 Article 165 of the Majella defines "Gross Fraud" as being deceived in respect of goods to the extent of one-tenth; in respect of animals and to the extent of one-fifth in respect of real property, and to the extent of one-twentieth in respect of goods. Article 163 (2) of the new Kuwaiti Civil Code (Law No. 67 of 1980) defines Gross Fraud as exceeding one-fifth.

46 Ibn Nujaym, *al-Baḥr al-Rā'iq*, Vol. VII, p.169. This position is reflected in the *Majella*, (Art. 357) and has been taken up by the modern legislation of Kuwait (Art. 151) and the UAE (Art.187)

47 Coulson, *Commerical Law, op.cit.*, p.69

48 Sanhūrī, *Maṣādir al-Ḥaqq*, II, 157-8

49 Sanhūrī, *Maṣādir al-Ḥaqq*, II, p.157

50 See previous chapter, "Mistake accompanied by Taghrīr and Tadlīs"; Sanhūrī, *Maṣādir al-Ḥaqq*, II, p.158

51 Coulson, *Commercial Law, op.cit.*, p. 70

to the trilogy of "residual" options.[52]

6.3.5 CONSTITUENT ELEMENTS

The Islamic jurists surmised that Fraud consisted of two elements :-

(a) Exploitation by means of trickery
(b) Inducement of the contracting party into contracting

Sanhūrī determines that in the first category, such trickery must be sufficient to deceive the contracting party. Therefore the case of each contracting party is looked into together with his personal circumstances.[53]

This stance is upheld by the modern legislation. Article 125 of the Egyptian Civil Code states :

> "A contract may be declared void on the grounds of fraudulent misrepresentation, when the artifices practiced by one of the parties, or by his representatives are of such gravity that, but for one of them, the other party would not have concluded the contract".[54]

Similarly, Article 151 of the Kuwaiti Code states:

> "The contract may be nullified because of fraud (*Tadlīs*) if one party consents to the contract as a result of subterfuge aimed at him by the other party with the intention of deceiving him and compelling him into the contract. It must be shown that the deceived party was not satisfied with the contract and would not have accepted it if it had not been for the treachery aimed at him."[55]

The fraud may be perpetrated by various means, among which are physical acts : for example, manifestations or advertisements which delude the general public; the production of forged documents; claiming assumed qualities or quantities, and so on. The Bahrain Code of Contract lists the acts which constitute fraud according to its constitution. These, it states, are "committed by a party to a contract, or with his connivance, or by his agent,

---

[52] For which, see chapter VII, below

[53] Sanhūrī, *Maṣādir al-Ḥaqq, op.cit.*, II, p.159

[54] Egyptian Civil Code, (Law No. 131 of 1948), Art. 125

[55] Civil Law of Kuwait (Law No. 67 of 1980), Art. 151

with intent to deceive another party thereto or his agent, or to induce him to enter into the contract". The acts are :-

> (a) the representation, as a fact, of that which is not true, by one who knows it to be false or recklessly does not care whether such representation be true or false;
> (b) the active concealment of a fact by one having knowledge or belief of the fact;
> (c) a promise made without, at the time of making, any intention of performing it;
> (d) any other act calculated to deceive;
> (e) any such act or omission as the law specially declares to be fraudulent."[56]

Article 185 of the UAE Civil Code states :

> "*Taghrīr* is when one of the two contracting parties deceives the other by means of trickery of word or deed which leads the other to consent to what he would not otherwise have consented to."[57]

The differences between these modern enactments are interesting. The Bahrain provisions are based loosely on the Common Law position, but the disparities between the Kuwaiti and UAE provisions are highlighted by their different sources. Whereas the Kuwaiti provisions have employed the term *Tadlīs*, the UAE codification uses *Taghrīr*, the term employed in the Jordanian Code.[58] This is despite the alledged Mālikī origins of the former term.[59] It might have been expected that *Tadlīs* would have been used in the UAE provisions therefore, in accordance with Article 1 of the same code, which directs that the most appropriate school of *Fiqh* for reference is the Mālikī school. The explanation for this clearly arises from the reliance of the UAE Civil Code on the Jordanian provisions. It might also be stated, however, that *Taghrīr* has been chosen as the more Arabic of the two terms,[60] and in conjunction with the model of the *Majella*, which has been followed closely in the whole of this section.

---

[56] Bahrain Law of Contract, 1969 : Article 20 (1)

[57] Derived from Jornanian Civil Code, Art. 143

[58] Jordanian Civil Code, Law No. 43 of 1976, Arts. 143, 144, 148, 149, 150

[59] See Section 2 : Terminology, *Supra*.

[60] See Section 1 *supra*, on the origins of the term *Tadlīs*.

The essential framework of the *Fiqh* remains in the modern legislation : the trickery which misleads the defrauded party into contracting is still the basic precept.[61] The Kuwaiti Code puts emphasis here on the intention to deceive,[62] whereas the UAE Code omits specific mention of 'deliberate' or 'intentional' fraud, even though the aspect of premeditation may be implicity derived from a construction of the provisions, and the uneasy distinction made between *Ghabn* and *Taghrīr*. The terms *Ghabn* and *Taghrīr* are interspersed throughout this section, without express distinction between the two; it is to be presumed that resort must be had to the earlier *Fiqh* texts for differentiation. We have already noted that *Ghabn* usually encompasses both intentional and unintentional misrepresentation leading to contractual imbalance; it may be construed, as a result of this omission, that the concept in the modern legislation of the UAE/Jordan reflects the generally wider concept of the original *Fiqh*, than is addressed by the Kuwaiti Code.[63] The Kuwaiti Memorandum, on the other hand, admits that in several of its articles on Fraud, it has considered the provisions from several other countries. Although the majority of its provisions are in perfect harmony with the precepts of the Sharī'a, the choice of the term *Tadlīs*, and the inclusion of non-*Sharī'a*, non-*Majella* provisions must reflect the multi-disciplinary references resorted to in its formulation.

The *Fiqh* holds that lying may also constitute sufficient cause for fraud, as long as such falsehoods have obscured the true facts from the contracting party, and have persuaded him to contract only through deceit and delusion.[64]

This is followed in modern legislation also. Article 152 of the Kuwaiti code declares : "Subsumed under the general heading of fraud is subterfuge consisting of lying with regard to the evidence, information and acts of the contract and its surrounding conditions".[65]

Alternatively, fraud may be perpetrated by passivity or omission, such as failing to disclose essential information. Mere concealment is considered a sufficient means of trickery in certain conditions and in certain contracts known as Trust Sale Contracts.

Finally, trickery and deception perpetrated by a third party may be regarded as fraud under certain conditions.

---

61 Kuwait, Memorandum to Civil Code No. 67 of 1980, p.143

62 *ibid.*, p.143

63 The Kuwaiti Memorandum expressly directs that where a contract cannot be avoided for *Tadlīs* because the deception is not sufficient to be thus entitled, protection may be sought by revocation for negligence or under the system of *Istighlāl*.

64 Sanhūrī, *Maṣādir al-Ḥaqq, op.cit.*, II, p.159

65 Kuwaiti Civil Code, (Law No. 67 of 1980), Art. 152; UAE Civil Code, Art. 186

For our purposes,[66] therefore, we shall divide the categories of Islamic fraud into four:-

(1) Fraudulent Acts
(2) Fraudulent Statements
(3) Failure to Disclose
(4) Fraud By A Third Party

6.3.6 FRAUDULENT ACTS (al-Taghrīr al-Fi'lī)

Arabic *fiqh* calls the first category of fraud, literally, "Active Fraud",[67] denoting a fraud produced by a positive act[68] as distinguished from fraudulent statements or failure to disclose. The act is intended to induce the contract by deceit (*Ghabn*)[69] and as such is regarded as fraud no matter how insignificant it may appear.[70]

Taşriyya

The law governing fraudulent acts was construed by analogy from a decision of the Prophet concerning a case of *Taṣriyya*,: "Do not tie up the udders of she-camels and sheep. If one among you buys a she-camel or sheep with its udders tied up, he has two options after milking it : either to retain it or to return it with a measure of dates".[71] *Taṣriyya*, therefore, is the act of binding the teats of female livestock (originally ewes, but extended by analogy to camels, nannygoats and cows)[72] in order to give the false

---

66 Sanhūrī recognises all four categories: *Maṣādir al-Ḥaqq, op.cit.*, II, p.161

67 Sanhūrī, *Maṣādir al-Ḥaqq, op.cit.*, II, p.161; Jazīrī, *Kitāb al-Fiqh*, II, p.200

68 P. Owsia, *op.cit.*, p.525

69 al-Ḥaṭṭāb, *Mawāhib al-Jalīl li Sharḥ Mukhtaṣar Khalīl*, (6 Vols. Tripoli 1329 AH; Cairo, 1928) IV, pp.437 ff.

70 Sanhūrī, *M. al-Ḥaqq, op.cit.*, II, p.161

71 Bukhārī 34:64; M.M. Ali, *A Manual of Hadith*, (London and Dublin, 1944; 1983), p.299, No.4; also attributed to be related by Abū Hurayra, See for instance, Jazīrī, *Kitāb al-Fiqh*, II, p.201. These are supported by a Prophetic tradition related by Ibn Māja, concerning the sale of *al-Mukhafalāt* (animals with cloven hooves), which he states is fraudulent (*Khallāb*). See also Sanhūrī, *Maṣādir al-Ḥaqq, op.cit.*, II, p.164

72 Sanhūrī, *M. al-Ḥaqq, op.cit.*, II, pp. 163-66; al-Jazīrī, *Kitāb al-Fiqh*, II, pp.200, 201. The extension by analogy to cow and camel is disputed in Shi'ite law if there is no consensus of opinion. This is due to the Shi'ite rules on Fiqh which do not recognise *Qiyās* as a source of law. Owsia, *op.cit.*, p.527, citing Shahīd al-Thānī, *Masālik al-Afhām*, (Tehran, 1273) I, 195.

impression to the intending purchaser of a very productive milk-yield. The so-bound livestock are called *Muṣarrāt.*[73]

The unknowing purchaser of *Muṣarrāt*, upon milking them, will discover the fraud that has been perpetrated against him. He may then opt to rescind the contract by returning the animal together with compensation for the milk used by him.[74] The suggested compensation in such cases is a *Ṣā'* of dates, or the equivalent staple food of the locality.[75]

From this precedent the jurists construed a doctrine of fraud or misrepresentation by conduct to cover all fraudulent acts deliberately contrived to create a false impression in the mind of the purchaser as to the existence, nature, quality or quantity of the object of contract. This doctrine exists equally in Shi'ite law.[76]

Ibn Qudāma writes in his *al-Mughnī* :

> "Every kind of *Tadlīs* which is the cause of a variation in the consideration payable....gives rise to the option of rescission....in the same way as *Taṣriyya*."

Tadlīs al-Mashātah

Examples of such acts which were held by the jurists to constitute fraud are numerous. The most frequently cited refer to the sale of slaves, where cosmetics or dyes have been used to improve the looks of the slave so as to delude the unwary buyer into misconceptions concerning the health, age or natural beauty of his intended purchase. Dyeing the hair black,[77] curling the

---

73 See, for example, 'A.R. al-Jazīrī, *Kitāb al-Fiqh 'alā al-Madhāhib al-Arba'a*, II, pp. 200-202

74 Not to give compensation for the milk used would amount to Ribā or unjustified enrichment

75 Ibn Qudāma, *al-Mughnī, op.cit.*, IV, 135-8; Sanhūrī, *Maṣādir al-Ḥaqq, op.cit.*, II, p.163-66; For Shi'ite authors, See P. Owsia, *op.cit.*, p.526; Ibn 'Abidīn, *op.cit.*, IV, 149; Also Ibn al-Hammām, *Sharḥ al-Taḥrīr*, (Būlāq, 1316 AH) *passim.* Ibn 'Amr and Abū Dāwūd, relating a Tradition of the Prophet suggest the equivalent value of the milk should be paid in wheat (the staple food of Egypt). Ibn al-Mawwāq, *al-Tāj wa al-Iklīl li Mukhtaṣar Khalīl*, in the margin of al-Ḥaṭṭāb, *op.cit.*, IV, 437, suggests the same.

76 P. Owsia, *op.cit.*, p.527

77 Ibn Qudāma, *al-Mughnī, op.cit.*, IV, 141; Ramlī, *Nihāyat al-Muḥtāj, op.cit.*, IV, 73-74

hair to make it appear frizzy,[78] applying blusher to the cheeks,[79] inserting cotton balls in the mouth corners to plump up the face, and padding clothes to imply a strong musculature[80] are sometimes referred to as *Tadlīs al-Mashatah* or "beautician's fraud"[81] and constitute fraud both in marriage contracts[82] and contracts for the sale of slaves, provided that the purpose of such actions is to induce the other party into contracting.[83] Ibn Qudāma considers such cosmetic alterations as fraud even if they are "accidental" or at least done without the intention to defraud.[84]

Some authors regard the deliberate act of splattering a slave's clothes or skin with ink, and placing an inkwell and pen in his hands as fraud, when it is done to mislead the buyer. The latter will think that the slave is literate when in reality the opposite is true.[85] Other jurists, however, hold that fraud such as this is discoverable by the purchaser and therefore do not concur with the former opinion.[86]

Ghushsh al-Khāfī

In a prototype of cases entitled *Ghushsh al-Khāfī*, or "concealed deception" the jurists determined that mixing or adding substances to the subject-matter in a way which is intended to defraud the other party, such as diluting milk with water, or cooling milk for the purpose of increasing its weight, constitutes active fraud.[87] This category covers cases where the seller does not actually conceal a defect, but merely attempts to create the impression

---

78 Ibn Qudāma, *ibid.*; Abū Ḥanīfa dissents here on the basis that the state of the hair cannot constitute a defect, even if it is fraudulent: Sanhūrī, *M. al-Ḥaqq, op.cit.*, II, p.163

79 al-Ramlī, *Nihāyat al-Muḥtāj, op.cit.*, IV, 73-74

80 al-Ramlī, *Nihāyat al-Muḥtāj, op.cit.*, IV, 73-74

81 The reference is found in Shi'ite Fiqh : Shahīd al-Thānī, *Masālik al-Afhām*, (Tehran, 1273) I, p.166, cited in Owsia, *op.cit.*, p.525

82 A woman may also seek annulment of her marriage according to Mālikī law on the basis of lack of marriage equality (*Kafā'a*) where the husband has fraudulently misrepresented his status : *Lum'ah*, and *Rawdah*, II, p.59, cited in Owsia, *op.cit.*, p.526

83 Shahīd al-Thānī, *Masālik al-Afhām*, I, p.166 in Owsia, *op.cit.*, p.525

84 Ibn Qudāma, *al-Mughnī*, (Cairo Third Edn., 1367 AH), IV, 142-3

85 Ibn al-Mawwāq, reciting that Ibn al-Ḥājib, dissented on this. Ibn al-Mawwāq, *al-Tāj wa al-Iklīl li Mukhtaṣar Khalīl*, in the margin of al-Ḥaṭṭāb, *Mawāhib al-Jalīl li Sharḥ Mukhtaṣar Khalīl*, (6 Vols. Tripoli 1329) IV, 437; Sanhūrī, *M. al-Ḥaqq, op.cit.*, II, p.162;

86 Notably the major Shāfi'ī jurists and Abū Ḥanīfa. See Sanhūrī, *Maṣādir al-Ḥaqq*, II, p.163, and *infra*.

87 Shahīd, I and II, p.236, cited in P. Owsia, *op.cit.*, p.525

that the object is free of defects, such as by painting, or dyeing a garment to make it appear as new;[88] or selling a stated number of articles which turn out to be less than the number or amount stated.[89]

Ibn al-Mawwāq, reporting Ibn Abī Zamanīn's opinion in this context, states that if the occurrence of such fraud turns out fortuitously for the buyer, he may return the object, but if not the value is returned to him.[90] In other words, we may presume that if the actual number exceeds the stated number, the buyer would, in Ibn Abī Zamanīn's opinion, be able to keep the excess because the mistake was the seller's.

Similarly, the act of damming off canal or mill water in order to direct it over A's land so that he may sell or lease water rights to B at excessive rates, is a case specifically mentioned by the Shāfi'ī jurist al-Ramlī.[91] The proviso here is that the buyer or lessee suspects that the cost exceeds its value. It is unlikely that any judge would consider the act of diverting water from its natural course as a fraudulent act, any more than he would construe the sale of water rights over private land to be an illegal contract. This category of fraud would therefore be better placed under the title of "gross disproportion of price to value (*Istighlāl*)".[92] The case would nevertheless probably meet with some dispute among the classical lawyers, for some of them do reject the sale or gift of a watercourse as invalid. The right of benefit from such water, they claim, is of a nature which cannot admit of its being precisely ascertained and cannot therefore constitute the legitimate object of a contract, even if that water is conveyed through a trough or trench.[93] It is difficult to understand their objection, however, if satisfactory means by which to measure the quantity of water can be provided. It is tempting to suppose that the real objection of these lawyers to the sale of such watercourses is based rather on the presumption of a public right of access to water. This supposition is understandable, given the particular geographical climate in which these doctrines were constructed.

88 al-Ḥaṭṭāb, *op.cit.*, IV, pp.437-8

89 al-Ḥaṭṭāb, *ibid.*

90 al-Mawwāq, citing Ibn Abī Zamanīn, in margin of al-Ḥaṭṭāb, *Mawāhib al-Jalīl li Sharḥ Mukhtaṣar Khalīl, op.cit.*, IV, 437; cited in Sanhūrī, *Maṣādir al-Ḥaqq*, II, p.162

91 al-Ramlī, *Nihāyat al-Muḥtāj Ilā Sharḥ al-Minhāj, op.cit.*, IV, pp.73-74

92 For which, See Chapter VI.5.1 below

93 Hamilton, *The Hedaya, op.cit.*, p.271

al-Najsh

The classical authors also highlighted the practice of *al-Najsh* as a particular case of illegal trickery. *Al-Najsh* occurs in two forms : In the first, a third party acting in collusion with the seller offers ficticious tenders for the goods without intending to buy them for himself. He does this solely in order to enhance the price of the goods by inciting his fellow offerees to offer higher bids.[94]

The second form of *al-Najsh* occurs when the buyer acts in collusion with his competitors to defraud the seller. He does this by agreeing with his fellow bidders not to proffer high bids so that they may buy the goods at a reduced price.[95]

Both forms of *al-Najsh* give rise to the right of option to the defrauded party when he learns of the fraud, and ownership has passed to the buyer.

6.3.7 EFFECTS

While there is agreement among the classical jurists that fraud or misrepresentation by conduct is forbidden, there is disagreement as to the effects of such fraud.[96]

The classical Ḥanafī doctrine, as exposed by Abū Ḥanīfa and his disciple Muḥammad, does not consider *Taṣriyya* to constitute a *Faskh* contract. These scholars state instead that the defrauded party is merely entitled to claim restitution (*Ta'wīḍ*) for the difference in value between the price paid and the true value of the object of contract.[97] According to these two jurists therefore, the right to avoid the contract at the option of the defrauded party does not exist if that party has converted the goods, or, in this case, milked the livestock.[98]

This school of thought by no means forms the absolute consensus even

---

94 Sanhūrī, *Maṣādir al-Ḥaqq*, II, p.166; Marghīnānī, *al-Hidāya*, (Hamilton), *op.cit.*, p.278; also, T.P. Hughes, *A Dictionary of Islam*, (London, 1885), p.428; E. Fagnan, *Additions Aux Dictionnaires Arabes*, (Algiers, 1923) p.169, who defines *al-Najsh* as "Le Fait de surenchérir un objet sans intention de l'acheter, pour en faire monter le prix"; and M.M. Ali, *A Manual of Hadith*, (London and Dublin 1944; Reprinted 1983), p.292

95 Sanhūrī, *ibid.*, p.166

96 Sanhūrī, *ibid.*, II, p.163; al-Jazīrī, *Kitāb al-Fiqh*, II, p.201

97 Maḥmaṣānī, *General Theory, op.cit.*, II, p.426; Sanhūrī, citing *Sharḥ al-Taḥrīr*, by Ibn al-Hammām, in *Maṣādir al-Ḥaqq*, II, p.164; al-Jazīrī, *Kitāb al-Fiqh*, II, p.202

98 Sanhūrī, *ibid.*, p.164

of the Ḥanafī School,[99] and is distinguished as a dissenting opinion among all the other schools. The reasoning of Abū Yūsuf and Muḥammad is that *Taṣriyya* does not constitute a defect on the grounds that if the beasts had not been bound and were to be found deficient in milk yield, the sale would not be revocable. Fraud not constituted by defect, they state, does not give rise to the option.[100] They acknowledge the existence of the Prophetic Ḥadīth (quoted above), but claim that the latter is contradicted by a *Qiyās* supported by the other primary sources. This *Qiyās* holds that "hostility (*'Udwān*) results in a liability to its equivalent or value".[101] In this matter where the seller has been hostile to the buyer by his act of fraudulent *Taṣriyya*, the buyer may demand damages from him to the value of his loss.

The Shāfi'īs,[102] Mālikīs,[103] Ḥanbalīs[104] Ibāḍīs,[105] Ibn Mas'ūd, Ibn 'Amr, Abū Hurayra and Anīs, Ibn Abī Layla, Isḥāq and Abū Yūsuf[106] however, give the victim of fraud the option of whether to cancel the contract or ratify it. The modern Ḥanafī school also succumbs to the majority opinion. In the words of Ibn Qudāma al-Maqdīsī,[107] the simple fact that the seller has deceived the buyer (by his act of binding in *Taṣriyya*) renders his actions as fraudulent as if he himself had told the buyer that the sheep were good milkers.[108]

This is the position taken up by modern legislation : where a contract is deemed to be tainted with fraud or *Ghabn al-Fāḥish* accompanied by Fraud, the defrauded party has the option whether to rescind or to ratify the contract, (providing that he has not converted, damaged, lost or altered the

---

99 Abū Yūsuf, dissenting, argues for the return of the beast together with the value of the milk. al-Jazīrī, *Kitāb al-Fiqh*, II, p.202

100 Sanhūrī, *ibid..*, p.164

101 *"Ḍamān al-'Udwān yakūn bi al-mithl aw bi al-Qīma" (Liability for 'Hostility' may be in kind or in value): al-Jazīrī, Kitāb al-Fiqh*, II, p.202

102 al-Jazīrī, *Kitāb al-Fiqh*, II, p.201

103 *idem.*, p.202

104 al-Jazīrī, *ibid.*, p.202; Maḥmaṣānī, *General Theory*, *op.cit.*, II, p.325; Sanhūrī, *M. al-Ḥaqq*, II, p.162, citing Ibn Qudāma al-Maqdīsī, *Sharḥ al-Kabīr 'Alā Matn al-Muqanna'*, in the margin of Ibn Qudāma, *al-Mughnī*, Vol. IV, pp. 80-81

105 al-Salīmī, *Jawhar al-Niẓām*, *op.cit.*, p.326; Saleh, *General Principles*, *op.cit.*, p.40

106 al-Jazīrī, *Kitāb al-Fiqh*, II, p.202; Sanhūrī, *ibid.*, p.164, citing *Sharḥ al-Kabīr*, on the margin of Ibn Qudāma's *al-Mughnī*, *op.cit.*, IV, pp. 80-81

107 *Sharḥ al-Kabīr 'Alā Matn al-Muqanna'*, in the margin of Ibn Qudāma, *al-Mughnī*, Vol. IV, pp. 80-81; and Sanhūrī, *ibid.*, II, p.164

108 Sanhūrī, *ibid.*, p.164

object in any way).[109]

The restriction on the duration of the option is also subject to variations of judgment. The Ḥanbalī and Ibāḍī schools extend the option to three days from the discovery of the fraud or misrepresentation.[110] Abū Ḥanīfa, meanwhile, relates a Tradition from the Prophet reporting to allow up to two inspections after milking.[111] Shāfi'ī's companions say that the option must be exercised "in the face of the news", just as a contract to marry may be abrogated on first sight of the intended spouse.[112] The Mālikīs, on the other hand, allow up to three milkings.[113]

There is also dispute as to whether compensation should be paid to the buyer by the seller in the case of *Taṣriyya* and its analogies, where fraud has been committed. Abū Ḥanīfa suggests that the seller should pay damages,[114] but the leading jurists of the three schools along with Abū Yūsuf and Ibn Qudāma insist that the sheep should be returned to the seller accompanied by the value of the milk.[115] Nor is this value impervious to variation. Established by the *Qur'ān, Sunna* and *Ijmā'* to be a *Ṣā'* of dates, the question of whether the compensation for the milk used should be returned in kind or value is still raised by the jurists.[116] Nevertheless, the majority opinion concurs with the sources on the latter,[117] and most schools agree that if the buyer discovers the fraud without milking, he may return the animal without the *Ṣā'* of dates compensation.[118]

---

109 See Article 125 (1) of the Egyptian Civil Code; Art. 151 of the Kuwaiti Civil Code; and Art. 187 of the UAE Civil Code.

110 al-Salīmī, *Jawhar al-Niẓām, op.cit.*, p.326; Saleh, *General Principles, op.cit.*, p.40

111 Sanhūrī, *ibid.*, p.165

112 Sanhūrī, *ibid.*, p.165

113 al-Jazīrī, *Kitāb al-Fiqh*, II, p. 201

114 Sanhūrī, *ibid.*, II, p.164

115 Sanhūrī, *ibid..*, II, p.164

116 For example, the Shāfi'īs accept money, land or anything else to its value, if the contractors so agree amongst themselves. The Mālikīs would accept only the equivalent of staple food of the respective country. al-Jazīrī, *Kitāb al-Fiqh*, II, p.201

117 Sanhūrī, *ibid.*, p.164

118 See, for example, Ibn Qudāma: "The Prophet said: You must milk your camels and sheep before you sell them. If you do not, the buyer has the right, after having milked the animal, either to keep it if it suits him, or to return it if not. In this second case, he must give to the seller a *Ṣā'* of dates. The buyer who knows, before having milked the beast himself, that she has not been milked, has the right to return her without being accountable for indemnity." Henri Laoust, *Le Précis de Droit d'Ibn Qudāma*, (Beirut, 1950), pp.98-99; See also al-Jazīrī, *Kitāb al-Fiqh*, II, p.201; and Sanhūrī, *Masādir al-Ḥaqq*, II, p.165.

When the milk itself is defective, the Shāfi'īs and Mālikīs state that the existence of this defect avoids the requirement of compensation for milk taken. The buyer is obviously required to prove this to the seller by producing the bad milk.[119] The Shāfi'īs and Mālikīs also concur on a further point, and this is that even if the buyer milks the animal more than once, the compensation remains a single *Ṣā'* of dates, or the equivalent. This is the case so long as he has not been unreasonable. Moreover, the Mālikīs go on to state that if a number of sheep are bought under the one contract and they are all ***Muṣarrāt***, the buyer can return them together with a *Ṣā'* of dates for each one milked. The Shāfi'īs add that where the sale occurs collectively, a *Ṣā'* must be provided for each seller by each buyer.[120]

6.3.8 CONDITIONS OF ACTIONABLE FRAUD

To determine whether *al-Tadlīs al-Fi'lī* may be actionable, the *Fiqh* provides guidelines in the form of conditions which are to be fulfilled :-

(1) The alleged defrauded party must have suffered material damage (*Ḍarār*) such as is recognised by commercial standards and practices; that is, the fraud must be significant[121] and an impetus to contract.[122]

(2) The fraud itself must be cunning to such a degree as to delude any ordinarily prudent member of the public.[123]

(3) One of the contracting parties must know of the fraud and have relied on its concealment.

(4) The other contracting party must be ignorant of the fraud and have had no other means of coming to know

---

119 al-Jazīrī, *Kitāb al-Fiqh*, II, p201

120 al-Jazīrī, *Kitāb al-Fiqh*, II, p.201

121 "*bi-Jasāma*" : the degree of significance is not determined by the extent of significance as an abstract, but rather on the effect that that fraud has on the particular contracting party in question, and the influence it played in deluding him into contracting. See al-Ramlī, *Nihāyat al-Muḥtāj, op.cit.*, IV, pp.73-74; and Kuwaiti Memorandum to the 1980 civil Code, p.143 : The Kuwaiti provision takes the Egyptian code as its model here.

122 Sanhūrī, *ibid.*, II, pp. 159, 165

123 Coulson, *Commercial Law, op.cit.*, pp.70-71; al-Ramlī, *Nihāyat al-Muḥtāj, op.cit.*, IV, pp.73-74

of it.[124]

The case often cited to illustrate these conditions is that of a transaction for a slave whose hands or clothes have been stained with ink. The buyer, alleging fraud, relies on the supposition that to bear ink stains is to denote literacy, and accuses the seller of deliberate misrepresentation. The jurists determined, however, that such a supposition is ill-founded, and one which any ordinarily prudent person is not likely to make. Therefore, even if the staining was deliberately intended to delude on the part of the seller, the buyer's claim of rescission would fail.[125] The Mālikīs do regard this as fraud however. The Shāfi'īs concur with the former decision, providing that there is no gross disproportion of balance between the parties benefits.[126]

A similar case given by the texts involves the purchase of a female animal on the assumption that her swollen stomach denotes pregnancy. The buyer here may not have recourse to the option to rescind if the expected results do not materialise. The swelling, it is reasoned, may have occurred for some cause other than as a result of breeding.[127]

The fourth condition is, naturally enough, that if the party alleging fraud was aware of the fraud at the time of contracting, then there is no rescission of the contract.[128] The position here is parallel to that of a defect which the affected party knew to exist at the formation of the contract. Ibn Qudāma states (again using the prototype case of *Taṣriyya*) : "The return of such an animal is allowed only to prevent the damage arising from a deficient milk-yield. Since no real deficiency exists in this case, there is no right to return the animal. No fault exists in the sale-object, and its qualities are as described at the time of contract. Therefore there is no *Tadlīs* because the

---

124 Sanhūrī, *Maṣādir al-Ḥaqq*, II, p.159

125 Coulson, *Commercial Law*, p.71; Similarly with a slave dressed as a baker : al-Ramlī, *Nihāyat al-Muḥtāj, op.cit.*, IV, pp.73-74.

126 Sanhūrī, *Maṣādir al-Ḥaqq*, II, p.162

127 Sanhūrī, *ibid.*, II, p.165 The situation, should the buyer's anticipation prove correct, would also be subject to dispute : Firstly, according to the Fiqh, the unborn foetus cannot constitute part of the object of sale and must therefore be returned to the seller; and secondly, is it not here the buyer who is attempting to defraud the seller, by obtaining something for nothing ? It could be argued therefore that the unlawful intention of the buyer would render the contract void on the grounds of unlawful *Maḥall*, or alternatively, a claim may be made on the basis of *Istighlāl*, and the contract would be *Fāsid*.

128 Coulson, *Commercial Law, op.cit.*, p.71; Kuwaiti Civil Code Art. 153 (2): The equivalent article does not appear in the UAE Civil Code.

purpose of the option is to prevent damage, and no damage exists."[129]

Similarly, if the trickery perpetrated is discoverable, such that any reasonable person would be deemed capable of learning of the fraud, but that the party in question was negligent therein, there is no option established for fraud.[130]

Although the maxim *Caveat Emptor* does not apply to Islamic law to the same degree as in English Common law,[131] the Sharī'a is nevertheless not inclined to treat any negligence or foolishness on the part of the buyer with indulgence. A purchaser will not be released from his obligations simply because an "apparent bargain", desired on his part by mere avarice rather than in exchange for legitimate consideration, has not been realised. This is despite the fact that he may have suffered material damage : his expectations of securing an object for less than its recognised value are not legitimate at law. The strict confines of the required conditions for actionable fraud are therefore such as to allow some scope for the reasonable hyperboles and windowdressing of normal commercial marketing and advertising.[132]

6.3.9 FRAUDULENT STATEMENTS

The majority opinion concerning Misrepresentation or lies during the period of contracting is that it renders the contract void, provided that it is accompanied by exorbitant inequality in the respective considerations,[133] or is annexed to *Ghabn*.[134]

---

129 Ibn Qudāma, *al-Mughnī, op.cit.*, IV, p.136; also cited in Coulson, *Commercial Law*, p.71

130 al-Ramlī, *Nihāyat al-Muḥtāj, op.cit.*, IV, pp.73-74; Sanhūrī, *Maṣādir al-Ḥaqq, op.cit.*, II, p.162

131 See, for example, *obiter* Cockburn CJ in *Smith v Hughes*, QB (1871) *LR*, 6QB 597; 40 *LJ*, QB 221; 25 *LT*, 329; 19 *WR*, 1059. Smith and Thomas, *A Casebook on Contract*, pp.95-96; P.S. Atiyah, *The Sale of Goods*, (5th Edn; 1975); Sale of Goods Act 1979; S.J. Stoljar, 'Growth of Implied Warranties in Sale of Goods' (1952), 15 *MLR*, p.425; Pollock on *Contracts*, (Thirteenth Edn; London, 1950) pp.264, 353, 451 ff; For Insurance Misrepresentations, see *ibid.*, pp.433, 599; G.H. Treitel, *Contract*, (Sixth Edn; London, 1983) pp. 262-7, 429-32. See also, E.J. Schuster, *The Principles of German Civil Law*, (Oxford, 1907) pp.109-110; 210-211, where (at p.211) he states that "under the teminology of English Law, a German agreement for sale would be deemed a contract *Uberrimae Fidei*.

132 See Kuwaiti Memorandum to the Civil Code of 1980, p. 145

133 Saleh, *General Principles, op.cit.*, p.40

134 Sanhūrī, *M. al-Ḥaqq*, II, pp.178-179.

Ibn 'Ābidīn states that where in *Taghrīr al-Qawlī* the fraud is accompanied by *Ghabn*, that *Ghabn* must exceed one third of the value of the object, before the deception necessitates restitution in normal circumstances.[135] Thus in the examples promoted by Ibn 'Ābidīn, if A tells B to follow a certain route, declaring that it is safe, and when B follows it, he is set upon by thieves, A will not be liable; Similarly, if C tells D that his intended spouse is a freewoman, and D marries her on the basis of that information, only to discover that she is not free, C will not be liable for restitution of the value of the child born from the marriage, if C is not her guardian.[136] In such cases liability arises only in three concerns :

(1) If the deception constitutes a condition, for instance, if D marries the girl only on condition that she is free;

(2) If the deception occurs in a commutative contract; for instance, if a buyer of a house builds upon that house subsequent to it passing into his possession, and thereafter a claim is made upon the original house. The buyer will be compensated for the building work he undertook on the structure. Similarly, if a father vouchsafes to the traders in the market that his son is authorised to trade, and it later appears that he has two sons, one of which does not have that authority, and he has neglected to distinguish the fact; He is thus liable for misleading the traders into engaging in commerce with the wrong son, and will be called upon to restitute the losses of the merchants for that deception.[137]

(3) If the contract contains such warranty; for instance, in a contract of Hire or Deposit, where the benefit must be returned intact to the obligor. If the object of the contract is destroyed or damaged in these cases, restitution may be claimed by the Depositor or Hirer. This does not apply in contracts of Gift, *'Arīya*, charitable donations (*Ṣadaqāt*), or Loan (*Rahn*), where warranties of soundness in the object do not exist.[138]

The Ḥanbalīs accord the option of fraud in any case to any gross disproportion between the value of the goods and that demanded by, and

---

135 Ibn 'Ābidīn, *Radd al-Muḥtār 'Alā al-Dhurr al-Mukhtār*, 8 Vols., (Cairo, 1386-89/1966-69) Vol. IV, pp.247-250. The same rule applies to contracts of Deposit and Hire, but not to the unilateral contracts of Gift and *'Arīya*.

136 Sanhūrī, *M. al-Ḥaqq*, II, p.179

137 Sanhūrī, *M. al-Ḥaqq*, II, pp.179-180; Kasānī, *al-Badā'i'*, VII, p.201; Ibn Nujaym, *al-Baḥr al-Rā'iq*, VI, p.144

138 Sanhūrī, *M. al-Ḥaqq*, II, pp.180-182; Ibn Nujaym, *al-Baḥr al-Rā'iq*, VI, p.145

paid to, the seller.[139] The Shāfi'īs accord the option where any fraud has resulted in such an imbalance.[140]

In other cases of fraudulent statements, however, the option of fraud (*Khiyār al-Tadlīs*) does not apply, for this option is restricted to fraudulent conduct.[141] This opinion applies to all except the Ḥanbalī and Ibāḍi schools. According to the scholars of the latter two schools, any fraudulent statements, together with failure to disclose, constitute actionable fraud sufficient to abrogate the contract.[142]

The difference which exists in the approach of the Islamic law system and, for example, the English Common Law system in relation to the concept of Mistake, is also evident with regard to Misrepresentation. Where common law treats the consent as vitiated[143] Islamic law regards the underlying contract as valid, but gives a remedy to the injured party under the trilogy of options of *Ru'ya, 'Ayb,* and *Wasf.*[144]

Apart from this difference, however, the Islamic approach to misrepresentation is closer to the objectivism of Western legal systems, in that the scope accorded by the law to remedy alleged misrepresentation is necessarily of a more limited nature. Misrepresentation manifested by fraudulent statements finds remedy in Islamic law only under two categories. The first is in sales entitled *Istirsāl*; the second is in sales of trust.[145]

Bay' al-Mustarsal

Any perusal of the Fiqh books on contract will inevitably lead to an encounter with a peculiarly Islamic example of misrepresentation. This particular case of misrepresentation fits uneasily under any one categorisation and therefore probably stands best on its own. It is dressed in rather archaic and nomadic robes, but in its modern analogies it assumes a continuing importance in commercial life.

This category of misrepresentation is usually referred to in English as

---

139 Ibn Qudāma al-Maqdīsī, *al-Sharḥ al-Kabīr 'alā Matn al-Muqanna'*, Vol. IV, p.79; Ibn Qudāma, *al-Mughnī, op.cit.*, IV, pp.80-81; Sanhūrī, *Maṣādir al-Ḥaqq*, II, pp.162, 182

140 Sanhūrī, *ibid.*, II, p.162

141 Coulson, *Commercial Law, op.cit.*, p.72

142 Sanhūrī, *Maṣādir al-Ḥaqq*, II, pp.168-169; Saleh, *General Principles, op.cit.*, p.72

143 Misrepresentation encompasses both acts and statements under English Common law : Treitel, *The Law of Contracts*, (6th Edn; London 1983), pp.252 ff.

144 Coulson, *Commercial Law, op.cit.*, p.72; For the options, see Chapter VII below.

145 Sanhūrī, *Maṣādir al-Ḥaqq*, II, p.178

"forestalling the market"[146] or "meeting the riders".[147] The practice was to ride out of the towns to intercept strangers (whether in trading caravans from afar, or villagers from the country) on their way to the markets. The town's tradesmen buy the wares at prices markedly lower than those in their local market, thereby exploiting the travellers' ignorance of local prices.[148] The Prophet is reported to have condemned such activities as "cheating "and "deceitful"[149] and gave the injured strangers the right to rescind their unfair contracts with the riders upon learning of the real value of their commodities in the market place. Just how practical these rescissions may have been, once the riders had left the company of the strangers, is open to speculation. However, the theoretical principle is sound and the justice of its consequences without question.

The *Bay' al Mustursāl*[150] has been developed by the Ḥanbalī[151] Mālikī Fiqh[152] to comprise a trust sale agreement where the contractor discloses a secret about himself (*Istaslama*), indicating that he has no knowledge pertaining to that particular object of contract.[153] By so confiding, he seeks indemnity and advice from his co-conractor, or may consult with, or appoint him to buy and sell in his stead.[154] The basis of this contract is not the original price,[155] but the market price. The advising contractor has a duty by virtue of the trust expressly placed in him, not to deceive his vulnerable co-

---

146 Hamilton, *The Hedaya, op.cit.*, p.278

147 eg. Coulson, *Commercial Law, op.cit.*, p.72

148 Ali, *A Manual of Hadith*, (London, Dublin, 1983) : Bukhārī 34:49, p.269, No. 9, regarding cereals bought from camel owners.

149 Coulson, *Commercial Law, op.cit.*, p.72; Ali, *ibid.*, Bukhārī 34:58, pp. 297-298 (No.12)

150 Also called *Bay' al-Musta'amana*: see Sanhūrī, *Maṣādir al-Ḥaqq*, II, p.175

151 See *al-Sharḥ al-Kabīr 'Alā Matn al-Muqanna'*, Vol. IV, p.79; and Sanhūrī, *Maṣādir al-Ḥaqq*, II, pp.177,182

152 Dardīr/Dasūqī, *al-Sharḥ al-Kabīr*, (Commentary by Dasūqī) Vol. III, pp.141-142; See also Dardīr's *Sharḥ al-Ṣaghīr*, (in bottom margin of al-Ṣāwī, *Bulghat al-Sālik lī Aqrab al-Masālik*, 3 vols. (Cairo, 1978) Vol. II, p.63; See also Ibn Juzayy, *al-Qawānīn al-Fiqhiyya*, (Beirut, 1977) p. 264; al-Khurshī, *Sharḥ Mukhtaṣar*, 8 Vols. in 4, (1318. Reprint, Beirut, n.d.) V, pp.152-153; al-Tasūlī, *al-Bahja Fī Sharḥ at-Tuḥfa*, 2 vols. in 1 (Cairo, 1370/1951) II, pp.106-107 (With commentary by al-Tāwudī)

153 Sanhūrī states that the Shāfi'īs also pertain to this doctrine: *Maṣādir al-Ḥaqq*, II, p. 182

154 Ibn Ḥanbal defines the party in such a sale as 'he who does not have the advantage in bargaining (*Yamākas*)'. There are no limits to *Ghabn* in this context in the Ḥanbalī *Fiqh*, although the Mālikīs stress that the *Ghabn* should exceed one-third of the value of the object. Others state one-sixth; while yet others refer the matter to custom. See Sanhūrī, *Maṣādir al-Ḥaqq*, II, p. 178

155 As in Trust Sale contracts; See next Section

contractor as to the true market prices. Should he be so fraudulent, the deceived party is granted the option to rescind the contract. This is in accordance with the Prophet's reported adage : " Deceit of a thing on trust is a sin".[156]

An explicit denial of fraud or deception by a contractor is also sometimes held to constitute a case of *Bay' al-Mustarsal*.[157] Therefore if A says to B "There is no fraud (*khilāba*) or dishonesty (*Ghushsh*) between us in our dealing", he is expected to abide by his statement.

Either the seller or the buyer may be the defrauded party. A seller may as easily say to the buyer "Pay what you would normally pay", as a buyer may ask the advice of a seller concerning his intended purchase.[158]

The rule meets with restrictions, however, even within the Mālikī school. The general maxim is "Where there is no ignorance, there is no revocation". Therefore, if the contractor can be proven to have known the true value of the object he will be precluded from rescinding the sale. Secondly, to be able to rescind, the *Ghubn* must have superceded one third of the value of the commodity. Thirdly, the sale must not fall into the category of *al-Mukāyasa* (Risk, bargaining) sales, such as include market bartering.[159]

6.3.10 FAILURE TO DISCLOSE

In general, deliberate silence or failure to disclose a fact or set of circumstances regarding a sale is not deemed fraudulent. In certain special cases however, silence may be deemed a fraud, and in these cases, the burden of proof is upon the defrauded party to show that he would not have concluded the contract had he been aware of that fact or set of circumstances.

Tadlīs Bi al-'Ayb

By analogy to the sale of *Muṣarrāt*, the *Fiqh* has established in all four schools that there is an implied warranty against defects in goods, and that

---

156 Sanhūrī, *ibid.*, p.175; al-Ḥaṭṭāb, *Mawāhib al-Jalīl li Sharḥ Mukhtaṣar Khalīl, op.cit.*, IV, 470 (The adage is reported by Ibn Ḥabīb)

157 al-Ḥaṭṭāb, *ibid.*, IV, 473. Ibn Ḥanbal states that *Ghubn* must be first established here for the option to arise. Others state that the option exists for three days if the buyer has yet to see the object of contract, and in the meantime learns that his fellow contractor has cheated him. Sanhūrī, *ibid.*, p.175

158 See, for example, among the Mālikī texts, *Sharḥ al-Kabīr*, by Dasūqī (In the margin of Dardīr, III, pp.141-142); and Sanhūrī, *Maṣādir al-Ḥaqq*, II, 176.

159 Dardīr/Dassūqī, *Sharḥ al-Kabīr*, III, pp.141-142

intentionally concealing a defect in goods is fraudulent. The Ḥanafīs consider such concealment as forbidden (*Ḥarām*); the Mālikīs explain that it constitutes *Tadlīs*; while the Shāfi'īs and the Ḥanbalīs consider it to be *Ghushsh* (Deception).[160]

In all schools the sale, again by analogy to *Taṣriyya*, is considered valid, but the option of *Tadlīs* is established for the buyer.

In the same way, rights and liens held over the objects of sales must also be declared. If A sells a house to B without disclosing the existing lease, Ibn Ḥanbal has stated that neglecting to disclose this fact amounts to *Tadlīs* or *Taghrīr*.[161] Therefore the concealment of rights interferes with the absolute sale obtaining the benefits of the object, and is considered as significant a concealment as that of a defect, thus affecting the severance of the bargain.[162]

By way of example, the *Fuqahā'* determine that in bargaining sales (*Bay' al-Mumākasa/al-Musāwama*), concealment may be considered as fraud if the seller deliberately conceals a defect in the object with the intention to defraud. This is called *Tadlīs bi al-'Ayb* (Fraud with Defect).[163] Zayla'ī states : "Soundness of the object is an [implied] condition of the contract. It is not permitted to sell a defective object (knowingly) unless that defect is disclosed". This Ḥanafī opinion is based on the Tradition of the Prophet related by Ibn Māja and Ibn Ḥanbal.[164]

Dardīr[165] states that the defect may not be alluded to generally, but must be specifically stated when discosure is made. Nor may the seller mention the real defect among a list of imaginary defects, so that the buyer, finding the object sound concerning the imaginary defects will discount also the real defect.[166]

In these cases the defrauded party is granted the option for fraud and this option operates in conjunction with the option of defect. The jurists allow

---

160 Sanhūrī, *Maṣādir al-Ḥaqq*, II, 183

161 Ibn Rajab, *al-Qawā'id al-Fiqhiyya*, (Cairo, 1391/1971) pp.41-42

162 Sanhūrī, *Maṣādir al-Ḥaqq*, II, 186

163 Sanhūrī, *Maṣādir al-Ḥaqq*, II, 185

164 "It is not permitted for a Muslim to sell to his brother a sale in which there is a defect, unless he discloses it to him". related in Zayla'ī, *Tabyīn al-Ḥaqā'iq : Sharḥ Kanz al-Daqā'iq*, (Būlāq, 1313-1315; Reprint Beirut, n.d.) Vol. IV, p.31; Sanhūrī, *Maṣādir al-Ḥaqq*, II, pp.183-184; Ibn Nujaym, *al-Baḥr al-Rā'iq*, Vol. VI, p.35 who states that it is forbidden to so conceal a defect in an object. See also Ibn Juzayy, *al-Qawānīn al-Fiqhiyya*, pp.263-264; and the Shāfi'ī author Shīrāzī, *al-Muhadhdhab*, Vol. I, pp.283-284.

165 Dardīr, *al-Sharḥ al-Ṣaghīr*, in margin of al-Ṣāwī, *op.cit*, vol. II, pp.53-54

166 Dardīr, *al-Sharḥ al-Ṣaghīr*, in margin of al-Ṣāwī, *op.cit*, vol. II, pp.53-54

that there might be some advantage in establishing the option of fraud in addition to the option for defect here, for in certain cases the latter defect may fail to arise, or the case may be that the object cannot be returned.[167]

Shīrāzī relates : "Abū Sabā' said :'I bought a she-camel from the house of Wā'ila Ibn al-Asqa', and when I went outside with it, 'Aqba b. 'Āmir said to me : 'Did he explain to you what was wrong with it?' I said, 'What is wrong with it? Its bearing indicates sound enough health.' He said: 'Do you want it for travel or for meat?' So I said, 'I want to perform the *Hajj* on her.' Then he said, 'Her hoof is broken'". Shīrāzī, relating the Prophetic Tradition, reaffirms that Abū Sabā' could claim restitution from the seller, and that the sale is valid, subject to his option to rescind for fraud on the same basis as *Taṣriyya*.[168] The principle is also held in certain circumstances by the modern legislation : Article 20 (2) of the Bahrain Contract Law of 1969 states, for example:

> "Mere Silence as to facts likely to affect the willingness of a person to enter into a contract is not fraud, unless the circumstances of the case are such that, regard being had to them, the law casts a duty on the person keeping silence to speak, or unless his silence amounts, in its context, to a representation that a material fact does or does not exist."

The UAE Civil Code format is slightly different. Article 186 states:

> "Deliberate silence concerning a fact or set of circumstances shall be deemed a misrepresentation (*Taghrīr*) if it is proved that the person misled thereby would not have made the contract had he been aware of that fact or set of circumstances."[169]

The burden of proof rests upon the party alleging fraud here, to show that non-disclosure of essential facts affected his will in contracting. The silence must also be deliberate, and presumably it is left to the Court to construe the exact implications of that phrase. It does indicate, however, that a negligence to disclose may not necessarily be deemed fraudulent.

---

167 Sanhūrī, *Maṣādir al-Ḥaqq*, II, 185

168 This is also upheld in the Ḥanbalī school: Ibn Qudāma al-Maqdīsī, *al-Sharḥ al-Kabīr 'Alā Matn al-Muqanna'*, Vol. IV, pp. 83-85; Sanhūrī, *Maṣādir al-Ḥaqq*, II, pp.185-186

169 This is taken from the Jordanian Civil Code of 1976, Art. 144. *cf.* also Art. 125 (2) Egyptian Civil Code; Art.152 Kuwaiti Civil Code;

Similarly, Misrepresentation or Silence which is determined as fraudulent within the the given definition,[170] does not avoid the contract where the Court determines that that fraud was known by, or discoverable with ordinary diligence to, the party whose consent has been so induced.[171]

Persons under Judicial Restriction and Tabarru'āt

The general rule that contracts formed on the basis of deception without fraud may not be annulled[172] finds exception, in both the *Fiqh* texts and modern legislation, where one of the parties is a person under judicial restriction (*al-Maḥjūr 'alayh*);[173] or the contract is a unilateral contract of gift (*Tabarru'āt*).[174] Thus the sale of property belonging to orphans is made invalid by the presence of *Ghabn al-Fāḥish*.[175]

The sale is *Bāṭil* unless the *Ghabn* in it is amended for the benefit of the protected party.[176] Thus the contracts are more properly described as *Fāsid*, for they may be amended or ratified by the tutor or guardian of the restricted party, so long as the amended contract is beneficial to the interests of that party.[177] This applies as much to persons under judicial restriction on account of bad debts,[178] or a person ill with death sickness when his liabilities exceed his assets.[179] Here the UAE Civil Code allows that the contract is suspended (*Mawqūf*), no matter how slight the *Ghabn*, until the *Ghabn* is redressed, or the authority of the creditors is attained. Otherwise, the contract is void.

Contracts involving *Waqf* property, the property belonging to the *Bayt al-Māl*, or the State are considered according to the same rules as the property of an orphan. The contract may be avoided for *Ghabn* unaccompanied by

---

170 Contained in Art. 20 of the Bahrain Law of contract, quoted above.

171 Article 22 (3) of the Bahrain Law of Contract of 1969

172 Sanhūrī, *Maṣādir al-Ḥaqq*, II, 175 ff; *Majella*, Art. 356; Contract Code of Bahrain, Art. 20 (2); UAE Civil Code, Art. 191

173 See Section on Capacity in Chapters V and VI above. Included here are the *Safīh* and the *Majnūn*.

174 *Majella*, Art. 356; Kuwait Civil Code, Art. 154; UAE Civil Code, Art. 191

175 *Majella*, Art. 356; Aḥmad, H.Ṣ, *Baḥth Muqārin*, *op.cit.*, p.88 specifies that this is so when the orphan makes a bequest or enters into an agricultural contract. See also Ibn Nujaym, *al-Baḥr al-Rā'iq*, Vol. VI, p.100. Ibn 'Abidīn, *op.cit*, III, p.72; al-Ḥaṭṭāb, *op.cit.*, Vol. IV, p.482

176 Aḥmad, *Baḥth Muqārin*, *op.cit.*, p.88

177 Aḥmad, *Baḥth Muqārin*, *op.cit.*, p.89

178 UAE Federal Civil Code, Art. 189

179 UAE Federal Civil Code, Art. 189

Tadlīs, and no matter how slight the *Ghabn*.[180] A contract formed with *Ghabn al-Fāḥish* is *Fāsid*, but if that *Ghabn* is superceded by the *Maṣlaḥa* of the Treasury or State, the contract is considered as validly concluded. If not the contract may be abrogated.[181]

The Mālikīs are the only major school whose scholars remain divided as to whether the option to rescind operates in favour of the deceived party here, or whether he has the right to claim the excess over the true value of the object.[182]

The recent Civil Code of the UAE includes within this section, contracts involving deceptions concerning real estate purchases (*'Aqār*) "and such like".[183] These contracts may also be annulled, according to the UAE provision, where the bargain would be deemed unconscionable by any person conversant with that market. The article is unique among the constitutions under study.

Bay'āt al-Amāna: Trust Sale Contracts

The exception to the majority opinion that 'lies alone do not constitute actionable fraud' occurs in all schools in the category of contracts entitled "Trust Sales". In such contracts, the buyer puts himself at the mercy of the seller and is obliged to rely upon the seller's representations. If the seller (here called an Agent of Trust : *Bayyā' al-Amāna*) thereby betrays that trust, Islamic fiqh treats him severely : to cheat in this case is *Ḥarām* (forbidden).[184]

The fiqh, in seeking to give the utmost protection to the vulnerable buyer, permits of no degree of dishonesty whatever on the part of the agent of trust.[185]

Sales of Trust are governed by two orders:

(1) The lack of falsehood in disclosing the original price

(2) The lack of concealment of anything which may be associated with the

---

180 *Majella*, Art. 356; UAE Civil Code, Art. 191; Aḥmad, *Baḥth Muqārin, op.cit.*, p.89. The Mālikīs add the contract of Agency to this list if the agent introduces *Ghabn al-Fāḥish* into the contract.

181 Aḥmad, *Baḥth Muqārin, op.cit.*, p.89

182 Aḥmad, *Baḥth Muqārin, op.cit.*, pp.89-91; al-Ḥaṭṭāb, *op.cit*, IV, p.472

183 "*Wa Ghayrihi*": this presumably alludes to other immovables only. UAE Federal Civil Code, Art. 188

184 Sanhūrī, *Maṣādir al-Ḥaqq*, II, pp.166, 183

185 Sanhūrī, *Maṣādir al-Ḥaqq*, II, p.166; al-Kāsānī, *al-Badā'i'*, V, p.223

price or the commodity.[186]

In the case of Trust Sales both lies and concealing essential information are considered tantamount to deception and fraud. The judge, in his determination of such cases must look to the conscience of the seller in question, and must seek reassurance of his integrity.[187]

The fiqh recognises various particular forms of trust sales, of which three form the core concern of the jurists. These are :-

(1) *Bay' al-Murābaḥa* : A sale conducted by the agent at cost price, with a declared additional profit;

(2) *Bay' al-Tawliyya* : A sale conducted by the agent at cost price;

(3) *Bay' al-Waḍī'a* : A sale conducted at cost price with a declared discount.[188]

In some works the category of *Bay' al-Najsh* is also included, but it is not strictly a trust sale contract.[189] Another category infrequently included in this list is that of *Shirka* or *Ishrāka*, which is a part sale with a reduction in price.[190]

In these contracts it is the original sale price which is of the essence. The seller has an absolute duty to disclose, firstly, the cost price; secondly, the agreed profit or discount;[191] and thirdly, any other factor which may have affected the price, such as defects, additions, or that the sale is the result of a bankruptcy order, or subject to payment arrangements such as credit, or payment by installments.[192] It is not sufficient to provide proof of the wholesale price alone, the breakdown of relevant concomitants is absolutely essential in these contracts.[193] Once a buyer has purchased an object on credit (*bi al-Nasīa*) for instance, he is not thereafter allowed to sell by

---

186 Sanhūrī, *Maṣādir al-Ḥaqq*, II, p.183

187 Sanhūrī, *Maṣādir al-Ḥaqq*, II, p.166

188 Sometimes also referred to as *Bay' al-Muwāḍa'a*, eg. Sanhūrī, *Maṣādir al-Ḥaqq*, II, p.171

189 Saleh, *General Principles, op.cit.*, p.41; See subsection 'Al-Najsh' *supra*.

190 Sanhūrī, *Maṣādir al-Ḥaqq*, II, p.167; and Kuwaiti Civil Code, Art. 462

191 Shīrāzī, *Kitāb al-Tanbīh, op.cit.*, p.104

192 Coulson, *Commercial Law, op.cit.*, p.73.

193 Sanhūrī, *Maṣādir al-Ḥaqq*, II. p.167

Murābaḥa, unless he discloses his previous credit agreement.[194] If he does not disclose his previous credit agreement, and the second purchaser comes to learn of it, that second purchaser is allowed to exercise his right of option to rescind the sale for fraud,[195] and is entitled to the value of the commodity (in cash) on the day of his taking possession of it.[196] The same reasoning applies to the case where he takes the object as reparation of a debt owed to him.[197]

If harm or damage occurs to an object prior to a *Murābaḥa* contract, such damage must be disclosed, incidentally of whether that harm was the fault of the seller or of a third party.[198] Similarly, any addition or increase of the intended object of a *Murābaḥa* sale must be declared.[199] According to the Fiqh, such increase forms the object of a sale; if it is not declared, the due processes of option and rescission may be inhibited, should defects or damage occur.[200] If, however, a Ḥanafī buyer purchases an object from someone as a debt on his own account (*bi-Dayn*), he may sell it by *Murābaḥa* without disclosure as to that debt and the subsequent buyer will be protected by his normal rights of option against the risks of buying.[201] The same does not apply in Mālikī law. Sanhūrī indites that if A takes something as reparation of a debt owed to him by B, he may not then sell it by *Murābaḥa* without disclosing the original circumstances.[202]

In all these sales of trust the failure of the seller to disclose all relevant and correct information concerning the price, is regarded as tantamount to

194 Mālik Ibn Anas, *al-Mudawwana*, X, pp.59-62; Sanhūrī, *Maṣādir al-Ḥaqq*, II, p.171

195 Sarakhsī, *al-Mabsūṭ*, XIII, p.78 (Ḥanafī); Sanhūrī, *M. al-Ḥaqq*, II, p.168; Mālik, *al-Mudawwana*, X, pp.59-62; Shīrāzī, *al-Muhadhdhab*, II, pp. 288-290

196 Mālik Ibn Anas, *al-Mudawwana*, X, 59-62

197 Sanhūrī, *M. al-Ḥaqq*, II, p.169

198 Mālik Ibn Anas said: "[A commodity] may not be sold by Murābaḥa until that which has befallen it by way of defect whilst in [the original purchaser's] possession has been declared." *al-Mudawwana*, X, pp.59-62; See also al-Shāfi'ī, cited in Sanhūrī, *op.cit.*, II, p.168; and *idem.*, II, p.172

199 In the Mālikī school, for example, property which is bought and worked upon or added to may not be sold as *Murābaḥa* without disclosure : eg. a slave-girl whose teeth have been gilded. See Mālik Ibn Anas, *al-Mudawwana*, X, pp.59-62. For trust sales in Mālikī Fiqh, see: Dasūqi/Dardīr, *al-Sharḥ al-Kabīr*, III, 160-171; al-Khurshī, *Sharḥ 'alā al-Mukhtaṣar*, V, 171-180; al-Ḥaṭṭāb, *Muwāhib al-Jalīl*, IV, 488-495; al-Tasūlī, *al-Bahja Fī Sharḥ al-Tuḥfa*, II, 150-155

200 Sanhūrī, *Ibid.*, p.168

201 For a more intricate explanation, See Sanhūrī, *M. al-Ḥaqq*, II, p.169

202 For example, if B buys a car for 1000 Dirhams, the payment of which the seller defers for one year, and B wanted to sell the car by *Murābaḥa*, he would have to disclose his deferred payment. Mālik, *al-Mudawwana*, X, 59-62; Sanhūrī, *M. al-Ḥaqq*, II, p.172

positive Misrepresentation[203] and enables the buyer to rescind the contract. According to Abū Ḥanīfa and Muḥammad, the option consists of a straightforward choice between taking the object for its full price or rejecting it.[204] Abū Yūsuf would prefer the price paid by the buyer to be decreased rather than to grant him an option to rescind.[205] The subtraction of surplus profit is also upheld by the majority Shāfi'ī and Ḥanbalī opinions.[206]

The trust sale contract of *Tawliyya* is found in various forms. That acknowledged by the Ḥanbalīs and the Mālikīs is called *Bay' al-Istidlāl*, which is a sale concluded at market price. The Ḥanbalīs declare that such a sale is void only if the misrepresentation perpetrated by the seller is accompanied by gross disproportion between the respective contributions.[207] The Mālikīs are, however, prepared to avoid the contract where this disproportion is only slight.[208] Sanhūrī also recognises *Ishrāka*, which is basically a *Tawliyya* trust sale where only a share of the commodity is exchanged in return for a proportionate amount of the price.[209]

According to Abū Ḥanīfa and Abū Yūsuf, fraud perpetrated in a *Tawliyya* contract allows the price paid to be decreased.[210] The resulting price, after the decrease, would then amount to the original cost price. It is characteristic of Islamic law here to seek to repair the damage rather than to

---

203 Coulson, *Commercial Law, op.cit.*, p.73

204 Ibn al-Hammām, *Fatḥ al-Qadīr*, V, p.256. This position is also held by some Mālikī and Shāfi'ī authors: see Ibn Juzayy, *al-Qawāwīn al-Fiqhiyya*, pp.263-264, who states that even if the seller offers to subtract the excess, the sale is nevertheless binding upon him subject to the option exercised by the other party. Abū Ḥanīfa does not regard it as binding in this case. cf. Sanhūrī, *Maṣādir al-Ḥaqq*, II, p.172. A minority opinion of the Shāfi'ī school likens it to a defect: see, for example, Shīrāzī, *al-Muhadhdhab*, II, pp.288-290.

205 Sanhūrī, *Maṣādir al-Ḥaqq*, II, 170; Ibn al-Hammām, *Fatḥ al-Qadīr*, V, 256

206 Sanhūrī, *ibid.*, pp. 172-173; Shāfi'ī Sources: Shīrāzī, *al-Muhadhdhab*, II, pp.288-290; al-Shirbīnī, *Mughnī al-Muḥtāj*, II, pp.76-80; Ramlī, *Nihāyāt al-Muḥtāj*, IV, 104-115; 'Amīra, *Ḥāshiyya 'Alā Sharḥ al-Maḥallā 'Alā Minhāj al-Ṭālibīn*, (Latter by al-Nawāwī) at bottom of page in al-Qalyūbī, *Ḥāshiyya 'Alā Sharḥ al-Maḥallā 'Alā Minhāj al-Ṭālibīn*, 4 Vols. (Cairo, n.d.). Ḥanbalī Sources: Ibn Qudāma, *al-Mughnī*, IV, 259-294; Ibn Qudāma al-Maqdīsī, *al-Sharḥ al-Kabīr 'alā Matn al-Muqanna'*, IV, 100-108

207 Saleh, *General Principles, op.cit.*, p.41; See alo Bahrain Law of Contract, Art. 85 (a)

208 Sanhūrī, *Maṣādir al-Ḥaqq, op.cit.*, II, p.; Saleh, *General Principles, op.cit.*, p.41

209 Sanhūrī, *M. al-Ḥaqq*, II, p.167; and Kuwaiti Civil Code, Art 462 (1)

210 For trust sale contracts according to the Ḥanafī school see Ibn al-Hammām, *Fatḥ al-Qadīr*, 252-263; Kāsānī, *al-Badā'i'*, V, 220-228; al-Sarakhsī, *Kitāb al-Mabsūṭ*, XIII, 78-91; Dammād Effendī, *Majma' al-Anhūr Sharḥ Multaqā al-Abḥur*, (Cairo, 1328 AH) 2 vols. Vol. II, 74-79; *Fatāwā al-Hindiyya*, III, 160-165; Ibn Nujaym, *al-Baḥr al-Rā'iq*, VI, 106-115; Ibn 'Abidīn, *al-Radd al-Muḥtār*, IV, 235-246

award compensation to the buyer for the seller's deception. As Abū Ḥanīfa insists, a contract cannot be *Tawliyya* if the subsequent purchase has been increased or diminished. This is in distinction to *Murābaḥa*, where if deception occurs, there is no change in its characteristics: it simply becomes a *Murābaḥa* contract with a larger profit margin. Muḥammad awards the option to rescind to the buyer, stating that *Murābaḥa* and *Tawliyya* are supply and demand contracts, the characteristics of which are that they are subject to change with time, therefore the buyer's right to reject the goods at a later date when he recognises the fraud must be recognised.[211] The Ḥanbalī school also recognises the option in *Tawliyya*, Murābaḥa, Muwāḍī'a and *Shirka* contracts.[212] If something should occur so as to prevent abrogation of the contract, as for instance, the loss of the object which would normally preclude the right of the buyer from his option of defect, then the Ḥanbalī buyer may seek restitution of the whole price on the basis of his stated option, such as his option of sight or conditional option.[213]

The contract of *Muwāḍa'a* is considered as having the same conditions and principles as the contract of *Murābaḥa*.[214] According to Abū Ḥanīfa therefore, the option operates for either the whole price, or for complete rejection of the contract.[215] The majority opinion of the Ḥanbalī school is that fraud does not invalidate a *Murābaḥa* contract and that it must be distinguished, for example, from an invalidation for defect. If A informs B that he bought his car for 100 Dirhams, and sells it to B by *Murābaḥa*, stating that the profit is for 1 dirham in 10, the purchaser, B, will pay 110 Dirhams. If B later discovers that the price paid by A was really 90 Dirhams, the sale is *Ṣaḥīḥ*, because an increase in price according to the Ḥanbalī school and Abū Yūsuf, does not preclude validity of the contract. Therefore B may demand the excess from A over the price paid (that is, 10 DH) and deduct from it the proportion of the profit (that is, 1 DH). Consequently, 99 Dirhams remain payable by the buyer, B.[216]

The position on *Muwāḍa'a* to be gleaned from the texts of Ibn Ḥanbal and al-Shāfi'ī indicate, however, that the same buyer may opt between taking the object for its principal price plus a share of the profit, or rejecting

---

211 Sanhūrī, *ibid.*, p.170; Ibn al-Hammām, *Fatḥ al-Qadīr*, V, 256

212 Ibn Qudāma al-Maqdīsī, *al-Sharḥ al-Kabīr 'alā Matn al-Muqanna'*, IV, 100-103

213 Sanhūrī, *ibid.*, p.170

214 Sanhūrī, *ibid.*, p.171

215 Sanhūrī, *ibid.*, p.174

216 Thus according to al-Thawrī amd Ibn Abī Layla, as cited in Sanhūrī, *ibid.*, p.174

it.[217]

The doctrine would seem to extend to any contract wherein one of the parties relies on the experience of the other party to a significant degree, and therefore needs protection from the law against harm and *Ghubn*.[218] It is questionable whether such reliance must be declared, or whether certain contracts apart from those mentioned above are automatically regarded as trust sale contracts. On the evidence of modern legislation, it would seem that the list of trust sales contracts is not closed. Without a doubt, the more general *uberrimae fidei* contracts of recent times, such as insurance contracts (where they are permitted) and certain banking contracts, may be comfortably accommodated into this category. Indeed, Sanhūrī, writing in the 1950's, acknowledged the parallel between the Islamic trust sale contracts and the contract of insurance in Western law.[219]

Failure to Disclose : Modern Legislation

The principle that fraud may be perpetrated by passive or non-action, such as failing to disclose essential information is taken up by modern legislation. In the Egyptian code, intentional silence on the part of one of the contracting parties as to a fact or as to the accompanying circumstances is deemed to constitute fraud if it can be shown that the contract would not have been concluded by the other party had he had knowledge thereof.[220] In the Kuwaiti code, reticence about certain conditions in or pertaining to the contract will be deemed fraudulent if such reticence impinges on the necessity for honesty or clarity imposed by the law, or the agreement, or the nature of the transaction, or in the special confidence which is derived by virtue of the circumstances of the case.[221]

The Bahraini code, however, places its emphasis not on the overriding invalidation of such contracts, but, conversely, on the validity of such contracts subject to certain exceptional circumstances. Article 20 (2) states :

> "Mere silence as to facts likely to affect the willingness of a person to enter into a contract is not fraud, unless the circumstances of the case are such that, regard being had to

---

217 Ibn Qudāma al-Maqdīsī, *al-Sharḥ al-Kabīr 'alā Matn al-Muqanna'*, IV, 100-103; Sanhūrī, *ibid.*, p.174. The seller has no option here.

218 Sanhūrī, *M. al-Ḥaqq*, II, p.166; 167

219 Sanhūrī, *M. al-Ḥaqq*, II, p.167; This is also mentioned in the Kuwaiti Memorandum to the 1980 Civil Code, p.145

220 Egyptian Civil Code, (Law No. 131 of 1948), Art. 125

221 Kuwaiti Civil Code, (Law No. 67 of 1980), Art. 152

> them, the law casts a duty on the person keeping silence to speak, or unless his silence amounts, in its context, to a representation that a material fact does or does not exist."[222]

The Kuwaiti and UAE Civil Codes recognise the specific Trust sale contracts of *Tawliyya, Ishrāka,*[223] *Murābaḥa* and *Waḍī'a.* Here, as in the *Fiqh* texts, the original cost price paid by the seller must be disclosed by him in addition to the profit percentage in *Murābaḥa* sales, or the rebate percentage in the case of *Waḍī'a* sales.[224] If it is later established that the price paid by the seller was less than disclosed, the buyer need only pay the real price.[225] If the seller seeks to hide concomitant details (*Mulābasāt*) which affect his sale, the Kuwaiti provisions state that this will be considered Fraud if these details are deemed to affect the will of the buyer in contracting.[226]

The UAE provisions state, additionally, that where the original cost price is not known at the time of contracting, the purchaser is given the option to rescind when he learns of it.[227] He shall also have the option to rescind if he learns that the seller conceals a matter affecting the object or the capital value, but he loses this right if he converts, consumes or disposes of the goods after delivery.[228]

6.3.11 THIRD PARTY FRAUD

al-Najsh

Islamic Fiqh, like Western jurisprudence, permits that fraud issuing from a third party may affect the consent of a party to a contract, so long as this third party is in connivance with the other contracting party.[229]

Al-Najsh sales fit into this category, for the person who is *al-Nājish* is acting in collusion with one of the contracting parties in order to raise or

---

222 Bahrain Law of Contract, 1969 : Art. 20 (2). The phaseology here carries echoes of the Common Law influence.

223 *Ishrāka* is only explicity recognised in the Kuwaiti Civil Code, Art. 462 (1)

224 Kuwaiti Civil Code, Art. 462 (1); UAE Civil Code, Art.506 (1)

225. Kuwaiti Civil Code, Art. 462 (2); UAE Civil Code, Art.506 (2)

226 Kuwaiti Civil Code, Art. 462 (3)

227 UAE Civil Code, Art.506 (3)

228 *Ibid.* Art.506 (3)

229 Sanhūrī, *Maṣādir al-Ḥaqq*, II, p.186

is not the seller, but the third party who is acting in collusion with him.

In the Ḥanbalī school, it is not conditional that the seller be in collusion with the perpetrator of the fraud of *al-Najsh*, and the buyer may rescind or ratify as normal. Dispute does exist within the school on this point, but the overriding argument is that the *Taghrīr* here is perpetrated against the innocent contracting party, nomatter from where that *Taghrīr* issues, and it is the duty of the law therefore to protect the innocent party by allowing him the option to rescind.[231] This condition of collusion does prevail, however, in the Mālikī and Shāfi'ī schools.[232]

Ghurūr

To be included in the categories of Fraud perpetrated by third parties is the deception (*Ghurūr*)[233] perpetrated by the father who tells the traders that his son has authority to engage in commercial transactions, without also informing them that he has a second son who is not so authorised. The fraud here issues from a stranger to the contract. If the fraudster is absent, and his whereabouts are unknown, the deceived party is permitted to demand restitution from the other contracting party, who may then reclaim it eventually from the fraudster.[234]

Agent or Guide

A third instance of fraud issuing from a third party which gives rise to the option to rescind is the case where the fraud issues from an agent, or a *Dalīl*, (Guide, Adviser).[235]

The agent is the representative of the party in question : fraud by the agent is therefore considered as fraud by the contracting party himself. The hypothesis is that agent and principal are acting in collusion to defraud the innocent party, or that the principal knows or has means of knowing of that fraud. The agent, in any case, is acting for the benefit of the principal, hence

---

231 Ibn Qudāma al-Maqdīsī, *Sharḥ al-Kabīr 'Alā Matn al-Muqanna'*, Vol IV, p.79

232 Sanhūrī, *Maṣādir al-Ḥaqq*, II, p.186

233 This is rather an archaic form of the Arabic, meaning 'deception', for the form *Taghrīr* is more commonly found these days. *Ghurūr* is more readily comprehended in its comptemporary use as 'having delusions of grandeur'.

234 Sanhūrī, *Maṣādir al-Ḥaqq*, II, p.187

235 Dalīl is referred to in Ibn Ḥanbal's *Musnad*, IV, 74 as the guide employed by owners of trading caravans to provide animals and facilities necessary for all trans-saharan journeys. This would therefore explain the frequent examples in the legal texts to guides in conjunction with lost or ill-advised routes.

it is incumbent that that principal bears the responsibility of the fraud, and that the innocent party is protected from that fraud by having resort to the option.[236]

Ibn ʻĀbidīn relates an example : "A man said to a spinner: 'I have no knowledge of spinning yarn. Bring me yarn so that I might buy some.' Meanwhile a third party sold some yarn to the spinner, but the buyer was unaware of this. The spinner then made himself an adviser between the other two, pretending that he was merely an intermediary, and advising the buyer to purchase the more expensive of the two sorts of yarn. The buyer did as he was advised, but he later learned of the deception.[237] Sanhūrī states that the seller is here more than a mere intermediary, for he already owns the expensive yarn himself, and is deceiving the buyer into thinking that he is an uninterested party. The buyer therefore has the right to return the goods, with compensation for any consumption or conversion, in exchange for restitution of the whole price.[238]

In al-Ramlī's opinion, (related by Ibn Ābidīn) if a foreigner acting without a broker (*Dallāl*) deceives him, he does not have the right to restitution (*Istirdād*). Furthermore, if the buyer deceives the seller in a contract concerning real estate (*ʻAqār*) where the buyer is claiming pre-emption, does the seller have the right to restitution upon discovering the deception ? Al-Ramlī states that he forgoes the right in such a case even though he was not the deceivor but was himself deceived.[239]

Modern Legislation

As far as the modern legislation is concerned, these conditions are outlined as follows:

Egypt : "A party who is the victim of fraudulent misrepresentation by a third party can only demand the avoidance of the contract, if it is established that the other contracting party was aware of, or should necessarily have been aware of the fraudulent misrepresentation."[240]

In the Iraqi legislation, Fraud is dealt with on a similar basis to *Ghalaṭ*. Article 121 (1) treats contracts tainted with fraud as suspended (*Mawqūf*) upon the authorisation of the deceived party. In contracts where the fraud

236 Ibn ʻĀbidīn, *Radd al-Muḥtār*, IV, p.246; Sanhūrī, *Maṣādir al-Ḥaqq*, II, pp.187-188

237 Ibn ʻĀbidīn, *al-Baḥr al-Rā'iq*, VI, pp.110-116

238 Sanhūrī, *Maṣādir al-Ḥaqq*, II, p.189

239 Ibn ʻĀbidīn, *Radd al-Muḥtār*, IV, p.246; Sanhūrī, *Maṣādir al-Ḥaqq*, II, p.188

240 Egyptian Civil Code (Law No. 131 of 1948), Art. 126

issues from a third party, however, the contract is not regarded as suspended unless, as in the Egyptian provision, it can be established that the contracting party had knowledge or means of knowing of that fraud at the conclusion of the contract.[241] The deceived party is therefore precluded from exercising his option to rescind when the other contracting party is unaware of the fraud perpetrated; the option also lapses when the deceived party has converted, consumed, lost or damaged the object of contract, even if this happened before he learnt of the fraud. The contract remains operative in these cases.[242]

The Kuwaiti Code follows the model set by the preceding Egyptian-prototypes :

> (1) "For a contract to be nullified on the grounds of fraud, it is necessary for the subterfuge to have come from the other party of the contract or his proxy or subordinate or one representing him in the ratification of the contract in his interests."
>
> (2) "If the subterfuge has come from another source, then the deceived party shall not retain the right to insist on nullifying the contract unless the other party, upon ratifying the contract is apprised of this subterfuge or it is within his capacity to find out about it."[243]

The provisions contained in the Egyptian Code-prototypes, including the Kuwaiti Civil Code, are also echoed in the UAE Civil Code, Article 190. It may be surmised therefore that the modern legislation is slightly more restrictive than are the ***Fiqh*** texts in relation to fraud perpetrated by third parties. Where, in the texts, the overriding intention is to provide protection to the innocent party, modern provisions do not extend the protection of the law to such an extent. Indeed, the rationale is that to allow the option to the deceived party in cases where the other contracting party has no knowledge of the fraud, would be detrimental to that other contracting party.

The Kuwaiti code provides two exceptions to these rules. The first is that in contracts of Gift or Donation, the unilateral right to annul the contract is

---

241 Iraqi Civil Code, Art. 122; See also : Syrian Civil Code, Arts.126 and 127; Libyan Civil Code, Arts. 125 and 126; Lebanese Civil Code, Arts. 208 and 209

242 Iraqi Civil Code, Art. 123

243 Kuwaiti Civil Code, (Law No. 67 of 1980), Art. 153; Also see The Bahrain Law of Contract, Art. 20 (1); and Jordanian Civil Code, Art. 147.

not superceded by these laws if consent to the contract has come about as a result of fraud, and this is so regardless from which party the fraud emanates.[244]

The second exception occurs when both parties have resorted to fraud against each other. When this takes place during the contracting, neither side is permitted the right to insist upon ratification of the contract.[245]

6.3.12 CONCLUSION

A doctrine of fraud may therefore be constructed from the pooling of the numerous exegeses of the Islamic jurists concerning general principles. Where application is concerned, however, the doctrine becomes more subjective, and each school must be consulted at length as to its particular construction of the doctrine. An example considered to constitute fraud by one school, or even one disciple of that school, may not always be deemed so by the jurists of another school. In this respect it may be stated that it is the Ḥanbalī school which is more inclined to construct a case of fraud. The Ḥanafīs, on the other hand, give the least consideration to the concept.[246]

Throughout all of the cases of fraud to be gathered from among the *fiqh* texts, it is clear that the guiding principle of the law here is simply to seek to repair the damage (*Ḍarar*) incurred by fraudulent behaviour.[247]

The cases cited in the texts and treatises, which have been reproduced above, smack somewhat of the antiquity of the law. The majority of exemplary cases, after all, concern slave-trading and the marketing of livestock. As Coulson sagely remarks, however, instead of a "slave-girl whose hair has been dyed black," we can easily read "a jet plane with a forged certificate of airworthiness."[248] The law here also suffers somewhat from the jurists' preoccupation with hypothetical cases. The nice distinctions of Common Law, based on precedent, are not to be found in the Sharī'a texts. Hence we do not encounter any distinction made by the jurists between misrepresentations to induce and misrepresentations in contractual statements, even though such distinctions clearly do exist at law, and differ in their effects. Nor do we find discussion of misrepresentation, whether of contractual force or not, where such misrepresentation is wholly innocent, or

---

244 See Article 154 of the Kuwaiti Civil Code of 1980; this is followed by Art. 191 of the UAE Civil Code

245 See Article 155 of the Kuwaiti Civil Code of 1980

246 Sanhūrī, *Maṣādir al-Ḥaqq*, *op.cit.*, II, p.163

247 Coulson, *Commercial Law*, *op.cit.*, p.73

248 Coulson, *ibid.*, p.73

merely negligent. The difficulties encountered in, for example, the Common Law concerning the relationship between rescission for a misrepresented term of the contract and rescission for breach, do not arise in the same context among the early Islamic jurists.

The hypothetical cases of classical law are outmoded, but the principles by which damage by fraud is rectified may be extended from their precepts, according to the traditional legal methods, to cover an infinite number of cases. The exact role played by these transactions in the economic life of early Islamic society is not clear. Yet it is discernible from the sources that the scope of the Islamic doctrine of *Tadlīs* encompasses a rather wide ambit in its general application. Incorporated into the doctrine of fraud, is a trilogy of options which may be applied where the stricter requirements of actionable fraud are not met. In this way, the Sharī'a is able to rectify any damage caused to a contracting party when his legitimate expectations of a contract have been disappointed.

In the realm of fraudulent statements, the requirements of actionable fraud are necessarily more stringent. Special contracts are earmarked for their vulnerablity to fraud, and particular protection is here afforded to the buyer and persons under judicial restriction. On the whole, however, the distinction is made in Islamic law, as in the Common Law doctrine of Misrepresentation,[249] between indiscriminate sales talk and specific promises or assertions of verifiable facts.

The scope and effects of the Islamic ambit of fraud can be discerned in the modern legislation to only a limited extent in the Kuwaiti and UAE Codes. Bahrain has fairly abandoned the Islamic formula in favour of the Common Law model, and where the codes coincide, it is the result of the fortuitous coincidence of International precepts rather than designed legislating. The Civil Code of Kuwait is concocted from a selection of Islamic and International principles, especially those of the French Civil Law and the Egyptian prototype codes. The provisions are also echoed in the Kuwaiti Commercial Code, as indicated in the Memorandum to the Civil Code. The provisions governing fraud in the UAE Civil Code, derived from the Jordanian Code, are closer to the Islamic tenets. The codes therefore diverge in certain respects, although neither of these two Codes make explicit mention of the rules pertaining to knowledge of the fraud by the respective contracting parties.

---

249 For which see G.H. Treitel, *The Law of Contract*, (6th Edn; London 1983), pp. 252, 253, ff.; The Misrepresentation Act, 1967; Smith and Jones, *A Casebook on Contract*, (7th Edn; London 1982), pp.271-275

Chapter 6.4

UNDUE INFLUENCE OR DURESS

6.4.1 Definition of Duress (Ikrāh)

The Islamic Law Doctrine of Duress has been developed to a rather more refined degree than that of fraud.[1] Sanhūrī states that the prominence of duress as a doctrine is that it is the most objective, and the least subjective, defect to consent and the will.[2] Its development may also be reflected by the fact that it is the least polonymous of the doctrines affecting the proper consent of the contracting parties.[3] The primary element of duress is the threat (*Tahdīd*). A party impugning his co-contractor or a third party with duress in order to rescind a contract, must prove that the person accused of either threatening to exert, or of exerting, duress is capable of implementing his threats, or of effecting that duress. Further, the victim of duress must give sufficient evidence that he was intimidated enough by this duress to act against his will. Muslim jurists apply subjective criteria in determining a said victim's fear in duress and each case is therefore judged on its own facts. The jurists recognise that duress may be exerted in manifold ways and they are therefore prepared to take verbal threats into as high consideration as physical force.

Duress is the only impediment to consent which is treated by Muslim jurists as a complete violation of the intention and the will. Ḥanafī law

---

1 Schacht, *Introduction, op.cit*, (1979) p.117

2 *Masādir al-Ḥaqq*, II, 198

3 cf., for instance, the doctrines of Fraud and Misrepresentation *supra*. The term is mentioned in *Qurān*, (II:256) in relation to compulsion in religion.

books usually devote a chapter to this subject alone,[4] and much effort has been applied in determining the exact definition of the term *Ikrāh*. Zayla'ī defines *Ikrāh* as: "An action directed against a person which suppresses his true consent."[5] Sarakhsī, similarly, states: "By duress, one means the action of a person against another which subrogates the consent (of the latter) or vitiates his choice (*Ikhtiyār*)."[6]

6.4.2 Effects

The effects of duress in Civil, and those in Criminal cases are not distinguished; nor is a great deal of discussion devoted to how far duress invalidates a declaration, or to what degree it diminishes the responsibility of the victimised party. The effects of a contract concluded under duress may be generally divided into two classes. The Shāfi'īs[7] and Ḥanbalīs[8] regard the act under duress as non-existent *ab initio*. The Shāfi'is argue that *Ikhtiyār* and consent are interdependent concepts, and cannot operate independently in the intention to create legal relations.[9] Therefore the contract is void (*Buṭlān*) as no consent is involved. In the second category, the Mālikīs[10] and the Ḥanafīs[11] regard such an act as more or less valid because it has been agreed to by intention of the party, even though the consent was not freely given. The distinction is both formalistic and psychological : a party under duress intends to pronounce the words but does not intend to create a legal relation with those words. Intention of the first category is present so that the contract may be concluded, but consent is defective so the contract will not be binding, but rather subject to the

---

4 For example, Sarakhsī, *Kitāb al-Mabsūṭ*, XXIV, pp.38 ff. Sarakhsī here (pp.38-39) confounds transactional consent (*Riḍā al-Ta'āmul*) with subjective contentment (*Riḍā al-Nafsī*) in that he equates the case of a person suffering under some anxiety with that of a person under duress. This has been noticed by Owsia *op.cit.*, p.567, and the passage is quoted in Sanhūrī, *Maṣādir al-Ḥaqq*, II, p.201; Ibn 'Abidīn, *Radd al-Muḥtār*, (Third Edn., Bulac), V, pp. 109 ff.; Kāsānī, *Badā'i'*, VII, pp.175 ff.; Sanhūrī, *Maṣādir al-Ḥaqq*, II, p.199;

5 Zayla'ī, *Tabyīn al-Ḥaqā'iq*, (6 Vols: Boulac, 1313 AH), Vol. V, 181

6 *Kitāb al-Mabsūṭ*, XXIV, p.38

7 Shāfi'ī, *Kitāb al-Umm*, III, 210 ff; Ramlī, *Nihāyat al-Muḥtāj*, V, 72 and VI, 48.

8 Ibn Qudāma, *al-Mughnī*, (Third Edn.) V, 139 and VII, 118 ff

9 Sarakhsī, *Kitāb al-Mabsūṭ*, XXIV, pp.36-39; Sanhūrī, *Maṣādir al-Ḥaqq*, II, pp. 201, 202-203; Owsia, *op.cit.*, p.571

10 Dardīr/Dassūqī, *al-Sharḥ al-Kabīr*, III, pp.5,6.

11 Chafik Chehata, *Le Droit Musulman*, (Paris 1970), p.129

authorisation of that consent which will be given upon ratification.[12] Duress, being deemed extrinsic to the will, does not render the contract void, but merely voidable; it is then possible for that party to either ratify or annul the act once he is free of duress.[13]

The element which is taken into consideration here is the subjective psychological effect of duress in the mind of the duressed party, and the compulsion thus affecting his choice (*Ikhtiyār*). Consent, states Sanhūrī, is always lacking in Duress. If the contractor remains independent in his aim, the *Ikhtiyār* is valid, and if not, it is *Fāsid*.[14] Thus in coercive duress (*al-Ikrāh al-Muljī'*), such as the threat to murder, beat or wound, the duressed person is so constrained as to lose his faculty of choice: the fear of harm to his person or members of his family instilled in his mind by the threat vitiates his freedom to choose. This lack of choice is, however, limited to the duration of that coercion.[15] The freedom to choose nevertheless remains valid in non-coercive duress such as confinement or imprisonment for long periods, which do not cause alarm for harm done to the person or members of his family and which do not vitiate his choice between suffering under the duress and making the unwanted contract.[16]

In the second category, a minor discrepancy exists between the methodology of the two schools' reasonings. The Mālikīs state that the act vitiated by duress is valid but may be annulled; whereas in the Ḥanafī school, discussions waiver between declaring a contract affected by duress as avoided (*Fāsid*) and those in the minority who consider it to be suspended, but which in either case may be ratified.[17] Ultimately the result is hardly very different. The term *Mawqūf* reflects a recurrent view in the Fiqh books in relation to the effects of duress. For those schools that categorise the contract as *Buṭlān*, *Mawqūf* here refers to 'suspended contracting'; for

---

12 Sanhūrī, *Maṣādir al-Ḥaqq*, II, p.200

13 The Majority view of the Shi'ite schools also hold the contract voidable subject to ratification, although minor dissenting philosophies also exist. See Owsia, *A Comparative Study of the Conclusion of Contracts, op.cit.*, p.563

14 Sanhūrī, *Maṣādir al-Ḥaqq*, II, p.202, Fn.1

15 al-Kāsānī calls coercive duress 'Complete duress : *al-Ikrāh al-Tām*', and non-coercive duress 'Incomplete duress : *al-Ikrāh al-Nāqiṣ) See his Badā'i'*, VII, p.175

16 It is only the Ḥanafī school which distinguishes between *Ikrāh Mulji'*, and *Ikrāh ghayru mulji'*. 'Members of the family' is interpreted to mean those within the proscribed degrees of both lineal ascent and descent. Sanhūrī, *Maṣādir al-Ḥaqq*, II, p.202; Ibn Nujaym, *Fatḥ al-Ghaffār bi Sharḥ Manār al-Anwār*, 3 Vols. in 1 (Cairo, 1355/1936) Vol III, p.119; See also Maḥbūbī, *Tawḍīḥ Fī Ḥall Jawāmiḍ al-Tanqīḥ*, in margin of al-Ṭaftazānī, *al-Talwīḥ Fī Kashf Ḥaqā'iq al-Tanqīḥ*, 2 Vols. in 1 (Cairo, 1377/1957) Vol. II, p.196

17 Sanhūrī, *Maṣādir al-Ḥaqq*, II, p.200

those who determine the contracts as ***Fāsid*** it signifies suspended validity; it signifies suspended operation for those who term it as ***Waqf***; and suspended of its binding quality for those who determine the contract as not binding.[18] In short then, the sale operating under duress is not valid according to those who recognise it as ***Buṭlān*** or ***Fāsid***; but it is valid, subject to ratification, to those who recognise it as ***Mawqūf*** or ***Ghayru Lāzim***.

6.4.3 Conditional Elements

Sanhūrī states that the Islamic scope of duress is more extensive than that in Western systems because it is not restricted to the objective operation of duress, and the two categories of Effects of Duress, and Remedies and Liabilities arising therefrom. The ***Fiqh***, however, incorporates a plurality of doctrines which distinguish it from Western parallels. These are, *inter alia*, Unlawful Acts; Necessity (***Ḍarūra***); Legal Defence (*Difā' Shar'ī*); Compulsory Bailment (*al-Waḍī'a al-Iḍṭirāriyya*): Simulation in the *Talji'a* sale; and Foreign Cause (*al-Sabab al-Ajnabī*).[19]

The generally accepted conditions which may be said to give rise to annulment under the Option of Duress (*Khiyār al-Ikrāh*) are derived from the nature of the duress itself and may be summarised as follows:

(1) The duress must be illicit;

(2) It must emanate from a party who has the power to execute his threats, that is, it must be realistically practicable (*Mutaḥaqqiq*);

(3) It must be of such a nature as to intimidate the victim: that is, it must be of significant and imminent danger (*Khaṭar Jasīm Muḥdiq*)[20]

Thus, duress may not arise from the exercise of a right or the threat to exercise that right. For example, a man ordered to pay his taxes under threat of imprisonment may not claim restitution under duress, for that 'duress' is theoretically legitimate.[21]

The duress is ascertainable only if the person under duress acted so as to defend himself against something more powerful than that which he has undertaken.[22] The threat must be real and engender fear that it will be carried out in the mind of the duressed party, in that he is unable to repel or

---

[18] Sanhūrī, *Maṣādir al-Ḥaqq*, IV, p.139; See also Ibn Nujaym, *al-Baḥr al-Rā'iq*, V, 277; and Ibn 'Abidīn, *Radd al-Muḥtār*, IV, pp.104-105

[19] That is, a cause not connected to the essence of the contract itself. Sanhūrī, *Maṣādir al-Ḥaqq*, II, pp.200-201

[20] Sanhūrī, *Maṣādir al-Ḥaqq*, II, p.203

[21] Sanhūrī, *Maṣādir al-Ḥaqq*, II, p.211

[22] Sanhūrī, *Maṣādir al-Ḥaqq*, II, p.203

avoid it.[23] Thus if he is only threatened verbally with a beating or short imprisonment, this is not considered significant duress unless his constitution is so weak as not to withstand such 'light' discomfort.[24] 'Significant' is something of a subjective adjective, in Islamic fiqh, as in its Western parallel :[25] It is a relative matter which depends upon the mental state of the person involved, his physique, and the means of duress applied.[26] Sanhūrī states, however, that coercive duress is more significant than non-coercive, such that it is regarded as affecting verbal, active and legal dispositions and is thus voidable because the law recognises it as an excuse to avoid the liability arising in the contractor. Non-coercive duress is considered as affecting verbal disposition, but is not regarded as an excuse sufficient to avoid liability in active dispositions because it does not amount to the 'significant' degree necessary for that. It is a presumption therefore, that a mere warning will not be construed as duress suffiently menacing to vitiate the choice of the duressed contractor; Nor will a threat to compound or cause the destruction of property, which will, in any case, find alternative remedy at law. If both types are present, consent is lacking and thus legal disposition is avoided.[27]

The general maxim of Islamic Duress may thus be stated that it is permitted for a man to accept the smaller matter in defence of the graver.[28] To this end, Sarakhsī furnishes us with an example unique to Muslim fiqh : If a man is threatened by duress which claims that he will suffer injury by eating *al-Mayyita*, or pork, or by drinking wine, and he does not eat so that he is killed, while he knows that it is possible for him to consume of these things without harm, then he is a sinner; and if he did not know that he would not suffer physical injury by their consummation, he would not be deemed a sinner because he paid heed to the warning against the prohibited commodities.[29] Thus the doctrine of duress illustrated here combines with the doctrine of *Ḍarūra* in accordance with the *Qurān* (VI:145) and the duressed person is directed towards choosing the lesser of the two evils.

---

23 Sarakhsī, *Kitāb al-Mabsūṭ*, *op.cit.*, XXIV, p.50

24 Sanhūrī, *Maṣādir al-Ḥaqq*, II, p.204; See also Sarakhsī, *Kitāb al-Mabsūṭ*, XXIV, pp.50,68

25 For a Resumé of the Western stance, see Sanhūrī, *Maṣādir al-Ḥaqq*, II, p.190-198; and Judge 'Abd el-Wahab Ahmad El-Hassan, 'The Doctrine of Duress (*Ikrah*) in *Shariā*, Sudan and English Law', *Arab Law Quarterly*, 1(2) (Feb. 1986) pp.321-236, particularly pp.235-236; *Chitty on Contract*, ch. VII generally;

26 Sanhūrī, *Maṣādir al-Ḥaqq*, II, p.203

27 Sanhūrī, *Maṣādir al-Ḥaqq*, II, p.203

28 Sanhūrī, *Maṣādir al-Ḥaqq*, II, p.205

29 Sarakhsī, *Kitāb al-Mabsūṭ*, XXIV, pp.151-154

The question arises nonetheless as to whether the threat to execute a right in order to gain an advantage which is not due, is legitimate duress. Subject to the lack of legal sanction on the abuse of rights, and basing opinion on Article 91 of the *Majella*,[30] it would seem that such a situation would not constitute true duress.

6.4.4 Modern Legislation

The *Majella* reflects the view of the Ḥanafīs and Mālikīs in that Duress will render the contract voidable rather than void.[31] But the definition given in the *Majella* of 'effective constraint' is more limited than the classical definition of duress. Effective constraint is defined as being present "If the person who is the subject of such constraint performs the act he has been forced to do in the presence of the person causing the constraint, or of his representative."[32]

Bahrain

In the Bahrain Law of Contract of 1969, a contract induced by Duress is also voidable at the option of the party whose consent has been so induced.[33] That party may then set the contract aside absolutely, or if he has already received any benefit from the contract, he may make arrangements for compensation as the court deems just.[34] *Ikrāh* is defined in this law as being "where the relations subsisting between the parties are such that one of the parties is in a position to dominate the will of the other and uses that position to obtain an unfair advantage over the other."[35] As in the original Islamic tenets, duress, as defined in the Bahrain Code of Contracts, affects the consent of the compelled contracting party, and may be subject to

---

30 *Majella*, Art.91: "The exercise of a right permitted by the Sharī'a cannot invoke liability for compensation".

31 *Majella*, Art.1006: 'Contracts of sale, purchase, hire, gift, transfer of real property, admission, release, postponement of debt, and renunciation of a right of pre-emption if entered into as a result of constraint are invalid, whether caused by major constraint or minor constraint. If the person subject to the constraint ratifies the contract after the cessation of the constraint, such contract is valid'.

32 *Majella*, Art. 1005. See also Ar-Rawi, 'Principles on the Islamic Law of Contracts', in *George Washington Law Review*, 22 (1953-4), p.34

33 Bahrain Law of Contract, 1969, Art. 22 (1) and 23 (1).

34 *ibid.*, Art. 23 (2).

35 *ibid.*, Art. 19 (1)

reasonably wide interpretation.[36]

Coercion, according to this code, means committing or threatening to commit, any act which is an offence under the Penal Code', or the lawful detaining or threatening to detain, any property to the prejudice of any person whatever, with the intention of causing any person to enter into an agreement.[37] Coercion affects the free consent of the contracting party in a similar way to *Ikrāh.*[38]

The principle definition given by the Bahrain legislation is very general, but particular specifications are provided in subsequent paragraphs, without prejudice to Article 19 (1). A person is deemed to be in a position to dominate the will of the other contracting party,

> (1) Where he holds a real or apparent authority over the other, or where he stands in a fiduciary relation to the other; or
>
> (2) Where he makes a contract with a person whose mental capacity is temporarily or permanently affected by reason of age, illness, or mental or bodily distress.

The conditions are therefore still general enough to allow for subjective determination by the court in each particular case, and here, as in other categories of vitiated consent, such as Fraud, the circumstances of the individuals involved will be taken into consideration.

When it appears that a contract has been brought about by undue influence because evidence adduced suggests that the bargain is unconscionable, the burden of proof falls on the the person who is in the position to dominate the will of the other, to show that he did not thus exert duress.[39]

Kuwait

It is noticeable that the Kuwaiti legislation regarding duress is not significantly removed from that of the classical *Fiqh.* Article 156 (1) of the Civil Code[40] states that a contract may be annulled on the grounds of *Ikrāh*

---

36 *ibid.*, Art. 16 (2)

37 *ibid.*, Art. 17

38 *ibid.*, Art. 16 (1)

39 *ibid.*, Art. 19 (3)

40 Kuwaiti Civil Code, Law No. 67 of 1980

when the contract has been entered into by a party under a fear which was induced in an unlawful manner, and which, if the fear which allegedly forced him into contracting had not been present, he would not have so contracted. The fear must still be of 'significant' (*Jasīm*) harm which intimidates him, or threatens to intimidate either himself or some other person, whether such intimidation be in mind or body, in good repute, honour or property.[41] The assessment of this fear remains subjective in Kuwaiti law, just as in Classical law, and consideration in this matter is given (in cases of both males and females) to the mental state; age; intelligence or ignorance; health or ill-health; and 'any other circumstance which may have been influential during the period in which the cause of fear was exerted over that person.'[42]

Article 157 (1) states that the duress must have been exerted by the other contractor, or by an act of his representative or assistant, or one commissioned by that contractor, or who is concluding the contract for his benefit. It stands to reason therefore, that the other contracting party must know of, or have means of knowing of, the duress exerted upon the duressed contractor.[43] A claim for annullment of the contract where the duress has issued from a third party, and the co-contractor has no knowledge of it, will fail on the grounds that that co-contractor would suffer disadvantage by that annullment. This applies to all contracts except the unilateral contract of Gift.[44]

The United Arab Emirates

The definition of Duress to be found in the UAE Civil Code is equally wide. Here, duress is "coercion of a person without the right of so doing to perform an act without his consent."[45] The UAE Code specifically rules that duress may be forcible, that is, a threat of grave or imminent nature to person or property;[46] or non-forcible, that is, if it involves a lesser threat;[47]

---

41 *ibid.*, Art. 156(2)

42 *ibid.*, Art.156 (3)

43 *Ibid.*, Article 157 (2)

44 Article 158 of the Kuwaiti Civil Code states: "Request to annul the contract of gift is permitted if consent thereto has been given as a result of duress, without consideration to the person from whom that duress issued."

45 UAE Civil Code, Art. 176

46 *ibid.*, Arts. 176, 177

47 *ibid.*, Arts. 176, 177

material; or moral.[48] Moreover, any threat to cause harm to close relations, or threat of a risk prejudicial to the person's own honour, whether of a forcible or non-forcible nature is to be regarded as duress.[49]

According the the UAE Code, forcible duress nullifies consent and vitiates free choice. Non-forcible duress also nullifies consent but is not considered as vitiating free choice.[50] Here, as in the classical *Fiqh*, the person threatening duress must be capable of carrying out his threat, and the victim must have believed in the imminence and gravity of that threat.[51]

In both cases, the subjective qualities of the person under duress are taken into consideration by the court, as in the Kuwaiti jurisdiction. Here the UAE code includes, in addition to the age, and physical stature of the person, his rank, position, influence, and the degree to which minor or major duress may hurt that person, or any element which may affect the gravity of that duress.[52]

As with the Classical Law, and Kuwaiti legislation, the UAE contractor issuing the duress may not enforce his contract, whether the duress is minor or major, forcible or non-forcible. The other contracting party is not bound by the contract so long as the duress continues. He may, however, ratify the contract once that duress has ceased.[53] An addition to this section in the UAE Code which is not to be found in the Kuwaiti or Bahraini Codes, concerns a husband's duress of his spouse into ceding to him rights or property to which he is not properly entitled. The UAE legislation thus recognises such duress as preclusion of rights (such as the husband precluding his wife from visiting her family, which is her natural and legal right).[54] This Code also recognises duress issuing from a third party, where the duressed party can prove that the other contracting party knew of, or could be presumed to have known of the duress. If the party claiming to have been coerced into contracting cannot prove the knowledge or complicity of his co-contractor, he remains bound by the contract, for the same principles as have been outlined in relation Article 157 (2) of the Kuwaiti Code above.[55]

---

[48] *ibid.*, Art. 176

[49] *ibid.*, Art. 178: "Close" relations are itemised as parents, children, spouse or sibling.

[50] *ibid.*, Art. 179

[51] *ibid.*, Art. 181

[52] *ibid.*, Arts. 180: Intelligence is conspicuously not mentioned here.

[53] *ibid.*, Art. 182

[54] *ibid.*, Art. 183

[55] *ibid.*, Art. 184.

Chapter 6.5

ISTIGHLAL AND IDH'ĀN

6.5.1 ISTIGHLĀL : Unfair Exploitation

A fourth impediment to consent, *Istighlāl*, was formed by the jurists in cases where a disproportion of obligation exists between the two contracting parties. *Istighlāl* is based on the principle of *Lā Ḍarār*: There must be a requisite balance between the rights and obligations of the contracting parties. In such cases the Ḥanafī and Shāfi'ī schools only asserted just cause for annulling the contract where fraudulent imputation had led to "gross" disproportion.[1]

Certain allowances are made where contracts involve orphans, *Waqf* property and state or public assets. The Mālikī and Ḥanbalī schools however, will allow rescindment of contract in the case of "innocent" or inexperienced victims of disproportionate misrepresentation contracts. It is this stance which was taken up by the modern codes, such as the Lebanese and Egyptian codes, the latter of which Sanhūrī had a hand in drafting.[2]

The Kuwaiti Code follows suit here, for it states :

> If a person exploits another through coercion, evident recklessness, apparent weakness, or defiant inclination, or if

1 For the interpretation of "gross", see below.

2 See, for example, Art. 214 of the Lebanese Code of Obligations and Contracts, Art. 125 of the Iraqi Civil Code ("If one of the contracting parties has been subjected to *Istighlāl* because of his need, heedlessness, or capriciousness, or lack of experience or weakness of knowledge, in such a way as to afflict his contracting with *Ghabn al-Fāḥish*, he is permitted, during the term of one year from the time of contracting, to request that the *Ghabn* be lifted from him to a reasonable degree. If the disposition issuing from him is in the form of a gift, he is permitted, within this time, to reduce it." Compare Art. 129 of the Egyptian Civil Code; Art. 130 of the Syrian Civil Code; Art. 129 of the Libyan Civil Code.

> he uses his moral authority or influence over another and thus forces him to ratify a contract for his interest or the interest of a third party; and if, upon ratification, this contract contains gross inequities between the obligations to be executed and the spiritual or material profit to be gained, such that the ratification is plainly offensive to the honour of the transaction and to the requirement of good faith, then the judge shall be empowered, upon request by the victim of the exploitation and in accordance with justice and taking the circumstances of the case into consideration, to reduce the obligations of the exploited party; or to increase the obligations of the other party; or to nullify the contract."[3]

The Civil Code of the UAE, following the Ḥanafī doctrine, does not treat *Istighlāl* as a distinct principle. The provision of unfair exploitation is restricted to the protection of the property of those under judicial restriction on account of debt or suffering from death sickness, where that person's liabilities exceed his assets.[4] In these cases any cheating (seen here as exploitation of the protected person), no matter how slight, must be redressed, or the consent of the creditors obtained, otherwise the contract is void.

Sanhūrī equates *Istighlāl* to Mistake in Value, where the wronged contractor is lacking in experience, or is ignorant or heedless. He states that the correlation is particularly striking in the Ḥanafī School.[5] Relating al-Ḥamawī, Sanhūrī shows that just as a right of option for *Ghabn* is established in the case of an agent and principle in this respect, it is also established in the case of a seller cheating a buyer by *Taghrīr*, insofar as the buyer is completely unaware of the fact that he has been cheated. If the seller testifies that he bought certain goods for a specific price, and that they are worth a specific amount, for instance, and the buyer purchases the goods on the basis of this information, if it can be established that he has been cheated, he is allowed to exercise an option of *Ghabn* to rescind the contract on the basis of *Istighlāl*.[6]

The Ḥanafī School also recognises the case where a contractor is exploited and deliberately deceived into contracting by virtue of the fact that

---

3 Art. 159 of the Kuwaiti Civil Code (Law No. 67 of 1980).

4 UAE Civil Code, Art. 189: in the section on *Ghabn*.

5 Sanhūrī, *Maṣādir al-Ḥaqq*, II, p.151. He also notes that *Istighlāl* finds its equivalent in Western Laws here in the categories of protected persons (*ibid.*, p.152).

6 Aḥmad b. Muḥammad al-Ḥamawī, *Ghamz 'Uyūn al-Baṣā'ir : Sharḥ al-Ashbāh wa al-Naẓā'ir*, (Cairo, 1290 AH) 2 Vols. Vol.II, p.195; Sanhūrī, *Maṣādir al-Ḥaqq*, II, p.151

his own requirements compel him into contracting. This is called a forced sale or *Bay' al-Muḍṭarr*, or purchase. According to Ibn 'Ābidīn, the forced sale and purchase is *Fāsid*. It occurs when a person is, for example, compelled to eat or drink the merchandise, or to don a garment or suchlike, and the seller will not subsequently sell the goods except for a price which far exceeds their true value. The forced purchase occurs when the buyer will not buy except for a price which is far less than the commodity's market value, and he accomplishes this by way of *Ghabn al-Fāḥish*.[7]

The reasoning is the same in the case where the judge has ordered the sale of property in discharge of a debt, or where a *Dhimmī* is ordered to sell a copy of the *Qur'ān*. But if the order issues from the Sulṭān or secular leader, and does not specify sale of his property, the sale is valid. The distinguishing factor then, is to ask from whom the compulsion came. If it is the iniquitous seller who is compelling the disadvantaged party into contracting, then the sale is treated as forced. Where there has been no compulsion exerted, even though the party has to contract, and there is no evidence of *Ghabn al-Fāḥish*, the contract is valid as normal, even where the goods are not contracted for at market price or where *ghabn ghayru fāḥish* has occurred.

Again, this stance has been taken up by the Kuwaiti and UAE Civil Codes. Article 162 of the Kuwaiti Code, and Article 191 of the UAE Code state that inequity alone is not sufficient to avoid the contract, except in certain cases specified by the law, such as contracts involving "gross" inequity between a party and the State or other public legal persons, persons of diminished competence, and the administration of a *waqf* contract.[8] In any event, there is no contesting inequitable auction or public tender contracts which have been carried out according to the rules set out by law.[9] In these itemised cases, the victim of the inequity may request amendment of his obligations, even if the contract has been ratified by his legal guardian, or approved by a court of law.[10] The interpretation given to "gross" in the Kuwaiti Code is any inequity which exceeds one-fifth of the value of the contract.[11] In cases where the other party (that is, not the victim of the inequity) is not contracting against the State or public legal person, and there is reason for suspecting that he may be unfairly disadvantaged by amendment of the victim's obligations, he may request nullification of the

7 Ibn 'Ābidīn, *Radd al-Muḥtār*, IV, p.146; Sanhūrī, *Maṣādir al-Ḥaqq*, II, p.151

8 Kuwaiti Civil Code, Art. 163 (1); UAE Civil Code, Art. 191

9 *ibid.*, Art.165

10 *ibid.*, Art.163 (3)

11 *ibid.*, Art.163 (2)

contract.[12]

In the Bahrain Contract Code of 1969, Article 85 (a) states that contracts cannot be enforced against a party "if the consideration to be received by him is so grossly inadequate, with reference to the state of things existing at the date of the contract, so as to be either by itself, or coupled with other circumstances, evidence of fraud or undue advantage taken by the plaintiff."

This Article must be taken in conjunction with Article 29 (2), which states that an agreement to which the consent of the promisor is freely given is not void merely because the consideration is inadequate; this will be taken into account by the court in determining whether the promisor gave his consent freely.

It is also for the court to determine the interpretation of the term "*grossly inadequate*" according to the circumstances of the particular case. Such determination will not take notice of market prices which have changed since the time of contracting, although remedies for this circumstance may be found, if sufficiently severe and unpremeditated, within the scope of *Force Majeure.*

Contracts of gift, motivated by the intention to exploit, are also expressly protected against in the Kuwaiti Civil Code. Here the judge is empowered, at the request of the donor, to nullify the contract or to reduce the substance of the gift. He is directed to do this in accordance with the circumstances of each case, justice and humaneness.[13]

One important distinction between the expositions of the Classical and modern laws in this context is that the modern Codes set a limitation period of one year after ratification of the contract on claims for *Istighlāl* where such exploitation has not been the result of defiant inclination, exertion of moral authority,[14] or diminished competence.[15]

In the latter cases, the one-year limitation period does not run until that defiant inclination or exertion of moral authority has been removed; or until the date of completion of competence or death. All claims, in any case, become null and void fifteen years after ratication of the contract.[16]

12 *ibid.*, Art. 164

13 Kuwaiti Civil Code, Art. 160

14 For example, *ibid.*, Art. 161 (1)

15 *ibid.*, Art. 166

16 *ibid.*, Art 161 (2), 166

6.5.2 IDH'ĀN : Contracts of Adhesion

In the modern context, the form of contract which receives particular attention under this category is the contract of Adhesion or *'Aqd al-Idh'ān.* Like the French *Contrat d'adhesion*, the *Idh'ān* is a contract with compulsory terms, usually in the form of a supply contract between large business enterprises offering goods and services, and the private consumer. The modern codes thus afford the private consumer protection against unjustifiable terms, and particularly against any clauses which exempt him from his normal legal rights, in consideration of his disadvantaged bargaining power.[17]

Article 81 of the Kuwaiti Civil Code provides in this respect :

> "If a contract is concluded by way of adhesion and it includes an onerous condition, the judge is permitted, on request of the obligor, to amend the condition according to the principles of justice, in order to alleviate him of the injustice, or to release him completely from the condition, whether or not he knew of (its onerousness). Any agreement to the contrary is void".

The UAE Code's article regarding Contracts of adhesion follows the Kuwaiti article almost to the letter.[18] The Code goes on to state that in cases where doubt exists in contracts of adhesion, the doubt is always construed in favour of the obliging party.[19]

---

17 See the discussion provided in Ballantyne, *Commercial Law in the Arab Middle East : The Gulf States*, pp.89-90; and Art. 80 of the Kuwaiti Civil Code.

18 UAE Civil Code, Art. 248

19 Kuwait Civil Code, Art. 82. See also *ibid.*, Art. 194 (1); and El-Hassan, 'Freedom of Contract, The Doctrine of Frustration, and Sanctity of Contracts in Sudan Law and Islamic Law', *Arab Law Quarterly*, Vol. I (1) (Nov. 1985) p.53

Chapter 6.6

FORCE MAJEURE

A contract may be prematurely terminated by susbequent clauses such as *Force Majeure* or supervening impossibility of performance. Although subsequent events are not strictly relevant to the system of Nullities at the formation of contract, the incidence of *Force Majeure* will be treated briefly here since the validity and effects of the contract may be affected by this concept.[1]

The concept in the Sharī'a corresponding to *Force Majeure* is *Qūwa Qāhira* or *Qūwat al-Qānūn*, but it is somewhat wider than the Western concept of Frustration.[2]

Here termination differs from the unilateral kind in that an external cause justifies the termination. The Sharī'a recognises basically any 'Act of God', or unforeseen condition as coming under the ambit of *Force Majeure*, and this includes any unforeseen changes in circumstances which are outside the control of the obligor, and which through no fault of that obligor, may constitute unfair loss or harm to the affected party. Thus a 'Misfortune from

---

1 See Saba Habachy, 'The System of Nullities in Muslim Law', *American Journal of Comparative Law*, Vol. 13 (1964) p.72

2 Compare, for instance, the doctrine of changed circumstances with the International law doctrine of ***Rebus sic stantibus***, the rules for which were defined by the International Law commission as follows:- "When a fundamental change has occurred with regard to a fact or situation existing at the time when the treaty was entered into, it may be invoked as a ground for terminating or withdrawing from the treaty if (a) the existence of that fact or situation constituted an essential basis of the consent of the parties to the treaty; and (b) the effect of the change is to transform in an essential respect the character of the obligations undertaken in the treaty". Draft Article 44 (2) of the International Law commission of 1963; *Yearbook of the I.L.C.*, (1963); and see Waldock in 1 *Yearbook of the I.L.C.*, (1966) pp.75-86. But cf. Harazti, 'Treaties and the Fundamental Change of Circumstances', ***Recueil Des Cours***, I (1973) III, pp.46-60, who acknowledges a wider application. See also Amin, *Islamic Law in the Contemporary world*, (Glasgow, 1985) pp.53-63; and *id.*, 'The Theory of Changed Circumstances in International Trade', (1982) 4 *LMCLQ*, pp.577-586, revised in *id.*, 'The Doctrine of Changed Circumstances in International Trade', *World Law*, (Sept-Oct 1984) pp.41-45

Heaven', such as rain or cold or drought which destroys a crop and therefore renders delivery of it impossible, is regarded as *Force Majeure*.[3]

Thus, a contractor in a Muslim jurisdiction hired under a contract of service to dig a well may rescind the contract should he strike rock after the first few feet of digging. Similarly, the lessor may terminate a lease to his property at any time should there occur any change in his financial position which requires that he sell the property; or any change to his circumstances, for instance, if he should need to travel.[4]

The Sharī'a extends its scope of *Qūwat al-Qānūn* not only to supervening impossibility of performance, but also to situations where the performance has been rendered materially different from what was originally contracted for by a change in the essential rights and obligations of the contractual agreement. The underlying theory of the doctrine of changed circumstances, which takes the Arabic nominature of *'Udhr*, or 'excuse; just cause', is based on the implication that any contract should cease to bind when :

(1) A wholly unforeseen fundamental change has occurred in events;

(2) The contract has become especially onerous on the obliging party as a result;

(3) There is a requisite duty to impose a just and reasonable solution.

Upon fulfilment of these conditions, the contract may be deemed frustrated and the parties will be released from their respective obligations.

When supervening circumstances have not rendered performance impossible, but have as their result, that the contractual obligation has become unreasonably burdensome on a party, that party may plead exemption from liability for non-performance by establishing the onerousness. He is then allowed to rescind the contract. Modern legislation is slightly more restrictive in addressing *Force Majeure*. Pre-determined by both the Kuwaiti and the UAE Civil Code, the circumstances must be unforeseen and of a public nature. The UAE code states, echoed almost exactly by the Kuwaiti Code :-

---

[3] Maḥmaṣānī, *al-Naẓariyya al-'Āmma li al-Mūjibāt*, I, p.499; Coulson, *Commercial Law*, pp.83-84; El-Hassan, 'Freedom of Contract, The Doctrine of Frustration, and Sanctity of Contracts' *op.cit.*, p.58

[4] Coulson, *Commercial Law, op.cit.*, pp.85-86, 91; Sloane, *Status of Islamic Law, op.cit.*, p.747

> "If exceptional circumstances of a public nature which could not have been foreseen occur as a result of which performance of the contractual obligation, even if not impossible, becomes oppressive for the obligor, so as to threaten him with grave loss, it shall be permissible for the judge, in accordance with the circumstances and after weighing up the interests of each party, to reduce the oppressive obligation to a reasonable level if justice so requires, and any agreement to the contrary shall be void."[5]

In cases of an unforeseen change of circumstances and *Force Majeure*, the Bahrain Contract Code also affords the court the discretionary power to decree specific performance or otherwise, "where the performance of the contract would involve some hardship on the defendent which he did not foresee, whereas its non-performance would involve no such hardship on the plaintiff."[6] The Code also affords this solution to cases "where the plaintiff has done substantial acts or suffered losses in consequence of a contract capable of specific performance."[7]

The differences in expression between the Codes highlights on the one hand, the Civil Law perspective of this concept, and on the other, in the Bahraini Code, the concept couched in English Law terms. Needless to say, the effects do not differ greatly from each other, both giving the court a discretionary power to alleviate the obligations of the parties. The remedy provided by the Classical law, to allow the party to rescind the contract almost as an "option for *Quwat al-Qānūn*", is neither objective enough nor practicable. It may be said therefore, that the new position adopted by these States is the more judicious.

The judicial basis underlying the doctrine of *Force Majeure* and changed circumstances in Islamic Law is the same requisite balance between the rights and obligations of the contracting parties which motivates the doctrine of *Istighlāl* and Unjustified Enrichment.[8]

---

5 UAE Civil Code, Art. 249; Kuwaiti Civil Code, Art 198

6 Bahrain Contracts Code of 1969, Art. 79 (b)

7 *ibid.*, Art. 79 (c)

8 Amin discusses several International law cases where the doctrine of Changed Circumstances has been successfully invoked. See his 'Iran-United States Claims Settlement' 32 *International and Comparative Law Quarterly*, (1983) pp.750-756; The *Iran-United States Agreement*, (1981) [Algiers declaration], Art. 5, relating to fundamental changes which had taken place in Iran due to the Revolution; and Amin's *Political and strategic Issues In the Gulf*, (Glasgow, 1984) pp.19023, 25-28 ff.

If the impossibility is the fault of the contractor himself, he will be debarred from pleading exemption from liability on the grounds of *Force Majeure*. Similarly, if that impediment is deemed foreseeable, avoidable, or resistable, he will not be permitted to plead exemption from liability for his contractual obligations on these grounds. A contractor who has been exempted performance on the basis of a *Force Majeure* may not claim counterperformance. Thus when the *Force Majeure* is total, as compared to partial or temporary, it can be considered a means of extinction of the contract.[9]

The difference that arises between Islamic Law and the English Common Law Doctrine of Frustration, is that in the latter, a *Force Majeure* terminates the contract.[10] In Islamic Law, however, the *Force Majeure* caused by the intervening impossibility renders the contract invalid for only so long as that inpossibility exists. When the *Force Majeure* ceases, therefore, the contract redeems its validity and may be enforced.[11]

The question concerning remedies for contracts terminated under this heading is somewhat obscure among the Fiqh books. If, as a result of *Force Majeure*, a contractor does not perform his part of the contract, he will not be liable for damages. If it is not entirely clear, however, at what time the contract became frustrated, the matter of partial fulfilment or partial liability arises, and it is in this context that difficulties of doctrine exist. It is likely that compensation would be awarded in proportion to work carried out or usufruct derived, but the certainty and amount remains unpredictable.

The concept of Islamic *Force Majeure* was one of the principles to be kept to the letter in the Egyptian Civil Code, the model for the Kuwaiti Civil Code.[12] Article 147 of this code[13] provides that "If as a result of exceptional and unpredictable circumstances, which are of a general nature, the performance of a contract would make performance onerous for a party,

---

9 See Libyan Civil Code, Art. 360; Amin, *Islamic Law in the Contemporary World, op.cit.*, p.52

10 As it does, in, for instance the Libyan Civil Code of 1953, Art. 360

11 Amin, *Islamic Law in the Contemporary World, op.cit.*, p.51, notes that this principle has been upheld by the Civil Law of Iran (1927-1932) Art. 229.

12 A comparison may be made here with Article 1148 of the French Code Civil which states : "There is no occasion for damages where, in consequence of *Force Majeure* or *Cas Fortuit*, the debtor has been prevented from conveying or doing that to which he was obliged, or has done what he was debarred from doing". Compare also article 360 of the Libyan Civil code

13 Law No. 131 of 1948

even though the performance is not impossible, the judge can reduce the onerous contractual obligation to a reasonable task, taking into account the relevant circumstances and the equivalence of benefits of both contracting parties. Any agreement contrary to this statutory provision is void." Thus the contract may be rescinded, but the condition is somewhat narrower than the extremely wide ambit of the Sharī'a. In addition, the Egyptian circumstance has to be 'exceptional'.[14]

The explanatory Memorandum, prepared by Sanhūrī and the Drafting Committee of the Egyptian Civil Code, clarifies that Article 147 applies to contracts generally, and is not limited to administrative contracts. There are, however, conditions limiting its application :-

(1) It must be an exceptional circumstance of general and not particular character;

(2) The circumstance must be unpredictable and unforeseeable;

(3) The circumstance must render the performance of the obligation so onerous that the debtor is threatened with exhorbitant loss.

The debtor must satisfy all three conditions before he may ask the Court to interfere and readjust the excessive obligation to reasonable limits. If the court accepts that all the necessary conditions have been complied with, it will adjust the contractual obligations according to the particular circumstances of the case in question, and taking into consideration the interests of both parties.[15]

The Court is not, however, empowered to terminate the contract: it may only reduce the obligation of the obligor. Nor is the party invoking this doctrine allowed to suspend performance of his obligation, or to unilaterally terminate the contract.[16]

---

[14] One of the sources of this provision is the *Théorie de l'Improvision* recognised by the French Administrative Courts, but rejected by the French Civil Code. The other is Art.269 of the Polish Civil Code of 1934. See also the Codes of Iraq (1951) Art. 146 (2); Libya (1953) Art.147 (2); and Syria (1949), Art. 148 and 148 (2) which all recognise the theory of unforeseen circumstances; for which, see Kourides, 'The Influence of Islamic Law on Contemporary Middle East Legal Systems :The Formation and Binding Force of Contracts', 9 *Columbia Journal of Transnational Law*, (1970) pp.420-421

[15] The Codes of Iraq (1951) Art. 146 (2); Libya (1953) Art.147 (2); and Syria (1949), Art. 148 and 148 (2) also all allow the Court to readjust the obligations of the contractor under these conditions.

[16] Sanhūrī, *al-Wasīṭ*, (1964) pp.280-286

Chapter 6.7

RIBĀ, GHARAR AND MAYSIR

6.7.1 RIBĀ

Of all the *Quaestiones Vexatae* of Islamic law, it is the prohibition of *Ribā* which reigns supreme.[1] The confusion surrounding the subject of *Ribā* originates from the fact that while conveying the prohibition, the Prophet did not go so far as to give the term *Ribā* any precise definition. Since its inception the prohibition has been subject to various interpretations, although the general axiom of *Ribā* has been modified to make a distinction between usury and interest.

Ibn Khaldūn, in his discussion of the proper relation of philosophy to society, and thereby to the law, states that the Divine Legislator is not bound by the limits of theoretical reason, unlike the philosopher. What the Former announces must be accepted and never doubted, even when surpassing, or apparently contradicting what has been known by human reason.[2] Reason, he says, must assent to authority, for positive sciences are ultimately based on the acceptance of the authority of the legislator; the goal of their search is to ascertain what the legislator has commanded, after which their search ends and reason must rest.[3] In order to ascertain precisely what the Divine Legislator has commanded by the prohibition of *Ribā* therefore, questions and solutions concerning the precise meaning of *Ribā*, the extent of its interpretation, and the force of its application, can only seek illustrative and investigative solutions. This study does not pretend to

---

1 An exhaustive exposition of this subject has been made by Nabil Saleh, in his *Unlawful Gain and Legitimate Profit in Islamic Law : Ribā, Gharar and Islamic Banking*, (Cambridge, 1986)

2 Ibn Khaldūn, *Muqaddimat*, ed. E.M. Quatremère, (Paris, 1858) III, pp. 27 ff.

3 Muhsin Mahdi, *Ibn Khaldun's Philosophy of History*, (London, 1957; Second Impression, 1971) pp. 78, 100-103

provide the answer to the *Ribā* enigma. Rather, it directs its regard to the role accorded to the prohibition throughout the centuries both in theory and in practice, and seeks to discover the importance accorded to *Ribā* today, as it is incorporated (or otherwise) into the modern legal codes.

Ribā is usually translated as 'Usury', 'Excessive Interest', or 'Usurious Interest'.[4] However, the Arabic term is usually held to constitute something wider than the mere prohibition of excessive interest.[5] Hughes defines Usury as : "An excess according to a legal standard of measurement or weight, in one or two homogeneous articles opposed to each other in a contract of exchange, and in which such excess is stipulated as an obligatory condition on one of the parties without any return."[6] Lane adds that in its legal sense, *Ribā* signifies an addition obtained in a particular manner (that is, in buying, selling, lending or giving), and that it is of two kinds : lawful and unlawful. The unlawful is any loan for which one receives more than the initial loan, or by means or gain for which profit is drawn therefrom. The lawful form of *Ribā* is a gift which is given in order to receive in return for it an addition over and above that of the initial gift. The addition must be given by the complete free will of the donee.[7] Additionally. it has been stated that *Ribā* can only attach to synallagmatic contracts, where reciprocal obligations are involved. Gifts and charitable bequests, therefore, cannot be tainted with *Ribā*.[8] *Ribā* literally means 'increase in' or 'addition to' anything. In its widest general implication it signifies 'any unjustified increase of capital for which no compensation is given'.[9] Such then, is the vagueness of the

---

4 See, for example, Wehr, *A Dictionary of Modern Written Arabic*, *op.cit.*, p.324; Faruqi, *Law Dictionary*, (Beirut, 1972) p.171, who includes 'Danism' as a translation. Lane, *Lex*, includes 'profit'. Also, Gibb and Kramers, (Ed.) *Shorter Encyclopoedia of Islam*, (London, 1953) p.471. See Saleh, *Unlawful Gain*, *op.cit.*, p.12 f.

5 'Interest' is defined in the Oxford Dictionary as: "The money paid for the use of money lent or for the forbearance of a debt according to a fixed ratio." 'Usury' is defined therein as: "The practice of changing, taking or contracting to receive, excessive or illegal rates of interest for money on loan." For a comprehensive discussion, See Ibrāhīm Zakī al-Dīn Badawī, *Naẓariyya al-Ribā al-Muḥarramu Fī al-Sharī'a al-Islāmiyya*, (Baghdad, 1966/1967)

6 T.P. Hughes, *A Dictionary of Islam*, (London, 1885). Here the definition of usury parallels the Hebrew *Neshec*, which includes gain of any kind.

7 Lane, See also R. Roberts, *Social Laws of the Qur'ān*, (London, 1925;fourth reprint, 1977) pp.102ff. On the grounds that the whole concept of *Ribā* is more comprehensive than mere 'interest' or 'usury', the arabic term is therefore much to be preferred over any attempts to provide an unsatisfactory English translation.

8 Ahmed, B.D., 'Ribā in Islamic Law', *Islamic and Comparative Law Quarterly*, VI:1 (March, 1986) pp.51-70, at p.52

9 Schacht, 'Ribā', *Encyclopoedia of Islam*, Vol. III, p.1148; *id.*, *Introduction*, (1964) at 145; Coulson *Commercial Law in The Gulf States*, (1979) p.11

prohibition, for further precision in the definition of *Ribā* is precluded by the very lack of such definition in the Qur'ān and Sunna.[10] The enigma rests on the fact that if *Ribā* is interpreted as usury, then transactions involving additional gains or profits are valid provided those gains are not usurious; but if *Ribā* is defined as interest then such transactions are all illegal.

While we may acknowledge the difficulty of defining *Ribā*, we may yet maintain one certainty among its characteristics. This is that all *Ribā* is banned absolutely by the Qur'ān.[11] The first verses concerning *Ribā* (like those concerning the imbibing of wine) were revealed in Mecca in the form of a moral exhortation, and only received outright condemnation at a later stage in Medina.[12] The Qur'ānic prohibition is to be found in *Sūrat al-Baqara*:

> "Those who devour *Ribā* will not stand except as he stands who has been driven to madness by the touch of Satan. That is because they say : 'Trade is only like *Ribā*, but God has permitted trade and forbidden *Ribā*.... God will deprive *Ribā* of all blessing"[13]

> "O ye who believe! Fear God, and give up what remains of your demand for *Ribā*, if you are indeed believers. If you do not, take notice of war from God and His Apostle : But if you turn back, you shall have your capital sums : Deal not unjustly, and you shall not be dealt with unjustly. If the debtor is in difficulty, grant him time till it is easy for him to repay. But if you remit it by way of charity, that is best for you if only you knew."[14]

> "O you who believe ! Devour not *Ribā*, doubled and multiplied; But fear God, that you may prosper."[15]

---

10 For the Qur'anic background and doctrine, See Saleh, *Unlawful Gain, op.cit.*, pp.8-12.

11 Fazlur Rahman, 'Ribā and Interest', *Islamic Studies*, 3 (1964), pp.3f.

12 Shaikh Draz, 'L'Usure en Droit Musulman', in *Travaux de la Semaine, Internationale de Droit Musulman*, (Sirey, France, 1953), pp.147-148; Saleh, *Unlawful Gain, op.cit.*, p.2

13 *Qur'ān*, (II:275-276)

14 *Qur'ān*, (II: 278-80)

15 *Qur'ān*, (III: 130)

It would appear that at the rise of Islam the practice of lending money was being exploited so as to reap excessive gains from the interest charged on loans. If borrowers could not meet the due date by which to return the capital borrowed, the lenders would double and then redouble the interest rates thus reducing the debtor to penury.[16] Such practices were deemed intimidatory, unjust and against social and economic welfare.

The Islamic code urges leniency towards debtors, and the Qur'ān specifies no punishment for unpaid debts.[17] If the debtor consistently fails to pay his debts, Islamic law provides that he should be imprisoned, unless he can furnish proof of his insolvency, whereupon he is set at liberty. If in good health, he could be required to work off the discharge of his debt, but not so that be becomes enslaved to the lender.[18] The Islamic interdiction of *Ribā* therefore fell into the net of social reform instituted by the Prophet upon pre-Islamic practices.[19] The earliest Qur'ānic prohibitions against *Ribā*

---

16 Compare *Leviticus* 25:39 ff., and Hammurabi Ss. 117,48,115f.,118f., where debtors are reduced to enslavement for the period it takes them to repay the outstanding debt.

17 *Qur'ān*, (II:280-282) Muirhead writes: "The tumults and seditions so frequent in Rome during the first two centuries of the republic are more frequently attributed by the historians to the abuses of the law of debt than to any other cause, social or political". *Historical Introduction to the Private law of Rome*, (Third ed. Revised and Ed. by A. Grant; London, 1916) pp. 84-85. As a result of the *Nexum* transaction, the debtor had to yield himself to *de facto* servitude. Laws to repress usury in Rome were established with the tribunate and its *jus auxilii*: a provision of the XII. Tables made the *Unciarium Fenus* half of the capital or eight and one-third per cent yearly the maximum rate, and imposed a fourfold penalty on its contravention. A law in the year 407 reduced it to Four and one-sixth, giving debtors three years grace to repay. The Genucian law of 412 made interest illegal, but the law soon became dead letter; it was reversed by the Poetilian law of 428 (326) which gave the creditor *de facto* right to enslave the debtor. The Nexal contract was not outlawed until the enactment of the *Julian cessio bonorum* in 706 A.U.C (well after the rise of Islam) whereupon a debtor would be formally discharged from his debt on handing over all his possessions to his creditor. (*id.* pp.86-87)

18 Roberts, *Social Laws of the Qur'ān*, *op.cit.*, p.102

19 Professor M.A. Shaban's economic historical theories, in his *Islamic History*, I, *op.cit.*, pp.1 ff.; A 1904 *al-Manār* Report held against *Ribā* as letting money yield profit without the intermediation of work, thus permitting the concentration of capital to remain in the hands of the few : thus perpetuating the economic exploitation of the poor by the rich. See 'Ṣundūq al-Tawfīr Fī Idārat al-Barīd', in *al-Manār*, Vol.VII (1904) p.28

are limited to the loan of fungible commodities (*Qarḍ*).[20] This kind of *Ribā* is termed *al-Ribā al-Nasī'a*.[21] In a *Qarḍ* loan the lender is not permitted to demand from the borrower any advantage or premium. The borrower may willingly grant an advantage to the lender only after settlement, and this may not form a condition of the contract.[22] Any demand or condition for interest in advance of settlement of a *Qarḍ* loan is regarded as a special case of unjustified enrichment, or "consuming the property of others for no good reason".[23]

As far as clarification by the Prophet is concerned, there is also little help to be gleaned from the Ḥadīth. One report states that in his last sermon, given on Mount Arafat during the pilgrimage the year before he died, Muḥammad said : "Remember that you will indeed reckon your deeds : Allāh has forbidden you to take *Ribā*, therefore all interest obligation shall henceforth be waived."[24] Schacht ascribes the prohibition of *Ribā* to the Prophet's acquaintance with Jewish doctrine and practice in Medina[25] rather than to an aversion to Meccan exploitative practices. Indeed, the same prohibition existed in the ancient Egyptian, Babylonian, Greek and the Roman legislations.[26] It also exists in the Talmud and Bible, thus subjecting

---

20 See also *Qur'ān*, (II:219), (V:90), (IV:161), (XXX:39). *Qarḍ* corresponds to the *Mutuum* loan for use of Roman law. Udovitch states that from all indications these forms of loans were "almost insignificant in Medieval Islamic commerce". See his 'Reflections on the Institutions of Credits and Banking In the Medieval Islamic Near East', *Studia Islamica*, (Paris, 1975) XLI, pp. 5-21. Cf. the Tradition of the Prophet related by Abū al-Faḍl Ja'far Ibn 'Alī al-Dimashqī, *On the Beauties of Commerce*, transl. in H. Ritter, *Der Islam*, VII (1917) pp.64-65; and generally see 'Alā' al-Dīn Khurūfa, *'Aqd al-Qarḍ Fī al-Sharī'a al-Islāmiyya*, (Beirut, 1982)

21 See B.D. Ahmed, 'Ribā in Islamic Law', *Islamic and Comparative Law Quarterly*, VI:1 (Mar.1986) pp.66 ff., who rejects the suggestion that *Ribā Nasī'a* should only apply to production loans, and not to consumption loans, on the basis that both were known at the inception of Islam and no distinction was made between them at that time (at pp.69-70).

22 See Khurūfa, 'Alā' al-Dīn, *'Aqd al-Qarḍ Fī al-Sharī'a al-Islāmiyya*, (Beirut, 1982); Saleh, *Unlawful Gain and Legitimate Profit in Islamic Law*, (Cambridge, 1986), pp. 35-44

23 *Akl Amwāl al-Nās bi al-Bāṭil*, which is forbidden in *Qur'ān*, (II:188), (IV:29), (IV:161), (IX:34); cf. Schacht, *Introduction*, *op.cit.*, p.12

24 Ninth Day of Dhū al-Ḥujja, 10 A.H. in the Uranah Valley of Mount Arafat.

25 Schacht, *Introduction*, *op.cit.*, p.13

26 See Cardahi, 'Le Prêt à Intérêt et l'Usure au Regard des Législations Antiques, de la Morale Catholique Du Droit Moderne et de la Loi Islamique', *Revue International de Droit Comparé*, VII (July-Sept. 1955) pp. 499-541; and Badawī, *Naẓariyya al-Ribā al-Muḥarramu Fī al-Sharī'a al-Islāmiyya*, (Baghdad, 1966/1967)

both Jewish and Christian doctrines to its tenets.[27] In the protestant church, the doctrine became officially modified during the course of the sixteenth century, thereby allowing the followers of its persuasion to legitimately indulge in the exploitative practices which remained legally out of bounds to the Muslims.[28]

"Throughout the Middle Ages", writes Bertrand Russell, "the law of nature was held to condemn 'usury'...but when Protestantism arose, its support - especially the support of Calvanism[29] - came chiefly from the rich middle class, who were lenders rather than borrowers. Accordingly first Calvin, then other Protestants, and finally the Catholic Church, sanctioned 'usury'."[30]

In contrast to the declining ambit of the Christian and Jewish prohibitions in the Medieval era, the interdiction against *Ribā* in Islam underwent such attempts at exegesis as were gradually to extend its scope. The Qur'ānic prohibition was amplified by several *Aḥādīth* to encompass the exchange of currencies and denominated articles termed "*Ribawī*." Variant versions of an *Ḥadīth* determine *Ribawī* commodities as gold and silver, and articles for human consumption, such as wheat, barley, dates and raisins. When these commodities are bartered against each other, there must be no inequality between the two lots, nor a delay in delivery.[31] The process of

---

27 *Talmud*, Baba M[e]zi'â, chpt. 5; See Exodus XXII:25; Leviticus XXV:36; Deuteronomy, XXIII:20-21 See McLaughlin, 'The Teaching of the Canonists on Usury', *Medieval Studies*, I (1939) pp.81-147; III (1940) pp.1-22; and Nelson, *The Idea of Usury From Tribal Brotherhood to Universal Otherhood*, (Chicago, 1969)

28 *Qur'ān*, (IV:161) accuses the Jews of taking *Ribā*, thereby illustrating that the practice was abounding even before modification of the Talmud prohibition. See also Goitein, *Letters of Medieval Jewish Traders: translated from the Arabic With Introduction and Notes*, (Princeton, N.Jersey, 1973)

29 Calvin refuted Aristotle's theory of the sterility of money with his "transvaluation of values". "He succeeded in legitimizing usury without seeming to impair the vitality either of the universalism or the fraternalism of the Christian ethic" (p.74) by exhorting that the Mosaic and Gospel rules should be interpreted in the light of the individual conscience, the equity of the Golden Rule, and the requirements of public utility. Nelson, *The Idea of Usury*, pp.73-82

30 Bertrand Russell, *History of Western Philosophy*, p.601. Borrowing their arguments from Calvin, the "marchaunts and occupiers" in 1571 pressed for the abrogation of the Bill against usury of 5 and 6 Edward VI, c.20 (1552) which had repealed the rate of 10% allowed by the Act of 37 Henry VIII c.9 (1545). A. Hyma, *Christianity, Capitalism and Communism*, (Michigan, 1937) ch.iii

31 The *Ḥadīth* exists in all the major *Ṣaḥīḥ* compilations, except Bukhārī's. Shīrāzī, *Kitāb al-Tanbīh Fī al-Fiqh*, (Ed. A.W.T. Juynboll: Leiden, 1879; Cairo, 1348) p.98; Bayḍāwī on *Qur'ān* (II:276). Bayḍāwī suggests that the prohibition against *Ribawī* commodities in loans predates Islam; Goldziher, *Zâhiriten*, *op.cit.*, pp.41ff. B.D. Ahmed, 'Ribā in Islamic Law', *Islamic and Comparative Law Quarterly*, VI:1 (Mar.1986) pp. 64-66

analogy was applied by the jurists to the *Ribā* rules of 'equality in quantity and quality, and immediate delivery', employing the *'Illa* of the *Ribā* prohibition to other commodities with the same characteristics as those specified by the Prophet. The varying interpretations of the *'Illa* among the schools not unnaturally resulted in diverging analogies.[32] The Ḥanafī school extended the list of *Ribawī* commodities to all fungible goods normally sold by weight or measure; The Malikīs extended it to all foodstuffs which could be preserved or stored; while the Ḥanbalī and Shāfi'ī schools applied the rules to the barter of all foodstuffs. The consensus of Muslim opinion settled on the area covered by general agreement, that is, the barter of foodstuffs capable of being preserved.[33]

The importance of the prohibition in economic terms, no less at the time of the Prophet as in modern-day financial transactions, renders his disinclination to define the precise boundaries of the prohibition somewhat of a mystery. Throughout the development of the law, the prohibition has remained prone to varied and subjective interpretation over and above the bounds of *Ribawī* commodities.[34] It has been suggested that the Meccans kept closer to the original circumstances of the Qur'ānic prohibition, for they held that there could be no usury unless there was a time lag in the transaction.[35] This would mean that the Meccans would be unlikely to object to unequal exchange if both lots were delivered immediately.[36]

One incidence where the Islamic lawyers may be accused of taking the *Ribā* prohibition to an illogical extreme is that related in a Tradition by

---

32 See Saleh, *Unlawful Gain, op.cit.*, p.15 f.

33 Coulson, *A History of Islamic Law*, (Edinburgh, 1964) p.79. B.D. Ahmed, 'Ribā in Islamic Law', *Islamic and Comparative Law Quarterly*, VI:1 (Mar.1986) p.66, remarks that as modern currencies do not possess the attribute of being weighable or measureable, they cannot be considered as *Māl Ribawī*, and therefore lie outside the scope of *al-Riba al-Faḍl*. See also, Saleh, *Unlawful Gain, op.cit.*, pp.19 ff.

34 For a general purview, See Wensinck and Kramers, *Handwörterbuch Des Islam*, (Leiden, 1941) pp.613-616; Fahim, 'La Riba et les Contrats Usuraires Dans le Droit et l'Économie de l'Islam', *Cahiers de l'Institut des Sciences Économiques Appliquées*, [Série V, n.3] (1961) pp.139ff.

35 Schacht, *Origins, op.cit.*, p.251 The doctrine was allegedly projected back to Ibn 'Abbās and his companions.

36 But cf. Goitein, *A Mediterranean Society*, (Berkeley/Los Angeles, 167-1972) Vol. I, pp.197 ff. who states that the granting of a two month delay for payment was considered normal business procedure as far as most commodities were concerned. See also Stillman, 'The Eleventh Century Merchant House of Ibn 'Awkal: (A Geniza Study)', *Journal of the Economic and Social History of the Orient*, XVI, part I (Leiden, April, 1973) p.73

Imām Mālik :[37]

> "I was with 'Abdallāh b. 'Umar when a goldsmith came to him and said: O Abū 'Abd al-Raḥman, I make jewellry from gold and then I sell the finished product for more than its weight, in consideration for my handiwork upon it. 'Abdallāh prohibited this and the goldsmith began to remonstrate. 'Abdallāh continued to forbid it until they arrived at the door of the mosque, or at his riding animal, and then 'Abdallāh said : 'A Dinar for a Dinar; A Dirham for a Dirham : There is no excess between them. This is the commission of our Prophet upon us and our commission upon you.'"

In the light of the Qur'anic verse (II:275-6)[38] and the invocation to all Muslims to pursue honest trade and business, the extension of the *Ribā* prohibition to the work of jewellers is somewhat incongruous. It is hard to envisage how they are supposed to profit by their trade if they are not permitted to charge for their labour.

As far as enforcement of the prohibition is concerned, the *Muḥtasib* could only deal with the incidence of *Ribā* if it was interest charged on a credit transaction, the reason being that this was the only kind of *Ribā* that carried the unanimity of the lawyers as to is prohibition. *Ribā* charged on lump sums in cash were not, in any case, so easily detectable by the Market Inspector.[39] Nevertheless, credit transactions could also help to avoid the *Ribā* regulations. Udovitch states that because of the price differential between a credit and a cash transaction, the prohibition was not restrictive to the conduct of commerce.[40] The price difference between these payments does not formally constitute interest. However some of the early legists regarded the credit sales as fulfilling the same economic function as interest by providing a return to the creditor for the risks involved in the transaction, and compensating him for the absence of his capital.[41] The same flexibility and licit fulfillment of the economic function of an interest-bearing loan could be achieved, from the point of view of both investor and trader, by

---

37 On the authority of Humayd b. Qays the Meccan from a *Mujtahid*: Suyūṭī, *Tanwīr al-Ḥawālik: Sharḥ Muwaṭṭa' al-Imām Mālik*, Vol II (Cairo, 1348 AH) p.59

38 Cited *Supra*.

39 Maqrīzī, *Khiṭāṭ*, 2 vols (Bulaq, 1270 AH) *passim.*; al-Dimashqī, *Kitāb al-Ishāra ilā Maḥāsin al-Tijāra*, (Cairo, 1318); Levy, *Social Structure of Islam*, p.337.

40 Udovitch, 'Reflections on the Institutions of Credits and Banking in the Medieval Islamic Near East', *Studia Islamica*, XLI (Paris, 1975) pp.9-10

41 Udovitch, 'Reflections', *op.cit.*, pp.9-10

highly developed and adaptable forms of partnership and commenda arrangements.[42]

The early Islamic jurists construed the prohibition extremely narrowly and condemned all contracts involving interest as illegal.[43] In this light it could be assumed that the above transactions would be tainted with the same illegality as those which openly courted *Ribā*. It may also be argued that the stringent Islamic rules for the Deposit contract are a reflection of the narrow interpretation of *Ribā*. The deposit involves no payment of a fee or any other compensation to either depositor or depositary. Its function was restricted to that of its title - the deposit and safeguarding of goods or money for the benefit of their owner. The depositary is severely proscribed from gaining benefit or use of the deposit[44] and this has been ascribed by Udovitch as the 'strong, inhibiting influence on the development in the Islamic world of any form of deposit banking, and contributed toward keeping credit and banking activities within rather narrow confines'.[45]

In fact, a restrictive interpretation of *Ribā* effectively resulted in three forms of reaction : The first was a disregard for the religious precept, where trade carried on according to local custom;[46] the second was a widespread use of subterfuges, such as *Ḥīla* (legal devices) or double sales[47] : these legal devices observe the letter of the law, while transactions continue as necessity and custom require, thereby avoiding the legal prohibition; the third reaction was a pious refusal to entertain any transaction which could

42 Udovitch, *ibid*., p.10

43 *Ribā* is regarded as the fourth of the seven Godly sins. G.M. Baroody, *Crime and Punishment Under Islamic Law*, [Transl. of *Manār al-Sabīl*, by Sheikh Ibrāḥīm Ibn Muḥammad Ibn Salīm Ibn Dūyān] (London, 1979: Second Edn.) The Qur'ānic retribution for the practice of *Ribā* is twofold: the loss of God's blessing and torture in Hell. Roberts, *Social Laws of the Qur'ān*, *op.cit*., p.108

44 Unlike the early western contract of deposit wherein, the depositary being able to keep the goods and use them for commercial purposes, the premium and deposit developed into a type of proto-banking. See Udovitch, 'Reflections', *op.cit*., pp.19-20

45 Udovitch, 'Reflections', *op.cit*., pp.19-20

46 See, for example, reports of Muslim women lending their *Mahr* or proceeds of their domestic poultry-keeping 'without pangs of conscience'. *The Times*, Newspaper (London, 17 Nov., 1931)

47 E. Sachau, *Muhammedanisches Recht*, (Berlin, 1897)

be construed as involving *Ribā*.[48] It was this latter reaction which resulted in the management of finance and banking practices passing to *Dhimmī* Jews and Christians living in the early Arab communities.[49]

The first of these reactions is best documented by the accounts of Ottoman commercial life and the Geniza records;[50] Gibb and Bowen, noting an interest rate of 7-12% suggest : "There is enough evidence in the Arabic sources to confirm that the placing out of money at interest was by no means uncommon amongst Moslems".[51]

Jennings has shown that in the seventeenth century Anatolian city of Kayseri "legal and moral practice had evolved to a point where an interest rate of 20% per year was accepted by the entire religious community as in accordance with the Shar'ia....There is no alternative but to conclude that the consensus of the Muslim community judged such practice acceptable before and approved by God".[52] No attempts were apparently made in Kayseri to either conceal the interest, or to resort to questionable *Ḥiyal* or other 'fraud', although the historical process by which this state of affairs evolved is not clear. Interest-free loans were still recognised as being ethically praiseworthy, but it is not known whether interest was automatically charged on those loans where no specific rate is mentioned.[53] Similarly, the Geniza documents of the merchant house of Ibn 'Awkal show the large importance given to imports of gold Dinars and silver Dirhams, despite their inclusion

---

48 See, for example, M.L. Darling, *Rusticus Loquitur*, (Oxford, 1930) who writes of unclaimed interest of deposits in Post Office Savings Banks in India, p.368. See also the debate conducted in Rashīd Riḍā's *al-Manār* between the Khedive of Egypt and Muḥammad 'Abduh in the early twentieth century over the Egyptian *Ṣundūq al-Tawfīr* affair : *al-Manār*, Vol VII (1904) pp.28-29; *ibid.*, Vol. IX (1906) pp.332-350; *ibid.*, (1917) pp. 526-528, as related in Mallat, 'The Debate on Riba and Interest in Twentieth Century Jurisprudence', pp.29-32 in *Islamic Law and Finance.*, (SOAS, London, 1988) [Ed. C. Mallat].

49 Çagatay asserts that the same monopolization of finance by the Jews and Christians occurred in the Ottoman Empire: 'Riba and Interest Concept in the Ottoman Empire', *Studia Islamica*, 32 (1972) p.58

50 See Udovitch, 'Theory and Practice of Islamic Law: Some Evidence from the Geniza', *Studia Islamica*, XXXII (Paris, 1970) pp.289 ff; Çagatay, 'Riba and Interest Concept In the Ottoman Empire', *Studia Islamica*, 32 (1972) pp.53-68

51 Gibb and Bowen, *Islamic Society and The West*, (Toronto/Oxford, 1957) V (Part I) p.301. A comparison may be made here with Ancient Greece, where despite the prohibition against interest-bearing loans (See, for example, Aristotle's *Politique*, Bk. I, Ch. 3, Para. 23) it continued to be practiced, and at extremely variable rates, with no maximum ceiling.

52 This included men of religion: See Jennings, 'Loans and Credit in Ottoman Records', *Journal of the Economic and Social History of the Orient*, 16 (73) pp.184-185: see also cases cited on p.189

53 *idem.*, pp. 190-191

in the accepted list of *Ribawī* commodities. In addition to being a means of exchange, coins were considered much as any other commodity, being bought and sold in a manner remarkably similar to today's currency markets.[54]

The resources of legists and lawyers alike in thinking up *Ḥiyal* to circumvent the obstacles posed by the *Ribā* prohibition are abundant.[55] Double sales (*Bay'atān fī bay'atin*) in the form of *Mukhāṭara and Murābaḥa* contracts were formulated on the premise that the prospective debtor sells an object for cash to the prospective creditor; the debtor immediately buys back the object for a greater amount payable at a future date: thus the transaction amounts to a loan with the object as security. The difference between the two prices represents the interest.[56] This stratagem was also formulated using real property as security for the debt and allowing the creditor such use of it as would represent interest payment. This would be equivalent to the sale of real property with the right of redemption (*Bay' al-Wafā'; Bay' al-'Uhda*) but is not strictly admissible as either a sale or pledge.[57]

Similarly, the *Muwāḍa'a* consisted of several transactions each recorded and attested in separate documentation and deposited with a Notary Public (*Thīqa*). An unofficial covering document would be drawn up setting out the real relationship between the parties to each other and the real purport of the agreement. The intermediary would hand the relevant documents to each party at given stages thereby preventing unauthorised use, and producing, if necessary, a compensating document or previously prepared acknowledgement for this use.[58] The 'Īna (credit) sales mentioned above were based on the transaction of *Nasī'a* (delay): The creditor sells to the debtor some object for the sum of the capital and interest, payable at a future date; immediately, the creditor buys back the same object for the capital which is payable immediately. This amounts, in effect, to an unsecured loan.

In seventeenth century Bursa, Ottoman Court Records show that an arrangement made by *Istiḥsān* outside the Islamic nominate contracts,

---

54 Stillman, 'The Eleventh Century Merchant House of Ibn 'Awkal', *Journal of the Economic and Social History of the Orient, op.cit*., pp.58-62

55 Khan, M.S., 'Mohammedan Laws against Usury and How They are Evaded', *Journal of Comparative Legislation*, 2 (1929) pp.233-244

56 Schacht, *Introduction*, p.79

57 Schacht, *Introduction*, p.79

58 Sarakhsī, *al-Mabsūṭ*, XXX, 150, (l.16ff on Ibn Abī Layla); Ikhwān al-Ṣafā', *Rasā'il Ikhwān al-Ṣafā wa-Khillān al-Wafā*, ed. Khayr al-Dīn al-Ziriklī, (Cairo, 1347/1928) iii, 155; Schacht, *Introduction*, p.83

enabled the creditor to lend money on interest in lieu of a mortgage of real estate.[59]

In recent times there have been frequent recurrences of support for the third stance. The Islamic Fiqh (Jurisprudence) Academy of the Islamic Conference, held in 1986, supported the restrictive interpretation of *Ribā* which had been adopted by the early jurists. Concordantly, it condemned all interest-bearing transactions as void.[60] Many discussions[61] have taken place as to the Islamic alternative to Western banking practices, which may avoid *Ribā*, and thereby a violation of the *Sharī'a*.[62] Several mechanisms, such as *Muḍāraba* (Equity sharing between client and bank; partnership),[63] *Muqaraḍa* (Islamic bonds on which no interest is earned, but whose market value varies with the anticipated [variable] profit share),[64] and Lease Financing,[65] have been put forward as means by which this may be achieved, and discussed by pro-Islamic economists with increasing optimism

---

59 H. Gerber, 'The Muslim Law of Partnerships in Ottoman Court Records', *Studia Islamica*, LIII, p.111. The UAE Civil Code prohibits "sham arrangements" as these : See Arts. 394 (1) and (2), and 395.

60 *Middle East Executive Report*, (March, 1986) p.7

61 See R. Wilson, *Banking and Finance In The Arab Middle East*, (London, 1983); A.F. Rahman, *Economic Doctrines of Islam: Banking and Finance*, vol 4 (London, 1979); S.N.H. Naqvi, *Ethics and Economics, An Islamic Synthesis*; Khalid A. Ahmad, *Al-Tafkīr al-Iqtiṣādī*, (Beirut, 1397 AH); Khurshid Ahmad, 'Economic Development In an Islamic Framework', in K. Ahmad, [Ed.] *Studies in Islamic Economics*; S.H. Homoud, *Islamic Banking: The Adaptation of Banking Practice to Conform with Islamic Law*, (London, 1985; Reprinted 1986)

62 In the commercial sphere the 'Islamic legal revolution' which promulgated the Civil Procedure Act in the Sudan in 1983, prohibited *Ribā* transactions, (See Gordan, 'The Islamic Legal Revolution : The Case of Sudan', 19 *International Lawyer*, (1985) p.801) although the implementations of the new interpretations have received criticism by legal authorities: cf. Mayer, 'Khartoum: After the Fall', *Middle East Executive Report*, (Oct.1985) pp.8, 22, who states that the Sudanese Civil Transactions Act is based on the Jordanian Civil Code rather than the *Sharī'a*. The position was relaxed in December 1987 by the new Government; See Reuters, 'Sudan Eases Shari'a Law', *Saudi Gazette*, (Dec. 12, 1987)

63 See M.N. Siddiqi, *Banking Without Interest*, pp.19 ff; Siddiqi, *Muslim Economic Thinking*, pp.30-31

64 see R. Wilson, 'Islamic Banking in Jordan', *Arab Law Quarterly*, 2(3) (Aug. 1987) p.211, n.8

65 See, for instance, W. Van Orden Gnichtel, 'Lease Financing in Saudi Arabia', *International Financial Law Review*, (Jan. 1984) pp.34-36

as to their financial efficacy.[66]

6.7.2 The Modern Enigma of Ribā

Modern jurists are just as varied in their opinions as to the exact interpretation of *Ribā*. In his *Tafsīr*, Ali accepts the definition as : "Undue profit made, not in the way of legitimate trade, out of loans of gold and silver, and necessary articles of food, such as wheat, barley, dates, and salt (according to the list mentioned by the Holy Apostle himself). My definition would include profiteering of all kinds but exclude economic credit, the creature of modern banking and finance."[67] Ali's proposition is upheld by *Qur'ān*, (II:275) where the distinction between *Ribā* and trade is clearly made.[68] Later jurists have tended to adopt the less rigourous approach to *Ribā* by interpreting it according to other Qur'ānic verses as "excessive interest" or "usury",[69] thereby allowing for a "fair" return on commercial capital.[70] According to the Ḥanafī doctrine Muslims may conclude transactions involving *Ribā* with non-Muslims in enemy territory.[71] This interpretation offers a somewhat extended reflection of the modifications made to the Jewish doctrine.[72] In the interests of the assumed solidarity of the clan, or *mishpaha*, pious Jews are prevented from seeking *Neshec* from their kin (*ah*) and may only exact it from aliens (*nokri*), who are in any case excluded from their fraternity.[73]

---

66 See generally, Tussing, 'Understanding Islamic Banking', *Middle East Executive Report*, (Dec. 1986) p.17; Roy, 'Islamic Banking: Rapid Growth and the Moral Dilemma', *Middle East Executive Report*, (April, 1986) p.8; Carlson, 'Trade Finance Under Islamic Principles : A Case Study', *Middle East Executive Report*, (Dec. 1986) p.9; Khan and Mirakhor, 'The framework and Practice of Islamic Banking', *Finance and Development*, (Sept. 1986) pp.32,34;

67 Ali, *The Holy Qur'ān*, *op.cit.*, Sura II, n.324

68 See B.D. Ahmed, 'Ribā in Islamic Law', *Islamic and Comparative Law Quarterly*, VI:1 (Mar.1986) pp. 53 ff., who distinguishes the four types of Spot transactions and the four types of Future transactions in relation to *Ribā*.

69 *Qur'ān*, (III:131): "O you who believe! Devour not usury by doubling and quadrupling."

70 See Kristan L. Peters Hamlin, 'The Impact of Islamic Revivalism on Contract and Usury Law in Iran, Saudi Arabia and Egypt', *Texas International Law Journal*, Vol. 22 (1987) pp.351-381

71 Schacht, *Introduction*, *op.cit.*, p.199

72 cf. *Deuteronomy*, 23:20 :'Unto a foreigner thou mayest lend upon usury'.

73 This double-edged moralism, a source of embarrassment to the medieval philosophers, was rejected by medieval Christianity. Aspiring to universalism, the church refuted the discrimination against the alien. Nelson, *The Idea of Usury*, *op.cit.*, pp.xix-xxii (Introduction)

In conjunction with the wave of European-inspired codification among the Arab Nation States during the present century, most modern Islamic States have either legislated for, or tacitly approved the role of interest within their economies. However, even in countries such as Egypt where express recognition is given to interest,[74] these provisions have not gone without challenge. In May 1985, the Constitutional Court of Egypt issued judgment against the claim that the change in Article 2 of the Constitution (which provides that the *Sharī'a* shall be the principal source of law) affected existing legislation, notably Article 226 of the Civil Code of 1948. The plaintiff, the Rector of al-Azhar University, argued that this article was contrary to the amended form of Article 2 of the Constitution, in that it provided for the payment of interest in the case of delayed payment of loans.[75] In rejection of his case, the court nevertheless directed the legislative powers to 'purify' provisions of past statutes so as to conform to the principles of the *Sharī'a.*[76]

A lateral philosophy to the medieval Judaïc and Christian distinctions between types of transactions in which usury is forbidden or permitted, is to be discovered in the modern Gulf codes.

---

[74] In the Egyptian Civil Code, Law No. 131 of 1948, Arts. 226,227,542 recognise contracts containing interest. This is confirmed as constitutional by the Civil Courts : *Arab Law Newsletter*, (June, 1986) pp.1-2. Similar recognition is given by Iraq and Qatar (See Ballantyne, *Legal Development In Arabia*, (1980) pp.114-115. See also 'Supreme Constitutional Court (Egypt) - Shari'a and Ribā : Decision in Case No. 20 of Judicial year No.1', *Arab Law Quarterly*, 1 (1) (Nov. 1985) pp.100-107; and Saba Habachy, 'Commentary on the Decision of the Supreme Court of Egypt given on 4 May 1985 concerning the legitimacy of interest and the constitutionality of Article 226 of the New Egyptian Civil Code of 1948', *Arab Law Quarterly*, 1 (2) (Feb. 1986) pp.239-241

[75] *Rector of Al-Azhar University v. President of the Arab Republic of Egypt, the Prime Minister, the President of the Council of Ministers, the President of the Legislative Committee of the People's Assembly, and Fuad Goudah*, Case No. 20 of Judicial Year of the Constitutional Court, and No.7 of the Supreme Court (No. 9): (Decision issued 16 Nov. 1985); See *Arab Law Newsletter*, No.1 (Nov 1985) pp.1-2; *Ibid.*, No.3 (Jan.1986) p.2; *Ibid.*, No.8 (June 1986) p.1; See also Saba Habachy, *Arab Law Quarterly*, 'Commentary on the Decision of the Supreme Court of Egypt given on 4 May 1985 concerning the legitimacy of interest and the constitutionality of Article 226 of the New Egyptian Civil Code of 1948', *Arab Law Quarterly*, 1 (2) (Feb. 1986) pp.239-241; and *Journal of International Banking Law*, I, (1) (1986) p.N9

[76] See *Arab Law Quarterly*, 1 (1985) p.100; and *Arab Law Newsletter*, No.3 (Jan. 1986) : Some 40 Cases questioning the Constitutionality of Article 226 were rejected on the grounds that it had already been decided that Art.226 was valid and binding in its judgment of 16 May 1985, and that precedent applies in matters of Constitutional Court judgment.

Bahrain

As might be expected from a civil code based on English Law principles, there is no mention of *Ribā* in the 1969 Contract Law of Bahrain, nor is a distinction made between civil and commercial loans. Fixed rates of interest on capital, and contracts involving interest are therefore enforceable in the courts.[77] There is a state ceiling, and although neither code mentions a specific figure, the local market rate is set at 9% maximum. Any commercial loan demanding in excess of 15% is void, whether or not the borrower objects to the excess. The High Civil Court of Bahrain, on at least one occasion, has obliged a plaintiff suing on an agreement carrying 40% compound rate to reduce it to the state ceiling of 15%.[78]

Kuwait

The recent enactments of the Kuwaiti Civil and Commercial Codes, for example, distinguish between *Ribā* in civil transactions, which is forbidden, and that in commercial transactions, which is permitted, subject to the State-declared ceiling. Kuwait Civil Code, Law No. 67 of 1980, states in Article 305 :'Any agreement providing for interest in respect of the use of an amount of money or delay in performance of an obligation shall be void.'[79]

The Kuwaiti Commercial Code distinguishes a commercial loan from a civil loan, in that the borrowed amounts are to be expended upon commercial activities.[80] Thus banking transactions and transactions involving negotiable instruments would clearly constitute commercial activities, whereas project consulting and design or other professional contracts would remain within the ambit of the Civil Code provisions.[81] Article 102 (1) of

---

77 See Art. 2(1) of the Bahrain Commercial Code, which gives priority to the agreement between the parties so long as it does not contradict the laws in force.

78 *International and Financial Law Review*, (Feb. 1989).

79 It is interesting to note that the term *Ribā* is avoided in this article. For the distinction between commercial and civil contracts, see Qalyūbī, Samīḥa al-, *al-Qānūn al-Tijārī al-Kuwaitī -Naẓariyya al-'Amāl al-Tijāriyya - al-Tājir - al-Maḥall al-Tijārī*, (Kuwait, 1974); and 'Id, Idwār, *al-'Uqūd al-Tijāriyya wa 'Amaliyāt al-Muṣārif*, (Beirut, 1968), Chapter One.

80 Law No. 68 of 1980, Art. 101.

81 Some categories still remain unclear : *Arab Law Newsletter*, No. 20 (July/Aug 1987) p.3 asks, for instance, whether specialised sub-contracts are to be treated as Civil or Commercial Law contracts ? Under the primary section of the Commercial Code, which sets out the definition of commercial companies and associations, the answer to this question would depend on an investigation of the sub-contractor's business practices, registration, books kept, and so on.

the Commercial Code declares : "The creditor shall have the right to receive an interest for any commercial loan unless otherwise is agreed upon (*sic*). If the rate of interest is not stated in the contract, the entitled interest shall be the legal one (7%)."[82] Agreements for interest in excess of the State limit will be reduced to the State maximum at the date of conclusion of the contract.[83] This applies to any excess payments agreed upon which, by implication, will be construed as interest, and reduced to the State maximum unless proof is given that it forms consideration for a service or disbursement.[84] Oman, Qatar and Bahrain similarly allow enforcement of interest claims.[85]

In Kuwait the distinction is therefore between merchants and non-merchants, implying that in business at least, money is no longer considered a barren commodity. The default position is that interest is to be charged, although the State has determined the ceiling of 7% beyond which interest demands will not be enforced. Subsection (2) of Article 102 provides that where interest has been agreed upon in a contract and the debtor fails to pay, the deferred interest shall be calculated on the basis of the agreed-upon rate. Compound interest is prohibited, and the sum of interest due should never exceed the sum of the loan capital, notwithstanding rates for long-term loans.[86]

The exceptions to this modern solution are Iran, Pakistan and Saudi Arabia, where the persistent fundamentalist approach dictates a continuation of the academic prohibition.[87] *Ribā* or interest for whatever amount, in whichever form or guise it may be paid or charged, is illegal, for instance, in Saudi Arabia, and will not be upheld either by the *Sharī'a* or the

---

82 See Arts. 110; 409 (which relates to Negotiable Instruments); and 5 (1) (which lists commercial activities, including Banking transactions) of the Kuwaiti Commercial Code. The State ceiling is set by the Central Bank, having been established by the Council for the Administration of the Bank after agreement with the Finance Minister (*ibid.*, Art.111)

83 Kuwaiti Commercial Code, Law No. 68 of 1980, Article 111 (1)

84 *ibid.*, Art. 111 (2)

85 Ballantyne, *Commercial Law In The Arab Middle East : The Gulf States*, (London, 1986) p.133

86 Kuwait Commercial Code, Law No.68 of 1980, Art.115

87 Khan and Mirakhor, 'The Framework and Practice of Islamic Banking', *Finance and development*, (Sept. 1986) p.35; Sloane, P.D., 'The Status of Islamic Law In The Commercial World', *International Lawyer*, (Fall 1988) 22(3) p. 756. The conclusion reached by the Islamic Fiqh (Jurisprudence) Academy of the Islamic Conference in Jeddah in 1986, stated that bank interest is unlawful no matter whether added to a loan when entering the agreement, or accrued over the period of repayment. The decision has no legislative effect however, merely persuasive influence. See *Arab Law Newsletter*, No.7 (May, 1986) p.1

Administrative Courts;[88] However, Islamic banking in Saudi Arabia is not mandatory, and, where requested, banks continue to pay interest to customers on their accounts.[89] In Pakistan and Iran, on the other hand, statutory enforcement of Islamic Banking systems does exist.[90]

The United Arab Emirates

The new Civil Code of the United Arab Emirates, which, unlike Kuwait, is as yet unaccompanied by an enacted Commercial Code,[91] has unearthed considerable controversy amongst its provisions concerning interest payments. The main provision is to be found in Article 714, which provides : "If a contract of loan stipulates a benefit in excess of the essence of the contract, *otherwise than a guarantee of the right of the lender*, that stipulation is void but the contract is valid".[92] The terminology of the Arabic is so obtuse as to invite the presumption that the article is deliberately ambiguous. This was perhaps in order to leave the onus of interpretation to the courts, thereby testing the judicial waters in what might have been an unprecedented trend in the movement to reaffirm the Sharīʻa principles within the commercial statutes of the Gulf States.

The intention to prohibit interest within the Civil Code may be presumed from several other articles : Article 575 lies very close to the *Ribawī* commodity prohibitions of the early Islamic scholars, in that it prohibits the sale of money in exchange for deferred payment of monies; Article 584 forbids sales in which the seller defers receipt of the consideration in

---

[88] *Middle East Executive Report*, (Jan. 1986) p.5; Andreas Haberbeck, 'Risk Sharing in an Islamic Society', *Arab Law Quarterly*, Vol. 2(2) (May 1987) p.139; Sloane, 'The Status of Islamic Law In The Commercial World', *International Lawyer*, (Fall 1988) 22(3) p.756

[89] Sloane, 'The Status of Islamic Law In The Commercial World', *International Lawyer*, (Fall 1988) 22(3) p.756. The publication of Saudi Decision No. 822 states that the Legal Committee of the Ministry of Commerce shall be entrusted with the settlement of disputes between banks and their customers arising out of contracts and banking transactions entered into from 10 Jan. 1986. (See *Arab Law Newsletter*, (May 1986) No.7 p.1). The Banking disputes are thereby removed from the *Sharīʻa* Courts, and official recognition is given to the need for dispute resolution on the matter of bank interest charges.

[90] Khan and Mirakhor, 'The Framework and Practice of Islamic Banking', *Finance and development*, (Sept. 1986) p.35

[91] A Draft Federal Commercial Code has been prepared and circulated informally among legal and judicial authorities in the UAE.

[92] Emphasis added. The author would like to express her thanks to Mr. James Whelan, Resident Partner of Clifford Chance, Sharjah, UAE, for his enlightening discussion of this article and the Civil Code in general.

exchange for an increase in that consideration for sale; Article 710 defines a loan, which, pertinent by its omission, precludes any accretion or interest payment; and Article 849 defines a loan as conferring ownership of property on another for a limited period without consideration. These four articles, taken in conjuction with the primacy of the *Sharī'a* as a general source of law in the absence of lacunae in the code,[93] assert at the very least that the legislators did not intend to give official sanction to interest claims; yet the manifest expression of these articles only serves to make the ambiguity of Article 714 all the more mysterious.

If the intention of an obscure wording of Article 714 was to cause reaction, it was highly successful. Whereas the courts and practitioners of the law continued to expect enforcement of commercial interest claims under the previous regulation of commercial contracts, namely in accordance with Arts. 61 and 62 of the Abu Dhabi Code of Civil Procedure, 1970,[94] the UAE Banking Association felt sufficiently threatened to commence active lobbying of the Central Bank, The Ministry of Justice and the National Consultative Committee, in order to ensure that the rights of banks to enforce interest payments by customers were upheld.[95]

In a 1979 decision, an Abu Dhabi court had declared void a provision of the Abu Dhabi Code of Civil Procedure which allowed the court to award pre-judgment interest as an element of damages. The decision was based on Federal Law No. 10 of 1973, Article 85, which declared void all agreements contrary to the *Sharī'a*. The court held the interest attested in this case contrary to the *Sharī'a* provisions on Ribā.[96] In *Abullāh Fāshid Ḥilāl v. International Bank of Credit and Commerce* the Abu Dhabi Court of Appeal held that even where interest on a loan made by the bank to Ḥilāl was one of the contractual provisions, interest was usurious, whatever the amount, and whether the beneficiary was a bank or a person. In support of this decision, the court relied on Article 85 of the 1973 Courts Law, and also a *Ḥadīth* of the Prophet that "people shall be bound by the terms of their agreement save where they allow a prohibited thing or prohibit a permissible thing." Needless to say, there was strong dissent to this decision by one of

---

93 UAE Civil Code, Arts. 1,2: which therefore reads for the prohibition of interest

94 This code formally applies only to the Emirate of Abu Dhabi, but in practice it is followed in other Emirates. See *Chadbourne and Parke Monthly Newsletter*, Oct. 15, 1986 p.1; Sloane 'Status' *op.cit*, p.760

95 *Arab Law Newsletter*, No. 7 (May 1986) pp.1,4

96 Ballantyne, *Commercial Law in the Arab Middle East: The Gulf States*, p.59; Sloane, 'Status of Islamic Law' *op.cit*, p.760, n.121

the three judges.[97]

Further decisions of the Federal Supreme Court, the *Janata case* in 1981, and *Bank of Baroda v. Abu Dhabi Electronics Trading Co.* in 1983, had established the rates of 12% and 9% (simple) respectively as maximum enforcement rates of interest.[98] The lobbying association therefore also sought the revision of these articles of the Abu Dhabi Code of Civil Procedure which had allowed the interpretation to limit the amounts of interest which may be legally enforced. The response of the National Consultative Committee was to state that the matter was properly the responsilibity of the Federal Cabinet.[99] This Cabinet duly convened to consider the question at length, during which time several contrary indications were given as to the course of their resolutions. The Governor of the UAE Central Bank was quoted in an interview as saying: "If there is a contract between a bank and its customer then the provisions of this contract will prevail. If there is no contract, interest will be charged at the rate of 12% for business loans and 9% for personal loans".[100] Despite the fact that the Federal Supreme Court upheld (also in 1986) the principle that interest once paid need not be refunded, it also held that if the interest on a loan had not been repaid by the borrower, but had been debited by the bank against a separate account held in the name of the borrower, then this principle did not apply. In such a case, the bank would be required to return the interest payments in excess of the statutory maximums of 12% and 9% respectively for commercial and civil (simple) interest payments.[101]

In May 1986 an army officer brought a case at the Court of First Instance in Abu Dhabi against a well-known bank, claiming that Article 714 of the Federal Civil Code prohibits interest on commercial loans. The court thereby held that the Civil Code applies exclusively to civil transactions and

---

97 Civ. Appeal No. 5 (Dubai 1979). See Ian Edge, 'Comparative and Commercial Law of Egypt and the Arabian Gulf', *Cleveland State Law Review*, Vol. 34:129, pp.143-144.

98 *Arab Law Newsletter*, No.10 (Sept 1986), p.4; 'UAE Bank Interest', *International Financial Law Review*, (Nov. 1986) Vol.V, No. 11, pp.42-43

99 *Arab Law Newsletter*, No.9 (Jul/Aug 1986), p.7

100 See *Arab Law Newsletter*, No.10 (Sept 1986) p.4. The Minister of State for Finance and Industry, Aḥmed Al-Tayer, also stated : "The policy of the Government is to have the banks operate at a profit." He denied that the Government supported the policy of *Ribā*, and stated that the religious prescription could not be enforced, therefore banks should not be required to repay interest already submitted by customers on loans. This is in accordance with the original understanding of Arts. 61 and 62 of the Abu Dhabi Code of Civil Procedure, 1970. See also *ibid.*, No.11 (Oct 1986) p.4 and *ibid*, No.12 (Nov 1986) p.3

101 See *Arab Law Newsletter*, No.12 (Nov. 1986) p.3

that a loan agreement with a bank is a commercial transaction.[102]

The expected appeal from this court was forestalled by an amendment to the Federal Civil Code (Law No.5 of 1985), signed and enacted by the President of the UAE with the approval of the Federal Cabinet and Supreme Council, to the effect that : "The attached law [the Civil Transactions Code] shall apply to Civil transactions in the United Arab Emirates. Commercial transactions shall continue to be governed by the respective laws and regulations applicable thereto until the Federal Commercial Code is issued".[103] The amendment gave certain indication that the proposed Federal Commercial Code would legalize interest payments for commercial transactions in much the same way as Kuwait has done. Meanwhile, the "respective laws and regulations applicable thereto" in the absence of a commercial code, presumably included the Civil Code.

The courts in Abu Dhabi have held in anticipation of this view in a number of reported cases. In 1986, a lawsuit was brought by a prominent local company owned jointly by several UAE and other Arab Nationals, as against two foreign banks, for the recalculation of interest payments charged over the period of 10-15 years, on the grounds that Abu Dhabi law prohibits interest in excess of the State ceiling of 12% (simple) per annum. Throughout the period, interest rates in the UAE had been invariably in excess of the ceiling, so that the effect of the suit would have had dire economic consequences for the banks.[104] In Abu Dhabi, the Code of Civil Procedure provides that interest may be awarded on judgment amounts at rates up to 12% for commercial transactions and 9% for other, non-commercial, transactions. These provisions have been upheld by decisions of the Federal Supreme Court in 1983[105] and have commonly been interpreted to apply directly to interest on the original principal amount claimed. A 1981 ruling of the Federal Supreme Court expressly found that interest at compound rates was illegal.

In mid-1987, in a letter addressed to the Chief Justice of Abu Dhabi *Sharīʻa* Court, the Director of the Presidential *Dīwān* stated that henceforth jurisdiction of disputes involving banks or negotiable instruments transactions is withheld from the *Sharīʻa* Courts, and that all pending cases are to be transferred to the Civil Courts.[106] This was followed by an

---

[102] *Arab Law Newsletter*, No.8 (June 1986) p.1

[103] *Arab Law Newsletter*, No.18 (May 1987) p.4

[104] *Arab Law Newsletter*, (May 1986) No.7 p.4

[105] *Arab Law Newsletter*, (May 1986) No.7 p.4

[106] This was already the case in Dubai and Sharjah, where Civil Courts are granted exclusive jurisdiction over banking transactions by Decrees of the Rulers. *Arab Law Newsletter*, No.20 (Jul/Aug 1987)

amendment to the Abu Dhabi Code of Civil Procedure[107] which expressly provided that in interest rate disputes the court should honour the rates contracted by the parties, or otherwise applied in practice, for the period up until the filing of the lawsuit. Thereafter courts will apply the commercial interbank rate of a maximum 9% (simple) in all transactions. The maximum statutory interest rates are therefore applicable only in absence of specific agreement between the parties.[108]

It retrospect, it seems doubtful that the Federal legislative powers of the UAE harboured any real hopes of re-introducing the *Ribā* prescription into commercial transactions. Certainly, Banking Institutions were adamant in their opposition; in addition, the Civil Courts of Dubai[109] award interest at variable rates according to the Kuwait dichotomy of Civil/Commercial contracts, while in Sharjah,[110] the Courts will authorise the award of interest in accordance with otherwise valid agreements between the parties. Similarly, in 1986, the Ruler of Umm al-Quwayn issued a Decree expressly to fill the lacuna in the Federal legislation, declaring that contractual interest payment on bank loans and deposits is lawful and effective, and will be enforced by the National Civil Courts. The decree also outlawed appeals from judicial decisions upholding contractual interest rates without prior approval of the Ruler or the Deputy Ruler.[111] Western-style banking methods are already so deeply engrained (and welcomed) into the structure of commercial life that it now seems unlikely that they will be replaced fully by Islamic Banking methods in the foreseeable future. Indeed, if such a project were ever to work, it would require the unanimity of the whole banking structure, not just on a national scale, but also on an international scale, for the prescription to work the whole length of the reinvestment chain. Until international banking systems can be persuaded of the advantages of Islamic Banking therefore, the prospect seems unlikely. With the latest submission to the Kuwaiti dichotomy of *Ribā* rulings in the Federal legislation of the UAE, it seems that any attempt to convince the West of the advantages of Islamic Banking by example, has suffered something of a defeat.

---

107 Abu Dhabi Law No. 3 of 1987 (Issued September 1987) Effective as of publication : *Official Gazette*, 1 Aug. 1987; *Arab Law Newsletter*, No.22 (Oct.1987) p.3

108 At Oct. 1987 separate Federal Legislation regarding bank interest was still under discussion; the procedure of Abu Dhabi is commonly followed meanwhile by the other Emirates.

109 But not the *Sharī'a* Courts.

110 Where Courts operate under a decree of the Ruler

111 *Arab Law Newsletter*, No.12 (Nov. 1986) p.3

Writing as one of the first Westerners on the subject, Schacht established the Western Orientalist approach to *Maysir* and *Ribā*. Although the prohibitions are directly concerned with certain types of legal transactions, he states, they are "not meant to lay down legal rules regulating the form and effects of these transactions, but to establish moral norms under which certain transactions are allowed or forbidden."[112] He goes on to say : "The idea that such transactions, if they are concluded notwithstanding the prohibition, are invalid and do not create obligations, does not, as yet, appear in the Koran." The point inclines towards the sublime : as with all "illegality", the question is a matter for the individual conscience. It cannot be expected, on the other hand, that constitutions claiming the *Sharī'a* as the principal source of law[113] would uphold such contracts, or make them invalid subject to the removal of offensive *Ribā* clauses. Nor is it safe to assume that such contracts would be upheld in constitutions where the *Sharī'a* is determined to be a source of law,[114] unless sanctioned either by express provision, or by an accompanying constitutional clause which dictates that freedom of contract has precedence over the laws of the *Sharī'a*. There is, of course, no such clause in any of the modern Gulf Constitutions, nor is there likely to be.

The only degree of predictability to be hoped for in this matter is derived from jurisdictions such as Kuwait, whose separate Codes provide unambiguous regulations concerning the matter of *Ribā* and the enforcement of *Ribawī* contracts by the Courts, setting out clearly the State-imposed limits where relevant. That does not mean to say, however, that the matter is as predictable in practice. Increasingly, also, there are lawyers and judges who refuse to entertain cases involving *Ribā* as a matter of conscience.

The problem of riba and interest rates is probably beyond prescription: in practice the matter can only be determined by the conscience of each

---

112 Schacht, *Introduction, op.cit.*, p.12

113 Such as Qatar, Egypt since 1980; Saudi Arabia and Oman (though the latter are without constitutions as such). But see Vogel, 'Decision No.822 on Banking Disputes: An Analysis', *Middle East Executive Report*, (April,1986) pp. 9, 22, where regulations or statutes contravening the *Sharī'a* are held as 'unconstitutional' in Saudi where the *Qur'ān* is the sole constitution. (Royal Decree '[O]ur Constitution is the Qur'ān': *Umm al-Qura*, No.1320 (July 19, 1950). See also, Asherman, 'Doing Business in Saudi Arabia: The Contemporary Application of Islamic Law', *International Lawyer*, (1982) pp.321, 322 n.5

114 For example, Kuwait, Bahrain and the UAE. See Ballantyne, 'The Shari'a : A Speech to the IBA Conference in Cairo', *Arab Law Quarterly*, 2(2), (Feb. 1987) p.14; and O'Sullivan, Edmund, 'Islamic Insurance', *Arabian Insurance Guide*, (1984) pp.44ff. and Jabsheh, 'UAE Insurance Market', *Arabian Insurance Guide*, (1984) pp.92-93

individual Muslim. Express legislation against *Riba* would require both a finite definition of the term, and, preferably, a multilateral declaration of the same among the Muslim Arab countries. It is perhaps only a consensus of the jurists which could settle the matter, but if the "doors of *Ijtihād*" remain open, there is nothing to suggest that a later concensus of jurists may not similarly reverse the decision. Savigny wrote, "Legislation can succeed only if it is in harmony with the internal convictions of the race to which it is addressed. If it goes farther, it is doomed to failure."[115] In the case of *Ribā*, legislation may be considered out of place for the very reason that a purely religious law, practised according to the individual conscience and interpreted in different ways by different people is not only difficult to prescribe in a hard and fast way, but would also, probably, be viewed as an imposition of the State. In religious terms, it could be argued as an equivalent to the prohibition of alcohol, presently the law in, *inter alia*, Kuwait and Sharjah. Moreover, the proscription of interest would be extremely difficult to enforce, given the proliferation of foreign financial institutions within the Gulf region: indeed, the effects on the economy would be significant.

The present status of *Ribā* in the Gulf States under study is actually quite liberal, for it allows a - limited - right to choose, whilst endeavouring to prevent the worst of corruption and exploitation.

The fact, therefore, that modern commercial legislation upholds the collection of interest and is prepared to award legal recognition to contracts which are undeniably *ribawī*, does not settle the problem once and for all. The legal protection for such contracts is, in any case, not predictably assured in any of the Gulf Constitutions, there being clear examples of the Courts' reluctance to avoid the Islamic prohibition, and a similar reluctance manifested by lawyers of these jurisdictions to defend cases seeking restitution of interest payments.[116] The consequence must, understandably, be that parties entering into any contract tainted with *Ribā*, should not automatically anticipate that the courts will enforce it, although where there are express provisions, it is likely that these will be upheld, subject to no other illegality. In this case, the courts would nevertheless apply 'equitable' remedies to restore the parties to the position they were in prior to contracting. Thus, in the *Sharī'a*, a buyer having derived benefits from the object of contract would be required to pay compensation to the seller for

---

115 Paton and Derham, *A Textbook of Jurisprudence*, p.19

116 The Kuwaiti legal journal *Majallat al-Qaḍā' wa'l-Qānūn*, Year 9: Issue Nos.1 + 2 cites a judgment given by the Court of Cassation in the High Court of Appeal, Session 25/6/1980 at p.127 : the plaintiff has to request interest payment, otherwise it will be waived by default.

those benefits he had enjoyed before avoidance of the contract.[117] The stance clearly reflects the ever-present dichotomy between legal theory and practice. It also reflects a dichotomy between the exerted efforts of the legislative councils to achieve a rational and acceptable compromise, wherein the stricter Islamic doctrines may lie comfortably alongside the tenets of modern commercial exigencies, and at the same time, respecting the desire of the judiciary and practising lawyers to uphold both their own Islamic convictions in their professional practices, and those of the majority of the communities for which they work.

6.7.3 GHARAR

The *Sharī'a* determined that in the interests of fair, ethical dealing in commutative contracts, unjustified enrichment should be prohibited. This policy precludes any element of uncertainty or risk (*Gharar*).[118] In a general context, the unanimous proposition of the jurists held that in any transaction, by failing or neglecting to define any of the essential pillars of contract relating to the consideration or the object, the parties undertake a risk which is not indispensable for them. This kind of risk was deemed unacceptable and tantamount to speculation due to its inherent uncertainty. Speculative transactions with these characteristics are therefore prohibited on the basis of *Maysir*, *Gharar* and *Ribā*. Contracts in this category are deemed null and void.[119]

All details as to consideration, the precise date of payment thereof if it is to be a deferred payment contract, the sum and the currency or commodity; the identification of the subject matter, its quality and quantity; the date of delivery if it is to be a *Salam* contract; and any other pertinent and necessary details of the contract must be established between the contractors at the time of contracting in order to prevent *Gharar*.[120] A certain

117 P.D. Sloane, 'The Status of Islamic Law In The Commercial World', *International Lawyer*, (Fall 1988) 22(3) p.746

118 *Gharar* is rarely definitively defined in the Classical texts. See Saleh, *Unlawful Gain, op.cit.*, pp. 50-51

119 On such grounds Ibn Taymiyya proscribed the contracts involving the purchase of a run-away slave, a strayed animal, or a foetus. In fact, these contracts are already precluded as contravening the *Sharī'a* in that they do not satisfy the precepts governing existence and delivery of the object. Ibn Taymiyya, *Fatāwā*, (Cairo, 1384-1386/1965-1966) I, 490; II,10

120 Hamilton, *The Hedaya, op.cit.*, p.274; Sanhūrī, *Maṣādir al-Ḥaqq*, III, 49; Ibn Juzayy, *Qawānīn*, pp. 282-3; Ibn Rushd, *Bidāyat al-Mujtahid*, II, pp.148, 172. See also Saleh, *Unlawful Gain, op.cit*, pp.51-52.

imprecision of date is allowed only when the period of repayment is ascertainable within the knowledge of both parties. A contract for payment "Three days after Harvest", for instance, would be invalid for *Gharar*. This rule does not apply to payments of bail and debts however. In these latter contracts a small degree of uncertainty is tolerated.[121]

In this context it is illuminating to compare three different hyperthetical cases:-

(A) A concludes a contract of sale with B for a commodity for immediate delivery, for which A agrees to pay B "three days after harvest".

(B) C concludes a contract of sale with D for a commodity to be delivered immediately and payment to be forty days hence. C subsequently agrees to receive the price "three days after harvest".

(C) E concludes a contract of sale with F for a commodity to be delivered immediately, and for payment to occur "on the return of the pilgrims". Subsequently, the parties jointly, or F alone either pays the price or affixes the time of payment to a specific date.

In case (A) the contract is clearly invalid on the grounds of *Gharar* for the unascertainability of the term of payment, "three days after harvest". In case (B) the original sale is valid for the term is precisely defined. But what of the subsequent uncertain clause ? Here the contract remains valid, since the additional stipulation was not included in the original contract of sale. It therefore becomes a stipulation with regard to payment of debt (not the price) which allows of a certain degree of uncertainty.[122] Case (C) is initially invalid on the same grounds as case (A). However, it is held by the majority of scholars that the subsequent ascertainment of the price, either by its actual payment or by assigning a definitive date for payment, removes the uncertainty and renders the contract perfectly valid.[123] The validation of this type of contract is arguable : the original justification for invalidating the uncertain contract is the apprehension of dispute. Once the uncertainty is removed, the scholars reason, there is no room for litigation and the sale remains valid. This is legitimate because the uncertainty in this case relates only to an "accidental circumstance" (the period at which the price is to be paid) rather than an essential pillar of the contract (for instance, the price itself).

Sales generally involving non-existent or future objects such as future crops are void on the ground of *Gharar*. By reason of expediency however, certain commercial exceptions in this domain have been permitted to slip

---

121 Hamilton, *The Hedaya, op.cit.*, p. 274

122 See supra, and Hamilton, *The Hedaya, op.cit.*, p.274

123 This is, however, subject to dissent: eg. Ziffer; cf. Hamilton, *ibid.*, p.275

through the blanket prohibition of *Gharar*. In cases where the value of the commodity is not precisely known, for example in *Muzābana* contracts,[124] or in certain barter contracts such as the barter of livestock for meat,[125] or the lease of land (for monetary payment),[126] the jurists attempted to circumvent the illegality of the contract by *Ḥiyal* or by re-terming the uncertainty as '*Mukhāṭara*' (risk).[127] *Mukhāṭara* by practice, therefore, came to purport acceptable or expedient risk. Socially indispensable transactions that cannot be entirely freed of uncertainty have generally been considered as permissible. Thus the contract of *Muḍāraba* is valid even though compensation (capital) and amount of labour might not be specified at the time of contracting.[128] If the uncertainty exceeds all reasonableness however, the transaction will be forbidden. Inevitably, the question arises as to where that acceptable level of uncertainty may be drawn; and just as inevitably, the opinions differ throughout the Schools. In consideration of jurisprudential problems such as 'whether it is permissible to sell fruits in an orchard before they have ripened' Muslim Fiqh delves into depths of hypothesis and casuistry which is more redolent of philosphy than law.

6.7.4 MAYSIR

The theory of *Gharar* is based on the Qur'ānic prohibition of *Maysir*.[129] The prohibition of *Maysir* arises from the premise that an apparent agreement between two parties is in actuality the result of immoral inducement provided by false hopes in the parties' minds that they will profit unduly by the contract. Little consideration is given by the parties to the risk of loss, nor would it be likely that they would participate in gambling contracts in

---

124 Contracts whereby dates growing on the tree are sold in exchange for those which have already been harvested.

125 Mālik, *al-Muwaṭṭa*; al-Qurṭubī, *al-Jāmi' li-Aḥkām al-Qur'ān*, (Cairo, 1967) II, 54

126 Ibn Ḥajar, *Fatḥ*, V, 423

127 Schacht, 'Ḥiyal', *Encyclopoedia of Islam*2, (New Edition, Leiden, 1971), vol. III, p.511. Also Suyūṭī, *Tanwīr al-Ḥawālik: Sharḥ Muwaṭṭa' al-Imām Mālik*, 3 Vols. (Cairo, 1348 AH) Vol. II, pp. 55,75

128 Coulson, *Commercial Law, op.cit.*, p.23; Saleh, *Unlawful Gain, op.cit.*, pp.101 f.

129 *Qur'ān*, (II:219), (V, 93-94), (IV, 29). cf. also al-Bukhārī, to *Sūra* LIII, concordance V, 466 a, 8-12 (Verses on gambling often also encompass prohibitions against wine and idolotry).

the expectation of loss.[130] This prohibition was extended by the jurists to cover all speculative and aleatory contracts, and also those where the obligations or advantages of either party are not fully defined at the time the contract is entered into. It is upon the prohibitions of *Maysir* and *Gharar* that the Western concept of Insurance is forbidden in Islamic law.

Muslim philologians have established that the term *Maysir* was originally applied to a pre-Islamic game of arrows in which seven participants gambled for shares of an allotted prize.[131] The term literally means a way of obtaining something too easily, and deriving unearned profit, hence gambling.[132] It was principally the ambiguity concerning the scope of the Qur'ānic precept which provided the impetus for the many subsequent discussions and references. Although the legal-religious term for 'forbidden' (*Ḥarām*) is not used in the *Qur'ān* in conjunction with *Maysir*, the severity of the prohibition is indicated by its close link to idolatry and wine,[133] and the use and consumption of pork.[134] The Qur'ānic disapprobations emphasize both the individual and social vices of *Maysir*.[135] Nevertheless, there is nothing in these verses to indicate that *Maysir* may mean anything more than the name of a particular game. Despite the Qur'ānic imprecision of the concept, the legal classification of *Maysir* was unassailable.[136] It was left to later jurists to designate the term specifically to all kinds of gambling,

---

130 Mawdūdī, *Tafhīm al-Qur'ān*, cited in Abdur Rahman I. Doi, *Shari'ah: The Islamic Law*, (London, 1984), p.351; See also Bakhūrī, *Taqṣīrāt Tafhīm*, (A Study of Abū 'Alā' Mawdūdī's *Tafhīm al-Qur'ān*, (Bijnaur, 1979). For the "immoral" reasoning, See Nawāwī's *Minhaj al-Ṭālibīn*, (Cairo, 1319 AH); Translated into French by L.W.C. Van der Berg, into English by E.C. Howard, (London, 1914), Bk. 62, P.483 ff.

131 Usually a camel, divided into ten parts. cf. A. Huber, *Über das "Meisir" Genannte Spiel der Heidnischen Araber*, (Doctoral Thesis: Leipzig, 1883); 'Abd al-Salām M. Harūn, *al-Maysir wa al-Azlām*, (Cairo, 1953). For descriptions of pre-Islamic gambling, cf. Ibn Ḥabīb, *Muḥabbar*, ed. I. Lichtenstaedter, (Hyderabad, 1361/1942).

132 Yusuf Ali, *The Holy Qur'ān, Text Translation, Commentary, op.cit.*, p.86 (Commentary to *Qur'ān*, (II,219); Fakhr al-Dīn Rāzī, *Mafātīḥ al-Ghayb*, known as *al-Tafsīr al-Kabīr*, (Cairo, 1324 AH; 1353-1381/1934-1962) II, p.231 (*Tafsīr Ṣūrat al-Mā'ida*, verse 90). The origin of the term has been subject to much conjecture by lexicographers : their inability to reach any unanimous theory would seem to indicate that its original meaning has been lost in antiquity. See also F. Rosenthal, *Gambling In Islam*, (Leiden, 1975), pp. 74-76

133 al-Zamakhsharī, *al-Kashshāf 'An Ḥaqā'iq al-Tanzīl wa 'Ayūn al-Aqāwīl Fī Wujūh al-Ta'wīl*, 4 Vols. (Bulaq, 1318-1319; Cairo, 1354 AH; 1385/1966) I, p.433

134 al-Bukhārī, *al-Adab al-Mufrad*, ed. M.F. 'Abd al-Bāqī, (Cairo, 1375), p.326

135 In the *Jāhiliyya*, it was not uncommon for men to gamble (*khaṭara*) recklessly with their property and family (*ahl*): al-Qurṭūbī, *al-Jāmi' li Aḥkām al-Qur'ān*, (Cairo, 1967), II, p. 52; and al-Ṭabarī, *Tafsīr*, (New Edn; Cairo, 1961?), X, p.573

136 Rosenthal, *Gambling*, *op.cit.*, p.84; *Qurān*, II:219

whether for a prize (*al-Mukhāṭara 'alā ju'l*) or betting for a stake (*al-Munāhaba 'alā rahn*).[137] They did this by projecting the *'Illa* (Cause) from the Qur'ānic prohibition to apply comprehensively to risk-taking and gambling (*Qimār*) based on certain authoritative statements attributed to the Prophet.[138] Thus *Maysir* and *Qimār* were established in their broader terms in a similar way to the general interdiction against alcohol. The jurists drew the simple conclusion that if a given activity could be declared to be, or in some way defined as, *qimār*, it was clearly illegal.[139] The legal principle to which the Islamic objection to gambling is attributed is that even if a gamble does not comprise fraud, the winner has not earned that which he has won, and the loser loses on the mere chance.[140] The comparable social consequences of gambling, such as the acquisition of property, charitable donations made by generous winners, and the pleasure of play, were considered insufficient to outweigh the harm and loss attendant upon its participation.[141] The influence of gambling on the public economy is a question open to speculation, although for private individuals the economic effects of this past-time, even on a comparatively small scale, might easily have led to financial ruin. Even so, it is not likely that such sporadic economic consequences of gambling ever translated into social terms.[142] It was fundamentally the effect of gambling upon the physical and spiritual constitution of the compulsive gambler which was given greatest consideration by the jurists : the effect of gambling was regarded as similar to that of alcohol. Speculation, like alcohol, they said, leads to the neglect of religious duties.[143]

In metaphysical terms, it could also be stated that the role accorded to chance (*Ittifāq*) and astrological determinism (*al-Sihām al-Falakiyya*) in

137 Fakhr al-Dīn al-Rāzī, *Mafātiḥ al-Ghayb*, (Cairo, 1353-1381/1934-1962), VI, pp. 48ff., who relates on the authority of Ibn Sirīn, Mujāhid and 'Ata: 'Everything involving a stake (*Khaṭar*) comprises *Maysir*, even the walnut game of children'. See also Kāsānī, *al-Badā'i'*, *op.cit.*, VI, p.206 f.

138 Rosenthal, *Gambling, op.cit.*, p.78 suggests that the *Maysir* game no longer existed at the time of the Prophet and that he used *Maysir* as a generic term for gambling. This may explain why the game was unknown by the late eighth century.

139 Rosenthal, *Gambling, op.cit.*, p.85

140 A. Yusuf Ali, *The Holy Qur'ān, op.cit.*, p.86; al-Qurṭūbī, *al-Jāmi' li-Aḥkām, op.cit.*, II, 57

141 See the views of the thirteenth century jurist, 'Abd al-'Azīz Ibn 'Abd al-Salām, *Qawā'id*, (Cairo, 1388/1968), I. p.98; and Fakhr al-Dīn al-Rāzī, *Mafātiḥ, op.cit.*, IV, 50; XII, 80

142 See Rosenthal, *Gambling, op.cit.*, p.157

143 Ibn Taymiyya, *Fatāwā*, (Cairo, 1384-1386/1965-1966), II, 16-21; al-Zamakhsharī, *al-Kashshāf 'An Ḥaqā'iq al-Tanzīl, op,cit.*, I, 433

gambling is in a sense a mockery of the divine purpose. The elements of hazard and risk themselves raised profound theological and philosophical questions relating to the clarification of important moot problems such as predestination (*Qadar*) and pre-determination (*Jabr*) versus free will and chance.[144]

Despite the *Sharī'a's* general acceptance of speculation in commerce, the Islamic prohibition did extend to certain business activities which were prevalent in the pre-Islamic Arabian Peninsular, and which contained extreme or unnecessary degrees of speculation.[145]

Sandwiched between the two poles of commerce and frivolous diversion are sporting contests, such as shooting and racing (*an-Nidāl wa al-Sibāq*). Sporting contests are expressly approved by the Ḥadīth and the Sunna, on the grounds of military and physical expedience,[146] and the presence of a *Muḥallil*[147] which eliminates gambling.[148] The prize money for such competitions became known by a commercial term, *'Iwād*, possibly in order to indicate 'compensation' for participants' expenses incurred by competing.[149] The establishment of an *'Iwād* was regarded as a contract, but its enforceability was subject to debate between the schools. The Shāfi'ī's regarded it as fully binding (*Lāzim*) but elsewhere the contract was treated as an award (*Ju'āla*), which became enforceable upon execution of the condition.[150] Alternatively, it was considered in the Mālikī school as a

---

144 This was only applied to gambling generally in the early history of Islam. Since the ninth century, it was applied solely to the games of *Nard* and chess. The metaphysical arguments involved nevertheless reflect sectarian differences between the Mu'tazilites, the Zoroastrians, the religionists, the dualists and the Sūfis. cf. Rosenthal, *Gambling, op.cit.*, pp.158-171

145 The contracts of *Muzābana, Muḥāqala, Mulāmasa, Munābaza*, and *Bay' al-Ḥiṣṣa*, will be dealt with in the next section.

146 See Tradition related in al-'Imrānī, *al-Bayān Fī al-Furū'*, MS Brit. Mus. Or.3739, fol. 77b, chapter on al-Sabq wa al-Rāmī

147 The *Muḥallil* is a person whose presence legalizes an activity which would otherwise be illegal, such as that of a *Wālī* in a marriage. cf. Ibn 'Abd al-Salam, *Qawā'id, op,cit.*, II, 184. The *Muḥallil* does not lose anything and may gain, but without incurring any risk. The distinction being that in gambling there are only winners and losers, but that in sporting contests there are other competitors too. cf. al-Subki, *Fatāwā*, (Cairo, 1355-1356), II, 421ff.

148 This distinction was rejected by both the Mālikīs [cf. Khalīl, *Mukhtaṣar*, trans. G.H. Bousquet (Algiers, 1956), I, 219ff.] and Ibn Taymiyya [*Fatāwā, op.cit.*, III, 121 ff] who was obviously supported by Ibn Qayyim al-Jawziyya [*Furūsiyya, op.cit.*, 20, 61, 74] despite his ostensible approval.

149 Rosenthal, *Gambling, op.cit.*, p.97

150 Rosenthal, *ibid.*, p.100

contract for service or hire (*Ijāra*).[151] The Ḥanbalī Ibn Qayyim al-Jawziyya, after fruitlessly attempting to compare it to contracts of *Ju'āla, Ijāra, Mushārika*, general vows and obligations (*Nudhūr, Iltizāmāt*) or promises and gifts (*'Idāt, tabarru'āt*), determined finally that it was analogous to none of these and classified it as a separate nominate contract.[152] In any event, the ingenious criterion of military expediency eliminated the stigma of *Bāṭil* from sporting contests as it could be extended to almost any competitive sport.[153] Gambling by participants and non-participants alike nevertheless remained completely illegal.[154]

As with certain other Islamic prohibitions, the sin of *Maysir* held no specified sanction. Such sanction as was given, was meted at the discretion of the judge. The effect of having been convicted of gambling however, was the loss of normal civil rights, for a gambler was regarded as lacking in *Murūwah* (Manliness).[155] As *Murūwah* constitutes one of the essential requirements for an individual to qualify as a witness (*Shāhid*), a gambler would automatically be precluded from giving legal testimony.[156] Needless to say, very little material is to be found relating to official sanctions given for convictions of gambling. The characteristic privacy of its pursuit and prevailing social conditions appear to have prevented most *Maysir* offences

---

151 The latter permitted unequal stakes. It is uncertain whether the donor of a stake may compete for and therefore possibly win the stake; al-Dimyāṭī seems to think that most *'Ulamā'* would approve this provided the donor donates the prize to charity if he wins. *Faḍl al-Khayl*, fol. 89 a [MS Bodleian Marsh, 889]

152 Ibn Qayyim al-Jawziyya, *Furūsiyya*, ed. 'Izzat al-'Attar al-Husaynī, (Beirut, n.d. [1974?], 75-78

153 See, for example, al-Imrānī, *al-Bayān Fī al-Furū'*, *op.cit.*, fols. 77b-78b; al-Nawāwī, *Minhāj*, ed. L.W.C. Van den Berg (Batavia, 1882-1884) III, 319f; al-Rāfi'ī, *Muhanar*, fol. 267 a-b MS Brit. Mus. Or. 4285, fol 110b. This is upheld by UAE Civil Code Arts. 1012-1020.

154 Rosenthal, *ibid.*, p.109

155 "*Laysa min ṣan'at ahl al-dīn wa-lā al-murūwah*" (Play is not what Muslims do; it does not go with true manliness) al-Shāfi'ī, *Kitāb al-Umm*, (Bulaq 1324) VI, p.213. For the legal understanding of *Murūwah*, See al-Nawāwī, *Minhāj*, (Batavia, 1882-1884), III, 402f. For *Sāqiṭ al-Murūwah*, See also al-'Amilī, *Miqlāt*, (Cairo, 1282 AH/ 1865; 1317) p.62

156 Rosenthal, *Gambling*, *op.cit.*, pp.10, 93-94: according to al-Shāfi'ī, a person would be precluded only if it was known that he had neglected the prescribed duty of prayer through disrespect (*Istikhfāf*) brought about by his absorption in the game. See the Ḥanafī Qāḍīkhān, *Fatāwā al-Khāniyya*, (Calcutta, 1835) III, 321. According to Mālik, if he played constantly, he was considered lacking in *murūwah*; if he only played occasionally, and was considered otherwise an *'Adl*, he was acceptable as a witness. cf. al-Shāfi'ī, *Kitāb al-Umm*, (Bulaq, 1924) VI, 213; Sahnūn, *Mudawwana*, (Cairo, 1323) XIII, 3; Ibn Qayyim al-Jawziyya, *Furūsiyya*, *op.cit.*, p.23

from ever having reached the courts.[157] In any event, there is little evidence in the sources to indicate that either the large merchant clans or the religious scholars indulged in gambling activitites to any inordinate extent.[158] Even though this must be seen in the light of the general sparsity of information available to us concerning the private lives of the merchant classes, it would not be unreasonable to assume that official action against gambling was rarely enforced or necessary. Al-Khuzā'i cites an official complaint sent by a secretary of the Caliph al-Mahdī to the governor of Mecca, about general gambling activities.[159] It may be presumed that on this occasion government intervention against gambling did occur. We are not told precisely what form it took. Nor are we informed as to the nature or extent of government sanctions meted in conjunction with raids upon gambling dens (*Dūr al-Muqāmirīn*) under the *Ikhshīd* of Egypt, other than a rather moralistic account of a *Mutammi'* (literally, "making greedy") being brought to account for his greed.[160] Al-Bukhārī recounts that 'Alī confined serious gamblers (*Yu'āmilūn bi al-warq*) for a day; those who played for fun he confined for half a day.[161] It is reported elsewhere that he also refused to acknowledge them,[162] a practice said to have been ordered by the Prophet.[163] In general it would appear that what worldly punishments are reported have a tendency to be directed more towards public humiliation than serious sanctions. Ibn

157 The likely guardian would have been the *Muḥtasib* or market supervisor whose authority was subject to restrictions related to transgressions committed in the privacy of the home. See al-Mawardī, *al-Aḥkām as-Sulṭaniyya*, (Cairo, 1298) pp.238f. On the Muḥtasib see Crone, *Roman, Provincial and Islamic Law, op.cit.*, pp.107-108

158 Rosenthal, *Gambling, op.cit.*, p.146. It may be noted that the reckless gambler lover of the *Thousand and One Nights* was set against a merchant background. See 49th and 846-847th Nights in [Ed.] Sir W.H. Macnaghten, *Arabian Nights: The Alif Laila; or the Book of the Thousand Nights and One Night*, (4 Vols: Calcutta, 1839-1842) I, 375; IV, 194ff.

159 "*Nard, qimār, Maysir*, chess and frivolous pursuits (*abāṭil*)": F. Wüstenfeld, *Die Chroniken der Stadt Mekka*, (Leipzig, 1857-1861) IV, pp. 163,168; also cited in Rosenthal, *Gambling, op.cit.*, pp.37,156

160 A *Mutammi'* encouraged other gamblers to gamble even when they had lost all they carried with them. He would recieve a daily salary from the concessionaire (*Mutaqābil*) of the dicing den. cf. Ibn Sa'īd, *Mughrib*, ed. and transl. K.L. Tallquist Text 30, trans. 63 (Leiden, 1899); transl. A. Mez, *Die Renaissance des Islams*, (Heidelberg, 1922) p.324; Rosenthal, *Gambling, op.cit.*, p.144

161 al-Bukhārī, *al-Adab al-Mufrad*, ed. M.F. 'Abd al-Bāqī (cairo, 1375) p.326

162 Literally :'extended the *Salām* to them'. Ibn Abī Shaybah, *Muṣannaf*, fol. 72b [MS. Istanbul Nuru Osmaniye, 1219]

163 Ibn Ḥajar al-Haythāmī, *al-Zawājir 'an Iqtirāf al-Kabā'ir*, (Cairo, 1370/1951) II, 189; al-Dhahābī, *al-Kabā'ir*, (Cairo, 1385/1965) p.89. It seems the Malikis did not object to extending the Salām to *Nard* and chess players. cf. Ibn Abī Zayd, *Risāla*, ed. and transl. L. Bercher, (Third Edn; Algiers, 1949) pp. 324ff.

al-Zubayr (d. 73/692) threatened gamblers with beatings and having their heads shaved.[164] Severe beatings and banishment are also occasionally reported as having been imposed by the secular authorities.[165] The poet al-Talla'fārī (593-675 AH) was banished from Damascus for a while because of his excessive gambling. Those caught gambling with him in Aleppo were threatened with amputation of a hand.[166]

It may be said that muslim society regarded *Maysir* less as a public nuisance or economic danger, than as a private vice. Whatever arguments were applied to the social, metaphysical or economic consequences of *Maysir* and risk-taking activities, the disapprobation of the practice would appear to relate less to material concerns than to the general muslim pre-occupation with the concept of *Murūwah*. The implicit perception of gambling as a practice belonging to the dregs of society and "the deep-rooted feeling of metaphysical guilt which tended to inhibit the natural instinct for it",[167] therefore seems to have influenced and controlled the actual practice of gambling and risk-taking to a far greater extent than any amount of legislation or punitive sanctions. The fact that commerce has not managed to escape this general aversion to risk-taking, despite the ostensible loop-hole so adroitly provided by the Qur'ān in (IV:29), is perhaps an indication in itself of precisely how deep-rootedly this aversive influence is engrained.

6.7.5 The Modern Exposition

The Islamic prohibition against gambling (*Qamara*) and risk-taking (*Gharara*) is therefore firmly established. There are comparable aspects, however, which remain controversial even in modern times, as they bear relation to risk-taking and the derivation of 'unearned profit'. The institutions of Mortgages and Insurance, and the combined concepts of

---

164 al-Bukhārī, *al-Adab al-Mufrad, op.cit.*, p.328; and the excerpt from *Kitāb al-Thamān (MS. al-Tamr) al-Rā'iq al-Mujtana min al-Hadā'iq*, MS. Dublin Chester Beatty 4759, fols. 20b-21b (anon.) cited in Rosenthal, *Gambling, op.cit.*, p.92

165 Ibn Sa'īd al-Maghribī, *Mughrib*, ed. transl. K.L. Tallquist Text 30, Transl. 63 (Leiden 1899); Transl. A. Mez, *Renaissance, op.cit.*, p.324; Rosenthal, *Gambling*, p.144

166 Rosenthal, *Gambling, op.cit.*, p.147

167 Rosenthal, *Gambling*, p.171

Share-trading, Financial Futures,[168] and spot-commodity purchases would clearly be *Bāṭil* on several grounds according to the strict tenets of the *Sharī'a* : For leaving open the payment term (whether amount or due date); tying the payment term to some fluctuating standard such as market price or the rate of interest; by not taking possession of the object before resale; by making a contract conditional upon the occurrence of some uncertain event.[169] These controversial areas therefore lie somewhat juxtaposed between the established prohibition of *qamara* and the recognised necessity of modern business practice. The Qur'ānic verse "O you who believe! Do not consume your property among yourselves in vanities![170] But let there be amongst you traffic and trade by mutual goodwill"[171] draws an unambiguous distinction between unnecessary risks taken for frivolous purposes, and necessary risks encountered in pursuit of business. The risks attendant upon business were regarded as unavoidable. Islam therefore, if somewhat reluctantly, accepted the legality of some commercial transactions which were aleatory in nature because it recognised that all business ventures anticipating yield of profit inevitably entail certain incalculable and unavoidable risks. To deny this form of speculation would be to stifle the essence of enterprise which forms an indispensable process conducive to productivity. Clearly, it would not be beneficial to the economy to prohibit such activities as lead to the availability of new products, expansion and diversification of business ventures; and the maintenance of supply in proportion to demand; all of which require a willingness to face degrees of risk. Thus Islam recognises the economic validity of such speculative

---

168 Leggatt, J., defines a Futures Contract as "a legally binding commitment to deliver at a future date, or take delivery of, a given quantity of a commodity, or a financial instrument, at an agreed price. The contract is standardised in all respects except with regard to price and terms of delivery. Standardisation of contracts allows interchangeability with all other contracts of the same delivery period. This allows buyers and sellers to offset or liquidate any of their open positions with an equal and opposite transaction of a futures contract. Less than 2% of futures contracts culminate in the actual delivery of the physical commodity." *SCF Finance v. Khalil Masri*, 1 *All ER* (1986) at p.44

169 Coulson cites the example of a construction contract, which specifies the job to be done and a completion date, which is void for *Gharar* based on the uncertainty of completion : *Commercial Law*, p.90. It may be arguable here that under the exception of contracts of *Istiṣnā'* (for which See Saleh, *Unlawful Gain, op.cit.*, p.61), the term for expected completion may be stipulated.

170 (*bi al-Bāṭilī*)

171 *Qur'ān*, (IV:29) : (author's own translation)

business ventures as *Salam* sales and investments in partnerships.[172] Recognition having been given to the serious livelihood of commerce, and denied to the frivolous diversion of gambling, which often gives rise to hostility, deception and impecunity,[173] the need arises for a clearer differentiation between the two. When dealing with business risks and uncertainties, there are two kinds of risk at issue. The first is the incalculable risk encountered, for instance, when manufacturing new articles to be produced in a virgin market.[174] The second is pure risk which involves only fear of loss, without chance of gain, and which may be calculated according to the laws of probabilities and averages.[175] Gambling is distinguished from these business risks by the very fact that the risks involved in gambling are deliberately sought out and are the result of voluntary choice. Gambling risks entail both loss and gain, the hope of gain motivating the choice towards risk. In all three states under study, contracts incorporating gambling are null and void.[176]

Insurance

The dividing line between commerce and speculation in these days of Insurance policies, Stock Exchanges and Futures Markets is thin and is becoming narrower with increasing technology, which provides celerity and accuracy in the calculation of statistical probabilities and which avoids the necessity for delivery of commoditites.[177]

Mutual insurance, for example, may arguably provide a community with such benefits as may be deemed permissible in Islamic Law according to the principles of *Istiṣlāḥ* or *Istiḥsān*,[178] in that it is designed primarily for the re-

---

172 Rosenthal, *Gambling, op.cit.*, p.139; A. Udovitch, *Partnership and Profit In Medieval Islam*, (Princeton, 1970). It is pertinent to note that the UAE Federal Civil Code recognises contracts of *Salam* (Art.568:"Contract for forward sale") and *Muḍāraba* partnership (Art.691)

173 Rosenthal, *Gambling, op.cit.*, p.140

174 See Siddiqi, *Insurance in an Islamic Economy*, (Leicester, 1985; Transl. of 1973 Urdu Edn.), p.14

175 *idem.*, pp.14-15, 17

176 Bahrain, Contract Law, 1969, Arts. 34 (1), (2) and (3); Kuwait Civil Law Art. ; UAE Civil Law, Art. 1021.

177 See FN 168 on Financial Futures above.

178 See subsections on *Istiṣlāḥ* and *Istiḥsān Supra*.

allocation of risk.[179] There are, however, many forms of Life Insurance, which are merely thinly disguised investment methods, and the majority of insurance companies conduct their business in such pursuit of profit, by investing collected premiums and reinsuring with other insurers, thereby contravening the Islamic laws regarding both *Ribā* and *Gharar*.[180]

This type of insurance is therefore effectively a gamble upon the incidence of the contingency insured against, because the interests of both parties are diametrically opposed.[181] The only type of insurance that would appear to be lawful according to the *Sharīʻa* is a mutual insurance, where both parties share an equal risk and therefore both hope that the contingencies insured against will not occur. The main objection to this contract is that, at the time of its conclusion, the insurer, in the majority of cases, will not know, firstly, whether he will ever be required to pay out the claim that he has contracted to insure; and secondly, the precise sum of that claim payment.[182]

---

179 Thus held at the 1986 conference of Islamic Fiqh Academy, that co-operative insurance results in no unjustified profits for the insurance company as against the policy holders because, (a) the company is one of the policy holders, and (b) the profits are shared among the policy holders, not taken solely by the company.

180 But Saudi Arabia, which objects to life insurance contracts on this basis, does operate a State Social Assurance Scheme, which was brought into force by Royal Decree No. M/22 of 1989 AH. Haberbeck suggests that if the contract provided for profit shares rather than fixed interest, it would circumvent the Islamic prohibition of *Ribā*. See her article, 'Risk Sharing in an Islamic Society', in *Arab Law Quarterly*, 2(2) (May 1987) pp.140-141. This is equivalent to operating Insurance on a *Muḍāraba* basis, as suggested by, *inter alia*, Prince Muḥammad al-Faisal, from 'An Economic Model', (Ed. Ibnul Hassan), *Arabian Insurance Guide*, [Ed. Shahrukh A. Husain] (Northampton, 1984) p.68; Siddiqi, *Banking Without Interest*, (Leicester, 1983) p.13 ff.; See also Klingmuller, E., 'The Concept and Development of Insurance in Islamic Countries', *Islamic Culture*, XLIII, No.1 (Jan. 1969) at p.27 f. 'Islamic Banking : Progress and Obstacles', *Islamic Finance*, (July, 1983) pp.31-35, at p.35

181 Thus was insurance rejected by Islamic Scholars at the First International Conference on Islamic Economics held in Mecca in 1976, and upheld by the Saudi 'Ulamā' in 1977; It was reaffirmed by the Islamic Fiqh (Jurisprudence) Council at its second session held at Mecca in 1986, but with the express proviso that mutual Insurance is recognised. See Haberbeck, 'Risk Sharing in an Islamic Society' 2 *Arab Law Quarterly*, (1987) pp.138, 141, who surmises that the chief objection to insurance for profit rests on the *Maysir* element since the *Gharar* and *Juhāla* elements also exist in mutual insurance (p.141). See also *Middle East Executive Report*, (March, 1986) p.7

182 Except in contracts for life insurance, which meet with disapproval on alternative grounds, in any case (See *supra*); and contracts where total payment under the policy may be limited. This latter category is not, however, cleared of the uncertainty : the maximum sum is set only in cases of total loss, and amounts for partial destruction, disabilities, and so on are still unknown at the time of contracting. cf. Haberbeck, 'Risk Sharing in an Islamic Society', *op.cit.*, p.140

The majority of Arab countries do, however, recognise the legality of insurance contracts for the purpose of profit, and regulate them by statute.[183]

Bahrain

Insurance contracts are not specifically referred to in the contract Law of Bahrain but are recognised by virtue of the articles governing conditional contracts[184] in conjunction with general sanctity of contract.[185]

Kuwait

The Kuwaiti Civil Code devotes a comprehensive section in Chapter 4[186] to Insurance, which follows general civil law provisions, outlining execution of the contract,[187] obligations of the insured and insuror,[188] and the transfer of rights and obligations arising out of such contracts.[189]

United Arab Emirates

The articles governing insurance in the UAE Civil Code are comprehensive and pertain more to internationally recognised precepts than to the *Sharī'a*. Starting with 'payments for life',[190] the Civil Code sets out in detail the general provisions covering contracts of insurance,[191] the effects and obligations,[192] Fire Insurance,[193] and Life Insurance.[194] The first UAE national

---

183 See Egyptian Civil Code, No. 131 of 1948, Art. 747; For Iraq, see Anderson, *Law Reform In The Muslim World, op.cit.*, pp.96-97; Kuwait Civil Code, No. 67 of 1980, Art. 773; Omani Royal Decree No. 12 of 1979 *OGSO*, No. 67 (1 April 1979): 'The Insurance Companies Law', [together with Ministerial Decree of the Ministry of Social Affairs and Labour, Decision No. 5 of 1980, *OGSO*, No.192 (15 April 1980)]; for which see Hill, T.W., 'The Commercial Legal System of The Sultanate of Oman', 17 *International Lawyer*, (1983) at 507, 527.

184 Bahrain Contract Law of 1969, Arts. 35-39

185 *Ibid*, Art. 12(1)

186 Kuwaiti Civil Code, Arts. 773-809

187 *Ibid*, Arts. 775-789

188 *Ibid*, Arts. 790-798 and Arts. 799-801 respectively.

189 *Ibid*, Arts. 802-809

190 UAE Civil Code, Arts. 1022-1025

191 *Ibid*, Arts. 1026-1031

192 *Ibid*, Arts. 1032-1036

193 *Ibid*, Arts. 1037-1045

194 *Ibid*, Arts. 1046-1055

Insurance Company was founded in Abu Dhabi as the Abu Dhabi National Insurance Company, under Amīrī Decree No. 1 of 1972, and has subsequently been joined by a plethora of other 'fringe' insurers. The Government has consequently issued requirements relating to the formation and operation of these companies, in order to introduce some form of rationalisation.[195]

Share-Trading

The situation as regards Stock Exchanges has been clarified by virtue of official sanction and direct legislation, in some of the constitutions under study. Kuwait, for instance, has long operated the Sūq al-Manākh exchange, even though it has modified stock exchange regulations frequently since the crash of 1981.[196] Bahrain issued legislation in 1987 ratifying a stock exchange, which also authorises dealings in all commodities, financial futures and precious metals, so long as the stock reflects the actual performance of the company.[197] The position of share-trading within the confines of Classical Islamic law is rather more open to question. A case can be construed equally successfully for its definition as mere speculation, as it can for the argument that the underlying principles of such investments (*viz.* sharing the risk of profit or loss) is in harmony with the *Sharī'a* and by promoting industrial development constitutes legitimate business. In acknowledgement of this, Saudi Arabia has not launched a stock market. Yet the Saudi Government Financial and Economic Agency does operate a Stock Index and provides facilities for domestic security dealing, and the trading of shares by banks.[198]

The position as regards the more recent institutions of Financial Futures and Spot Markets is less certain; indeed, it seems to harbour a widespread and unmitigated suspicion towards speculation. There is little evidence to be found in the Gulf States, however, that any Financial Futures Exchange

---

195 See Jabsheh, 'UAE Insurance Market', *Arab Insurance Guide*, (1984) pp.92-93.

196 See, for example, Decree 1492 of 1983 (Regulating the Stock Market); Law 100/83 (regarding certain specific provisions concerning settlement of transactions relating to company shares concluded on credit); Decree 1505/83 Council of Ministers Resolution 46/83 amending certain provisions of Decree 57/82 (Concerning Credit Share Guarantee Documents); Ministerial Resolution 47/83 amending certain provisions of Resolution 5/83; Ministerial Resolution 35 of 1983 issuing the Internal Regulations of Kuwaiti Stock Market; Decree 1595/85 Resolution No. 1/75 (on composition of Stock Market Disciplinary Board)

197 Decree Law No. 4 of 1987, which permits trade in non-Bahraini securities listed by the exchange.

198 *Arab Law Newsletter*, No. 19 (June 1987) p.1

contract would be avoided on the grounds of *Maysir* or *Gharar.*

In a law suit brought within the United Kingdom, a Jordanian National sought to avoid payment of a loan given by his brokers (a British branch of an American corporation) for the purpose of further speculations on the Financial Futures Market, on the grounds that his speculations were unlawful according to Islamic law.[199] His suit failed in the English courts, not least because of a reliance upon an argument (dismissed on the basis of, *inter alia*, jurisdiction) which, had it been upheld, would have made a mockery of Western commercial regulations.

6.7.6 Conclusion

In conclusion, the comparative analysis *Ribā, Gharar* and *Maysir*, with regard to their former Classical expositions and the modern legislation of the Arab Gulf States under study, brings to light a re-emergence of the old dilemna of the dichotomy between practice and theory of the law. Yet it may be seen that in the modern codifications of these states, the position of the legislation with regard to *Ribā* and *Gharar* is emerging from the haze of uncertainty; it is, nevertheless, not crystal clear in all respects. Further, it is likely to be subject to change, depending on the expressed public and legal consensus of each locality. While the concepts of commercial interest and insurance are permitted, for instance, in theory, there remain a significant number of practising lawyers who will not defend cases whose main cause is the pursuit of *Ribā.* In addition, the contemporary trend of public opinion is largely against *Ribā*, despite the legality afforded by modern liberal interpretation of the concept.

In the short term at least, the legal status is quite clear. The civil laws, although sometimes ambiguously worded, nevertheless all give recognition to interest payments up to the relevant state ceiling, and to insurance contracts. The commercial laws are of necessity more amenable to the concepts of Freedom of contract, stipulations, and general international precepts, and all support interest payments up to the relevant higher commercial state ceiling. While in the narrower scheme, the parties may restrict their own contracts, it seems unlikely that these laws, in their present spirit, would seek to restrict further the freedom of commercial parties to enter into contracts of their own choosing.

The situation with regard to Islamic banking is presently somewhat tenuous. The divergence of opinions between the commercial bankers and the public customers, the Islamic bankers and the international community is resulting in a calvacade of new suggestions for an interest-free,

---

199 *SCF Finance Co. Ltd.* v. *Khalil Masri*, QB 1 *All ER* (1986) at p.40

internationally compatible system of banking. Whatever else may be said, the reintroduction in the post 1970's of operations traditional to the *Fiqh* within these sectors, and the increasing volume of Islamic banking methods since, is significant indication to the West that the Islamic provisions governing *Ribā, Gharar* and *Maysir* are not obsolete. There are at large, many Islamic financial institutions both within the Arab world and without, which offer an alternative, if not a challenge, to Western banking systems. By and large, the West has viewed the emergence of these institutions with a degree of scepticism and suspicion. While it is true that the western banking operating deficits have a lot to answer for, and that in their shadow, Islamic banking offers a clearer perspective, there is no reason to doubt that both systems can become fully operable on an international scale.

The legislative changes in the last four decades have shown that the *status quo* in Kuwait and the UAE is not stagnant as regards these Islamic concepts of *Ribā and Gharar*. The present legislation in these States belies the rift between the extremes of interpretation, and for the time being it represents a compromise based on civil law precepts. The very most to be hoped for is that any future course of this enigma may be determined in the light of a more constructive response from the West. Ideally, the outcome would be a transformation of both *Sharī'a* principles and secular precepts into an harmonious combination, to form a new individual system which finds acceptance within Islam and the West alike. The very least to be hoped for is that the legislation of the individual States will reflect the consensus of opinion in those States, couched in clear and unambiguous terms.

Chapter 7

THE ISLAMIC RIGHTS OF OPTION

The right of Option is accorded by the *Fiqh* as a unilateral "Choice" to cancel (*Faskh*) or to ratify (*Imḍā'*) a contract, in particular, a contract of sale.[1] If the option is to cancel, the effect is to render the situation as if the contract had never existed, although these acts are not void *ab initio* as in the case of contracts tainted with nullity. The *Fuqahā'* simply categorised them as valid legal acts subject to ratification. Until ratification or rejection, therefore, the acts are *Ghayr Lāzim*, or *Mawqūf*. Sanhūrī and Bellefonds draw a parallel here between acts giving rise to an option and the occidental acts affected by a condition; whether it consists of a suspended condition, or a condition of avoidance depends on the nature of the option.[2] Ratification, on the other hand, renders the obligation *Lāzim*.

The Islamic Rights of Option may be divided into two categories:

(1) Those which are created by the mutual consent of the contracting parties affecting the formation of the contract, such as the Option of acceptance or Rejection within the *Majlis*, the Option of Distinction, and the Option to defer payment within a specified time limit.

(2) Those which are created by operation of law affecting the binding force of the contract, such as the option for Misdescription, the Option of Inspection and the Option of Defect.[3]

1 See Schacht, *Introduction, op.cit.*, (1979) p.152

2 Sanhūrī, *Maṣādir al-Ḥaqq*, IV, p.216; Bellefonds, *Traité*, I, p.309

3 Bellefonds, *Traité*, (Paris, 1965) pp.309-311; Kourides, 'The Influence of Islamic Law on Contemporary Middle East Legal Systems: The Formation and Binding Force of Contracts', *Columbia Journal of Transnational Law*, 9:2 (1970) p.407; Hooper, *The Civil Law Of Palestine and Trans-Jordan*, (Jerusalem, 1936) pp.113-114

Bellefonds also recognises two categories of options, and determines them as "Conventional Options", which consist of *Khiyār al-Sharṭ* and *Khiyār al-Ta'yīn*; and "Legal Options", consisting of the Options of *'Ayb, Ru'ya, Tadlīs* and *Ghalaṭ*. Thus the "Conventional Options" are two, of which only one is recognised by all four Schools, while the other is only recognised by the Mālikī and Ḥanafī Schools. Coulson, on the other hand, divides options into the two categories of (1) those two options which "have the purpose of allowing the parties time for reflection", namely, the *Khiyār al-Majlis* and the *Khiyār al-Sharṭ*; and those which "concern contracts involving a blemish or irregularity and are therefore *fasid*", namely, the remaining four.[4]

The *Majella* recognises six options. These are the options of : Acceptance, which takes place within the *Majlis*;[5] Misdescription;[6] Non-Payment of the price (khiyār al-Naqd);[7] Selection (*Ta'yīn*);[8] Inspection;[9] and Defect.[10]

Sanhūrī, on the other hand, only recognises four options. These are the options of *Sharṭ*,[11] *Ta'yīn*,[12] *Ru'ya*,[13] and *'Ayb*.[14] The Options which arise in consequence of *Ghalaṭ* and *Tadlīs* and *Ikrāh* have been discussed already in

---

4 Coulson, *Commercial Law in the Gulf States*, p.57 *et seq.*

5 *Majella*, Art. 182

6 *Majella*, Art. 310 "If the vendor sells property as possessing a desirable quality and such property proves to be devoid of such quality, the purchaser has the option of either cancelling the sale or of accepting the thing sold for the whole of the fixed price". Hooper, *op.cit*, pp.310-311; and Introductory Remarks of the Report of the Committee drafting the Majella, p.ix; see also Art. 72 where no validity is attached to conjecture which is obviously tainted by error; and Saba Habachy, 'The System of Nullities In Muslim Law', *American Journal of Comparative Law*, 13 (1964) p.72

7 *Majella*, Arts. 313-315: If the payment of the price is not made within the term, or if the buyer dies within the term, the sale is cancelled. This option is also recognised by the UAE Federal Civil Code, Arts. 556-557 (2); and the Kuwaiti Civil Code, Arts. 329-335

8 *Majella*, Arts. 316-318; Also called 'Distinction', 'Designation' or 'Determination'. Here it is permissible to stipulate a term within which to make a selection and determine the choice from among a number of objects.

9 *Majella*, Arts. 320-335

10 *Majella*, Art. 336-355. See Hooper, *op.cit*., (1933) pp.248-266

11 Sanhūrī, *Maṣādir al-Ḥaqq*, IV, pp.217 ff.

12 Sanhūrī, *ibid*., IV, pp.234 ff.

13 Sanhūrī, *ibid*., IV, pp.248 ff.

14 Sanhūrī, *ibid*., IV, pp.268 ff.

their relevant Chapters.[15] The Option of Description (*Khiyār al-Waṣf*), which is occasionally referred to by Sanhūrī, is not discussed in a separate section, but is included in the section on *Khiyār al-'Ayb*, due to the concurrence of its principles with the latter.

The first Option which arises from the natural rights of the contracting parties during their contractual negotiations is called the Option of the Contractual Session.

7.1 KHIYĀR AL-MAJLIS

Shāfi'ī claims that the Option of *Majlis* originated with the Ḥijāzīs, and was taken up by the majority of the traditionists in most Muslim countries. Schacht, on the other hand, concludes that the idea of the *Khiyār al-Majlis* originated in Mecca, was taken up by the traditionists and was eventually acknowledged on the strength of the traditions from the Prophet, by al-Shāfi'ī.[16] In any event, the institution did not exist in the common doctrine of the Iraqis or Medinese, and may well have been the result of Meccan custom as Schacht suggests.[17] The Option of *Majlis*, does occur in Mālik, but the *Isnād* of the earliest Tradition is generally thought to be unreliable.[18] Thus the option is not generally recognised by the Ḥanafī and Mālikī schools. It does not, in any case, apply to unilateral contracts such as gift, *Waqf*, or *Ḥawāla* or *Shuf'a*; contracts of Agency; *Ju'āla* (reward); partnerships which are revocable by either partner, (including in the Ḥanbalī School, the partnerships of *Muḍāraba* and *Muzāra'a*);[19] or contracts of pledge and deposit which only become binding after delivery of the object and which are revocable by the owner of the object.

The option of *Majlis*, where it is recognised, exists during the period of the meeting for bargaining (*Majlis*), and commences with the offer, lasting for the period of the *Majlis*.[20] The option is available to either of the parties concerned, but various opinions exist as to whether the option may continue, either once the offer and acceptance have been made, or once it has been exercised. The rules pertaining to this option presuppose that the parties are

---

15 See Chapters 6.2, 6.3 and 6.4 respectively. Sarakhsī discusses *Khiyār al-Ikrāh* in his *Kitāb al-Mabsūṭ*, vol. XXIV, pp.135-144.

16 Schacht, *Introduction into Muslim Law*, (Oxford, 1979), pp.160-161

17 Schacht, *ibid.*, p.161

18 The *Isnād is : Nāfi'ī - Ibn 'Umar - The Prophet. This Isnād* is suspected of being the product of later collectors. See Schacht, *ibid.*, p.167

19 Ibn Qudāma, *al-Mughnī*, III, p.595. In the other schools these two contracts are classed in the category of contracts for service or hire, and do allow the option to operate.

20 *Majella*, Art. 182, subject, however, to Arts. 183 and 185

contracting *inter presentes*; by analysis, it should follow that the option is not available *inter absentes*, but, as has been noted earlier, the rule is hardly enforcable.[21]

The option is extinguished by :

(1) Natural termination of the *Majlis*;

(2) Unilateral renunciation of the option, whether express or implicit by conduct such as conversion or disposition;

(3) The death of either of the contracting parties;[22]

(4) Loss of the object during the *Majlis*. Ownership and risk pass with the conclusion of the contract except where fungible goods sold by weight or measure have not been transferred;

(5) By agreeing to a *Khiyār al-Sharṭ*.[23]

The *Majella* does not recognise the right of option if either party shows any sign of dissent, whereupon the offer becomes void.[24] The option also ceases according to the *Majella*, once the offer has been withdrawn.[25]

In the UAE Civil Code, the Option of *Majlis* is allowed until the end of the *Majlis*, and the offeror may retract prior to acceptance, or if either party gives any indication of resiling from the contract. It is not apparent, however, whether the party may retract after acceptance before the *Majlis* has ended, but the presumption must be that he may not.[26] The UAE legislation is constructed on the Shāfi'ī/Ḥanbalī doctrine, rather than the expected Ḥanafī, which would not have recognised the option.[27]

This Option has been discussed more fully in relation to the contractual Session above.[28]

---

21 See Chapter V, 'The Contract of Sale', Section 2.2.4, subsection 'Option of *Majlis*'. Sanhūrī, *Maṣādir al-Ḥaqq*, II, p.59; Hamid, 'Mutual Assent in the Formation of Contracts in Islamic Law', *JICL*, VII, p.52

22 Except in contracts of hire or service, which will be frustrated due to lack of subject.

23 Coulson, *Commercial Law in the Gulf States*, pp.59-60

24 *Majella*, Art. 183

25 *Majella*, Art. 184

26 See UAE Civil Code No.2 of 1987, Art. 136

27 Coulson seems to have expected this. See his *Commercial Law*, p.58

28 See Chapter V, 'The Contract of Sale', subsection 'Option of *Majlis*'.

7.2 KHIYĀR AL-SHARṬ

7.2.1 Incidence

Either or both parties to a contract may insert a condition into the contract giving them an option, within a fixed period of time, to either cancel or ratify the sale.[29] The clause containing the Option must be inserted or stated either simultaneously with the determination of the principal obligation, or immediately afterwards. The option here is equivalent to a suspended condition, and may thereafter be exercised by the party stipulating the condition as desired. That party is not, however, permitted to subordinate his option to some future, uncertain event, for this would amount to *Gharar*, and render the contract void.[30]

This Option operates solely upon the will of the stipulating contractor. As Bellefonds remarks, therefore, if, in a contract of sale, the seller stipulates that the sale will be concluded only after payment of the price, and that this payment must have taken place within the permitted delay,[31] we would not here be dealing with a sale accompanied by a stipulated option, but rather, a suspended condition. The operation of the obligation depends here upon a conditional element, namely, payment of the price within the permitted period, and not solely on the will of the contractor who stipulates the option.[32]

The origins of the Stipulated or Conditional Option appear to derive from an *Ḥadīth* of the Prophet : "The Prophet said to Habbān al-Anṣārī, who was complaining of being cheated in his transactions : When you buy or sell, at the moment of sale make a declaration to the effect 'that there shall be no cheating (*Lā khilāba*), and I reserve for myself the Option for three days.'"[33]

Stipulation of the *Khiyār al-Sharṭ* is permitted in any transactions whose obligation may be abrogated. It is therefore precluded from :

(1) Contracts which are irrevocable, for instance, marriage contracts and affranchisement of slaves;

---

29 *Majella*, Art. 300

30 A. d'Emilia, 'Il Ḥiyār aš-Šarṭ nel Aṣl di Šaibānī', *Rivista Degli Studi Orientali*, 32 (1957) pp.633-640

31 For which, see below.

32 Bellefonds, *Traité*, I, p.312

33 See Shawkānī, *Nayl al-Awṭār*, V, 155 for other variants of this *Ḥadīth*. Also Bellefonds, *Traité*, I, p. 313. The origins of this *Ḥadīth* seem directed at hasty transactions, and designed to afford both contracting parties time for reflection, hence the Mālikī title for the Option, "*Khiyār Sharṭ al-Tarawwā*: Option for Reflection".

(2) Contracts which are always subject to rescission by their author, for instance, contracts of Gift, 'Ārīya, and Deposit;

(3) Contracts which become binding upon the transference of possession, for instance *Salam* contracts.[34]

Third Party

The Option may be stipulated in favour of a third party.[35] This ruling is contrary to the conclusion determined by *Qiyās*, but is allowed on the basis of *Istiḥsān*, for the facility is requisite especially in cases of agents acting on behalf of their absent principals. The same rules apply as when the option is stipulated in favour of one of the contracting parties, therefore the option in favour of the third party must be declared at the same time as the principal obligation. Additionally, the third party must be designated precisely, to prevent the contract being tainted with *Gharar*.[36]

The third party is considered, in judicial reasoning, as the designated agent of the principal contractor, and benficiary of the option. Because of this reasoning, the relevant rules pertaining to Agency naturally apply. Certain difficulties do arise, however, when the principal and 'Agent' make simultaneous and contradictory decisions, and these will be discussed under 'Effects of the Option'.

Term of the Option

The Ḥanafī and Shāfi'ī schools state that the term of the Option of Sharṭ should not exceed three days.[37] There is, however, a certain amount of dispute among and within the schools on this matter.[38]

---

[34] Ibn Qudāma, *al-Mughnī*, III, pp.594 ff.; Ibn 'Ābidīn, *Radd al-Muḥtār*, IV, p.50; Bellefonds, *Traité*, I, p.314; Coulson, *Commercial Law*, p.63

[35] Sanhūrī. *Maṣādir al-Ḥaqq*, IV, p.220

[36] Sanhūrī. *Maṣādir al-Ḥaqq*, IV, p.220; Marghīnānī, *Hidāya*, III, p.23; Ibn Qudāma, *al-Mughnī*, III, p.587; Kāsānī, *Badā'i'*, V, p.271; Bellefonds, *Traité*, I, p.315; Ramlī, *Nihāyat al-Muhtāj*, IV p.11

[37] By analogy with the option of *Tadlīs*, which allows three days for inspection of the *Muṣarrāt*. See Shāfi'ī, *Kitāb al-Umm*, VII, pp.87-150; Schacht, *Origins*, p.270, 299, 326-327.

[38] The *Majella* does not take up the Ḥanafī specificity of term: the term may be determined by the contracting parties, but must be stipulated. See Art. 301

Schacht states that neither the ancient Medinese or Iraqi Schools originally put a time limit to this right of option,[39] and this is followed in the Mālikī School.[40] Within the Ḥanafī School, the Disciples, dissenting, hold that the term should be unlimited.[41] This opinion contradicts the normal rules establishing the boundaries of certainty in contracts, for it threatens normal and straightforward binding obligations with prolonged suspension, making them conditional upon the expiry of an unlimited term. It therefore renders the contract vulnerable to the very kind of exploitation which Islamic legal principles characteristically try to preclude. It may be argued that even allowing a term of three days provides the opportunity for fraud or exploitation. The most persuasive rejoinder to this is the argument for allowing the restricted term in the interests of commercial requisites. Three days, after all, seems not to be an unreasonable term, in which the contractor or purchaser may survey the results of his contract, and determine any incidence of mistake, misdescription, defect or fraud.[42] In any case, from the view-point of legal reasoning, the facility of the restricted option far outweighs the disadvantages of a limited suspension of obligation. The opportunity this option affords to the beneficiary for inspecting the object and determining the advantages of his transaction, means that very few jurists would thereafter entertain claims on his behalf for fraud or error in the contract.[43] Ultimately, therefore, the contract which has become binding upon the expiry of a three-day Option of Stipulation, is less likely to be disputed.

An alternative solution, adopted by the Mālikī School, varies the term of the option according to the requirements, and the nature of the object of each transaction. In a sale of cloth, for example, two days is deemed adequate time for the purchaser to assess the sale; whereas a week is deemed reasonable for assessing a purchased slave; and a month or thereabouts is considered more suitable for assessing a Real Estate

---

39 Schacht, *Origins*, p. 299

40 *al-Muwaṭṭa'*, (1310) III, p.137; Emilia, A.d', 'Il *bai al-hiyār* nella *Mudawwanah*', *Revista degli Studi Orientali*, XXIV (1949) pp.45-58; and *idem.*, 'La Struttora della Vendita Sottoposta a *Khiyār* Secondo la *Sedes Material dell' al-Mudawwanah* (Nota Preliminairie)', *Oriente Moderno*, XXI (1941) pp.86-98

41 Sarakhsī, *Kitāb al-Mabsūṭ*, (1324-1331) XIII, p.41

42 These may, in any case, be operable under their specific options. For option of misdescription see chapter on Mistake, the *Majella*, Arts. 310, 311, 312 and 325. This option is hereditary; it is also covered by the *Khiyār al-Ru'ya*.

43 Bellefonds, *Traité*, I, pp.313-314

purchase.[44]

According to the Mālikī School, if, at the conclusion of the contract, the parties omit to state the specific duration of the term of the option, or if that delay is uncertain in any other way, for instance, if it is based on the occurrence of unknown events such as 'when it rains', the contract is nevertheless valid. In this case, it is for the Judge to determine a reasonable term for the option to continue. The Judge is directed to establish this term according to custom and in consideration of the object of the contract.

According to Abū Yūsuf, Muḥammad, Shāfi'ī and Ibn Ḥanbal, omitting to determine the duration of the option annuls the option, and renders the contract *Fāsid.* According to Abū Ḥanīfa, whereas in theory the whole contract should be *Fāsid* due to the irregular condition, in actuality he holds that if the option is exercised within three days (the 'legal default'), the contract remains valid. Otherwise, the contract becomes *Fāsid.*[45] The option is operable only when it is reserved in good faith by the contractors. If it is exercised merely to secure a short-term benefit in which to profit, for instance, from the usufruct of the object, the motive of the reservation is illegal, for the contractor will be gaining an advantage without consideration. The option here will be void, on the grounds that it has been reserved as a *Ḥila.*[46]

7.2.3 Effects

If both parties stipulate the option, possession does not usually pass. If only one party stipulates, however, possession passes within the term of the option, whether or not that party has given consideration. After inspection of the object during the term of the Option, that party then announces his decision whether to go ahead with the contract, or to revoke. Upon revocation, he naturally returns the object to the other party.

When the option has been stipulated in favour of a third party, and that party declares his decision within the term of the option, normal effects ensue. The same is true when both the contractor (the Principal) and the third party (the agent or beneficiary) come to the same decision, and either both ratify, or both revoke the contract. When, however, the decisions of these two differ, the situation becomes a little more complicated. It is generally held that the first of these decisions (to reach the notice of the co-

---

44 Ibn Rushd, *Bidāyat al-Mujtahid*, II, p.207; Sanhūrī, *Maṣādir al-Ḥaqq*, IV, p.221; Bellefonds, *Traité*, I, p.317

45 Sanhūrī, *Maṣādir al-Ḥaqq*, IV, p.222; Bellefonds, *Traité*, II, p.317

46 Couslon, *Commercial Law*, p.64

contractor ?) is the applicable one.[47] If the principal gives his decision first, he is effectively revoking the agency; if it is the decision of the third party which comes first, this amounts to an effective confirmation of the agency.

Where the decisions made by the principal and third party/agent are simultaneous and contradictory, the law is uncertain, for there is no established opinion as to the course of effects. One opinion states that only the contractor's decision will be valid, whereas another opinion only recognises revocation of the contract as the ensuing result.[48]

The Option of Stipulation is extinguished by four processes :

(1) When the stipulated, legal or customary duration has elapsed, without the option having been exercised by the party/ies. While the option remains open, the contract is regarded as *Ghayr Lāzim*; if no decision is declared after the lapse of the term, this is interpreted as ratification of the contract, which therefore becomes retroactively binding.[49]

(2) On the death of the beneficiary of the option, according to Ḥanafī and Ḥanbalī *Fiqh*.[50] These two Schools attach the right of option, in the case of the stipulated option, strictly to the person of the designated beneficiary. The right is not, therefore, allowed to pass to his heirs on his death. When such beneficiary dies within the duration of the option, the sale becomes obligatory upon his heirs and they have no right to revoke the contract.

 The Shāfi'īs and Mālikīs, on the other hand, allow the right of option of stipulation to pass to his heirs as in the case of normal patrimonial and property rights. The question of an intervening death of the beneficiary naturally assumes rather more importance within the Mālikī School, where, because there are no limitations on the term, there is more likelihood of such an occurrence, than within the three-day term allowed by the Ḥanafī and Shāfi'ī Schools.

(3) Upon the beneficiary's exercise of the Option within the stipulated or legal limits.[51]

---

47 Sanhūrī, *Maṣādir al-Ḥaqq*, IV, p.221; Bellefonds, *Traité*, I, p.316

48 Sanhūrī, *Maṣādir al-Ḥaqq*, IV, 221; Bellefonds, *Traité*, I, p.316

49 *Majella*, Art. 305

50 Marghīnānī, *al-Hidāya*, III, p.24; Ibn Qudāma, *al-Mughnī*, IV, p.77; Bellefonds, *Traité*, I, p.318; *Majella*, Art. 306.

51 *Majella*, Art. 307

7.2.4 Exercise of the Option

The contracting party who has stipulated the *Khiyār al-Sharṭ* may exercise his option either by express confirmation or revocation, or by tacit means.

As Bellefonds remarks,[52] it would seem logical to infer that the party benefitting from the option should be obliged to inform the other contracting party of his final decision. In fact, the doctrinal stance of the jurists is not so easy to determine here. It is only the Shāfi'ī School which categorically recognises the validity of the decision to ratify in cases where the beneficiary of the option has let the term expire without informing his co-contractor of his decision.[53]

Abū Yūsuf also recognises the validity of the contract in this case, but he will not allow this process to operate in certain contracts, such as Agency, and Limited Partnership contracts. In these contracts, he states, the co-contractor must be informed of the decision made by the beneficiary of the option.[54]

Abū Ḥanīfa and Shaybānī determine that omission to inform the co-contractor of the decision at option cancels the contract. Yet another Ḥanafī jurist, Zayla'ī, distinguishes between ratification and revocation here, and it is this opinion which forms the mainstream concensus of the Ḥanafī School. In the case of ratification of the contract, Zayla'ī surmises that it is not necessary to inform the other contractor. The latter's assumption of ratification is a natural consequence of not having had the object returned to him, nor having been given express notification of cancellation. If the beneficiary decides to revoke the contract, he must, according to the dominant Ḥanafī opinion, inform his fellow contractor of that decision. If he does not do so, the option is considered as never having been stipulated, and the contract is binding on him.[55]

It is thus established that allowing the duration of the option to elapse without declaration amounts to tacit acceptance of the contract. This is the stance that was adopted by the *Majella*.[56] Similarly, certain dispositions by the beneficiary will amount to tacit ratification, such as the seller's discharging of a fungible before the lapse of the option, or before it has passed into his possession.[57] A party selling an object in exchange for valuable consideration is not, however, allowed to dispose of that consideration in a sale to a third party before he has received it from the buyer. The second sale is theoretically invalid because it has been formed on the basis of

---

52 Bellefonds, *Traité*, I, p.318

53 Kāsānī relates this in his *Badā'i'al-Ṣanā'i'*, V, pp.267 ff.

54 This opinion was reached by *Ijmā'*.

55 The same divergence occurs in the Ḥanbalī *Fiqh*. The *Majella* holds that the option may be by words or action (Arts. 302, 303, 304)

56 *Majella*, Art. 305

57 But see Kāsānī, *Badā'i' al-Ṣanā'i'*, V, 267 for instances which do not amount to tacit confirmation.

credit, and necessitates the ratification of the first sale to be valid.[58]

If a seller who has stipulated the Option in the sale of an object to A (who has also elected for an Option of Stipulation for three days), makes a second disposition to B during the course of that option, such as another sale or a lease, the second disposition annuls the primary sale and effectively amounts to a tacit delaration of revocation of the contract between the seller and A. Similarly, if B makes any disposition which is incompatible with his primary role as buyer, such as taking the same object on bail, or borrowing it, this also amounts to a revocation of the first contract.

In the case of exchange or barter, if the object of exchange is disposed of, for instance, by sale, before the expiration of the term of option, the exchange is avoided.

7.2.5 Loss or Damage

Where loss or damage occurs to the object during the option, that option is extinguished. This is also the case when the object has perished prior to passing of possession, but here not only is the option extinguished, but also the contract itself, for it no longer has an object. When the object has perished after the passing of possession, and the option has been declared for the benefit of the seller, the buyer is still bound to pay the seller the equivalent value of the object, but he is released from paying the stipulated contract price. Where it is the buyer who has reserved the option, and the object is totally lost whilst in his possession, he is bound to deliver up the stipulated contract price.[59]

Where both contractors have stipulated the right of option, the jurists regard each as strictly independent of the other. In reality, as pointed out by Bellefonds, the option to annul the contract is the one which necessarily pre-dominates, as an act which has been revoked and which therefore does not exist, cannot subsequently be ratified.[60] Similarly, a primary ratification is annulled by a subsequent cancellation. Thus the maxim of this option in these circumstances is that Revocation supercedes Ratification : *al-Faskh aqwā min al-Ijāza.*[61]

Both revocation and ratification operate retroactively from the time of the conclusion of the contract. Thus if both seller and buyer have each reserved the option, and the object is lost or destroyed, no efects of the sale will ensue. Until the moment when the two parties conclude the contract, the property of the object rests with the seller. The risks therefore devolve on him, and the buyer is not held

---

58 Bellefonds, *Traité*, I, p.320

59 Kāsānī, *Badā'i' al-Ṣanā'i'*, V, 272; Bellefonds, *Traité*, I, p.320 and authors cited there.

60 Bellefonds, *Traité*, I, p.321; Muḥammad Y. Mūsā, *al-Amwāl wa Naẓariyyat al-'Aqd*, (Cairo, 1953) p. 478; Kāsānī, *Badā'i' al-Ṣanā'i'*, V, 271; *Majella*, Art. 307

61 Kāsānī, *Badā'i' al-Ṣanā'i'*, V, 272; Bellefonds, *Traité*, I, p.321

accountable for the price. If either of the contractors opts to revoke the contract, the sale is regarded as never having existed because of the retroactive effect of the option once exercised.[62]

Where only the seller has reserved the option, the sale is *Ghayr Lāzim*, and as long as the option endures, the property of the object is not transferred to the buyer. The buyer is, however, bound to pay the price from the conclusion of the contract because for him the sale is perfectly binding. Abū Ḥanīfa, somewhat perturbed by this result, and basing his reasoning on the case of Barter, decided that in this case the object of contract leaves the ownership of the seller, but does not pass into the ownership of the buyer.[63] This thesis was rejected by the two disciples and the remainder of the Ḥanafī School.[64]

If the sale is ratified by the seller, whether such ratification be express or tacit, or if certain circumstance intervene so as to invalidate the ratification (such as the death of a contractor), the transferal of property from seller to buyer will nevertheless be effective. The buyer in this case will be regarded as the retroactive proprietor, commencing from the conclusion of the contract. It is therefore from this time that he has the right to the fruits or produce of the object of contract. The rules pertaining to intervening dispositions and third parties are also applicable here.

In the case where the buyer opts to annul the contract, he must restitute to the seller whatever he has received from him and the risk remains with the latter.[65]

If the buyer alone has reserved the right of the option, the situation is inversely symmetrical to the preceding one. The property of the object of contract is immediately transferred to the buyer,[66] who is not, however, bound to pay the price so long as his option endures. Risk naturally rests with him, as the object remains in his possession.[67]

Bellefonds states that what the *Fuqahā'* term a "Stipulated Option" is nothing other than a *Condition Potestative*, that is, a condition which depends on the will of the contracting parties. Bellefonds thus poses the question as to whether the other party is bound by the optional decision ? As Bellefonds points out, in French Civil Law, a condition which is purely *potestative* is not forbidden if it depends solely on the will of the 'Creditor'.[68] A contract affected by a similar condition which is merely suspensive, does not immediately produce any effect, either with regard to the 'creditor' or the 'debtor' of the contract.

---

62 Bellefonds, *Traité*, I, p.322

63 This is the stance upheld by the *Majella*, Art. 308

64 al-Marghīnānī, *al-Hidāya*, III, p.22; Bellefonds, *Traité*, I, p.323

65 Bellefonds, *Traité*, I, p.323

66 Abū Ḥanīfa dissents here.

67 As upheld by the *Majella*, Art.309

68 French Civil Law, Art. 1174; Bellefonds, *Traité*, I, p.321

In Islamic Law, the situation is different. Each contractor's obligations are regarded separately from the other's. The only obligations which are suspended are those of the contractor who has reserved the option for himself. The other contractor is bound by his obligations from the time of the conclusion of the contract. Thus, as Bellefonds remarks, the contract is a hybrid : *Lāzim* for one party, and *Mawqūf* for the other.[69]

7.2.6 Modern Legislation

No mention is made of options in the Contract Law of Bahrain. However, in the Dubai Contract Law of 1971, a law based on English law principles and often very similar to the Bahrain Code, mention is given to Options in relation to their effects. Article 66 states that "when a person at whose option the contract is voidable rescinds it, the other party thereto need not perform any promise therein contained in which he is promisor." This is a general effect to which the Classical Law and modern statutes generally pertain. Article 66 goes on to state, "The party rescinding a voidable contract shall, if he has received any benefit thereunder from another party to such contract, restore such benefit, so far as may be (possible) to the person from whom it was received". Thus although individual options are not mentioned specifically in this Code, we may presume that they are recognised as in the classical law.

In the Federal Civil Code of the UAE and the Kuwaiti Civil Code, the Option of Stipulation is expressly recognised.[70] Article 218 (1) of the UAE Code primarily states that where a contract contains a condition that a party may cancel without the mutual consent of the co-contractor, or an order of the court, the contract will not be binding on one or both of the parties. Each party may then act unilaterally in cancelling the contract when it is not binding upon him, or when he has reserved an option in his own favour.[71] The reservation of the Option of Stipulation may be made, according to the UAE Civil Code, by either of the parties, and either in advance or subsequent to contracting, in favour of that party himself or of a third party.[72] The term of the Option of stipulation is to be agreed upon between the parties (the Mālikī stance), and where they have not agreed upon a particular

---

69 Classical and modern authors alike regard the condition as *Mawqūf*. See Ibn al-Hammām, *Fatḥ al-Qadīr*, V, p.115; Kāsānī, *Badā'i' al-Ṣanā'i'*, V, 264; *al-Sharḥ al-Kabīr 'Alā Matn al-Muqanna'*, in the margin of Ibn Qudāma's *al-Mughnī*, IV, pp.70,71; Chehata, *Essai d'une Théorie Générale de l'Obligation en Droit Musulman*, p.83; Sanhūrī, *Maṣādir al-Ḥaqq*, IV, p.223

70 The Kuwaiti Code, Arts. 322-328 treat the Option in relation to its effects as does the Bahraini Code. See also KCC Art. 458.

71 UAE Federal Civil Code, No. 2 of 1987, Art. 218 (2)

72 UAE Federal Civil Code, No. 2 of 1987, Art. 219; Kuwaiti Civil Code, Arts. 205,206

period, the judge is expected to specify the most appropriate period in accordance with custom.[73] Where both parties have reserved the option of *Sharṭ* for themselves, the ruling follows the Classical principle, in that property of the object does not pass.[74] If one party first elects to cancel the contract, while the other elects to affirm, it is the cancellation which is of effect, for the same reasoning as has been described above in relation to the Classical exposition. If, on the other hand, one party confirms the contract, the other party retains his option to cancel throughout the period laid down for the option.[75] The effect of this option in the UAE and Kuwaiti Codes is limited to confirmation or cancellation of the contract.[76] Confirmation or cancellation may be express or by implication, by any act, word, or disposition indicating the same.[77] Once the option has been exercised to confirm the contract, it becomes binding retroactively to the date of contracting. The option to cancel is of immediate effect and renders the contract void *ab initio*.[78]

As in the classical Law, the option must be exercised within the term agreed upon by the parties, and the other contracting party must be informed if the elected option is to cancel the contract and is effected by words rather than by mutual consent or an order of the court.[79] If the option is to ratify the contract, there is no requirement that the other contracting party should be informed, for it is thus assumed.[80]

The contract with conditional option becomes binding on both parties when the term of the option expires without the option having been exercised.[81] The option lapses upon the death of the beneficiary contracting party, (the Ḥanafī and Ḥanbalī stance) and the contract therefore becomes binding on his heirs, whether or not the term has expired. The other contracting party who has also reserved an option of condition retains his right to cancel the contract, notwithstanding the death of his co-contractor, and the binding nature of the contract on the latter's heirs.

From this exposé, it may be seen therefore, that the Federal UAE Civil Code has retained the Islamic character of the *Khiyār al-Sharṭ*, and adheres closely to the mainstream school of thought. It is not, however, consistently adherent to the doctrine of one school, but pertains to doctrines of different schools where this would enable it to follow the most flexible and permissive stance. The legitimacy of

---

73 UAE Federal Civil Code, No. 2 of 1987, Art. 219; Kuwaiti Civil Code, Art. 458

74 UAE Civil Code, Art. 220

75 *ibid.*, Art. 222

76 *ibid.*, Art. 221 (1); Kuwaiti Civil Code, Art. 458

77 UAE Civil Code, Art. 223 (1)

78 *ibid.*, Art. 221 (2)

79 *ibid.*, Art. 224 (1)

80 *ibid.*, Art. 224 (2)

81 *ibid.*, Art. 223 (2); Kuwaiti Civil Code, Art. 458

this exercise is still somewhat questionable, even if it has long been practised.

7.3 KHIYĀR AL-TA'YĪN

In cases of Indetermination, the Ḥanafī and Mālikī schools provide for a second "conventional" option.[82] This is the "Option of Designation" (*Khiyār al-Ta'yīn*), which takes effect in contracts in which the object is partially undetermined at the time of contracting. One of the parties therefore reserves the option to choose, or designate from among several objects, the true object of that contract during a prefixed term. The same party may, instead, choose to cancel the contract. Therefore the option consists of two possible decisions:

(1) To ratify by choosing from among the alternative objects

(2) To cancel the contract entirely

In effect, the Option of *Ta'yīn* is merely a variation of the *Khiyār al-Sharṭ*.[83] The difference between the two options does not lie in the result, whether it be to ratify or cancel the contract, nor in the fact that the terms of the option must be satisfied to confirm the transaction; it merely lies in the nature of the term : in the *Khiyār al-Sharṭ*, it is in the very existence of the legal act; in the *Khiyār al-Ta'yīn*, it is in determining the object of a legal act already in existence. Because of the similarity in nature between the two options, the Ḥanafī School affords only incidental attention to this option.[84] In the Mālikī School, the liaison between the two is less apparent. In this option, as in the previous one, whatever decision the party makes, takes effect retroactively from the time the contract was concluded. If the contract is cancelled, therefore, it is regarded as never having taken place.

The option is accompanied by a string of conditions, which must be fulfilled in order for such an option to be exercised. These conditions are quite onerous, indicating the jurists' concern to prevent loop-holes for exploitation of the principle, and to reconcile it as far as possible with the previous condition of precise determination of the object of contract. The Shāfi'ī and Ḥanbalī Schools do not recognise the option of Determination for this very reason. If the object of the contract is insufficiently determined, they state, it does not conform to the basic principles of Islamic contract. If the obligatory force of the contract is to be

---

82 See Emilia, 'Il *bai al-hiyār* nella *Mudawwanah*,' *op.cit.*, pp.45-58

83 Sanhūrī, *Maṣādir al-Ḥaqq*, IV, p.234; Bellefonds, *Traité*, I, p.324

84 The Ḥanafī texts do not always distinguish between these two options. Kāsānī is one of the authors who does treat them separately (*Badā'i'*, V, p.157 ff.), and Sanhūrī follows his example, discussing them in two succeeding chapters (*Maṣādir al-Ḥaqq*, IV, p.234 ff.)

suspended while the contractor makes his choice of object, that object is obviously not as precisely defined as the rules of contract otherwise stipulate. The *Khiyār al-Sharṭ*, they say, finds precedent in an *Ḥadīth* of the Prophet, and is rendered necessary through legal convenience, but the same cannot be said for the *Khiyār al-Ta'yīn*.

In justification of the *Khiyār al-Ta'yīn*, the Ḥanafīs and Mālikīs employ the same argument used to support their use of the *Khiyār al-Sharṭ*. True, this time the option finds no authority in a Prophetic Ḥadīth, but where the incidence does not conform to *Qiyās*, they suggest that it is justified by resource to *Istiḥsān*.[85] The options have been introduced, they say, for the benefit of individuals in order to counter prejudice which may otherwise result from a defect, *Ghabn*, or some other such cause. To enable the contractor to choose upon sight the most suitable object of his contractual intentions would be the best way to avoid such prejudice. The sale will thereby be concluded at the moment in which the contractors conclude the agreement, together with the facility and terms of the option, but it will only become definitive and binding when the contractor who has reserved the option of Determination has made his choice of object.[86]

The Ḥanafī and Mālikī jurists were nevertheless anxious to prevent exploitation of the uncertainty created by the introduction of this option, and enumerated stringent conditions for its employment :-

(1) The option can only be exercised in synallagmatic contracts for valuable consideration and in which property is transferred. It is therefore restricted to the contracts of Sale, Barter, Gift in trust, and other such synallagmatic transactions.[87]

(2) The option may be exercised by either contracting party, but not by a third party.[88] It is difficult to envisage what advantage a seller may have in such an option, but the option is founded on equity, and so the facility must be available to both parties.[89]

(3) The option must be precisely and expressly stipulated. Whether or not it should be stated in conjunction with the stipulated option is a point of dispute

---

85 Zayla'ī, *Tabyīn al-Ḥaqqā'iq*, IV, p.21

86 Bellefonds, *Traité*, I, p.325

87 The classical authors restricted it to Sale, but modern authors have extended it to assimilated contracts. See Mūsā, *al-Amwāl wa Naẓariyyat al-'Aqd, op.cit*, p.464; and Khafīf, *Aḥkām al-Mu'āmalāt*, (Third Edn.) p.430

88 Kāsānī, *Badā'i'*, V, p.262; Zayla'ī, *Tabyīn al-Ḥaqqā'iq*, IV, p.22; Ibn al-Hammām, *Fatḥ al-Qadīr*, V, p.131; Ḥaṭṭāb, *Mawāhib al-Jalīl*, IV, p.424

89 *Majella*, Art. 316; Bellefonds, *Traité*, I, p.326

within the Ḥanafī School.[90]

(4) The choice of designation may only be exercised between a maximum three objects, otherwise the contract will be *Fāsid* on the grounds of *Gharar*.[91]

(5) There is also the implicit condition that this option can only be brought into effect when the subject-matter of the contract presents complexities or uncertainties which it would have been preferable to avoid.[92]

(6) The Ḥanafīs require that the objects from which the choice is made must be of the same class, but must be of different quality or kind (*Mutafāwata*) for the option to be of any consequence.[93]

(7) The Ḥanafīs require that the price of all objects of choice, and the allowed delay in designation of the object must be fixed precisely in advance. The Mālikīs apply a global price for all objects.

7.3.1 Duration of Option

(8) Within the Mālikī doctrine, the question of duration of the option is not given much attention. The same Mālikī liberalism as accorded to the Option of Stipulation is here given to Designation : Delay varies according to the nature of the transaction and its object, and according to usage and local custom. Ḥaṭṭāb queries whether this should be the case even if the beneficiary of the option allows the time accorded for it to elapse ? He determines that if the term has long elapsed, that beneficiary should not be allowed to exercise the option; but if the term has only recently expired, then the facility should still be his.[94] "Recent" (*Qarīb*) is interpreted here by Abū Ḥassan to mean one, two or three days after the lapse of the option term.[95]

The Ḥanafī authors are at odds in this matter. Some do not stipulate a fixed term within which the option must be exercised, on the gounds that it is, after all, only a matter of choosing between the objects. In claiming that it is not here a question concerning the existence of the legal act itself, one

---

90 Mūsā, *al-Amwāl wa Naẓariyyat al-'Aqd, op.cit.*, p.467; Bellefonds, *Traité*, I, p.326

91 Kāsānī, *Badā'i'*, V, p.157

92 Kāsānī, *Badā'i' al-Ṣanā'i'*, V, p.261; Dardīr, *al-Sharḥ al-Ṣaghīr*, (2 Vols., Boulac, 1298 AH), II, p.46

93 This condition finds no mention in the Mālikī School, but it may be deduced from their application of a global price (see next paragraph), that the objects may be identical according to Mālikī doctrine.

94 Ḥaṭṭāb, *Mawāhib al-Jalīl, op.cit*, IV, p.425; Bellefonds, *Traité*, I, p.327; Emilia, A.d', 'Il *bai al-hiyār* nella *Mudawwanah*', *op.cit*.

95 Schacht says that three days is the prevailing opinion, but does not provide references. See his *Introduction*, p.153

wonders whether the facility of the option also to cancel the contract has either been forgotten, or is disputed by some Ḥanafī authors ? In any case, a comparison cannot be made here with the *Khiyār al-Sharṭ*, which suspends the actual contract until the stipulation of the option has been satisfied, and in which it is undisputed within the Ḥanafī School that the term must be determined. Other Ḥanafī authors adopt the same solution to the duration of term as in the *Khiyār al-Sharṭ*, by reason of the similarities between the two options.[96] This is the solution which appears to predominate within the Ḥanafī School. We may state, on the basis of Abū Ḥanīfa's opinion, therefore, that the term for the option of *Ta'yīn* is set at three days; in this matter however, as has been noted, he was not followed by his disciples.[97]

7.3.2 Extinction of the Option

The option itself is extinguished :-

(1) By the beneficiary of the option exercising his choice between the objects. The choice may be express or implicit. If, for instance, in a contract of sale, the buyer disposes of one of the objects of choice, it may be assumed that this was his designated object in the primary contract of sale. If it is the seller who has reserved the option, and he disposes elsewhere of one of the objects, he must indicate to the buyer that that object is no longer for sale and must be excluded from his choice.

(2) The lapse of the term of option extinguishes the option of *Ta'yīn*, but is subject to the different interpretations within the two Schools. If the option has been allowed to pass without a choice of object having been made, the Mālikīs will determine that the contract is annulled.[98] The Ḥanafīs, on the other hand, interpret this as confirmation of the contract, and the beneficiary of the option is held to have determined his choice of object.

The death of the beneficiary is without relevance to this particular option, and the right of option passes to his heirs as a normal right.[99] The distinction between the *Khiyār al-Ta'yīn* and the *Khiyār al-Sharṭ* in this case rests on the more objective choice to be made. In the former, the option which passes to the heirs of the beneficiary is not strictly a question of the existence of the legal act, but merely

---

96 Kāsānī, *Badā'i'*, V, p.157 presents the two arguments. See also Bellefonds, *Traité*, I, p.327

97 See Ibn al-Hammām, *Fatḥ al-Qadīr*, V, p.132; Bellefonds, *Traité*, I, p.327

98 Ḥaṭṭāb, *Mawāhib al-Jalīl*, IV, p.425; Bellefonds, *Traité*, I, p.327

99 Kāsānī, *Badā'i'*, V, 262; UAE Federal Civil Code, Art. 236

a choice concerning the object. In the Option of Stipulation, the choice of whether to affirm or cancel the contract itself is regarded as too subjective to be inherited by what are, effectively, strangers to the contract; the option of Stipulation must remain, therefore, solely dependent upon the will of the original contracting party.[100]

7.3.3 Loss or Damage

Loss or damage to one of the objects of contract, whether by accident or by *Force Majeure*, has different effects depending on whether the beneficiary of the option has already taken possession of the objects concerned. The jurists go into great detail on the variation of situations which may prevail here, according to the different contracts and circumstances. Taking the case of a contract of sale in which the option of designation is to be exercised between two objects, where a total or partial loss is sustained, the effects may be enumerated in brief according to three categories :-

Before Passing of Possession

(1) If both objects are lost, the sale is void for lack of object, and the risks remain with the seller;[101]

(2) If only one object is lost and the buyer has reserved the option, he then has the option either to revoke, or to confirm the contract with the remaining object as the object of contract;[102]

(3) Where only one object is lost and it is the seller who has reserved the option, it is he who may annul or confirm the sale on the basis of the remaining object.

After Passing of Possession

(1) Where the buyer has stipulated the option and only one of the objects is lost whilst in his possession, this lost object becomes the object of the contract and the buyer must pay the seller the price of that object. Meanwhile, he holds the second object in trust and must return it to the seller.[103]

---

100 Sanhūrī, *Maṣādir al-Ḥaqq*, IV, p.240; Bellefonds, *Traité*, I, p.328

101 UAE Federal Civil Code, Art.235 (1)

102 UAE Federal Civil Code, Art.235 (1)

103 UAE Federal Civil Code, Art.235 (1)

(2) Where both objects perish, and the loss has been successive, the sale is valid with regard to the first of these objects to perish. The buyer owes the price of that object, and the value of the second to the seller.[104]

(3) Where both objects perish simultaneously, the sale becomes binding and the price is constituted by half the value of each object, as it is no longer possible to ascertain the object of contract.[105]

Option Belonging to Seller

(1) If one of the objects perishes, whether before or after passing of possession, the seller has the option to confirm the sale with the remaining article as the object; or he may cancel the sale.[106]

(2) If the loss of both objects after passing of possession is successive, the first object lost is regarded as held in trust, and the second as the object of the contract.[107]

(3) If both objects have perished simultaneously, before passing of possession, the contract is void for lack of object, as 1 (1) above.[108]

(4) If both objects are lost simultaneously after the passing of possession, the purchaser must pay half the price of each object.[109]

7.3.4 EFFECTS

The effects of the option of *Ta'yīn* depend on the party who has reserved that option. Where the option is reserved by the buyer (which is naturally the more common), the sale is immediately concluded and is considered *Nafīdh* (Operative), but not binding on the buyer.[110] Therefore, if possession is passed immediately, whether of one or of all the objects, the buyer is not bound to pay the price immediately. When, during the term of the option, he chooses his object, this affirms the contract of sale by establishing the precise object and the choice renders

---

104 UAE Federal Civil Code, Art.235 (1)

105 Sanhūrī, *Maṣādir al-Ḥaqq*, IV, p.240; Bellefonds, *Traité*, I, p.328; UAE Civil Code, Art. 235 (1)

106 UAE Federal Civil Code, Art.235 (2)

107 UAE Federal Civil Code, Art.235 (2)

108 Bellefonds, *Traité*, I, p.329; UAE Civil Code, Art. 235 (2)

109 UAE Federal Civil Code, Art.235 (2)

110 Thus termed *Nafīdh Ghayru Lāzim*. See Sanhūrī, *Maṣādir al-Ḥaqq*, IV, pp.216 ff (who spells it *Nāfidh*, but this is erroneous).

the contract retroactively sound as from the time of contracting. At the moment the choice is made, the price becomes payable by the buyer, and he must return the alternative unchosen objects (if they are in his possession) to the seller. If these objects have become lost or damaged whilst in his possession, he must compensate the seller for their value.

Sanhūrī interprets the option here as a suspended condition.[111] This does not seem unreasonable, bearing in mind the facility within the option to cancel the contract. The distinction between this option and the suspended condition of Civil Law systems is, however (as Bellefonds remarks), that in the latter, transfer of property is suspended and the risk remains with the seller.[112] In this option though, property may be transferred immediately, while the risk remains with the buyer so long as the objects are in his possession. Moreover, the option exercised by the buyer does not give rise to the obligation of the contract, but merely confirms that obligation. The choice exercised in the suspended condition is to be distinguished here, for the choice gives rise to the obligation itself, and that contractor may cancel the contract by deciding not to choose any of the objects of contract. The principles of the suspended condition thereby bear more resemblance to those of the *Khiyār al-Sharṭ*. Chehata and Bellefonds, rejecting the direct correlation between the *Khiyār al-Ta'yīn* and the suspended condition, suggest instead that the Islamic Option rather conceals within the whole what is termed in French Civil Law as a *Condition potestative tacite*, that is, a simple condition which depends on the will of the contracting party.[113]

When the option is stipulated in favour of the seller, the sale is also concluded from the moment of contract, but it is not binding (*Ghayr Lāzim*) on the seller, and therefore excludes transfer of ownership to the buyer of any of the possible objects.

The option to designate which particular object will be that of the contract in this case belongs to the seller, and his choice is binding upon the buyer. Once made, the choice confirms the contract and becomes retroactive from the conclusion of the principal agreement. Thus if the buyer has already disposed of the designated object, or constructed rights over it, these acts are ratified by the seller's choice. If, on the other hand, he has disposed of, or constructed rights over, an object which does not become the designated object of the seller, these acts of disposal are null and void, and without existence.

One concluding important point is that where the seller has reserved the option to designate the object of contract, he is not bound to exercise that option. Unlike the buyer who has to exercise the option reserved to him, the seller may abstain from making a choice of object, and therefore from the contract which he

---

111 Sanhūrī, *Maṣādir al-Ḥaqq*, IV, p.217 Note

112 Bellefonds. *Traité*, I, p.329; See also French Civil Code, Art. 1182

113 Sanhūrī, *Maṣādir al-Ḥaqq*, IV, p.420; Chehata, *Essai d'une Théorie Générale de l'Obligation en Droit Musulman*, p.65; Bellefonds, *Traité*, I, p.329;

concluded. In this respect, where the seller has the right of option, the *Khiyār al-Ta'yīn* resembles the *Khiyār al-Sharṭ*.

7.3.5 Modern Legislation

The option of *Ta'yīn* is recognised in the modern legislation of the Federal State of the Emirates, on condition that the consideration of each object of choice is determined, and that the term of the option is stipulated.[114] If the contracting parties do not stipulate this term, or if the term laid down for one of them (by the court) expires without the option having been exercised, the other party may apply to the court to determine the term or the subject-matter of the transaction.[115]

Here, as in the classical law, the contract is not binding on the beneficiary of the option until he has exercised his right within the term. Once the election is made, whether expressly or implicitly, the contract becomes binding upon him, effective as with regard to the object he has chosen,[116] retroactively to the time of contracting.[117]

With regard to loss or damage of the object or objects of choice, the solutions provided for by the UAE Civil Code are exactly commensurate with the Classical law expositions. The relevant articles have therefore been indicated within the respective subsections, above.[118]

It may be seen, therefore, that the UAE Code has adhered religiously to the doctrine of *Khiyār al-Ta'yīn* as it is set out in the *Fiqh*. It may be said that the articles of the UAE Civil Code are cursory, but in the event of any lacunae arising with respect to this doctrine, it must be apparent to any presiding judge that the source of these principles lies within the *Fiqh*, rather than in the Kuwaiti/Egyptian Codes, and it is therefore to this source that further reference may be expected to be made.

---

114 UAE Federal Civil Code, Art. 231

115 *ibid.*, Art. 232

116 UAE Federal Civil Code, Art.233

117 UAE Federal Civil Code, Art.234

118 See subsection 3.3 above.

7.4 KHIYĀR AL-'AYB

The first of the residuary legal options is that of defect (*'Ayb*). Here the buyer is automatically entitled to choose to annul the contract if he discovers upon transfer of possession, that the object of contract is so defective as to diminish its value. The same option is granted to contracts of hire and in any transfer of property for valuable consideration. Thus a party hiring property is bound to return that property without defect to its owner.[119]

Because the Option of Defect is a legal right, the buyer does not need to stipulate a reservation of the option at the time of contracting in order for him to be able to resort to it later.[120] Bellefonds regards this option as the transition between the two conventional options already discussed, and the remaining options of Inspection, Fraud and Mistake, which are not based on express reservations by the parties concerned.[121] As Saleh points out, the option of defect is specifically pertinent in contracts to manufacture (*istiṣnā'*) in the Ḥanafī School.[122]

The Option of Defect is distinguishable from the two preceding options, firstly, by its unconventionality : it does not operate as a suspensive condition; and secondly, because it, like the remaining legal options, operates in the same way as a condition of avoidance. Together with the three other legal options, therefore, the option of defect fulfils the role which would have been exercised by express conditions of avoidance, had Islamic law generally tolerated them. As it is, conditions relating to the transfer of real rights cannot, in principle, and without exceptions, be coupled with express conditions, whether these are resolutory or suspensive. It is in the light of this fact, that the legal options of Islamic law may be accorded their true import in the dissolution of inequitable contracts.[123]

---

119 Kāsānī, *Badā'i'*, V, pp.274 ff.; *Hidāya*, III, pp.27-31; Ramlī, *Nihāyat al-Muḥtāj*, (Cairo, 1935) IV, pp.24 ff.; Ibn Rushd, *Bidāya*, II, 72 ff.; Ḥaṭṭāb, *Mawāhib al-Jalīl*, pp.IV, 428 ff.; Santillana, *Instituzioni*, II, pp.140-154; Ibn Qudāma, *al-Mughnī*, IV, pp.134 ff. (Third Edn.); *idem, Kitāb 'Umdat al-Aḥkām Fī al-Fiqh 'Alā Madhhab al-Imām Aḥmad b. Ḥanbal.*, (Transl. Laoust) pp. 98-99; Bellefonds, *Traité*, I, p.331;

120 Kāsānī, *Badā'i'*, V, p.274; Sanhūrī, *Maṣādir al-Ḥaqq*, II, p.130. For the not dissimilar position of the Shi'a doctrine in the Option of Defect, See Parviz Owsia, *op.cit*, pp.481 ff.

121 Bellefonds, *Traité*, I, pp.331-332

122 Saleh, *Unlawful Gain and Legitimate Profit in Islamic Law : Riba, Gharar and Islamic Banking*, (Cambridge, 1986) p.61

123 Sanhūrī, *Maṣādir al-Ḥaqq*, IV, p.216; Bellefonds, *Traité*, I, p.332. See also the explanatory remarks in Coulson, *Commercial Law*, pp.56 *et seq*, and 65.

7.4.1 Origins

The origins of the Option of Defect are somewhat obscure, but they are generally thought to have evolved from the Tradition concerning *Muṣarrāt.*[124] In any case, the origins of this option are more likely to have been the result of juristic reasoning. The need for an equitable institution to cover for the incidence of dissolution in contracts, where express avoidance of inequity by coupling conditions to the contract is precluded by the law, is apparent. The jurists may have developed the series of legal options along the lines of other comparable equitable devices which also do not find their origins in the primary sources. The historical course of their evolution is lost to us, but Santillana, taken up by Bellefonds, suggests that this option developed from pre-Islamic Medinan custom.[125] The majority of examples proffered by the earliest authors whose works are extant concern, almost exclusively, defects occurring in slaves after purchase.[126] This is evidence which was suggestive enough to prompt Santillana to the thesis that the Option of Defect developed in conjunction with slave trading.[127] The theory is acceptable, although there is little reason to suppose that the institution should have been restricted to defects in slaves, other than the mass of examples available in the early sources. The defects occurring with regard to slaves are indeed usually more complex than those occurring in relation to livestock, real estate or inanimate objects, for they involve complications of a succinct nature, relating to liens, paternity, and rights in ownership.[128] The facility to cancel the contract for defect has, in all events, been developed, whether simultaneously or subsequently, to include all goods. This has

---

124 Ibn Qudāma, *al-Mughnī*, IV, p.134 (Third Edn.); Kāsānī, *Badā'i'*, V, pp.274 ff.; Bellefonds, *Traité*, I, p.332; J. Schacht, *Origins*, p.125. For *Muṣarrāt*, see Chapter on Fraud, *Supra*.

125 Santillana, *Instituzioni*, II, p.140; Bellefonds, *Traité*, I, p.333

126 Defects which are the particular objects of extended discourse are : (1) The dispensation to flee or steal; (2) Nocturnal incontinence; (3) Madness; (4) Being married (which may lead to absenteeism through the desire to join the spouse). See Kāsānī, *Badā'i'*, V, p.274 ff.; and Bellefonds, *Traité*, I, p.336; and Schacht, *Origins*, pp.325, 326

127 Santillana, *op.cit.*

128 Kāsānī, *Badā'i'*, V, p.274 ff. lists examples of physical defects in slaves, such as blindness, whether in one eye or both, outward and inward squints (Strabysmus), falling eyelids, night-blindness, narrow-angled eyes, or eyes which are too deeply set; swollen lacrymal glands; leprosy; scrofula; struma or baldness; excessive halitosis in males, mild in females; hernia; white or greasy hair; tuberculosis; ulcers; any illness; obesity in females; licentiousness in females (although not in males unless it proves disadvantageous to his work). See the note regarding slaves in the Introduction. Here, some of the defects may be applicable, for instance, to livestock, although it is to be noted that obesity is an advantage in livestock. See generally, Santillana, *Instituzioni*, II, 143; and Bellefonds, *Traité*, I, pp. 334-335.

been done most extensively by the Mālikīs, and now includes anything from defects in goods on hire, to the sale of real estate inhabited by Djinn![129]

Any buyer in Islamic law has an automatic implied warranty against latent defects in the goods purchased.[130] The buyer is also permitted to expressly renounce a defect which might develop in the object during a restricted period after having been taken into possession by him.[131]

7.4.2 Constituent Elements of Defects

The primary element which constitutes a defect which may give rise to an option to cancel the contract, is that it must be a latent defect. A "latent" defect is defined in the Ḥanafī School as "Everything which results in a diminution of value, according to commercial custom, whether this diminution is gross or minimal."[132] The other Schools simply require that the defect is of a certain gravity. The Mālikīs, for example, who term this option *Khiyār al-Naqīṣa*, state that the defect must be of such a nature as to cause a "discernible" diminution in the value of the goods, or to render the object less suitable for the use to which it was intended to be put, whether such intention be discernible from the nature of the object, or from the intention of the party concerned.[133] The Mālikīs can be seen, therefore, to distinguish between major and minor defects, and it is only the former which give rise to the Option for Defect. Where defects of a minor nature occur, the Mālikīs allow for a reduction in the price to be made.[134]

The Shāfi'ī School is more inclined to treat every defect as latent by definition, due to the implied warranty against defects. The Shāfi'īs do not, in principle, therefore, entertain the possibility of reducing the price of the object due to defects discovered in it. Nevertheless, the Shāfi'ī jurists do not recognise defects in the goods as giving rise to the option to annul the contract, except where such defects

---

129 See, for example, Ḥaṭṭāb, *Mawāhib al-Jalīl*, IV, 136; and *Majella*, Arts. 352, 353, 354 and 355 for comestibles; Arts. 513-521 for hire contracts.

130 *Majella*, Art. 336

131 This is a condition which is not permitted in the Option of Inspection. See Kāsānī, *Badā'i'*, V, 297

132 Ibn 'Ābidīn, *Radd al-Muḥtār*, IV, pp.109-153; Sarakhsī, *Kitāb al-Mabsūṭ*, XIII, pp.91-121; Ibn Nujaym, *al-Baḥr al-Rā'iq*, VI, pp.35-68; Ibn al-Hammām, *Fatḥ al-Qadīr*, V, pp.151-183; Marghīnānī, *al-Hidāya*, III, p.27; Kāsānī, *Badā'i'*, V, p.273-291; Zayla'ī, *Tabyīn al-Ḥaqā'iq*, IV, p.31-43; Bellefonds, *Traité*, I, p.333

133 Sanhūrī, *Maṣādir al-Ḥaqq*, IV, p.270, 272 f.; Santillana, *Instituzioni*, II, p.143 gives a resumé of the Mālikī doctrine according to Mālik Ibn Anas and Bukhārī.

134 Dasūqī/Dardīr, *al-Sharḥ al-Kabīr*, IV, p.365; Dasūqi, *Ḥāshiyya 'alā Sharḥ al-Kabīr*, III, pp.109-140; al-Ḥaṭṭāb, *Mawāhib al-Jalīl*, IV, pp.428-466; al-Khurshī, *Sharḥ Mukhtaṣar Sīdī Khalīl*, V, pp.125-152; al-Ṣāwī, *Bulghat al-Sālik li Aqrab al-Masālik*, (Cairo, 1978) II, pp.49-63; Santillana, *Instituzioni*, II, p.143; Bellefonds, *Traité*, I, p.334

have prevented the purchaser from achieving his legal aims.[135]

The definition given by the *Majella* is "anything which reduces the value of property in the opinion of persons competent to judge that property".[136]

In brief then, the position may be stated thus: the defect must exist; in the Ḥanafī School, it must have a detrimental effect on the value of the object, howsoever slight such diminution in value may be. This is so even if the diminution corresponds to a defect which does not render the object unsuitable for its intended purpose. In the remaining Schools, the defect must be of a certain gravity according to the Mālikīs, and must have prevented the purchaser from exercising his legal intentions according to the Shāfi'īs.

The scope for anulling a contract for defect is therefore liberally wide, although the determination of its conditions, namely that the defect exists, and that the object has suffered a diminution in value due to it, are easily and objectively ascertainable. The price of like goods on the open market is the normal point of comparison for assessing any devaluation. Likewise, assessing an object's suitability for its natural or declared intentional use is straightforward.[137] The Ḥanafī criterion relating to diminution of value is rather too rigid, however, when referring to contracts of Hire. The parties to a hire contract have no ready source of price quotations which are established as precisely and fairly as those in the markets relating to contracts of sale.

It is not generally a requirement that the defect must be hidden in order to give rise to the option to cancel the contract.[138] Defects may be readily apparent, but the majority of jurists hold that the buyer must not have known of, or noticed, that defect at the time of contracting. If he did know of the defect, and this can be proven, he is held to have renounced his right of Option. It is somewhat difficult to reconcile this reasoning in the case where a buyer has been staring at a glaring defect in the object at the time of concluding the contract, when it would have been expected that his subsequent claims not to have noticed it would have met with the response of *Caveat Emptor*. To allow resource to the Option in this case is surely giving licence to negligence in contracting ? It is more readily comprehensible in the case where the contractor contracts *in absentia*, or without seeing the object, in which case, he may have resort to the Option of Inspection.

In response to the former reasoning, Santillana has established that a defect which is evidently apparent, in other words, which only reqires summary

135 Shīrāzī, *al-Muhadhdhab*, I, pp.282-288; Bellefonds, *Traité*, I, p.334

136 *Majella*, Art. 338; See also Arts. 336-355; and arts. 513-521 for hire-contracts in the *Majella*.

137 The Shāfi'ī Jurist, al-Ramlī, lists a series of recognisable latent defects which frequently result in diminution in price and value. Ramlī, *Nihāyat al-Muḥtāj*, IV, 32.

138 The Mālikī authors define hidden defects as "Any other defect not mentioned by customs".

examination of the object in order to be discovered, cannot in principle be ignored by the buyer. If a buyer in this case continues with the contract and takes the object into his possession, he is deemed to have renounced his right to the Option.[139] It is in the light of such reasoning that modern authors such as Sanhūrī bring the option of Defect into line with the French Civil Law theory of error.[140]

7.4.3 Conditions

The conditions required for exercise of the option are four :-

(1) The existence of the defect must antecede the contract, or where passing of possession is not immediate, it must antecede this;[141]

(2) The defect must still be in existence when the purchaser wishes to annul the contract: if the defect has disappeared (for instance, a medical condition in livestock has been cured) the sale may not be dissolved;[142]

(3) The buyer must be unaware of the defect at the time of contracting, and of taking the object into his possession. Therefore, if the seller indicates the defect to the buyer, or the defect is so manifestly obvious as not to escape detection, and the buyer accepts it without protest, he is considered to have renounced his right to the option. The burden of proving that an apparent defect escaped his notice falls upon the buyer;[143]

(4) The contract must not have been made subject to an agreement excluding guarantee. If the buyer has exonerated the seller from his responsibility for defects, he may not have subsequent resource to the option. According to Shaybānī, a waiver of this nature only covers defects existing at the time of sale, and cannot encompass defects arising thereafter.[144] Abū Yūsuf, however, interprets such waivers as applicable to all defects

---

139 Santillana, *Instituzioni*, II, p.147

140 Sanhūrī, *Maṣādir al-Ḥaqq*, II, p.112 f.; *idem.*, IV, p.276; Owsia, *op.cit.*, p.483

141 Except in Hire contracts, where defects occurring after transfer of possession nevertheless give rise to the option: Ibn Abidīn, *Radd al-Muḥtār*, IV, p.78

142 Sanhūrī, *Maṣādir al-Ḥaqq*, IV, p.274

143 Sanhūrī, *Maṣādir al-Ḥaqq*, IV, p.276; Bellefonds, *Traité*, I, p.338

144 Kāsānī, *Badā'i'*, V, pp.276-277; Bellefonds, *Traité*, I, p.338

> present and future, without the need for express declaration of this meaning. The variation of opinion presumably has something to do with the Islamic preclusion of contracting for future occurrences, *Gharar*, and existence of the object of contract at the time of contracting. The remaining Schools are reluctant to authorise general clauses of non-guaranty, but differences of opinion still occur.[145]

Despite the variations in opinion among and within the schools, the nature of the exceptions is so restrictive that, given the principles governing the exercise of the option, it would seem that there is no general remedy in Islamic Law to the buyer for defects arising after transfer of possession, except in accordance with these conditions. There are, however, a few exceptions which relate ostensibly again to slaves, but some of which may easily be applied to goods in general.

An exception to the first condition occurs in Mālikī *Fiqh*, where the theory of *'Uhda*, or legal guarantee, determines that where a defect develops (in a slave) shortly after the sale and transfer of possession, that defect is considered anterior to the passing of possession. It may therefore give rise to the buyer's right of option to annul the contract.[146]

In fact, there are two kinds of *'Uhda*. One kind allows that all defects appearing in the object within the course of three days subsequent to the passing of possession, are considered as occurring prior to the transfer; the second kind establishes the term at one year from the passing of possession, and concerns the onset of three particular diseases: leprosy (*al-Juzām*); vitiligo (*al-Baraṣ*);[147] and madness.[148] In all these cases the buyer may avail himself of the option to annul the contract on the basis of defect, even though that defect did not exist at the time of transfer of ownership. The example lends itself to a comparative situation arising in relation to the sale of real estate, where defects undiscovered at the time of sale, manifest themselves at some considerable time thereafter, but which may be ascribed to faults existing, if not apparent, prior to the contract.

---

145 In the Shāfi'ī School, for example, Shīrāzī notes a minimum of three opinions : (1)That the clause covers all defects; (2) That it is completely inoperable; (3) That it is only valid in relation to hidden defects in animals and slaves, of which the seller is ignorant. Shīrāzī, *Kitāb al-Tanbīh Fī al-Fiqh, op.cit.*, II, p.16; *idem., al-Muhadhdhab Fī Fiqh Madhhab al-Imām al-Shāfi'ī, op.cit.*, I, p.288; see also al-Ḥaṭṭāb, *Mawāhib al-Jalīl*, IV, p.439; Ramlī states that where the waiver is operable, it is absolute: *Nihāyat al-Muḥtāj*, IV, p.33; and Santillana, *Instituzioni*, II, p.149.

146 Ibn Rushd, *Bidāyat al-Mujtahid*, II, p.175; Bellefonds, *Traité, I, p.336*

147 Or leucodermia : A kind of piebald skin disorder.

148 Ibn Rushd, *Bidāyat al-Mujtahid*, II, p.175; Bellefonds, *Traité, I, p.336*

The second condition is the subject of a certain amount of controversy in the Ḥanafī School, notably in relation to the four defects mentioned above.[149] There is a minority contingent of authors who maintain that it is not necessary that such defects are manifestly still in existence when the contractor seeks to annul the sale, and that prior existence of these defects is sufficient to establish his option to annul. The view is forthright, for example, in relation to the case of madness, which is commonly regarded as incurable. This view does, however, remain the minority opinion, the majority holding that the principles of existence apply to these defects as to any others.

7.4.4 Effects

The buyer who discovers a defect in accordance with the conditions stated above, is granted the right by law, to either annul or confirm the contract. In cases where the defect is only minor, the Mālikī buyer is only permitted a third option : He may only affirm the sale and demand restitution of the price proportional to the gravity of the defect in the object.

If the buyer affirms the sale after discovery of the defect, the sale, which is *ghayr lāzim* prior to his exercising the option, becomes binding upon him. His confirmation may be express, or tacit as the result of some disposition made by him, or his use of the object. Once the buyer has affirmed the contract, he may not then reclaim from the seller; this is accordance with Ḥanafī and Shāfi'ī *Fiqh*, and Mālikī *Fiqh* in the case of grave defects. The Ḥanbalī jurists grant the buyer an indemnity (*Arsh al-'Ayb*) equivalent to the difference between the price of the non-defective article and that for which the defective article would be sold on the market.[150] This last solution is considered the most judicious by Bellefonds.[151] It is rejected outright by the remaining schools on the basis that allowing the buyer to collect restitution merely obscures the indemnity which the Ḥanbalī law claims the seller should pay.

If the buyer opts to annul the contract, a distinction is made here in Ḥanafī *Fiqh* in order to establish the procedure of this annulment, according to whether the defect has been discovered prior, or subsequent, to the transfer of possession. If discovery is made prior to transfer, the annullment may be effected without either

---

149 In relation to adult slaves (not minors, where they are not regarded as serious defects) namely, habitual escaping, stealing, nocturnal incontinence and madness. Through deductive logic, it has been stated that if a child slave suffering from incontinence continues with the defect into adulthood, it does not constitute a defect as viewed judicially, because the defect occurred after the transfer of possession. See Kāsānī, *Badā'i'*, V, pp.275-276; Bellefonds, *Traité*, I, p.337

150 Ibn Qudāma, *Kitāb 'Umdat al-Aḥkām Fī al-Fiqh, op.cit.*, ; and Maqdisī, *al-Sharḥ al-Kabīr*, in the margin of Ibn Qudāma's *al-Mughnī*, (Second Edn.) IV, p.86;

151 Bellefonds, *Traité*, I, p.339. This is also the case in Shi'a law; See Owsia, *op.cit*, p.482

the acquiescence of the seller, or the intervention of the courts. The buyer's declaration of annullment, and his having made all reasonable efforts to ensure that his decision reaches the seller, is sufficient.[152]

If the defect is discovered after transfer of possession, and the buyer requires to annul the sale, according to the Ḥanafī and Mālikī Schools, he must procure the acquiescence of the seller.[153] If the seller declines to restitute the price, the buyer's remedy lies with the courts. The solutions here are judicious, for so long as the object has not been delivered to the buyer, it is unlikely that he himself has paid the price; the annulment is therefore practically and straightforwardly effected without the need for recourse to a judge. In the latter case, where property and consideration have changed hands, the situation becomes more complicated, and each case should be judged according to its own circumstances.

When annulment has been granted by either the seller, or the court, the buyer must return the object to the seller, and may demand restitution of the price if he has already paid it. It is only in the Ḥanbalī school that he may adopt the intermediary option of retaining the object for partial restitution in proportion to its decreased value due to the defect.

If, however, the buyer is prevented from returning the object to the seller, for one of the various reasons which terminate the option, he is then allowed by all schools to demand such restitution from the seller, so long as he himself has not contributed to the impossibility of returning it.[154]

7.4.5 Extinction of the Option

The numerous situations which terminate the Option of Defect may be divided into two categories :

(1) Those relating to the presumed will, or formal will of the buyer to confirm the sale, despite the defects contained in the object;[155]

(2) Those in consequence of a change in the object or in its legal condition.[156]

---

152 Bellefonds, *Traité*, I, pp.339-340

153 This is not so in the Shāfi'ī and Ḥanbalī Schools, where the buyer may annul without recourse to the seller or, on his default, to a judge. See Ramlī, *Nihāyat al-Muḥtāj*, IV, 41.

154 Bellefonds, *Traité*, I, p.340

155 Sanhūrī, *Maṣādir al-Ḥaqq*, IV, p.279 f.

156 *ibid.*, IV, p.283 f.

Waiver of Right

The buyer may renounce his right to the Option. This may be effected in advance by agreement, or at the time of discovery of the option. Renunciation may be tacit, as the result of an act of conversion which manifests the buyer's intention to accept the object with its defect;[157] or by any disposition once he has been notified of the defect; or in general, any non-action by the buyer once he has been notified of the defect.[158]

Disposition, Change, Conversion

Any change, conversion or disposition of the object extinguishes the Option, whether such change, conversion or disposition is of a legal or material nature. For example, if the buyer himself sells, makes a gift of, pledges, or places the object on bail, the object has been made the subject of a legal disposition; it is no longer in the buyer's possession, and may not be returned to the original seller.[159] The result is the same whether the buyer has converted or disposed of the object in knowledge of its defect, or whether he was unaware of it. Thus it is of no effect whether the change, conversion or disposal was made prior, or subsequent to the conversion. If, however, the object is eventually restored to him, for example, in the case of a pledge, Hire, or bail contract, and whether or not the second party of the second disposition has taken advantage of his own option of Defect, Inspection, Sharṭ, or any other solution available to him, the right to annul the first contract on the basis of the defect is restored to that first buyer, if he can show that he was unaware of the defect prior to his subsequent disposition.[160] If it can be proven, however, that the buyer disposed of the object with full knowledge of its defect, this is taken as tacit acceptance of the defect and he is denied the option to rescind the first contract.

Where the change is of a material nature, for example, by total or partial loss, damage or conversion, certain additional principles apply for the exercise of the option :-

(1) **Conversion** : In principle, any conversion of the goods by the buyer precludes his right of option to rescind for defect. There is a certain amount of disagreement on this matter, however, as some authors declare that conversion

---

157 For example, dyeing or cutting material; building on land; grinding corn: See Sanhūrī, *Maṣādir al-Ḥaqq*, IV, p. 287

158 At least to the extent that his non-action is neither self-explanatory, nor justified otherwise. Ramlī, *Nihāyat al-Muḥtāj*, IV, 42; Bellefonds, *Traité*, I, p.341

159 Sanhūrī, *Maṣādir al-Ḥaqq*, IV, p.287

160 Bellefonds, *Traité*, I, p.341, citing Ḥaṭṭāb, *Mawāhib al-Jalīl*, IV, 444-445

in the form of addition is without effect on the option, and that it is only by way of exception that the option is denied to the buyer on discovery of a latent defect. In its simplest exposition, the authors distinguish the effects of the right to opt for defect in four different kinds of "addition" :-

(a) Where defect occurs with any inherent increase of the object (*Ziyāda Muttaṣila Mutawallada min al-Aṣl*), for instance an increase in the size or weight of an animal. The option operates as normal, irrespective of whether the defect is discovered before or after passing of possession. Whatever option the buyer may choose, he must include the increase, and may not claim compensatory indemnity for the defect from the seller, without having to pay a supplement for the increase.

(b) Where the defect occurs with any addition which is non-inherent, but which is inseparable, for instance, dying a purchased material, or building on purchased land. The buyer does not have the right to opt, irrespective of whether the defect is discovered before or after transfer of possession. He may, however, claim from the seller a diminution in price corresponding to the gravity of the defect concerned.

(c) Any inherent addition which is separable (*Munfasila*), for example, natural fruits, milk, farm stock produce.[161] In this case, where the defect has been discovered prior to passing of possession, the buyer retains his right to option. The example of livestock bearing young falls into this category : the buyer in this case may annul the sale completely, rejecting the original defective animal of the contract and the young, or he may opt to confirm, for the original sale-price agreed, which means that he takes both animals.[162] This decision does not altogether concord with the general principles of object of contract, which dictate that objects not originally agreed upon in the contract, cannot be retained by the buyer. In accordance with general Islamic principles of *Ribā*, it would have been expected that the buyer would be required to contract separately for the young, or at least to have paid valuable consideration for the increase, so that he would not be gaining 'something for nothing'. The distinction here is that the addition is discovered prior to passing of possession, and the addition of the young is considered compensation for the defect; likewise, acceptance of the defect may be regarded as consideration for the additional object, despite the fact that defect and addition are unlikely to be of equal value. The transfusion of 'two' contracts into one here is an

161 Sanhūrī, *Maṣādir al-Ḥaqq*, IV, p.285 f.

162 *ibid.*, p.285

uncharacteristic solution of Islamic *Fiqh*.

Where the defect is discovered subsequent to passing of possession, the buyer's right of option is extinguished.[163] He may, however, claim from the seller, restitution of the price proportional to the gravity of the defect.[164] Returning to the case of the animal bearing young, if the buyer were to return both to the seller, the seller would himself acquire goods (the additional young animal) for which he was not a guarantor. If the buyer were to retain the young, and return only the animal to the seller, he would be benefitting from the illicit gain, because he has not paid consideration for it, either valuable, or by accepting the defect. The addition of the young, which occurred after transfer of possession, is rightfully his property. If, however, he were entitled to revoke the contract, he would have to do it completely, returning the object and the addition. As it is, the true object of the contract is defective, and for this he may claim restitution from the seller. In effect, in this case, he is not required to pay consideration for the young in kind, by forfeiting his compensation for the defect, because the addition is legally his property.

(d) A defect occurring in conjunction with any distinct and non-inherent additions, for example, revenues and profit derived from usufruct. Here, there is no obstacle to the exercise of the option for defect. If the object is still in the seller's possession when the increase occurs, he keeps the profit when the contract is dissolved, because the option is of retroactive effect, and the seller is regarded as never having lost ownership of the object. If the increase occurs when the object has been delivered to the buyer, and the buyer opts to annul the contract for defect, he must restitute the defective goods, adding to it the profit he has made from the addition. This is the opinion of the two Ḥanafī disciples, Muḥammad and Abū Yūsuf, which forms the majority opinion of that School.[165]

(2) **Total Loss** : If the object has been totally lost or damaged, there is no question of the right of option arising. Where destruction of the object occurs whilst it is in the possession of the seller, the risk falls on him, and he cannot claim from the buyer. If the object perishes after transfer of possession to the buyer, the risk falls on him, but he may reclaim from the seller the difference in price resulting from the discovery of the defect in the object prior to its destruction.[166]

---

163 *ibid.*, p.273

164 *ibid.*, p.286

165 Bellefonds, *Traité*, I, p.342-344

166 Sanhūrī, *Maṣādir al-Ḥaqq*, IV, p.284

(3) **Partial Loss** : If loss occurs before passing of possession, and the buyer is not responsible, the buyer may resort to his usual right of option to confirm or rescind the contract. He may also elect to take possession of the object at a reduced price, proportional to the partial loss or damage.[167]

If the partial loss occurs before passing of possession through some fault of the buyer's, that buyer may elect to confirm the sale for the originally agreed sale price, or to claim a reduction in price from the seller, in which case, the latter has the right to annul the contract.

Where partial loss has occurred subsequent to the passing of possession, the buyer forfeits his right to the option, but he may claim an indemnity from the seller, representing the decrease in value of the object due to the defect. From the moment of transfer of possession, the seller is no longer the guarantor, and the risk falls on the buyer, but the seller may agree to restitute the total price to the buyer in return for the goods in their original state.[168]

(4) **Death of the Beneficiary** : The option of Defect is not extinguished by the death of the beneficiary. The right to opt passes to his heirs on condition that the deceased's death occurs before the discovery of the defect.[169]

7.4.6 Alternative Forms of Defect

The Option for defect may be held to operate in situations in which a characteristic of the contract, although not immediately recognisable as a defect insofar as it affects the value of the object for the contractor, nevertheless causes him some loss.[170] Such would be the case, for instance, where the buyer discovers that the object he has bought has hitherto been placed on bail or pledge and thus has liens attached to it; or where a right of pre-emption attaches to real estate. The existence of liens and pre-existing rights manifestly affect the value of the goods for the buyer, and the law will afford him the right of option to rescind his contract in such cases.

In some works, the options of Description and Inspection are treated simultaneously, and in conjunction with Mistake in contracts. In others they are treated separately.[171] On the whole, it is easier to treat the option for misdescription under the subject of Mistake, as an impediment to consent, and this is where

---

[167] *ibid.*, p. 284

[168] *ibid.*, p.285

[169] Bellefonds, *Traité*, I, p.344

[170] Ibn Ābidīn, *Radd al-Muḥtār*, IV, pp.49 ff.; Bellefonds, *Traité*, I, p.344

[171] See Kāsānī, *Badā'i'*, V, p.292; *Majella*, Arts. 310-312 (Description); and 320-325 (Inspection)

reference is made to it both in this work and in Sanhūrī's treatise.[172]

The Ḥanafīs and Shāfi'īs hold that Options for dispossession (*Khiyār al-Istiḥqāq*), whether partial or whole, also come into this category. Whether it is the buyer who is dispossessed of a part of the object or whether it is partial loss of the object whilst in the seller's possession, the situation affords the buyer the right to rescind the contract by Option of Defect. If he confirms the contract, he is not liable to compensate the seller for the decrease in value due to dispossession or partial loss.[173] In this case, the Mālikīs distinguish between total or majority dispossession, where the buyer may rescind the contract; and partial dispossession, where the buyer may only claim a reduction in price.[174]

7.4.7 Modern Legislation

In the modern Civil Code of the UAE, the warranty against defects in objects of contracts is recognised as a natural legal right in contracts susceptible to cancellation,[175] "save as are within the customary tolerance".[176] The general rules relating to the option for defects apply, namely, the defect must affect the value of the object, it must be unknown to the purchaser, and there must not be any waiver in favour of the seller, exempting him from liability for that defect.[177] The option is operable for "old"[178] defects, that is, latent[179] defects which were present in the goods prior to the sale, or which arise prior to delivery,[180] or which are new but attributable to an old cause which existed prior to delivery.[181]

Where these conditions apply, the contract is not binding upon the beneficiary of the option, who may exercise his right to opt before delivery, or may cancel thereafter.[182] As in the Classical exposition, the option to avoid before delivery may be affected by any demonstration of cancellation without requiring the mutual consent of the other contracting party, or an order of the court, so long as the co-

---

172 *Maṣādir al-Ḥaqq*, II, p.112 f.; and Chapter 6.2 above

173 Ḥaṭṭāb, *Mawāhib al-Jalīl*, V, p.304; Shīrāzī, *al-Muhadhdhab*, I, p.296

174 Ibn Rushd, *Bidāyat al-Mujtahid*, II, p.320; Ḥaṭṭāb, *Mawāhib al-Jalīl*, V, pp.303ff. Bellefonds, *Traité*, I, p.344

175 UAE Federal Civil Code, No.2 of 1987, Art.237

176 *ibid.*, Art. 543 (1) and (2) and Art. 237

177 *ibid.*, Art.238

178 UAE Civil Code, Art. 238

179 That is, which cannot be observed by an external inspection of the goods, or which would not be apparent to the ordinary man, or which would only be apparent upon testing. *ibid.*, Art. 544 (4)

180 *ibid.*, Arts. 544 (19 and (2), and 238

181 *ibid.*, Art. 544 (3)

182 *ibid.*, Art. 239 (1)

contractor has been notified of that cancellation.[183] But after the passing of possession, cancellation must be by mutual consent or by order of the court.[184]

There are certain circumstances in which the seller is not responsible for old and latent defects, however; these are itemised as follows :

(1) If the seller discloses the defect to the purchaser at the time of sale;

(2) If the buyer accepts the defect after he has seen it, or it has been disclosed to him;[185]

(3) If the buyer knows of the defect;[186]

(4) If the seller inserts a condition into the contract waiving his liability for defects, or for specific defects, except where the seller deliberately conceals the defect or the buyer is prevented from seeing it;[187]

(5) If the sale is by public auction by judicial or administrative authorities.[188]

A strange anomaly exists in the UAE Code with regard to precisely what may constitute the option. Article 544 (1) in the section "Effects of Sale : (iii) Liability for latent defects", states that the option is either to confirm or to cancel the sale. The purchaser does not have the facility within this Code to accept them in return for a reduction in the stipulated price.[189] However, Article 242 in the subsection entitled 'The Option to Reject for Defects', states : "The person having the option to reject for a defect may also retain the thing contracted for and claim for the reduction in value". As the option for defect arises as a natural legal right, and does not require previous stipulation within the contract, this anomaly is perplexing. It remains to be seen how a court of law would interpret the inherent contradiction between these two articles.

Where the party with the right of option elects to cancel, he must return the object to the seller and he may recover the price paid.[190] As in the Classical *Fiqh*, the option lapses by non-exercise; by acceptance of the defect after becoming aware of it; by any disposition of the object whether or not prior to knowledge of the defect; by loss or destruction of the object after passing of possession; by conversion, or increase prior to receipt which does not arise from the object itself,

---

183 *ibid.*, Art. 239 (2)

184 *ibid.*, Art.239 (2)

185 *ibid.*, Art.238

186 *ibid.*, Art.238

187 *ibid.*, Art.238

188 *ibid.*, Art. 545

189 *ibid.*, Art. 544 (1)

190 *ibid.*, Art. 240

or after delivery, "by way of a single increase arising out of the thing itself".[191] The option is similarly not avoided by the death of the party having that option and the right passes to his heirs.[192]

The right to return the goods to the seller for defect is not prevented by reason of a change in market value of the goods.[193] The option lapses if the buyer converts or disposes of the goods subsequent to realisation of the defect.[194] But if he converts or disposes of them prior to such knowledge, his recourse against the seller is by way of reduction in the price proportional to the defect.[195] If, however, he has created third party rights over the object prior to his knowledge of the defect, but the object still remains in his ownership, he may return it to the seller free of the third party rights so long as the object has not been altered in the interim.[196] But if the third party rights are created after his knowledge of the defect he forfeits his right to return it. If any addition has been made in the above case, it is treated as a new alteration with an old defect.[197]

Where a new defect arises while the object is in the buyer's possession, his option to cancel the sale on the basis of an old defect has lapsed. He may not return the object to the seller unless the latter specifically agrees to take them back; but he again may have recourse against the seller by means of a reduction in the price of the object proportional to the defect.[198] This rule applies where any addition has been made by the seller to the object.[199] It that new defect later disappears, the option for the old defect once again becomes operable.[200]

If several items are sold under one agreement and a defect becomes apparent in one of them, prior to delivery, the purchaser may accept the whole for the whole price, or reject the whole.[201] Where the defect in one of the items becomes apparent after delivery, that individual item may be returned to the seller, so long as it may be separated from the rest without harm, for a proportional reduction in the price of the whole. He may not, however, return all the goods unless the seller so agrees, or unless harm would be caused to the goods by separation. In the latter case, the party has the option of returning all for the full price, or accepting all for the full

---

191 *ibid.*, Art. 241 (1) This is an innovative condition.

192 *ibid.*, Art. 241 (2)

193 *ibid.*, Art. 552

194 *ibid.*, Art.546

195 *ibid.*, Art.547

196 *ibid.*, Art.552 (1)

197 *ibid.*, Art.552 (2)

198 *ibid.*, Art.548 (1)

199 *ibid.*, Art.549 (1)

200 *ibid.*, Art. 548 (2)

201 *ibid.*, Art.550 (1)

price.[202]

Liability and risk pass on delivery of the object to the buyer. When the buyer rejects the sale, or his right to reject is established by a court of law by virtue of a proven defect, that liability passes back to the seller, whether or not the object is back in his possession, unless the court has ordered immediate return if the seller is present.[203] Where the object yields, therefore, and that yield is not deemed to be part of the property, the yield remains with the party in possession, just as in the Classical Law exposition. In this respect, the buyer cannot have recourse against the seller for monies expended on the property in the interim between delivery and cancellation.[204] Where there is no yield, the buyer does have recourse against the seller for monies so spent.[205] Where the yield is deemed part of the property, it belongs to the seller.[206]

If a third party claim arises over part of the goods sold prior to the buyer taking possession of the whole, that buyer is permitted to return the goods he has already taken and to recover the price paid; or he may accept the sale and have recourse in respect of that part of the goods which is subject to the third party right.[207]

If the third party claim arises after delivery, and this gives rise to a defect, the buyer may opt to return the goods and recover the price; or he may retain the remainder (that is, that part which is not affected by the third party claim) and recover proportional value from the price. Where the third party right does not give rise to a defect, and the part over which that claim has arisen is the lesser part of the contract, the purchaser may only have recourse over that part.[208] If it becomes apparent after the sale that there is a right over the goods sold in favour of a third party, the purchaser has the option either to wait for that third party right to expire, or to cancel the contract and recover the price from the seller.[209]

In any event, all claims for rescission of a contract, or for reduction in, or supplement to the purchase price are debarred after the expiration of one year from the date of delivery of the goods.[210]

The UAE Code therefore, in regard to the option of defect, is in close harmony with the majority opinions of the Classical *Fiqh*. The only major difference which is apparent between these systems, is that the modern legislation of the UAE

---

202 *ibid.*, Art.550 (2)

203 *ibid.*, Art.554

204 *ibid.*, Art.553 (1)

205 *ibid.*, Art.553 (3)

206 *ibid.*, Art.553 (2)

207 *ibid.*, Art. 540 (1)

208 *ibid.*, Art. 540 (2)

209 *ibid.*, Art. 540 (3)

210 *ibid.*, Art. 524

debarrs claims for defects in goods six months after delivery to the purchaser has taken place.[211] This is, of course, except where the seller himself has undertaken to be responsible for the goods for a longer period, in which case he will probably issue a certificate of guarantee at the time of delivery, with its stipulated term. The idea of bars by limitation is totally alien to the Classical Law, but the practicality of such limitation in modern times is readily apparent. Separate rules apply for immovables and real estate in this context, which may require longer periods of limitation, and in any event, the seller cannot rely on this limitation where he has fraudulently concealed the defect from the buyer.[212]

7.5 KHIYĀR AL-RU'YA

Where parties are contracting *in absentia*, or the object is not present at the *Majlis*, and the buyer has given valuable consideration, he is granted the right to rescind or confirm the contract by the Option of Inspection, when the object is eventually delivered into his possession, and does not meet with his contractual expectations.[213] This Option also provides a useful resource in the case of contractual Mistake, where the will of the contracting parties has not been disclosed, or in relation to Mistake as to a difference in the desired (insubstantial) quality of the object;[214] in the *Salam* contract,[215] or in contracts of sale by sample,[216] or "lump" sales.[217]

The doctrines pertaining to this option are manifestly different according to the various Schools of law. The Ḥanafī School, for instance, regards this option as a legal option granted to any contractor who has not seen the object at the time of

[211] *ibid.*, Art.555 (1)

[212] *ibid.*, Art.555 (2)

[213] al-Kāsānī, *al-Badā'i'*, V, pp.291-299; Sanhūrī, *Maṣādir al-Ḥaqq*, II, pp.132-135 : Sanhūrī quotes a Tradition of the Prophet in support of this doctrine : "Whoever buys something without seeing it has the option upon seeing it". See also Chapter on Mistake, Section 'Non-Disclosure of the Will'; and Mistake in Value; and *Ghabn*. Also, *ibid.*, IV, 248

[214] See Sanhūrī, *Maṣādir al-Ḥaqq*, II, p.114; and Chapter V.5.4 ("Precise Determination of the Object); and Chapter VI above.

[215] See Chapter V.2.1 above

[216] See *Majella*, Arts. 324-325. Samples of immovables are not generally valid representations.

[217] Where each lump item must be viewed separately. See *ibid*, Arts. 327-328

contract.[218] As a legal right, he does not need to stipulate the characteristics of the option at the time of contracting, but should he do so, the option nevertheless remains open to him, and those characteristics become enforceable.[219]

The Mālikīs, on the other hand, regard it as a conventional option, for which the contractor who wishes to benefit by it must usually reserve the option at the time of contracting. Here, the object must be precisely defined, and if the characteristics thus described are present at inspection, or if they are not defined at the time of contracting, and the option is mentioned in the contract, the sale is binding.[220]

The Shāfi'ī position ranges from the more modern absolute prohibition of the option, - on the basis of Phophetic Tradition prohibiting aleatory sales, and sales where the object is not present.[221] If the sale of an object which is not present at the *Majlis* is invalid, they say, there can be no option to rescind the contract - to one which again resembles the Ḥanafī doctrine.

Al-Ṭaḥāwī relates a Tradition (originally related by Bakkār b. Qutayba) of a dispute between Talha b. 'Ubaydallāh and 'Uthmān b. 'Affān : Talha bought property in Kūfa from 'Uthmān. After the sale it was claimed that 'Uthmān had been cheated, but he claimed option of Inspection, for he had not seen the object before selling it. Talha said the option was his right for he had bought something which he had not seen. Jubayr b. Mat'am, ajudicating, decided that the option was the right of Talha (the buyer) and was not available to 'Uthmān.[222]

Although it is difficult to detect the predominant Ḥanbalī doctrine, the discernible consensus seems to hold with a position which, although it approaches the Shāfi'ī doctrine, is less absolute. Discernible also, are more liberal opinions concerning the Option of Inspection, which bear closer resemblance to the position of the Ḥanafī School. The predominating opinion seems to be, then, that the Option is permitted so long as the buyer has either seen the object at some recent point

---

218 According to Abū Ḥanīfa, Abū Yūsuf, Zafar and Muḥammad, who do not accord the option to the seller, who is assumed to have seen the object before. See al-Ṭaḥāwī, *Kitāb al-Shuf'a*, Arabic Text in part IV of Wakin, *The Function of Documents in Islamic Law*, I, 2.78; Others (Sawwar b. 'Abdallāh al-'Anbarī, for example) give the option to both buyer and seller if neither have seen the object previously. See *idem.*, I, 2.79-80

219 Sarakhsī, *Kitāb al-Mabsūṭ*, XIII, pp.68-78; Ibn al-Hammām, *Fatḥ al-Qadīr*, V, pp.137-151; Ibn Nujaym, *al-Baḥr al-Rā'iq*, VI, pp.26-35; al-Zayla'ī, *Tabyīn al-Ḥaqā'iq*, IV, pp.24-31; Sanhūrī, *Maṣādir al-Ḥaqq*, IV, p.248, 249 f.

220 The Mālikī jurist, Ibn Rushd, in his *Bidāyat al-Mujtahid*, II, (Cairo, 1952) p.154, gives a useful account of the position in the Schools; he does not, however, mention the Ḥanbalī doctrine. See also Sanhūrī, *Maṣādir al-Ḥaqq*, IV, pp.259-261

221 "Do not sell what you do not have". This has been interpreted by all Schools except the Ḥanafī to mean "actually in possession". See al-Shīrāzī, *al-Muhadhdhab*, I, pp.263-264; and Sanhūrī, *ibid.*, IV, p.262 f.

222 al-Ṭaḥāwī, *Kitāb al-Shuf'a*, I, 2.81; in Wakin, *The Function of Documents*, p. 18 of the Arabic Text.

prior to the contract, or that the object has been precisely defined in the contract. In this way, the risk that the object has changed in the interim, or will not meet with his contractual expectations, is reduced. If the object has changed, deteriorated, or does not meet with its contractual description, the reasoning is that the buyer may dissolve the contract on the basis that the stipulations of the contract have not been complied with. Thus the Option of Inspection is effectively rejected also by the Ḥanbalī School.[223]

The predominant Ḥanafī doctrine on the Option of Inspection is clearly the most liberal, and has due consideration for the practicalities of trading without necessarily being in the presence of the object of contract. It is, for this reason, a particularly useful reference for modern *Fiqh*, in relation to Stock Market and Financial Futures trading.

The Ḥanafī School interprets the Prophetic Tradition "Do not sell what you do not have", to mean "what you do not own", thereby averting what the other Schools have interpreted as a preclusion to the Option of Inspection. In addition, the Ḥanafī jurists claim that to allow the Option is to avert the very *Gharar* which the other Schools claim is introduced by the option. The sale is saved from risk, they state, because it does not become binding until after the object has been seen. Thus the option which is exercised before the object has been seen would be invalid and of no effect. More positively, the Ḥanafīs promote an alternative *Ḥadīth*, whose origins are somewhat dubious, stating that "He who buys a thing without having seen it, has the Option at the moment he sees it".[224]

7.5.1 Conditions

According to the Mālikī School, if the object is situated in the vacinity of the *Majlis*, it is indispensible for the buyer to have seen it before contracting. If it is situated too far away, or in a place which is too difficult of access, the sale is possible on condition either that the object is precisely described, or that the buyer has inspected it at some short time prior to contracting.[225]

If, at the passing of possession, the object differs from its previous viewing or its description, the contract may be annulled by the buyer on the basis that the object does not conform with the seller's contractual promise. Thus the right of Option *per se* does not exist in the Mālikī School, unless the parties have specifically agreed in their contract that the buyer may opt to rescind the contract upon inspection of the object. The right of the buyer in this case is automatic, and there is no requirement for him to establish that the object differs from the one he

---

223 Sanhūrī, *Maṣādir al-Ḥaqq*, IV, p.265 f.; Bellefonds, *Traité*, I, p.346

224 Marghīnānī, *al-Hidāya*, III, p.25 (Cairo, 1936); Bellefonds, *Traité*, I, p.348

225 Sanhūrī, *ibid.*, IV, p.259

intended to purchase.[226]

The conditions applicable to the Ḥanafī Option of Inspection are similar to those of the Mālikī School : the object must be precisely defined as to its kind, genre and value in order to preclude any imbalance between the parties' obligations, and to prevent the facility of the option becoming prone to exploitation, fraud or mistake. The Ḥanafī school does, therefore, recognise the inherent difficulties of this option, but does not consider these difficulties sufficient justification for prohibiting the facility, and denying the buyer who has not seen the goods, the advantage of being able to trade immediately.

The Option is, however, strictly limited to contracts for valuable consideration which transfer ownership; or hire contracts. Thus it may be exercised in contracts of sale, barter, or partition of real property, for example, in allotment of goods forming the capital of a company. It may not be exercised, for example, in payments of *Mahr*, or compensation for *Khul'*, or ransom, which are all acts which may not be revoked.[227]

The option is only available to the buyer in a contract of Sale; the seller may not have resource to this option.[228] The situation is parallel in contracts of Hire, Lease, and Bail. The reasoning is that the seller, Hirer or Bailor have already viewed the object, and that if the option were to be granted to these parties, ostensibly the consideration or price would become the object of the obligation, for which the option is expressly precluded. It would seem that these parties are denied the facility of the Option of Inspection, therefore, even in situations where it is conceivable that the Hirer, Lessor or Bailor have not previously seen the object, for instance, where the object has been inherited from a distant relative, and rented out, or otherwise, through agents of that locality. The matter remains uncertain, however, following a judgment invoked for the benefit of the Caliph 'Uthmān : 'Uthmān claimed to be able to exercise the Option of Inspection in a sale of goods which he had not seen prior to selling them, and this claim did not meet with objections from the Companions. It has since acquired a certain amount of authority through *Ijmā'*.[229] The established position of the Ḥanafī School, however, adheres to the original opinion regarding the seller and bailor who have not previously seen the object, and does not grant them the right to annul the contract of sale or bail. This rule does not apply to the contract of exchange or barter, where effectively both parties are buyer and seller, and therefore both may exercise the option.

---

226 The Mālikī doctrine is like that of the Ḥanafī School in this respect alone. See Sanhūrī, *Maṣādir al-Ḥaqq*, IV, p.260

227 Kāsānī, *Badā'i'*, V, p.292; Bellefonds, *Traité*, I, p.349

228 Abū Ḥanīfa originally concluded that the option would be available to the seller if the sale is concluded without him having seen the object. He later changed his opinion to the one adopted by the majority of the Ḥanafī jurists. Bellefonds, *Traité*, I, p.349

229 The judgment was delivered by Jabī b. Mat'am; See Bellefonds, *Traité*, I, p.349

In the Ḥanafī School, it is essential that the beneficiary of the Option should not have seen the object either at the time of contracting, or previously.[230] It is not sufficient, in other words, that the object should just have been absent at the time of contracting. If the buyer has seen the object previously, the burden falls on him to establish that it has changed since he last inspected it. It is of no matter how insignificant this change may have been.

The option becomes operable upon first sight of the object.[231] "Sight" has been subject to variable interpretation, but in principle, it amounts to the same as if the object had been present at the time of contracting. The situation can obviously vary due to the nature of the object in question, and it has been accepted that some objects of necessity require longer and more demanding examination than others : Real estate contracts, livestock purchased for meat, comestibles and such like are prime examples. Nevertheless, the established rule is that the option becomes operable on first **sight** of the object, for instance a glimpse of the facade of a house, or courtyard of a property, and continues for however long that particular inspection reasonably requires. The beneficiary may therefore decide to exercise his right of option on only part-inspection of the object.[232]

The duration of the option therefore depends on the object concerned. The *Fiqh*, quite naturally, seeks to limit this duration as much as is possible and reasonable, in order to restrict the uncertainty of the contract and its vulnerability to exploitation. The Mālikī School holds that the beneficiary's silence, after a certain delay which is sufficient in the circumstances for a rapid examination, is construed as confirmation of the contract. The Ḥanafī construction does not accord with this view, and where express ratification or annullment is not forthcoming, the beneficiary is considered as retaining the option in default until that option is extinguished, either by forfeiture, or by eventual lapse.

Where the party of a contract is blind and cannot view the object at the time of contract or subsequently, he may appoint a third party to inspect it for him. Where that third party has been given ostensible authority to contract on his principal's behalf, in other words, he is acting as the blind party's agent, it is his (the third party/Agent's) declaration which determines the nature of the contract, and the same conditions apply here as for normal sales by sighted parties.[233] If the third party has

---

230 Sanhūrī, *ibid.*, IV, p.260

231 Sanhūrī, *ibid.*, IV, p.255; *Majella*, Arts. 320 and 332 : Where the property has been seen at any time prior to contracting and the buyer is aware that it is that property, there is no option unless a change has susequently occurred in the object. The option also applies to contracts of Hire : see *ibid*, Arts. 507-512

232 Kāsānī, *Badā'i'*, V, p.295-296; Ibn al-Hammām, *Fatḥ al-Qadīr*, VI, p.141; Sanhūrī, *ibid.*, IV, p.256; Bellefonds, *Traité*, I, p.352; The *Majella*, defines inspection as 'becoming acquainted with the situation and condition of the object, so as to make known the principal thing desired in it'. (Art. 323)

233 See *Majella*, Art. 333

not been given authority to act on the principal's behalf, the option remains open to the blind principal, despite the fact that the object might now be in his possession.[234] The *Majella* takes up this solution for a messenger without authority sent to collect the object or suchlike.[235] The blind beneficiary may also inspect the object by use of alternative senses such as smell, touch, or taste, whichever is the most suitable in the circumstances, and again, the rules applying to the normal Option of Inspection are followed here.[236]

7.5.2 Effects

Because the option is of a legal nature, it does not have to be stipulated at the time of the contract. It functions in much the same way as the Civil Law *Condition Resolutoire*, in other words, as a condition of avoidance. Moreover, any agreement between the parties, either in advance, or at the time of contract, to deprive the buyer (or equivalent party) of his legal right to the Option of Inspection, is null and void.

Upon the agreement of the parties, ownership of the object is transferred to the buyer (or possession is transferred to the bailee, hirer). Thus in Ḥanafī *Fiqh*, the sale of an object which is not present or which has not been seen prior to contracting is valid, but not binding (*Nafīdh Ghayru Lāzim*).[237]

The option endures continually and up to the party's first sight, or cursory examination, of the object. In theory, the option should not be operable until the party has seen the object, although this matter is subject to dispute. The prevailing opinion determines that the buyer may exercise his right of option, and annul the contract before he sees the object. The contract, between agreement and seeing the object, is not binding, and therefore, in essence, it is revocable.[238]

Upon seeing the object for the first time, therefore, the beneficiary of the option may annul or confirm the contract. If he chooses to annul, the sale is considered as never having existed; If he chooses to confirm, the sale becomes binding as normal. The beneficiary is not required to justify his option to annul, for there is no burden of proof on him to show that the object does not meet with his contractual

---

[234] Abū Ḥanīfa disputes this opinion, on the basis that the mandate to receive into his possession, gives the third party the authority to exercise the option. See Marghīnānī, *al-Hidāya*, III, p.26. Either way, the situation is not altogether certain for the seller.

[235] *Majella*, Art. 334

[236] Kāsānī, *Badā'i'*, V, p.293; Marghīnānī, *al-Hidāya*, III, p.26; Bellefonds, *Traité*, I, p.351; *Majella*, Arts. 329-331. The blind man according to the *Majella* may not avail himself of the option if he has been provided with a correct description of the object prior to contracting, including 'descriptions' gained by tasting etc. prior to sale.

[237] Sarakhsī, *Kitāb al-Mabsūṭ*, XIII, p.199

[238] Kāsānī, *Badā'i'*, V, p.295; Bellefonds, *Traité*, I, p.350-351

expectations, providing he has not seen that object previously. This is the case even when the object has been precisely defined and appears in all respects to have met with those descriptions. Unlike the alternative Option of Description, the buyer in the Option of Inspection may retain his right of option even if the descriptions are satisfied. The option is thus operable without requiring justification, the acquiescence of the other contracting party, or the intervention of the courts.

7.5.3 Extinction

The option is extinguished :

(1) When the beneficiary has seen the object and made his declaration of option. Declaration may be express or tacit, by disposition. Silence does not, in all circumstances, mean confirmation, and cannot, in any case, be construed as annulment of the contract.

(2) If the beneficiary, before inspection, disposes of the object, either partially or completely, this may be construed as confirmation of the contract under certain circumstances. In general, however, it it not considered as ratification, as the option cannot generally come into operation until the object has been seen.[239] The authors allow that in contracts of sale to a third party, hire, affranchisement, gift accompanied by actual passing of possession, and actual pledge, the option is (temporarily) extinguished due to the superceding rights of the third party concerned : These rights cannot be jeopardised by a continuation of the option. The beneficiary's right to opt is therefore considered as having expired, not because his disposition is construed as ratification, but because one of the terms of the option itself has been suppressed. By virtue of the passing of possession of the object to a third party, the beneficiary himself has become a guarantor in respect of that third party. He may not, therefore, exercise the option unless the object is returned to him, for whatever reason, be it annulment of the second sale for latent defect, or expiry of the term of a bail contract.[240] The right of option does remain to the beneficiary when the subsequent disposition is itself revocable by nature (for instance, resale under a condition dependent upon the will of a contracting party; or gift before passing of possession).

3) Partial or total destruction of the object extinguishes the right to option. The principle is parallel to that discussed in relation to the Option of Defect, where

---

[239] This rule applies also to the primary seller. See *Majella*, Arts. 322 and 335; and Sanhūrī, *ibid.*, IV, p.257

[240] In general, rights which have been extinguished may not be rekindled subsequently. See Sanhūrī, *Maṣādir al-Ḥaqq*, IV, p.258; Bellefonds, *Traité*, I, p.354

the object is reduced in value, or has been converted.[241]

(4) The death of the beneficiary extinguishes the Option of Inspection. Heirs remain bound by the contract notwithstanding the fact that the beneficiary himself, if not deceased, would still have the facility to revoke the contract.[242]

7.5.4 Modern Legislation

The Option of Inspection has been incorporated into the majority of modern codes. Among the codes which were enacted during the first wave of legislative reform and which have been influenced by the work of 'Abd al-Razzāq al-Sanhūrī, the principles of the Ḥanafī *Fiqh* have been followed. Of the prototype codes of the 1950's, it is the Iraqi code which adheres closest to the Classical law exposition,[243] but similar principles may also be found in the Egyptian,[244] Syrian,[245] Lebanese,[246] and Libyan Codes.[247]

The option is also to be found in the UAE Civil Code. The Code reinforces the rules applicable in the classical law, that the option arises from a natural legal right that the object must not have been seen prior to contracting, and that it must be specified.[248] The term of the option in this code lasts until the object is seen within the agreed period, or until anything ocurrs which causes it to lapse,[249] such as confirmation of the contract, the death of the beneficiary[250] destruction of the object in whole or part, or their becoming defective; or an irrevocable disposition by the beneficiary, or a disposition which rights to a third party.[251] The option does not become binding on the beneficiary until he exercises his option,[252] nor does it lapse by non-exercise.[253]

---

241 See Section 4.5 above; Sanhūrī, *ibid.*, IV, pp.257-8; Kāsānī, *Badā'i'*, V, pp.296-297.

242 *Majella*, Art. 321; Sanhūrī, *ibid.*, IV, p.257

243 Iraqi Civil Code, 1953, Arts. 517-523

244 Egyptian Civil Code, Law No. 131 of 1948, Art. 419

245 Syrian Civil Code, Arts. 387, 389

246 Lebanese Civil Code, Art. 408

247 Libyan Civil Code of 1953, Art. 408

248 UAE Civil Code, No. 2 of 1987, Art. 226. The Option of Inspection is also expressly prescribed as a legal right in the Draft Commercial Code of the UAE, Art. 304

249 *ibid.*, Art. 227, 229 (2)

250 *ibid.*, Art. 229 (2)

251 *ibid.*, Art. 229 (2)

252 *ibid.*, Art. 228

253 *ibid.*, Art. 229 (1)

Cancellation or confirmation may be express or by implication, on condition that in the case of cancellation, the beneficiary informs his co-contractor of his decision.[254]

The contractual option of Inspection in the UAE Code is clearly seen, therefore, to adhere closely to the predominant line of the Classical *Fiqh* expositions. This may be taken as a general rule for the whole system of options as exposed in the modern Civil Code of the UAE. In general, therefore, we may summarise the position of modern legislation as regards options as follows :-

The Bahraini Code does not expressly allude to the Islamic system of Options, but this does not necessarily preclude certain facilities for avoiding or cancelling the contract due to the causes which give rise to the options. The Kuwaiti Code, taking its model from the Civil Law/Egyptian model, deals with Options briefly but not comprehensively; and not in the Classical Law methodology. As with the Bahraini Code, however, this does not mean that the same causes will not give rise to equitable remedies at law. The UAE Civil Code, as we have seen, is modelled on the Classical law, and mainly on the Ḥanafī School, but with exceptions. That a predominantly Mālikī State should opt for the Ḥanafī doctrinal exposition would be surprising if it were not for the fact that the Ḥanafīs are generally more tolerant of the number of recognised options (although they are not always the most liberal concerning the rigidity of the doctrines themselves); secondly, the Ḥanafī *Fiqh* treatises are by far the most expansive on this subject, and therefore provide a better source reference. Again, it would have been interesting to read from the legislative committee itself the reasoning behind its judicious choice of doctrines : the absence of a Memorandum here is, once more, unfortunate.

Nevertheless, the evident and directly Islamic source of this Code is pleasing, for it recaptures exactly the spirit and the letter of the Classical contractual law, and endorses the fact that these equitable systems of Options are eminently as relevant today as they were twelve to thirteen centuries ago.

---

254 *ibid.*, Art. 229 (2) and 230

Chapter 8

EXTRINSIC CONDITIONS

Extrinsic Conditions constitute part of the formation and binding force of contracts (like options) which admit of limitations and exceptions. The views of the main Schools regarding the extent of the freedom enjoyed by the contracting parties to insert conditions are widely divergent. On the one hand, the Ibāḍīs, Ḥanafīs and Shāfi'īs are cautiously restrictive, and argue that conditions are generally invalid subject to the stringent principles laid down by the jurists of these Schools. While on the other hand, the Mālikī and Ḥanbalī Schools (the latter propounded forcibly by Ibn Taymiyya) argue that the basic rule is to admit whatever conditions the parties deem requisite, subject to exceptional cases of invalidity.

8.1 Ḥanafī and Shāfi'ī Schools

According to the Ḥanafī and Shāfi'ī Schools, every contract clause (*Sharṭ*) which does not comply exactly to the rules laid down, or which introduces a modification to such rules, is null and void.[1] The narrow ambit of the term *Sharṭ* encompasses the general prerequisites for the validity of legal acts, as opposed to their essential elements (*Arkān*).[2] The wider ambit covers the extrinsic clauses which are increasingly appended to modern contracts. The Ḥanafīs generally recognise three types of condition, in accordance with their recognition of the three main categories of validity. These are : *Shurūṭ*

---

1 Chehata, *Droit Musulman*, (Paris, 1970) p.136

2 Schacht, *Introduction*, (Oxford, 1979) p.118

Ṣaḥīḥa, Fāsida, or *Bāṭila.*[3] When a condition is *Fāsid, it renders the whole contract Fāsid.* The *Fāsid* condition upsets the balance of equality between the contracting parties and since injury to one party is prohibited in contracts, the contract must be considered as voidable.[4] When the condition is *Bāṭil,* in that it does not confer additional advantage on any of the parties,[5] it does not affect the validity of the contract and the condition is severed from the contract.[6] Thus where the seller makes a condition that the buyer should not resell the goods, or that the buyer should destroy them, the condition can be severed and the contract remains valid.[7]

The rules of *Shurūṭ,* structured as they are upon the narrow interpretation, are severly restrictive: *Shurūṭ* are permitted so long as they are either :

(1) Implied in the nature of the contract (*Sharṭ yaqtaḍīhā al-'Aqd*) such as appointing the term of future delivery in a *Salam* contract;[8]

(2) Intimately connected with the contract (*Sharṭ mulāyama; Muwāfaqa*) such as a pledge of security in a contract of

---

3 Ibn al-Hammām, *Fatḥ al-Qadīr,* V, 214; Kāsānī, *Badā'i',* V, p.170; Sanhūrī, *Maṣādir al-Ḥaqq,* III, p.121; Abdalla Mohamed, 'Stipulations for the Benefit of Third Parties in Islamic Law of Contracts', *Journal of Islamic and Comparative Law,* vol.9 (1980) pp.7-20, at p.9; *Report of the Commission Appointed to Draft the Mejella,* in Hooper, *The Majella, op.cit.,* (1933) at p.7

4 Musa, 'The Liberty of the Individual in Contracts and Conditions According to Islamic Law', *Islamic Quarterly,* II (4) (1955) pp.253-255; Bellefonds, 'Les Actes Juridiques Valables et les Actes Nuls en Droit Musulman', 75 *Revue Algérienne, Tunisienne et Marocaine de Législation et de Jurisprudence,* 1 (1959); Chehata, 'Le Système des Nullités en droit Musulman Hanéfite et en Droit Comparé', *Rapports Généraux au VIe Congrès International de droit Comparé,* (Hamburg, 1962) at 91 (Brussells, 1964); and in 5 *Revue al-'Ulūm al-Qānūniyya wa al-Iqtiṣādiyya,* 1 (1963); Habachy, 'The System of Nullities in Muslim Law', 13 *American Journal of Comparative Law,* (1964) pp.69-71; Kourides, 'The Influence of Islamic Law on Contemporary Middle Eastern Legal Systems : The Formation and Binding Force of Contracts', *Columbia Journal of Transnational Law,* 9 (2) (1970) p.408

5 Definition given by Kāsānī, *Badā'i',* V, p.170

6 Kourides, 'The Influence of Islamic Law on Contemporary Middle East Legal Systems : The Formation and Binding Force of Contracts', *Columbia Journal of Transnational Law,* 9 (2) (1970) p.408

7 Kāsānī, *ibid.,* p.170

8 Shīrāzī, *al-Muhadhdhab,* I, p.268

surety;[9]

(3) Requirements for the incidence of a legal duty (*Sharṭ Wujūb*) such as the payment of *Zakāt*;[10]

(4) Have been established by custom or sanctioned by the *Fiqh*, such as *Khiyār al-Sharṭ*.[11]

The Ḥanafī and Shāfi'ī jurists disclose the incidence of terms and conditions in the process of their casuistic dicussions on contracts. From these discussions, three general rules may be surmised :-

(1) A contract containing any condition which is deemed to be advantageous or disadvantageous to either party, or repugnant to the requisites of the contract, is invalid.[12]

(2) The insertion of any condition which may occasion legitimate contention by involving an advantage to the subject of the sale is also invalid.[13]

Such sales were forthrightly condemned by the Prophet. The principles of their condemnation were taken up by the *'Ulamā'* on the grounds that additional or extraneous acts which do not naturally result from the contract, require consideration or recompense to balance the advantage they provide for the party demanding them. Without such recompense the contract would be of a usurious nature.

There are, however, exceptions to this quite stringent rule. The exceptions pertain to aspects where custom prevails over the auspices of *Qiyās*. Such a case, for instance, would be where C buys unsewn leather for shoes from D on condition that D sew them or have them made up for

---

9 Kāsānī, *Badā'i'*, V, p.171; Ibn al-Hammām, *Fatḥ al-Qadīr*, V, p.215. This is the general rule rather than an exception in the Shāfi'ī School. See Shīrāzī, *al-Muhadhdhab*, I, p.268

10 Shīrāzī, *Kitāb al-Tanbīh*, *op.cit.*, p.97; Levy, *Social Structure of Islam*, *op.cit.*, p.256; Musa, 'The Liberty of the Individual in Contracts and Conditions According to Islamic Law', 2 *Islamic Quarterly*, (1955) p.7

11 Ibn al-Hammām, *Fatḥ al-Qadīr*, V, p.214 f. The Ẓāhirīs will not recognise any condition unless it has been expressly permitted by a rule of law: Ibn Ḥazm, *al-Muḥallā*, (Cairo, 1347-1352) II, p.299, on the basis of a Prophetic Tradition, "How can men stipulate conditions which are not in the book of God ? All conditions that are not in the book of God are invalid, be it a hundred conditions, God's judgment is more binding."

12 Kāsānī, *Badā'i'*, V, p.169; Ramlī, *Nihāyat al-Muḥtāj*, III, p.433 ff.; Hamilton, *The Hedaya*, p.273; Schacht. *Introduction*, (Oxford, 1979) p.152

13 Marghīnānī/Hamilton, *ibid.*; Kāsānī, *ibid.*; Ramlī, *ibid.* The example given is the sale of a slave on condition that he is to be emancipated.

him.[14] The contract is initially *Fāsid*, but has generally been adopted by the process of *Istiḥsān* for practical purposes. It therefore represents a divergence from the rigid adherence of the Ḥanafī proposition that the effects of every contract are prescribed by law.[15]

Another such example concerns the *Khamīsa* contract, where the condition that the share-cropper deliver up one-fifth of the land-produce as a portion of the rent is properly void. Due to the intrinsic nature of the condition it would properly render the contract also void.[16] The Mālikī School recognises this condition, however, on the basis of *Ḍarūra*, as an exception, and in that School, at least, the contract is valid despite the non-conforming condition.

(3) The insertion of a clause which has no obvious advantage to either party, and yet is not a natural result of the contract, does not render the contract invalid. The condition itself is lawful but unenforceable, such as a contract to sell an animal on the condition that the purchaser shall sell it again.[17]

The anomaly which occurs in *Fāsid* contracts of this type in the Ḥanafī school is that if such a condition which renders the contract invalid is performed, then the contract redeems its validity. The purchaser who has emancipated the slave he has bought is therefore still responsible for its price to the seller.[18] Abū Ḥanīfa regards the complete and established sale as perfectly valid, and would even allow the purchaser legal effects naturally ensuing from the sale, such as compensation in the case of defect.[19]

(4) Any condition made by the seller reserving for himself any advantage from the sale is invalid. Thus a condition that "he shall reside in it for the space of two months after the sale" renders invalid a contract for the sale of a house.[20] Any reduction in the sale price here (viz. the prolonged residence in the house) implies the interweaving of a contract for rent in with the sale

---

14 Ibn al-Hammām, *Fatḥ al-Qadīr*, V, p.215; Hamilton, *The Hedaya*, p.273; Schacht, *Introduction*, p.152

15 Abdalla Mohamed, 'Stipulations for the Benefit of Third Parties in Islamic Law of Contracts', *JICL, op.cit.*, p.10

16 See Chapter V.5 above

17 Hamilton, *The Hedaya*, p.273; Other examples given are: the sale of an animal on condition that the purchaser ride it (Kāsānī, *Badā'i'*, V, p.171); or of a house on condition that the purchaser dwell in it : Ibn al-Hammām, *Fatḥ al-Qadīr*, V, p.215; Shīrāzī, *Kitāb al-Tanbīh*, p.97

18 Hamilton, *The Hedaya.*, p.273. With dissent by the two disciples.

19 *ibid.*, p.274

20 Kāsānī, *Badā'i'*, V, p.169; Ibn al-Hammām, *Fatḥ al-Qadīr*, V, p.215

contract. Islamic law is not fond of combination or double contracts.[21] Likewise, a contract of sale on condition that the purchaser lend the seller some sum of money or make him a gift, is also illegal; firstly, because the Prophet has forbidden a sale on condition of a loan;[22] and secondly, because the interweaving of different categories of contracts in this way is also prohibited due to the uncertainty which it creates with regard to apportionment of the consideration between the two distinct contracts.[23]

(5) Stipulations concerning suspension with respect to the delivery of the goods, which are extant and specific, invalidate a contract in transactions which aim at the immediate transfer of ownership (*Tamlīk fī al-Ḥāl*).[24] The only suspension accorded by law in respect of time is in the case of a debt. Here, for the purpose of granting respite to the debtor to collect his monies together in order to repay his debt, a prescribed period is allowed. In respect of other extant goods, however, such delay is not permitted.[25]

(6) The insertion of an invalid condition renders the whole contract invalid.[26] The general rule is that nothing, the sale of which is by itself invalid, can be made an exception to a contract of sale, or *mutatis mutandis* of hire or pawn brokerage.[27]

(7) A stipulation which implicates the subject of another contract renders the contract invalid. Thus a contract to buy cloth on condition that the seller sew it into a garment implicates a contract of service into the original contract of sale, and is illegal. It must be remarked here, however, that the ideals of the primary *Fiqh* regulations have been superceded (in the interests of custom) and that sales for purchase and manufacture are now recognised as valid in the form of contracts of *Istiṣnā'*.[28]

---

21 Ibn al-Hammām, *Fatḥ al-Qadīr*, V, p.218: *Ṣafqatāni fī Ṣafqa*. Doi recites the Tradition: " The Messenger of Allāh has forbidden making one contract of sale into two contracts of sale." Doi, *Shari'ah: The Islamic Law*, (1984) p.363

22 Hamilton, *ibid.*, p.274. "The Messenger of Allāh has forbidden to attach an extra condition with a sale transaction". Doi, *ibid.*, p.363

23 *ibid.*, p.274. This is also forbidden according to the Mālikī and Ḥanbalī Schools; See, for example, Ibn Qudāma, *al-Mughnī*, IV, p.95

24 Schacht, *Introduction*, (Oxford, 1979) p.119. This is particularly true in the case of monetary exchange, due to the incidences of *Ribā*. Delivery is, in any case, a natural legal effect, and is the right of the buyer. See Sanhūrī, *Maṣādir al-Ḥaqq*, V, p.189

25 Hamilton, *The Hedaya*, p.274. For instance, a condition or stipulation of a term in a contract of suretyship (which gives rise to obligations of immediate effect) is not permissible. See Schacht, *Introduction*, p.159

26 Schacht, *Introduction*, *op.cit.*, p.119

27 Hamilton, *The Hedaya.*, p.274

28 And see the application of *Istiḥsān*, *supra* under para. 2

(8) Any stipulation concerning imprecise deferment of the consideration is invalid. The period of deferment must be absolutely determined within the knowledge of both parties for the condition to be valid. Any degree whatsoever of uncertainty in the payment of the price renders the contract of sale null and void.This would not be the case if the stipulation were to be agreed upon subsequent to the contract of sale. A condition agreed between the parties after the contract would become a stipulation with regard to the payment of a debt, in which the jurists allow a certain degree of indetermination.[29]

Specific contracts allow of variant solutions. In certain contracts, for instance, (such as marriage, or the unilateral contract of gift) a condition may be stipulated, but not a term; Whereas in contracts of hire and lease, the stipulation of a term is permitted, but not that of a condition.[30] Both however, are admitted in the unilateral 'contracts' of repudiation, manumission and bequest.[31] Similar disparities also hold in relation to contracts of association. In the agricultural contracts of *Muzāra'a* and *Musāqāt*[32] the stipulation of a term is permitted while that of a condition is not. The situation exists to the contrary in the contract of *Sharika/Shirka* (Mercantile Partnership), while both a condition and a term may be stipulated in *Muḍaraba* (Sleeping Partnership) contracts.[33] It remains to be noted that any clause or condition purporting to waive or exclude a contracting party's natural right to revoke (such as arises under the system of legal options) is void.[34] This is not, however, always the case as regards the option of defect. Subject to the rules of fraud and concealed defects, the parties may agree to waive the seller's liabilities for certain defects in the object.[35]

8.2 Mālikī and Ḥanbalī Schools

The position adopted by the Mālikī and Ḥanbalī Schools in relation to

---

29 Hamilton, *The Hedaya*, p.274

30 Technological rules are laid down for the interpretation of terms mentioned by the parties in their contractual declarations. Generally speaking the term or *Ajal* must be certain (Ma'lūm).

31 Taking 'contract' as the Islamic umbrella term :see section one *supra*, and Schacht, *Introduction*, p.119.

32 Special contracts for the lease of agricultural land with profit-sharing.

33 Schacht, *Introduction*, p.119

34 Coulson, *Commercial Law in the Gulf States*, (London, 1984) p.66

35 See Option of Defect, Chapter 7.4 above.

conditions in contracts is rather more liberal.[36] These schools recognise two types of validity of *Shurūṭ*, in accordance with their general recognition of validity of contracts into valid and invalid.[37] These schools have gone a stage further than the Ḥanafī and Shāfi'ī Schools in their degree of permissibility, and have widened the scope of conditions to a significant extent as to diverge radically in doctrine. A condition in these schools is therefore valid according to the same terms as previously itemised for the Ḥanafī and Sāfi'ī Schools, in that it may prescribe the natural effects of the contract, and include effects which are neither in accordance nor against the natural effects of the contract,[38] but in addition to recognising conditions established by custom,[39] they will also recognise a condition by which one of the parties purports to secure a benefit either for himself, or for a third party.[40]

It is this third category which diverges so radically from the Ḥanafī and Shāfi'ī stance. As can be seen, the Mālikīs and Ḥanbalīs do not differ in that they do not distinguish between conditions made in favour of third parties or those for the benefit of the contracting parties themselves. They do differ, however, in allowing a certain advantage to one of the parties over the other. In the Mālikī School, the advantage may only be reasonable or "inexcessive". In the Ḥanbalī School, there is no such limitation. A condition inserted into a contract for the sale of a house which stipulates that the seller may be allowed to remain in residence for an extended period, would therefore be upheld by the jurists of both Schools.[41] Similarly, a contract for the sale of land may include the condition that the sale is subject to the buyer building a mosque upon that land, or bequeathing it as a *waqf* trust.[42]

Of necessity, the additional permissibility afforded by this third category must be carefully restricted. In the Mālikī school, the balance to be attained by allowing a certain advantage to a party and yet restricting that advantage in order to avoid exploitation and *Istighlāl* is necessarily a delicate one. In the Ḥanbalī School, there is no equivalent rule stating that the advantage conferred on one of the contracting parties by means of the condition must

---

36 Ibn Rushd, *Bidāyat al-Mujtahid wa Nihāyat al-Muqtaṣid*, (Cairo, 1966) II, pp.174-179; Khurshī, *Sharḥ Mukhtaṣar Sīdī Khalīl*, V, pp.80-84; Sanhūrī, *Maṣādir al-Ḥaqq*, V, p.155

37 Ibn Rushd, *Bidāyat al-Mujtahid wa Nihāyat al-Muqtaṣid*, (Cairo, 1966) III, p.174;

38 Khurshī, *Sharḥ Mukhtaṣar Sīdī Khalīl*, V, pp.80-84

39 *ibid.*

40 Ibn Rushd, *Bidāyat al-Mujtahid*, III, p.175

41 *ibid.*

42 *ibid.*

be "inexcessive". The scope afforded to a single condition is thus unlimited.[43]

The justification of the divergent interpretation of doctrine here lies in the fact that while the Ḥanbalī jurists also recognise the Traditions of the Prophet prohibiting 'sales combined with loan contracts', and combination contracts, they do not accept the authority of the Tradition attributed to the Prophet in which a sale combined with a condition is prohibited. Instead, the Ḥanbalīs accept as authoritative another Prophetic Tradition prohibiting the combination of a sale with two conditions. Thus where a contract for the sale of cloth to be made into a specific garment would be valid in the Ḥanbalī school, as in the other schools, the same contract with the extra condition that the cloth should be dyed red would not be valid.[44] The reasoning for this is that a contract which carries a plurality of conditions (not counting those which merely reinforce the natural legal effects of the contract), lacks unity and risks becoming a source of conflict.[45]

The restriction of the Mālikī School that the condition should be "inexcessive", and that of the Ḥanbalī School that the condition should be singular provide empirical evidence to the effect that these two schools are no less concerned with averting exploitation and *Istighlāl* in contracts. A contractor of these schools is still not allowed to insert conditions which contradict the prescribed effects of the contract, a rule of law,[46] or which result in any uncertainty regarding object or consideration. This rule applies whether the condition is for the benefit of the contracting parties of for a third party.[47] Thus where the seller makes a condition that if the buyer wished to resell the object, then he (the seller) must have first refusal at the original cost-price, this condition is invalid in all schools except the Ḥanbalī school. If, on the other hand, the seller stipulates that the buyer should pay him the price of the goods plus a loan, the condition is invalid for *Gharar* in all schools. The consideration for the goods has become indeterminable, because it also constitutes consideration for the loan obtained. The buyer therefore redeems the consideration he would otherwise have paid for the goods and the sale is invalid.[48]

---

43 Ibn Qudāma, *al-Mughnī*, IV, p.95; Abdalla Mohamed, 'Stipulations' *op.cit*, p.16; Hamid, 'The Freedom to Make Stipulations', *op.cit*, p.30 f.

44 Ibn Qudāma, *ibid.*

45 Sanhūrī, *Maṣādir al-Ḥaqq*, III, p.186; Bellefonds, *Traité I, p.231.*

46 Ibn Qudāma, *al-Mughnī*, IV, p.95

47 Abdalla Mohamed, 'Stipulations', *op.cit*, pp.15-16

48 Ibn Rushd, *Bidāyat al-Mujtahid*, III, p.176; Ibn Qudāma, *al-Mughnī*, IV, p.95

In more recent times, the tendency of the Ḥanbalī School has been to become even more liberal towards conditions in contracts. This movement has chiefly been expounded by the neo-Ḥanbalī jurists Ibn Taymiyya and Ibn Qayyim al-Jawziyya. According to these scholars, the freedom to make stipulations is the general rule of Islamic Law, in the same context that freedom of contract is the general rule.[49] The same Qur'ānic verses are cited as authority for the two arguments : If God has commanded us to undertake agreements and to fulfil them as agreed, then we are perfectly free to stipulate whatever we deem suitable in such undertakings, so long as these conditions do not contravene the law (including the laws of *Ribā*),[50] or prescribe effects which are contradictory to those naturally arising from the contract.[51] The only requirement, therefore, is for the mutual consent of the parties, for there is no verse in the *Qur'ān*, they state, which prohibits the making of contracts and conditions.[52] This is the rule also applied to conditions made for the benefit of third parties.

8.3 Conditions In Favour Of Third Parties

Although there is no specific rule to be found in any of the texts of Classical Jurisprudence, the general principle which has been inferred by the majority of contemporary authors from the various types of contracts is that Islamic law does not recognise the validity of conditions made in favour of third parties.[53]

In the classical texts, there is, in fact, no distinction made between conditions in favour of third parties and those for the benefit of the contracting parties themselves.[54] Therefore, the validity of conditions in favour of third parties would seem to be rather more dependent on fulfilling the rules laid down by each School than on the person of the beneficiary. Nevertheless, as the distinction is not made, validity of conditions for the

---

49 See Chapter IV above. Ibn Taymiyya, *Fatāwā*, III, pp.323-347

50 *Qur'ān*, (II:275), (IV:25), (V:1), (VI:120); Ibn Taymiyya, *Fatāwā*, III, pp.331-334

51 For example, a condition that the buyer may not sell or use the object of the contract: Ibn Taymiyya, *ibid.*

52 Ibn Taymiyya, *Fatāwā*, III, p.334

53 See Chafiq Chehata, *al-Naẓariyya al-'Āmma li al-Iltizāmāt Fī al-Sharī'a al-Islāmiyya*, p.156; Maḥmaṣānī, *al-Naẓariyya al-'Amma li al-Mūjibāt wa al-'Uqūd Fī al-Sharī'a al-Islāmiyya*, II, pp.639 ff.; Sanhūrī, *Maṣādir al-Ḥaqq*, V, p.16; Qadrī Pasha, *Murshid al-Ḥayrān ilā Ma'rifāt Aḥwāl al-Insān Fī al-Mu'āmalāt al-Sharī'a 'alā Madhhab al-Imām al-A'ẓam Abū Ḥanīfa*, (Cairo, 1933) p.58; Abdalla Mohamed, 'Stipulations for the Benefit of Third Parties in Islamic Law of Contracts', *JICL*, 9 (1980) p.7

54 Kāsānī, *Badā'i'*, V, p.170 ff.; Ibn al-Hammām, *Fatḥ al-Qadīr*, V, 218; Abdalla Mohamed, 'Stipulations' *op.cit.*, p.8

benefit of third parties is bound to be formed in accordance with the validity of normal conditions. Thus in the Ḥanafī and Shāfi'ī Schools, a condition by the buyer for an additional advantage to himself is *Fāsid*, and the result would be the same if the condition was stipulated in favour of a third party.[55]

The modern interpretation that conditions in favour of third parties are not generally valid in Islamic Law may be assumed to have been constructed on the basis of the Ḥanafī and Shāfi'ī doctrines, for the assumption of these Schools is for invalidity subject to validity for all conditions. The Ḥanafī and Shāfi'ī schools, with their rigid adherence to the principle that the proper legal effects naturally arise out of every contract, are unlikely to accept the validity of conditions which confer advantages and effects upon a third party, which would not otherwise have been conferred by law. Thus if a seller of a commercial property which has been rented out to a tenant sells the property to B on condition that B does not evict the tenant presently residing in the property, he is attempting to confer an additional advantage upon the tenant third party which is not prescribed by the legal effects of the contract, and which would be treated by the Ḥanafī jurists as *Fāsid*.[56] Whereas in the Mālikī School a party may validly confer an "inexcessive" advantage upon a third party, the Ḥanbalī School will not restrict such an advantage. A stipulation by the seller to the effect that the buyer should give it in trust to a certain category of people or a charity would thus be recognised by these schools as a valid condition for the benefit of a third party.[57] Likewise, the condition inserted by the seller that the buyer should emancipate the slave sold to him would be valid.[58] It is with regard to the Ḥanbalī School, therefore, that it may be said that conditions for the benefit of third parties are uncategorically recognised.[59]

Two modern authors at least have recognised this principle. Madkur alleges that recent Ḥanbalī authors recognise conditions in favour of third parties,[60] and this is in accordance with the Ḥanbalī disposition to recognise

---

55 Ibn al-Hammām, *Fatḥ al-Qadīr*, V, p.218

56 Abdel Wahhab Salah El-Din and J.H. Brinsley, 'The Stipulation For a Third Person in Egyptian Law', 10 *American Journal of Comparative Law*, (1961) p.78: Abdalla Mohamed, 'Stipulations', *op.cit.*, pp.12-13. See also Ibn al-Hammām, *Fatḥ al-Qadīr*, V, p.215

57 Ibn Rushd, *Bidāyat al-Mujtahid*, III, p.175-6

58 *ibid.*

59 Ibn Taymiyya, *Fatāwā*, III, pp.327-348; Ibn Qudāma, *al-Mughnī*, IV, p.95; Abdalla Mohamed, 'Stipulations', *op.cit.*, pp.14-17;

60 Madkur, *al-Madkhal li al-Fiqh al-Islāmī*, cited in Abdalla Mohamed, 'Stipulations', *JICL*, 9 (1980) p. 7

the general validity of conditions subject to certain exceptions. The second author is Abdalla Mohamed, who also differentiates between the diverging doctrines of the schools rather than between conditions made in favour of the contracting parties or of third parties, including the degrees of tolerance towards conditions exhibited between the *Jamhūr al-Ḥanābila*, and the neo-Ḥanbilīs, Ibn Taymiyya and Ibn Qayyim al-Jawziyya.[61]

Nevertheless, the same exceptions exist here as they do in normal conditions, and this includes conditions recognised by custom in the Ḥanafī School.[62]

Thus a typical creditor/beneficiary condition, where the seller stipulates that the buyer shall guarantee payment of the price to one of the seller's creditors is perfectly valid, even in the Ḥanafī School.[63] But the condition that a buyer should emancipate a slave he has just bought, or should give the newly purchased land to a charitable trust is only valid in the Ḥanbalī School.[64]

It may be seen, therefore, that there is no one general rule which prevails in Islamic Law pertaining to conditions in contracts, other than the fact that there is no distinction made between conditions for the benefit of the contracting parties and those made for the benefit of third parties. The principle categories of rules are tripartite, with the Ḥanafī and Shāfi'ī Schools in the first, most restrictive category, followed by the Mālikīs and the main body of the Ḥanbalī School in the second less restrictive category. In the third are the neo-Ḥanbalī authors, Ibn Taymiyya and Ibn Qayyim, who afford an almost unrestricted tolerance towards the concept.

The recognition of conditions established by custom is an important loophole in the *Fiqh*. This, together with the liberal attitude manifested by the Mālikī and Ḥanbalī Schools has resulted in the acceptance of the majority of innovative conditions which are required by contemporary transactions. Where in theory, the law may seem to preclude the greater proportion of conditions, it is, in fact, possible that a single legal condition may be validly incorporated into a contract by means of the Ḥanafī exceptions established according to custom, or by pertaining to the neo-Ḥanbalī doctrine. Because

---

61 See his article 'Stipulations for the Benefit of Third Parties in Islamic Law of Contracts', *Journal of Islamic and Comparative Law*, 9 (1980) pp. 7-20

62 The Shāfi'īs do not recognise conditions established by custom. Madkur, *op.cit*, p.647; and Mohamed, *op.cit.*, p.14. Abdalla Mohamed (p.13) gives the example of Governments making conditions with corporations rendering some kind of public service for the benefit of a certain class of people or the public at large.

63 Ibn al-Hammām, *Fatḥ al-Qadīr*, V, p.215; Sanhūrī, *Maṣādir al-Ḥaqq*, V, p.644; Ibn Taymiyya, *Fatāwā*, III, pp.327-348

64 Ibn Taymiyya, *Fatāwā*, III, pp.327-348

of the loop-hole in the Ḥanafī *Fiqh*, therefore, the exigences of modern contractual negotiations may validy be incorporated into jurisdictions which would not otherwise pertain to the more liberal Ḥanbalī School of Law.

8.4 Modern Legislation

The position with regard to extrinsic conditions in the modern codifications of the three Gulf states has become greatly modified. The tendency has been to become more tolerant of appended conditions, and this is likely to be a reflection both of modern Western legislation and of the increasing complexity and documentation of contracts in the modern age. The *Majella* does adhere to the generally restrictive rules of the Ḥanafī and Shāfi'ī Schools, and will recognise a condition if it is essential to the contract, assures due performance of the contract, or is sanctioned by local custom.[65]

The narrow and restrictive clauses of paragraphs 1-4 pertaining to the Ḥanafī and Shāfi'ī schools, above, are nevertheless generally ignored in the present Kuwaiti Civil Code, even though the *Majella* has previously been of relevance in this jurisdiction. Its narrow interpretations have been replaced successively by wider connotations, culminating in Article 175 (1) of the 1980 Code which states : "The contract must of necessity include any condition upon which the contracting parties have agreed, as long as there is no legal impediment or that it does not contradict public order or public morals." The onus now then, is on inclusion of conditions, rather than their mere implication or natural incidence arising from the contract.[66]

The inclusion of an invalid condition, moreover, (according to the present Kuwaiti legislation) no longer avoids the whole contract, as in certain cases dictated by the uncodified rules of the *Madhāhib* stated above. The position now is closer to that of the *Bāṭil* condition of the Ḥanafī school, in that the invalid condition is severable, and the contract remains *Ṣaḥīḥ* so long as neither of the parties has specified that his consent to the whole of the contract rests upon that condition. It is only where a party has specified that he will not agree to the contract without the condition, that the contract itself becomes void.[67]

The UAE Civil Code more readily reflects the *Sharī'a* position pertaining to conditions in contracts. In stating that such conditions should be in accordance with the tenor of the contract, be sanctioned by custom or usage, or be beneficial to either of the contracting parties, (subject as usual to the

---

65 Hooper, *The Majella*, (Jerusalem, 1933) Arts. 186-188

66 Kuwaiti Civil Code, Law No 67 of 1980, Art. 175 (1)

67 Kuwaiti Civil Code, Law No. 67 of 1980, Art. 175 (2). See also the Explanatory Memorandum to the Civil Code, p.166

considerations of public policy and morals),[68] the UAE Civil Code is adhering closely to the Ḥanafī and Shāfi'ī doctrines.

The article also recognises the principle of severance in accordance with Ḥanafī doctrine, along with the same conditions as the equivalent Kuwaiti provision mentioned above,[69] and conditions made in favour of Third Parties, so long as they conform to the rules laid down for normal conditions.[70] By virtue of Part III of the Contract Law of Bahrain, concerning Conditional Contracts, it may be surmised that the Bahraini Statute, following the Common Law rather than the Islamic *Fiqh*, recognises contracts containing conditions. The main emphasis in the Bahrain Code is given to conditional contracts subject to the occurrence of events which are collateral to such contracts. In this respect the law of Bahrain is not in accordance with orthodox Islamic Law.[71]

A great number of the contemporary disputes brought in the courts of the Gulf States under study concerning *Shurūṭ*, are in relation to insurance contracts. Obviously, with the strictures of *Ribā* and *Gharar* here, and the idiosyncrasies of Insurance Law itself, this is an area of the law which provides a fair degree of uncertainty and controversy. A few examples will suffice for the purposes of demonstrating the effect of such clauses and conditions, and their treatment by the courts.

In mid-1987, the Bahrain Court of Appeal held that a Bahraini Insurance Company was not liable for payment in accordance with its policy, by virtue of a contractual condition that if the insured had violated traffic laws, hence causing the accident, it would invalidate the contract.[72] This decision was echoed by a similar ruling in the UAE Federal Supreme Court, which upheld an exclusionary clause in a "comprehensive" contract for automobile insurance, which disclaimed coverage where the insured had violated traffic law. In a suit brought by the insured against his insurance company, it was held that the insured had exceeded the speed limit prior to his involvement in an accident resulting in a fatality. Thus his policy was deemed invalid by virtue of the exclusionary clause, and the Insurance Company was held not liable for payment of the *Diyya* on his behalf.[73]

---

68 UAE Civil Code, Law No. 2 of 1987, Art.206

69 See Ballantyne, 'The New Civil Code of the United Arab Emirates', 1 (3) *Arab Law Quarterly*, (May 1986) p.263

70 UAE Civil Code, Law No. 2 of 1987, Art.206

71 Bahrain Law of Contract, Arts. 35-40

72 *Arab Law Newsletter*, (Oct. 1987) No. 22, p.1

73 *Arab Law Newsletter*, (Nov. 1987) No.23, p.3

An earlier judgment by the Court of Appeal in Abu Dhabi had relied on the Insurer's description of the policy as "comprehensive", and had rejected the insurer's reliance on a similar exclusion clause. The Abu Dhabi ruling is puzzling in itself, for it appears to be contrary to the provision of the UAE Civil Code, which states that a condition in an insurance contract which deprives an insured of coverage because of a violation of law is invalid, except where such a condition is limited to violations of law which constitute felonies or intentional misdemeanours.[74] It is arguable that the excession of the speed limit in the above case could have been construed as a felony, or intentional misdemeanour, although the Appeal Court in Abu Dhabi clearly did not interpret it as such. It is not clear how extensive the effects of such rulings may be, but the contention that similar judgments may impose injurious effects on innocent third parties[75] may well be avoided by a provision of the Abu Dhabi Traffic Law, which makes coverage for Third Party Insurance mandatory, and avoids such exclusionary clauses in insurance policies seeking to escape liability for these payments in cases of accident.[76]

It remains to be seen whether the UAE courts will enforce subsequent policy terms which vary with the standard terms, or whether the latter will be applied as a matter of law, or in default of contrary provisions. It appears, at present, as though the courts are not reluctant to honour individual contractual terms in the light of these cases, at least where the conditions are not contrary to the law or inconsistent with the spirit of the law, and so long as the formalities of such contracts are complied with.[77] Clauses to limit the maximum coverage for liability arising out of Third Party claims for personal injury or death are invalid according to a decision of the UAE Federal Supreme Courts. This ruling upholds a provision of Ministerial Decision No. 54 of 1987 issued by the Ministry of Economy and Commerce, and relating to the adoption of standard automobile insurance policies. The insurers are held to be liable for all ajudicated amounts, including court costs and expenses, but excluding fines. Similar clauses for

---

74 UAE Civil Code, No. 2 of 1987, Art. 1028 (a)

75 See Ballantyne [Ed.], *Arab Law Newsletter*, No.22 (Oct. 1987) p.1

76 The same law upholds the right of the insurer to seek indemnity from the insured for such payments. See *Arab Law Newsletter*, No.23 (Nov. 1987) p.3. The problem has been resolved with the adoption of standard automobile insurance policies. Ministerial Decision No. 54 of 1987 of the Ministry of Economy and Commerce; Effective as of 1 Dec. 1987 (which does not effect policies already issued).

77 For example, the new standard policy provides that exclusion clauses must be clearly set out in red ink. See *Arab Law Newsletter*, (Nov. 1987) No. 23 p.4

property damage, however, are recognised.[78]

Actual previous rulings in the UAE Courts seem to be in contrast to the new decisions. In late 1987, for example, the Federal Supreme Court allegedly rejected an insurer's defence that a clause requiring notification of the accident within seventy-two hours was not complied with, and effectively amounted to breach of contract. The court held that the clause was arbitrary and ordered the insurer to pay the coverage as agreed.[79] This judgment merely followed the tendency of previous judgments, for instance, emphasising the insurers' obligations to pay coverage in exchange for premiums paid.

In cases where the contract has been concluded with an additional 'essential' condition, which is, however, not customary in such contracts, and yet does not coincide with inherent conditions of the goods, the Kuwaiti courts have sought to interpret the goods in such disputes as objects of a contract of lease (*Ijār*). Conditions in contracts of lease are automatically severable, and do not, consequently, avoid the whole contract.[80]

An important corollary to this subject concerns Arbitration clauses. It is commonly held that although the *Sharī'a* recognises the Institution of Arbitration, in principle arbitration clauses are unenforcable. An agreement to arbitrate can only strictly be made after the dispute arises, because an arbitration clause (especially in Saudi Arabia) would constitute *Gharar*. This is because the nature or occurrence of a future dispute is uncertain.[81]

The Law of Contract applicable in Dubai and Sharjah provides, *inter alia*, that if the contract contains a clause regarding arbitration, this remedy must be exhausted before invoking the jurisdiction of the courts.[82] *Qāḍīs* in Dubai courts have occasionally held for the dismissal of such court actions as premature, by recognition of the arbitration clause laid out in small print on the reverse of bills of lading, and have compelled the parties to proceed to arbitration.[83]

---

78 *Arab Law Newsletter*, (Nov. 1987) No. 23 p.4

79 *Arab Law Newsletter*, (Oct. 1987) No. 22 p.4

80 Appeal No. 124/81: Commercial : Session 30/1/82, *Majallat al-Qaḍā' wa al-Qānūn*, (*Wazīrat al-'Adl*, Supreme Court of Kuwait) Issue No.3, Year 10 (June, 1984) p.135; Rule No. 40

81 An agreement to arbitrate an existing dispute is revocable by either party up until the point at which an award is made. See Saleh, S., *Commercial Arbitration in the Middle East*, (London, 1984) pp.49-50

82 Dubai Law of Contract, 1971, Art. 32

83 See Feulner and Khan, 'Dispute Resolution in the United Arab Emirates', *Arab Law Quarterly*, 1 (3) (May, 1986) p.314

Similarly, a clause attempting to exclude the jurisdiction of a UAE Court, or to confer exclusive jurisdiction in a foreign court would not be recognised in the UAE. However, the Civil Courts would not ordinarily refuse *ex facte* a choice of foreign law to govern a contract provided that that choice is otherwise legal.[84]

Conclusion

The unanimity of the Ḥanafī and Shāfi'ī jurists against the addition of adjoining clauses or suspensive conditions to contracts is an extension of the proposition that there should be no interference with the natural effects arising out of legal transactions. The effects of every contract are determined by law irrespective of the intention of the parties, and the formation of the contract is a mere cause for achieving certain objectives which have already been dictated by the law.[85] The adherence of these two Schools to this proposition is sufficiently rigid to render the logic somewhat perplexing at first : The unanimity of these Schools in favour of the *Khiyār al-Sharṭ* is equally strong. How is it, then, that the Option of stipulation is wholly acceptable, whilst attaching conditions to contracts is wholly unacceptable ? The answer lies in the degree of uncertainty which either of these institutions permits to permeate the contract. In a contract with an option to stipulate, the rules are so restrictive that uncertainty is avoided as far as is possible; A suspensive condition is itself an element of uncertainty, for it provides, in general, for effects which would not otherwise arise naturally from the legal transaction undertaken. While it must be admitted that the *Khiyār al-Sharṭ* does weaken the obligatory force of the contractual tie, in that the contract is not binding on the beneficiary until the option is exercised, it does offer the supervening advantage of flexibility which the contractual institution would lack otherwise. Toleration of the Option of *Sharṭ* may then be seen in conjunction with the disavowell of the facility to make contractual conditions in these Schools. Allowing the one without the other provides sufficient flexibility within the law to cover most

[84] Feulner and Khan, 'Dispute Resolution in the United Arab Emirates', *Arab Law Quarterly, op.cit.*, pp.313-314. UAE Courts do not usually require proof of foreign law as a question of fact: they often apply the law with which they are most familiar, which may give rise to unpredicted results (but see Feulner, *op.cit.*, p.314). Such clauses are, of course, subject to mandatory provisions of applicable local laws: for example, the Commercial Agencies Law, Law No. 18 of 1981, which states that commercial agency disputes are to be governed by the Ministry of Economy and Commerce; the courts do not exercise primary jurisdiction here.

[85] Abdalla, 'Stipulations for the Benefit of Third Parties in Islamic Law of Contracts', *Journal of Islamic and Comparative Law*, vol. 9 (1980) p.8

requirements, whilst not allowing the law to become so flexible as to render it vulnerable to exploitation.

CONCLUSION

Specific conclusions relating to the subject areas of Islamic contracts and their comparison with modern legislation in the Gulf States of Bahrain, Kuwait and the United Arab Emirates, have been drawn at the end of each of the preceding chapters. The purpose of this short conclusion is therefore to give a final overview of the general transition of the system of contracts from the Classical to the modern theory. It also aims to identify certain areas and directions in which it may be possible for this sphere of the law to develop in the future.

The shortfalls of the Classical exposition of the law as a whole, with its unsystematic collection of diverse opinions and arbitrary rulings, has already been highlighted. To draft the regulations of practically every aspect of the contractual system in Islam, including all the diverging views of even just the four Sunni Schools is a project so ambitious as to have defied all attempts. In Arabic, the feat was undertaken by the great Egyptian legist, Professor Sanhūrī, in his treatise *Maṣādir al-Ḥaqq fī al-Fiqh al-Islāmī*. Sanhūrī's collection of material is probably the most comprehensive that we can ever expect to attain, but his commentaries on, and objective analyses of that material allow scope for further study.

So far, the full task has not been undertaken in an English exposition, although Professor Coulson has provided a brief outline of the Islamic contractual system in his *Commercial Law in the Gulf States*; and Parviz Owsia has completed a detailed comparative analysis of the Shi'a and Common law systems, with additional Sunni law comparisons; while Y. Linant de Bellefonds has attempted an analysis of the four Sunni schools from a Civil law perspective, in *Traité de Droit Musulman Comparé*. Other authors have touched upon individual subject areas of Contracts with varied success, but to date, there has been no attempt to provide a detailed exposition of modern legislation in the Gulf in the light of traditional contractual concepts.

Using Sanhūrī's work as a "backbone", the present study has attempted to provide that exegesis in the English language, using mainly, although not exlusively, Arabic sources. It is, however, of necessity limited in scope, and for this reason has been restricted to the "theory" of the contractual systems, leaving mention of breach and subsequent effects to another study.

The traditional laws form the basis of the comparative theme, and are placed against the backcloth of an investigation into the historical and social evolution of the commercial and doctrinal milieux of early Islam. In this way it has sought to discover the sources, whether eclectic or of "Divine Origin", and the possible catalysts of the developing Islamic system of Contracts. It has attempted to analyse the extent of influence these sources and catalysts have had on the Islamic system of contracts, and inversely, the responses it formulated to them.

Once the Classical law of Islam has been detailed in relation to each doctrine, the present status of these doctrines within the three Gulf States of Bahrain, Kuwait and the Federal state of The United Arab Emirates has then been set against it and compared.

The apparent net result of such a procedure seems, above all, to highlight a two-fold transition from Classical into modern law. The first of these is that the law regarding Contracts has undergone a "tightening-up" of its tenets into clearer, single exegeses. The idiosyncratic and casuistic meanderings of the Classical treatises make difficult reading to an enquirer who just wants to discover the law relating to a specific topic. He has to consider geographical location, the School of law to which the author adheres, his stance within that School, and the era in which the author was writing - and then he has to wade through hypotheses, pages of tenuous examples, and all the variant opinions expounded by that school for each doctrine exposed. To boot, few of the treatises are blessed with an index! The present day Civil Codes of the Gulf States are, in comparison, straightforward. They expound single doctrines, without variant opinions, and are not so prone to over-embellish certain principles to the cost of others. The "tightening-up" process was begun by the *Majella.* Its development can be traced through the Civil-Egyptian-Kuwaiti model. With careful application this process can be furthered in several ways, the most important of which appear to be filling the gaps in the law, and clarifying the language.

The second consequence of the transition from Classical to modern is also, in a way, a result of the "tightening-up" process. It is that a certain degree of unification among the contract codes of the Arab Middle East has occurred. Naturally, the geographical and tribal/political boundaries of the past are of less consequence now in regard to access, while codification itself will incline towards this result. Nevertheless, we find that the prevalence of the Civil/Egyptian Contract Code model of the 1970's codifications has resulted in limited unification of the Contract Codes in the Arab world. The laws are not, however, unified within the Arab world, nor yet within the Arab Gulf : Bahrain continues to retain a Contract Law based on English Law; Kuwait has followed the Civil/Egyptian model; while the

Federal State of the United Arab Emirates has adopted the more 'Islamic' format initiated by Jordan.

The divergences between these three codes therefore present interesting scope for analysis and comparison, and to this end, it is even questionable whether complete unification of the contract laws within the Arab Muslim world could be preferable at this stage. For the National and International lawyer, the plaintiff and layman, and certainly the scholar, unification would, no doubt, be welcomed as a grace to lighten their burden of discovering the law. In terms of searching for the true modern, Arab, Islamic legal system, however, any narrowing of the field at this nascent stage would be premature.

It is hoped that the comparative analysis will have raised some important questions and indicated the occasional ambiguities and uncertainties both within the Classical expositions and the modern legal codifications. In this respect it may be said, and in particular with reference to the Civil Code of the United Arab Emirates, that whatever conflicts, whether real or apparent, arise within these modern codes, they are the result of lacunae or ambiguous articles. They may also be the result of the fact that while Islam prohibited certain socio-economic practices in a vague and inconclusive manner, it also allotted to these practices the stigma of *Ḥudūd* malefactions, but without the definitive penalties. As such, the "freedom of conscience" has resulted in a "confusion at law". It is only by systematic analysis and highlighting of these principles, that the codification process within the Arab Muslim jurisdictions may be amended to reflect the true intentions of the original doctrines. In the same manner, by analysing the present codifications themselves, the incongruities of ambiguous and vaguely couched articles may be amended to more truthfully reflect the original intention of the legislators.

Sceptical western critics might argue here that this process is without point for laws in the Arab Middle East are becoming less Islamic, or that in any case, Islamic law came into being as a purely idealistic system. However, this polemic cannot be argued convincingly. Turning aside from the purely religious purpose of the Islamic infrastructure, the reasoning and "Divine Legislation" that constitutes the social rationale behind the more idiosyncratic of the Islamic tenets has long been cause for speculation and attempted justfications. In the majority of cases, the religious tenets carry clear community benefits and, with historical hindsight, it is not problematic to divine their original social implications.

It is true to say that the majority of cases tackled by the Muslim jurisprudents from the tenth century AD were purely hypothetical questions posed of themselves in order to clarify problematic aspects of their teaching.

It is also true to say that the officially recognised sources of traditional law did not encompass the whole spectrum of methodology instituted by the practitioners of the law. Moreover, the fact is that certain notions of Islamic law, such as the prohibitions of *Ribā* and *Gharar*, have never been universally applied; while others, such as certain Criminal, Tax, Family and Constitutional laws have been blandly put aside.

As a legal system Islam has kept a prominent but variable significance within the socio-political schemes of Middle Eastern Societies. In the Gulf States, it may be described as the cultural epicentre, the heritage and nucleus of identity in Arab Muslim life. There is an inter-relation and reciprocal influence between its legal, religious and ethical aspects. These aspects derive from a common source, and their interaction is inevitable. It is therefore impossible, in the real sense, to talk about a secular legal system within the Arab Gulf States : the legislation may appear to be secular in most respects, but the sources of reference for these laws, and the consciences of its interpreters are innately religious.

To the interested observer, who has watched the twentieth century phoenix-like eruption of the *Sharī'a* from the ashes of the mid-nineteenth century western cultural dominance, the premise that the *Sharī'a* is an idealistic system ever divorced from practice, does not, therefore, ring true. The overwhelming argument against this polemic is that to be purely idealistic, the system must never have had any relevance in practice. Such cannot be said of the system of Islamic contracts, nor of the system of law in general, for as Nabil Saleh states, "Islamic law was not a purely idealistic program never put to the test".[1]

A parallel criticism that the expositions of the *Sharī'a* are now archaic, especially in the subject matter of their *exempla*, would strike a truer note. This is not to say that the *Sharī'a* itself is archaic; but if it could be expounded in a modern form, much as the *Majella* attempted to do in its time, then perhaps the merger between traditional law and modern applications would not seem so forced.

The recent trend against wholesale adoption of western legal principles (which was the pattern of codification in the nineteenth century), together with the desire to regulate a merger of the Islamic ethos with general international principles and twentieth century requirements, is proof of the pervasive relevance of the *Sharī'a* within the systems of law in the Muslim world. In addition, the historical resource of adapting practical legal methodologies to render the theory of the law more flexible is continuing.

---

1 Nabil Saleh, 'Financial Transactions and the Islamic Theory of Obligations and Contracts,' in *Islamic Law and Finance*, [Ed. C. Mallat] (Proceedings of the Conference held on 8 April 1988, SOAS; London, 1988) p.1

The enigma of *Ribā* and *Gharar* also survived the spate of codification.

In fact, the *Sharī'a* has never once been redundant; all parts of it have, at some stage and to varying degrees, been applied to regulate the social life of Muslim communities. Even the recent example of Turkey proves the impossibility of replacing the *Sharī'a* in a wholesale way by another legal system within a Muslim country. The *Sharī'a* is a system which encompasses all elements of Muslim life and community. It is not a system which can be packaged up and kept in a law court, for formal reference by academic lawyers. Its religious nature requires that it is integrated into the daily round of Muslim life. In this respect the nature of the *Sharī'a* highlights the ultimate dichotomy between law and practice. Modern law, for instance, states that interest payments on capital sums may be legally collected. A large proportion of practising Muslims, however, under the dictates of their own consciences, support the Islamic financial institutions operating according to the strict doctrine of *Ribā*. It may be asked of these Muslims which law they regard as paramount, the codified law of two decades or the Divine law of fourteen centuries.

By looking into the history of the development of the Islamic system of contracts, it has been hoped to glean a clearer perspective of the law in its present state. The process of discovering the traditional material of Islamic history and combining it with contemporary analysis and comparative study will inevitably lead to new interpretations. In the realm of contracts in Islamic law, the process is still important, for the origins of the system are still partially veiled by lack of knowledge of the first two centuries of Islamic legal development. Through further research, or through the discovery of new documentation, or even by continual plucking at the paradigms of the law, the original shape of the *Sharīa* within these lost two centuries may eventually be discovered and its applications shown in their true context. It will then be possible to appreciate the interpretation of the Islamic contract laws as they were originally practised within the earliest community of believers. By so doing, we may advance a little further towards achieving the harmonious merger between traditional *Sharī'a* principles and modern day needs within the legal codes of the Muslim Middle East.

GLOSSARY OF ARABIC TERMS

Adl	Respectable; Noble
Amal	Judicial Practice
Aqada	To Contract
Aqār	Real Estate; Immovable Property
Aqd	Contract
Āriya	Contract of Hire
Aufū bi al-'Uqūd	Fulfil all contracts
Ayb	Defect
Ibādāt	Religious Ethics
Idāt	Promises
Illa	Cause; Underlying Reasoning
Īna	Double Sale
Iwāḍ	Compensation
Udhr	Excuse; Just cause
Udwān	Hostility
Uhda	Legal Guarantee (Mālikī)
Ukāẓ	Pre-Islamic annual fairs
Ulūm	Sciences (Pl. of 'Ilm)
Ulamā'	Religious Scholars
Umra	Archaic form of unconditional donation in perpetuity
Uqūd	Contracts (pl. of 'Aqd)
Uqūd Mu'ayyana	Nominate contracts
Uqda	Contract (Qur'ānic derivation)
Urf	Custom, practice
Abāṭil	Frivolities
Ahl	Family
Ahl al-ḥadīth	Traditionists
Ahl al-Ibāḥa	Advocates of Freedom of Contract
Ahliyya	Capacity
Ajal	Term; Delay
Akl Amwāl al-Nās bi al-Bāṭil	"Consuming the property of others for no good reason".
Al-A'māl bi al-Niyya	Acts are judged by their intention

Amīn	Mercantile Agent; Trustworthy
Arkān	Pillars (of Contract)
Arsh al-'Ayb	Indemnity for Defect
Aṣl	Source. Origin; Root
al-Baraṣ	Vitiligo, leucodermia, piebald skin
Bāṭil	Void, Null and Void
Buṭlān	Void, Null and Void
Bay'	Sale
Bay' al-Amāna	Trust sale
Bay' al-Dayn	Sale of a debt
Bay' al-Ḥiṣṣa	Sale by Allotment or Share
Bay' al-Istidlāl	Mālikī and Ḥanbalī term for *Tawliya*: sale concluded at market price
Bay' al-Malāqiḥ	Sale foetus in the womb or unborn (Prohibited)
Bay' al-Mudāmin	Sale of the seed of male animals for fecundation
Bay' al-Murābaḥa	Sale at cost price, with a declared additional profit
Bay' al-Mustarsal	Sale by forestalling the Market; 'Meeting the Riders'
Bay' al-Musta'amana	Sale by forestalling the Market
Bay' al-Muwāḍa'a	Sale conducted at cost price with a declared discount
Bay' al-Najsh	Sale whose price is raised/ diminished by Ficticious tenders
Bay' al-Tawliyya	Sale at Cost price
Bay' al-'Uhda	Sale of real property with the right of redemption
Bay' al-Wadī'a	Sale conducted at cost price with a declared discount
Bay' al-Wafā'	Archaic Sale with Redemption/ Loan for usufruct
Bay'āt al-'Amāna	Trust Sale Contracts
Bay' bi al-Ma'nā al-'Āmm	General Sale
Bay' bi al-Ma'nā al-Khaṣṣ	Special Sale
Bay'tuka	'I have sold you'
Bayt al-Māl	Treasury
Bayyā' al-'Amāna	Agent of Trust
Bi al-Bāṭilī	Frivolously; Triflingly
Bi al-Dayn	On credit; on own account

Bi al-Ma'nā 'l-'Ām	In a general context
Bi al-Nāṣīa	On Credit
Dūr al-Muqāmirīn	Gambling or Dicing Den
Daf' Mafsada	Aversion of corruption
Dalīl,	Guide, Adviser
Dallasa	To swindle or cheat; Defraud
Dallasa	To conceal a fault or defect in an article of merchandise
Ḍamān	Liability; Tort; Guarantee;
Ḍamān al-'Udwān yakūn bi 'l-mithl aw bi'l-Qīma	"Liability for 'Hostility' may be in kind or for Value"
Ḍamān	Tacitly
Ḍarūra	Necessity
Ḍarar	Harm; Damage; Disadvantage
Dhimmī	Non-Muslim Subject
Dhū al-Ghafla	Negligent Person
Difā' Shar'ī	Legal Defence
Diyya	Bloodmoney
Fā'ida	Additional
Faqīh (pl. Fuqāha')	Legal Scholar
Furū'	Branches
Farḍ al-'Ayn	Duty of the Individual
Farḍ al-Kifāya	Duty of the Community
Fāsid	Voidable; Void
Faskh	Cancellation; Abrogation
al-Faskh aqwā min al-Ijāza	Revocation supercedes Ratification
Fatwā (pl. Fatāwā)	Formal Legal Opinion
Fawāt al-Waṣf al-marghūb	Lapse of a desired characteristic/ quality
Fi'l	Deed
Fi'liyya	Active, Actual
Fiqh	Islamic Jurisprudence
Fuḍūlī	Unauthorised Agent
Ghabn	Misrepresentation
Ghabn (Ghubn) Fāḥish	Gross Misrepresentation
Ghalaṭ	Error, Mistake
Ghalaṭ al-Ma'nā	Mistake in meaning
Gharar	Uncertainty
Gharara	To deceive, delude
Ghurūr	Deception
Ghushsh	Dishonesty
Ghushsh al-Khāfī	Concealed Deception

Ghayru Lāzim	Not Binding
Ghayru Muta'aqqid	Contract which has not been formed
Ghayru Tamyīz	Without Distinction (eg.Minor)
Ḥadīth (pl. Aḥādīth)	Tradition
Ḥīla (pl. Ḥiyal)	Legal Stratagem; Ruse
Habl al-Habla	Sale of Impregnated Livestock (Prohibited)
Ḥālan	Immediately
Ḥalāl	Lawful
Ḥarām	Forbidden
Ḥasharāt	Vermin, small animals, insects
Ḥawāla	Bill of Exchange; payment of a debt through the transfer of a claim
Hazl, Hāzil	Jest; simulated contracts
Hiba	Gift
Ḥijr	Interdiction
Ḥisba	Office of Market Inspector
Ḥudūd	Islamic penal sanctions
Ḥuqūq	Rights; laws
Iḥtiyāl	Trickery, Deception, Fraud
Iḥtiyāliyya	Trickery, Deception, Fraud
Ibāḥa	Freedom of Contract
Īhām	Deception, Fraud
Ījāb	Acceptance
Ijāra	Contract for Service or Hire
Ijār	Hire, Rent
Ijmā'	Concensus
Ijtihād	Independent Interpretation
Ikhtiyār	Free Will; Freedom of Choice
Ikhtiṣāṣ	Special Interest; Lien
Ikrāh	Duress, Undue Influence
al-Ikrāh al-Muljī'	Coercive Duress
al-Ikrāh at-Tām	Coercive or 'Complete' Duress
al-Ikrāh al-Nāqiṣ	Non-coercive duress
Īlāf	Īlāf Pact or Treaty (for access through territory)
Iltizām, pl. Iltizāmāt	Obligation(s)
Imḍā'	Ratification
Ishāra, pl. Ishārāt	Gestures
Ishrāka	Part sale with a reduction in price.

Isnād	Chain of Transmission in a Ḥadīth
Ista'jara	Engaging of services
Istidlāl	Reasoning; Inference
Istighlāl	Unfair advantage
Istiḥsān	Preferences
Istikhfāf	Disrespect
Istirdād	Restitution
Istirsāl	"Forestalling the Market"
Istiṣḥāb	Presumption
Istiṣlāḥ	Interpretation for the public good or benefit
Istaslama	To submit oneself; ie. in Trust Sales to the expertise of the seller
Istisnā'	Contract to Manufacture
Ittifāq	Chance
Ittiḥād	Unity (of *Majlis*)
Jā'iz	Permissible; Legal
Jabr	Pre-determination
Jahl	Ignorance
Jāhilī (Jāhiliyya)	Pre-Islamic
Jamā'a	Republic
Juzāf	Sale whose object is of an uncertain amount
al-Juzām	Leprosy
Jins	Species, kind
Jizya	Islamic Poll Taz
Ju'āla	Award
Ka'ba	The Ka'ba Stone at Mecca
Kafā'a	(Marriage) Equality
Khadī'a	Deceit, Trickery
Khalal	Imbalance; Defect
Khalīfa	Caliph
Khallāb	Deception
Khamīsa	Sharecropping with one-fifth of crop as land rent
Khamr	Wine; Alcohol
Khaṭa'	Error
Khaṭar	Risk; Stake
Khaṭar Jasīm Muḥdiq	Significant and Imminent Danger
Khāṭara	To Risk
Khilāba	Fraud
Khilāf	Differences of Opinion

Khiyāna	Deception
Khiyār (pl. Khiyārāt)	Option (s)
Khiyār al-'Ayb	Option of Defect
Khiyār al-Ghalaṭ	Option of Mistake
Khiyār al-Majlis	Option of the contractual session
Khiyār al-Ru'ya	Option of Inspection
Khiyār al-Sharṭ	Option of Condition or Stipulation
Khiyār Sharṭ al-Tarawwā	Option for Reflection (Mālikī term)
Khiyār al-Tadlīs	Option of Fraud
Khiyār al-Waṣf	Option of Description
khiyār at-Ta'yīn	Option of Determination
Khiyār fawāt	Lapsed Option
Khiyārāt al-Istiḥqāq	Options for dispossession
Khul'	Judicial Divorce granted to Wife
Kināya	Allusory
Kitāb al-buyū'	Chapter on Sales
Kitāba	Clerk
Lā ḍarāra wa lā ḍirāra fī 'l-islām	In Islam there is no injury or malicious damage
Lā yaftarad fī aḥad innahu yajhal al-Qānūn	"Ignorance of the Law is no excuse"
Laysa min ṣan'at ahl al-dīn wa-lā al-murū'a	(Play) is not what Muslims do; it does not go with true manliness.
Lāzim	Fully Binding
Ma'lūm	Certain
Ma'nā	Meaning
al-Ma'qūd alayh	Object of contract
Ma'tūh	Partially or temporarily insane person
Mabhath	Research
Mafālis	Insolvent
Maḥall	Subject matter; Object (of Contract)
Majlis	Contractual Session; Council
Maḥjūr 'alayh	Person under Judicial Restriction
Mahr	Marriage Dower
Majnūn	Lunatic; Madman
Makhū'	A horse with a mark on its chest
Makrūh	Blameworthy; Disapproved (of)
Māl	Property
Māl Mutaqawwim	Object of contract with permissible usufruct
Mala'	General assembly

Manqūl, pl.Manqūlāt, Manqūla	Movable Property, Movables
Marḍ al-Mawt	Death Sickness
Mashhūr	Predominant; Well known
Mashrū‘	Legal
Maṣlaḥa	Human good or benefit
Mawqūf	Suspended
Maysir	Pre-Islamic Gambling Game; Gambling
al-Mayyita	Flesh of animals killed without ritual
Mu‘āṭāh	By conduct (Disposition)
Mu‘āwadāt	Synallagmatic Transactions
Mubāḥ	Legal
Mubham	Ambiguous
Muḍāraba	Commenda Partnership Agreement; Equity sharing between bank and client
Mufāwaḍa	Unlimited mercantile partnership
Muflis	Insolvent
Muftī	Official Expounder of Islamic Law
al-Muḥāfaẓa ‘alā Maqsūd al-Sharī‘a...min al-Khalq	Consideration for what is aimed at for mankind in the law
Muhāqala	Sale of grain while still growing in exchange for a like quantity of wheat by conjecture
Muḥallil (pl. Muḥallilāt)	Legalising Expedients
Muḥtasib	Market Inspector
Mukhafalāt	Animals with Cloven Hooves
Mukhāṭara	Risk
Mukhāṭara ‘alā ju‘l	Gambling for a Reward
Mulābasāt	Concomitant details pertaining to contract
Mulāmasa	Pre-Islamic Sale by Touching (Prohibited)
Mumākasa	Bargaining; Haggling
al-Mumtana‘	Impossible
Munābadha	Sale by throwing the goods to the purchaser
Munāhaba ‘alā rahn	Betting for a stake
Munāẓara	Public disputation
Munfasila	Separable

Muqaraḍa	Islamic bonds on which no interest is earned, but whose market value varies with the anticipated [variable] profit share
Muqāwala	Piecework
Muqāyaḍa	To Barter
Murū'a	Manliness
Musāqāt	Contracts for the lease of agricultural land with profit-sharing.
Muṣarrāt	Animals whose udders have been tied
Musāwama	Resale without reference to original cost price; Bargaining; Haggling
Mushāraka	Partnership
Mushāwara	Mutual Consultation
Muta'awwah	Person diseased beyond competence
Mutaḥaqqiq	Positive; Realistically Practicable
Mutafāwita	Different; Varying
Mutammi'	(literally, "making greedy") : Encourager of Gambling
Mutanajjis	Impure
Mutaqābil	Concessionaire of Gambling Den
Muṭlaq	Absolute sale of object for money
Muwāḍa'a	Sale of multiple transactions
Muzābana	Selling dates growing upon the tree in exchange for dates which have already been harvested
Muzāra'a	Agricultural Contract where landlord provides seed, land and plants, and the worker provides labour
Nafaqa	Maintenance
Nafīdh	Operative
Nājis	Impure
Najsh	Bartering to deliberately raise or diminish price of goods
Naqliyya	Transmitted (Sciences)
Nard	Pre-Islamic Gambling Game
Naṣb	Swindling

Nasī'a	Credit
Naẓar fī Maẓālim	Investigation of Complaints
Niḍāl wa al-Sibāq	Shooting and Racing
Nikāh	Marriage
Nisbī	Relative
Niyāba	Agent, Representative, Attorney
Niyya	Intention
Niẓām (pl. Anẓima)	Regulation (partic. Saudi Arabia)
Nuḍūr	Vows
Qābilan li'l-Ibṭāl	Voidable
Qabūl	Acceptance
Qadar	Predestination
Qāḍī	Judge
Qamara	To Gamble, Gambling
Qarḍ	Loan of fungible commodities
Qarīb	Recent
al-Qaṭl al-khaṭā'	Accidental Homicide
Qaul	Saying; speech
Qimār	Gambling
Qirāḍ	Commenda Agreement; loan
Qasās	Retribution
Qiyās	Analogical Deduction
Qunya/Qinya	Aquisition, Property
Qur'ān,	The Holy Qur'an/Koran
Qūwa Qāhira/ Qūwat al-Qānūn	Force Majeure
Ra'y	Opinion
Rahn	Pledge; Loan
Ribā	Usury; (excessive) interest
Rabawī	Pertaining to Ribā; Ribā commodity
Riḍa	Consent
Riḍā at-Ta'āmul	Transactional consent
Riḍā al-Nafsī	Subjective contentment
Ru'ya	Sight; inspection
Ruqa'a	Instructional Credit Paper
Rushd	Integrity; discernment; probity; Prudence
Ṣā'	Cubic measure of varying magnitude
Sabab	Motivating Cause
al-Sabab al-Ajnabī	Foreign Cause
Ṣabiyy Mahjūr	Minor

al-Sabtiyya	Levantine Saturday-installment custom
Ṣadaqāt	Charitable Donations
Safīh	Prodigal; Spendthrift
Ṣaghīr Ghayr al-Mumayyiz	Minor without discretion
Ṣaghīr Ma'dhūn	Minor granted limited capacity
Ṣaḥīḥ	Sound; Legally Valid
Ṣalāḥ	Ripen
Salam	Future Contract
Sāqiṭ al-Murū'a	Lacking in Manliness
Ṣarf	Money-changing; Currency Exchange
Sarīḥan	Express
Shādhdh	Anonymous opinion
Shāhid, Shahīd	Witness
Shakk	Instructional credit paper; cheque
Sharī'a	The Sacred Law of Islam
Sharika/Shirka (pl.-āt)	Mercantile Partnership; Company
Sharīk	Partner; Co-Owner
Sharṭ	Condition
Sharṭ Mulāyama	Condition intrinsic to contract
Sharṭ Muwāfaqa	Condition intrinsic to contract
Sharṭ yaqtaḍīhā al-'Aqd	Condition implied in Contract
Shirka	Part sale with a reduction in price
Shuf'a	Pre-emption
Shurṭa	Police
Shurūṭ	Conditional clauses; conditions
Sihām al-Falakiyya	Astrological determinism
Siyāsa Shar'iyya	Canonical Statecraft
Suftaja	Letter of credit or bill of exchange
Sunna	Sayings and Exemplary Behaviour of the Prophet
sunna	Custom
Sūra	Qur'anic Verse
Ta'addad	Plurality of contractors
Ta'wīḍ	Restitution
Ta'zīr	Discretionary Islamic Punishments
Ṭabā'i' al-Ashyā'	Nature of things
Tabarru'āt	Contracts of Gift
Ṭabi'iyya	Natural (Sciences)
Tāb'iūn	Adherents, Followers, Disciples
Tadlīl	Deception

Tadlīs	Fraud
al-Tadlīs al-Fi'lī	Active Fraud
Tadlīs al-Mashātah	Beautician's Fraud
Tafsīr	Exegesis
Taghrīr	Misrepresentatuon; Fraud
Taḥāyul	Trickery, Deception, Fraud
Taḥayyul	Trickery, Deception, Fraud
Tahdīd	Threat
Taḥlīl	Dissolution; Resolution
Takhṣīṣ al-Quḍā	Judicial Interpretation
Ṭalāq	Unilateral Declaration of Divorce
Talji'a	Fictional Sale
Tamlīk al-'Ayn bi-'Iwaḍ	Right of ownership passes for consideration
Tamlīk al-'Ayn bilā 'Iwaḍ	Right of ownership passes without consideration
Tamlīk Fī al-Ḥāl	Immediate transfer of ownership
Tamyīz	Distinction
Taqlīd	Imitation
Taqrīr	Prophetic example
Taqṣīr	Negligence, Neglect
Taṣarruf (pl.Taṣarrufāt)	Right of Possession; Right of Disposal; Disposition
al-Taṣarrufāt al-Qawliyya	Oral Dispositions; Manifest expressions of the Will
al-Taṣarrufāt al-Fi'liyya	Material or actual dispositions
Tasmiya	Nomination
Taṣriyya	Fraudulent tying-up of udders of female livestock
Taṭfīf	Fraud (Qur'ānic derivative)
Tauliya	Sale at cost price
Thīqa (Muwaththiq)	Notary Public
Umm al-Kitāb	Mother Book
Umra	Small pilgrimage
Uṣūl al-Fiqh	Principles of Islamic Jurisprudence
Waḍī'a	Deposit; Bailment
Waḍī'a Iḍṭirāriyya	Compulsory Bailment
Wājib	Obligatory
Wakāla	Agency
Wakīl	Mercantile Agent
Walī	Guardian

Waqf	Testamentary Bequest of Real Estate
Waṣf	Characteristic; Quality
Waṣf marghūb	Quality which is lacking
Wasq	Measure : a camel-load equivalent to 60 *Ṣā'ṣ.*
Wathā'iq	Formularies
al-Wazn al-Ṣāfī	Net weight
Wujūh	Dignitaries
Yu'āmilūn bi al-Warq	Serious Gamblers
Zakāt	Alms Tax
Ẓann	Conjecture
Zawāj	Marriage
Zinā	Adultery
Ziyāda Muttaṣila Mutawallada min al-Aṣl	Inherent increase to object

BIBLIOGRAPHY

1. CODES & LAWS

Abu Dhabi Code of Civil Procedure, 1970.
Abu Dhabi Law No. 3 of 1987 (Issued September 1987) Effective as of publication : *Official Gazette*, 1 Aug. 1987 (Amendment to Abu Dhabi Code of Civil Procedure of 1970).
Abu Dhabi Amīrī Decree No. 1 of 1972, founding the Abu Dhabi National Insurance Company
Bahrain Contract Law, 1969; in force as from 25 D/Quida, 1389, corresponding to 1 Feb. 1970; Article 24 (2)
Bahrain Commercial Code, No. 7 of 1987 : Official Gazette 26 March, 1987
Bahrain Decree Law No. 4 of 1987 (Regulating the Stock Exchange)
British Nationality Act, 1948
British Protectorates, Protected States and Protected Persons Order In Council 1949/140; 1961/2325; 1965/1864; 1969/1832
British Protected States (Fujaira and Kalba) Order, 1952/141
Corpus Iuris Civilis, of Justinian
Dubai Contract Law, of 15 July 1971
Egypt : Draft Civil Code, 1949
Egyptian Civil Code, Promulgated 16 July 1948; Came into Force 15 Oct. 1949. Issued as Law No. 131 of 1948; Published in Official Gazette, *Jarīda al-Ra'smiyya*, No. 108, Extraordinary Edition of 29 July 1948 (French Translation by the Ministry of Justice, 1952)
Egyptian Commercial Code, 1883 (Heavily Modified by specific Statues)
Egyptian Code of Civil and Commercial Procedure, Law No. 13 of 1968, published in the *Egyptian Official Gazette : Al-Jarīda al-Ra'smiyya*, No. 19 of 9/5/1968.
Egyptian Criminal Code, 1927
England : Sale of Goods Act 1979
England : The Misrepresentation Act, 1967
England : Acts 5 and 6 Edward VI, (1552)
England : Act 37 Henry VIII (1545).
French Civil Code, 1790 (*Code Civil Napoléon*) with Subsequent

Amendments

German Civil Code, 18 Aug. 1896, (*Bürgerliches Gesetzbuch*) with subsequent Amendments and Amplifications.

Iraqi Civil Code, 1953

Iraqi Law of Commerce, Law No. 30 (1984)

Iranian Civil Law (1927-1932)

Jordanian Civil Code, Law No. 43 of 1976

Kuwait Constitution : *Al-Kuwait Al-Yaum*, Spec. Issue of 12 Nov. 1962. (English Translation in *International Encyclopoedia of Comparative Law*, 'Kuwait')

Kuwait Commercial Code, Law No. 2 of 1961

Kuwait Commercial Companies Code, Law No. 15 of 1960,

Kuwaiti Law No. 6 of 1961, recognising liabilities arising out of unlawful acts ('The Tort Law').

Kuwait : The Civil Code, Law No. 67 of 1980 (Law No. 1335, issued 29 Safar 1401 AH; Law No. 2 of Jan 5, 1981)

Kuwait Commercial Code, Issued by Decree Law No. 68 of 1980, Effective as of 25 February, 1981

Kuwait Code of Maritime Commerce, Law No. 28 of 1980.

Kuwait: Decree 1492 of 1983 (Regulating the Stock Market)

Kuwait: Law 100/83 (regarding certain specific provisions concerning settlement of transactions relating to company shares concluded on credit)

Kuwait: Decree 1505/83 Council of Ministers Resolution 46/83 amending certain provisions of Decree 57/82 (Concerning Credit Share Guarantee Documents)

Kuwait: Ministerial Resolution 47/83 amending certain provisions of Resolution 5/83

Kuwait: Ministerial Resolution 35 of 1983 issuing the Internal Regulations of Kuwaiti Stock Market

Kuwait: Decree 1595/85 Resolution No. 1/75 (on composition of Stock Market Disciplinary Board)

Lebanese Code of Obligations and Contracts, 1932

Libyan Civil Code of 1953

al-Majella, Commission of Ottoman Jurists (1867-1877) (Constantinople, 1305 AH); also transl. by C.A. Hooper, *The Civil Law of Palestine and Trans-Jordan*, (2 vols., Jerusalem, 1933); also transl. by Tyser, C.R., Demetriades, D.G., and Haqqi, Ismail, *The Mejelle*, (Lahore, 1967; Cyprus, 1901)

Oman : Ministerial Decree of the Ministry of Social Affairs and Labour, Decision No. 5 of 1980, *OGSO*, No.192 (15 April 1980)

Omani Royal Decree No. 12 of 1979 *OGSO*, No. 67 (1 April 1979): 'The

Insurance Companies Law'
Polish Civil Code of 1934
Qatar Civil and Commercial Law, Law No. 16 of 1971
Ra's al-Khaima Courts Law, 1971
Saudi Arabia : Negotiable Instruments Regulation, Royal Decree No. 37 (11.X. 1383 AH)
Saudi Arabia : Royal Decree '[O]ur Constitution is the Qur'ān': *Umm al-Qura*, No.1320 (July 19, 1950).
Saudi Arabia: Cabinet Decree No. 16-3-1336, issued on 20-10-81 AH.
Saudi Arabia : Decree No. M/22 of 1989 AH (State Social Assurance Scheme)
Sudanese Civil Transactions Act, 1984 (Repealing Contracts Act, Sales Act)
Sudanese Civil Procedure Act, 1983 (Repealing 1974 Act)
Syrian Civil Code, 1949
Termination of Special Treaty Relations Between The United Kingdom and Bahrain, 1971 Cmnd. 4827
Termination of Special Treaty Relations Between The United Kingdom and The Trucial States, dated 1 December 1971, Cmnd. 4941
Tunisian Code of Obligations and Contracts, 1906
Turkish Criminal Code, 1926
United Arab Emirates, Federal Law No. 10 of 1973
United Arab Emirates Federal Rule No.4 of 1980 'Regarding categorization of contractors'.
United Arab Emirates : Union Law No. 5 of 1985 Issuing the Code of Civil Transactions for the United Arab Emirates, [Effective as from March 1986], *UAE Official Gazette*, No 158, (Dec. 1985)
United Arab Emirates, The Federal Civil Code, No. 2 of 1987
United Arab Emirates, Commercial Agencies Law, Law No. 18 of 1981
UAE : Ministerial Decision No. 54 of 1987 of the Ministry of Economy and Commerce; Effective as of 1 Dec. 1987 (regarding Insurance)
United States I *Restatement (Second) of Contracts*, (1981)

2. CASES

Abullah Fashid Hilal v. International Bank of Credit and Commerce, (Abu Dhabi Court of Appeal), Civ. Appeal No. 5, Dubai 1979
Appeal No. 124/81: Commercial : Session 30/1/82, *Majallat al-Qaḍā' wa al-Qānūn*, (*Wazīrat al-'Adl*, Supreme Court of Kuwait) Issue No.3, Year 10 (June, 1984) p.135; Rule No. 40
Appeal No. 119/1987 [Kuwait Appeal Court] Appeal from Commercial Court of 27/1/82, *Majallat al-Qaḍā' wa al-Qānūn*, Rule No.39, p.130

Abdul Hussein v Sona Dero, (1917) 45 *IA*. 10; Cases 94

Associated Japanese Bank (International) Ltd v. Crédit du Nord SA, (1988), Q.B.

Bank of Baroda v. Abu Dhabi Electronics Trading Co., 1983, Federal Supreme Court, Abu Dhabi, [Cited in *Arab Law Newsletter*, No.10 (Sept 1986), p.4]

Bell v. Lever Bros. Ltd., (1932), A.C.

Hotchkiss v. Nat'l City Bank of New York, 200 F. 287, 293 (1911),

Janata case, 1981, Federal Supreme Court, Abu Dhabi [Cited in *Arab Law Newsletter*, No.10 (Sept 1986), p.4]

SCF Finance Co. Ltd. v. Khalil Masri, QB 1 All ER (1986) at p.40

Ra's al-Khaima Civil Court, Suit No. 397/78, September 1978 Arabic court record of the Ra's al-Khaima Civil Court, Suit No. 397/78

Rector of Al-Azhar University v. President of the Arab Republic of Egypt, the Prime Minister, the President of the Council of Ministers, the President of the Legislative Committee of the People's Assembly, and Fuad Goudah, Case No. 20 of Judicial Year of the Egyptian Constitutional Court, and No.7 of the Supreme Court (No. 9): (Decision issued 16 Nov. 1985)

Smith v Hughes, QB (1871) *LR*, 6QB 597; 40 *LJ*QB 221; 25 *LT*329; 19 *WR*1059.

Villa Jacqueline, (French Cass. Civ. 23.11.1931)

The Geneva Award of 23 August 1958 between *Saudi Arabia and ARAMCO*, is deposited in the archives of the Republic and Canton of Geneva. This quotation refers to the Onassis Agreement of 20 Jan 1954 (15 Jumad I, 1373) as quoted on pp.146-7 of the official typewritten English version of the Award, and pp.101-2 of the printed version.

3. ḤANAFĪ

Abū Yūsuf, Ya'qūb Ibn Ibrāḥīm, *Ikhtilāf Abī Ḥanīfa wa Ibn Abī Laylā*, [ed. Abū al-Wafā' al-Afghānī], (Cairo, 1357 AH)

idem., *Kitāb al-Kharāj*, (Cairo, 1302 AH)

'Ālamgīr, Awrangzeb, *al-Fatāwā al-'Ālamgīriyya*, (Calcutta, 1828); also published as *al-Fatāwā al-'Ālmakīriyya*, 6 vols., (Cairo, 1323 AH); and *Fatāwā al-Hindiyya*, (Cairo, al-Muniyya ed.)

Dammād Effendī, Muḥammad Ibn Sulaymān, *Majma' al-Anhūr Sharḥ Multaqā al-Abḥur*, (Cairo, 1328 AH) 2 vols.

Ḥamawī, Aḥmad b. Muḥammad al-, *Ghamz 'Uyūn al-Baṣā'ir : Sharḥ al-Ashbāh wa al-Naẓā'ir*, (Cairo, 1290 AH) 2 Vols.

Ibn 'Ābidīn, Mḥd. Amīn b. 'Umar b. 'Abd al-'Azīz b. (1198/1784-

1258/1842), *Radd al-Muḥtār 'alā al-Durr al-Mukhtār*, 8 Vols., (Cairo, 1386-89/1966-69)
idem., *Radd al-Muḥtār 'alā al-Durr al-Mukhtār*, (1252 AH), 5 Vols: vol.IV; (First Ed., Boulac, 1316), V; (Cairo, 1324: Dār al-Sa'āda; also in 7 vols)
idem., *Taḥbīr al-Taḥrīr Fī Ibṭāl al-Qaḍā' bi al-Faskh bi al-Ghabn al-Fāḥish bilā Taghrīr.*
Ibn Amīr al-Ḥājj, Mḥd. b. Mḥd., *al-Taqrīr wa al-Taḥbīr*, commentary on *al-Taḥrīr*, by Ibn al-Hammām (Būlāq, 1316 AH)
Ibn al-Hammām, Kamāl al-Dīn (d.861/1457) *Fatḥ al-Qadīr: Sharḥ al-Hidāya*, (Cairo, 1315-1318 AH) 8 Vols.
idem., *Sharḥ al-Taḥrīr*, (Būlāq, 1316 AH)
Ibn Nujaym, Zayn al-'Abidīn b. Ibrāḥīm, *al-Ashbāh wa al-Naẓā'ir*, (Cairo, 1298 AH)
idem., *al-Baḥr al-Rā'iq: Sharḥ Kanz al-Daqā'iq*, (Cairo, 1334 AH) 8 Vols.
idem., *Fatḥ al-Ghaffār bi Sharḥ Manār al-Anwār*, 3 Vols. in 1 (Cairo, 1355/1936)
Kāsānī, 'Alā' al-Dīn Abū Bakr b. Mas'ūd al-, *Kitāb al-Badā'i' al-Ṣanā'i' Fī Tartīb al-Sharā'i'*, (Cairo, 1909-1910; 1327-1328 AH), 7 Vols
Khaṣṣāf, Aḥmad b. 'Umar al-, *Kitāb al-Ḥiyal wa al-Makhārij*, (Cairo, 1314 AH; Hanover, 1923).
Maḥbūbī, 'Ubayd Allāh b. Mas'ūd al-, (d.747/1346) *Tawḍīḥ Fī Ḥall Jawāmiḍ al-Tanqīḥ*, in margin of al-Ṭaftazānī, *al-Talwīḥ Fī Kashf Ḥaqā'iq al-Tanqīḥ*, 2 Vols. in 1 (Cairo, 1377/1957)
Marghīnānī, Burhān al-Dīn al-, *al-Hidāya : Sharḥ Bidāyat al-Mubtadi'*, 4 Vols. (Cairo, 1326-1327 AH); Transl. Hamilton, (2nd Ed.: Lahore, 1957)
idem., *Kifāya*, (Bombay, 1863)
Qāḍīkhān, Maḥmūd, *al-Fatāwā al-Khāniyya*, (Calcutta, 1835)
Sarakhsī, Shams ad-Dīn, *Kitāb al-Mabsūṭ: Sharḥ al-Kāfī*, (Cairo, 1913; 1324-1331 AH) 16 vols.; 30 vols.
Shaybānī, 'Abd al-Qādir b. 'Umar al-, *Dalīl al-Ṭālib*, with commentary by Mar'ī b. Yūsuf (Cairo, 1324-1326)
idem., *Kitāb al-Aṣl*, [Kitāb al-Sharika], MS. Dār al-Kutub al-Miṣriyya, Fiqh Ḥanafī, 34 folios, 57b and 61b; (Cairo, 1954)
Shaybānī, Muḥammad b. al-Ḥasan al-, *Kitāb al-Kasb*, ed. S. Zakkār, (Damascus, 1980)
idem., *Kitāb al-Makhārij Fī al-Ḥiyal*, Ed. Joseph Schacht (Leipzig, 1930)
Suyūṭī, Imām 'Abd ar-Raḥmān Ibn Mḥd. Jalāl ad-Dīn al-, *al-Ashbāh wa al-Naẓā'ir*, (Cairo, 1359 AH; 1936; 1378/1959)
Ṭaḥāwī, Aḥmad al-, *Kitāb al-Shuf'a Min al-Jāmi' al-Kabīr Fī al-Shurūṭ*, (Ed. J. Schacht) in 20 *Heidelberger Akademie der Wissenschaften*, 3

(1929-1930)
Zayla'ī, 'Uthmān Ibn 'Alī, *Tabyīn al-Ḥaqā'iq: Sharḥ Kanz al-Daqā'iq*, (6 Vols: Cairo/Boulac, 1313 AH)
Zubaydī, Aḥmad b. Aḥmad, *al-Tajrīd al-Ṣarīḥ li-Aḥādīth al-Jāmi' al-Ṣaḥīḥ*, (Būlāq, 1287 AH)

4. SHĀFI'Ī

'Amīra, al-Burullusi Shihāb al-Dīn, *Ḥāshiyya 'Alā Sharḥ al-Maḥallā 'Alā Minhāj al-Ṭālibīn*, (Latter by al-Nawāwī) at bottom of page in al-Qalyūbī, *Ḥāshiyya 'Alā Sharḥ al-Maḥallā 'Alā Minhāj al-Ṭālibīn*, (Latter by al-Nawāwī) 4 Vols. (Cairo, n.d.)
Anṣārī, Abū Yahyā Zakarīyā b. Mḥd. b. Z. al-, *Sharḥ al-Bahja al-Wardiyya*,
Bayhaqī, Aḥmad b. al-Ḥusayn, *Kitāb al-Sunan al-Kubrā*, (Hyderabad, 1344-1355)
Ghazālī, Abū Ḥāmid Mḥd., *al-Iqtiṣād fī al-I'tiqād*, (Cairo, 1320 AH)
idem., *al-Wajīz*, (Cairo, 1317)
idem., *Iḥyā' 'Ulūm al-Dīn*, (Cairo, 1933) 4 vols. (Transl. Behari:1972)
idem., *Kitāb al-Mustasfā min 'Ilm al-Uṣūl*, 2 Vols. (Būlāq, 1322 and 1324; Cairo, 1937/1356)
Ibn Ḥajar al-Haythāmī, Aḥmad Ibn Mḥd. b. 'Alī, *Tuḥfa al-Muḥtāj*, (Cairo, 1282)
idem., *Fatḥ al-Jawād bi-Sharḥ al-Irshād*, (latter by al-Muqri' al-Shawarī al-Yamānī) 2 Vols. (Cairo, 1347)
idem., *al-Zawājir 'an Iqtirāf al-Kabā'ir*, (Cairo, 1370/1951)
Māwardī, Abū al-Ḥasan 'Alī b. Muḥammad b. Ḥabīb al-, *Kitāb al-Aḥkām as-Sulṭāniyya wa al-Wilāyāt al-Dīniyya*, (Cairo, 1393/1973); also transl. by Count Léon Ostrorog, *El-Aḥkām Es-Soulthania : Traité de Droit Public Musulman d'Abou'l Ḥassan 'Alī Ibn Moḥammad Ibn ḥabīb El-Mawerdi*, 2 Vols., (Paris, 1900, 1901, 1906): [New Edn.: *Le Droit du Califat*, (Paris 1925)]; also transl. by E. Fagnan, *Les Statuts Gouvernementaux ou Règles de Droit Public et Administratif*, (Algiers, 1915)
idem., *al-Aḥkām al-Sulṭāniyya wa al-Wilāyāt al-Dīniyya*, (Cairo, 1298)
Nawāwī, Muḥyī al-Dīn al-, *Minhāj aṭ-Ṭālibīn*, (Cairo 1319 AH). Translated into French by L.W.C. Van der Berg (Batavia, 1882-1884); and into English by E.C. Howard, (London, 1914)
idem., *al-Majmū' : Sharḥ al-Muhadhdhab*, and its continuation by Taqī al-Dīn al-Subkī (Cairo, 1344-1353 AH) 12 Vols.
Qalyūbī, Shihāb al-Dīn al-, *Ḥāshiyya 'Alā Sharḥ al-Maḥallā 'Alā Minhāj al-Ṭālibīn*, (Latter by al-Nawāwī) 4 Vols. (Cairo, n.d.)
Qazwīnī, *Kitāb al-Ḥiyal Fī al-Fiqh*, edited by J. Schacht, (Hanover, 1924)

Rāfi'ī (al-Qazwīnī), al-, *Muhanar*, fol. 267 a-b MS Brit. Mus. Or. 4285, fol. 110b

Ramlī, Khayr al-Dīn, *Nihāyat al-Muḥtāj ilā Sharḥ al-Minhāj*, (8 Vols; Cairo 1304/1938)

Shāfi'ī, Muḥammad b. Idrīs al-, *Kitāb al-Umm*, (7 vols. Cairo, 1321-1326 AH; Būlāq 1324)

idem., *Ikhtilāf al-Ḥadīth*, printed in the margin of *Kitāb al-Umm*, (Cairo, 1325 AH)

idem., *Kitāb al-Risāla Fī 'Ilm al-Uṣūl*, (Cairo, 1321)

Shīrāzī, A. Isḥāq Ibr. b.'A.b.Yu. al-Fayrūzabādī al-, *al-Muhadhdhab Fī Fiqh Madhhab al-Imām al-Shāfi'ī*, 2 Vols., (Cairo, 1343 AH)

idem., *Kitāb al-Tanbīh Fī al-Fiqh*, (Ed. A.W.T. Juynboll; Leyden, 1879; and Cairo, 1348 AH)

Shirbīnī al-Qādirī al-Khaṭīb, Shamsaddīn M.b.M.b.A al-, *Mughnī al-Muḥtāj: Sharḥ Minḥāj al-Ṭālibīn*, 4 Vols. (Cairo, 1308; 1377/1958)

Subkī, Tāj al-Dīn al-, *Jam' al-Jawāmi'*, 2 vols. (Cairo, 1354 AH)

Subkī, Taqī al-Dīn al-, *al-Fatāwā*, (Cairo, 1355-1356), 2 vols.

Sulāmī , 'Abd al-'Azīz b. 'Alī b. 'Abd as-Salām, (d.1262) *Qawā'id al-Aḥkām Fī Maṣāliḥ al-Anām*, 2 Vols in 1, (1388/1968)

Suyūṭī, *Tanwīr al-Ḥawālik: Sharḥ Muwaṭṭa' al-Imām Mālik*, (Cairo, 1348 AH) 2 Vols.

Ṭaftazānī, *al-Talwīḥ Fī Kashf Ḥaqā'iq al-Tanqīḥ*, 2 Vols. in 1 (Cairo, 1377/1957)

Zamakhsharī, Imām Maḥmūd b. 'Umar al-, *al-Kashshāf 'An Ḥaqā'iq al-Tanzīl wa 'Ayūn al-Aqāwīl Fī Wujūh al-Ta'wīl*, 4 Vols. (Būlāq, 1318-1319; Cairo, 1354 AH; 1385/1966)

5. MĀLIKĪ

Dardīr, Abū al-Barakāt A.b.N.b.A., (1201/1786) *al-Sharḥ al-Ṣaghīr*, 5 Vols. in 2, (Cairo, 1385/1965; vol.I; 1383/1963 Vol. II; 1391/1971 Vol.III; 1382/1962 Vols. IV,V; Reprint 1972); Also at bottom margin of al-Ṣāwī, *Bulghat al-Sālik li Aqrab al-Masālik*, 3 vols. (Cairo, 1978)

Dasūqī, M.b.A.b. 'Arafa, (1230/1815) *Ḥāshiyya 'Alā al-Sharḥ al-Kabīr li Abī al-Barakāt Sīdī Aḥmad al-Dardīr ['Alā Khalīl]*, (4 vols.; Boulac, 1295; Reprint 1331 AH)

Ḥaṭṭāb, Abū 'Abdallāh, *Mawāhib al-Jalīl li Sharḥ Mukhtaṣar Khalīl*, (6 Vols. Tripoli/Cairo, 1329 AH; Cairo, 1928)

Ibn 'Āṣim al-Mālikī, Abū Yaḥyā M.b.M. *Tuḥfat al-Ḥukkām Fī Niqāṭ al-'Uqūd wa al-Aḥkām*, (Cairo, 1355 AH) 2 vols. Also known as *Matn al-'Āṣimiyya*. (Also transl. by Bercher, *Al 'Acimiyya or Tuh'fat al-H'ukkam fi Nukat al-'Uqoud wa'l-Ah'kam : "Le Present Fait aux*

Juges Touchant Les Points Délicats des Contrats et des Jugements", (Algiers, 1858)

Ibn Juzayy, Muḥammad, *al-Qawānīn al-Fiqhiyya Fī Talkhīṣ Madhhab al-Mālikiyya*, (Beirut, 1977)

Ibn al-Mawwāq, Abū M.b.Yu.b.al-Q. al-'Abdānī, (897/1492) *al-Tāj wa al-Iklīl li Mukhtaṣar Khalīl*, in the margin of *al-Ḥaṭṭāb, Mawāhib al-Jalīl li Sharḥ Mukhtaṣar Khalīl*, (6 Vols. Tripoli 1329)

Ibn Rushd (Averroes), Abū Walīd M. b. A., *Tahāfut al-Tahāfut*, (Incohérence de l'Incohérence) ed. M. Boryges [Bibliotheca Arabica Scholasticorum, Séries Arabe, Vol. III], (Beirut, 1930)

idem., *al-Muqqadamāt al-Muḥamidāt Libayān mā 'qtadathu al-Rusūm al-Mudawwana min al-Aḥkām al-Sharī'a wa at-Taḥsīlāt al-Muḥkamāt (al-Shār'iyāt) li Ummahāt masā'ilhā al-Mushkilāt*, 2 vols. in 1; (Cairo, 1325; 1332 AH)

idem., *Bidāyat al-Mujtahid Wa Nihāyat al-Muqtaṣid*, (Cairo, 1966), 2 Vols.

Isḥāq, Khalīl b., *Mukhtaṣar*, (Paris, 1318/1900); Trans. G.H. Bousquet (Algiers, 1956)

Khurshī, (al-Kharashī) Abū 'Abdallāh Mḥd. al-, *Sharḥ Mukhtaṣar Sīdī Khalīl*, 8 Vols. in 4, (Cairo 1307-1308; 1316-1317 AH.; Reprint, Beirut, n.d.)

Mālik Ibn Anas, *al-Mudawanna al-Kubrā*, [Narrated by Saḥnūn] (Cairo, 1323 AH) 16 vols.

idem., *al-Muwaṭṭa'*, (Translated by 'Aisha 'Abdarahmān at-Tarjumana and Yu'qūb Johnson : Cambridge, 1982)

idem., *al-Muwaṭṭa'*, (With Commentary by al-Zurqānī: Cairo, 1280 AH; 1310) 4 Vols.

Qarāfī, Shihāb al-Dīn Abū al-'Abbās Aḥmad b. Idrīs al-, *Kitāb al-Ummiyya Fī Idrāk al-Niyya*, (Cairo, 1344 AH)

idem., *Sharḥ Tanqīḥ al-Fuṣūl Fī Ikhtiṣār al-Maḥṣūl Fī Uṣūl*, (Cairo, 1393/1973)

idem., *Tanqīḥ al-Fuṣūl Fī 'Ilm al-Uṣūl*, published as Chapter II in *al-Dhakhīra*, (A Collection of Qarāfī's writings) (Cairo, 1961)

Saḥnūn, 'Abd al-Salām b. Sa'īd, *al-Mudawwana al-Kubrā*, (Cairo, 1323) [Narration of the same work by Mālik Ibn Anas] (Cairo, 1323-1324)

Ṣāwī, al-Shadhilī al-Khalwaṭī al-Mālikī al-, (1241/1825) *Bulghat al-Sālik li-Aqrab al-Masālik*, 3 vols. (Cairo, 1978)

Shāṭibī, Abū Isḥāq Ibrāhīm al-, *al-Muwāfaqāt Fī al-Uṣūl al-Shar'iyya*, 4 Vols. (Cairo, 1341 AH)

idem., *Kitāb al-I'tiṣām*, 2 vols. (Cairo, 1295 AH)

Tasūlī al-Sabrārī, 'A.b. 'Abd al-Salām al-, *al-Bahja fī Sharḥ al-Tuḥfa*, (Latter by Ibn 'Āṣim) 2 vols. in 1; (Cairo, 1370/1951)

Tāwudī, M.b. Sudā al-, (12-7/1792) *Ḥilā al-Ma'āṣim*, (In margin of Tasūlī's

al-Bahja fī Sharḥ al-Tuḥfa, (Cairo, 1370/1951)
Zaqqāq, Abū al-H.'A.b.Q.b.M al-Tujaybī al-, *Lāmiyyat al-Zaqqāq*, on pp.129-152 following text in Ibn 'Āṣim, *Matn al-'Āṣimiyya*, (Cairo, n.d.). Also transl. by Merad Ben 'Ali Ould Abdelkader, 'La "Lāmiyya" ou "Zaqqāqia" du Jurisconsulte Marocain : Zaqqāq', (Casablanca, 1927) *Revue Algérienne, Tunisienne et Marocaine de Législation et de Jurisprudence*, 41 (1925) pp.35-54; 42 (1926) pp.1-8, 17-42
Zurqānī, Mḥd. b. 'Abd al-Bāqī al-, *Sharḥ 'Alā Mukhtaṣar Khalīl*, (8 vols.; Cairo, 1307 AH)
idem., *Sharḥ 'Alā Muwaṭṭa' al-Imām Mālik*, (n.p., 1936)

6. ḤANBALĪ

Ibn Ḥanbal, Abū 'Abdallāh Aḥmad b., *al-Musnad*, 6 Vols; (Cairo, 1313 AH)
Ibn Qayyim al-Jawziyya (d.751/1350-1), *al-Furūsiyya*, ed. 'Izzat al-'Aṭṭar al-Ḥusaynī, (Beirut, n.d. [1974?])
idem., *I'lām al-Muwaqqi'īn 'An Rabb al-'Ālamīn*, 4 Vols; (Cairo, 1968-1980)
Ibn Qudāma, Shaikh Muwaffaq al-Dīn b. (d.620/1223) *Kitāb al-Mughnī*, (Cairo, Third Ed. 1367 AH; 9 vols.), III, IV (Cairo, 1341-48 AH) 12 Vols.
idem., *Kitāb 'Umdat al-Aḥkām Fī al-Fiqh 'Alā Madhhab al-Imām Aḥmad b. Ḥanbal*, (Damascus, 1352 AH), fo. 66b; (Cairo Edition of 1352 AH)
idem., *Rawḍat al-Naẓīr*, MSS in the al-Azhar Library, 284
Ibn Rajab, Abū al-Faraj 'Abd al-Raḥmān b. (d.795/1393) *al-Qawā'id al-Fiqhiyya*, (Cairo, 1933; Reprint 1391/1971).
Ibn Taymiyya, Sheikh al-Islām Taqī al-Dīn Aḥmad (d.728/1328), *Fatāwā*, 5 Vols, (Cairo, 1326-1329 AH; (Cairo, 1384-1386/1965-1966)
idem., *al-Qiyās Fī al-Shar' al-Islāmī*, (Cairo, n.d.)
idem., *Majmū'at al-Rasā'il wa al-Masā'il*, 5 Vols. (Cairo, 1341-1349/1923-1931)
idem., *Majmū'*, Ẓāhiriyya Library, Damascus, 91 Folios 325a-333b (n.d.; n.p.)
idem., MS *Uṣūl al-Fiqh*, Egyptian National Library [Dār al-Kutub] 150, Folios 178b-180a.
Maqdisī, Shams al-Dīn Abī al-Faraj 'Abd al-Raḥmān Aḥmad b. Qudāma al-, *al-Sharḥ al-Kabīr 'Alā Matn al-Muqanna'*, in the margin of Ibn Qudāma's *al-Mughnī*, (Second Edn.; and Beirut, 1392/1972)
Sijistānī, Abū Dāwūd sulaymān al-, (d.275/888-9) *Kitāb al-Sunan*, (Cairo n.d.) 4 Vols
Tawfī, Najm ad-Dīn, *Risāla Fī al-Maṣāliḥ al-Mursala (Majmū' Rasā'il Fī*

Uṣūl al-Fiqh), (Beirut, 1324)
idem., 'Sharḥ al-Ḥadīth al-Thānī wa al-Thalāthīn Min al-Arba'īn al-Nawāwiyya,' published in *Majmū' al-Rasā'il Fī Uṣūl al-Fiqh*, (Beirut, 1324 AH).

7. IMĀMĪ

Ibn Bābūyah, Muḥammad b. 'Alī, *'Ilal al-Sharā'i'*, (Najaf, 1963)
idem., *Man Lā Yaḥḍuruhu al-Faqīh*, Ed. H.M. Al-Khurshān, (Tehran, 1390)
Ṭūsī, Muḥammad b. al-Ḥasan al-, *Masā'il al-Khilāf*, (Iran, n.d.)
idem., *Tahdhīb al-Aḥkām*, ed. H.M. al-Khurshān (Tehran, 1390)
idem., Kitāb al-Istibṣār, Ed. H.M. al-Khurshān (Tehran, 1390)

8. IBĀḌĪ

Salīmī, 'Abdallāh b. Ḥamīd b. Sallūm al-Sām al-, *Jawhar al-Niẓām Fī 'Ilmai al-Adyān wa al-Aḥkām*, (Cairo, 1334 AH)
idem., *Kitāb Sharḥ Ṭal'at al-Shams 'Alā al-Alāfiyāt*, (2 Vols.: Egypt, n.d.)
Shamakhī, Sheikh 'Amr b. 'Alī al-, *Kitāb al-Īḍāḥ*, IV Vols., (Libya and Beirut, 1971)

9. ẒĀHIRĪ

Ibn Ḥazm, Abū Mḥd. 'Alī b. Aḥmad, *al-Muḥallā*, Ed. M.M. al-Dimashqī, (Cairo, 1347-52 AH), 11 Vols.
idem., *al-Iḥkām Fī Uṣūl al-Aḥkām*, (Cairo, 1347 AH) 8 Vols.
idem., *Mulakhkhaṣ Ibṭāl al-Qiyās wa al-Ra'y wa al-Istiḥsān wa al-Taqlīd wa al-Ta'līl*, (Damascus, 1960) [Introduction by al-Afghānī]
Ibn Shahīd al-Thānī, Zayn al-Dīn b.'Alī b. Aḥmad al-'Āmilī, (d.966/1559), *Ma'ālim al-Uṣūl*, (Tehran 1379 AH)
idem., *Ma'ālim al-Dīn*, (Lucknow, 1301 AH)
idem., *Masālik al-Afhām*, (Tehran, 1273)

10. ARABIC SOURCES

Abū Zahra, Muḥammad, *al-Milkiyya wa Naẓariyyat al-'Aqd*, (First Ed. 1939)
Aḥmad, Ḥasan Ṣubḥī, *Baḥth Muqārin Mawḍū'uhū 'Uyūb al-Riḍā Fī 'Uqūd al-Mu'āwaḍāt al-Māliyya Fī al-Sharī'a al-Islāmiyya: al-Ghubna wa al-Tadlīs*, Vol. I, (Dār al-Maṭbū'āt al-Jāmi'iyya: College of Law, Alexandria University, Egypt, n.d.)
Aḥmad, Khālid A., *al-Tafkīr al-Iqtiṣādī Fī al-Islām*, (Beirut, 1397 AH)
'Akīlī, 'Azīz al-, *al-Mūjiz fī Sharḥ Qānūn al-Tijāra al-Kuwaitī*, (Kuwait,

1978),
Al-Kuwait al-Yawm, (Kuwaiti Official Gazette) Supp. No.s 253-373 (Dec. 1959 - April 1962)
'Āmilī, Muḥammad Baha al-Dīn al-, *Miqlāt*, (Cairo, 1282 AH/ 1865; 1317)
'Arafa, Muḥammad 'Alī, *al-Taqnīn al-Madanī al-Jadīd*, (Cairo, 1949)
Azraqī, Muḥammad b. 'Abdallāh al-, *Kitāb Akhbār Makka*, ed. F. Wüstenfeld (Leipzig, 1858)
Badawī, Ibrāhīm Zakī al-Dīn, *Naẓariyya al-Ribā al-Muḥarramu Fī al-Sharī'a al-Islāmiyya*, (Baghdad, 1966/1967)
Baghdādī, 'Abd al-Qāhir al-, *Uṣūl al-Dīn*, (Istanbul, 1928)
Bakhūrī, *Taqṣīrāt Tafhīm*, (A Study of Abū 'Alā' Mawdūdī's *Tafhīm al-Qur'ān*, (Bijnaur, 1979)
Buḥturī, *Ḥamāsa*, (Cairo, 1929)
Bukhārī, Abū 'Abdallāh Mḥd. b. Ismā'īl, *al-Jāmi' al-Ṣaḥīḥ*, (Cairo, n.d.) 9 vols.
idem., *al-Adab al-Mufrad*, ed. M.F. 'Abd al-Bāqī, (Cairo, 1375)
Burr, Zakī 'Abd al-, *Majallat al-Qānūn wa al-Iqtiṣād*, XXV, pp.116-121
Chehata, (Shahāṭa) Chafik, *al-Naẓariyya al-'Amma li al-Iltizāmāt Fī al-Sharī'a al-Islāmiyya*, (Cairo, 1939)
Dhahabī, al-, *al-Kabā'ir*, (Cairo, 1385/1965)
Dimashqī, Abū al-Faḍl Ja'far b. 'Alī al-, *Kitāb al-Ishāra ilā Maḥāsin al-Tijāra*, (Cairo, 1318 AH)
Dimyāṭī, al-, *Faḍl al-Khayl*, fol. 89 a [MS Bodleian Marsh, 889]
Fārābī, al-, *Iḥṣā' al-'Ulūm*, (La Statistique des Sciences), ed. Osman Amine, (Second Edn; Cairo, 1949)
idem., *Kitāb Taḥsīl al-Sa'āda*, (Hyderabad, 1345 AH)
Fāsī, 'Allāl al-, *Risālat al-Maghrib*, (Rabat, 7 Nov. 1949) Fr. transl. in *Échanges*, (Rabat) French Series No. 8 of 25 Dec. 1949
Hajjwī, *al-Fikr al-Sāmī*, (Fez, n.d.) Transl. J. Berque, *Essai Sur La Méthode Juridique Maghrébine*, (Rabat, 1944)
Harūn, 'Abd al-Salām M., *al-Maysir wa al-Azlām*, (Cairo, 1953)
Haykal, Muḥammad Ḥusayn, *Ḥayāt Muḥammad*, (Cairo 1358 AH/ 1939; 13th Ed., n.d.)
Hilāl, Jawdat, 'Istiḥsān wa Maṣāliḥ Mursalat' in *Usbū' al-Fiqh al-Islāmī Mahrajān Ibn Taymiyya*, (Damascus, 1961; Reprint 1966)
Ibn Abī Shayba, 'Abdallāh b. Muḥammad, *Kitāb al-Muṣannaf Fī al-Aḥādīth wa al-Āthār*, ed. M.A. al-Nadwī, (Bombay, 1979-1983)
idem., *al-Muṣannaf*, fol. 72b [MS. Istanbul Nuru Osmaniye, 1219]
Ibn Abī Zayd, *Risāla*, ed. and transl. L. Bercher, (Third Edn; Algiers, 1949)
Ibn Duyān, Sheikh Ibrāhīm Ibn Muḥammad Ibn Sālim, *Manār al-Sabīl*, in explanation of the Ḥanbalī text *al-Dalīl*, transl. by George M. Baroody as *Crime and Punishment Under Islamic Law*, (London,

1979; Second Edn.)
Ibn Ḥabīb, Muḥammad, *Kitāb al-Munammaq*, ed. K.A. al-Fāriq (Hyderabad, 1964)
idem., *Muḥabbar*, ed. I. Lichtenstaedter, (Hyderabad, 1361/1942).
Ibn Hishām (d.834), *Kitāb Sīrat Rasūl Allāh*, (Eg. Ed. Būlāq, 1295 AH) ; Ed. F. Wüstenfeld, *Das Leben Muhammeds Nach Muhammed Ibn Ishâk*, (Göttingen, 1858-60)
Ibn Khaldūn, 'Abd al-Raḥmān, *Muqaddimāt Ibn Khaldūn (Prolégomènes d'Ebn Khaldoun)*, ed. É.M. Quatremère ('Notice et extraits des Manuscrits de la Bibliothèque du Roi et autres Bibliothèques, publiés par l'Institut Impérial de France', Vols. 16-18), (Paris 1858), corresponding to *Kitāb al-'Ibar wa Dīwān al-Mubtada' wa al-Khabar Fī Ayyām al-'Arab wa al-'Ajam wa al-Barbar wa man 'Āṣarahum min Dhawī al-Sulṭān al-Akbar*, ed. Naṣr al-Ḥūrīnī, (7 vols.;Būlāq, 1284/1867)
Ibn Sa'd, Muḥammad, *al-Ṭabaqāt al-Kubrā*, 8 vols (Beirut, 1957-60)
Ibn Sa'īd al-Maghribī, Abū al-Ḥasan 'Alī b. Mūsā b. Mḥd b. 'Abd al-Mālik b., (b.610/1213) *Mughrib*, ed. transl. K.L. Tallquist Text 30, Transl. 63 (Leiden 1899); Vol.IV Publ. and Transl. into German by T.C. Tallquist, under the Title, *al-'Uyūn al-Du'dj Fī Ḥulā Dawlat Banī Ṭughdj*, (Leiden, 1898)
Ibn Sīnā, (Avicenna) Abū 'Alī al-Ḥusayn b. 'Abdallāh b., (b.370/980), *Fī Aqsām al-'Ulūm al-'Aqliyya*, in *Tis' Rasā'il Fī al-Ḥikma wa al-Ṭabi'iyyāt*, (Cairo, 1326/1908)
Ibrāhīm, Aḥmad, *al-Qānūn wa al-Iqtiṣad*, (1934)
'Īd, Idwār, *al-'Uqūd al-Tijāriyya wa 'Amaliyāt al-Muṣārif*, (Beirut, 1968)
Ikhwān al-Ṣafā, *Rasā'il Ikhwān al-Ṣafā wa-Khillān al-Wafā*, ed. Khayr al-Dīn al-Ziriklī, (Cairo, 1347/1928)
Imrānī, al-, *al-Bayān Fī al-Furū'*, MS Brit. Mus. Or.3739, fol. 77b, 78b
Iraq Ministry of Justice, *Legal System Reform*, *al-Waqai al-Irāqiyya*, (Official Gazette) (1977) No.37 (in Arabic)
Jazīrī, 'Abd al-Raḥmān al-, *Kitāb al-Fiqh 'alā al-Madhāhib al-Arba'a*, (5 Vols.; Sixth Edn.; Beirut, n.d.), Vol. II (7th Edn.:Dar 'Ahya' al-Turāth al-'Arabī: Cairo); Vol. III (Seventh Printing: Beirut, n.d.)
Jihāẓ, Al-, (d. 255 AH) MSS. in British Museum OR. 3188, fo. 267
Kalā'ī, (al-Balansī) Sulayman b. Mūsā al-, *Kitāb al-Iktifā'*, part I, Ed. H. Massé, (Algiers/Paris, 1931)
Khaffīf, 'Alī al-, *Aḥkām al-Mu'āmalāt*, (Cairo, 1941)
Khallāf, 'Abd al-Wahhāb, *al-Siyāsa al-Shar'īyya*, (Cairo, 1977)
idem., *Maṣādir al-Tashrī' al-Islāmī Fī-Mā Lā Naṣṣa Fīh*, (Cairo, 1955; Kuwait, 1970)
Khurūfa, 'Alā' al-Dīn, *'Aqd al-Qarḍ Fī al-Sharī'a al-Islāmiyya*, (Beirut,

1982)
Kitāb al-Thamān (MS. al-Tamr) al-Rā'iq al-Mujtanā min al-Ḥadā'iq, MS. Dublin Chester Beatty 4759, fols. 20b-21b (anon.)
Lu' lu' wa al-Marjān, (Cairo, 1949)
Maḥmaṣānī, Ṣubḥī, *al-Naẓariyya al-'Āmma li al-Mūjibāt wa al-'Uqūd Fī al-Sharī'a al-Islāmiyya*, 2 vols., (Beirut, 1948)
idem., *Falsafat al-Tashrī' Fī al-Islām*, (1975 Edn. in Arabic) [3rd Ed. Arabic (Beirut 1961)]
Maqrīzī, *al-Mawā'iz wa al-I'tibār fī Dhikr al-Khiṭaṭ wa al-Āthār*, 2 Vols., (Būlāq, 1270 AH) and Ed. G. Wiet, 5 vols. (Cairo, 1911-1922)
Mas'ūdī, *Murūj al-Dhahab wa Ma'ādin al-Jawāhir*, Ed./Transl. C. Barbier de Meynard and P. de Courteille, as *Maçoudi, Les Prairies d'Or*, (Paris, 1861-77)
Majallat al-Qaḍā' wa al-Qānūn, [Official Kuwaiti Law Reports]
Morcos, Soliman, and Faraq, W., in *al-Qānūn wa al-Iqtiṣād*, (Sept. 1952)
Mūsā, Muḥammad Yūsuf, *al-Amwāl wa Naẓariyyat al-'Aqd*, (Cairo, 1953)
Muslim, Abū al-Ḥusayn b. al-Hajjāj al-Nīsābūrī, *Ṣaḥīḥ*, (Cairo, 1334 AH) 8 vols.
Nūr al-Islām, (Cairo, n.d.)
Nūrī Bey, Jalāl, *Ijtihād al-Islām*, (Constantinople, 1913; Arabic transl. Cairo, 1920)
Pasha, Qadrī, *Murshid al-Ḥayrān ilā Ma'rifāt Aḥwāl al-Insān Fī al-Mu'āmalāt al-Sharī'a 'alā Madhhab al-Imām al-A'zam Abū Ḥanīfa*, (Cairo, 1933)
Qālī, Ismā'īl b. al-Qāsim al-, *Kitāb Dhayl al-Amālī wa al-Nawādir*, (Cairo, 1926)
Qalyūbī, Samīḥa al-, *al-Qānūn al-Tijārī al-Kuwaitī -Naẓariyya al-'Amāl al-Tijāriyya - al-Tājir - al-Maḥall al-Tijārī*, (Kuwait, 1974)
Qurṭubī, Muḥammad b. Aḥmad al-, *al-Jāmi' li-Aḥkām al-Qur'ān*, (Cairo, 1967)
Rafi'ī, al-, *Muhanar*, fol. 267 a-b MS Brit. Mus. Or. 4285, fol 110b
Rāzī, A. Bakr A.b.'A. al-Jassās al-, *Sharḥ Kitāb Ādāb al-Qāḍī*, (Latter work by al-Khaṣṣāf) Edited by F. Ziadeh (Cairo, 1978)
Rāzī, Fakhr al-Dīn Mḥd. al-, *Mafātīḥ al-Ghayb*, known as *al-Tafsīr al-Kabīr*, (Cairo, 1324 AH; 1353-1381/1934-1962) 8 vols.
Riḍa, Rashīd, (Ed.) *al-Manār*, VII, (1904); IX (1324/1906); (1917)
idem., *Ta'rīkh al-Ustādh al-Imām al-Shaikh Muḥammad 'Abduh*, (Cairo, 1931), 3 Vols
Saḥḥār, 'Abd al-Ḥamīd Jawda al-, *Khadīja Bint Khuwaylid*, (Cairo, 1967)
Samdān, Aḥmad al-, 'Muslim Private International Law', *Majallat al-Ḥuqūq*, (Kuwait Univ. Faculty of Law and Shar'īa: Jumāda I, 1402/ March 1982)

Ṣan'ānī, 'Abd al-Razzāq b. Hammām al-, *al-Muṣannaf*, Ed. H.-R. al-A'ẓamī, 11 Vols. (Beirut, 1970-1972)

Sanhūrī, 'Abd al-Razzāq Aḥmad, *al-'Ālim al-'Arabī*, (Cairo, 1953)

idem., *al-Wasīṭ Fī Sharḥ al-Qānūn al-Madanī al-Jadīd*, (Beirut, n.d.; Cairo, 1952)

idem., *Document No.1, Sale and Barter, Selected Sample from Western Legislation III and IV Majallat al-Qaḍā'*, (Cairo, 1936)

idem., *Maṣādir al-Ḥaqq Fī al-Fiqh al-Islāmī*, (6 Vols.; Cairo 1954-9)

Shaṭṭī, Muḥammad Jamīl, *Mukhtaṣar Ṭabaqāt al-Ḥanābila*, (Damascus, 1339 AH)

Shayzarī, 'Abd al-Rahmān b. Naṣr al-, *Nihāyat al-Rutba Fī Ṭalab al-Ḥisba*, ed. al-Bāz al-'Arīnī, (Cairo, 1365/1946); Transl. by W. Behrnauer in *Journal Asiatique*, 5me Sér. XVI, pp.347-352; XVII, pp.1-76

Shawkānī, Muḥammad Ibn 'Alī al-, *Nayl al-Awṭār: Sharḥ Muntaqā al-Akhbār*, (Cairo, 1347 AH), 8 Vols.

Subul al-Salām, (Cairo, 1372 AH)

Sulāmī (d.941-1021), *Kitāb Ādāb al-Ṣuḥba*, ed. M.J. Kister (Jerusalem, 1954)

Ṭabarī, Muḥammad b. Jarīr al-, *Jāmi' al-Bayān Fī Tafsīr al-Qur'ān*, 30 vols. (Būlāq, 1905-12; New Edn; Cairo, 1961?)

idem., *Ta'rīkh al-Rusul wa al-Mulūk*, Ed. M.J. de Goeje *et al.*, (Leiden, 1879-1901)

Tha'ālibī, 'Abd al-Mālik b. Muḥammad al-, *Thimār al-Qulūb*, Ed. M.A.-F. Ibrāhīm (Cairo, 1965)

Thābit, Ḥassān b., *Dīwān*, Ed. W.N. 'Arafat (London, 1971)

Tirmidhī, Muḥammad b. 'Īsa b. Sahl al-, *Sunan*, (Cairo, n.d.)

Umm al-Qurā, No.1320 (July 19, 1950). [Saudi Official Gazette]

Wāqidī, Muḥammad b. 'Umar al-, *Kitāb al-Maghāzī*, (Ed. M. Jones; Oxford, 1966)

Ya'qūbī, Aḥmad b. Abī Ya'qūb al-, *Ta'rīkh*, ed. M.T. Houtsma, 2 vols. (Leiden, 1883)

Yāqūt b. 'Abdallāh, *Kitāb Mu'jam al-Buldān*, Ed. F. Wüstenfeld, 6 Vols. (Leipzig, 1866-1873)

Zayd, Muṣṭafā, *al-Maṣlaḥa Fī al-Tashrī' al-Islāmī wa Najm al-Dīn al-Tawfī*, (Cairo, 1954)

Zabaydī, Imām Aḥmad b. 'Umar al-, *al-Tajrīd al-Ṣarīh li-Aḥādīth al-Jamī' al-Ṣaḥiḥ*,

Zarqā', Muṣṭafā Aḥmad al-, *al-Madkhal al-Fiqhī al-'Āmm ilā Ḥuqūq al-Madaniyya*, (Damascus, 1952; Reprinted 1961; 1965)

11. GENERAL SOURCES

Abel, A., 'La djizya: tribut ou rancom?', *Studia Islamica*, XXXII, (1970) pp.5f.

idem., 'L'Incidence de l'Activité Commerciale de la Mekke Sur Son Développement Urbain', in *Dalla Tribu Allo Stato* (Academie Naz. dei Lincei; Rome, 1962)

Abi-Saab, G.M., 'The Newly Independent States and the Rules of International Law: An Outline', *Howard Law Journal*, Vol. VIII (1962) pp.95-121

idem., 'The Newly Independent States and The Scope of Domestic Jurisdiction', *American Society of International Law Proceedings*, (1960)

Abu Zayyad, Fuad S., 'Kuwait', in *Yearbook of Commercial Arbitration*, (The Netherlands, 1979) pp.139-147

Adams, C.C., *Islam and Modernism in Egypt*, (Oxford, 1933)

Aghnides, N.P., *Mohammedan Theories of Finance (With an Introduction to Mohammedan Law and a Bibliography)*, (New York, 1916; 1969)

Ahmad, Anis, 'Scientific Approach to Fiqh and Social Sciences in Islam', in: *International Conference on 'Science in Islamic Polity-Its Past, Present and Future', 19-24 Nov. 1983: Abstracts of Papers*, (Islamabad: Ministry of Science)

Ahmad, Khurshid, 'Economic Development In an Islamic Framework', in K. Ahmad, [Ed.] *Studies in Islamic Economics*, (Jedda/Leicester, 1400/1980)

Ahmed, Badar Durrez, 'Ribā in Islamic Law', *Islamic and Comparative Law Quarterly*, VI:1 (March, 1986) pp.51-70

Ali, A. Yusuf, *The Holy Qur'ān : Text, Translation and Commentary*, (Islamic Foundation; Leicester, 1975)

Ali, Muhammad I., and Sulaiman, Abdul W.A., 'Recent Judicial Developments in Saudi Arabia', *Journal of Islamic and Comparative Law*, vol. 3 (1968)

Ali, M.M., *A Manual of Ḥadīth*, (London and Dublin, 1944; 1983)

Ali, S.A., *Economic Foundations of Islam*, (Calcutta, 1964)

Amedroz, H.F., 'The Ḥisba Jurisdiction in the Aḥkām Sulṭaniyya of Mawardi', *The Journal of the Royal Asiatic Society*, (1916) pp.77-101, 287-314

idem., 'The Maẓālim Jurisdiction in the Aḥkām Sulṭaniyya of Mawardi', *The Journal of the Royal Asiatic Society*, (1911) pp.635-674

idem., 'The Office of Kadi in the Ahkam Sultaniyya of Mawardi', 2 *The Journal of the Royal Asiatic Society*, (1910) pp.761-796

Amin, *International and Legal Problems of the Gulf*, (London, 1981)

idem., *Islamic Law in the Contemporary World*, (Glasgow, 1985)

idem., *Middle East Legal Systems*, (Glasgow, 1985)

idem., 'The Doctrine of Changed Circumstances in International Trade', *World Law*, (Sept-Oct 1984) pp.41-45

idem., 'The Theory of Changed Circumstances in International Trade', (1982) 4 *Lloyd's Maritime and Commercial Law Quarterly*, pp.577-586

Amos, Sheldon, *The History and Principles of The Civil Law Of Rome*, (London, 1883)

Anderson, J.N.D., 'Codification in the Muslim World: Some Reflections', *Rabels Zeitschrift für Ausländisches und Internationales Privatrecht*, XXX (Tubingen, 1966) pp.241-153

idem., 'Islamic Law and Structural Variations in Property Law', *International Encyclopoedia of Comparative Law*, 2, (1975) pp.103 ff.

idem., *Law Reform In The Muslim World*, (London, 1976)

idem., 'Law as a Social Force In Islamic Culture and History', *Bulletin of the School of Oriental and African Studies*, 20 (1957)

idem., 'Law Reform In Egypt: 1850-1950' in *Political and Social Change in Modern Egypt*, Ed. P.M. Holt (Oxford, 1968) pp.209-230

idem., 'The Sharī'a and Civil Law (The Debt Owed by the New Civil Codes of Egypt and Syria to the Sharī'a)', *Islamic Quarterly*, (April, 1954) pp.29-46

idem., 'The Movement Towards Codification in Turkey, Cyprus and The Arab World', *Indian Yearbook of International Affairs*, (1958) pp.125-142.

Anees, M.A., and Athar, A.N., *Guide to Sira and Ḥadīth Literature In Western Languages*, (London and New York, 1986)

Ansari, Z.I., 'Islamic Juristic Terminology Before Shāfi'ī - A Semantic Analysis With Special Reference To Kufa', *Arabica - Revue d'Études Arabes*, (Oct. 1972) vol. XIX (3), pp.255-300

Ansay, Tugrul, *et al*, *Introduction to Turkish Law*, (Ankara, Society of Comparative Law, 2nd Ed., 1978)

Arab Law Newsletter, No.1 (1985)

Arab Law Newsletter, No.2 (1985)

Arab Law Newsletter, No.3 (Jan. 1986)

Arab Law Newsletter, No.6 (April 1986)

Arab Law Newsletter, No.7 (May, 1986)

Arab Law Newsletter, No.8 (June 1986)

Arab Law Newsletter, No.9 (Jul/Aug 1986)

Arab Law Newsletter, No.10 (Sept 1986)

Arab Law Newsletter, No.11 (Oct 1986)
Arab Law Newsletter, No.12 (Nov. 1986)
Arab Law Newsletter, No.18 (May 1987)
Arab Law Newsletter, No.19 (June 1987)
Arab Law Newsletter, No.20 (Jul/Aug. 1987)
Arab Law Newsletter, No.22 (Oct.1987)
Arab Law Newsletter, No. 23 (Nov. 1987)
Aristotle, *Nicomathean Ethics*, (Oxford, 1980)
idem., *Politique*, (Oxford, 1946) Bk. I
Asherman, 'Doing Business in Saudi Arabia: The Contemporary Application of Islamic Law', *International Lawyer*, (1982) pp.321, 322 n.5
Atiyah, P.S., *The Sale of Goods*, (5th Edn; 1975)
Ayub, Muhammad (Allama Hafiz), 'Mischief against Hadith Exposed - (Maulana Ayub's) Crushing Reply to Rejectionists,' *Islamic Order*, (Karachi, 1984) 6 (3) pp.47-65
Aziz, Ahmad, 'Iṣlāḥ', *Encyclopoedia of Islam*, Vol IV (Leiden, 1978) p.154
Baaklini, Abdo I., 'Legislatures in the Gulf Area : The Experience of Kuwait, 1961-1976', *International Journal of Middle Eastern Studies*, 14 (1982) pp. 359-379
Babylonian *Talmud*, (Baba M^{e}zi'a, chpt. 5)
Badr, Gamal Moursi, 'Islamic Law : Its Relation to Other Legal Systems', *The American Journal of Comparative Law*, vol.26 (1978) pp.187-198
idem., 'Law in the Middle East: Origin and development of Islamic Law : A Review', *Tulane Law Review*, 30 (1955-1956) pp.451-460.
idem., 'The New Egyptian Civil Code and the Unification of the Laws of the Arab Countries', *Tulane Law Review*, 30 (1955-1956) pp.299-304
Bagby, Ihsan A., 'The Issue of Maṣlaḥa in Classical Islamic Legal Theory', *International Journal of Islamic and Arabic Studies*, Vol. II (1985) No.2 (Bloomington, Indiana, USA) pp.1-11
Bajwa, M.A., 'Islam on the Law of Evidence', *The Review of Religions*, [Ed. A.Q. Niaz] Vol. XL, No.8 (Aug. 1941)
Baharna, Husain M. al-, *The Legal Status of the Arabian Gulf States*, (Manchester, 1981)
idem., 'United Arab Emirates', in *International Encyclopoedia of Comparative Law: National Reports*, pp. U:53-U:57.
idem., 'United Arab Emirates', in *International Encyclopoedia of Comparative Law: National Reports*, pp. U:53-U:57
Ballantyne, W.M., 'An Overall View: The Common Elements and A Comparative Study (Excluding Iran)', *Proceedings of the Seminar on Middle Eastern Law. International Bar Association, Hamburg*, (London, 1981) pp.1-17

idem., *Arab Law Quarterly*, 2(4), Nov. 1987, pp.352-356

idem., [Ed.], 'Supreme Constitutional Court (Egypt) - Shari'a and Ribā : Decision in Case No. 20 of Judicial year No.1', *Arab Law Quarterly*, 1 (1) (Nov. 1985) pp.100-107

idem., *Commercial Law In The Arab Middle East : The Gulf States*, (London, 1986)

idem., *Legal Development in Arabia*, (London, 1978; Reprint 1980)

idem., *Proceedings of the Seminar on Middle Eastern Law. International Bar Association*, (Hamburg, 1981) pp.93-111

idem., *Register of Laws of the Arabian Gulf : A Register of the Laws of the States Members of the Gulf Cooperation Council*, (London, 1985)

idem., 'The Constitutions of the Gulf States: A Comparative Study', *Arab Law Quarterly*, vol. I(2) (Feb. 1986) pp. 158-176

idem., 'The New Civil Code of the United Arab Emirates: A Further Reassertion of the Shari'a', *Arab Law Quarterly*, vol. I (3) (May 1986) pp.245-264

idem., 'The Shari'a: A Speech to the IBA Conference in Cairo, on Arab Comparative and Commercial Law, 15-18 Feb. 1987', *Arab Law Quarterly*, 2 (1) (Feb. 1987) pp.12-28

idem., 'The States of the GCC: Sources of Law, the Shari'a and the extent to which it applies', *Arab Law Quarterly*, vol. I(1) (Nov. 1985) p.3 *et seq.*

idem., 'The States of the GCC: Sources of Law', *Arab Law Quarterly*, vol. I(3) (1985) p. 11 *et seq.*

idem., 'Note on the New Commercial Code of Bahrain (Decree Law 7/1987)', *Arab Law Quarterly*, vol.2 (4) (Nov. 1987) pp.352 ff.

Baroody, G.M., *Crime and Punishment Under Islamic Law*, Transl. of *Manar al-Sabīl*, by Sheikh Ibrahīm Ibn Muḥammad Ibn Salīm Ibn Dūyūn, (London, 1979 :Second Edition)

Bassiouni, Cherif, and Dyba, M.E., in A.P. Blaustein and G.H. Flanz (Eds.), *Modern Constitutions of the World*, VII, (New York, Dec. 1985) 'United Arab Emirates', Vol. XVI (8/82)

Bellefonds, Y. Linant de, 'Ḳanun', *Encyclopoedia of Islam*, Vol.IV (New Edition: Leiden, 1978) pp.556-557

idem., 'Volonté Interne et Volonté Déclarée en Droit Musulman', in *Revue Internationale de Droit Comparé*, (July-Sept.1958), No.3

idem., *Traité de Droit Musulman Comparé*, (Paris, 1965) 2 Vols;

idem., 'Immutabilité du Droit Musulman et Réformes Législatives en Égypte', *Revue International de Droit Comparé*, Vol. VII (Paris, Jan-Mar 1955) pp.5-34

idem., 'Les Actes Juridiques Valables et les Actes Nuls en Droit Musulman', 75 *Revue Algérienne, Tunisienne et Marocaine de Législation et de*

Jurisprudence, 1 (1959)
Bergsträsser, G., *Grundzüge des Islamischen Rechts*, publ. by J. Schacht (Berlin, 1935)
Berque, J., *''Amal'*, in the *Encyclopaedia of Islam*, (New Edition), Vol.I, (Leiden, 1960), pp.427-429
idem., *Essai sur la Méthode Juridique Maghrébine*, (Rabat, 1944).
Birks, J.S., and Sinclair, C.A., *The Nature and Progress of Labour Importing : The Arabian Gulf States*, (International Labour Office Working Paper, Geneva, 1977)
Bishop, Eric E.F., 'Al-Shāfi'ī (Muḥammad Ibn Idrīs) Founder of a Law School', *The Moslem World*, 19 (1929) pp.156-175
Blaustein, A.P., and Flanz, G.H., (Eds.) *Modern Constitutions of The World*, Vols. II, V, VIII, XV, XIV
Blaustein, Eric B., 'Kuwait', in *Modern Constitutions of The World*, Blaustein, A.P., and Flanz, G.H., (Eds.) Vol. VIII (12/71) (New York, Dec. 1985)
Bonderman, D., 'Modernization and Changing Perceptions of Islamic Law', *Harvard Law Review*, 81 (1968) pp.1169-1193
Bousquet, G.-H., 'Le Mystère de la Formation et des Origines du Fiqh', *Revue Algérienne, Tunisienne et Marocaine de Législation et de Jurisprudence*, 66 (1947) pp.66-81
Bousquet, G.-H., and Schacht, J., (Eds.), *Selected Works of C. Snouck Hurgronje*, (Leiden, 1957)
Brinton, J.Y., *The Mixed Courts of Egypt*, (Second Edn: New Haven/London, 1968)
Brockelmann, Karl, *Geschichte der Arabischen Litteratur*, (Weimar, 1898-1902; Leiden, 1937-1942; 1943-1949; Leipzig, 1901)
Brown, L. Carl, 'The Middle East: Patterns of Change, 1947-1987', *The Middle East Journal*, 41 (1) (Middle East Institute, Washington, D.C., Winter, 1987) pp.26-39.
Brunschvig, R., 'De la Fiction Légale dans L'Islam Médiéval', *Studia Islamica*, XXXII, (Paris, 1970) pp.41-51
idem., 'La Preuve en Droit Musulman', 2 *Études d'Islamologie*, (Paris, 1976) pp.201-216.
idem., 'Polémique médiévales autour du rite de Malik,' *al-Andalus*, XV, (1950); and *Études d'Islamologie: Droit Musulman*, 2 (1976) pp.65-101
idem., 'Théorie Générale de la Capacité Chez Les Hanéfites Mediévaux', *Études d'Islamologie : Droit Musulman*, 2 (1976) pp.37-52
Buckland, W.W., *A Textbook of Roman Law: From Augustus to Justinian*, (Third Edn: Revised by P. Stein; Cambridge, 1975)
Bulliet, R.W., *The Camel and The wheel*, (Cambridge, Mass., 1975)

Çagatay, N., 'Riba and Interest Concept In the Ottoman Empire', *Studia Islamica*, 32 (1972) pp.53-68

Cahen, Claude, 'Body Politic,' in Grunebaum, *Unity and Variety in Muslim Civilization*, (Chicago, 1955) pp.132-158

Cardahi, Choukri, 'Le Prêt à Intérêt et L'Usure au Regard des Législations Antiques, de la Morale Catholique, du Droit Moderne et de la Loi Islamique', *Revue International de Droit Comparé*, VII (Paris, July-Sept 1955) pp.499-541

idem., 'Le Projet de Code des Obligations du Liban', 60 *Bulletin de la Société de Legislation Comparée*, (1931) at p.611

Carlson, 'Trade Finance Under Islamic Principles : A Case Study', *Middle East Executive Report*, (Dec. 1986)

Carter, L.N., 'Gulf Cooperation Council', *Persian Gulf States : Country Studies*, Ed. R.F. Nyrop (Second Edn. Washington, 1985)

Chehata, Chafik 'Le Droit du Contrat et des Obligations Musulmans', *Droit Musulman: Applications au Proche-Orient*, (Dalloz: Paris, 1970)

idem., 'Volonté Réelle et Volonté Déclarée dans le Nouveau Code Civil Égyptien', [Lecture given at the Institute de Droit Comparé at the University of Paris on 5 March 1953] in *Revue Internationale de Droit Comparé*, (April-June 1954) pp.242-249

idem., *Droit Musulman*, (Paris, 1970)

idem., *Théorie Générale de l'Obligation en Droit Musulman Hanéfite*, (Cairo, 1936; reprinted Paris 1969)

idem., 'La Notion d'Incapacité en Droit Hanéfite' in *Études de Droit Musulman*, (Paris, 1971) pp.77-155

idem., 'L'Équité en Tant que Sources du Droit Hanafite' II *Studia Islamica*, XXV (1966)

idem., 'Le Code Civil Français et son Influence dans le Bassin Méditerranéan', *Egypt: La Semaine Internationale de Droit*, (Paris, 1954)

idem., 'Les Survivances Musulmanes dans La Codification du Droit Civil Egyptien', *Revue International de Droit Comparé*, (1965) pp. 839-853

idem., 'Le Système des Nullités en droit Musulman Hanéfite et en Droit Comparé', *Rapports Généraux au VIe Congrès International de Droit Comparé*, (Hamburg, 1962) at 91 (Brussells, 1964); and in 5 *Revue al-'Ulūm al-Qānūniyya wa al-Iqtiṣādiyya*, 1 (1963)

Chelhod, J., 'La Place de la Coûtume dans le Fiqh Primitif et sa Permanence dans Les Sociétés Arabes à Tradition Orale', *Studia Islamica*, LXIV (1986) pp.19-37

Cheshire G.C., *Cheshire and Fifoot's Law of Contract*, (Tenth Edn; London, 1981)

Chitty, Joseph, *Chitty on Contracts*, (25th Edn.) Gen. Ed. A.G. Guest (London, 1983)

Cohen, Claude, 'Economy, Society, Institutions' in *The Cambridge History of Islam*, Ed. P.M. Holt, A.K.S. Lambton, B. Lewis, (First Edn, Cambridge, 1977) Vol. 2B, pp. 524 ff.

Cohen, H.J., 'The Economic Background and Secular Occupation of Muslim Jurisprudents and Traditionalists in the Classical Period of Islam', *The Journal of the Economic and Social History of the Orient*, (1970)

Cook, M., *Early Muslim Dogma*, (Cambridge, 1981)

Cottrell, A.J., *et al*, *The Persian Gulf States: A General Survey*, (Baltimore/London, 1980)

Coulson, N.J., 'Doctrine and Practice in Islamic Law : One Aspect of the Problem', *Bulletin of the School of Oriental and African Studies*, XVIII, 2, (1956) pp.211-226

idem., *A History of Islamic Law*, (Edinburgh, 1964)

idem., *Commercial Law in the Gulf States*, (London, 1984)

idem., *Conflicts and Tensions in Islamic Jurisprudence*, (Chicago U.P., 1969)

idem., 'Muslim Custom and Case-Law', *Die Welt Des Islams*, N.S. 6 (1959) pp.13-24

Crone, P. and Cook, M., *Hagarism the Making of the Islamic World*, (Cambridge, 1977)

idem., *Meccan Trade and The Rise of Islam*, (Oxford/Princeton, 1987)

idem., *Roman, Provincial and Islamic Law*, (Cambridge, 1987)

idem., *Slaves On Horses, The Evolution of the Islamic Polity*, (Cambridge, 1980)

Dalloz, Malinvaud, (1972) 'Chronique'

Daoualibi, M., *La Jurisprudence dans le Droit Islamique*, (Paris, 1941)

Daniels, John, *Kuwait Journey*, (London, 1971)

Darling, M.L., *Rustiqus Loquitur*, (Oxford, 1930)

Daura, Bello, 'A Brief Account of the Development of the Four Sunni Schools of Law, and Some Recent Developments', *Journal of Islamic and Comparative Law*, 2 (1968) pp.1-12

David, René, *French Law : Its Structure, Sources, and Methodology*, (Transl. by Michael Kindred), (Louisiana State University Press, 1972),

David, René, and Brierley, John E.C., *Major Legal Systems In The World Today: An Introduction to the Comparative Study of Law*, (London, 1968; 1985)

Davies, Michael, *Business Law in Egypt*, (Deventer: Netherlands, 1984)

Davis, Helen M., *Constitutions, Electoral Laws, Treaties of States in the*

Near and Middle East, (Durham, N. Carolina, 1947)
De Lacy O'Leary, *Arabia Before Muhammad*, (London, 1927)
Dekmejian, R. Hrair, *Islam In Revolution : Fundamentalism In The Arab World*, (New York, 1985)
Dennett, Daniel C. Jnr., *Conversion and the Poll Tax in Early Islam*, (Cambridge, 1950)
Dickson, *Kuwait and Her Neighbours*, (1956)
Dimashqī, Abū l-Faḍl Ja'far Ibn 'Alī al-, 'On the Beauties of Commerce', transl. in H. Ritter, *Der Islam*, VII (1917) pp.64-65
'Document: The Provisional Constitution of the United Arab Emirates', *Middle East Journal*, 26 (3) (1972) pp.307-325
Doi, Abdur Rahman I., *Non-Muslims Under Shārī'ah*, (London, 1983)
idem., *Shārī'a: The Islamic Law*, (London, 1984)
Donner, F.M., *The Early Islamic Conquests*, (Princeton, 1981)
Dougherty, James E., 'Religion and Law', *The Persian Gulf States: A General Survey*, [Ed. A.J. Cottrell *et al*] (Baltimore/London, 1980) pp. 281 ff.
Draz, Shaikh, 'L'Usure en Droit Musulman', in *Travaux de la semaine Internationale de Droit Musulman*, (Sirey, France, 1953)
Driver, G.R., and Miles, J.C., *The Babylonian Laws*, (2 Vols.:Oxford, 1953-1955)
Du Margoliouth, *Mohammad and The Rise of Islam*, (London, 1906; 1971)
idem., 'Omar's Instructions to the Qadi', in *The Journal Of The Royal Asiatic Society*, (London, April 1910) pp.307-326
Ducati, B., 'Rationalismus und Tradition im Mohammedanischen Recht - Die am Meisten Juridische der Muslimischen Rechtschulen', *Islamica*, (Leipzig, 1927), 3, pp. 214-218
Dwyer, Daisy Hilse, 'Is Middle Eastern Behaviour Distinctive? Toward a Political Analysis of Knowledge of the Law.' (Paper published by Columbia University)
Ebraheem, Hasan Ali al-, 'Jurisdictional Changes in Kuwait', *World Today*, (1960)
Edge, Ian, 'Comparative Commercial Law of Egypt and The Arabian Gulf', *Cleveland State Law Review*, Vol. 34, No.1 (1985-1986)
Emary, Ahmad el-, *La Conception de l'Impôt Chez Les Musulmans*, (Paris, 1930)
Emilia, A. d', 'Intorno Alla Moderna Attiuità Legislativa di Alcuna Paesi Musulmani nel Campo del Diritto Privato', 33 *Oriente Moderno*, (1953) pp.301-321
idem., *Annuario di Diritto Comparato e di Studi Legislativi*, XXXII (1957) pp.82-117
idem., 'Il Ḥiyār aš-Šart nel Aṣl di Šaibānī,' *Rivista Degli Studi Orientali*, 32

(1957) pp.633-640

idem., 'Il *bai al-hiyār* nella *Mudawwanah*', *Revista degli Studi Orientali*, XXIV (1949) pp.45-58

idem., 'La Struttora della Vendita Sottoposta a *Khiyār* Secondo la *Sedes Material dell' al-Mudawwanah* (Nota Preliminairie)', *Oriente Moderno*, XXI (1941) pp.86-98

Enger, M, (Ed.) *Maverdii Constitutiones Politicae*, (Bonn, 1853)

Europa Publications Limited, 'Kuwait', in *The Europa Yearbook : A World Survey*, (London, 1984)

Fagnan, E., *Additions Aux Dictionnaires Arabes*, (Algiers, 1923)

Fahim, Adel S., 'La Riba et Les Contrats Usuraires Dans Le Droit et L'Économie de l'Islam', *Cahiers de l'Institut des Sciences Économiques Appliquées*, [Série V, n.3] (1961) pp.139 ff

Faisal, Prince Muhammad al-, 'An Economic Model', (Ed. Ibnul Hassan), *Arabian Insurance Guide*, [Ed. Shahrukh A. Husain] (Northampton, 1984)

Faris, N.A., (Ed.), *The Arab Heritage*, (New Jersey, 1946)

Faruqi, H.S., *Law Dictionary*, (Librairie du Liban, Third Edn : Beirut, 1986)

Fattal, A., *Le Statut Légal des Non-Musulmans en Pays d'Islam*, (Beirut, 1958)

Feulner, Gary R., and Khan, Amjad Ali, 'Dispute Resolution in the United Arab Emirates', *Arab Law Quarterly*, 1 (3) (May, 1986) pp. 312 ff.

Finet, A., *Le Code de Hammourabi*, (Paris, 1973)

Finkelstein, J.J., 'The Ox That Gored', (Prepared for Publication by M. de J. Ellis) *American Philosophical Society*, Vol.71, Part 2 (Philadelphia, 1981)

Fischel, W.J., *Jews In the Economic and Political Life of Medieval Islam*, (London, 1937)

idem., 'The Origin of Banking in Medieval Islam', *Journal of the Royal Asiatic Society*, (1933), pp. 339-352.

Fitzgerald, S.V., 'The Alleged Debt of Islamic to Roman Law', *The Law Quarterly Review*, (1951) pp.81-102

Flanz, G., and Shafik, F., in A.P. Blaustein and G.H. Flanz, (Eds.), *Modern Constitutions of the World*, (New York, Dec. 1985) 'Egypt', Vol. V (11/84)

Foster, B.R., 'Agoranomos and Muhtasib', *Journal of the Economic and Social History of the Orient*, (1970)

Fransman, L., *British Nationality Law*, (London, 1989)

Friedmann, W., *Law in a Changing Society*, (London, 1964)

Furuqi, *Law Dictionary*, (3rd Edn.; Beirut, 1986)

Fyzee, A.A.A., 'The *Adāb al-Qāḍī* in Islamic Law', *Malaya Law Review*, 6 (1964) pp.406-416

idem., *Outlines of Muhammedan Law*, (3rd Ed.: London 1964; 4th Edn. Delhi, 1974)
Gatteschi, Domenico, *Manuale Di Diritto Pubblico e Privato Ottomano*, (Alexandria, 1865)
Gaudefroy-Demombynes, M., 'Sur Les Origines de la Justice Musulmane', *Mélanges Syriens Offerts á René Dussaud*, (Paris, 1939) vol. II, p.828
idem., 'Un Magistrat Musulman = Le Mohtasib', *Le Journal des Savants*, (Paris, 1947) pp.36ff.
Geiger, Abraham, *Was Hat Mohammed Aus Dem Judentum Aufgenommen*, (Bonn, 1823). Translated by F.M. Young, under the title *Judaism and Islam*, (New York, 1970)
Gerber, H., 'Sharia, Kanun and custom in the ottoman Law: the Court Records of Seventeenth Century Bursa', *International Journal of Turkish Studies*, 2(1) (1981) pp.131-147
idem., 'The Muslim Law of Partnerships in Ottoman Court Records', in *Studia Islamica*, LIII, pp. 111-119
Ghestin, J., *La Notion D'Erreur Dans Le Droit Positif Actuel*, (Paris, 1971)
Gibb, H.A.R., 'An Interpretation of Islamic History', *Muslim World*, XIV, (1955) 4-15, 121-133
idem., and Bowen, H., *Islamic Society and The West*, Vol I, part 2 (Toronto/Oxford, 1957)
idem., 'Constitution Organization', in Ed. Khadduri and Liebesny, *Law In The Middle East*, (Washington, D.C., 1955) PP.3f.
idem., *Mohammedanism*, (New York, 1962)
idem., 'Some considerations on the Sunni Theory of the Caliphate', 3 *Archives d'Histoire du Droit Oriental*, (1948) pp.401-410
idem., *Modern Trends in Islam*, (Chicago, 1947)
Gibb and Kramers, (Ed.) *Shorter Encyclopoedia of Islam*, (London, 1953)
Gilmore, G., *The Death Of Contract*, (Ohio, 1974; 17th Reprint 1986)
Gnichtel, W. Van Orden, 'Lease Financing in Saudi Arabia', *International Financial Law Review*, (Jan. 1984) pp.34-36
Goetze, A., 'The Laws of Eshnunna Discovered at Tell Harmal', *Sumer*, 4 (1948) pp.63 ff.
idem., The Laws of Eshnunna, (Annual of the American Schools of Oriental Research) 31 (New Haven, 1956)
Goitein, S.D., 'A Turning Point in the History of the Muslim State', *Islamic Culture*, (1949)
idem., *Letters of Medieval Jewish Traders: Translated from the Arabic with an Introduction and Notes*, (Princeton, 1973)
idem., *Mediterranean Society*, 2 vols (Berkeley and Los Angeles, 1967-1972)

idem., *Studies in Islamic History and Institutions*, (Leiden, 1966)
idem., 'The Cairo Genîza as a source for the History of Muslim Civilization', *Studia Islamica*, III (1955)
idem., 'The Documents of the Cairo Genîza, as a Source for Mediterranean Social History', *Journal of the American Oriental Society*, LXXX (1960)
Golb, Norman, 'Legal Documents from the Cairo Genizah', *Jewish Social Studies*, XX (1958)
Goldziher, I., *Muslim studies*, transl. by C.R. Barber and S.M. Stern, from *Muhammedanische Studien*, vol. II, (London, 1971)
idem., 'A Muhammadán jogtudomány eredetéröl', *A Magyar Tudományos Akadémia*, Ertehezéseh a nyelv-és széptudományok köréböl kötet XI, (Budapest, 1884)
idem., 'Das Prinzip des Istiṣḥāb in der Muhammedanischen Gesetzwissenschaft', *Wiener Zeitschrift fur die Kunde des Morgenlandes*, (1887) I: pp.228-236
idem., *Introduction to Islamic Theology and Law*, Transl. by A. and R. Hamori, (1910; transl. Princeton, 1981)
idem., 'Die Religion des Islams' in P. Hinneberg (ed.), *Die Kultur des Gegenwart*, vol. I, part iii, (Berlin and Leipzig, 1906)
idem., 'Fikh' in *Encyclopaedia of Islam* [1], (written c. 1913) pp.102-107
idem., *Die Zâhiriten, Ihre Lehr-System und Ihre Geschichte*, (Leipzig, 1884)
idem., *Muhammedanische Studien*, (Halle, 1889-1890) (reprint 1961)
idem., 'The Principles of Law in Islam', in H.S. Williams (ed.), *The Historians' History of the World*, (London, 1907), vol. VIII
idem., *Vorlesungen Über den Islam*, (Heidelberg, 1910, 1925)
Gordan, 'The Islamic Legal Revolution : The Case of Sudan', 19 *International Lawyer*, (1985)
Grohmann, *From the World of Arabic Papyri*, (Cairo, 1952)
idem., *Einführung Und Chrestomathie Zur Arabischen Papyruskunde*, (Prague, 1955)
Guidi, I., *et al*, (Eds. & Transl.) *Chronica Minora*, CSCO, Scriptores Syri:Third Series, Vol. IV (Louvain, 1903-1907)
Guillaume, A., *The Traditions of Islam: An Introduction to the Study of the Ḥadīth Literature*, (Oxford, 1924)
Habachy, Saba, 'Property, Right and Contract in Muslim Law', *Columbia Law Review*, 62 (1962) pp.450 ff.
idem., 'The System of Nullities In Muslim Law', *American Journal of Comparative Law*, 13 (1964) pp.61-72
idem., 'Commentary on the Decision of the Supreme Court of Egypt given on 4 May 1985 concerning the legitimacy of interest and the constitutionality of Article 226 of the New Egyptian Civil Code of

1948', *Arab Law Quarterly*, 1 (2) (Feb. 1986) pp.239-241

Haberbeck, Andreas, 'Risk Sharing in an Islamic Society', *Arab Law Quarterly*, 2 (2) (May 1987) p.138 *et seq.*

Hakima, Ahmad Mustafa Abu, *The Modern History of Kuwait : 1750-1965*, (London, 1983)

Hall, Marjorie J., (Ed.) *The Business Laws of the United Arab Emirates*, (London, 1979)

Hallaq, Wael B., *The Gate of Ijtiḥād :A Study in Islamic Legal History*, (Ann Arbor, Michigan: University Microfilms International, 1983)

Hamid, M.E., 'Does the Islamic Law of Contract recognize a doctrine of Mistake?' in *Journal of Islamic and Comparative Law*, Vol.IV (1972), pp. 1-16

idem., 'Islamic Law of Contract or Contracts?' in *Journal of Islamic and Comparative Law*, vol.3 (1969), p.1-10

idem., 'Mutual Assent in the Formation of Contracts in Islamic Law', *Journal of Islamic and Comparative Law*, Vol.7, (1977) pp.41-53

idem., 'Mutual Consent in the Formation of Contracts', *Journal of International and Comparative Law*, vol.VII, (1977), p.48

idem., 'The Role of Consent in the Formation of Contracts - A Comparative Study in English and Islamic Law', (Unpublished Ph D. Thesis, University of London, 1971)

idem., 'The Freedom to Make Stipulatiuons In The Islamic Law of Contract', *Journal of Islamic and Comparative Law*, Vol. VI (1976) pp.22-32

Hamidulla, M., *Muslim Conduct of State*, (Revised Ed. Hyderabad, 1945)

idem., 'Sources of Islamic Law, A New Approach', 1 *Islamic Quarterly*, No. 4, (1954) pp. 207-208

idem., 'Influence of Roman Law on Muslim Law', *Journal of the Hyderabad Academy*, (Madras, 1943)

Hamlin, Kristan L. Peters, 'The Impact of Islamic Revivalism on Contract and Usury Law in Iran, Saudi Arabia and Egypt', *Texas International Law Journal*, Vol. 22 (1987) pp.351-381

Haque, Ziaul, 'Some Forms of Ribā al-Faḍl', *Islamic Studies*, 22: IV (1983)

Harazti, 'Treaties and the Fundamental Change of Circumstances', *Recueil Des Cours*, I (1973) III, pp.46-60

Hasan, Ahmad, 'The Critique of *Qiyās*', *Islamic Studies*, XXII

Hassan, Ahmad, 'Al-Shāfi'ī's Role in the Development of Islamic Jurisprudence', *Islamic Studies*, 5 (1966) pp. 239-273

idem., *The Doctrine of Ijmā' in Islam*, (Islamabad, 1978)

Hassan, H.I. 'Judiciary System from the Rise of Islam to 567 A.H. (A.D. 1171)', *The Islamic Quaterly*, 7 (1963) pp.23-30

Hassan, Judge 'Abd El-Wahab Ahmed El-, 'Freedom of Contract, The

Doctrine of Frustration, and Sanctity of Contracts in Sudan Law and Islamic Law', *Arab Law Quarterly*, Vol. I (1) (Nov. 1985) pp.51-59

idem., 'The Doctrine of Duress (*Ikrah*) in *Shariā*, Sudan and English Law', *Arab Law Quarterly*, 1(2) (Feb. 1986) pp.321-236

Heller, P.B., in A.P. Blaustein and G.H. Flanz, (Eds.), *Modern Constitutions of the World*, (New York, Dec. 1985) 'Syria', Vol. XV (6/74)

Heyd, Uriel, *Revival of Islam in Modern Turkey*, [Lecture delivered 28 March, 1968 : Jerusalem Hebrew University, 1968)

Hijazi, A., 'Kuwait : Development From a Semitribal, Semicolonial Society to Democracy and Sovereignty', 13 *American Journal of Comparative Law*, (1964) pp. 428-437

Hill, D.J., and Abbas, Abulbakar Sadiq, 'Comparative Survey of the Islamic Law and the Common Law Relating to the Sale of Goods,' in *Journal of Islamic and Comparaitve Law*, Vol.2 (1968)

Hill, T.W., 'The Commercial Legal System of The Sultanate of Oman', 17 *International Lawyer*, (1983)

Hitti, Philip K., *Capital Cities of Arab Islam*, (Minneapolis, 1973)

idem., *The History of The Arabs*, (New York, 1967)

Holmes, *The Common Law*, (1881: Ed. Howe, 1963)

Holt, P.M., Lambton, A.K.S., Lewis, B., (Eds.) *Cambridge History Of Islam*, (Cambridge, 1977)

Homoud, S.H., *Islamic Banking: The Adaptation of Banking Practice to Conform with Islamic Law*, (London, 1985; Reprinted 1986)

Hooper, C.A., *The Civil Law of Palestine and Trans-Jordan*, (Jerusalem, 1933).

Hourani, A., *Arabic Thought in the Liberal Age, 1798-1939*, (London, 1970)

idem., *The Ottoman Background of the Modern Middle East*, (University of Carreras Arabic Lecture, 1969)

idem., *The Emergence of the Modern Middle East*, (London, 1981)

Hourani, George F., 'The Basis of Authority of Consensus in Sunnite Islam', *Studia Islamica*, 21 (1964) pp.13-60

idem., *Arab Sea-Faring*, (Princeton, 1951)

Hoyle, Mark S.W., 'The Structure and Laws of the Mixed Courts of Egypt', *Arab Law Quarterly*, 1 (3) May 1986, pp. 327-345

idem., 'The Mixed Courts of Egypt 1916-1925' *Arab Law Quarterly*, 2 (3) August 1987, pp. 292-310

'The Mixed Courts of Egypt 1926-1937' *Arab Law Quarterly*, 2 (4) November 1987, pp. 357-389

idem., 'The Mixed Courts of Egypt 1938-1949' *Arab Law Quarterly*, 3 (1) February 1988, pp. 83-115

Hrair, Dekmejian R., 'The Anatomy of Islamic Revival: Legitimacy Crisis, Ethnic Conflict and the Search for islamic Alternatives', *Middle East*

Journal, 34 (Winter, 1980) pp.1-12

Huber, A., *Über das 'Meisir' Genannte Spiel der Heidnischen Araber*, (Doctoral Thesis: Leipzig, 1883)

Hugues, H., 'Les Origines du Droit Musulman', *La France Judiciaire*, (1879-1880)

Hughes, T.P., *A Dictionary Of Islam*, (London, 1885)

Huneidi, Isa A., 'Twenty-Five Years of Civil Law System in Kuwait', *Arab Law Quarterly*, 1 (2) (Feb.1986) pp.216-219

Hurgronje, C.Snouk-., *Revue de l'Histoire des Religions*, XXXVII (1898), Reproduced in Bousquet and Schacht, *Selected Works of C. Snouk Hurgronje*, (Leiden, 1957).

idem., *Verspreide Geschriften*, (Leipzig, 1923-1927) 6 Vols.

Husaini, Ishāq Mūsa al-, 'Ḥisba In Islam', *The Islamic Quarterly*, 10 (1966) pp.69-83

Hussein, Raef T.A., 'The Early Arabian Trade and Marketing', *Islamic Culture*, Vol. LIX, No.4 (Hyderabad, Oct. 1985) pp.365-376

Huzayyin, S., *Arabia and the Far East*, (Cairo, 1942)

Hyma, A., *Christianity, Capitalism and Communism*, (Michigan, 1937)

Inalcik, Halil, 'Bursa and the Commerce of the Levant', *Journal of the Economic and Social History of the Orient*, 3, (1960), 133ff.

idem., 'Bursa', in *Encyclopaedia of Islam*[2] (Ed. Lewis, Pellat and Schacht) Vol. I, Fasc. 12 (London/Leiden, 1958) pp.1333-1336

International Encyclopoedia of Comparative Law, Vol. I, 'National Reports', (Completed Dec. 1972)

International Encyclopoedia of Comparative Law, Vol. IB (Completed July 1972)

Iqbal, Muhammad, *The Reconstruction of Religious Thought in Islam*, (First Edn. Lahore, 1930; Reprinted 1968)

Ishaq, Khalid M., 'Islam and Law In The Twenty-First Century', *Islamic and Comparative Law Quarterly*, (Sept.-Dec. 1985)

'Islamic Banking : Progress and Obstacles', *Islamic Finance*, (July, 1983) pp.31-35

Islamic Research Institution, *Landlord and Peasant in Early Islam*, (Islamabad, 1977)

Jabsheh, 'UAE Insurance Market', *Arabian Insurance Guide*, (1984) pp.92-93

Jennings, R., 'Loans and Credit in Early Seventeenth Century Ottoman Judicial Records', *Journal of the Economic and Social History of the Orient*, 16 (1973) pp.168-216

Jolowicz, *Historical Introduction to the Study of Roman Law*, (Second ed., Cambridge 1952)

Journal of International Banking Law, I, (1) (1986) p.N9

Justinian, *Corpus Iuris Civilis*, (1908) = Scott, S.P., (Transl.) *The Civil Law*, (Cincinnati, 1932) 17 Vols.

Juynboll, G., *Muslim Tradition: Studies in Chronology, Provenance and Authorship of Early Ḥadīth*, (Cambridge, 1983)

idem., *The Authenticity of the Tradition Literature; Discussions in Modern Egypt*, (Leiden, 1969)

Juynboll, Th. W., 'Salam', in *Encyclopaedia of Islam*, (London, 1934), p.89

idem., 'Ḥadīth' *Shorter Encyclopoedia of Islam* (Leiden, 1961), pp.116-121

Jwaideh, Zuhair E., 'The New Civil Code of Iraq', *Goerge Washington Law Review*, 22 (1953-1954) pp.176-186

Kabalan, Hasan, 'La Maladie de la Mort et la Peur de la Mort en Droit Musulman (Selon l'Ecole Hanafite)', 2 *Revue Judicaire Libanaise*, 33

Kabeel, Soraya M., *Select Bibliography on Kuwait and the Arabian Gulf*, (Kuwait, 1969)

Kassim, 'The New Civil Code of Kuwait', *Middle East Executive Report*, (Feb. 1962)

Kerr, M.H., *Islamic Reform : The Political and Legal Theories of Muḥammad 'Abdūh and Rashīd Riḍā*, (Berkeley, 1966).

idem., 'Rashīd Riḍā and Legal Reform', *Muslim World*, L (1960) pp.99-108; 170-181

idem., 'The Emergence of a Socialist Ideology in Egypt', 16 *Middle East Journal*, (1962) pp.127-144

Khadduri, Majid, *Islamic Jurisprudence : Shaf'i's Risala*, (Baltimore, 1961)

idem., 'The Maslaha (Public Interest) and 'Illa (Cause) in Islamic Law', *New York Journal of International Law and Politics*, 12 (1979) pp.213-217

idem., 'Nature and Sources of Islamic Law : Customary Law and Islamic Law,' Symposium on Muslim Law, I, *The George Washington Law Review*, XXII, (Oct. 1953-1954) pp.3-23

Khadduri, M., and Liebesny, H.J., (eds.) *Law In The Middle East*, (Washington, DC., 1955)

Khafīf, Sheikh Alī al-, 'Sunna's Role in Expounding Islamic Rulings and Refutation of Suspicions cast on its Authenticity', *Islamic Culture*, (Oct. 1968) pp.242 ff.; and Vol. XLIII, No.1 (Jan. 1969) pp.55-65

Khalīl, M.I., 'Wālī al-Maẓālim or the Muslim Ombudsman ', *Journal of Islamic and Comparative Law*, 6 (1969-1976) pp.1-9

Khalīl, *Mukhtaṣar*, trans. G.H. Bousquet (Algiers, 1956)

Khan, M.S., 'Mohammedan Laws against Usury and How They are Evaded', *Journal of Comparative Legislation*, 2 (1929) pp.233-244

Khan and Mirakhor, 'The framework and Practice of Islamic Banking', *Finance and Development*, (Sept. 1986)

Khany, Riad, 'The Legal System of Syria', *Comparative Law Yearbook*,

Vol. I, 1977 (Center For International Legal Studies, The Netherlands, 1978) pp. 137-152

Khoury, Philip S., 'Islamic Revivalism and the Crisis of the Secular State in the Arab World: An Historical Appraisal,' in *Arab Resources: The Transformation of a Society*, I.Ibrahim, (Ed.), (London; Center for Contemporary Arab Studies, Washington, D.C., 1983)

Kiran, B., and Jain, 'Constitution and the Law in the State of Kuwait : Highlights and Sidelights', *Islamic and Comparative Law Quarterly*, Vol. VI (4) (Dec. 1986) Ed. T. Mahmood pp.231 ff.

Kister, M.J., 'Mecca and Tamim: Aspects of Their Relations', *Journal of Economic and Social History of the Orient*, (1965), pp.116-163

idem., 'Some Reports Concerning Mecca from Jahiliyya to Islam', *Journal of the Economic and Social History of the Orient*, 15 (1972) p.76

Klingmuller, Ernst, 'Le Concept de Légalité dans le Droit Islamique', in *Rapports Généraux au VIe Congrès International de Droit Comparé*, at Hambourg, 30 July-4 August, 1962 (Brussels, 1964)

idem., 'The Concept and Development of Insurance In Islamic Countries', *Islamic Culture*, Vol. XLIII, No.1, (Hyderabad, Jan. 1969), p.36

Knoun, Abdallah, 'Ḥadīth its Scientific and Religious Value', *Islamic Culture*, Vol. XLIII, No.3, (July 1969, Hyderabad) pp.215-231

Kourides, P. Nicholas, 'The Influence of Islamic Law on Contemporary Middle Eastern Legal Systems : The Formation and Binding Force of Contracts', *Columbia Journal of Transnational Law*, vol.9 (2) (Fall, 1970) pp.384-435

Kramers, J.H., 'Droit de l'Islam et Droit Islamique', *Analecta Orientalia, Posthumous writings and Selected Minor Works of J.H. Kramers*, (Leiden, 1956)

Kremer, A. Von, *Culturgeschichte Des Orients Unter Den Chalifen*, (Vienna, 1875-1877), Vol.I

Lammens, H., *La Meque à la Veille de l'Hégire*, (Reprinted from Mélanges de l'Université St. Joseph, Vol. IX) (Beirut, 1924)

idem, La Cité Arabe de Ṭāif à la Veille de l'Hégire, (Reprinted from Mélanges de l'Université St. Joseph, Vol. VIII) (Beirut, 1922)

idem., *L'Arabie Occidentale Avant L'Hégire*, (Beirut, 1928)

idem., 'La République marchande de la Mecque vers l'an 600 de notre Ère', *Bulletin de L'Institute Égyptien*, 5th Series, 4 (1910) pp.23-54

idem., *Islam: Beliefs and Institutions*, (London, 1968)

Lane, E., *An Arabic-English Lexicon*, (London, 1872)

Laoust, Henri, *Le Traité de Droit Public d'Ibn Taimiyya, Traduction Annotée de La Siyassa Šar'iya*, (Beirut, 1948)

idem., *Essai sur les Doctrines Sociales et Politiques de Taki-D-Din Ahmad B. Taimiya*, (Cairo, 1939)

idem., *Le Précis de Droit d'Ibn Qudama*, (Beirut, 1950)
idem., *Contribution á Une Étude de la Méthodologie Canonique de Taki-d-Din Ahmad B. Taimiya*, (Cairo, 1939)
Larkin, Patricia E., in A.P. Blaustein and G.H. Flanz, (Eds.), *Modern Constitutions of the World*, (New York, Dec. 1985) Vol. II (6/85)
Leage, R.W., *Roman Private Law*, (London, 1932; Third Edn: New York, 1967)
Lee, *The Elements of Roman Law*, (Fourth Edn; London, 1956)
Leeman, W.F., *Foreign Trade in the Old Babylonian Period*, (Leiden, 1960)
Levy, *The Social Structure of Islam*, (Cambridge, 1969)
Lewis, A., *Naval Power and Trade In The Mediterranean AD 500 to 1100*, (Princeton, New Jersey, 1951)
Lewis, B., *The Arabs In History*, (Fourth Edn; London, 1966)
Liebesny, H.J., 'Administration and Legal Development in Arabia: The Persian Gulf Principalities', *Middle East Journal*, X (1) (1956) pp.33-42
idem., 'Comparative Legal History: Its Role In The Analysis Of Islamic and Modern Near Eastern Legal Institutions', in *American Journal of Comparative Law*, 20 (1972) pp.38-52
idem., 'International Relations of Arabia: The Dependent Areas', *The Middle east Journal*, Vol. I (Washington, D.C., 1947) pp. 148-165
idem., *Law of The Near and Middle East: Readings, Cases and Materials*, (Albany, 1975)
idem., 'Religious Law and westernisation in the Moslem Near East', *American Journal of Comparative Law*, Vol. 2 (1953) pp.492-504
idem., 'Impact of Western Law In the Countries of the Near East', *George Washingtom Law Review*, 22 (1953-1954) pp.127 ff.
Lopez, R.S., and Raymond, I.W., *Medieval Trade in the Mediterranean World*, (London, 1955)
Macdonald, D.B., *Development of Muslim Theology, Jurisprudence and Constitutional Theory*, (Beirut, 1965)
Macnaghten, Sir William Hay [ed.], *Arabian Nights: The Alif Laila; or the Book of the Thousand Nights and One Night*, (4 Vols: Calcutta, 1839-1842)
Madina, Maan Zilfo, *The Classical Doctrine of Consensus in Islam*, (Chicago: Dept. of Photoduplication, University of Chicago Library, 1957)
Maḥmaṣānī, Ṣubḥī, 'The Principles of International Law in the Light of Islamic Doctrine', *Recueil Des Cours*, I (1966) pp.201-328
idem., *General Theory*, (1972 Edn)
idem., *Philosophy of Jurisprudence In Islam*, (Engl. Transl. by F. Ziadeh : Leiden, 1961)

idem., 'Transactions In The Sharī'a in *Law In The Middle East*, ed. Khadduri and Liebesny, (Washington, 1955), pp.179-202

Mahdi, Muhsin, *Ibn Khaldun's Philosophy of History*, (London, 1957: Second Impression 1971), p.75

Maine, Sir H., *Ancient Law*, (First Edition: 1917; London,1977)

Makdisi, G., *The Rise of Colleges: Institutions of Learning In Islam and The West*, (Edinburgh, 1981)

idem., 'The Scholastic Method in Medieval Education: An Inquiry Into its Origins in Law and Theology,' *Speculum*, 49 (1974) pp.640-661

idem., 'Interaction between Islam and the West', *Revue des Études Islamiques*, 44, (1976) pp.287

idem., 'Ibn Taiymīya's Autograph Manuscript on Istiḥsān: Materials for the Study of Islamic Legal Thought', in *Arabic and Islamic Legal studies in Honour of H.A.R. Gibb*, (Leiden, 1965)

Makdisi, John, 'An Objective Approach to Contractual Mistake In Islamic Law', *BUILJ*, No. 2, (Summer, 1985), pp. 325; 333-334

idem., 'Islamic Law Bibliography', *Law Library Journal*, 78 (1986) pp.103-189

idem., 'Legal Logic and Equity in Islamic Law' in *The American Journal of Comparative Law*, vol.33 (1985) pp.63-92

Mallat, Chibli, 'The Debate on Riba and Interest in Twentieth Century Jurisprudence', pp.27-45 in *Islamic Law and Finance.*, (SOAS, London, 1988) [Ed. C. Mallat].

Mantran, R., 'Ḥisba', *Encyclopoedia of Islam*, (New Edition, Leiden, 1971) Ed. B. Lewis, V.L. Ménage, Ch. Pellat and J. Schacht. Vol III, pp.485-490

Marghīnānī, *The Hedāya*, transl. by Charles Hamilton, (Delhi, 1982 ed.)

Masud, Muhammad Khalid, *Islamic Legal Philosophy : A Study of Abū Isḥāq al-Shāṭibī's Life and Thought*, (Islamabad: Pakistan, 1977)

Mayer, 'Khartoum: After the Fall', *Middle East Executive Report*, (Oct.1985)

McKeag, 'Mistake In Contract : A Study In Comparative Jurisprudence', 23/2 *Studies In History, Economics and Public Law*, (Columbia University, 1905), 3, pp. 23-24.

McLaughlin, T.P., 'The Teaching of The Canonists on Usury', *Medieval Studies*, I, (1939) pp. 81-147; II (1940) pp.1-22

Meron, Y., 'Points de Contact des Droits Juif et Musulman', *Studia Islamica*, vol.LX (1984) pp.83-117

idem., 'The Development of Legal Thought In Hanafi Texts', *Studia Islamica*, 30 (1969) pp.73-118

Mez, A., *Die Renaissance des Islams*, (Heidelberg, 1922); and Transl. S. Khuda Bakhsh and D.S.Margoliouth, (Patna, 1937)

Middle East Executive Report, (Jan. 1986)
Middle East Executive Report, (March, 1986)
Miles, *The Countries and Tribes of the Persian Gulf*, (London, 1966)
Milliot, L., *Introduction à l'étude du Droit Musulman*, No. 221
idem., 'Coûtume et Jurisprudence Musulmans ('Orf et 'Amal)' in *Rapports Généraux au Ve Congrès International de Droit Comparé*, (Brussels, 1960) pp.179-183
idem., *Démembrements du Habous*, (Paris, 1918)
idem., *Introduction à l'Etude de Droit Musulman*, (Paris, 1953)
idem., 'La Pensée Juridique de l'Islam', *Revue Internationale de Droit Comparé*, (1954)
Mitteis, L., *Reichsrecht und Volksrecht in den Östlichen Provinzen des Römischen Kaiserreichs*, (Leipzig, 1891)
idem., 'Zwei Griechische Rechtsurkunden aus Kurdistan', *Zeitschrift der Savigny-Stiftung für Rechtsgeschichte*, (1915)
Mittwoch, *Zur Entstehungsgeschichte des Islamischen Gebets und Kultus*, (Berlin, 1913)
Mohamed, Abdalla I., 'Stipulations for the Benefit of Third Parties in Islamic Law of Contracts', *Journal of Islamic and Comparative Law*, vol. 9 (1980) pp.7-20
Morand, M., *Avant-Projet de Code Présenté à la Commission de Codification du Droit Musulman*, (Algiers, 1916)
idem., *Introduction à l'Étude du Droit Musulman Algérien*, (Algiers, 1921;1961)
Musa, 'The Liberty of the Individual in Contracts and Conditions According to Islamic Law', *Islamic Quarterly*, II (4) (1955) pp.252-263
idem., 'The Liberty of the Individual in Contracts and Conditions According to Islamic Law', *Islamic Quarterly*, II (Dec. 1955) pp.79-85
Muslehuddin, Muhammad, *Islamic Jurisprudence and The Role of Necessity and Need*, (Islamabad, 1975)
idem., *Philosophy of Islamic Law and the Orientalists*, (Lahore, n.d.)
Nallino, C.A., 'Considerazioni sui Rapporti fra diritto romano et diritto musulmano' in his *Raccolta di Scritti editi e inediti*, vol. IV, (Rome, 1942)
idem., *La Littérature Arabe*, (trad. into the French by Ch. Pellat (Paris 1950)
idem., *Raccolta di Scritti*, (Rome, 1939)
Naqvi, S.N.H., *Ethics and Economics, An Islamic Synthesis*, (Leicester, c.1981)
Nelson, B.N., *The Idea of Usury, From Tribal Brotherhood to Universal Otherhood*, (Chicago, 1969)
Nicholas, B., *An Introduction to Roman Law*, (Oxford, 1962)
idem., *French Law of Contract*, (London, 1982)

Nolte, R.H., (Ed.) *The Modern Middle East*, (New York, 1963)

Nyazee, 'The Scope of Taqlīd', *Islamic Studies*, XXII (4) (1983) pp.1-29.

Nyrop, R.F., (Ed.) *Persian Gulf States : Country Studies*, (Washington, 1985)

Onar, S.S., 'The Majalla', *Law In The Middle East*, [ed. Khadduri and Liebesny] (Washington, D.C., 1955) pp. 292-308

Oriente Moderno, VIII (1928) pp.36-38

O'Sullivan, Edmund, 'Islamic Insurance', *Arabian Insurance Guide*, (1984)

Owsia, P., *A Comparative Study of the conclusion of contracts in Persian, Islamic French and English Law*, (Unpublished Ph D Thesis; London SOAS, 1965)

Paret, R., '*Istiḥsān* and *Istiṣlaḥ*', *Shorter Encyclopaedia of Islam*, (New Edition : Leiden, 1978), Vol.IV, pp.255-259; (Leiden, 1961 Edn. : pp.184-186)

Parry, C., *Nationality and Citizenship Laws of the Commonwealth and of the Republic of Ireland*, (London, 1960) Vol. II

Pearl, D.S., *A Textbook on Muslim Law*, (London, 1979)

idem., 'Codification in Islamic Law', *Jewish Law Annual*, Vol. II (1979)

Persian Gulf Gazette, No.s 1-32 (1953-1961)

Philby, H., *The Background of Islam*, (Alexandria, 1937)

Pillar and Kumar, 'The Political and Legal Status of Kuwait', II *International and Comparative Law Quarterly*, (1962) at p.108

Polanyi, Karl, Avensberg, Conrad M., and Pearson, Harry W., *Trade and Market in the Early Empires*, (Illinois, 1957)

Pollock on *Contracts*, (Thirteenth Edn; London, 1950)

Powers, D.S., 'The Will of Sa'd b. AbîWaqqâṣ: A Reassessment', *Studia Islamica*, (1983) pp.34-53

Pringsheim, Fritz, *The Greek Law of Sale*, (Weimar, 1950)

Qureshi, Dr. Anwar, *The Economic and Social System of Islam*, (Lahore, 1979)

Rahman, A.F., *Economic Doctrines of Islam: Banking and Finance*, vol 4 (London, 1979)

Rahman, Fazlur, 'Riba and Interest', *Islamic Studies*, 3 (1964) pp.3f.

idem., 'Towards Reformulating the Methodology of Islamic Law : Sheikh Yamani on 'Public Interest' in Islamic Law', *New York University Journal of International Law and Politics*, 12 (1979) pp.219-224

Ramadan, Said, 'Islamic Law: Its Scope and Equity, (First Edn., London?, 1961; Second Edn., 1970)

Rawi, al-, 'Principles on the Islamic Law of Contracts', in *George Washington Law Review*, 22 (1953-4)

Reland, H., *Dissertationes Miscellaneae*, trajecti ad Rhenum, (1706-1708), vol. III

Reuters, 'Sudan Eases Shari'a Law', *Saudi Gazette*, (Dec. 12, 1987)
Ripert, Georges, *La Régle Morale dans les Obligations Civiles*, (Fourth Edn; Paris, 1949)
Ripert, Georges, et Boulanger, Jean, *Traité de Droit Civil D'après le Traité de Planiol*, Vol. II, (Paris, 1957)
Ritter, H., 'Ein Arabisches Handbuch der Handelwissenschaft,' *Der Islam*, VII, (Berlin, 1917)
Roberts, R., *Social Laws of the Qur'ān*, (London, 1925; Fourth Reprint, 1977)
Rodinson, M., *Mohammad*, (London, 1971)
Rosenthal, F., *Gambling In Islam*, (Leiden, 1975)
idem., (Transl.) *Ibn Khaldun :The Muqaddimah :An Introduction To History*, (1958)
Roy, 'Islamic Banking: Rapid Growth and the Moral Dilemma', *Middle East Executive Report*, (April, 1986)
Sachau, E., (ed. and transl.) *Syrische Rechtsbücher*, (Berlin, 1907-1914)
idem., *Muhammedanisches Recht Nach Schafiitischer Lehre*, (Stuttgart and Berlin, 1897)
Salah El-Din, Abdel Wahhab, and Brinsley, J.H., 'The Stipulation For a Third Person in Egyptian Law', 10 *American Journal of Comparative Law*, (1961)
Saleh, Nabil, *Unlawful Gain and Legitimate Profit in Islamic Law : Riba, Gharar and Islamic Banking*, (Cambridge, 1986)
idem., 'Financial Transactions and the Islamic Theory of Obligations and Contracts', *Islamic Law and Finance*, [ed. C. Mallat] (London, 1988)
idem., *The General Principles of Saudi Arabian and Omani Company Laws (Statutes and Shar'ia)*, (London, 1981)
idem., 'Les Lois Régissant Le Commerce Dans Le Sultanat d'Oman', *Revue Trimestrielle De Droit Commercial*, (Paris, 1974)
Saleh, Samir, *Commercial Arbitration in the Arab Middle East*, (London, 1984)
Samhaber, Ernst, *Merchants Make History*, (New York, 1964)
Sanhūrī, 'Abd al-Razzāq al-, 'Le Droit Comme Élément de Reforme du Code Civil Égyptien', 2 *Recueil d'Études en l'Honneur d'Edouard Lambert*, (Paris, 1938) pp.621-642.
Santillana, D., *Code Civil et Commercial Tunisien. Avant-Projet Discuté et Adopté au Rapport de M. D. Santillana*, (Imprimérie Générale; Tunis, 1899), known as the *Code Santillana.*
idem., Review of M. Fathy in *Revista degli Studi Orientali*, (1916-1918)
idem., *Instituzione di Diritto Musulmano Malichita*, (Rome, 1926-1938)
Sauser-Hall, *La Réception des Droits Européens en Turquie, Extrait du Recueil de Travaux publié par la Faculté de L'Université ge Genève,*

(1938)
Sauvaget, J., *Introduction à l'Histoire de l'Orient Musulman*, (Paris, 1961)
Savvas-Pacha, *Etude Sur la Théorie du Droit Musulman*, 2 vols. (First Edn: Paris 1898; Second Edn. 1902; Reprinted 1982)
idem., *Le Tribunal Musulman*, (Paris, 1902)
Scarce, J.M., 'Preserving the Arab Gulf Culture', 1 *The Arab Gulf Journal*, Vol. 6, No. 1 (April 1986) p.60
Schacht, Joseph, 'Die Arabische Ḥiyal-Literature,' in *Islam*, XV, (1926), pp.211-232.
idem., 'Foreign Elements In Ancient Islamic Law', *Mémoires de l'Académie Internationale de Droit Comparé*, (1955)
idem., 'Ḥiyal', *Encyclopoedia of Islam*, (New Edition: Leiden, 1971), Vol. III, pp.511-512
idem., 'Abū 'l-Su'ūd', *Encyclopoedia of Islam*, Ed. H.A.R. Gibb, J.H. Kramers, E. Lévi-Provençal, J. Schacht (New Edn.; Leiden 1960) p.152
idem., 'Droit Byzantin et Droit Musulman', *Accademia Nazionale dei Lincei, Fondazione Allesandro Volta, Atti dei Convegni*, no. 12, (Rome, 1957)
idem., 'Fikh', *Encyclopoedia of Islam*, Second Edn., (Leiden, 1965) II, pp.886-891
idem., 'The Present State of the Studies in Islamic Law', in *Atti del Terzo Congresso di Studi Arabi e Islamici*, (Naples, 1967)
idem., 'Foreign Elements in Ancient Islamic Law', *Journal of Comparative Legislation and International Law*, (1950) 32 [Series III] 3-4
idem., 'Islamic Law', *Encyclopedia of Social Sciences*, (Old Edition), (New York, 1932), Vol. VIII, pp.344-349
idem., *Introduction to Islamic Law*, (Oxford, 1964; Reprinted 1966; 1979)
idem., *The Origins of Muhammadan Jurisprudence*, (Oxford, First Edn 1950, with corrections 1953)
idem., 'Modernism and Traditionalism in a History of Islamic Law', (Review of N.J. Coulson) in *Middle East Studies*, (1965)
idem., 'Pre-Islamic Background and Early Development of Jurisprudence', in M. Khadduri and H.J. Liebesny (eds.), *Law In The Middle East*, vol. I (Washington, 1955)
idem., 'Problems of Modern Islamic Legislation', in R.H. Nolte (Ed.) *The Modern Middle East*, (New York, 1963)
idem., 'Remarques Sur La Transmission De La Pensée Greques Aux Arabes', *Histoire De La Médicine*, (1952).
idem., 'Ribā', *Encyclopoedia of Islam*, Vol.III, pp.1148-1150
idem., 'Sharī'a', *Encyclopoedia of Islam*, Vol. IV pp.320-324
idem., 'Vom Babylonischen Zum Islamischen Recht', *Orientalistische*

Literaturzeitung, (1927)

idem., 'Problems of Modern Islamic Legislation,' *Studia Islamica*, XII, (1960) pp.99-129

Schacht, Lewis and pellat, (Eds.), *Dustūr: A Survey of the Constitutions of the Arab and Muslim States*, (Leiden, 1966)

Schiller, 'Coptic Documents', *Zum Gegenwärtigen Stand der Juristischen Papyrusforschung, ZVRW*, LX (1957)

idem., 'Coptic Law', *The Juridical Review*, XLIII (1931)

Schimmel, A., 'Chalif und Qādī im Spätmittelalterlichen Ägyptien', *Welt Islams*, vol. 24 pp.1 ff.

Schram-Nielson, E., *Studier Over Erstatningsloeren i Islamisk Ret*, (Copenhagen, 1945)

Schreiber, Hermann, *Merchants, Pilgrims and Highwaymen*, (New York, 1962)

Schuster, E.J., *The Principles of German Civil Law*, (Oxford, 1907)

Schwartz, Andreas B., 'Der Einfluss der Professoren auf die Rechtsentwicklung im Laufe der Jahrhunderte', in Elemer Balogh, Ed. 3 *Mémoires de l'Académie Internationale de Droit Comparé*, (1953)

idem., 'La Reception et l'Assimilation des Droits Étrangers', 2 *Introduction à l'Étude du droit Comparé; Recueil d'Études en l'Honneur d'Edouard Lambert*, (1938) pp.581-590

Seaman, Bryant W., 'Islamic Law and Modern Government : Saudi Arabia Supplements the Shari'a to Regulate Development', *Columbia Journal of Transnational Law*, Vol. XVIII (1980) No.3, pp.413-481

Seagle, W., *The quest for Law*, (New York, 1941)

Sebeos (attrib.) *Histoire d'Héraclius*, transl. F. Macler (Paris, 1883; 1904)

Seignette, N., *Code Musulman par Khalil: (Rite Malékite)*, (Algiers/Paris, 1878)

Shaban, M.A., *Islamic History : New Interpretation*, I (Cambridge, 1971)

Shāfi'ī, *al-Risāla*, (Cairo, 1321 AH), translated in Khadduri, *Islamic Jurisprudence*, (Baltimore, 1961)

Shamma, 'Law and Lawyers in Saudi Arabia', 14 *International and Comparative Law Quarterly*, (1965) pp.1034-1039

Siddiqi, H., 'Iqbal's Legal Philosophy and the Reconstruction of Islamic Law', 2 *Progressive Islam*, No.s 3-4 (Amsterdam, 1955) pp.14 ff.

Siddiqi, M.N., *Insurance in an Islamic Economy*, (Leicester, 1985; Transl. of 1973 Urdu Edn.)

idem., *Banking Without Interest*, (Leicester, 1983)

idem., *Muslim Economic Thinking*, (Jedda/Leicester, c.1981)

Siddiqi, M.Z., *Ḥadīth Literature; Its Origins, Development, Special Features and Criticism*, (Calcutta University, 1961)

Droit Musulman', *Annales de L'École Française de Droit de Beyrouth*, (Beirut, 1945; Leiden, 1959; Second Edn 1967-1968)

idem., 'Méthodologie et Sources du Droit en Islam (*Istiḥsān, Istiṣlāḥ, Siyāsa Sar'iyya)*', *Studia Islamica*, X (1959) pp.79-109

Tyser, C.R., Demetriades, D.G., and Haqqi, Ismail, *The Mejelle*, (Lahore, 1967; Cyprus, 1901)

'UAE Bank Interest', *International Financial Law Review*, (Nov. 1986) Vol.V, No. 11, pp.42-43

Udovitch, Abraham L., 'Reflections on the Institutions of Credits and Banking In The Medieval Islamic Near East,' *Studia Islamica*, XLI (Paris, 1975) pp.5-21

idem., *Partnership and Profit in Medieval Islam*, (Princeton, 1970)

idem., 'Theory and Practice of Islamic Law: Some Evidence from the Geniza', *Studia Islamica*, XXXII (Paris, 1970) pp.289ff.

idem., 'At the Origin of the Western Commenda: Islam, Israel, Byzantium?' *Speculum*, 37 (1962) pp.198-207

idem., [Ed.] *The Islamic Middle East, 700-1900 : Studies in Economic and Social History*, (Princeton, N.J., 1981)

Van den Berg, L.W.C., *De Contractu 'do ut des' Iure Mohammedano*, (Leiden and Batavia, 1868)

idem., *Minhâdj aṭ-Ṭālibīn, Texte Arabe Publié avec Traduction et Notations*, (Batavia, 1862-1884)

Varga, Csaba, 'Modernization of Law and its Codification Trends in the Afro-Asiatic Legal Development', *Studies In Developing Countries*, No.88 (Institute for World Economics of the Hungarian Academy of Sciences: Budapest, 1976)

Velidedeoglu, Hifzi Verdet, 'Le Mouvement de Codification dans les Pays Musulmans - Ses Rapports avec les Mouvements Juridiques Occidentaux', (Rapport Général Présenté au Ve Congrès de l'Académie Internationale de Droit Comparé à Bruxelles : 4-9 Aug. 1958) [Annales de la Faculté de Droit d'Istanbul], VIII (1959) pp.130-178 (Brussels, 1960)

Vida, G. Levi Della, 'Dominant Ideas In The Formation of Islamic Culture', *The Crozier Quarterly*, 21 (July, 1944) p.215 f.

Vidal, José, *Essai D'une Théorie Générale de la Fraude en Droit Français*, (Paris, 1957)

Viré, F., 'Kalb', *The Encyclopaedia of Islam*, [1] Vol. IV (Leiden, 1978) Ed. E. Van Donzel, B. Lewis and Ch. Pellat, pp.489-492

Vogel, 'Decision No.822 on Banking Disputes: An Analysis', *Middle East Executive Report*, (April,1986)

Wakin, J.A., *The Function of Documents in Islamic Law : The Chapters on sales from Ṭaḥāwī's Kitāb al-Shurūṭ al-Kabīr; [Edited with an*

Introduction and Notes by J.A. Wakin], (Albany, Lebanon pr., 1972)

Waldock, 1 *Yearbook of the International Law Commission*, (1966) pp.75-86.

Warmington, E., *The Commerce Between The Roman Empire and India*, (Cambridge, 1928)

Wassel, Mohamed, 'The Islamic Law, Its Application as it was Revealed in the Qur'ān and its Adaptability to Cultural Change', *Hamdard Islamicus*, 6(1) (1983) pp.53-61

Watt, W. Montgomery, *Muhammad, Prophet and Statesman*, (London, 1961; Oxford, 1964)

idem., *Islam and The Integration of Society*, (London, 1961)

idem., *Islamic Philosophy and Theology*, (Edinburgh, 1962)

idem., *Muhammad at Mecca*, (Oxford, 1953)

idem., *Muhammad at Medina*, (Oxford, 1956)

Wegner, Judith R., 'Islamic and Talmudic Jurisprudence :The Four Roots of Islamic Law and Their Talmudic Counterparts', *The American Journal of Legal History*, 26 (1982) pp.25-71

Wehberg, Hans, 'Pacta Sunt Servanda', *The American Journal of International Law*, vol.53, (1959) p.775-786

Wehr, Hans, *A Dictionary Of Modern Written Arabic*, (Ed. J.M. Cowan; Third Edn.; New York, 1976)

Weill, Alex, and Terré, François, *Droit Civil : Les Obligations*, (Dalloz: Second Edn; Paris, 1975),

Wensinck, A.J., and Kramers, J.H., *Handwörterbuch Des Islam*, (Leiden, 1941)

Wensinck, 'Sunna', in *Encyclopoedia of Islam*,[1], Vol. IV, p.557.

Whelan, James, Translation of The Federal Civil Code of The United Arab Emirates, No. 2 of 1987. Published in 3 *Business Laws of the United Arab Emirates*, (Suppl. 2, 1987)

Wickens, G.M., 'Al-Jarsifī on the *Ḥisba*', *The Islamic Quarterly*, 3 (1956) pp.176-187

Williston, S., 13 *A Treatise On The Law Of Contracts*, (First Edn. 1920; Ed. by Prof. Walter Jaeger since 1957: Third Edn.: 1970)

Wilson, R., *Banking and Finance In The Arab Middle East*, (London, 1983)

idem., 'Islamic Banking in Jordan', *Arab Law Quarterly*, 2(3) (Aug. 1987) pp.205-229

Winstone, H.V.F., *Kuwait : Prospect and Reality*, (London, 1972)

Wüstenfeld, F. (Ed.) *Das Leben Muhammads Nach Muhammad Ibn Ishâk*, (Göttingen, 1858-60)

idem., *Die Chroniken der Stadt Mekka*, (Leipzig, 1857-1861)

Yearbook of the International Law Commission, (1963) (UN: New York, 1964)

Yunus, As'ad, *Commercial Arbitration and Legal System in Kuwait*, (Kuwait, 1978)

Ziadeh, F.J., 'Shufa'ah: Origins and Modern Doctrine', *Cleveland State Law Review*, 34 (1) (1985-1986) pp.35-46

INDEX

A

B

D

H

I

K

L

N

Q